May 24–26, 2017
Singapore

**Association for
Computing Machinery**

Advancing Computing as a Science & Profession

SIGSIM-PADS'17

Proceedings of the 2017 ACM SIGSIM Conference on
Principles of Advanced Discrete Simulation

Sponsored by:
ACM SIGSIM

**Association for
Computing Machinery**

Advancing Computing as a Science & Profession

The Association for Computing Machinery
2 Penn Plaza, Suite 701
New York, New York 10121-0701

ISBN: 978-1-4503-4489-0 (Digital)

ISBN: 978-1-4503-5471-4 (Print)

Additional copies may be ordered prepaid from:

ACM Order Department
PO Box 30777
New York, NY 10087-0777, USA

Phone: 1-800-342-6626 (USA and Canada)
+1-212-626-0500 (Global)
Fax: +1-212-944-1318
E-mail: acmhelp@acm.org
Hours of Operation: 8:30 am – 4:30 pm ET

Printed in the USA

Message from the Conference Chairs

A warm welcome to SIGSIM PADS'17, the 5th ACM SIGSIM Conference on Principles of Advanced Discrete Simulation. SIGSIM PADS is the flagship conference of ACM's Special Interest Group on Simulation and Modeling (SIGSIM). It provides a unique forum for reporting and discussing research results and important topics of interest to the modeling and simulation (M&S) community. The annual PADS conference has a long history dating back to 1985. Over the years PADS has broadened its scope beyond its origins in parallel and distributed simulation and now encompasses virtually all research that lies at the intersection of the computer science and the M&S fields. Built on its strong history, PADS became the ACM SIGSIM's flagship conference and renamed as SIGSIM PADS in 2013. This year is the 5th edition of the conference under its new brand name.

PADS was first held in Singapore in 2006. We are very pleased that after 11 years PADS returns to Singapore under its new brand name. Singapore is a dynamic city rich in contrast and color, where you will find a harmonious blend of culture, cuisine, arts and architecture. With its friendly and welcome people, state-of-the-art infrastructure and spectacular events, Singapore has everything to make your stay a most memorable experience.

This year's SIGSIM PADS received a large number of submissions, further strengthening its status as a leading conference in its area. All papers submitted to the conference were rigorously reviewed with at least 3 reviewers for each paper. We would like to thank the program committee and additional reviewers for their diligent efforts to provide timely, critical reviews and feedback to the authors. The two and half day conference consists of 2 keynote speeches, 2 invited talks, and presentations of 21 full papers and 2 short papers. The first keynote will be given by Dr. Marc-Oliver Gewaltig on "Towards Simulating the Human Brian", and the second keynote will be given by Prof. Young-Jun Son on "An Integrated Human Decision Making Model under Extended Belief-Desire-Intention Framework". We hope that you enjoy this exciting program that we have arranged for you.

There are 8 students participating in this year's Ph.D. Colloquium. They will give brief presentations as well as showing posters concerning their research. Prof. Philip Wilsey will give a keynote presentation for the PhD Colloquium.

In keeping with the PADS tradition, a Best Paper Committee will select the SIGSIM PADS'17 Best Paper Award from the most highly ranked papers by reviewers. The candidates for this year's best paper are (in no particular order):

- Julius Higiro, Meseret Gebre and Dhananjai Rao. "Multi-tier Priority Queues & 2-tier Ladder Queue for Managing Pending Events in Sequential & Optimistic Parallel Simulations"

- Yulin Wu, Xiangting Hou, Wenjun Tan, Zengxiang Li and Wentong Cai. "Efficient Parallel Simulation over Social Contact Network with Skewed Degree Distribution"

- Md Shafiur Rahman, Nael Abu-Ghazaleh and Walid Najjar. "PDES-A: a Parallel Discrete Event Simulation Accelerator for FPGAs"

The Best Paper Award will be announced during the banquet at the conference. On behalf of the SIGSIM PADS'16 Program Chair, we are pleased to report that the winner of the SIGSIM PADS'16 Best Paper was "Automated Memoization for Parameter Studies Implemented in Impure Languages" by Mirko Stoffers, Daniel Schemmel, Oscar Soria Dustmann and Klaus Wehrle.

The success of this conference is due to the efforts of many people. We would like to thank other organizing committee members for their contributions to the conference: Misbah Mubarak and Wenjie Tang (Publicity Co-Chairs), Jason Liu (PhD Colloquium Chair), Elvis Liu (Publication Chair), and Irene Goh (Registration and Local Arrangement Chair). As always, Osman Balci did a great job with the web site, providing a very responsive service. We would also like to thank the ACM SIGSIM for their support and for providing travel grants to students.

We hope you enjoy the conference and have a wonderful time in Singapore!

SIGSIM PADS'17 General Co-Chairs
Wentong Cai
Nanyang Technological University, Singapore

Yong Meng Teo
National University of Singapore, Singapore

SIGSIM PADS'17 Program Co-Chairs
Philip A. Wilsey
University of Cincinnati, USA

Dong (Kevin) Jin
Illinois Institute of Technology, USA

Table of Contents

Keynote I
Session Chair: Wentong Cai *(Nanyang Technological University)*

Paper Session 1: Parallel Simulation I
Session Chair: Richard Fujimoto *(Georgia Tech)*

Keynote II
Session Chair: Kevin Jin *(Illinois Institute of Technology)*

Paper Session 2: Parallel Simulation II
Session Chair: Dhanajai Rao *(Miami University, Ohio)*

Paper Session 3: Performance Modeling and Simulation
Session Chair: David Nicol *(University of Illinois at Urbana-Champaign)*

Paper Session 4: GPU and Hardware Acceleration
Session Chair: Francesco Quaglia *(University of Rome)*

Paper Session 5: Simulation Application I: Networking and Communication
Session Chair: Nael Abu-Ghazaleh *(University of California, Riverside)*

Paper Session 6: Modeling and Simulation Methods
Session Chair: Christopher Carothers *(RPI)*

Paper Session 7: Simulation Application II
Session Chair: Jiaqi Yan *(Illinois Institute of Technology)*

Paper Session 8: Miscellaneous

Session Chair: Jared Ivey *(Georgia Tech)*

Author Index

Organizing Committee
ACM SIGSIM PADS 2017

General Co-Chairs

Wentong Cai
Professor,
School of Computer Science & Engineering,
Nanyang Technological University,
Singapore

Teo Yong Meng
Associate Professor,
School of Computing,
National University of Singapore,
Singapore

Program Co-Chairs

Philip Wilsey
Professor,
School of Eletric and Computing Systems,
University of Cincinnati,
Cincinnati, Ohio, USA

Kevin Jin
Assistant Professor,
Department of Computer Science,
Illinois Institute of Technology,
Chicago, Illinois, USA

Publicity Co-Chairs

Misbah Mubarak
Postdoctoral Fellow,
MCS Division,
Argonne National Laboratory,
Chicago, Illinois, USA

Wenjie Tan
Assistant Professor,
College of Information System & Management,
National University of Defense Technologies,
China

Proceeding Chair

Elvis Liu
Assistant Professor,
School of Computer Science and Engineering,
Nanyang Technological University,
Singapore

Ph.D. Colloquium Chair

Jason Liu
Associate Professor,
School of Computing and Information Sciences,
Florida International University,
Miami, Florida, USA

Registration & Local Arrangement

Irene Goh
School of Computer Science and Engineering,
Nanyang Technological University,
Singapore

Program Committee
ACM SIGSIM PADS 2017

Nael Abu-Ghazaleh, University of California at Riverside, USA
Anastasia Anagnostous, Brunell University, UK
Peter Barnes, Lawrence Livermore National Laboratory, USA
Fernando J. Barros, University of Coimbra, Portugal
Laurent Capocchi, University of Corsica, France
Christopher D. Carothers, Rensselaer Polytechnic Institute, USA
David Eckhoff, TUM CREATE, Singapore
Paul Fishwick, University Texas at Dallas, USA
Richard Fujimoto, Georgia Institute of Technology, USA
Philippe J. Giabbanelli, University of Cambridge, UK
Drew Hamilton, Mississippi State University, USA
Maâmar El-Amine Hamri, Aix-Marseille University, France
David R. Jefferson, Lawrence Livermore National Laboratory, USA
Laxmikant V. Kale, University of Illinois at Urbana-Champaign, USA
Darren Kerbyson, Pacific Northwest National Laboratory, USA
Yun-Bae Kim, Sungkyunkwan University, South Korea
Elvis S. Liu, Nanyang Technological University, Singapore
Jason Liu, Florida International University, USA
Ning Liu, IBM, USA
Margaret Loper, Georgia Tech Research Institute, USA
Madhav Marathe, Virginia Tech, USA
Yahaya Md. Sam, Universiti Teknologi Malaysia, Malaysia
Misbah Mubarak, Argonne National Laboratory, USA
Navonil Mustafee, University of Exeter, UK
David M. Nicol, University of Illinois at Urbana-Champaign, USA
Ernest Page, MITRE Corporation, USA
Alessandro Pellegrini, University of Rome, Italy
Kalyan Perumalla, Oak Ridge National Laboratory, USA
Francesco Quaglia, Sapienza University of Rome, Italy
George F. Riley, Georgia Institute of Technology, USA
Hessam S. Sarjoughian, Arizona State University, USA
Young-Jun Son, University of Arizona, USA
Steffen Strassburger, Technical University of Ilmenau, Germany
Claudia Szabo, University of Adelaide, Australia
Wenjie Tang, National University of Defense Technology, China
Satoshi Tanaka, Ritsumeikan University, Japan
Simon Taylor, Brunel University, UK
Andreas Tolk, Old Dominion University, USA
Stephen Turner, King Mongkut's University of Technology Thonburi, Thailand
Adelinde Uhrmacher, University of Rostock, Germany
Gabriel A. Wainer, Carleton University, Canada
Yiping Yao, National University of Defense Technology, China
Levent Yilmaz, Auburn University, USA
Lin Zhang, Beihang University, China
Yuhao Zheng, Data Visor, USA

SIGSIM PADS 2017 Sponsor

Towards Simulating the Human Brain

Marc-Oliver Gewaltig
Blue Brain Project
Ecole Polytechnique Fédérale de Lausanne
Campus Biotech, CH-1202 Geneva, Switzerland
Marc-Oliver.Gewaltig@epfl.ch

ABSTRACT

Understanding the human brain is still one of the biggest scientific challenges. The European Human Brain Project tries to tackle this challenge, by integrating a wide range of neuroscientific data into large multi-scale models and simulations of the brain. In this talk, I will highlight recent results and challenges that we face in our endeavour to reconstruct and simulate models of entire brains. The human brain is comprised of 80 billion neurons and 100*1012 synapses, each with dynamic properties that are governed by many differential equations. Representing the dynamic state of a complete human brain thus is still outside the reach of even the largest super-computers. Models of a mouse brain, still comprise 75 million neurons and 80 billion connections, but these are accessible with model supercomputers. In the first part of the talk, I will outline how high-resolution imaging data can be used to semi-automatically reconstruct 3D the positions of different neuron types as well as their connections. Next, I will discuss the challenges of representing and simulating such large-scale models using hybrid time and event driven simulation techniques. Finally, I will discuss applications of large-scale brain models for neuroscience, medicine, robotics and computing technology.

CCS Concepts/ACM Classifiers

• Networks~Network simulations • Computing methodologies~Massively parallel and high-performance simulations • Hardware~Emerging simulation
• Hardware~Neural systems

Author Keywords

Large-scale simulation; neural and brain modelling

BIOGRAPHY

Marc-Oliver Gewaltig investigates the simulation-aided reconstruction of sensory-motor loops, using data-driven whole brain models and muscoloskeletal body models. Marc-Oliver Gewaltig has been working in the field of large-scale parallel distributed simulations since the 1990s, when he started working on the Neural Simulation Tool NEST (www.nest-simulator.org), a popular open source tool for large-scale simulations of spiking neural networks. Marc-Oliver Gewaltig heads the Neurorobotics Section of the Blue-Brain Project at the EPFL in Lausanne and in the EU Flagship "Human Brain Project" (www.humanbrainproject.eu), he is responsible for the design and implementation of the HBP Neurorobotics Platform (www.neurorobotics.net), a cloud-based simulation platform for virtual robotics. Before joining the EPFL in 2011, Marc-Oliver Gewaltig was Principal Scientist (2003-2011) and Project Leader (1998-2002) at the Honda Research Institute Europe in Offenbach, Germany.

SIGSIM-PADS'17, May 24–26, 2017, Singapore.
ACM ISBN 978-1-4503-4489-0/17/05.
http://dx.doi.org/10.1145/3064911.3064935

Multi-tier Priority Queues and 2-tier Ladder Queue for Managing Pending Events in Sequential and Optimistic Parallel Simulations

Julius Higiro, Meseret Gebre, and Dhananjai M. Rao
Computer Science & Software Engineering (CSE) Department
Miami University, 510 E. High Street, 205 Benton Hall
Oxford, Ohio 45056-6221
raodm@miamiOH.edu

ABSTRACT

The choice of data structure for managing and processing pending events in timestamp priority order plays a critical role in achieving good performance of sequential and parallel Discrete Event Simulation (DES). Accordingly, we propose and evaluate the effectiveness of our novel multi-tiered (2 and 3 tier) data structures and our 2-tier Ladder Queue, for both sequential and optimistic parallel simulations, on distributed memory platforms. Our assessments use (a fine-tuned version of) the Ladder Queue, which has shown to outperform many other data structures for DES. The experimental results based on 2,500 configurations of PHOLD benchmark show that our 3-tier heap and 2-tier ladder queue outperform the Ladder Queue by 10% to 50% in simulations, particularly those with higher concurrency per Logical Process (LP), in both sequential and Time Warp synchronized parallel simulations.

CCS Concepts

•Theory of computation → **Data structures design and analysis**; •Computing methodologies → **Discrete-event simulation; Distributed simulation;**

Keywords

Discrete Event Simulation (DES); Optimistic Parallel Simulation; Time Warp; Binary Heap; Fibonacci Heap; Ladder Queue

1. INTRODUCTION

Sequential and parallel DES are designed as a set of logical processes (LPs) or "agents" that interact with each other by exchanging and processing timestamped events or messages [6]. Events that are yet to be processed are called "pending events". Pending events must be processed by LPs in priority order to maintain causality, with event priorities being determined by their timestamps. Consequently, data structures for managing and prioritizing pending events play a critical role in ensuring efficient sequential and parallel simulations [3, 7, 4, 10]. Effectiveness of data structures for event management is a conspicuous issue in larger simulations, where thousands or millions of events can be pending [1, 9]. Overheads in managing pending events is magnified in fine grained simulations where the time taken to process an event is very short – *i.e.*, LPs use only few 100s to 1000s of instructions per event. Furthermore, the synchronization strategy used in PDES, Time Warp in particular, can further impact the effectiveness of the data structure due to additional operations required for rollback-based recovery.

1.1 Motivation

Many investigations have explored the effectiveness of a wide variety of data structures for managing the pending event set, as discussed in Section 5. Among the various data structures, the Ladder Queue proposed by Tang *et al* [10] has shown to be the most effective data structure for managing pending events [3, 2], particularly in sequential DES. Accordingly, we aimed to replace the heap-based data structures (discussed in Section 4) used in our Time Warp synchronized parallel simulator with the Ladder Queue. Section 4.5 discusses our Ladder Queue implementation and its fine-tuning.

The Ladder Queue outperformed our multi-tier heap-based data structures in certain sequential simulations, consistent with observations by other investigators [3, 10]. However, as detailed in Section 6, the Ladder Queue was substantially slower in two cases – ❶ high concurrency: larger number of concurrent events (*i.e.*, events with same timestamp) per LP, and ❷ Time Warp synchronized parallel simulations conducted on a distributed memory computing cluster. Conversely, our multi-tier data structures performed well in parallel simulations.

To provide a good balance for both sequential and optimistic parallel simulations, we propose a significant change to the design of the Ladder Queue. Our revised data structure, discussed in Section 4.6, is called 2-tier Ladder Queue (`2tLadderQ`). Various configurations of the standard PHOLD benchmark are used to assess the effectiveness of the multi-tier data structures vs. our fine-tuned implementation of the Ladder Queue. Results from our experiments discussed in Section 6 data shows `2tLadderQ` provides comparable perfor-

SIGSIM-PADS'17, May 24–26 2017, Singapore

© 2017 ACM. ISBN 978-1-4503-4489-0/17/05. . . $15.00

DOI: http://dx.doi.org/10.1145/3064911.3064921

mance in sequential simulations but outperforms the Ladder Queue in optimistic parallel simulations. Our 3-tier heap (`3tHeap`) outperforms our `2tLadderQ` in high concurrency scenarios.

2. PARALLEL SIMULATOR OVERVIEW

The implementation and assessment of the different data structures has been conducted using our parallel simulation framework called MUSE. It has been developed in C++ and uses the Message Passing Interface (MPI) library for parallel processing. MUSE uses Time Warp and standard state saving approach to accomplish optimistic synchronization of the LPs. A conceptual overview of a parallel simulation is shown in Figure 1. A MUSE simulation is organized as a set of Logical Processes (LPs) that interact with each other by exchanging virtual timestamped events. The simulation kernel implements core functionality associated with LP registration, event processing, state saving, synchronization, and Global Virtual Time (GVT) based garbage collection.

The kernel uses a centralized Least Timestamp First (LTSF) scheduler queue for managing pending events and scheduling event processing for local LPs. With a centralized LTSF scheduler, event exchanges between local LPs do not cause rollbacks. Only events received via MPI can cause rollbacks. The scheduler is designed to permit different data structures to be used for managing pending events. This feature is used to experiment with the different pending event scheduler queues. A scheduler queue is required to implement the following key operations to manage pending events:

❶ **Enqueue one or more future events**: This operation adds the given set of events to the pending event set. Multiple events are added to reprocess events after a rollback.

❷ **Peek next event**: This operation returns the next event to be processed. The event is used to update an LP's LVT and schedule it. Note that peek does not dequeue events.

❸ **Dequeue events for next LP**: In contrast to peek, this operation dequeues concurrent events (*i.e.,* events with the same receive time) to be processed by an LP. Concurrent events could have been sent by different LPs on different MPI-processes. A total order within concurrent events is not imposed but can be readily introduced if needed.

❹ **Cancel pending events**: This operation is used as part of rollback recovery process to aggressively remove *all pending events* sent by a given LP (LP_{sender}) to another LP (LP_{dest}) at-or-after a given time ($t_{rollback}$). In our implementation, only one anti-message with send time $t_{rollback}$ is dispatched to LP_{dest} from LP_{sender} to cancel prior events sent by LP_{sender} to LP_{dest} at-or-after $t_{rollback}$. This feature short circuits the need to send a large number of anti-messages thereby enabling faster rollback recovery. This feature also reduces scans required to cancel events in Ladder Queue data structures discussed in Section 4.5 and Section 4.6.

2.1 Experimental Platform

The design of MUSE and the experiments reported in this paper were conducted using a distributed-memory compute cluster consisting of 80 compute nodes interconnected by 1 GBPS Ethernet. Each compute node has two quad-core Intel Xeon ® CPUs (E5520) running at 2.27 GHz with hyperthreading disabled. Each compute node has 32 GB of RAM

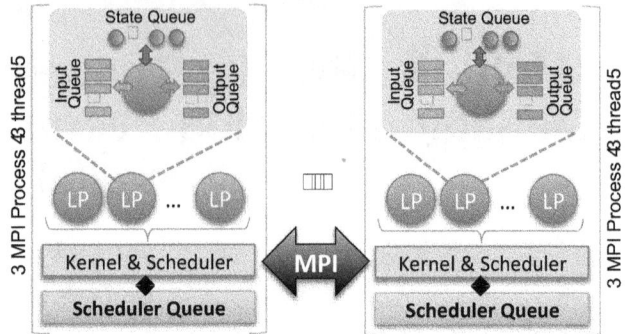

Figure 1: Overview of a parallel MUSE simulation

(4 GB per core) in Non-Uniform Memory Access (NUMA) configuration. The cluster has an independent 1 GBPS Ethernet network to support a shared file system. The nodes run Red Hat Enterprise Linux 6, with Linux (kernel ver 2.6.32) and the cluster runs PBS/Torque. The simulation software was compiled using GCC version 4.9.2 (`-O3` optimization level) with OpenMPI 1.6.4. All debug assertions were turned off for maximum performance.

3. PHOLD BENCHMARK

The experimental analysis have been conducted using a parallelized version of the classic Hold synthetic benchmark called PHOLD (see Section 7.1). It has been used by many investigators because it has shown to effectively emulate the steady-state phase of a typical simulation [3, 10]. Our PHOLD implementation developed using MUSE provides several parameters (specified as command-line arguments) summarized in Table 1. The benchmark consists of a 2-dimensional toroidal grid of Logical Processes (LPs) specified via the `rows` and `cols` parameters. The LPs are evenly partitioned across the MPI-processes used for simulation. The `imbalance` parameter influences the partition, with larger values skewing the partition as shown in Figure 2(a). The `imbalance` parameter has no impact in sequential simulations.

Table 1: Parameters in PHOLD benchmark

Parameter	Description
`rows`	Total number of rows in model.
`cols`	Total number of columns in model. #LPs = `rows` × `cols`
`eventsPerLP`	Initial number of events per LP.
`delay` or λ	Value used with distribution – Lambda (λ) value for exponential distribution *i.e.,* $P(x) = \lambda e^{-\lambda x}$.
`%selfEvents`	Fraction of events LPs send to self
`granularity`	Additional compute load per event.
`imbalance`	Fractional imbalance in partition to have more LPs on a MPI-process.
`simEndTime`	GVT when simulation logically ends.

The PHOLD simulation commences with a fixed number of events for each LP, specified by the `eventsPerLP` parameter. For each event received by an LP a fixed number of trigonometric operations determined by `granularity` are performed to place CPU load. The impact of increasing

4

the `granularity` parameter (no unit) is summarized in Figure 2(b) – smaller values result in finer grained simulations. For each event, an LP schedules another event to a randomly chosen adjacent LP. The `selfEvents` parameter controls the fraction of events that an LP schedules to itself.

The event timestamps are determined by a given `delay-distrib` and `delay` or λ parameters. Our experiments use an exponential distribution for timestamps, because it has shown to reflect *steady state* event distribution commonly found in a broad range of simulation models (but not all models obviously) [10]. Timestamp of events is computed as $t_{recv} = \text{LVT} + 1 + \lambda e^{-\lambda x}$, where the +1 ensures that events are always scheduled into the future as per MUSE API requirement discussed in Section 2. The impact of changing the λ (*i.e.*, `delay`) is shown in Figure 2(c) – smaller values of λ provide a broader range of timestamp value for future events resulting in fewer concurrent events per LVT. Conversely, larger λ values cause timestamps to be close to the current epoch, increasing both the number of concurrent events per LVT and the possibility of rollbacks. Section 6 explores impact of these parameters on scheduler queue performance using 2,500 different configurations.

4. SCHEDULER QUEUES

The pending events are managed by different scheduler queues that utilize different data structures to implement the key operations discussed in Section 2, namely: enqueue, peek, dequeue, and cancel. In this study we have compared the effectiveness of 6 different non-intrusive queuing data structures (see Section 7.1 for link to source code) namely: ① binary heap (`heap`), ② 2-tier heap (`2tHeap`), ③ 2-tier Fibonacci heap (`fibHeap`), ④ 3-tier heap (`3tHeap`), ⑤ Ladder Queue (`ladderQ`), and ⑥ 2-tier Ladder Queue (`2tLadderQ`). The queues are broadly classified into two categories, namely: single-tier and multi-tier queues. Single-tier queues such as `heap` use only a single data structure for accomplishing the 4 key operations. Conversely, multi-tier queues use organize events into tiers, with each tier implemented using different data structures. Table 2 summarizes the asymptotic time complexities of the 6 data structures discussed in the following subsections.

4.1 Binary Heap (`heap`)

The binary heap based (`heap`) is a commonly used data structure for implementing priority queues. It is a single-tier data structure and is implemented using a conventional array-based approach. A `std::vector` is used as the backing container and C++11 algorithms (`std::push_heap`, `std::pop_heap`) are used to maintain the heap. The heap is prioritized on both timestamp and LP's *ID* (to dequeue batches of events), with lowest timestamp at the root of the heap. Operations on the heap are logarithmic in time complexity – given l LPs each with e events/LP, the time complexity of enqueue and dequeue operations is $O(\log(l \cdot e))$ as shown in Table 2. If event cancellation requires z events to be removed from the heap, the time complexity is $O(z \cdot \log(e \cdot l))$. Consequently, for long or cascading rollbacks the cancellation costs is high.

4.2 Two-tier Heap (`2tHeap`)

The `2tHeap` is designed to reduce the time complexity of cancel operations by subdividing events into two distinct tiers as shown in Figure 3. The first tier has containers for

Table 2: Comparison of asymptotic time complexities (*i.e.*, Big O) of different data structures

Legend – l: #LPs, e: #events / LP, c: #concurrent events, z: #canceled events, $_{t2}k$: parameter, 1: amortized constant

Name	Enqueue	Dequeue	Cancel
`heap`	$\log(e \cdot l)$	$\log(e \cdot l)$	$z \cdot \log(e \cdot l)$
`2tHeap`	$\log(e \cdot l)$	$\log(e \cdot l)$	$z \cdot \log(e)+$
`fibHeap`	$\log(e) + 1$	$\log(e) + 1$	$z \cdot \log(e) + 1$
`3tHeap`	$\log(\frac{e}{c}) + \log(l)$	$\log(l)$	$e + \log(l)$
`ladderQ`	1	1	$e \cdot l$
`2tLadderQ`	1	1	$e \cdot l \div {}_{t2}k$

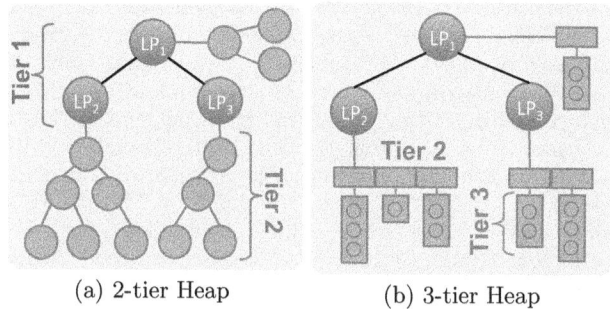

(a) 2-tier Heap   (b) 3-tier Heap

Figure 3: Structure of 2-tier & 3-tier heap

each local LP on an MPI-process. Each of the tier-1 containers contain a heap of events to be processed by a given LP. In `2tHeap` both tiers are maintained as independent binary heaps. Consequently, given l LPs and e pending events per LP, enqueue and dequeue operates require $O(\log e)$ time to insert in tier-2 followed by $O(\log l)$ time to reschedule the LP. Note that the tier-1 heap is updated only if the root event in tier-2 changes after an operation. Consequently, the best case time complexity becomes $\log e$ when compared to $O(\log(e \cdot l))$ for the `heap`. Furthermore, cancellation of events for an anti-message is restricted to just the tier-2 entries of LP_{dest} (see Section 2) with utmost 1 tier-1 operation to update schedule position of LP_{dest}. A `std::vector` is used as the backing storage for both tiers and standard algorithms are used to maintain the min-heap property for both tiers after each operation.

4.3 2-tier Fibonacci Heap (`fibHeap`)

The `fibHeap` is an extension to the previous `2tHeap` data structure and uses a Fibonacci heap for scheduling LPs. The Fibonacci heap is a slightly modified version from the BOOST C++ library. The Fibonacci heap has an amortized constant time for changing key values and finding minimum. Consequently, we use it for the first tier which is responsible for scheduling LPs and use a standard binary heap for the second tier. We do not use Fibonacci heap for the second tier because we found its runtime constants to be higher than a binary heap. Accordingly, the time complexity for enqueue and dequeue operations is $O(\log(e) + 1)$.

4.4 Three-tier Heap (`3tHeap`)

The `3tHeap` builds upon `2tHeap` by further subdividing the second tier into two tiers as shown in Figure 3(b). The binary heap implementation for the first tier that manages LPs for scheduling has been retained from `2tHeap`. However,

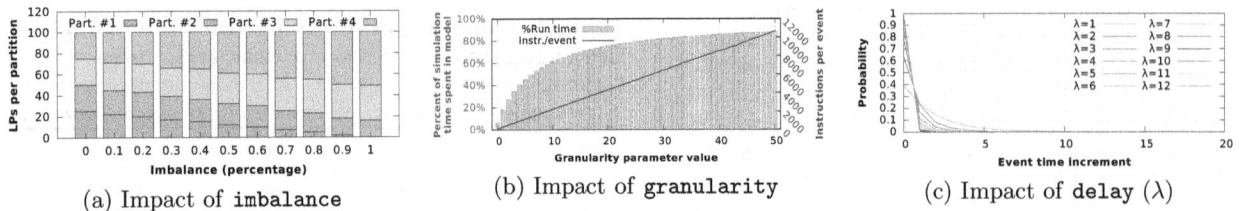

(a) Impact of `imbalance` (b) Impact of `granularity` (c) Impact of `delay` (λ)

Figure 2: Impact of varying key parameter values in the PHOLD model

the 2nd tier is implemented as a list of containers sorted based on receive time of events. Each tier-2 container has a 3rd tier list of concurrent events. Assuming each LP has c concurrent events on an average, there are $\frac{e}{c}$ tier-2 entries with each one having c pending events. Inserting events in the `3tHeap` is accomplished via binary search at tier-2 with time complexity $O(\log \frac{e}{c})$ followed by an append to tier-3, a constant time operation. Enqueue to tier-2 is followed by an optional heap fix-up of time complexity $O(\log l)$ as summarized in Table 2. Dequeue operation for a LP removes a tier-2 entry in constant time followed by a $O(\log l)$ heap fix-up for scheduling. Event cancellation has time complexity of $O(e + \log l)$ as it requires inspecting each event in tier-3 followed by heap fix-up. As an implementation optimization, we recycle tier-2 containers to reduce allocation and deallocation overhead.

4.5 Ladder Queue (`ladderQ`)

The `ladderQ` is a priority queue implementation proposed by Tang *et al* [10] with amortized constant time complexity as summarized in Table 2. Several investigators have independently verified that for sequential DES the `ladderQ` outperforms other priority queues, including: simple sorted list, binary heap, Splay tree, Calendar queue, and other multi-list data structures [2, 3, 10]. There are two key ideas underlying the Ladder Queue, namely: ① minimize the number of events to be sorted and ② delay sorting of events as much as possible. The multi-tier data structures also aim to minimize the number of events to be sorted. However, in contrast to the `ladderQ`, the other data structures always fix-up and maintain a minimum heap property.

The ladder queue consists of the following 3 substructures:

1. *Top*: An unsorted list which contains events scheduled into the distant future or epoch.

2. *Ladder*: Consists of multiple rungs, *i.e.*, list of buckets. Each bucket contains list of events with a finite range of timestamp values. Hence, although events within a bucket are not sorted, the buckets on a rung are organized in a sorted order. The `ladderQ` minimizes the number of events to be finally sorted by recursively breaking large buckets into smaller buckets in lower rungs of its ladder. Lower rungs in the ladder have smaller buckets with smaller time ranges.

3. *Bottom*: This substructure contains a sorted list of events to be processed. Inserts into *Bottom* must preserve sorted order. Hence, the `ladderQ` strives to maintain a short bottom by moving events back into the ladder, as needed [10].

4.5.1 Fine tuning Ladder Queue performance

Our implementation closely followed the design in the original paper by Tang *et al* [10]. However, to minimize runtime constants, we have explored different configurations for the buckets and the *Bottom* in the `ladderQ`. Specifically, we have explored the following 6 configurations – ❶ L.List-L.List: using a doubly-linked list (L.List) implemented by `std::list`) for buckets and bottom. Events are inserted into bottom via linear search as proposed by Tang *et al*. ❷ L.List-M.Set: L.List for buckets and a Multi-set ($O(\log n)$ operations) for bottom, ❸ L.List-Heap: a L.List and a binary heap (backed by a `std::vector`) for bottom, ❹ Vec-M.Set: a dynamically growing array (*i.e.*, `std::vector`) for buckets and Multi-set bottom, ❺ Vec-Heap: Vector buckets and binary heap for bottom, and ❻ Vec-Vec: Vector for buckets and bottom. This configuration enables using quick sort (*i.e.*, `std::sort`) for sorting buckets and binary search for inserting events into bottom.

Runtime comparison of the 6 `ladderQ` configurations is summarized in Figure 4. The data was obtained using PHOLD with different parameter settings. The ❻th Vec-Vec configuration was the fastest and performance of other configurations are shown relative to it in Figure 4(a). The L.List-L.List configuration was generally the slowest and performed 85× (or ~98%) slower than the Vec-Vec configuration. The peak memory used for simulations is shown in Figure 4(b), in comparison with the Vec-Vec configuration. As shown by the charts in Figure 4, the increased performance of Vec-Vec comes at about a 6× increase in peak memory footprint when compared to L.List-L.List configuration. This increased footprint arises because the `std::vector` internally doubles its capacity as it grows. With many buckets in the `ladderQ`, each implemented using a `std::vector`, the overall peak memory footprint is higher. Certainly, the increased capacity is used if the number of events in buckets grow. However, the Vec-M.Set and Vec-Heap configurations consume a bit more memory in some configurations, showing that Vec-Vec is not the worst in memory consumption. Consequently, we use the Vec-Vec configuration as it provides the fastest performance among the 6 configurations (see Section 7.1).

The maximum number of rungs in the *Ladder* also influences the overall performance of the `ladderQ` [10]. The chart in Figure 5 illustrates the impact of limiting the maximum number of rungs in the `ladderQ`. When the rungs are too few, the timestamp-based width of buckets is larger and more events with many different timestamps are packed into buckets. This also causes the *Bottom* to be longer with events spanning a broader range of timestamps. Consequently, when inserts happen into *Bottom*, many *Bottom*-to-*Ladder* re-bucketing operations are triggered to ensure bottom is short. These re-bucketing operations with many events significantly degrade performance. However, once sufficient number of rungs (6 rungs in this case) are permitted the events are better subdivide into smaller timestamp-

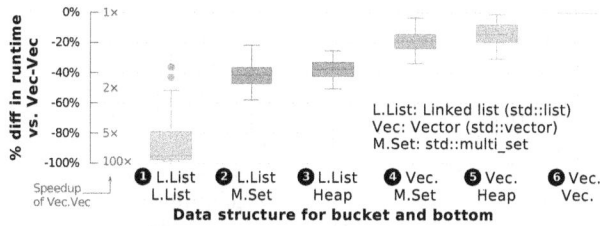

(a) Comparison sequential runtimes

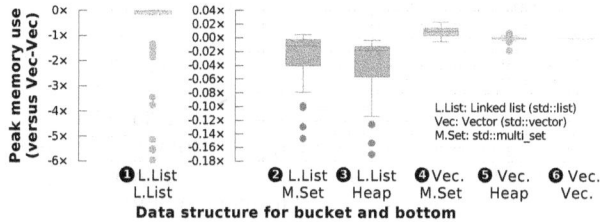

(b) Peak memory used

Figure 4: Comparison of execution time and peak memory for PHOLD benchmark (different parameter settings) using 6 different `ladderQ` configurations

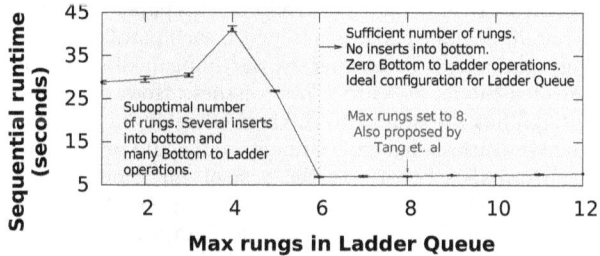

Figure 5: Impact of limiting rungs in Lader

based bucket widths. Small bucket widths in turn minimize inserts into bottom and *Bottom*-to-*Ladder* operations, ensuring good performance.

The chart in Figure 5 shows that a minimum of 6 rungs is required. For some select configurations of larger models we observed (data not shown) that 5 rungs would be sufficient. However, the number of rungs cannot exceed beyond a threshold to avoid infinite spawning of rungs [10]. Moreover, it limits the overheads involved in re-bucketing events from rung-to-rung [10]. Accordingly, based on the observations in Figure 5, we decided to adopt a maximum of 8 rungs, consistent with the threshold proposed by Tang *et al* [10]. Furthermore, we trigger *Bottom*-to-*Ladder* re-bucketing only if the *Bottom* has events at different timestamps to further reduce inefficiencies.

4.5.2 *Shortcoming of Ladder Queue for optimistic PDES*

The amortized constant time complexity of enqueue and dequeue operations enable the `ladderQ` to outperform other data structures in sequential simulations [2, 3, 10]. However, canceling events, requires a linear scan of pending events because *Top* and buckets in rungs are not sorted. In practice, scans of *Top*, *Ladder* rung buckets, and *Bottom* can be avoided based on cancellation times. Nevertheless, in a

general case, event cancellation time complexity is proportional to the number of pending events – *i.e.*, $O(e \cdot l)$ as summarized in Table 2. This issue is exacerbated in large simulations where thousands of events are typically present in *Top* and buckets in various rungs.

In this context, it is important to recollect from Section 2 that – as an optimization, MUSE utilizes only one antimessage to from LP_{sender} to LP_{dest} to cancel all n events sent after $t_{rollback}$ (rather than sending n individual antimessages) which reduces overheads. Furthermore, with our centralized scheduler design, only events received from LPs on other MPI-processes can trigger rollbacks. Consequently, the number of scans of the `ladderQ` that actually occurr is significantly fewer in our case, despite the aggressive cancellation strategy.

4.6 2-tier Ladder Queue (`2tLadderQ`)

A key shortcoming of the Ladder Queue for Time Warp based optimistic PDES arises from the overhead of canceling events used for rollback recovery. Our experiments (see Section 6) show that event cancellation overhead of `ladderQ` is a significant bottleneck in parallel simulation. On the other hand, our multi-tier data structures, where pending events are more organized, performed well.

Consequently, to reduce cost of event cancellation, we propose a 2-tier Ladder Queue (`2tLadderQ`) in which each bucket in *Top* and *Ladder* is further subdivided into $_{t2}k$ sub-buckets, where $_{t2}k$ is specified by the user. Figure 6 illustrates an overview of the `2tLadderQ` with $_{t2}k = 3$ sub-buckets in each bucket. Given a bucket, a hash of the sending LP's ID (or the receiver LP ID, one or the other but not both) is used to locate a sub-bucket into which the event is appended. Currently, we use a straightforward LP_{sender} modulo $_{t2}k$ as the hash function. Consequently, enqueue involves just 1 extra modulo instruction over regular `ladderQ` and hence retains its amortized constant time complexity. Similar to buckets, the sub-buckets are implemented using standard `std::vector` with events added or removed only from the end to ensure amortized constant-time operation.

The dequeue operations for a bucket require iterating over each sub-bucket. However, for a small, fixed value of $_{t2}k$, the overhead becomes an ammortized constant. The constant overhead is determined by the value of $_{t2}k$. Consequently, dequeue also retains the amortized constant characteristic from regular `ladderQ` as summarized in Table 2. Currently, we do not subdivide *Bottom* but leave it as a possible future optimization (link to source code in Section 7.1).

4.7 Performance gain of `2tLadderQ`

The primary performance gain for `2tLadderQ` arises from the reduced time complexity for event cancellation. Since each bucket is sub-divided, only $1 \div _{t2}k$ fraction of events need to be checked during cancellation. For example, if $_{t2}k=32$, only $\frac{1}{32}$ of the pending events are scanned during cancellation. This significantly reduces the time constants in larger simulations enabling rapid rollback recovery.

The value of $_{t2}k$ is a key parameter that influences the overall constants in `2tLadderQ`. For sequential simulation, where event cancellations do not occur, we recommend $_{t2}k=1$. With this setting the performance of `2tLadderQ` is very close to that of the regular `ladderQ`. However, in parallel simulation, the value of $_{t2}k$ must be greater than 1 to realize benefits of its design. Figure 7 shows the effect of chang-

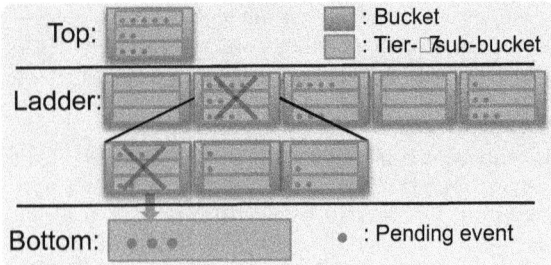

Figure 6: Structure of 2-tier Ladder Queue (2tLadderQ) with 3 sub-buckets / bucket (*i.e.*, $_{t2}k$=3)

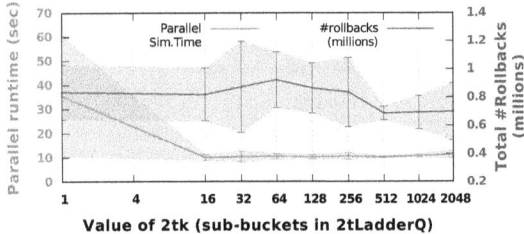

Figure 7: Effect of varying $_{t2}k$

ing the size of $_{t2}k$ in a parallel simulation with 16 MPI processes. The total rollbacks in the simulations were with 10% (except for $_{t2}k$=512, which for this model experienced fewer rollbacks). Nevertheless, for $_{t2}k$=1, the simulation has *much* higher runtime due to event cancellation overheads. The runtime dramatically decreases as $_{t2}k$ is increased. The runtime remains comparable for a broad range of values, namely: $64 \leq _{t2}k < 512$. However, for $_{t2}k \geq 512$, we noticed slow increase in runtime due to overhead of larger sub-buckets. Consequently, we have used a value of $_{t2}k$=128 for parallel simulation. We anticipate $_{t2}k$ value to vary depending on the hardware configuration of the compute cluster used for parallel simulation.

5. RELATED WORK

This paper proposes and explores multi-tier data structures for managing the pending event set in sequential and optimistic parallel simulations. Specifically, we compare effectiveness of the data structures against our fine-tuned version of the Ladder Queue [10] because it has shown to be very efficient for sequential Discrete Event Simulation (DES). Recently, Franceschini *et al* [3] compared several priority-queue based event list data structures to evaluate their performance in the context of sequential DEVS simulations. They found that the Ladder Queue outperformed every other priority queue based event lists data structure such as Sorted List, Minimal List, Binary Heap, Splay Tree, and Calendar Queue. We refer readers to the work by Tang *et al* [10] and Franceschini *et al* [3] for comparative discussion on the different data structures. They both use the classic Hold benchmark used in this study.

In contrast to earlier work, rather than using a linked list based implementation, we propose alternative implementation using dynamically growing arrays (*i.e.*, `std::vector`). Furthermore, we trigger *Bottom* to *Ladder* re-bucketing only if the *Bottom* has events at different timestamps to reduce inefficiencies. Our 2-tier Ladder Queue (`2tLadderQ`) is a

novel enhancement to the Ladder Queue to enable its efficient use in optimistic parallel simulations.

Dickman *et al* [2] compare event list data structures that consisted of Splay Tree, STL Multiset and Ladder Queue. However, the focus of their paper was in developing a framework for handling event list data structures in shared memory PDES. A central component of their study was the identification of an appropriate data structure and design for the shared event list. Gupta *et al* [4] extended their implementation of Ladder Queue for shared memory Time Warp based simulation environment, so that it supports lock-free access to events in the shared event lists. The modification involved the use of an unsorted lock-free queue in the underlying ladder queue structure. Quaglia [8] proposes a Low-Overhead Constant-Time (LOCT) secheduler that uses tree-like bitmaps which enables quick retrieval of events to be scheduled in a Time Warp simulator. Quaglia's experiments on multithreaded, shared memory architecture shows that the LOCT scheduler can outperform ladder queue, but the ladder queue has better overall efficiency [8]. Marotta *et al* [7] have contributed to the study of event list data structures in threaded PDES through the design of the Non-Blocking Priority Queue (NBPQ) data structure. An event list data structure that is closely related to Calendar Queues with constant time performance.

In contrast to aforementioned efforts, this paper focuses on distributed memory platforms in which each parallel process is single threaded. Consequently, our implementation does not involve thread synchronization issues. However, our 2-tier design has the ability to further reduce lock contention issues in multithreaded environments and could provide further performance boost. To the best of our knowledge, at the time of this paper, the Fibonacci heap (`fibHeap`) and our 3-tier Heap (`3tHeap`) are unique data structures that have potential to be effective in simulations with high concurrency.

6. EXPERIMENTS & DISCUSSIONS

Assessments of the effectiveness of the six scheduler queues from Section 4 have been conduced using different configurations of the PHOLD benchmark discussed in Section 3. The experiments were conducted on the distributed memory compute cluster described in Section 2.1. Our initial experimental analysis proved to be time consuming due to the large number of PHOLD parameters (see Table 1) and combinations of their values. Consequently, we pursued strategies to focus on most influential PHOLD parameters that impacted relative performance of the scheduler queues using Generalized Sensitivity Analysis (GSA) [5]. Section 6.1 discusses GSA experiments used to reduce the PHOLD parameter space and subsequent PHOLD configurations, called `ph3`, `ph4`, and `ph5`, used for further experiments. Section 6.2 and Section 6.3 discuss the results from sequential and parallel simulations conducted using `ph3`, `ph4`, and `ph5`.

6.1 Parameter reduction via GSA

Generalized Sensitivity Analysis (GSA) is based on two-sample Kolmogorov-Smirnov Test (KS-Test) and yields a $d_{m,n}$ statistic that is sensitive to differences in both central tendency and differences in the distribution functions of parameters [5]. The $d_{m,n}$ statistic is the maximum separation between cumulative probability distribution observed in a two-sample KS-Test. The KS-Test is performed with data from Monte Carlo simulations involving combinations of parameter values from a specified range or probability distribution. The simulation result is then classified into number of "success" (m) or its converse "failure" (n) to compute cumulative probability distribution and $d_{m,n}$ statistic for each parameter. In this study we have defined "failure" to be parameter values for which the `2tLadderQ` runs slower when compared to another scheduler queue. For sequential and parallel simulations we use $_{t2}k{=}1$ and $_{t2}k{=}128$ respectively.

An important aspect of GSA is to ensure that the values for each parameter covers its full range of values. Consequently, we use Sobol random numbers to select a combination of PHOLD parameter values to be used for simulation. Sobol random numbers are quasi-random low-discrepancy sequences that provide uniform coverage of a multidimensional parameter space for PHOLD (see Figure 2). Our parameter ranges also ensure that the peak memory consumption do not cross NUMA threshold, which in our case is 4 GB of RAM. Exceeding the 4 GB NUMA threshold introduces a lot of variance in runtimes requiring many runs to reduce variance to acceptable limits.

The randomly (using Sobol sequences) selected parameter set is used to run the model using two different scheduler queues. Average simulation execution time from 3 different replications is recorded for each scheduler queue along with the parameter-set. The process is repeated for 2,500 different Sobol sequences. The 2,500 data set is then collectively analyzed to compute the $d_{m,n}$ statistics for the different parameters. The results from sequential and parallel GSA are discussed in the following subsections.

6.1.1 GSA results for Sequential simulations

The charts in Figure 8 shows the cumulative m, n, and the $d_{m,n}$ statistics for the 9 different parameters explored using GSA for sequential simulations. The orange impulses show the parameter values and number of samples used for Monte Carlo simulation. Note that the distribution of samples varies depending on the nature of the parameter – *i.e.*, `eventsPerLP` varies in discrete steps of 1 from 1–20 while `imbalance` varies from 0 to 1.0 in small fractional steps.

The chart in Figure 9 shows the summary of the $d_{m,n}$ statistic or influence of each parameter (see Table 1) on the outcome – *i.e.*, `2tLadderQ` performs better or worse than `3tHeap`. The lightly shaded bands show the 95% Confidence Intervals (CI) computed using standard bootstrap approach using 5000 replications with 1000 samples in each. As expected, the `imbalance` (*i.e.*, skew in partition) has no impact in sequential simulation and has a low impact score of 0.037. Similarly, the GVT computation rate does not impact pending events and consequently its influence is low at 0.051.

Interestingly, other model parameters such as `rows`, `cols`, `self-events`, `simEndTime`, and `granularity` have no influence on relative performance of `2tLadderQ` vs `3tHeap`. The parameter with most influence is `eventsPerLP` with a score of 0.774. This parameter determines total number of concurrent events which influences bucket sizes and number of rungs in `2tLadderQ` as well as the third tier size in `3tHeap`. The parameter λ for exponential distribution has a marginal influence because it influences number of concurrent events as discussed in Section 3 and shown in Figure 2(c).

We have also conducted GSA to determine influential parameters impacting performance of other scheduler queues versus the `2tLadderQ` in sequential simulations (charts via

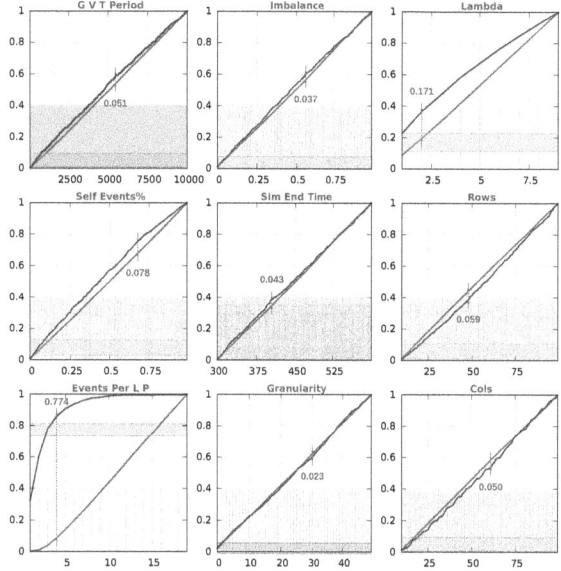

Figure 8: Results from Generalized Sensitivity Analysis (GSA) comparing 3tHeap and 2tLadderQ for sequential simulation (see Section 7.1 for more stats)

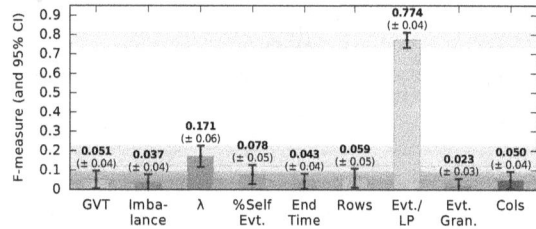

Figure 9: Summary of influential parameters from Figure 8 that cause performance differences between 2tLadderQ and 3tLadder in sequential simulations.

link in Section 7.1). Our analysis showed that none of the parameters play an influential role and the `2tLadderQ` performed consistently better or the same when compared to `ladderQ`, `2tHeap`, `fibHeap`, and `heap`. Only `3tHeap` and in few cases `2tHeap` outperformed our `2tLadderQ` in certain configurations. The performance of `ladderQ` and `2tLadderQ` was practically indistinguishable in sequential simulations (with $_{t2}k{=}1$).

<u>Summary</u>: GSA shows that for comparing event queue performance in sequential simulations using our PHOLD benchmark, we just need to focus on 1 or 2 parameters. Other aspects such as: model size, event granularity, fraction of self-events, GVT rate, etc., do not matter for comparison of scheduler queues. The scheduler queues to focus further analysis are: `ladderQ`, `2tLadderQ`, and `3tHeap`.

6.1.2 GSA results for Parallel simulations

GSA for parallel simulations were conducted using the same procedure discussed earlier but using 4 MPI-processes for parallel simulation. These analysis focused only on `ladderQ`, `2tLadderQ`, and `3tHeap` based on the inferences drawn from the earlier analyses. The average simulation execution time from 3 replications is recorded for each scheduler

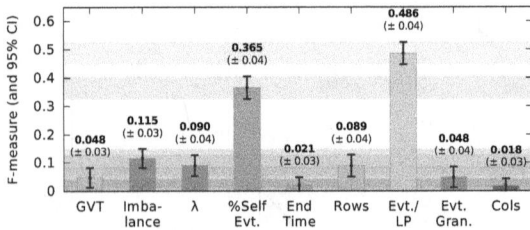

Figure 10: GSA data from parallel simulations (4 MPI-processes) showing influential parameters (2tLadderQ vs. 3tHeap).

Table 3: Configurations used for further analysis

Name	#LPs (Rows×Cols)	Sim. End Time	
		Seq	Parallel
ph3	1,000 (100×10)	5000	20000
ph4	10,000 (100×100)	500	5000
ph5	100,000 (1000×100)	100	1000

queue along with the parameter set. Initially, we observed that the `ladderQ` timings showed a lot of variance in runtime depending on number of rollbacks that occur. Consequently, to reduce variance, we have used a time-window of 10 time-units to curtail optimism and reduce rollbacks. The time-window restricts the simulation kernel from scheduling events that are more than 10 time-units ahead of GVT. We use the same time-window for all scheduler queues for consistent comparison and analysis.

The chart in Figure 10 shows the summary of the $d_{m,n}$ statistic or influence of each parameter (see Table 1) on the outcome – *i.e.*, `2tLadderQ` performs better or worse than `3tHeap`. The lightly shaded bands show the 95% Confidence Intervals (CI) computed using standard bootstrap approach using 5000 replications with 1000 samples in each. The parallel results are consistent with the sequential results and the `eventsPerLP` is the most influential parameter. However, in parallel simulation, the percentage of `selfEvents` (*i.e.*, LPs schedule events to themselves) has a more pronounced influence when compared to λ. The increased impact of `self-Events` arises due to the use of optimistic synchronization. The self-events are local and can be optimistically processed, with some being rolled back, causing more operations on a larger pending event set. The data also shows that conspicuous `imbalance` in partitioning or load balance has some influence on the outcomes. However, in this study we explore typical parallel simulation scenarios in which load is reasonably well balanced.

6.1.3 PHOLD *configurations for further analysis*

The Generalized Sensitivity Analysis (GSA) enables identification of influential parameters, thereby substantially reducing the parameter space. However, GSA data does not provide an effective data set to analyze trends, such as: scalability, memory usage, rollback behaviors, etc. In order to pursue such analysis we have used 3 different PHOLD configurations called `ph3`, `ph4`, and `ph5`. The fixed characteristics for the 3 configurations with non-influential parameters is summarized in Table 3. We use larger simulation end times for parallel simulation so obtain sufficiently long runtimes using 32 cores. The value of influential parameters, namely: `eventsPerLP`, `%selfEvents`, and λ is varied for comparing different settings, similar to the approach used by other investigators [10, 3].

6.2 Sequential simulation results

Sequential simulations were conducted to assess the effectiveness of the different data structures. We pursued sequential simulations to compare the base case performance of

the data structures, consistent with prior investigations [10, 3]. The sequential simulations also serve as a reference for potential use in conservatively synchronized PDES. The sequential experiments were conducted using 3 PHOLD configurations (see Section 6.1.3) on one compute node of our cluster described in Section 2.1. The simulations use only 1 MPI-process and states are not saved. Number of sub-buckets in `2tLadderQ` was set to 1, *i.e.*, t_2k=1. For these experiments, the influential parameters `eventsPerLP`, λ, and `%selfEvents` were varied to explore their impact on relative performance of the data structures. Event `granularity` was set to zero resulting in a fine grained simulation. For each configuration, data from 10 independent replications were collected and analyzed.

The charts in Figure 11(a)–(c) show change in runtime characteristics as the most influential parameter `eventsPerLP` is varied, for λ=1 (widest range of timestamps) and `%self-Events` = 0.25. This configuration was generally the best for `ladderQ`. As illustrated by Figure 11(a)–(c), the performance of `ladderQ` and `2tLadderQ` (t_2k=1) is comparable as expected. However, the `2tLadderQ` performs slightly (paired *t*-test p-value $\ll$ 0.05, *i.e.*, averages are not equal) better in some cases possibly due to improved caching resulting from smaller tier-2 sub-buckets. These two queues outperform the other queues for lower values of `eventsPerLP`.

However, the `3tHeap` generally outperforms the other queues (except for `2tHeap` in some cases) for higher values of `events-PerLP`. In all cases, there were no inserts into *Bottom* or *Bottom*-to-*Ladder* operations (discussed in Section 4.5.1) that degrade `ladderQ` performance. The size of the *Bottom* rung was proportional to the number of LPs and `eventsPerLP` – *i.e.*, with larger models, *Bottom* has more events for many LPs with the same timestamp to be scheduled. In the larger configurations, the maximum of 8 rungs were fully used. The maximum rung threshold of 8 was determined to be an effective setting as discussed in Section 4.5.1 and the same value proposed by Tang *et al* [10].

Profiler data (see Section 7.1) showed that the bottleneck in `ladderQ` arises from the overhead of re-bucketing events from rung-to-rung of the Ladder. On the other hand, in `3tHeap` re-bucketing does not occur. Consequently, the overheads of $O(\log \frac{e}{c})$ operations in `3tHeap` are amortized as number of concurrent events c increases.

The chart in Figure 11(d) shows the correlation between the 3 influential parameters and the performance difference between `3tHeap` and `ladderQ`. Consistent with the GSA results, the corellogram shows that the most influential parameter is `eventsPerLP` (R=0.93, p=0) followed by λ (R=0.19, p=0.192) with a very weak corellation. The `%selfEvents` has practically no impact on performance. The corellogram also shows that these parameters are independent and have no covariance between each other (R~0, p >0.95).

The charts in Figure 12 shows the peak memory usage

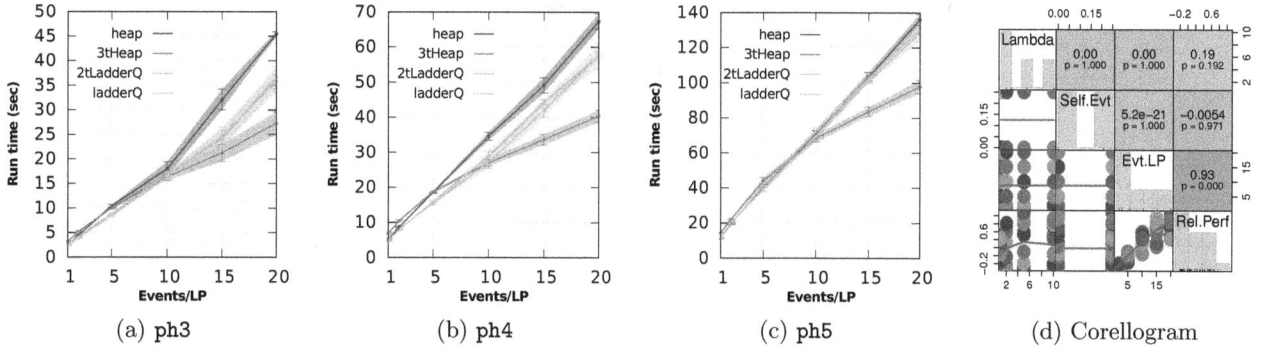

Figure 11: Sequential simulation runtimes and correlation of 3tHeap performance with PHOLD parameters

corresponding to the runtime data in Figure 11. The memory size reported is the "Maximum resident set size" value reported by GNU /usr/bin/time command on Linux. The memory usage of heap is the lowest in most cases. Since $t_2k=1$, the memory usage of ladderQ and 2tLadderQ is comparable as expected. The 3tHeap initially uses more memory than the other data structures because of many small std::vectors and due to std::vector doubling its capacity. However, the memory usage is amortized as the eventsPerLP increases. Consequently, the improved performance of 3tHeap over ladderQ is realized without significant increase in memory footprint.

6.3 Parallel simulation assessments

The sequential simulation assessments indicated that ladderQ, 2tLadderQ, and 3tHeap performed the best for a broad range of PHOLD parameter settings. Consequently, we focused on assessing the effectiveness of these 3 queues for Time Warp synchronized parallel simulations. The experiments were conducted on our compute cluster (see Section 2.1) using a varying number of MPI-processes, with one process per CPU-core. In order to ensure sufficiently long runtimes with 32-cores, we increased simEndTime for parallel simulations as tabulated in Table 3. The following subsections discuss results from the experiments.

6.3.1 Throttling optimism with a time-window

Initially we conducted experiments with fine-grained setting (*i.e.*, granularity = 0) from sequential simulations. We noticed that the ladderQ had a large variance in runtimes, particularly when it experienced many rollbacks. In several cases, cascading rollbacks significantly slowed the simulations – *i.e.*, ladderQ simulations required over 1 hour while 2tLadderQ would consistently finish in a few minutes. In order to avoid such debilitating rollback scenarios for ladderQ and to streamline experimental analysis timeframes (otherwise we would have to run 100s of replications for each configuration to reduce variance) we have throttled optimism using a time-window of 10 time-units. The time-window restricts the simulation kernel from scheduling events that are more than 10 time-units ahead of GVT – *i.e.*, the kernel spins (without optimistically processing pending events but performing other operations) waiting for GVT to advance. The time-window value of 10 is 50% of the maximum timestamp of events generated by exponential distribution with $\lambda = 1$. Consequently, most events in current schedule cycle will fit within this time-window with limited

impact on concurrency. We use the same time-window for all scheduler queues for consistent comparison and analysis.

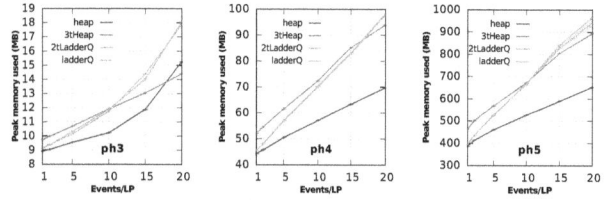

Figure 12: Comparison of peak memory usage

6.3.2 Efficient case for ladderQ

The charts in Figure 13 show key simulation statistics for low value of eventsPerLP = 2 and $\lambda=1$ for which ladderQ performed well, consistent with the observations in sequential simulations. The statistics show average and 95% CI computed from 10 independent replications for each data point. The peak rollbacks among all of the MPI-processes is shown as it controls overall progress in the parallel simulations. As illustrated by the data in Figure 13, both the ladderQ and 2tLadderQ perform well for all three models. In this configuration, overall the ladderQ experienced the fewest rollbacks. Nevertheless, the 2tLadderQ continues to perform well despite experiencing more rollbacks as shown in Figure 13(b). The good performance of 2tLadderQ under heavy rollback is consistent with its design objective to enable rapid event cancellation and improve rollback recovery. The maximum of 8 rungs on the ladder was reached in all the simulations, but with only few (1 to 3) buckets per rung. On average, the number of *Bottom* to Ladder operations (that degrade performance) were low per MPI process, about – ph3: {9144, 8911}, ph4: {1904, 1448}, and ph5: {53, 84} for {ladderQ, 2tLadderQ} respectively. We did not observe a strong correlation between number of these operations and rollbacks (see Section 7.1 for additional statistics).

In this configuration, the 3tHeap runs experienced a lot of rollbacks when compared to the other two queues despite the time-window. For ph5 data in Figure 13(c), 3tHeap experienced about 114805 rollbacks on average while ladderQ experienced only 2341, almost 50×fewer rollbacks. Consequently, it was slower than the other 2 queues, but its performance is not significantly degraded – ~1.5× slower despite 50× more rollbacks. The peak memory usage for all the 3 queues was comparable in these configurations.

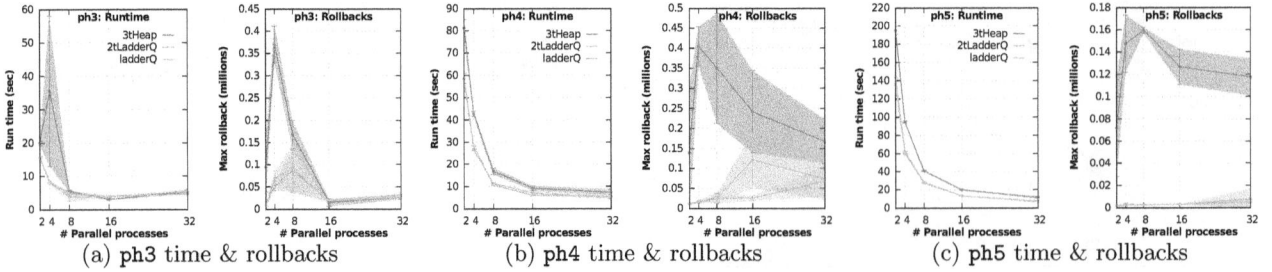

(a) ph3 time & rollbacks   (b) ph4 time & rollbacks   (c) ph5 time & rollbacks

Figure 13: Statistics from parallel simulation with `eventsPerLP=2`, $\lambda = 1$, %selfEvents=25%

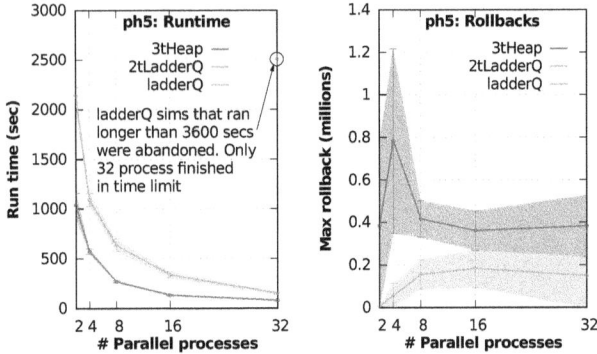

Figure 15: ph5 Statistics (best case for 3tHeap)

6.3.3 Knee point for 3tHeap vs. ladderQ

The charts in Figure 14 show key simulation statistics for the configuration where `3tHeap` and `ladderQ` performed about the same in sequential (see Figure 11). For `ph3`, both `ladderQ` and `2tLadderQ` experienced comparable number of rollbacks but the `2tLadderQ` performs better due to its design advantages. In the case of `ph4` and `ph5`, both the `ladderQ` and `3tHeap` experienced a comparable number of rollbacks, but much higher than the `2tLadderQ` despite having a time-window. Nevertheless, the `3tHeap` conspicuously outperforms the `ladderQ` because it is able to quickly cancel events and complete rollback processing. For `ph5`, the `3tHeap` outperforms the other 2 queues despite the high number of rollbacks. The peak memory usage for all the 3 queues was comparable in these configurations.

6.3.4 Best case for 3tHeap

Figure 15 shows simulation time and rollback characteristics in high concurrency configuration with `ph5`, with `eventsPerAgent=20`, $\lambda=10$, and %Self Evt.=25%. The `ladderQ` runs exceeded 3600 seconds in most cases even with a time-window, except for 32 processes. Consequently `ladderQ` experiments with fewer than 32 processes were abandoned. On the other hand `2tLadderQ` performed well due to its design. The `3tHeap` outperformed the other 2 queues despite experiencing $2\times$ more rollbacks.

7. CONCLUSIONS

Efficient data structures, *i.e.*, priority queues for managing pending event sets play a critical role in overall performance of both sequential and parallel simulations. In the context of this study, we broadly classified the queues into single-tiered (`heap`) or multi-tiered (`2tHeap`, `fibHeap`,

`3tHeap`, `ladderQ`, and `2tLadderQ`) data structures based on their design. Multi-tier data structures organize pending events into tiers, with each tier possibly implemented differently. Organizing events into multiple tiers decouples event management and Logical Process (LP) scheduling permitting different algorithms and data structures to suit the different needs.

The comparative analysis used a significantly fine-tuned version of the Ladder Queue (`ladderQ`) [10]. The objective of fine-tuning was to reduce the runtime constants of the `ladderQ` without significantly impacting its amortized $O(1)$ time complexity. Reduction in runtime constants is primarily realized by minimizing memory management overheads – *i.e.*, ❶ favor few bulk operations via `std::vector` than many small linked list nodes in `std::list` and ❷ recycle memory or substructures rather than reallocating them. Using `std::vector` (*i.e.*, dynamically growing array) enables use of algorithms with lower time constants, such as: `std::sort`, over `std::multiset` or binary heaps. The bulk memory operations do consume additional memory, but our analysis shows that the performance gains significantly outweigh the extra memory used. Ergo other simulation kernels can significantly improve overall performance by replacing linked lists with dynamically growing arrays.

One challenge that arose during design of experiments was exploring the large multidimensional parameter space in the PHOLD synthetic benchmark. Large parameter spaces may also arise with actual simulation models. We propose the use of Generalized Sensitivity Analysis (GSA) to reduce the parameter space. We also propose the use of Sobol random numbers to enable consistent exploration of the parameter space. GSA does require many simulations to be run to fully explore the parameter space. In our case, we ran 2,500 × 3 = 7,500 replications. However, GSA was able to significantly narrow the parameter space, *i.e.*, from 9 down to 2, in a scientific manner. GSA data shows that concurrency per LP indicated by `eventsPerLP` parameter (*i.e.*, batch of events scheduled per LP), plays the most dominant role in our benchmark. The data was cross-verified using corellograms from longer simulations. Similar GSA analysis can be applied to other models and benchmarks enabling consistent and focused analyses.

The sequential and parallel simulation results showed that `2tLadderQ` performs no worse than our fine-tuned `ladderQ` in sequential simulations (with $_{t2}k=1$). Furthermore, our `2tLadderQ` outperforms our `ladderQ` in parallel simulations because of its design that enables rapid cancellation of events during rollbacks. In fact, the `ladderQ` required aggressive throttling of optimism without which `ladderQ` was impractical to use in scenarios with many cascading rollbacks. These

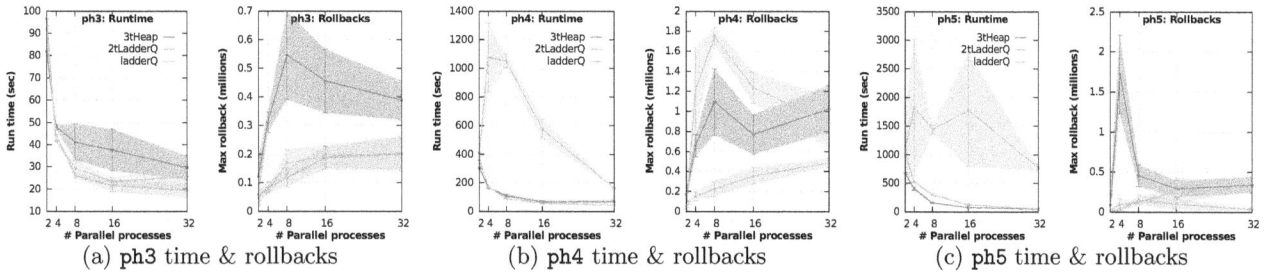

(a) ph3 time & rollbacks   (b) ph4 time & rollbacks   (c) ph5 time & rollbacks

Figure 14: Statistics from parallel simulation with eventsPerLP=10, $\lambda = 10$, %selfEvents=25%

experiments were conducted with fine-grained settings (*i.e.*, granularity=0) and results may vary with granularity. However, GSA data suggests that the variation with changing granularity would be small. However, increased granularity may allow relaxation of the time-window. The results strongly favor the general use of 2tLadderQ over the ladderQ. Furthermore, the multi-tier organization of 2tLadderQ can further reduce lock contention and consequent synchronization overheads in multithreaded simulations.

The experiments show that the runtime constants play an important role – for example, the Fibonacci heap with its $O(1)$ time complexity for many operations still did not perform well in our benchmarks. The 3tHeap has a much lower runtime constants enabling it to outperform the fibHeap in almost all cases. In sequential simulations, the advantages of 3tHeap are realized in simulations that have higher concurrency (*i.e.*, larger batches of events) per LP. Figure 16 summarizes the effective regions observed for the 3 queues. The advantages of 3tHeap is realized only when each LP has 10 or more concurrent events at each time step. Such scenarios with high eventsPerLP arises in epidemic models [9] and detailed simulation models such as packet-level network simulations [10]. However, further experimental analysis with a broader range of models and configurations is needed to formally verify effectiveness of 3tHeap. Moreover, different implementations, possibly in different programming languages will provide rigorous validation to ensure the results are algorithmic and not an artifact of one specific implementation.

The multi-tier data structures enjoy lower runtime constants for event cancellation operations which play an influential role in

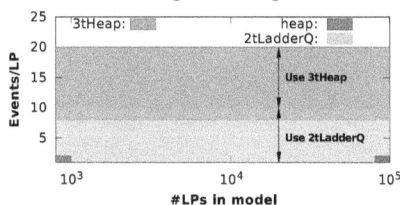

Figure 16: Effective regions of use

Time Warp synchronized parallel simulations. Therefore, the multi-tier data structures perform consistently better in optimistic parallel simulations.

In overall summary, our analysis strongly favor broad use of our multi-tier queues, specifically 2tLadderQ and 3tHeap, replacing all existing DES data structures. The 2tLadderQ and 3tHeap are consistently effective in sequential and parallel simulations, with sequential results also bearing potential application to conservative and multithreaded simulations.

7.1 Supplementary Material

Source code for MUSE and supplementary material available online at http://pc2lab.cec.miamiOH.edu/muse/

Acknowledgments
Support for this work was provided in part by the Miami University Global Health Research Innovation Center.

8. REFERENCES

[1] C. D. Carothers and K. S. Perumalla. On deciding between conservative and optimistic approaches on massively parallel platforms. In *Proceedings of the Winter Simulation Conference*, WSC '10, pages 678–687, Baltimore, Maryland, 2010.

[2] T. Dickman, S. Gupta, and P. A. Wilsey. Event pool structures for pdes on many-core beowulf clusters. In *Proceedings of ACM SIGSIM PADS*, pages 103–114, New York, NY, USA, 2013. ACM.

[3] R. Franceschini, P.-A. Bisgambiglia, and P. Bisgambiglia. A comparative study of pending event set implementations for pdevs simulation. In *DEVS Integrative M&S Symposium*, pages 77–84, San Diego, CA, USA, 2015. SCS.

[4] S. Gupta and P. A. Wilsey. Lock-free pending event set management in time warp. In *Proceedings of the ACM SIGSIM PADS*, pages 15–26, New York, NY, USA, 2014. ACM.

[5] B. Guven and A. Howard. Identifying the critical parameters of a cyanobacterial growth and movement model by using generalised sensitivity analysis. *Ecological Modelling*, 207(1):11 – 21, 2007.

[6] S. Jafer, Q. Liu, and G. Wainer. Synchronization methods in parallel and distributed discrete-event simulation. *Simulation Modelling Practice and Theory*, 30:54–73, 2013.

[7] R. Marotta, M. Ianni, A. Pellegrini, and F. Quaglia. A non-blocking priority queue for the pending event set. In *Proceedings of the 9th EAI International Conference on Simulation Tools and Techniques*, SIMUTOOLS'16, pages 46–55, ICST, Brussels, Belgium, Belgium, 2016.

[8] F. Quaglia. A low-overhead constant-time lowest-timestamp-first CPU scheduler for high-performance optimistic simulation platforms. *Simulation Modelling Practice and Theory*, 53:103–122, 2015.

[9] D. M. Rao. Efficient parallel simulation of spatially-explicit agent-based epidemiological models. *Journal of Parallel and Distributed Computing*, 93-94:102–119, 2016.

[10] W. T. Tang, R. S. M. Goh, and I. L.-J. Thng. Ladder queue: An O(1) priority queue structure for large-scale discrete event simulation. *ACM Trans. Model. Comput. Simul.*, 15(3):175–204, July 2005.

A Conflict-Resilient Lock-Free Calendar Queue for Scalable Share-Everything PDES Platforms

Romolo Marotta, Mauro Ianni, Alessandro Pellegrini, Francesco Quaglia
Sapienza, University of Rome
{marotta,mianni,pellegrini,quaglia}@dis.uniroma1.it

ABSTRACT

Emerging share-everything Parallel Discrete Event Simulation (PDES) platforms rely on worker threads fully sharing the workload of events to be processed. These platforms require efficient event pool data structures enabling high concurrency of extraction/insertion operations. Nonblocking event pool algorithms are raising as promising solutions for this problem. However, the classical non-blocking paradigm leads concurrent conflicting operations, acting on a same portion of the event pool data structure, to abort and then retry. In this article we present a conflict-resilient nonblocking calendar queue that enables conflicting dequeue operations, concurrently attempting to extract the minimum element, to survive, thus improving the level of scalability of accesses to the hot portion of the data structure—namely the bucket to which the current locality of the events to be processed is bound. We have integrated our solution within an open source share-everything PDES platform and report the results of an experimental analysis of the proposed concurrent data structure compared to some literature solutions.

1. INTRODUCTION

The advent and large diffusion of multi-core machines has impacted the way Parallel Discrete Event Simulation (PDES) platforms are built. They still adhere to the archetypal organization [6] where the overall simulation model is partitioned into interacting distinct entities—the so called simulation objects—yet they do no longer necessarily follow the classical multi-thread organization [27] where objects are (temporarily) bound to specific worker threads. Indeed, the possibility to share any PDES-engine data structure across threads, as well as the actual simulation objects' state, has led to the raise up of new architectural paradigms.

A current trend is the one of building PDES platforms as "share-everything" systems [14]. In this paradigm, an event (which may target any simulation object) can be picked by any worker thread for actual processing. As an extreme,

multiple worker threads can even pick events destined to the same simulation object at the same time [19], leading the simulation object to no longer figure out as a sequential entity [17]. Clearly, share-everything PDES platforms allow concentrating the computing power—namely, the worker threads which are operating within the PDES environment—on the higher-priority pending events. Indeed, each worker thread picks events with lower timestamps without considering any partial view of the pending event set—the view generated by partitioning simulation objects across threads. PDES platforms adhering to the share-everything paradigm, or at least tending to this type of architectural organization, can be found in [4, 19, 10, 5, 14].

This re-organization demands for some efficient *global pool* of pending events. Indeed, a core challenge when designing share-everything PDES platforms is to ensure that fully-shared data structures—most notably, the ones used at the level of the simulation engine—guarantee scalability of concurrent accesses. In particular, the pool keeping the pending events destined to whichever simulation object plays a core role to enable scalability of the overall PDES platform. Such a pool should in fact guarantee high concurrency of the accesses for both extraction of the events to be processed, and insertion of newly-scheduled events that result from the processing activities at some object.

Handling concurrent accesses to a fully-shared event pool by relying on critical sections protected via locks (e.g. spin-locks) does not ensure scalability, thus figuring out as an adequate approach limited to a reduced number of threads. For this reason, recent studies [10, 5, 14] have targeted the design of event pool data structures based on the lock-free paradigm. Here concurrent threads attempt to perform their operations—either an extraction or an insertion—without the need to take any lock. To leave the data structure in a consistent state, threads determine whether the operation can be correctly finalized by relying on atomic Read-Write-Modify (RMW) machine instructions [20], offered by off-the-shelf architectures, such as Compare-and-Swap (CAS). These instructions are used to determine whether the snapshot of the data structure (or a portion of it) accessed by a thread has been concurrently altered by some other thread. If this occurs, the operation has observed a stale snapshot, and is therefore deemed invalid. Therefore, it is aborted and then retried. In some sense, the operation is seen like an in-memory transaction, which is committed or aborted depending on whether it faces a conflict with a concurrent operation. Although this approach explicitly avoids blocking

SIGSIM-PADS '17, May 24–26, 2017, Singapore.

© 2017 ACM. ISBN 978-1-4503-4489-0/17/05. . . $15.00

DOI: http://dx.doi.org/10.1145/3064911.3064926

threads, thus enabling resilience versus thread reschedules, it may still be considered sub-optimal in scenarios where the likelihood of conflicts among concurrent operations is non-minimal. In fact, we may still experience a significant volume of operation aborts/retries.

In this article, we take the lock-free calendar queue presented in [14] as our reference and present the design of an innovative version that has the property of being conflict-resilient[1]. Conflict resilience is achieved in relation to concurrent extractions. This is a relevant objective since, in share-everything PDES, concurrent extractions are highly likely bound to the same bucket of the calendar—thus touching the same portion of the whole data structure—namely the bucket containing the event with the minimum timestamp. This bucket is somehow the "hot" one in the whole calendar, since any thread will attempt to pick its next event exactly from that bucket. On the other hand, newly-produced events will more likely carry timestamps associated with different buckets (i.e., buckets in the future), which automatically decreases the likelihood of conflicting on concurrent insertion operations.

As opposed to the approach in [14], the lock-free calendar queue we present in this article makes an extraction operation still valid (i.e., committable) in scenarios where some concurrent extraction has changed the snapshot of the currently hot bucket. Rather, the extraction will be aborted only in case the hot bucket becomes (logically) empty while attempting to extract from it. This is the scenario where a new bucket becomes the hot one, meaning that the locality of the processing activities within the simulation model has moved to a subsequent logical time interval.

We also discuss (and investigate experimentally) how to dynamically resize the width of the buckets in the calendar, which in turn affects the length of the chain of events that are expected to fall within the hot bucket. As we will show, when allowing conflict-resilient lock-free concurrent accesses to the calendar queue, classical policies for resizing the buckets (like the one proposed in the context of sequential accesses to the classical calendar queue presented in [3]) are no longer optimal. This is because the length of the chain of events associated with the buckets affects both:

- the time complexity for the access to the bucket chain, which in our case still stands as amortized constant time; this aspect was already captured by the work in [14];
- the actual number of concurrent extractions from the same bucket which are allowed to be still committable, even if the snapshot of that bucket-chain concurrently changes; this aspect is intrinsically new and specifically related to our conflict-resilient lock-free calendar queue proposal.

The experimental data we report in support of the effectiveness of our proposal, in terms of scalability in face of concurrent accesses, have been collected in differentiated scenarios: one where we test the conflict-resilient lock-free calendar queue as a stand-alone component via synthetic workloads based on the hold model [26], and a second one where the calendar queue has been integrated with a share-everything PDES platform [4], allowing us to test its effects on scalability and performance via both the PHOLD synthetic benchmark for PDES [7] and an agent-based simulation model [12].

The remainder of this article is structured as follows. In Section 2, we discuss related work. The baseline implementation of the lock-free calendar queue we take as the reference for our work is discussed in Section 3. Our conflict-resilient lock-free calendar queue is presented in Section 4. Experimental data are provided in Section 5.

2. RELATED WORK

Event pools constitute core components in both sequential and parallel simulation engines, and the literature on this topic offers a set of differentiated solutions, each one aimed at optimizing the effectiveness of the event pool data structure under specific workloads or execution scenarios. The original Calendar Queue presented in [3] is a timestamp-ordered data structure based on multi-lists, each one associated with a time bucket, which offers amortized constant time insertion of events with generic timestamps and constant time extraction of the event with the minimum timestamp. The Ladder Queue [24] is a variant of the Calendar Queue which is more suited for skewed distributions of the timestamps of the events, thanks to the possibility of dynamically splitting an individual bucket in sub-intervals (i.e., sublists of records) if the number of elements associated with the bucket exceeds a given threshold. The LOCT Queue [16] is an additional variant which allows reducing the actual overhead for constant time insertion/extraction operations thanks to the introduction of a compact hierarchical bitmap indicating the status of any bucket (empty or not). None of these proposals has been devised for concurrent accesses. Therefore, their usage in scenarios with sharing among multiple threads would require a global lock for serializing the accesses, which would be detrimental to scalability, as shown in [8].

The work in [2] provides an event-pool data structure enabling parallel accesses via fine-grain locking of a sub-portion of the data structure upon performing an operation. However, the intrinsic scalability limitations of locking still lead this proposal to be not suited for large levels of parallelism, as also shown in [18].

As for lock-free management of sets by concurrent threads, various proposals exist (e.g., lock-free linked lists [9] or skip-lists [21]), which anyhow do not offer constant time operations. The lock-free linked list pays a linear cost for ordered insertions, while the skip-list pays logarithmic cost for this same type of operation. The proposal in [13] is based on lock-free access to a multi-bucket data structure, and provides amortized $O(1)$ time complexity for both insertion and extraction operations. However, it does not provide a lock-free scheme for the dynamical resize of the bucket width. Hence, to achieve adequate amortizing factors, all the threads would need to (periodically) synchronize to change the bucket width and redistribute events over the reshaped buckets. On the other hand, avoiding at all the synchronized reshuffle of the buckets might give rise to non-competitive amortizing factors (say too many elements associated with a bucket). The proposal in [14] enables non-blocking reshuffle of the bucket width, but does not guarantee conflict resilience of extraction operations targeting the "hot" bucket to which the locality of the activities within the simulation model is bound. Hence as soon as two or more extraction operations are executed concurrently and conflict, just one

---
[1]The source code of our implementation can be found at https://github.com/HPDCS/CRCQ

of them is allowed to be finalized with no retry cycle. Our present proposal exactly tackles this problem.

Lock-free operations in combination with constant time complexity have also been studied in [8], which presents a variation of the Ladder Queue where the elements are at any time bound to the correct bucket, but the bucket list is not ordered. Constant time is achieved since the extraction from an unordered bucket returns the first available element, which does not necessarily corresponds to the one with the minimum timestamp. This proposal is intrinsically tailored for PDES systems relying on speculative processing, where unordered extractions leading to causal inconsistencies within the simulation model trajectory are reversed (in terms of their effects on the simulation model trajectory) via proper rollback mechanisms. However, still for speculative PDES, a few recent results [4, 19] have shown the relevance of fetching events from the shared pool in correct order, as a means to build efficient synchronization schemes able to exploit alternative forms of reversibility, which stand aside of the traditional Time Warp protocol [11]. Correct order of delivery is guaranteed in our proposal, since we always deliver the highest priority event currently in the event pool, which has been inserted by any operation that is linearized prior to the extraction.

The recent proposal in [10] explores the idea of managing concurrent accesses to a shared pool by relying on Hardware Transactional Memory (HTM) support. Insertions and extractions are performed as HTM-based transactions, hence in non-blocking mode. However, the level of scalability of this approach is limited by the level of parallelism in the underlying HTM-equipped machine, which nowadays is relatively small. Also, HTM-based transactions can abort for several reasons, not necessarily related to conflicting concurrent accesses to a same portion of the data structure. As an example, they can abort because of conflicting accesses to the same cache line by multiple CPU-cores, which might be adverse to PDES models with, e.g., very large event pools. Our proposal does not require special hardware support, thus fully eliminating the secondary effects caused by, e.g., HTM limitations on the abort rate of the operations.

3. RECAP ON THE REFERENCE SOLUTION

As mentioned, our reference solution is the one presented in [14]. The main idea behind this work is to build a lock-free pending event set directly inspired to the classical calendar queue [3]. More in detail, the presented variant is composed of an array of entries referred to as *physical buckets*, each of which is the head element of a lock-free ordered linked list implemented according to [9], with some modifications. The list in [14] relies on the two least-significant bits of the pointer to the next node[2] to represent four different states of a node. The time axis is divided into equal slots, called *virtual buckets*, each of which covers a time interval bw called bucket width. Each virtual bucket is associated with a physical bucket in a circular fashion.

In order to ensure consistency with concurrent accesses, the operations on the lock-free calendar queue rely on atomic RMW instructions, in particular CAS and Fetch-and-Add (Fetch&Add). The first type of instruction is used to update a given memory location only if its current content is equal

---

[2] 4-bytes alignment ensures that such bits are always set to zero.

to a given value, otherwise no memory update takes place and we say that the CAS instruction fails. The second type of instruction gathers the value stored in a given memory location, while atomically incrementing it of a given amount, so any read on that same memory location that is linearized after the execution of Fetch&Add necessarily observes the updated value.

When a new event e with timestamp T_e is enqueued, the index I_{pb} of the target physical bucket for the insertion is computed as $I_{pb} = (I_{vb} \mod L)$, where L is the calendar length, namely the number of physical buckets, and I_{vb} is the index of the virtual bucket associated with the time slot TS such that $T_e \in TS$. I_{vb} is computed as $I_{vb} = \lfloor \frac{T_e}{bw} \rfloor$. Finally e is inserted into the I_{pb}-th physical bucket applying the lock-free list-insertion logic defined in [9]. In more detail, the enqueue scans the physical bucket list and when it finds the correct position in the list, it inserts the new event by executing a CAS instruction that manipulates the pointer of the node that must precede the one to be inserted. Clearly, given the execution semantic of CAS, two concurrent conflicting attempts to manipulate that same pointer will lead one of the operations to fail, thus ensuring consistency of the manipulated list—namely, correct linking of its nodes. The failed insertion operation, if any, is then retried.

An integer C is associated with the calendar, which stores the index of the virtual bucket containing the event with the minimum timestamp, namely the event with the highest priority. A dequeue operation starts by retrieving the value C in order to extract the first node stored into the C-th virtual bucket, which is actually stored into the C_{phy}-th physical bucket, where $C_{phy} = (C \mod L)$. A node is removed by marking it as invalid, flipping the least significant bit of the pointer to the next node with a CAS instruction. Clearly, if two concurrent extractions of the minimum try to mark the same node as invalid, then one of them will fail. When the virtual bucket identified by C is empty, the event to extract has to be searched on the next one, then C is incremented by one and the whole operation is restarted.

Going back to enqueue operations, an additional challenge consists in handling insertions in the past of the current minimum timestamp, which may occur either in the current bucket or in a previous one. Although it is known that this type of insertion will never occur for the case of sequential simulation engines, where there is a guarantee of model-wide causality of the generation of the events during model execution, one needs to face this issue when adopting a lock-free calendar queue as the shared pool in the context of PDES systems. As an example, if speculative processing schemes are enabled by the PDES engine, then the current minimum timestamp stored by the calendar queue might not correspond to an event which is causally safe. To cope with such a scenario the proposal in [14] makes the enqueue that inserts an event with timestamp lower than the currently queued minimum repeatedly try to update the value of C with $I_e = \lfloor \frac{T_e}{bw} \rfloor$ by CAS, until it has assumed a value $C' \leq I_e$.

Anyhow, this is not sufficient to guarantee correctness. Let us consider an execution where a process P_1 is executing a dequeue and reads a value C_1 of current. After that, P_1 is descheduled and a second process P_2 takes control and executes two consecutive enqueues. The first enqueued event e_a has a timestamp T_a such that $I_a = \lfloor \frac{T_a}{bw} \rfloor$ and $I_a < C_1$. The second event e_b has a timestamp T_b such that $I_b = \lfloor \frac{T_b}{bw} \rfloor$ and $I_b = C_1$. Moreover, let us assume that e_b is now the event

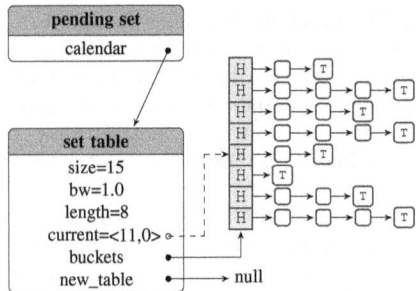

Figure 1: Scheme of the data structure.

with the minimum timestamp in the C_1-th virtual bucket. At this point P_1 is scheduled and continues its operation. In particular it scans the C_1-th bucket and returns e_b. This execution is incorrect since it violates the priority queue semantics, in fact there is a dequeue which returns e_B while e_A was the minimum. For this reason in [14] a dequeue operation re-checks the value of C after it has retrieved the first node from the bucket. If it is unchanged, it means that there has been no enqueue which has been finalized, namely has passed its *linearization point*, and has inserted a node in a previous bucket.

Clearly, any concurrent priority queue has an inherent bottleneck in the retrieval of the element with the minimum timestamp, since at any time it is materialized in a single element, located into a specific bucket [1], while insertion operations can be scattered across different buckets depending on the distribution of the timestamps of the events that are dynamically generated. Given that concurrent dequeues in the approach in [14] try to update the same pointer in the lock-free list via CAS, once hit a same node for extraction, just one of them can succeed, leading any other to fully restart. This problem is clearly exacerbated when increasing the level of concurrency of extraction operations. In other words, such concurrent dequeues always try to commit by hitting the first node of the current bucket, thus not attempting to adopt a fall back on the extraction of a subsequent node, without the need to fully restart the dequeue operation. This type of fall back behavior is what we term conflict resilience, which would lead an ongoing extraction operation to slide towards the subsequent element of the bucket list. The complexity of this type of approach stands in how we still allow linearizability of the concurrent operations on the calendar queue, including the possible mix of dequeues and enqueues bound to the same bucket, as we shall discuss.

4. THE CONFLICT-RESILIENT LOCK-FREE CALENDAR QUEUE

The basic organization of the data structure of our conflict resilient calendar queue, which is similar to the one presented in [14], is provided in Figure 1. Essentially it consists of a pointer to a table called *Set Table* which maintains the metadata required for its management. In particular: i) bw stores the actual bucket width of the data structure; ii) length is the number of buckets in the calendar; iii) size keeps the number of stored events; iv) current is a pair $\langle index, epoch \rangle$ such that *index* is the index of the virtual bucket containing the minimum and *epoch* is a value whose

role will be explained later; v) buckets is a pointer to the array that keeps the physical buckets; vi) new_table is a reference initialized to null which is used only during the resize phase of the calendar. To ensure consistency of concurrent accesses to our data structure, we rely on three different RMW instructions, namely CAS, Fetch&Add and *Fetch and Or* (Fetch&Or).

To avoid the effects of conflicts while concurrently extracting elements from the current bucket, we have introduced a set of capabilities oriented to reduce the need to fully restart the operations, reducing in this way the amount of wasted work. Indeed, reducing the CPU-time required to actually extract a node, by avoiding fully restarting the extraction in case of conflicts, we can reduce the negative performance effects possibly caused by a larger number of conflicting threads.

To achieve this target, we have exploited the newly introduced data-structure field, called *epoch*. As hinted it is stored inside current and is used to identify the instant in time at which an operation is performed, in order to reconstruct a partial temporal order among operations. A new epoch starts each time a new node is inserted in the past or in the current virtual bucket. This represents a critical instant in the state trajectory of the calendar queue since it means that a change in the minimum, or in the recorded timestamps that can be close to the minimum, is happened.

When enqueue or dequeue operations are invoked, the READTABLE() procedure is performed to retrieve a pointer to a valid set table. The objective of this procedure is to check if there is a resize operation currently in place on the calendar queue with the goal to assist the threads involved in this operation until it is completed. When no resize operation is in place, the reference to the current valid version of the table can be returned for actually performing extractions or insertions. All the operations on the lock-free calendar queue, including the resize, are described in detail in the next sections.

4.1 Enqueue Operation

The pseudo-code for the ENQUEUE() operation is shown in Algorithm 1. This operation takes in input an event e and the timestamp T_e associated with it. Once retrieved a valid set table reference using the READTABLE() procedure, the enqueue determines the correct physical bucket associated with the timestamp T_e, computing it as $i = (\lfloor \frac{T_e}{BW} \rfloor \mod B)$ where BW is the (current) bucket width and B is the size of the calendar, namely the number of physical buckets. Since the i-th bucket is a lock-free linked list implemented according to the indications in [9], we can use the provided search procedure to identify the right point for the insertion of the new node, with minimal changes due to the different states a node can pass through in our implementation. Executing the search procedure we retrieve a couple of nodes, called *left* and *right*, that would surround the new one. When performed, the search procedure tries to compact the nodes marked as deleted that are between the left and the right one, with the aim to return a coherent snapshot of the list. To manage events with the same timestamp, each event stores an increasing sequence number, unique with respect to the nodes with the same timestamp. In this way the couple $\langle timestamp, sequence\_number \rangle$ provides a total order among all stored nodes.

Algorithm 1 lock-free ENQUEUE

```
 1: procedure ENQUEUE(event e)
 2:     tmp ← new node(e)
 3:     repeat
 4:         h ← READTABLE( )
 5:         nc ← ⌊ n / h.bw ⌋
 6:         bucket ← h.table[nc mod h.length]
 7:         ⟨left, right⟩ ← bucket.SEARCH(tmp.t, VAL | MOV)
 8:         tmp.next ← right
 9:         old ← h.current
10:         tmp.epoch ← old.epoch
11:     until CAS(&left.next, UNMARK(right), tmp)
12:     repeat
13:         old ← h.current
14:         if nc > old.value then
15:             break
16:     until CAS(&h.current, old, ⟨nc, old.epoch + 1⟩)
17:     Fetch&Add(&h.size, 1)
```

Algorithm 2 lock-free DEQUEUE

```
 1: procedure DEQUEUE( )
 2:     while true do
 3:         h ← READTABLE()
 4:         oldCur ← h.current
 5:         cur ← oldCur.value
 6:         myEpoch ← oldCur.epoch
 7:         bucket ← h.table[cur + + mod h.t_size]
 8:         left ← bucket.next
 9:         min_next ← left
10:         if ISMARKED(left,MOV) then
11:             continue
12:         while left.local_epoch ≤ myEpoch  do
13:             right ← left.next
14:             if ¬ISMARKED(right) then
15:                 if left.ts < cur · h.bw then
16:                     right ← Fetch&Or(&left.next, DEL)
17:                     if ¬ISMARKED(right) then
18:                         Fetch&Add(&h.size, -1)
19:                         return left.event
20:                 else
21:                     if left = tail ∧ h.t_size = 1 then
22:                         return null
23:                     CAS(&bucket.next, min_next, left)
24:                     CAS(&h.current, oldCur, ⟨cur, myEpoch⟩)
25:                     break
26:             if ISMARKED(right,MOV) then
27:                 break
28:             left ← UNMARK(right)
```

Once retrieved the surrounding nodes, the node to be inserted is updated with a reference to the *right* node and with the epoch number retrieved from the **current** field. Finally the node is physically inserted into the list by performing a **CAS** operation on the next field of the *left* node making it point to the new one. If the **CAS** fails, the whole operation starts again from scratch. However, concurrent insertion operations, as we discussed, are typically less critical in terms of conflicts since they likely span different buckets of the calendar, or different surrounding nodes within a bucket.

To complete the update of the structure, the procedure checks if the inserted node belongs to a virtual bucket less than or equal to the one pointed by **current**, namely if the new event stands in the past or around the minimum. In the positive case, it updates the index kept by **current**. As hinted before, the enqueue of a node in the past modifies the minimum element of the queue. Therefore, the epoch number kept by **current** is incremented by one when updating this variable, starting in this way a new epoch of the whole calendar queue. As last operation, the **size** field is incremented by one to reflect the fact that the queue has been increased, in terms of kept elements. Atomicity of all these operations is guaranteed by relying on **CAS** and **Fetch&Add** instructions.

4.2 Dequeue Operation

Compared to the work in [14], the DEQUEUE() operation has been fully reshuffled so that the largest amount of carried-out work is useful also in case of conflicts, thus achieving conflict resilience. The pseudo-code of the DEQUEUE() operation is shown in Algorithm 2. Similarly to the enqueue operation, a dequeue starts by issuing a call to READTABLE(), in order to retrieve a valid table reference. It then fetches the **current** field, in order to extract the *index* of the virtual bucket storing the minimum-timestamp event and the current *epoch*. The physical bucket from which to start the extraction procedure is determined as $i = (index \bmod B)$, where B is the size of the calendar. Once the correct physical bucket is identified, it is scanned from the head, looking for a node valid for extraction.

However, we must ensure that the pointed node belongs to the current virtual bucket, since the list associated with a physical bucket might cover multiple virtual buckets. To this end, for each node, we check if the timestamp of the node belongs to the current virtual bucket. Moreover, to avoid the extraction of a node which has just been deleted (unlinked) or marked as invalid (logically deleted), we check whether the two last bits of the next field of the node keep some mark. Finally, according to the new conflict-resilient organization of the queue, we also need to check whether the node is valid with respect to the semantic of the dequeue operation. To this end, we must verify that the node belongs to an epoch earlier than the one read from **current** at the begin of the dequeue operation, or it belongs to the same one. If this condition is true, then the node was inserted before the beginning of the dequeue operation or, alternatively, it was placed in the future (with respect to the current bucket). In this scenario the state of the node is compliant to the semantic of the dequeue operation, thus it can be safely dequeued. In fact, its insertion was correctly linearized before the current (concurrent) extraction. Differently, if the above condition is not verified, then the node was inserted after the beginning of the current dequeue procedure, in particular after the initialization of a new epoch. Therefore, its insertion might have occurred after that a new minimum has been enqueued. In this latter case, the node cannot be extracted.

If the end of the current virtual bucket is reached without finding a valid node, either the current physical bucket is empty or the present nodes belong to a future time slot. In both cases, the procedure must continue the search for the minimum in the next bucket. Hence, **current** is atomically updated using a **CAS**. Regardless of the outcome of the **CAS** machine instruction, the procedure is restarted from the beginning. In this way, if **current** is concurrently updated, the new value becomes visible, even if it identifies a bucket in the past. Moreover, before updating the current bucket, the procedure tries to compact the virtual bucket, by cutting off (unlinking) all the traversed nodes that are found to be marked as invalid.

The search for a valid node halts when it finds a node which respects all the following properties: i) it is not marked, ii) it belongs to a correct epoch, iii) it is associated with the minimum timestamp in the current virtual bucket. Then, the dequeue operation tries to mark it as logically deleted (DEL), in order to finally extract and deliver it to the requesting worker thread. Differently from the proposal in [14], the node is marked by relying on Fetch&Or. The advantage coming from the reliance on this RMW instruction, rather than the classical CAS, is that it successfully completes even if the address of the node is concurrently updated (e.g., due to a concurrent enqueue of a new node). This is clearly favorable to concurrency since we are interested just in marking the node, regardless of a possible next node's update. Fetch&Or returns as well the value stored in the target memory location, therefore it is possible to verify the outcome of the marking attempt: if the original value is unmarked, the procedure has successfully marked the node obtaining the event, otherwise the worker thread detects that a concurrent takeover by another thread took place. In this case, the dequeue operation doesn't have to be restarted. Indeed, it is enough to continue the bucket list traversal, since the epoch field can tell whether the enqueue of a node is serialized before or after the current dequeue. Finally, the size field is decremented to signal the extraction of an element from the queue.

4.3 Resizing the Queue

$O(1)$ amortized time complexity is guaranteed by the fact that, on average, the number of elements within each bucket is balanced, in a way similar to the original calendar queue. As said before, every time an operation on the queue is performed, a READTABLE() procedure is called to retrieve a reference to a valid table. During this procedure, the number of elements per bucket is checked to determine whether it is still balanced. If this is not the case, a *resize* operation is executed. In particular, the resize is executed if size oversteps a certain threshold. The value of this threshold is a function of the desired number of events per bucket (denoted as $DEPB$), and the percentage of non-empty buckets.

The pseudocode of the READTABLE() operation (where the resize operation is implemented) is shown in Algorithm 3. When the *resize* condition is met, to announce its upcoming execution, the new_table field of the old set table is pointed to a new (just-allocated) set table. This somehow "freezes" the old table, preventing any new insertion/extraction operation into/from it. From now on, any thread executing a READTABLE() operation will be aware that a resize operation is taking place, and will start to participate.

Once the reference to the new table is published (preventing any thread from using the old one), before starting to migrate the nodes from the old to the new table, we must mark as MOV every entry of the bucket array, and all the first valid nodes of the associated lock-free lists. This is necessary to abort the execution of any dequeue operation. In fact, dequeue operations are restarted any time a node marked as MOV is found. In particular, a dequeue operation is restarted (and possibly joins the queue resize operation) if it attempts to dequeue any first valid node, or it tries to insert a new node to a list's head.

Algorithm 3 lock-free READTABLE

```
 1: procedure READTABLE( )
 2:     h ← array
 3:     curSize ← h.size
 4:     if h.new = null ∧ resize is NOT required then
 5:         return h
 6:     compute newSize
 7:     CAS(&h.new, null, new array(newSize))
 8:     newH ← h.new
 9:     if newH.bw ≤ 0 then
10:         begin ← RANDOM()
11:         for j ← 0 to h.t_size−1 do
12:             i ← (begin + j) mod curSize
13:             retry-loop to mark i-th head as MOV
14:             retry-loop to mark first node of i-th bucket as MOV
15:         MST ← compute bucket width
16:         CAS(&newH.bw, −1.0, MST)
17:     for i ← 0 to h.length−1 do
18:         while j-th bucket of h is non-empty do
19:             i ← (begin + j) mod curSize
20:             get first node of bucket i as right
21:             get the next node of right as right_next
22:             if right = tail then
23:                 break
24:             if right_next ≠ tail then
25:                 retry-loop to mark it as MOV
26:             create a copy of the right node
27:             while true do
28:                 search for right.ts in a virtual bucket vb of newH
29:                 if found node n with same key then
30:                     release copy
31:                     copy ← n
32:                     break
33:                 else if successful to insert copy as INV with a CAS then
34:                     break
35:             if CAS(&right.replica, null, copy) then
36:                 Fetch&Add(&newH.size, 1)
37:             else if right.replica ≠ copy then
38:                 try-loop to mark copy as DEL
39:             retry-loop         to         ensure         that newH.current.value ≤ vb
40:             retry-loop to mark right.replica as VAL
41:             retry-loop to mark right as DEL
42:     CAS(&q.array, h, newH)
43:     return newH
```

We are therefore sure that no one will extract nodes from the queue, making stable the portion of the time axis close to the minimum. This assumption allows us to safely determine the new bucket width, and the length of the bucket array—how to determine the bucket width will be discussed in Section 4.4. To this end, in a way similar to [3], a certain amount of events (starting from the minimum) is inspected to compute the *mean timestamp separation*. This is the average distance between the timestamps of consecutive events along the time axis. This value is multiplied by the desired number of events per bucket, in order to compute the bucket width. The result is stored in the bw field of new_table, by relying on a single-shot CAS (i.e., the operation is not retried if it fails).

In order to ensure lock-freedom during the resize operation (without introducing multiple copies of the same node), we rely on a mark-and-clone strategy. Before migrating a node, a thread must ensure that the node itself and its successor are marked as MOV. If they are not, it tries to do so by relying on CAS. This is done in order to avoid any interference with concurrent threads, executing any enqueue/dequeue operation, which did not notice that a resize operation is taking place. If the CAS succeeds (or if the nodes are already marked as MOV), the thread allocates a copy of the node, this time marked as invalid (INV). This copy is placed in the new structure, and the node (marked as INV) is ignored by any other dequeue operation until it is validated. By using a copy of the node, it is guaranteed that no node is lost. When placing the node's copy into new_table, if a copy of the same node is already present, it means that some other thread has already performed this operation. In this case, the copy is released and a reference to the one already installed into new_table is returned. Then, the node in the old structure is atomically updated so as to keep a reference to the found new copy. By traversing this reference, the node's copy in new_table is transitioned to the valid state VAL, and the original node is marked as logically deleted (DEL). It will be later physically deleted (i.e., unlinked from the list), still using CAS. To understand the reason behind this protocol, we should consider the insertion of a copy of one node performed by a delayed thread. In this scenario, the resize operation might be already finished, and a copy of the node could be already placed in new_table. Thanks to the validation of the new copy, realized by publishing a pointer to it in the original node, we are sure that the new copy will be not validated. In fact, until the original node is not removed, it will reference its copy. This copy-based pattern allows to enforce lock-freedom. In fact, any thread can take on the job of concurrently migrating the same node, trying to finally flag the original node and its new copy.

4.4 Varying the Bucket Width

In the original calendar queue [3], a strategy is defined to compute the bucket width, which estimates the mean separation time (MST) between two consecutive events. The obtained MST is then multiplied by a constant equal to 3, which represents the desired number of events per bucket (denoted as $DEPB$). This guarantees that the number of events in a bucket is bounded by a constant and thus the calendar queue delivers O(1) amortized time complexity for its operations. The value of $DEPB$ is chosen according to an experimental evaluation performed by Brown, which shows that such a value delivers good performance under different distributions of the timestamps.

Anyhow, the original calendar queue might suffer from reduced performance in at least two pathological scenarios. The first one occurs when the queue has reached a steady size, but the priority increment distribution changes over time, leading to a different MST compared to the one measured during the last resize. It follows that the bucket width is inappropriate and performance deteriorates. In the second case, the priority increment distribution makes events be clustered into two buckets distant from each other and reduces the efficiency, since enqueues traverse a significant amount of events during insertions and dequeues scan a large number of empty buckets.

There are several works that try to resolve these issues by triggering the data-structure reshuffle more frequently and designing new strategies to individuate a more accurate bucket width. In particular, the authors in [15] state that the sampling of events should be obtained from the most dense buckets, namely, those that contain the highest percentage of events stored into the queue. An analytical model is presented in [23] for computing a scale factor for the actual bucket width such that the new bucket width minimizes (in the model) the cost of queue operations. The final bucket width computation resorts to a combination of the sampling technique described in [15] and a minimization technique. Moreover the condition triggering the data-structure reshuffle is checked periodically. The time period is selected accurately in order to maintain O(1) amortized access time. The authors in [24] define a new data structure able to recursively split individual and dense buckets, making the bucket width be chosen properly for each bucket.

Anyhow, these works define heuristics and algorithms for computing MST, $DEPB$ and the bucket width for the case of sequential accesses. So they do not account for the effectiveness of the proposals with concurrent, scalable, conflict-resilient multi-list event pools, like the one we are presenting. They try to minimize the average cost of queue operations by modeling properties of events, in particular MST, so they cannot capture dynamics and behaviors connected to interactions between concurrent threads. In order to cope with such aspects, so as to determine a suited bucket width for our concurrent event pool, we had to take into account the impact of retries on the cost of queue operations, which lead to repeat some computational steps, such as atomic instructions. In particular, when a dequeue finds an empty bucket, it tries to increase current with a CAS instruction. Updating such variable is an expensive operation, since it is likely contended among threads, and might at worst lead to thrashing behaviors, just like for the Treiber Stack [25]. Consequently, it is reasonable that the number of events in a bucket should be at least T_d in our approach, where T_d is the number of cores expected to concurrently access a bucket for dequeue operations, which can be clearly less than the total number of cores available for running the share everything PDES system, which we denote as n. Anyhow, T_d can be much greater than the value of $DEPB$ used to compute the bucket width according to the rule proposed with, e.g., the original calendar queue. On one hand, this should not affect the asymptotic cost of dequeue operations, since a wider bucket width decreases the probability to scan a large amount of empty buckets. On the other hand, longer bucket lists affect the enqueue access time, since the enqueue has to scan an increased number of events before finding the position for the insertion. However, as shown in [13], a highly concurrent event pool based on a multi-list approach can have $O(n^2)$ times longer bucket lists than a baseline solution relying on spinlocks, and obtain comparable performance under high concurrency levels. Therefore, it follows that an average number $DEPB$ of elements within a bucket such that $T_d < DEPB << n^2$ can be a desirable value for optimizing the cost of both enqueue and dequeue operations in our proposal. Given that $T_d \leq n$ independently of the actual access pattern to the queue by concurrent threads, we suggest a value $DEPB \approx n$ as a suited one. In any case, in the experimental section, we report data with different configurations of the parameter $DEPB$, just to capture the effects of possibly different parameterizations while determining the bucket width.

5. EXPERIMENTAL DATA

We experimentally evaluated the performance of our data structure with two different test settings. In the first one

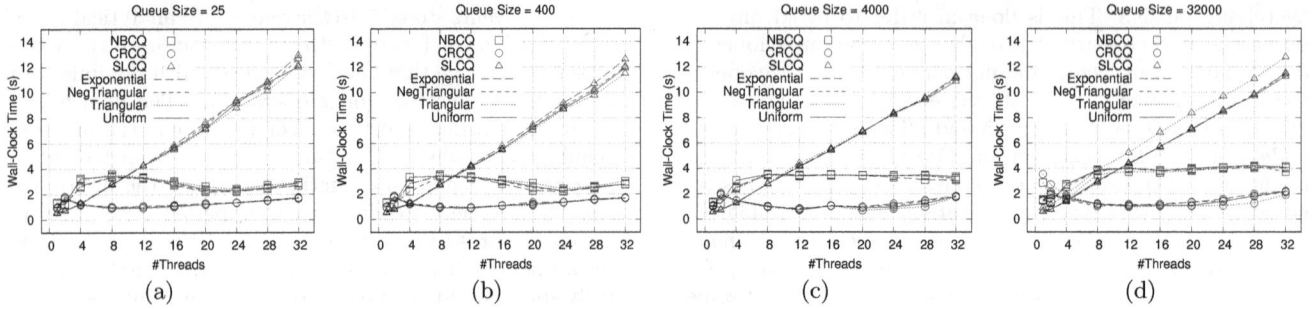

Figure 2: Results with the Hold-Model (each plot refers to a different queue size).

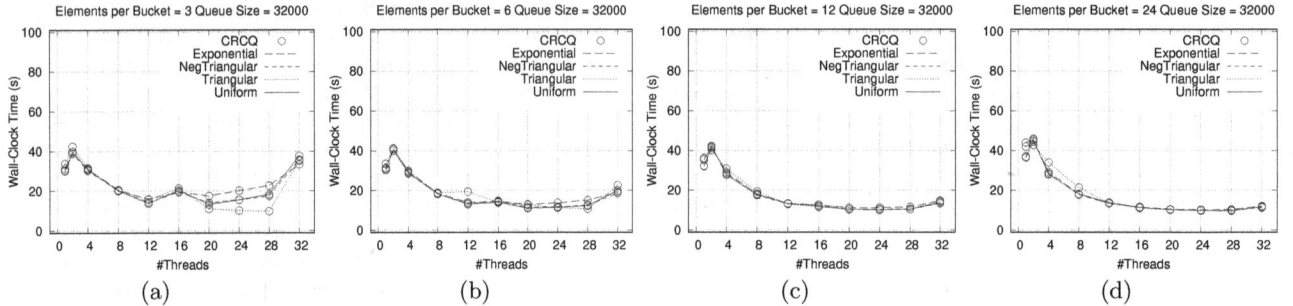

Figure 3: Hold-Model wall-clock times with queue size equal to **32000** and varied *DEPB*.

we exploited a synthetic workload based on the well known *Hold-Model*, where *hold* operations, namely a dequeue followed by an enqueue, are continuously performed on top the queue, which is pre-populated with a given number of items at startup (referred to as queue size). This test allows evaluating the steady-state behavior of the queue and, when executed in a multi-threaded fashion, its scalability and resilience to performance degradation in scenarios with scaled up volumes of concurrent accesses. The second test settings is related to the integration of the presented lock-free queue within an open source share-everything PDES environment, on top of which we run both the classical PHOLD benchmark for PDES systems and a multi-robot exploration model, called TCAR. The platform used in all the experiments is a 32-core HP ProLiant machine running Linux (kernel 2.6) equipped with 64 GB of RAM. The number of threads running the test-bed programs has been varied from 1 to 32.

5.1 Results with the Hold-Model

With the Hold-Model workload, the event pool is gradually populated with a given number of elements (queue size) and then each concurrent thread performs dequeue/enqueue operations with equal probability set to 0.5. Each run terminates when the total number of operations executed by the threads reaches 10^6. We run experiments with 4 different distributions of the priority increment for the generation of new elements to be inserted into the queue, which are shown in Table 1. For each distribution, we executed 4 tests with varies queue size, say 25, 400, 4000 and 32000. The performance of the proposed conflict-resilient calendar queue (CRCQ) is compared with the classical Calender Queue [3] (SLCQ), whose concurrent accesses are synchronized via

spin-locking, and the lock-free $O(1)$ event pool presented in [14] (NBCQ).

The results are shown in Figure 2, where each sample is obtained as the average of 10 different runs of the same configuration. We report the wall-clock times required to perform the target number of operations while varying the number of threads from 1 to 32. As expected the evaluated data structures have $O(1)$ access time, in fact, once the number of running threads is fixed, the wall-clock time is constant for different combinations of queue sizes and priority increment distributions. Both the two tested lock-free solutions outperform SLCQ. However, our new proposal CRCQ shows an improved performance wrt the NBCQ in almost every scenario, just thanks to conflict resilience on dequeues. Moreover, any number of threads larger than 4 is enough to make CRCQ be the most efficient implementation among all the tested alternatives.

Although the wall-clock time shown by CRCQ slightly increases with more than 12 threads, it is reasonable to think that the flat line of NBCQ in Figures 2(c) and 2(d) does not reveal a behavior similar to the ones in Figures 2(a) and 2(b) just because the minimum wall-clock time is expected with a higher number of threads compared to the maximum we could experiment with[3]. In other words, the higher efficiency of CRCQ allows to sense earlier the inherent bottleneck represented by retrieving the minimum from the event pool since, with reduced queue size, each bucket

---

[3]In fact, experimenting with a number of threads greater than the number of available CPU-cores in the underlying platform would have generated scenarios of interference on CPU usage, possibly leading to unclear motivations for winning or loosing on the comparison among the different solutions.

Table 1: **Employed Timestamp Increment Distributions.**

PROBABILITY DISTRIBUTION	FORMULA
Uniform	$2 \cdot \mathbf{rand}$
Triangular	$\frac{3}{2} \cdot \sqrt{\mathbf{rand}}$
Negative Triangular	$3 \cdot (1 - \sqrt{\mathbf{rand}})$
Exponential	$-\ln(\mathbf{rand})$

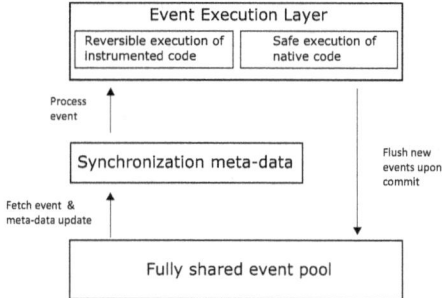

Figure 4: **High level structure of the employed share-everything PDES platform.**

contains few items and consequently the probability that a dequeue finds an empty bucket is higher.

To confirm this hypothesis, we have run a synthetic test with a queue size equal to 32000, but this time with different values of $DEPB$, namely 3, 6, 12, 24. As shown in Figure 3, an increased number of items in a bucket allows to increase the performance improvement obtained by a scaled up number of threads with CRCQ, since this reduces the probability to find an empty bucket. Consequently the amount of "wasted" local work of a thread is also reduced, thanks to conflict resilience of the proposed data structure, and at the same time there are less conflicts in updating/reading the value of **current**. Moreover, longer buckets act as an implicit back-off mechanism, exalting the resilience capability of our proposal to conflicting concurrent accesses to the hot spot of the queue, namely the minimum timestamp event. We recall again this is materialized in only one item at any time. This also confirms the deductions in [13] related to the fact that the optimal bucket width in scenarios with concurrent accesses can be significantly different from the one characterizing sequential implementations.

5.2 Share-everything PDES Results

In order to test our proposal in a pragmatic PDES scenario, we have integrated it with the last generation share-everything PDES engine standing at the core of the RAMSES speculative simulation framework [4]. The basic architecture of this engine is shown in Figure 4.

A meta-data layer is used to track the simulation object currently being run by any thread and the timestamp of the corresponding event. Thanks to the share-everything nature of the platform, there is only one event pool shared among all threads. Each extraction from the underlying event pool by some worker thread entails a meta-data update, which allows to compute the *commit horizon* of the simulation and to distinguish if an event can be affected by other events in the past or not. In the first case, the

extracted event can be safely executed by triggering the native version of the application code. Otherwise, the worker thread speculatively processes the event by running a modified version of the event handler obtained thanks to a transparent instrumentation (an ad-hoc compile/link procedure) of the native code. The instrumented code generates at runtime undo blocks of machine instructions, which can be used to rollback updates performed by the event processing. Moreover the simulation engine exploits lookahead in order to pinpoint events (after the commit horizon) that will not eventually be affected by causality errors and thus can be executed safely. The events produced by a speculative execution are locally stored waiting for the commitment of the event that generated them. If that event is not eventually committed because of a causality error, the local buffer of events is simply discarded without affecting the pending event set. Consequently, the event pool keeps only the *schedule committed* events, namely those generated by events that will never be rolled back. The concurrent extraction of events targeting the same simulation object leads to conflicting accesses by multiple threads to the state of that same object. These are resolved by synchronizing the worker threads via read/write spin-locks (giving higher priority to lower timestamp events). The original implementation of this simulation engine has been based on a shared event pool implemented as a calendar queue protected via spin-locks. Thus, resorting to the proposed conflict-resilient, lock-free and constant-time event pool has the advantage of confining the explicit synchronization across threads via spin-locks (e.g. in case of concurrent accesses to the same object) outside the lowermost layer. This is expected to provide significantly enhanced scalability.

5.2.1 Results with PHOLD

The first test-bed application we run on top of the share-everything engine is the classical PHOLD benchmark [7]. We configured it with 1024 simulation objects. The execution of an event leads to update the state of the target simulation object, in particular statistics related to the advancement of the simulation, such as the number of processed events and average values of the time advancement experienced by simulation objects. It also leads to executing a classical CPU busy-loop for the emulation of a given event granularity. There are two types of events: i) *regular* events, whose processing generates new events of any type; ii) *diffusion* events that do not generate new events when being processed. The number of diffusion events generated by regular ones (denoted as Fan-Out) is set to 1 and 50 in our evaluation. This varied event pattern leads to scenarios where the average number of events in the event pool is stable, but there are punctual fluctuations, which are more or less intense. In turn, these can allow assessing the effects of our proposal in scenarios where the actual locality of the activity (in particular extraction activities) bound to the hot bucket of the calendar queue can be more or less intense.

The timestamp increments are chosen according to an exponential distribution with mean set to one simulation-time unit. We selected two different lookahead values, respectively 10% and 0.1% of the average timestamp increment, in order to observe the impact of more safe vs more speculative processing on the run-time dynamics. Finally, the busy loop while processing an event is set to generate different event granularity in different tests, namely $60\mu s$, $40\mu s$ and $22\mu s$, in order to emulate low to medium granularity events proper of a large variety of discrete event models.

In Figure 5 and Figure 6 we show the speedup achieved by the parallel runs wrt the sequential execution of the same model. Speedup values are shown while varying the number of threads in the share-everything PDES system from 1 to 32, and with different lookahead values (respectively 10% and 0.1% of the average timestamp increment). Whenever the event granularity is larger and the lookahead is large enough to make threads process events safely with high probability (Figure 5(c)), we observe that both the lock-free event pools allow an almost linear speedup with coefficient 1 (ideal speedup). This is observed up to 16 threads. When running with more threads, the speedup coefficient is 0.8 for CRCQ and 0.7 for NBCQ. Conversely, the spin-locked calendar queue has scalability problems with more than 8 threads and its efficiency is further negatively affected by an increased Fan-Out value. Reduced lookahead (Figure6(c)) does not affect significantly the behavior of lock-free solutions and makes the spin-lock protected calendar queue to achieve an increased speedup when the Fan-Out is set to 1. The reason behind this behavior is that a smaller lookahead increases the probability to extract an unsafe event, that has to be executed speculatively and requires an explicit synchronization (possibly with rollback) in the worst case, reducing the actual concurrency in accessing the shared event pool.

A reduced event granularity leads to a higher pressure on the shared event pool by increasing concurrent accesses. In particular an event granularity equal to $40\mu s$ and a lookahead set to 10% (Figure 5(b)) makes the spin-locked calendar queue deteriorate after 8 threads and NBPQ after 24 threads (mostly because of conflicts and retries on dequeue operations), while CRCQ still delivers linear speedup. A reduced lookahead (Figure 6(b)) leaves almost unaltered the speedup of both the lock-free queues, but leads to a trend reversal. In particular, a larger Fan-Out makes lock-free solutions achieve higher performance (conversely the spin-locked calendar goes worse) since it balances the trend of reduction of concurrency in accessing the shared event pool due to synchronization at the meta-data layer (thanks to more intense bursts of enqueue operations). Anyhow also in this adverse scenario the proposed solution still delivers an almost linear speedup.

Finally, a very fine grain event, namely $22\mu s$, leads to a scenario quite similar to the tests with the Hold-Model, where increasing the number of threads leaves unaltered the wall-clock time spent into the conflict-resilient calendar queue. In Figure 5(a) it is shown how the speedup slope is reduced when moving from 24 to 32 threads in our solution (anyhow the speedup is still 0.5 of the ideal one with 32 threads), while a smaller lookahead (see Figure 6(a)) makes our proposal still achieve the same speedup of larger lookahead scenarios when Fan-Out set to 50, and gives no speedup advantages when moving from 24 to 32 number of threads with the smallest Fan-Out, thus indicating how CRCQ does not negatively impact the absolute performance when moving towards the usage of the maximum admitted parallelism level.

5.2.2 Results with TCAR

As the second PDES test-bed, we used a variant of the Terrain-Covering Ant Robots (TCAR) model presented in [12].

In this model, multiple robots (say agents) are located into a region (the terrain) in order to fully explore it. TCAR simulations are usually exploited to determine tradeoffs between the number of employed robots, and the latency for exploring the target region, e.g., for rescue purposes. Factors such as the speed of movement (depending on, e.g., environmental conditions within the region, or even obstacles) can be also considered.

In our implementation of TCAR, the terrain to be explored is represented as an undirected graph, therefore a robot is able to move from one space region to another in both directions. This mapping is created by imposing a specific grid on the space region. The robots are then required to visit the entire space (i.e., cover the whole graph) by visiting each cell (i.e., graph node) once or multiple times. Differently from the original model in [12], we have used hexagonal cells, rather than squared ones. This allows for a better representation of the robots' mobility featuring real world scenarios since real ant robots (e.g., as physically realized in [22]) have the ability to steer to any direction.

The TCAR model relies on a node-counting algorithm, where each cell is assigned a counter that gets incremented whenever any robot visits it. So the counter tracks the number of *pheromones* left by ants, to notify other ones of their transit. Whenever a robot reaches a cell, it increments the counter and determines its new destination. Choosing a destination is a very important factor to efficiently cover the whole region, and to support this choice the trail counter is used. In particular, a greedy approach is used such that, when a robot is in a particular cell, it targets the neighbor with the minimum trail count. A random choice takes place if multiple cells have the same (minimum) trail count.

The original TCAR model adopts a *pull* approach for gathering trail counters from adjacent cells. Considering the traditional PDES programming model, based on data separation across the simulation objects, such an approach would result in sending query/reply events across objects modeling adjacent cells each time a robot needs to move to some new destination cell.

To reduce the interactions across the simulation objects (by reducing the volume of events to be scheduled along the model lifetime) we adopted a *push* approach, relying on a notification event (message) which is used to inform all neighbors of the newly updated trail counter whenever a robot enters a cell. Then, each simulation object modeling a cell stores in its own simulation state the neighbors' trail-counters values, making them available to compute the destination when simulating the transit of a robot. In the used TCAR configuration, we included the evaluation of a new state value for the cell whenever a robots enters it, so as to mimic the evolution of a given phenomenon within the cells. This computation has been based on a linear combination of exponential functions (like it occurs for example when evaluating fading on wireless communication systems due to environmental conditions). Further, to model the delay robots experience when entering a cell for correctly aligning itself spatially, a lookahead of 10% of the average cell residence time has been added when generating new events used to notify the update of the local trail counter to the neighbors. We configured TCAR with 1024 cells, and we studied two alternative scenarios with different ratios between the number of robots exploring the terrain and the number of

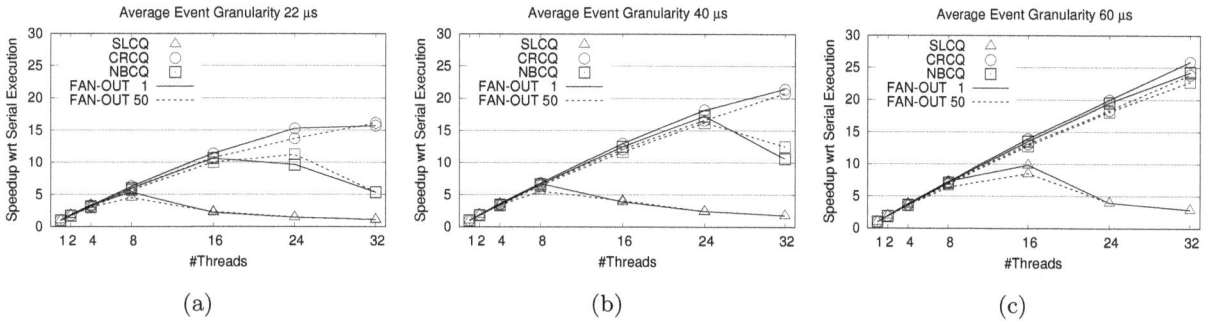

Figure 5: Results with PHOLD and lookahead 10% of the average timestamp increment.

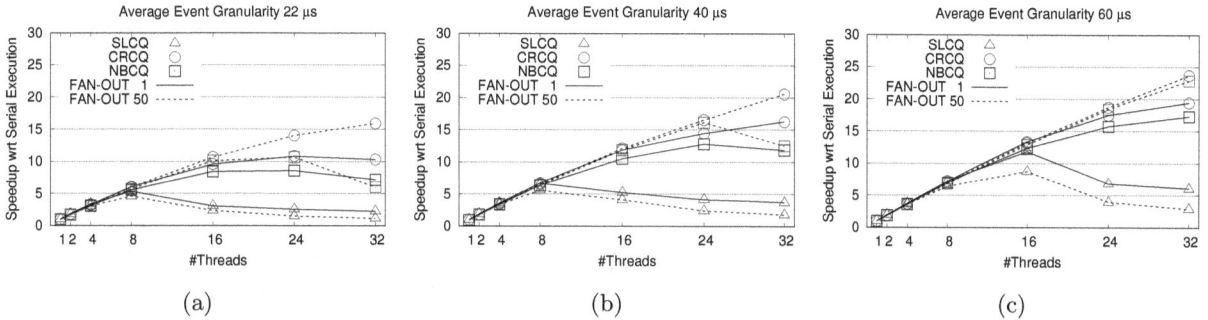

Figure 6: Results with PHOLD and lookahead 0.1% of the average timestamp increment.

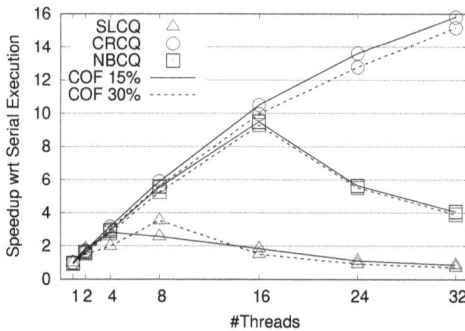

Figure 7: Results with TCAR.

cells, say 15% and 30%. We refer to this parameter as Cell Occupancy Factor (COF).

Speedup results are shown in Figure 7, where we still keep the PDES engine configuration with spin-lock protected calendar queue as the reference. By the plot we see how, also for this application, the maximum thread count leading the spin-lock protected calendar queue to be competitive is between 4 and 8, depending on the value of COF. Beyond 8 threads, such configuration rapidly degrades. NBCQ scales well up to 16 threads, but then degrades, while CRCQ provides close to linear speedup up to 32 threads, jointly guaranteeing at least 50% of the ideal speedup value even for larger thread counts.

6. CONCLUSIONS

In this article we have presented a conflict-resilient non-blocking calendar queue suited for share-everything PDES systems. Our proposal allows multiple worker threads that

attempt to extract the element with the minimum timestamp from a fully shared event pool to survive in their operations, despite the conflicting access to (and attempt to modification of) the same portion of the data structure—namely the hot bucket containing the unprocessed events with lower timestamps. With our solution, we experimentally determined excellent scalability of the shared-everything PDES engine on a machine with 32 CPU-cores, thus running the PDES applications with up 32 concurrent worker threads. We also tested our proposal with workloads related to concurrent accesses aside of the one generated by thread operating within the share-everything PDES platform. Besides the achievement of such scalability levels, our proposal also opens a new way of looking at non-blocking data structures, since it leaves the classical path where a non-blocking concurrent data structure is implemented by having a conflicting operations to be necessarily aborted and then retried from scratch.

7. REFERENCES

[1] D. Alistarh, J. Kopinsky, J. Li, and N. Shavit. The SprayList: a scalable relaxed priority queue. In *Proceedings of the 20th ACM SIGPLAN Symposium on Principles and Practice of Parallel Programming*, PPoPP, pages 11–20, 2015.

[2] R. Ayani. LR-Algorithm: concurrent operations on priority queues. In *Proceedings of the 2nd IEEE Symposium on Parallel and Distributed Processing*, SPDP, pages 22–25, 1990. IEEE Computer Society.

[3] R. Brown. Calendar queues: a fast O(1) priority queue implementation for the simulation event set problem. *Communications of the ACM*, 31(10):1220–1227, 1988.

[4] D. Cingolani, A. Pellegrini, and F. Quaglia. RAMSES: Reversibility-based agent modeling and simulation

environment with speculation support. In *Proceedings of Euro-Par 2015: Parallel Processing Workshops*, PADABS, pages 466–478. LNCS, Springer-Verlag, 2015.

[5] T. Dickman, S. Gupta, and P. A. Wilsey. Event pool structures for PDES on many-core Beowulf clusters. In *Proceedings of the 2013 ACM/SIGSIM Conference on Principles of Advanced Discrete Simulation*, pages 103–114. ACM Press, 2013.

[6] R. M. Fujimoto. Parallel discrete event simulation. *Communications of the ACM*, 33(10):30–53, 1990.

[7] R. M. Fujimoto. Performance of Time Warp Under Synthetic Workloads. In *Proceedings of the Multiconf. on Distributed Simulation*, pages 23–28. Society for Computer Simulation, 1990.

[8] S. Gupta and P. A. Wilsey. Lock-free pending event set management in time warp. In *Proceedings of the 2014 ACM/SIGSIM Conference on Principles of advanced discrete simulation*, PADS, pages 15–26. ACM Press, 2014.

[9] T. L. Harris. A pragmatic implementation of non-blocking linked-lists. In *Proceedings of the 15th International Conference on Distributed Computing*, DISC, pages 300–314. Springer Berlin/Heidelberg, 2001.

[10] J. Hay and P. A. Wilsey. Experiments with hardware-based transactional memory in parallel simulation. In *Proceedings of the 2015 ACM/SIGSIM Conference on Principles of Advanced Discrete Simulation*, PADS, pages 75–86. ACM Press, 2015.

[11] D. R. Jefferson. Virtual Time. *ACM Transactions on Programming Languages and System*, 7(3):404–425, 1985.

[12] S. Koenig and Y. Liu. Terrain coverage with ant robots: a simulation study. In *Proceedings of the fifth international Conference on Autonomous agents*, AGENTS, pages 600–607. ACM Press, 2001.

[13] R. Marotta, M. Ianni, A. Pellegrini, and F. Quaglia. A Non-Blocking Priority Queue for the Pending Event Set. In *Proceedings of the 9th EAI International Conference on Simulation Tools and Techniques*, SIMUTools, pages 46-55.ICST, 2016.

[14] R. Marotta, M. Ianni, A. Pellegrini, and F. Quaglia. A lock-free O(1) event pool and its application to share-everything PDES platforms. In *Proceedings of the 20th IEEE/ACM International Symposium on Distributed Simulation and Real Time Applications*, DS-RT, pages 53–60, 2016.

[15] S. Oh and J. Ahn. Dynamic calendar queue. In *Proceedings 32nd Annual Simulation Symposium*, pages 20–25, 1999.

[16] F. Quaglia. A low-overhead constant-time lowest-timestamp-first CPU scheduler for high-performance optimistic simulation platforms. *Simulation Modelling Practice and Theory*, 53:103–122, 2015.

[17] F. Quaglia and R. Baldoni. Exploiting Intra-Object Dependencies in Parallel Simulation. *Inf. Process. Lett.*, 70(3):119–125, 1999.

[18] R. Rönngren and R. Ayani. A comparative study of parallel and sequential priority queue algorithms. *Transactions on Modeling and Computer Simulation*, 7(2):157–209, 1997.

[19] E. Santini, M. Ianni, A. Pellegrini, and F. Quaglia. Hardware-transactional-memory based speculative parallel discrete event simulation of very fine grain models. In *2015 IEEE 22nd International Conference on High Performance Computing*, HiPC, pages 145–154. IEEE Computer Society, 2015.

[20] D. J. Sorin, M. D. Hill, and D. A. Wood. A Primer on Memory Consistency and Cache Coherence. *Synthesis Lectures on Computer Architecture*, 6(3):1–212, 2011.

[21] H. Sundell and P. Tsigas. Fast and lock-free concurrent priority queues for multi-thread systems. *J. Parallel Distrib. Comput.*, 65(5):609–627. Academic Press, Inc., 2005.

[22] J. Svennebring and S. Koenig. Building Terrain-Covering Ant Robots: A Feasibility Study. *Autonomous Robots*, 16(3):313–332, 2004.

[23] K. L. Tan and L.-J. Thng. Snoopy calendar queue. In *Proceedings of the 32nd Conference on Winter simulation*, WSC, pages 487–495, 2000.

[24] W. T. Tang, R. S. M. Goh, and I. L. Thng. Ladder queue: An O(1) priority queue structure for large-scale discrete event simulation. *Transactions on Modeling and Computer Simulation*, 15(3):175–204, 2005.

[25] R. K. Treiber. Systems programming: coping with parallelism. Technical report, IBM US Research Centers, Yorktown, San Jose, Almaden, US, 1986.

[26] J. G. Vaucher and P. Duval. A comparison of simulation event list algorithms. *Communications of the ACM*, 18(4):223–230, 1975.

[27] R. Vitali, A. Pellegrini, and F. Quaglia. Towards symmetric multi-threaded optimistic simulation kernels. In *Proceedings of the 26th Workshop on Principles of Advanced and Distributed Simulation*, PADS, pages 211–220. IEEE Computer Society, 2012.

Quantitative Driven Optimization of a Time Warp Kernel

Sounak Gupta
Dept of EECS, PO Box 210030
Cincinnati, OH 45110–0030
sounak.besu@gmail.com

Philip A. Wilsey
Dept of EECS, PO Box 210030
Cincinnati, OH 45110–0030
wilseypa@gmail.com

ABSTRACT

The set of events available for execution in a Parallel Discrete Event Simulation (PDES) are known as the pending event set. In a Time Warp synchronized simulation engine, these pending events are scheduled for execution in an aggressive manner that does not strictly enforce the causal relations between events. One of the key principles of Time Warp is that this relaxed causality will result in the processing of events in a manner that implicitly satisfies their causal order without paying the overhead costs of a strict enforcement of their causal order. On a shared memory platform the event scheduler generally attempts to schedule all available events in their Least TimeStamp First (LTSF) order to facilitate event processing in their causal order. By following an LTSF scheduling policy, a Time Warp scheduler can generally process events so that: (i) the critical path of the event timestamps is scheduled as early as possible, and (ii) causal violations occur infrequently. While this works effectively to minimize rollback (triggered by causal violations), as the number of parallel threads increases, the contention to the shared data structures holding the pending events can have significant negative impacts on overall event processing throughput.

This work examines the application of profile data taken from Discrete-Event Simulation (DES) models to drive the simulation kernel optimization process. In particular, we take profile data about events in the schedule pool from three DES models to derive alternate scheduling possibilities in a Time Warp simulation kernel. Profile data from the studied DES models suggests that in many cases each Logical Process (LP) in a simulation will have multiple events that can be dequeued and executed as a set. In this work, we review the profile data and implement group event scheduling strategies based on this profile data. Experimental results show that event group scheduling can help alleviate contention and improve performance. However, the size of the event groups matters, small groupings can improve performance, larger groupings can trigger more frequent causal

violations and actually slow the parallel simulation.

Keywords

Pending event set; Profile Guided Optimization; Event Scheduling; Lock contention; Parallel and distributed simulation; Time warp

1. INTRODUCTION

The set of events available for execution in a Parallel Discrete Event Simulation (PDES) are known as the *pending event set*. In an Time Warp synchronized simulation engine, these pending events are scheduled for execution in an aggressive manner that does not strictly enforce the causal relations between events [6, 10]. One of the key principles of Time Warp is that this relaxed causality will result in the processing of events in a manner that implicitly satisfies their causal order without paying the overhead costs of a strict enforcement of their causal order. Unfortunately, the event processing granularities of most discrete event simulation models are generally quite small which aggravates contention to the pending event shared data structures of a parallel simulation engine on a multi-processor platform. To alleviate this, some researchers have attempted to exploit lock-free methods [7], hardware transactional memory [8, 16], or synchronization friendly data structures [5]. Unfortunately, lock-free methods have additional overheads when incorporating sorting and deletion operations. While hardware transactional memory does reduce overhead this is mostly due to higher performing locking methods rather than providing any significant overall reduction in contention. Restructured data structures can be helpful to reduce contention, but even then we have found that contention remains an issue that needs to be addressed.

The work in this paper attempts to draw on the success of the computer architecture community in the use of application profile data to optimize the design and implementation of a compute platform [9]. In particular, we examine profile data from discrete event simulation models to help guide the design and optimization of scheduling strategies for the pending event set in a Time Warp synchronized simulation kernel. In this study, we focus on a single node shared memory platform to demonstrate the application of quantitative based design optimization. The profile data we use comes from previous work to build a system to profile discrete event simulations [20]. In this work, we will focus specifically on the data regarding *event chains* as reported in [20]. From that work, the event chain data data illustrates how many events could potentially be dequeued and

SIGSIM-PADS'17 May 24-26, 2017, Singapore, Singapore

© 2017 ACM. ISBN 978-1-4503-4489-0/17/05. . . 15.00

DOI: http://dx.doi.org/10.1145/3064911.3064932

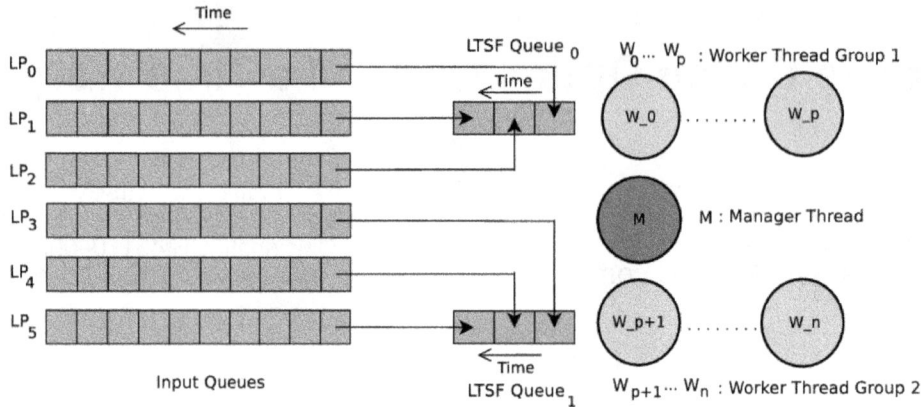

Figure 1: Pending Event Set in warped2

scheduled together such that they could be guaranteed ready to be executed. The data from that paper suggests that for some simulation models, a Time Warp simulator could dequeue multiple events with each event scheduling activity and successfully commit those events without triggering many rollbacks. In this paper, report on our experiences to leverage this event chain data into two different possible event scheduling strategies.

The remainder of this paper is organized as follows. Section 2 reviews some of the work related to scheduling events in parallel simulation. Section 3 reviews the previous work that quantifies the event organization in several discrete event simulation models. The data from this quantification motivations the approaches for scheduling events from the pending event set studied in this paper. Section 4 reviews the organization of the pending events in the WARPED2 parallel simulation engine which is the platform that our experimental analysis is performed. Section 5 describes the different methods that are explored for organizing, managing, and optimizing the pending event set to support LTSF event scheduling. Section 6 presents a performance results comparison between the different scheduling strategies for the pending event set. Finally, Section 7 contains some concluding remarks.

2. RELATED WORK

The Georgia Tech Time Warp (GTW) [4], a parallel discrete event simulator, is an implementation of the Time Warp mechanism proposed by Jefferson [10]. It was designed for discrete-event simulation applications having relatively small event granularity that could be executed on cache-coherent, shared-memory multiprocessors. GTW system consists of a group of logical processes (LPs) that communicate among themselves by exchanging time-stamped events (messages). The execution of each LP is message driven. Positive messages sent between LPs are directly inserted into the *Message Queue* while the negative (or anti) messages are similarly inserted into the *Cancel Queue*. Frequent access to message and cancel queues can lead to drastic increase in contention. To alleviate this problem, GTW designers introduced the concept of batch processing several unprocessed events within a specified batch interval. Several events would be processed in a batch by temporarily ignoring any rollbacks or cancellations. Though this ap-

proach would have reduced contention in the message and cancel queues, it can lead to the problem of overly optimistic execution in Time Warp. This refers to the situation where some LPs may progress too far ahead of others thereby leading to inefficient memory use and/or longer rollbacks. The authors, predicting this, implemented a 3-fold mechanism to tackle this problem. Blocking I/O events prevent LPs from progressing beyond a stated simulation time. Thus, an over-optimistic LP could be blocked from progressing by introducing a "dummy" blocking I/O event. The second mechanism employs the coarser approach of *simulated time barrier*. The idea borrows heavily from Bounded Time Warp synchronization protocol [17] which is a window-based simulation mechanism. The third mechanism deals with the frequency of fossil collection, which is a way to reclaim memory from events and states that are no longer being used.

WARPED [12, 14], built at University of Cincinnati, is a faithful implementation of Jefferson's classic model. Here LPs have their own input, output, and state queues. The initial kernel was designed for a distributed compute platform and the only parallelism available was among processes communicating by message passing. With the advent of newer generation of multicore processors, WARPED was re-designed (and renamed to WARPED2) such that is supported both fine-grained parallel threaded execution (pthreads) as well as process based parallelism that uses message passing. The pending event set in WARPED2 follows the design suggested by Ronngren *et al* [15] (and also used in several other kernels). There are two event pools, namely **Unprocessed** and **Processed** events. Events that are yet to be executed are stored in the **Unprocessed** pool. **Processed** pool stores processed events till the next fossil collection (*i.e.,* until the next GVT calculation). Adhering to the Time Warp mechanism, WARPED2 greedily processes events without strict adherence to their causal order. The simulation rolls back to the last known consistent state on detecting causal violations in any LP.

WARPED2 uses a two-level hierarchical organization for the *Pending event set* (Figure 1). On the first level, unprocessed events for each LP are stored in separate timestamp-sorted *Input Queue*. The second level is the timestamp-sorted *Schedule Queue* (often referred to as the Least Timestamp First or LTSF queue). The smallest unprocessed event from each LP is enqueued into this data structure. Dickman *et al* [5] proposed the use of multiple *LTSF Queues* to reduce

---
Algorithm 1: Event execution loop schematics
---
1 Lock the LTSF Queue linked to the worker thread;
2 Dequeue the smallest event e_m from that LTSF Queue;
3 Unlock that LTSF Queue;
4 **while** e_m *is a valid event* **do**
5   Process e_m (assume e_m belongs to LP_i);
6   Lock Input Queue for LP_i;
7   Move e_m from Input Queue to the Processed Queue;
8   Read the next smallest event e_n from Input Queue;
9   Lock the LTSF Queue linked to the worker thread;
10   Insert e_n into LTSF Queue;
11   Dequeue the smallest event e_m from the LTSF Queue;
12   Unlock the LTSF Queue;
13   Unlock Input Queue;
14 **end**

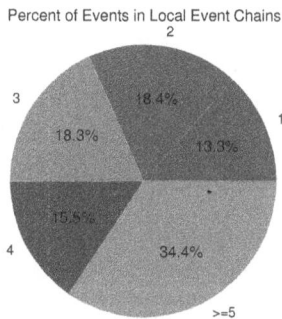

Figure 3: **Percent of Events in the Event Chains in a Portable Cellular Service Model**

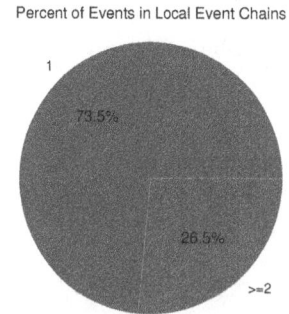

Figure 4: **Percent of Events in the Event Chains in a Model of Disease Propagation through a Population**

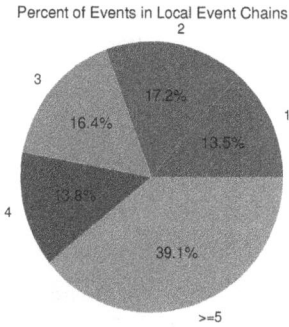

Figure 2: **Percent of Events in the Event Chains in an Automobile Traffic Model**

contention on a many-core processing platform. The main event processing loop in the WARPED2 simulation kernel is depicted in Algorithm 1. In WARPED2, each event processing thread is called a *worker thread* that continuously executes events from the pending event set until some termination condition is satisfied. A separate *manager thread* processes remote communication and Time Warp housekeeping functions, including termination detection.

3. MOTIVATING RESULTS FROM QUANTITATIVE STUDIES

Contention for access to the pending event set is a problem that we have studied for several years in the WARPED2 simulation kernel. We have explored various approaches such as: different organizations of data structures [5], model partitioning [1], lock-free algorithms for the pending event set[7], and transactional memory to access the pending event set [8]. While each provides a measure of relief for the contention, each have either limited success or disadvantages that inhibit their widespread use.

In a related study, we have pursued the development of methods to quantify the runtime profile of events in a discrete event simulation model [20]. This study developed tools to analyze the runtime traces of events processed by a simulation engine in order to discover certain properties about the events generated and processed by the simulation model. While the work profiled various characteristics such as events available for execution and the communica-

tion density of objects in the simulation, one characteristic that was captured called *event chains* suggested an optimization to the pending event set in a parallel simulation engine.

In particular, event chains are the collection of events from the pending event set of an LP that could potentially be executed as a group. That is, at a specific simulation time, an event chain would contain all of the events that time would be available in the pending event set for immediate execution at that time. Thus, we independently examine the pending event set of each LP. Beginning at time zero, the a chain of events is constructed and its maximum length counted. All of the events in that chain are treated as one and the algorithm then advances to the next event following the last in the chain to determine the length of the next chain. While the previous paper [20] classifies chains into three types (*local*, *linked* and *global*), in this paper we consider only local chains.

Our hypothesis is that if event chains of length greater than one are common, an interesting optimization to a simulation kernel might be to dequeue multiple events with each execution thread to execute as a block. Using the data from the previous study [20], Figures 2, 3, and 4 show the percentages of total events within each chain class. This data shows that events in two two of the simulation models (Figures 2 and 3) are in chains of length ≥ 2 and that they should therefore be candidates for scheduling in groups. However, the third simulation model (Figure 4) has nearly 74% of events in chains of length 1.[1]

---
[1]The pie chart of Figure 4 aggregates data for chains of length greater than two are nearly zero. Because the plotting

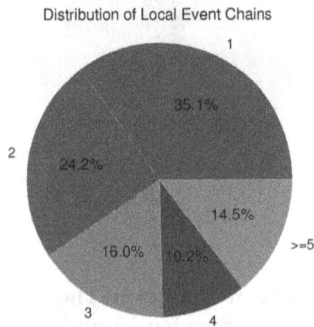

Figure 5: Event Chains in an Automobile Traffic Model

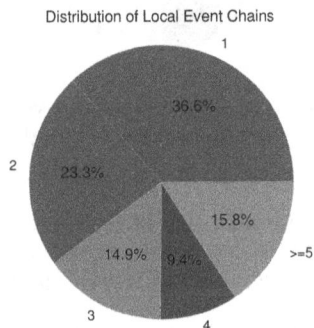

Figure 6: Event Chains in a Portable Cellular Service Model

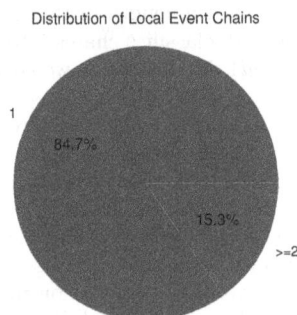

Figure 7: Event Chains in a Model of Disease Propagation through a Population

An alternate view of the event chain data is to show the number of chains of various lengths that occur throughout the simulation. This will help to demonstrate the percentages of multi-event scheduling opportunities that exist in the simulation. This organization of the data is shown in Figures 5, 6, and 7. The data in these pie charts highlight the percentage of chains of length 1 to 4 and greater than or equal to 5 that were found in each simulation model. Examining the first two simulation models (Figures 5 and 6), we can see that if two events are dequeued for each event scheduling activity, the simulator should find two immediately committable events more than 64% of the time; if three events are dequeued per scheduling activity then the simulator should find three immediately committable events approximately 40% of the time. As before, the third simulation model (Figure 7) shows that the simulator would only see two committable events approximately 15% of the time and nearly zero opportunities for finding chains of committable events greater than length two.

The profile data suggests that some simulation models will benefit from an event scheduler that distributes more than one event at a time from the pending event set. However, this analysis is from a conservative viewpoint of the event's availability. In part, optimistic synchronization benefits when causal relations are not strictly limited by a global time order in the simulation. Therefore, it could very well be that experimentation will show benefits from even larger counts of events being scheduled as a group than the profile data suggests.

4. PENDING EVENTS IN WARPED2

The WARPED2 Time Warp simulation kernel [19] is designed for execution on a single SMP processor or on a Beowulf cluster of SMP processors communicating with each other using MPI. WARPED2 uses a two-level hierarchical data structure to maintain the pending event set, namely: (i) a sorted list of pending events for each Logical Process (LP), and (ii) a set of one or more more scheduling pools of events called the LTSF queues. Each LP contains its list of pending events. This is a shared data structure with a unique lock assigned to each LP. The lowest timestamped event from each LP is placed into one of the LTSF queues. Each LTSF is also assigned a unique lock. Figure 1 presents an overview of this hierarchical design. A static partitioning of the LPs to the different nodes of the cluster is achieved using a profile guided partitioning process that optimizes a min-cut of the number of events exchanged between LPs [1]. This profile data is also used to assign LPs within a node to one of the LTSF queues. If there is only one LTSF queue, all LPs are assigned to that LTSF queue.

The number of LTSF queues on each compute node of the simulation is a runtime configuration parameter. The collection of threads that execute events (called worker threads) on each node are then statically assigned to a specific LTSF queue on that node. The worker threads process events from its assigned LTSF queue and inserts any generated events di-

---

software overwrites the labels making the graphic difficult to visualize, all chains longer than two are shown together. Likewise Figure 7 (discussed in the next paragraph) also aggregates the chain data for all chains of length two and above. For all practical purposes, the measurable number of chains in the epidemic model are limited to sizes of one or two events.

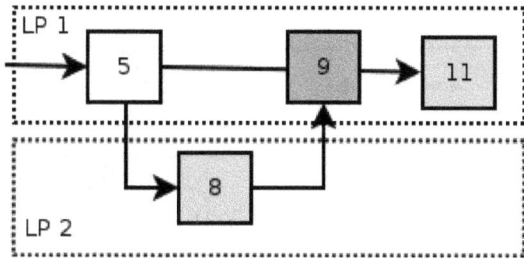

Figure 8: Event Causality

rectly into the corresponding LP event queue (events generated for remote nodes are placed into a message send queue). If a newly generated event defines a new lowest event for the LP, the worker thread also replaces the entry in the LTSF queue containing events for that LP. Finally there exists a manager thread on each node that performs housekeeping functions such as GVT and termination management [6]. The manager thread also performs the remote communication (sending and receiving) of events with other nodes. Thus, the manager thread must also sometimes access the shared data structures of the pending event set.

The hierarchical structure of the pending event set in WARPED2 provides for a highly effective scheduling of events that leads to infrequent rollbacks for many simulation models [5, 19]. On a single multi-core compute node using one LTSF queue, the WARPED2 simulator will generally experience zero rollbacks. However, as the number of worker threads increases beyond 4-6, contention for the LTSF queue diminishes overall performance as additional threads are added. In these situations, a multi-LTSF queue configuration can regain scalability [5]. However, with more than one LTSF queue, the scheduling of events on each node to follow the critical path of timestamped event execution becomes more problematic and rollbacks can increase. In this paper, we examine structuring the worker threads to dequeue multiple events per access to the shared pending event list data structures. This should further reduce contention and provide improved scalability with a fewer number of LTSF queues. The strategies explored and the results of experiments with them are described in the next two sections.

5. GROUP SCHEDULING: BLOCKS AND EVENT CHAINS

Group Scheduling is a opportunistic approach to scheduling pending events. Processing events in groups helps to reduce the frequency of access to the key shared data structure in the pending event set and therefore should help reduce contention contention to this critical resource. That price is increased risk of causal violation. Figure 8 contains an example illustrating a causal chain. Certain events in the pending event pool have a chronological order and cannot be processed greedily out of order. If such events are processed out of order, it leads to a *Causal Violation*. The benefits gained from scheduling schemes such as *Group Scheduling* rests on the rationale that time saved from reduced contention exceeds time wasted on rollbacks due to increased causal violations.

In this paper, we explore two different approaches to scheduling groups of events from the pending event set. In particular we consider scheduling groups of events from the

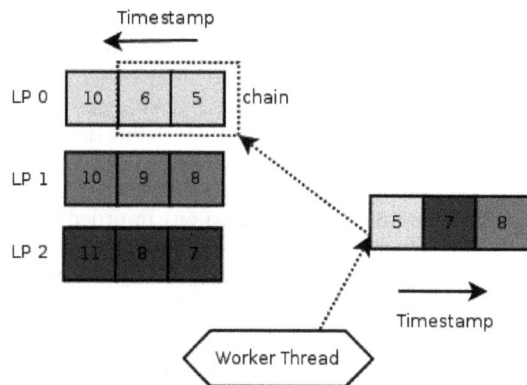

Figure 9: Chain Scheduling

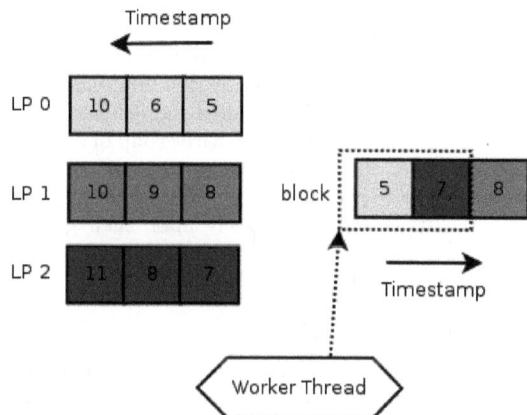

Figure 10: Block Scheduling

LPs as outlined in the profile study reported in [20]. We call this *chain scheduling*. Based on our initial success with chain scheduling, we restructured the solution to simply pull groups of events from the LTSF queue. We call this *block scheduling*. Each is described more fully in the next subsections.

5.1 Chain Scheduling

Figure 9 shows the schematics of *Chain Scheduling*. In this scenario, the smallest event from a LTSF Queue is considered. A group of consecutive events from the *Logical Process* linked to that smallest event forms the *chain*. The size of this chain (also referred to as *chain size*) is a configurable parameter. All events from this *chain* are processed in the same execution cycle. Output events, generated due to processing of these events, are either sent immediately or stored and sent in bulk but with a delay. Both these output event sending schemes have been studied in Section 6.2.

5.2 Block Scheduling

Figure 10 shows the schematics of *Block Scheduling*. In WARPED2, the smallest events from each *Logical Process* are placed in a timestamp-ordered priority queue (generally referred to as LTSF pool). Instead of pulling out one event per processing cycle (as is the usual scenario) from the LTSF pool, each worker thread dequeues a group of consecutively ordered events to form an event *block*. The size of this block (also referred to as *block size*) is a configurable parameter.

All events in a *block* are processed in the same execution cycle. The output events, generated as a result of this block processing, are sent out immediately after being created in order to minimize the effect of causal violations.

While the current version of block scheduling dequeues the next N consecutive events, we have considered dequeuing N at some unit distance forward in the LTSF queue (*e.g.*, every other event, every 3rd event, and so on) in order to better distribute the lowest events in the `LTSF queue` throughout the various worker threads. The distance between events dequeued is referred to as *skip distance*.

6. EXPERIMENTAL RESULTS

In the experimental analysis of group scheduling, we use the three models examined in Section 3 of this paper. The next section describes these models and then results from the block and chain scheduling studies with these models are reported. Furthermore, the distribution of output events with group scheduling is treated in two different ways. In particular, in the first method (called the *delayed* method), output events were held until the entire group of events were executed and then the output events were distributed. In the second method (called the *immediate* method), output events were distributed immediately upon their generation from event processing. Overall the immediate method consistently outperformed the delayed results.

6.1 Simulation Models

This section describes the three WARPED2 simulation models used as benchmarks to study the performance implications of the changes discussed in Section 5. Both these models are based on similar simulation models used by other researchers in parallel simulation.

6.1.1 Traffic

This model simulates the flow of cars through a grid of intersections. It models how cars move through and between the intersections. The intersections in our model are four way with three lanes in each direction. This model has been adapted for WARPED2 simulator from the ROSS [3] simulator.

The intersections here are modeled as Logical Processes and cars moving through and between intersections have been modeled as Events. As shown in Figure 11, there are three event phases at every intersection: **Arrival**, **Direction Select**, and **Departure**. The **Direction Select** event triggers the model to determine the direction a particular car should travel on next in order to reach its target intersection. The departure and direction select events are self-generated while the arrival event is received from an adjacent intersection.

Each car in this model is randomly assigned a specific intersection as destination. Cars are initially distributed uniformly across all intersections. A car, after arriving at an intersection, tries to go in the direction that would get it closer to its target. The flow of cars going through an intersection is regulated using thresholds to spread out the traffic and limit congestion on certain roads. If a car is denied permission to travel in the direction of its choice, it randomly chooses either to wait or take an alternate route. Events follow an exponential distribution and a new event is generated when an event is processed.

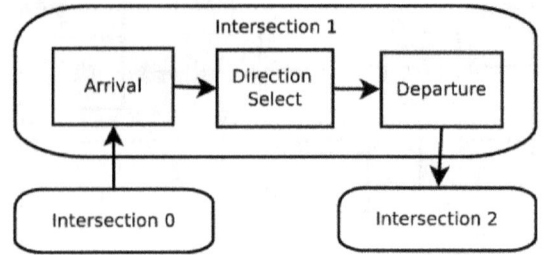

Figure 11: Sequence of events at each intersection

The State of a Logical Process keeps track of the status of traffic at each intersection. It consists of:

- the number of cars coming in from each direction,

- the number of cars going out in each direction,

- the total number of incoming cars at the intersection, and

- the total number of outgoing cars at the intersection.

To improve scalability of the traffic model, the grid has been modeled as a rectangular mesh (as is also done in ROSS). The grid size used for this simulation equals *1024 x 1024* which translates to a total of *1,048,576* LPs.

6.1.2 Portable Cellular Service (PCS)

This model simulates a wireless communication network that provides services for a number of subscribers (or *portables*). The service area of the network is divided into *cells*, each cell having a certain number channels that can be allocated for calls. A channel from the cell is allocated for an incoming or outgoing call. If no channels are available for allocation, the call is *blocked* [11]. Cells are the logical processes in this simulation and they are organized in the form of a rectangular grid as shown in Figure 12. The grid size used for this simulation equals *256 x 256* which translates to a total of *65,536* LPs.

Portables are allowed to move across adjacent cells with a wrap around occurring at the edges. The portables migrate to an adjacent cell after a time period that follows a Poisson distribution. The call is dropped if all the channels are busy on a cell to which the portable migrates to while on a call. This is called a *handoff block*. Call requests to a portable also follow a Poisson distribution. The State of a Logical Process keeps track of the channel count and call statistics at each cell. It consists of:

- Idle channel count,

- Call attempts count,

- Channel blocks count, and

- Handoff blocks count.

`NextCall`, `CallCompletion`, `PortableMoveOut`, and `PortableMoveIn` are the four event types in this simulation. `NextCall`, `CallCompletion`, and `PortableMoveOut` events are self-initiated by a cell whereas the `PortableMoveIn` event is sent to an adjacent cell with uniform randomness.

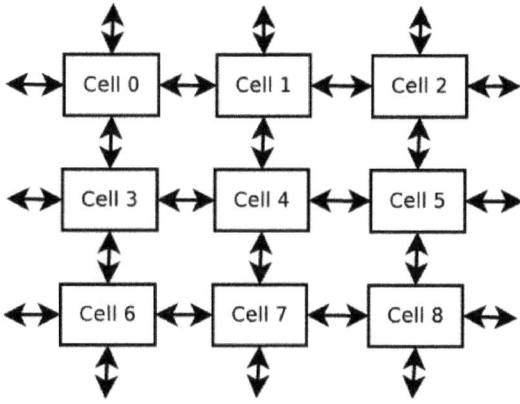

Figure 12: PCS Model Logical Processes

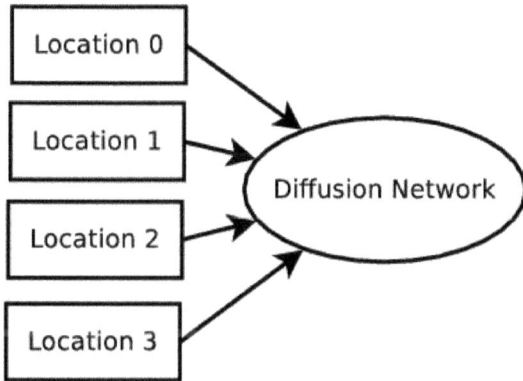

Figure 13: Epidemic Model

6.1.3 Epidemic

This models the spread of an infectious disease across a set of geographic locations, each housing a subset of the total population. It is based on a reaction-diffusion epidemic model proposed by Perumalla *et al* [13].

Each geographic location is represented in the simulation model as a logical process. Intra-location transmission of the disease between people is modeled as a probabilistic reaction function [2]. A finite state machine called *Probabilistic Timed Transition System (PTTS)* [2] models the spread of disease within an individual. Inter-location migration of population is modeled as a diffusion network based on the β model proposed by Watts *et al* [18]. Events in the epidemic model follow an exponential distribution. The number of logical processes used for this simulation model is *100,000*. Figure 13 presents an overall illustration of this model.

6.2 Performance Data

These experiments were run on an Intel® Core™ i7-4770 (a quad core processor with two hardware threads per core) machine equipped with 32 GB of memory. All simulations were run using `STL MultiSet` as LTSF queue. A single LTSF Queue is used for all experiments discussed in this paper.

The performance metrics used in this study are:

- `Overall Speedup` for a particular configuration of worker thread and group size equals

$$\frac{\text{Max runtime among all configurations}}{\text{Runtime for that configuration}} \quad (1)$$

This metric is useful to compare the overall performance of a configuration and to study the combined effect worker thread count and group size has on group scheduling.

- `Relative Speedup` for a particular configuration of worker threads and group size equals

$$\frac{\text{Runtime for same thread count while using group size 1}}{\text{Runtime for that configuration}} \quad (2)$$

This metric is useful to study the effect of group size only on group scheduling by isolating the results from the effects of worker thread count.

- `Commitment Rate` for a particular configuration of worker threads and group size equals

$$\frac{\text{Total number of events processed for that configuration}}{\text{Total number of committed events}} \quad (3)$$

Total number of committed events is independent of effect of worker thread count and group size. This metric is useful to understand how the greedy aspect of group scheduling adversely impacts the simulation through causal violations.

6.2.1 Traffic

The model configuration mentioned in Subsection 6.1.1 was used for this series of experiments. The total count of events committed equals **14,881,335** in all cases.

Figure 14 contains the speedup results with the Traffic model using event scheduling. It shows a speedup of nearly 3 when groups of 2 and 4 events are scheduled using 8 threads and the trends with 4 and 2 threads mostly mirror 8 threads. Beyond a chain size of 4 events, however, performance begins to steadily degrade. The simulation runs slower for all threads when output events are sent out in `Delayed` mode compared to that in `Immediate` mode. Figure 15 shows similar relative speedup behavior until event chain size of 4 beyond which the relative performance degrades. Figure 16 plots the commitment rate for event chains and shows the steady increase in causal violations due to increase in size of event chains. The performance of event chain improves in spite of higher causal violations till a certain point. Beyond that event chain size, the benefit of lower contention in event chain management is offset by the increasing number of causal violations. It is worth noting that the commitment rate is nearly the same for different number of worker threads and output event sending modes. Though we have not yet analyzed this behavior thoroughly, our speculation is that the scope of causal conflict remains unchanged for the chain sizes considered for this experiment.

Figure 17 contains the speedup results with the Traffic Model using block scheduling. It shows that performance in case of 2 worker threads remains invariant when there is a change in event block size. It is to be noted that, due to large LP count, there are no causal violations for blocks of small

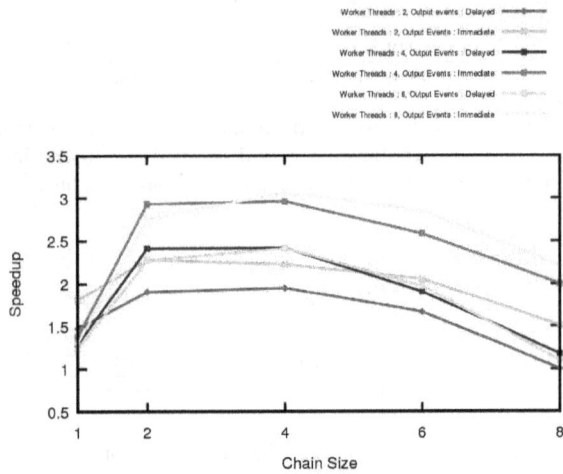

Figure 14: **Overall Speedup of Traffic using Event Chains**

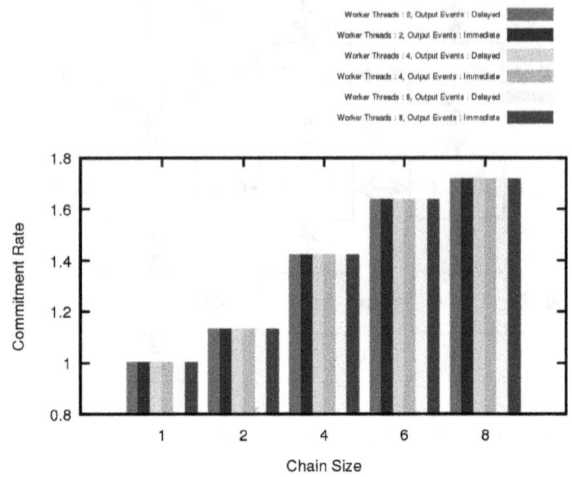

Figure 16: **Commitment Rate of Traffic using Event Chains**

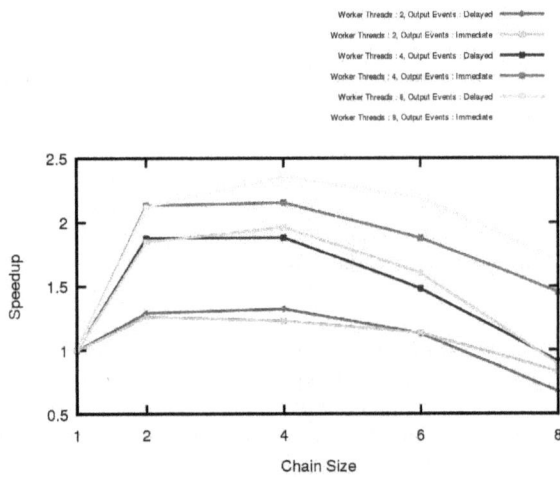

Figure 15: **Relative Speedup of Traffic using Event Chains**

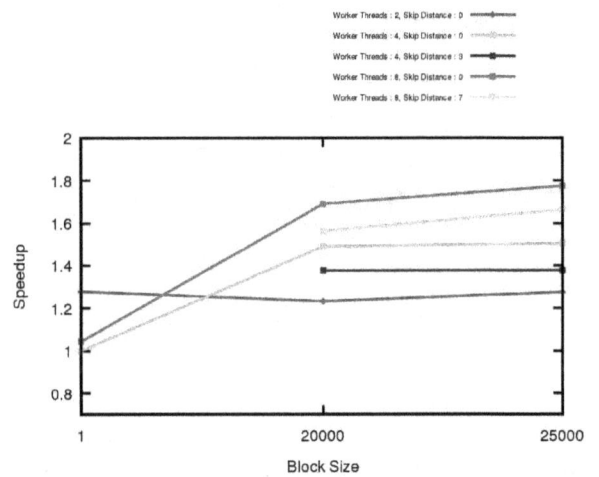

Figure 17: **Overall Speedup of Traffic using Block Scheduling**

sizes. Since one of the goals of this study is to study the impact of greedy processing of event blocks on event causality, the block size was increased to a point where causal violations could be observed. There is good overall speedup in case of 4 and 8 worker threads. However event blocks formed using `skip distance > 0` performs worse than event blocks formed using `skip distance = 0`. The same observations are true for relative speedup as shown in Figure 18. Figure 19 shows a relatively low number of causality violations when `skip distance = 0` and it increases when `skip distance > 0`.

6.2.2 PCS

The model configuration mentioned in Section 6.1.2 was used for this series of experiments. The total count of events committed equals 45,484,953 in all cases.

Figure 20 contains the speedup results with the PCS model when using chain scheduling. It shows decent good overall speedup for all threads. However, with the increase in event chain size, the performance steadily falls in case of 2 worker

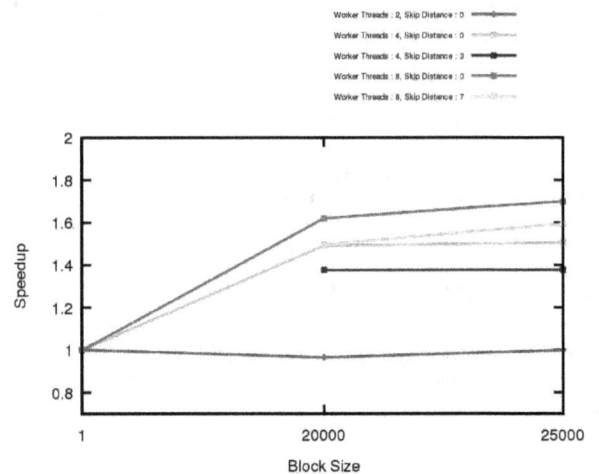

Figure 18: **Relative Speedup of Traffic using Block Scheduling**

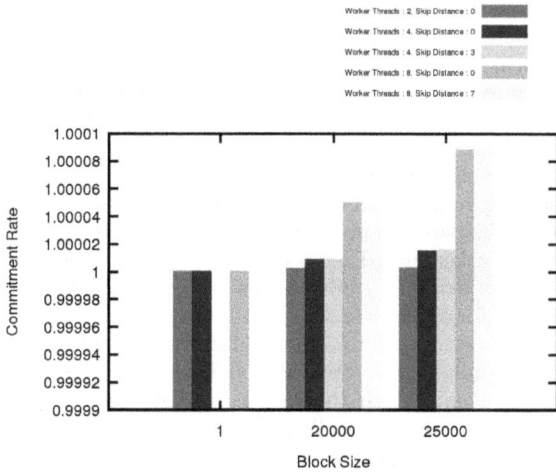

Figure 19: Commitment Rate of Traffic using Block Scheduling

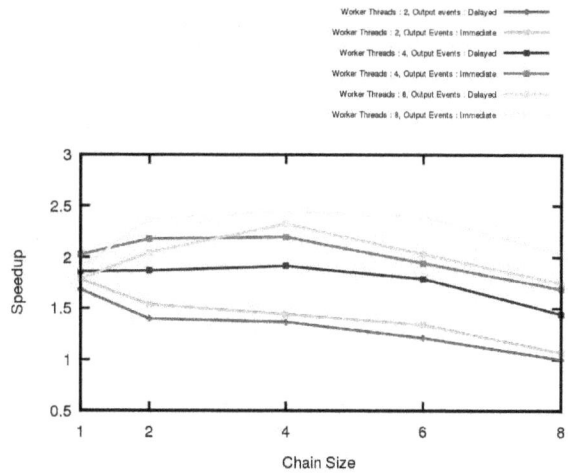

Figure 20: Overall Speedup of PCS using Event Chains

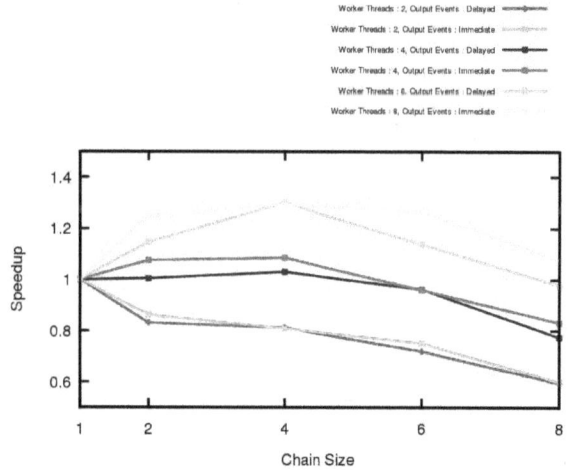

Figure 21: Relative Speedup of PCS using Event Chains

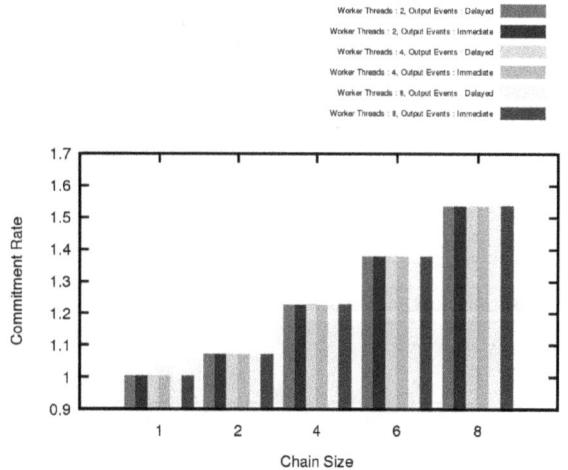

Figure 22: Commitment Rate of PCS using Event Chains

threads. This makes sense as contention should be minimal with only 2 worker threads. The performance remains fairly stable in case of 4 worker threads until the event chain size reaches 8. In case of 8 worker threads, the performance actually improves and peaks for event chain size of 4 before steadily degrading beyond that. Figure 21 shows that there is minimal or adverse relative speedup in case of 2 and 4 threads with increase in size of event chains. Only 8 worker threads shows improvement for event chain size of 4 before steadily degrading. Figure 22 plots the commitment rate for event chains and shows the steady increase in causal violations due to increase in size of event chains. The performance of event chain improves in spite of higher causal violations till a certain chain size. The benefit of lower contention in event chain management is offset by the increasing number of causal violations at that point. Similar to `Traffic` model, the commitment rate here is nearly the same for different number of worker threads and output event sending modes.

Figure 23 contains the speedup results with the PCS model when using block scheduling. Similar to the `Traffic` model, results presented are only for large block sizes in order to study the effect of greedy processing of event blocks on event causality. It shows that increase in event block size adversely affects overall performance in case of 2 worker threads. There is good overall speedup in case of 4 and 8 worker threads. However, event blocks formed using `skip distance > 0` performs worse than event blocks formed using `skip distance = 0`. The same observations are true for relative speedup as shown in Figure 24. Figure 25 shows relatively low number of causality violations when `skip distance = 0` and it increases marginally when `skip distance > 0`.

6.2.3 Epidemic

The model configuration mentioned in Subsection 6.1.3 was used for this series of experiments. The total count of events committed equals 30,676,881 in all cases.

If we review the profile results from Section 3, the evidence for the application of group scheduling in the Epidemic model is not encouraging. In fact, reviewing Figure 7

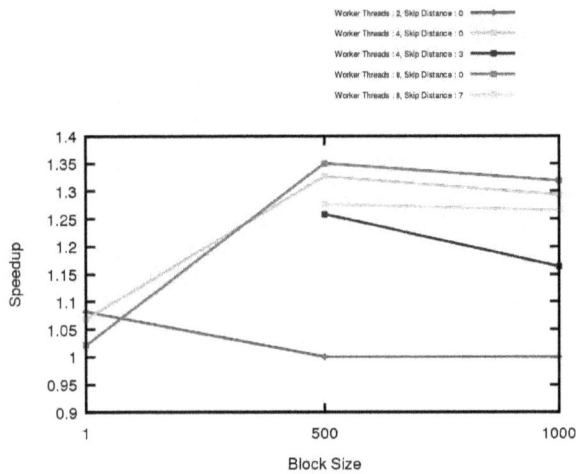

Figure 23: Overall Speedup of PCS using Block Scheduling

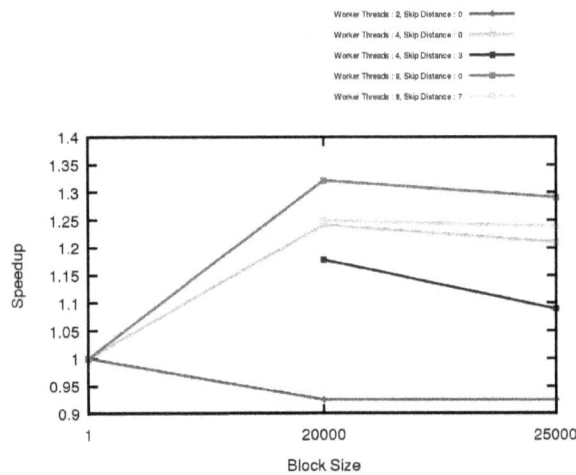

Figure 24: Relative Speedup of PCS using Block Scheduling

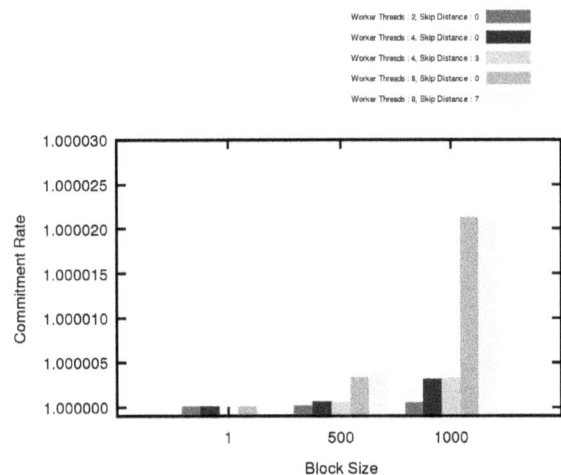

Figure 25: Commitment Rate of PCS using Block Scheduling

we can see that nearly 85% of the event chains in the Epidemic model are of length 1. As will be seen below, the experimental results mostly follow this result. While some modest improvements are seen, the results are not as dramatic as they are with the Traffic and PCS models shown above.

Figure 26 contains the speedup results with the Epidemic model using event scheduling. It shows minor speedup for all threads. The performance improves for event chain size of 2 in case of worker thread count of 4 and 8. Beyond this point performance degrades and remains stable. The simulation runs slower for all threads when output events are sent out in Delayed mode compared to that in Immediate mode. Figure 27 shows similar relative speedup behavior till event chain size of 2 beyond which the relative performance degrades and remains stable. Figure 28 plots the commitment rate for event chains and shows the increase in causal violations due to increase in size of event chains. The commitment rates in case of event chain sizes 4–8 are relatively similar. Since the overall and relative speedup values are also stable for event chain sizes 4–8, it indicates the benefit of using event chains to offset the contention problem when there are high number of worker threads. Similar to Traffic and PCS models, the commitment rate is nearly the same for different number of worker threads and output event sending modes. Though we have not yet analyzed this behavior thoroughly, we speculate that the scope for causal conflict remains unchanged when the chain size is considered for this experiment.

Figure 29 contains the speedup results with the Epidemic model using event scheduling. Similar to the Traffic and PCS models, results discussed are for large block sizes only since the focus of this study is the effect of greedy processing of event blocks on event causality. It shows that performance in case of 2 worker threads remains invariant when there is a change in event block size. There is much better speedup in case of 4 and 8 worker threads than was achieved with chain scheduling. The same observations are true for relative speedup as shown in Figure 30. Figure 31 shows no causality violations for worker thread count 2 and 4. Causality violations are observed in case of 8 worker threads. This indicates that causal chains do not occur frequently in the epidemic event stream.

7. CONCLUSION

The use of profile data from Discrete Event Simulation Models to develop pending event set scheduling strategies for a Time Warp synchronized simulation kernel is studied. The profile data suggested that two of the studied simulation models should benefit from the scheduling of multiple events during the event scheduling step of the simulation engine. Profile data from a third simulation model suggested that the opportunity to gain speedup from group scheduling would not be profitable. Experimental analysis of these group scheduling strategies for the corresponding models delivered results consistent with the results of the profile data analysis.

The two scheduling strategies (chain and block) of this study were examined in isolation and treated separately. The block scheduling method occurred to us more as a generalization of the chain scheduling approach rather than a direct derivation from the profile data. However, the results with block scheduling have encouraged us to go back to the profile data for a deeper study of the available parallelism

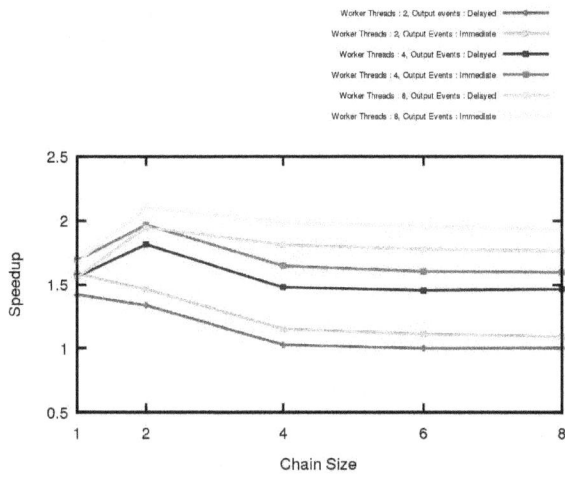

Figure 26: Overall Speedup of Epidemic using Event Chains

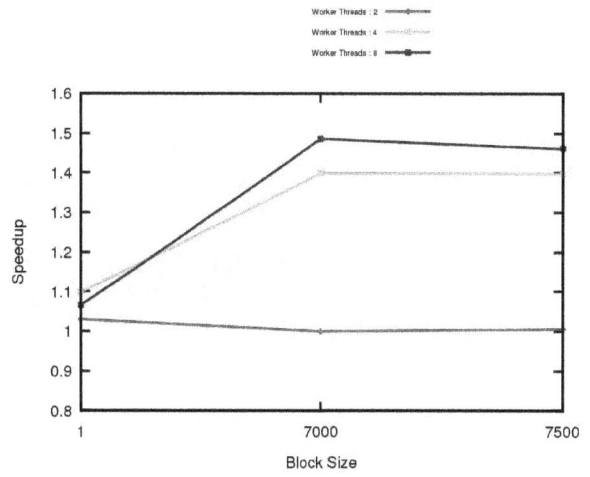

Figure 29: Overall Speedup of Epidemic using Block Scheduling

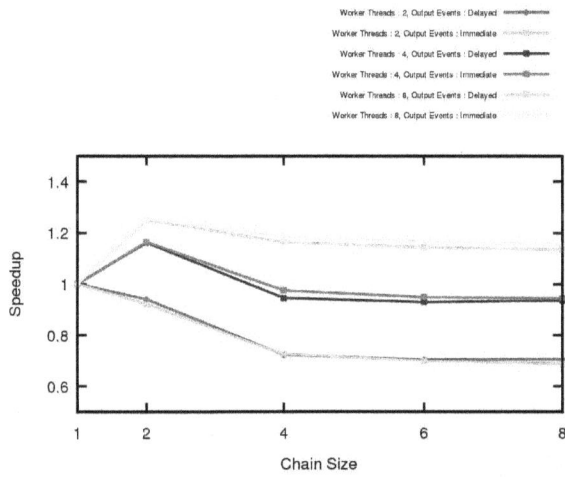

Figure 27: Relative Speedup of Epidemic using Event Chains

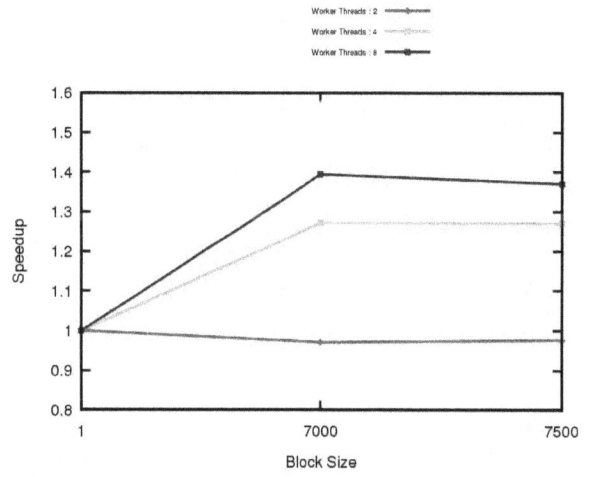

Figure 30: Relative Speedup of Epidemic using Block Scheduling

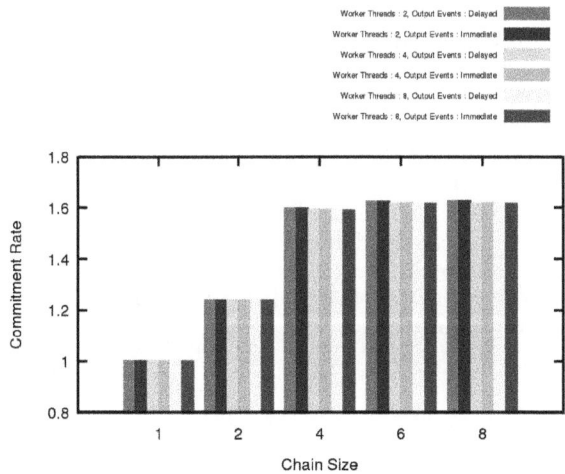

Figure 28: Commitment Rate of Epidemic using Event Chains

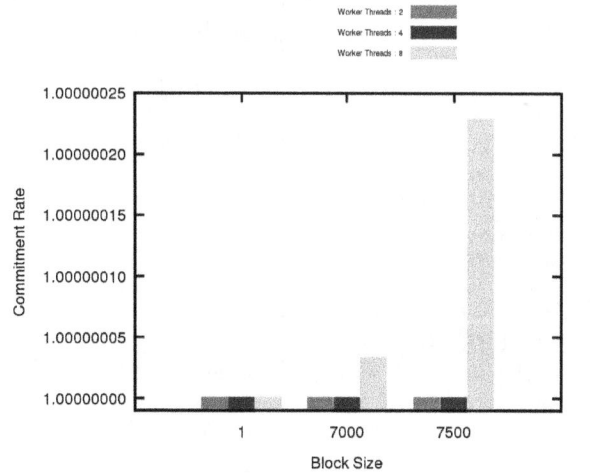

Figure 31: Commitment Rate of Epidemic using Block Scheduling

results. Our next question from this study is "Should we consider the average parallelism results *and* the chain results, to suggest that block and chain scheduling can be combined to achieve even better performance results?". This remains a question that we have yet to explore.

While the idea of scheduling multiple events during each scheduling event is not new and has already been explored by others, it is encouraging to have the performance results follow the profile data results. Ideally we will be able to discover additional new optimization strategies and techniques that are yet to be derived from a continued and extended profiling of simulation models.

8. ACKNOWLEDGMENTS

This material is based upon work supported by the AFOSR under award No FA9550–15–1–0384.

9. REFERENCES

[1] A. Alt and P. A. Wilsey. Profile driven partitioning of parallel simulation models. In *Proceedings of the 2014 Winter Simulation Conference*, pages 2750–2761, Savannah, GA, USA, 2014. IEEE Press.

[2] C. L. Barrett, K. R. Bisset, S. G. Eubank, X. Feng, and M. V. Marathe. Episimdemics: An efficient algorithm for simulating the spread of infectious disease over large realistic social networks. In *Proceedings of the 2008 ACM/IEEE Conference on Supercomputing*, SC '08, pages 37:1–37:12, Piscataway, NJ, USA, 2008. IEEE Press.

[3] C. D. Carothers, D. Bauer, and S. Pearce. ROSS: A high-performance, low memory, modular time warp system. In *Proceedings of the Fourteenth Workshop on Parallel and Distributed Simulation*, PADS '00, pages 53–60, Washington, DC, USA, 2000. IEEE Computer Society.

[4] S. Das, R. Fujimoto, K. Panesar, D. Allison, and M. Hybinette. Gtw: a time warp system for shared memory multiprocessors. In *Proceedings of the 26th conference on Winter simulation*, pages 1332–1339, Orlando, Florida, USA, 1994. Society for Computer Simulation International.

[5] T. Dickman, S. Gupta, and P. A. Wilsey. Event pool structures for pdes on many-core beowulf clusters. In *Proceedings of the 1st ACM SIGSIM Conference on Principles of Advanced Discrete Simulation*, pages 103–114, Montreal, Canada, 2013. ACM.

[6] R. M. Fujimoto. *Parallel and Distribution Simulation Systems*. John Wiley & Sons, Inc., New York, NY, USA, 1st edition, 1999.

[7] S. Gupta and P. A. Wilsey. Lock-free pending event set management in time warp. In *Proceedings of the 2nd ACM SIGSIM Conference on Principles of Advanced Discrete Simulation*, pages 15–26, Denver, CO, USA, 2014. ACM.

[8] J. Hay and P. A. Wilsey. Experiments with hardware-based transactional memory in parallel simulation. In *Proceedings of the 3rd ACM SIGSIM Conference on Principles of Advanced Discrete Simulation*, pages 75–86, London, UK, 2015. ACM.

[9] J. L. Hennessy and D. A. Patterson. *Computer Architecture: A Quantitative Approach*. Morgan Kaufmann Publishers Inc., San Francisco, CA, USA, 5th edition, 2012.

[10] D. Jefferson. Virtual time. *ACM Transactions on Programming Languages and Systems*, 7(3):405–425, July 1985.

[11] Y.-B. Lin and P. A. Fishwick. Asynchronous parallel discrete event simulation. *IEEE Transactions on Systems, Man and Cybernetics, Part A: Systems and Humans*, 26(4):397–412, July 1996.

[12] D. E. Martin, T. J. McBrayer, and P. A. Wilsey. Warped: A time warp simulation kernel for analysis and application development. In *System Sciences, 1996., Proceedings of the Twenty-Ninth Hawaii International Conference on,*, volume 1, pages 383–386, Hawaii, USA, 1996. IEEE.

[13] K. S. Perumalla and S. K. Seal. Discrete event modeling and massively parallel execution of epidemic outbreak phenomena. *Simulation*, 88(7):768–783, July 2012.

[14] R. Radhakrishnan, D. E. Martin, M. Chetlur, D. M. Rao, and P. A. Wilsey. An object-oriented time warp simulation kernel. In *International Symposium on Computing in Object-Oriented Parallel Environments*, pages 13–23, Berlin, Germany, 1998. Springer Berlin Heidelberg.

[15] R. Rönngren, R. Ayani, R. M. Fujimoto, and S. R. Das. Efficient implementation of event sets in time warp. In *Proceedings of the Seventh Workshop on Parallel and Distributed Simulation*, pages 101–108, San Diego, California, USA, 1993. ACM.

[16] E. Santini, M. Ianni, A. Pellegrini, and F. Quaglia. Hardware-transactional-memory based speculative parallel discrete event simulation of very fine grain models. In *Proceedings of the 2015 IEEE 22Nd International Conference on High Performance Computing (HiPC)*, pages 145–154, Washington, DC, USA, 2015. IEEE Computer Society.

[17] S. J. Turner and M. Q. Xu. Performance evaluation of the bounded Time Warp algorithm. *Proceedings of the SCS Multiconference on Parallel and Distributed Simulation*, 24(3):117–126, 1992.

[18] D. J. Watts and S. H. Strogatz. Collective dynamics of 'small-world' networks. *Nature*, 393:440–442, June 1998.

[19] D. Weber. Time warp simulation on multi-core processors and clusters. Master's thesis, University of Cincinnati, Cincinnati, OH, 2016.

[20] P. A. Wilsey. Some properties of events executed in discrete-event simulation models. In *Proceedings of the 2016 annual ACM Conference on SIGSIM Principles of Advanced Discrete Simulation*, pages 165–176, Banf, Alberta, Canada, 2016. ACM.

An Integrated Human Decision Making Model under Extended Belief-Desire-Intention Framework

Young-Jun Son
University of Arizona
Tucson, AZ 85721-0020
son@sie.arizona.edu

ABSTRACT

In this keynote talk, we discuss an extended Belief-Desire-Intention (BDI) framework for human decision making and planning, whose sub-modules have been developed using Bayesian belief network (BBN), Decision-Field-Theory (DFT), and a probabilistic depth first search (DFS) technique. A key novelty of the proposed approach is its ability to represent both the human decision-making as well as decision-planning functions in a coherent framework. In this talk, the proposed framework is illustrated and demonstrated for human's evacuation behaviors under a terrorist bomb attack situation. To mimic realistic human decision-planning and decision-making behaviors, attributes of the extended BDI framework are calibrated from the human-in-the-loop experiments conducted in the Cave Automatic Virtual Environment (CAVE) available at The University of Arizona. A crowd simulation is then constructed, where individual human behaviors are modeled based on what was learned from the CAVE experiments. In this work, the simulated environment (e.g. streets and buildings) and humans conforming to the extended BDI framework are implemented in AnyLogic® agent-based simulation software, where each human entity calls external Netica BBN software to perform its perceptual processing function and Soar software to perform its real-time planning and decision-execution functions. The constructed crowd simulation is used to evaluate the impact of several factors (e.g. number of policemen, information sharing via speakers/mobile phones) on the evacuation performance. Finally, we briefly discuss other applications (e.g. driver's behaviors) and research extensions (e.g. human learning/forgetting and human interactions) for the extended BDI framework.

Keywords

Extended Belief-Desire-Intention modeling

BIO

Dr. Young-Jun Son is a Professor and the Head of Systems and Industrial Engineering Department at The University of Arizona. He is a Department Editor of the IISE Transactions, and serve on the editorial board for six other international journals. He is the Vice Chair and Secretary of CMDS (Core Manufacturing Simulation Data) Standard Product Development Group at Simulation Interoperability Standards Organization.

He is an IISE Fellow, and has received several research awards such as the SME 2004 Outstanding Young Manufacturing Engineer Award, the IIE 2005 Outstanding Young Industrial Engineer Award, the Industrial and Systems Engineering Research Conference Best Paper Award (in 2005, 2008, 2009, 2016), and the Best Paper of the Year Award (2007) in International Journal of Industrial Engineering. He can be reached at son@sie.arizona.edu.

SIGSIM-PADS'17, May 24-26, 2017, Singapore, Singapore
ACM 978-1-4503-4489-0/17/05.
http://dx.doi.org/10.1145/3064911.3064936

Dealing with Reversibility of Shared Libraries in PDES

Davide Cingolani
Sapienza, University of Rome
cingolani@dis.uniroma1.it

Alessandro Pellegrini
Sapienza, University of Rome
pellegrini@dis.uniroma1.it

Markus Schordan
Lawrence Livermore National
Laboratory
schordan1@llnl.gov

Francesco Quaglia
Sapienza, University of Rome
quaglia@dis.uniroma1.it

David R. Jefferson
Lawrence Livermore National
Laboratory
jefferson6@llnl.gov

ABSTRACT

State recoverability is a crucial aspect of speculative Time Warp-based Parallel Discrete Event Simulation. In the literature, we can identify three major classes of techniques to support the correct restoration of a previous simulation state upon the execution of a rollback operation: state checkpointing/restore, manual reverse computation and automatic reverse computation. The latter class has been recently supported by relying either on binary code instrumentation or on source-to-source code transformation. Nevertheless, both solutions are not intrinsically meant to support a reversible execution of third-party shared libraries, which can be pretty useful when implementing complex simulation models.

In this paper, we present an architectural solution (realized as a static C library) which allows to transparently instrument at runtime any third party shared library, with no need for any modification to the model's code. We also present a preliminary experimental evaluation, based on the integration of our library with the ROOT-Sim simulation engine.

1. INTRODUCTION

In Parallel Discrete Event Simulation (PDES) [15], various synchronization protocols have been proposed in the literature. Among them, the Time Warp speculative one [19] has been proven to be particularly effective, as it is relatively independent (in terms of its run-time dynamics) of both the simulation model's lookahead and the communication latency for exchanging data across simulation platform's threads/processes. This allows Time Warp systems to guarantee a high performance, as well in systems that are not tightly coupled and/or encompass millions of processors [5].

The speculative nature of Time Warp allows simulation events to be processed at any Logical Process (LP) independently of their safety (or causal consistency). If an event is a-posteriori detected to be violating causality, its effects on the simulation state are undone via the *rollback operation*. Correctly and efficiently rolling back the simulation state is therefore a fundamental building block for an effective optimistic simulation platform.

Among the different approaches proposed in the literature to rollback the simulation state, the main two families which are considered are *checkpoint-based* [19] and *reverse computing-based* [7], depending on the algorithmic technique which is used to bring one simulation state to a previous (consistent) snapshot. The checkpoint-based rollback operation has been thoroughly studied to reduce its cost (both in terms of memory and CPU usage), either by reducing the checkpointing frequency (the so-called *sparse* or *periodic state saving*) [22, 6, 24, 31, 13, 35, 29] or by reducing the amount of data copied into a state snapshot (the so-called *incremental state saving*) [36, 26].

The reverse computing-based rollback operation, which tries to cancel the non-negligible memory footprint of the state saving technique, relies on *reverse events*, which can be generated either manually [7] or automatically [20, 8, 32, 33]. With respect to automatic generation of reverse events, the various proposals address it by relying either on binary instrumentation [20, 8] or on source-to-source transformation [32, 33]. Nevertheless, none of these solutions is able to deal with third-party shared libraries, which could be regarded as an important building block for the development of complex simulation models. To mention some, libraries such as ALGLIB [34], GSL [16], FFTW [14], LAPACK [11], or BLAS [21] might be necessary for the description of statistical or algebraic processes, proper of a large number of simulation scenarios.

These third-party shared libraries are not *optimism-aware*. In fact, they are devised for application scenarios which always operate on *committed* data. This is something that speculative synchronization protocols, such as Time Warp, intentionally do not provide anytime. While static binary instrumentation and source-to-source transformation could be directly used on these shared libraries to make them *reversible*, their applicability might fall either due to the lack of source code (in the case of closed-source libraries) or due to the fact that instrumenting shared objects could produce system-wide effects to other programs not related to optimistic simulation. In particular, non-speculative applications have no need to rely on shared libraries enabled for reversibility, which can introduce a non-necessary overhead. Moreover, it would be required to instrument the whole

SIGSIM-PADS 17, May 24 26, 2017, Singapore.

© 2017 ACM. ISBN 978-1-4503-4489-0/17/05...$15.00

DOI: http://dx.doi.org/10.1145/3064911.3064927

shared library, even if only a small subportion is actually used by the simulation model, reducing the maintainability of the program.

In this paper, we propose an alternative technique, based on the concept of *lazy instrumentation*, to complement static and source-to-source instrumentation, for x86 systems. This technique allows to intercept any call to any third-party shared library function, allowing to create (transparently to the simulation model developer) an instrumented version which could be easily coupled with any reversible simulation engine. Moreover, our technique allows to quickly switch between instrumented and non-instrumented (original) functions, opening to the possibility of fine-grained runtime self-optimization of the simulation run (similarly to the technique proposed in [27]) and to a different behavior of the engine when dealing with model vs. platform code. Overall, by relying on the approach proposed in this paper, we enable speculative execution of any third-party library within a Time Warp-based simulation engine, significantly increasing the degree of programmability offered to simulation models' developers. This is done transparently for any combination of third-party libraries: libraries which rely on additional libraries are managed as well, thanks to the simple organization of our library-call detection system.

Our technique allows to be easily embedded into any Time Warp-based simulation engine, equipped with a reversible memory management module, via a set of API functions which allow to tune its functioning at simulation startup. No change to the simulation model's code is required for the integration. To assess the viability of our proposal, and to illustrate as well its operating simplicity, we present a preliminary experimental evaluation by integrating our approach with the ROme OpTimistic Simulator (ROOT-Sim) [25]. The experimental evaluation strives to assess the overhead introduced by our proposal when relying on third-party libraries in simulation models.

The remainder of this paper is structured as follows. In Section 2 we discuss related work. Section 3 presents the design choices behind our proposal, and its implementation. The experimental assessment is finally reported in Section 4.

2. RELATED WORK

Despite the fact that reversibility grounds its roots in the 1970's [37], to the best of our knowledge no one has explicitly targeted instrumentation of third-party shared libraries for software reversibility purposes, in any computer science application.

The idea of supporting the rollback operation in the context of Time Warp systems by relying on reverse computation rather than on snapshot restoration dates back to 1999 [7], but at the time the reverse code was hand-generated. A first attempt to automatically generate reversibility code can be found in [20], where control flow analysis is used to generate code which allows to reconstruct the execution path taken in the forward code. Differently to our proposal, reverse code is generated at compile time, preventing the possibility on any number of third-party libraries.

In the recent work in [32], the authors perform source-to-source transformation of C++ code based on the ROSE compiler infrastructure [30], intercepting all operations which modify memory and recording information about the performed updates in a data structure that is used to reverse the effects of memory updates. As mentioned, our proposal

specifically targets all the scenarios where source code of third-party libraries is not available, thus preventing source-to-source transformation from being a viable solution.

The works in [36, 26], similarly to what we do, rely on static binary instrumentation to track memory updates during the forward execution of the events. Nevertheless, their goal is to use this information to generate periodic incremental checkpoints, which we avoid by design in our proposal.

Static binary instrumentation is used in [8] to generate so-called *undo code blocks*, which are packed data structures which keep machine instructions generated on the fly to undo the effects of the forward execution of events. While this is a proposal similar in spirit to our work, the authors in [8] do not account for the presence of third-party libraries, therefore limiting the degree of programmability of simulation models. In particular, the technique presented in [8] could not be used out-of-the-box to instrument third-party libraries. Indeed, static binary instrumentation cannot be used at runtime to intercept generic library calls. This is exactly the focus of this paper.

An approach similar in spirit to our proposal is the one of Valgrind [23]. This framework gains control of the program's execution in a way similar to what we do, in order to generate (in a JIT fashion) instrumented versions of the program code. Nevertheless, since the goal of Valgrind is debugging, it relies on a virtualized CPU which runs the client program. This introduces a slowdown which can be afforded when debugging, but cannot be tolerated when running high-performance simulations. Conversely, we generate instrumented code which is run by physical cores, and interacts with the library only when needed, without relying on any kind of virtualization.

Our proposal is also related to a number of works in the field of program execution tracing (see, e.g., [1, 4, 28, 38]) for debugging, vulnerability assessment and repeatability. These approaches provide detailed analysis of changes in the state of the program, and of the execution flow. Nevertheless, these works do not explicitly deal with the possibility to reverse a portion of the program's execution by relying on runtime-generated reverse instructions.

The US patent in [18] explicitly deals with reversibility of shared libraries within executables. Yet, differently from our proposal, the goal is to make reversible the linking process, thus allowing for different versions of the library to be attached to the same program. Differently, we are interested in undoing the effects of shared libraries on the memory map, to support a reversibility-based rollback operation.

3. SHARED LIBRARIES REVERSIBILITY

Before discussing the approach that we undertake to enact software reversibility of generic third-party shared libraries, let us summarize how third-party libraries interact with an executable, taking as reference Linux systems relying on the Executable and Linkable Format (ELF). Whenever the compiler determines that some function referenced in the source belongs to a shared library, it introduces in the program's image additional pieces of information to let the system, at runtime, *resolve* any reference to that function towards its actual implementation. In particular, the compiler:

- Records the name of the shared library in the program's image. This name often comes with the actual version of the library in it, so that if the executable

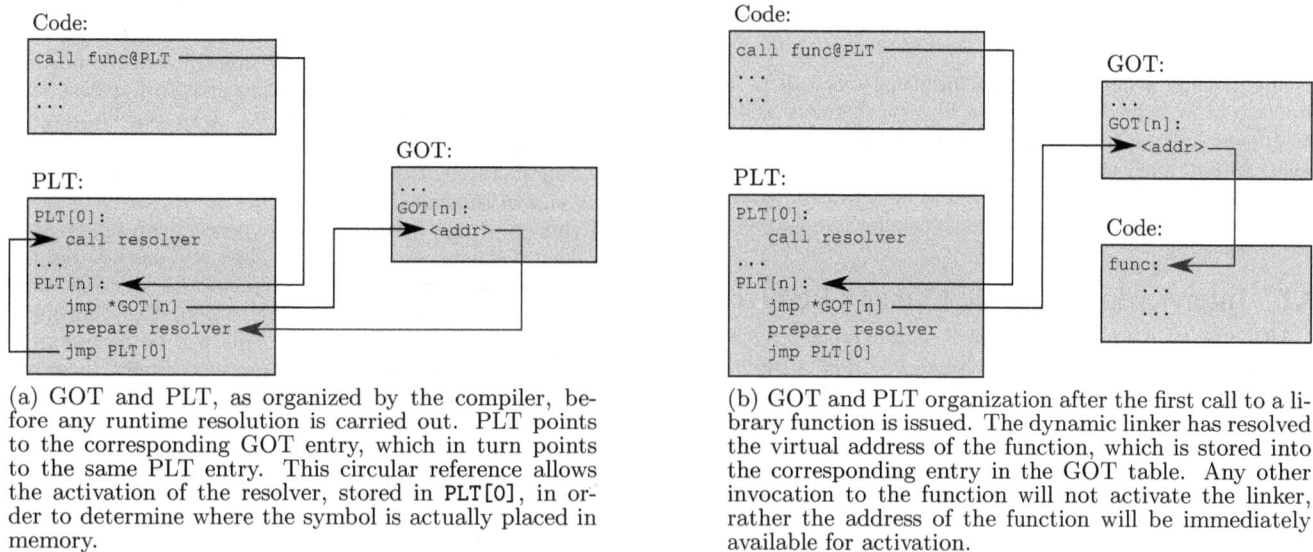

(a) GOT and PLT, as organized by the compiler, before any runtime resolution is carried out. PLT points to the corresponding GOT entry, which in turn points to the same PLT entry. This circular reference allows the activation of the resolver, stored in PLT[0], in order to determine where the symbol is actually placed in memory.

(b) GOT and PLT organization after the first call to a library function is issued. The dynamic linker has resolved the virtual address of the function, which is stored into the corresponding entry in the GOT table. Any other invocation to the function will not activate the linker, rather the address of the function will be immediately available for activation.

Figure 1: Resolver, GOT, and PLT hooking.

is moved to a different environment where a compatible library's version is not present, the loader fails to resolve any call, so as to avoid undefined behaviors;

- Reserves an entry in a special table, called the *Procedure Linkage Table* (PLT), for the specific library function. Any call to that function will actually refer the associated PLT's entry, which keeps enough space to host a couple of machine instructions;

- For any entry in the PLT, it reserves the corresponding entry in the *Global Offset Table* (GOT), which only stores a memory pointer.

The need for two tables arises due to the *lazy binding* policy adopted by dynamic loading. In fact, PLT and GOT reference each other in a way that allows the system to know whether a library function is being called for the first time. If it is so, the library symbol is resolved, otherwise the (already-resolved) function is simply called.

This is exactly where our proposal acts so as to generate reversibility-enabled copies of third-party library functions. To illustrate this mechanism, let us suppose that a program relies on the shared library's function func. The GOT and PLT tables are organized as in Figure 1(a). As mentioned, the call to func is actually a call to an entry of the PLT table, namely PLT[n], where n is the entry associated with func. The first entry of this table, namely PLT[0], is a special entry, which keeps an instruction to call the resolver, i.e. the function of the dynamic linker which is in charge of determining where the entry point of any library function is in memory. Once the first call to func is issued, the code in PLT[n] takes control. By PLT contruction, the code jumps to the address pointed by the corresponding GOT[n] entry. At program startup, this address points to PLT[n] itself, specifically to a code snippet which prepares (on the stack) the parameters needed by the dynamic linker to determine what library call caused its invocation. Then, the actual resolver is called, by jumping to PLT[0]. The resolver performs the resolution of the actual address of func, places it into GOT[n], and calls func. The GOT/PLT organization, after the symbol's resolution, is depicted in Figure 1(b). Any other call to func will not cause the activation of the dynamic resolver, as the address stored in GOT[n] now points to the actual virtual address of func.

In order to instrument third-party library function calls, we specifically intercept the above-described mechanism. In particular, our approach relies on a static library to be linked to the executable, which we call libreverse[1]. This library contains a *program constructor*, namely a function which is activated by the program loader before giving control to the actual main program. The goal of this constructor is to replace the call to resolver to a different function, exposed by the library itself, which alters the behavior of the latter part of the dynamic linking process. In particular, the custom resolver takes the following steps:

1. Similarly to the dynamic linker's resolver, it determines what is func's entry point virtual address;

2. Once func's address is identified, it creates a copy of the whole function in memory, instrumenting any instruction which has a memory operand as the destination (namely, a *memory-write* instruction);

3. The instrumentation is carried in a way such that before executing the actual memory write operation, control is given to a *trampoline* which activates a module of libreverse;

4. An entry in a custom table, called *Library Activation Trampoline* (LAT), is reserved. This entry keeps a small portion of code to determine whether the instrumented version of the library should be called or not;

5. The address of LAT[n] is stored into GOT[n], allowing any future activation of func to directly give control to the code in LAT[n];

---

[1]The source code of the library is available at https://github.com/HPDCS/libreverse.

43

6. Control is given to `LAT[n]`, in order to perform the actual function call.

This general scheme allows to intercept *any* call to *any* function in *any* third-party shared library, therefore making them aware of the reversibility requirements of Time Warp-based simulations, necessarily to support the rollback operation. All these points above demand special care, and we therefore describe in the following how they are supported by `libreverse`.

3.1 Intercepting Dynamic Linker s Resolver

Although the steps taken by the dynamic linker's resolver are mostly standardized, there could be some variability across systems and versions of the linker with respect to the actual steps taken. To make `libreverse` of general availability, we want our custom resolver to take the same steps as the system's dynamic linker. To this end, we use the following strategy to ensure portability across systems and linker versions.

As mentioned, when the program is launched, `libreverse`'s constructor is activated, which replaced in `PLT[0]` the address of the resolver with a custom one. Nevertheless, since this custom one should be compliant with the system's one, `libreverse` does not contain the custom resolver's code. Rather, it generates it at program startup. In particular, any dynamic linker's resolver has to perform these tasks:

- Determine whether the image of the shared library is mapped into the program's image, if not it has to be `mmap`'ed;

- Determine where is the function's entry point in the library image. This is commonly done by relying on a fast hash-function based mechanism, relying on the data stored in the `.dynsym` section in case of an ELF executable;

- The address is stored in `GOT[n]`, where `n` is passed as an argument on stack;

- The function is activated directly by the resolver.

The last point is where we hook our custom code. In particular, the activation of the library function is made by relying on an *indirect jump*. On x86 systems, this is implemented by an instruction in the form `jmp *%reg`, i.e. the address of the target function is stored into a register, which is used as the destination of the jump instruction. Once `libreverse`'s constructor takes control, it creates a copy of the system resolver's code, and starts scanning its bytes until such an instruction is found. This jump is then replaced with a *direct jump*, whose target is a function within `libreverse` which takes care of instrumenting the target function, before the control is given to it.

This strategy allows `libreverse` to attach itself to any version of the dynamic loader's resolver, independently of the actual way the identification of the function's symbol within the shared library's image is carried out.

3.2 Instrumentation of Library Functions

Once a library function is first called, by the above interception of the dynamic linker's resolver, we are able to take control right after the address of the function is identified.

At this point, in order to perform the actual instrumentation of the function, we must determine its size. To this end, we recall that the executable keeps track of the library file on disk storage. We are therefore able to navigate the path of the library file, and open it. A shared library on Linux systems is represented as an ELF file. By inspecting the symbol's table of this file, we can determine what is the actual size of the called function.

At this point, the instrumentation process can take place. We allocate a memory area of the same size as the original function via an `mmap()` call, making it both writable and executable. We then copy the whole content of the functions' binary representation in it. This will be its working copy, which we can inspect and alter accordingly, in order to enable reversibility of its actions.

The instrumentation process requires two *logical steps*. The first one entails determining the total number of assembly instructions which compose the function. The second one relates to identifying, among all the instructions, those which write on memory. These instructions should be properly altered to generate *reverse instructions* on the fly, namely assembly instructions whose execution undoes the effects of the original instructions in memory. To this end, we must determine both the destination address of the memory write instruction, and its size.

We note that these two steps require two different levels of detail (and, consequently, of complexity). Indeed, to determine the number of instructions which compose the library, we do not need to get into the *semantics* of the instructions themselves, which is a non-minimal optimization given that our target is the x86 architecture. In fact, the x86 ISA is a variable-size one. This means that the length in bytes of a single assembly instruction cannot be determined beforehand. Only by interpreting the opcode it is possible to determine the exact amount of parameters to the instruction, and therefore its length.

For the sake of performance, `libreverse` is equipped with two different disassemblers. The first one, which we call a *length disassembler*, is a fast table-based routine which only tells what is the length of the actual instruction in bytes, and gives a reference to the actual opcode[2]. The second disassembler which is included into `libreverse` is a *full disassembler*: it fully decodes the bytecode representation of the instruction, evaluating all its fields, allowing to extract the data of interest. The execution of the length disassembler is 3 times faster than the full disassembler, on any x86 instruction (i.e., independently of its length).

Therefore, `libreverse` enacts the instrumentation process in the following way. The length disassembler is invoked on the initial address of the function, returning the size of the first instruction and a pointer to its actual opcode. This opcode is matched against a table which tells whether the instruction *could* entail a memory-write operation. In the negative case, the next instruction can be identified by inspecting the bytecode located n bytes after the initial address, where n is the length returned by the length disassembler. In the positive case, the full disassembler is invoked on the same memory location. This allows to determine whether the involved instruction is *actually* a memory-write one and, if it is so, it allows to extract the size of the memory write

---

[2]In fact, x86 instructions can be preceded by an arbitrary number of *prefixes*, so that the first byte in a given instruction is not necessarily the opcode.

```
save CPU context (except RIP)
call reverse
restore CPU context (except RIP)
<original instruction>
jmp <address>
```

Figure 2: The instruction trampoline

(which in case of a simple `mov` instruction is encoded in the binary representation of the instruction itself) and the destination address of the memory-write operation.

At this point, the instrumentation process *replaces* the memory-write instruction with a *jump* to a code snippet (which we call the *instruction trampoline*) generated on the fly. This snippet is placed into an additional table, called the `INSTRUCTIONS` table. This is a table which, for each memory-write instruction, keeps a portion of code to prepare the required information to generate the associated reversible instruction. Since the number of memory-write instructions is not known beforehand, the `INSTRUCTIONS` table is pre-allocated keeping the space for a certain number of trampolines. If the space in the `INSTRUCTIONS` table is exhausted, a new table is silently allocated.

The instruction trampoline's code is organized as in Figure 2. The first required action is to save the CPU context. This is because the original library function must be unaware of the execution of all the injected code. Unfortunately, since the code was placed after the program's compilation, standard `setjmp/longjmp` functions cannot be used, as we are explicitly breaking System V ABI's calling conventions [2, 3] and *caller save* registers are not saved by the code. Therefore, our solution is to perform a fast CPU-context save by pushing all required general-purpose registers and the flags register. Since the code is crafted directly in assembly language, we use only *caller-save* registers, after having pushed all of them on stack. In this way, we do not need to concern about registers used by functions called by the trampoline, as their code is compiler-generated, and therefore respects the calling conventions. In this way, the consistency of the program's execution is preserved.

After having saved the CPU context, we issue a call to `reverse`, a `libreverse` internal function which computes the target memory-write address and generates the corresponding reverse instruction. According to the addressing mode of the x86 architecture, each memory address is identified by the expression *base address* + (*index* ∗ *scale*) + *displacement*. The parameters *scale* and *displacement* are already encoded in the instruction binary representation, while *base address* and *index* refer to the content of registers, which can be evaluated only at runtime. Therefore, once the control is given to the trampoline of a certain instructions, some data to allow the computation of the memory-write target address (and the size of the write, when available) are placed on stack. These data are the outcome of the instrumentation process, and are organized as in the following structure:

```
struct insn_entry {
        char flags;
        char base;
        char idx;
        char scale;
        int  size;
        long long offset;
}
```

where `flags` tells which are the relevant fields to recompute the target address, or to identify the class of data-movement instructions, as we will explain later in details; `base` keeps the (3 or 4 bits) base register binary representation; `idx` keeps the (3 or 4 bits) index register binary representation; `scale` is used to store the scale factor of the addressing mode; `size` holds the size (in bytes) of the memory area being affected by the memory-write instruction (when available at disassemble time); `offset` keeps the displacement of the addressing mode[3]. By relying on this information, the `reverse` function can determine the size and the target address of the memory-write instruction. This information is used to generate the corresponding reverse instruction, as we will discuss later.

As mentioned, the original instruction's bytecode is replaced with a jump to the corresponding entry in the `INSTRUCTIONS` table. In order to execute the original instruction, we copy the binary representation of the instruction directly within the corresponding `INSTRUCTIONS`' entry, after the call to the `reverse` function. Nevertheless, the original instruction might require contextual information in order to execute properly. This is due to the fact that many instructions in the x86 ISA use *relative* references. As an example, consider an operation used to store a value into a *local* variable. These variables are stored on the stack, and are often referenced using a displacement from either the base frame pointer, or from the stack pointer. Therefore, before giving control to the copy of the original memory-write instruction withing the `INSTRUCTIONS` entry, we restore the CPU context (except for the value of the `RIP` register, the program counter). This allows to correctly execute a large set of instruction, although we must explicitly account for the fact that the value kept by `RIP` is different from the original execution context.

This latter point deserves an additional discussion. Indeed, in the 64-bit version of the x64 architecture, a special addressing mode, which is called `RIP`-relative, allows to target symbols (e.g., variables) encoding in the instruction a displacement from the current value of the `RIP` register. This addressing mode is particularly important for library functions. Indeed, a shared library can be remapped to any virtual memory address range, depending on the set of libraries and/or runtime dynamics. Therefore, to reduce the overhead related to library loading, shared libraries code is generated by compilers as *position-independent code* (PIC). A PIC library has no indirect reference to any library or variable. This means that *any* reference within a library is expressed as a displacement with respect to the current instruction. In the 64-bit x86 ISA, this entails a huge usage of the `RIP`-relative addressing mode.

To cope with this issue, we cannot simply restore the whole CPU context, including the value of `RIP`. In fact, at the original address we no longer have the original instruction. To execute its copy, `RIP` *must* point to the copy, which is at a different address. Therefore, to correctly execute memory-write operations which rely on `RIP`-relative addressing, the only option is to *fix* the displacement. To this end, we rely on the length disassembler. In particu-

---

[3]We provide 64-bits space in the `insn_entry` structure due to the fact that the x86_64 assembly language allows one single instruction, namely `movabs`, to directly use a 64-bits addressing mode. In all the other cases, only 32 bits of the `offset` field are actually used.

45

```
        mov     %fs:platform_mode@tpoff,%eax
        cmpb    $0x0,%eax
        jz      1f
        call    original_function
        ret
    1:  call    instrumented_function
        ret
```

Figure 3: Entry of the LAT table (x86 64-bit version)

lar, this disassembler sets a global (per-thread) flag whenever it encounters an assembly instruction which is using the RIP-relative addressing mode. Once such an instruction is found, the full disassembler is invoked on it, allowing to determine whether this addressing mode is used in the source or in the destination operand. In both cases, the offset is corrected. This correction is trivial: we can at any time determine what is the *additional offset* (either positive or negative) introduced by the fact that the instruction is being moved to a different location. Anyhow, the correction of RIP-relative addressing cannot be limited to instructions copied into the INSTRUCTIONS table. In fact, since we create a whole copy of the original library function, all RIP-relative addressing must be corrected. Anyhow, by relying on the above-described scheme, the correction can be actuated in place on the copy of the instructions.

To complete the instrumentation process of the library function, we iterate over all the instructions carrying on the aforementioned steps, until we reach the end of the function. As mentioned, we can identify the end of the function by inspecting the library's ELF symbol table, to determine its total length in bytes. The final instruction of the instruction trampoline must give control back to the library function. Since there is a one-to-one mapping between the memory-write instruction and the entry in the INSTRUCTIONS table which keeps its instruction trampoline, the return to the function's flow can be implemented with a direct jmp instruction to the correct address.

After that the whole function is instrumented, we have to hook the altered version to the GOT/PLT invocation mechanism. As hinted before, we want to give the possibility to activate both the original version and the instrumented one, depending on the execution context. In particular, the reversibility facilities are only related to the execution of the simulation models' event handlers, while when executing in *platform mode* (i.e., when the control is taken by the simulation engine) we do not need to generate reverse instructions. In this latter case, for the sake of performance, we want to rely on the original version of the library functions, if they are used. To allow a fast switching between the two versions, we rely on the aforementioned LAT table. In particular, the *n*-th entry in the LAT, which corresponds to the current function being instrumented, is organized (for the case of 64-bit x86 Linux systems) as in Figure 3 (for a total of 24 bytes). The goal of this code is to check a (per-thread) global variable called platform_mode which tells whether a library function is invoked from the simulation engine level or from the application-level code. In the former case, the original (non-instrumented) library function is activated, while in the latter the instrumented version is called. To change the execution mode, libreverse offers an internal API function,

named platform_mode(bool) which tells whether control is being passed to an event handler or it is returning from such a handler. It is the responsibility of the simulation engine, when integrating with libreverse, to properly use this function. Overall, the integration with the GOT/PLT invocation mechanism is simply done by placing, after the LAT entry is properly crafted, its address within the corresponding entry of the GOT table.

There are two classes of instructions which cannot be directly dealt with according to the aforementioned instrumentation scheme, rather require special management. One is the cmov instruction, which is managed directly in the trampoline. Specifically, in case of a cmov, we use 4 bits of the flags field to record what is the check to be emulated. The trampoline checks whether the bits are different from zero, and in the positive case the corresponding status bits are checked to determine whether the condition is met or not. Nevertheless, the values of status bits might have been already altered during the execution of the previous injected operations. To this end, the trampoline's code looks on the application stack for the old value, as stored during the CPU-context save phase. If the condition is met, the cmov is managed exactly like a standard mov.

The second one is the movs instruction, for which we use one bit of the flags field to let the trampoline know whether its invocation is related to such an instruction. In this specific case, the size flag tells only the size of one single iteration of the movs instruction. Therefore, to compute the total size, the trampoline's code checks the value of the rcx register, and multiplies it by size. The starting address of the write is then computed by first checking the *direction flag* of the flags register. In case this flag is cleared, the destination starting address is already present in the rdi register. If the flag is set, then the movs instruction will make a backwards copy, and therefore the (logical) initial address of the move is computed as rdi - rcx * size.

An additional note must be discussed to complete our overview of the instrumentation mechanism. In fact, in order to link the place where a library function has a memory-write instruction with the corresponding INSTRUCTIONS entry, a jmp instruction is used to replace the actual mov. Nevertheless, the x86 ISA has a variable length. If the size of the jmp (which is 5 bytes) is smaller than the size of the actual intercepted memory-update instruction, the remaining space can be easily filled using a nop. On the other hand, the memory-write instruction's representation might be shorter than 5 bytes—the classical example is the aforementioned movs, which is only 1-byte long.

In this case, libreverse "makes room" for the jump instruction by coalescing multiple consecutive instructions in the same INSTRUCTIONS entry. This is done by continuing the disassembly of the library function, until enough room for the jmp is found. Nevertheless, there could be the possibility that the end of the function is reached before finding enough room. In this case, libreverse "backtracks" its execution by coalescing instructions *before* the memory-write instruction, until enough space is found. Anyhow, since the length of an assembly instruction is variable, it could be resource intensive to perform this latter action. To this end, while performing the forward instrumentation, libreverse builds an *instruction index*. This index keeps, for each instruction, its size in bytes. Therefore, if the end of the function is reached while coalescing instructions, it is possible to

Index Entry — Instruction size — Instrumented Flag — Reference Pointer

```
1  5  2  2
T  F  F  F
3  1  2  5  6
F  F  F  F  T
2  2  1  4  3
F  T  T  F  F
4  2  4  5  5
F  F  F  F  F
8  9  1  4  2
T  F  F  T  F
```

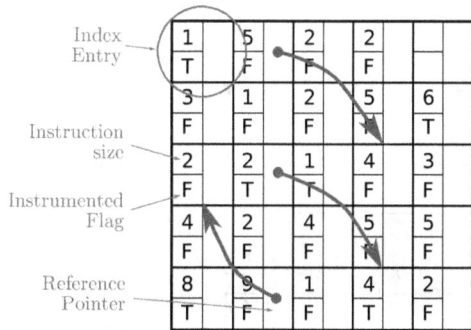

Figure 4: The index of assembly instructions built while instrumenting a library function.

increase the size up to the required amount of 5 bytes by simply inspecting this index. Since the number of instructions that compose the function is not known beforehand, the instruction index is implemented as a wait-free resizable array, as described in [10].

While this approach solves the problem related to the needed amount of bytes to insert the jmp to the INSTRUCTIONS' table entry, it might pose an additional problem. Let us discuss the following code snippet:

```
    jmp 1f
    movl $0x0, %eax
    movsl
1:  leave
    ret
```

The instrumentation process will detect that the movs is a memory-write instruction, and will trigger the replacement with a jmp. Since movs is only 1-byte long, the coalescing procedure will try to expand over subsequent instructions. The next is the 1-byte long leave, so the coalescing procedure continues, until the end of the function is reached. At this point, since the total amount of bytes found amounts to three, the coalescing procedure inspects the instructions' index to determine how many instructions behind the movs should be taken to make enough room to the jmp. Since the movl $0x0, %eax is 5-byte long, the coalescing procedure takes it and halts. This gives a grand total of 8 bytes (with respect to the 5 needed) to place the jmp. Nevertheless, this action will completely break the functioning of the program. In fact, the initial instruction in the example is a jmp which targets one of the instructions which will be moved into the INSTRUCTIONS' table entry, having the jmp target the middle of the (newly-inserted) assembly instruction.

To overcome this issue, we extend the aforementioned instructions index, adding (for each instruction) a reference. In particular, the opcode retrieved by the length disassembler is matched against a second table, which tells whether the instruction could have as a parameter a reference to a different instruction (e.g., the case for a jmp instruction). In the positive case, the instruction index keeps a reference to the instruction. In case it is a reference to a future instruction, we keep track of this by relying on a fast hash table. Once the target instruction is reached, the link between the two is completed.

Whenever an instruction is moved to an entry of the INSTRUCTIONS table, the corresponding entry in the instructions index is flagged. At the end of the instrumentation process, a fast scan of the instructions index is performed,

so as to determine whether some instruction referenced by, e.g., a jmp instruction has been moved into an entry of the INSTRUCTIONS table. In the positive case, the referencing instruction's offset is corrected, simply applying the corresponding shift to the displacement. The final organization of the instruction index is depicted in Figure 4.

The instructions index becomes handy to solve a couple of additional issues, related to the way shared libraries are built. In particular, any library function within a library can reference any other function within the library itself. Since a call instruction, to invoke another function in the library, uses an offset in a way perfectly similar to a jmp, but this reference will not be found during the instrumentation process of the current function. Here, two situations might arise:

1. *The function is exposed to the application and is actually used*: in this case, an entry in the PLT is present. This can be verified by inspecting the ELF symbol table of the running application. The call, therefore, is redirected to the corresponding PLT entry. While this might reduce a bit any optimization internal to the library, allows to perform a lazily instrumentation according to the scheme that we are presenting in this paper;

2. *The function is exposed to the application but is not used by the program, or is an internal one*: in this second case, we cannot rely on the PLT to carry on the lazy instrumentation. We rather keep within libreverse a list of functions internal to this library which have already been instrumented due to this specific scenario taking place. If the target function is present in this list, then the call is redirected to this already-instrumented symbol. If it is not, then the target function is instrumented (exactly according to the whole aforementioned scheme) and then the symbol is added to libreverse's internal list.

As a last note, since libraries are often implemented with high performance in mind, nothing prevents to "break" the common idea of function—this is something that, e.g., happens extensively in glibc. In particular, one function might jump into the middle of another one, just to execute a portion of its code in case some optimized condition of the host system is detected. While this scenario can be detected in a way similar to calls to different library functions (i.e., the reference of the jmp is not resolved while scanning the function), handling this condition is less trivial, as it would entail some code flow analysis like the ones presented in [12]. Since such an analysis is out of the scope of this paper, and considering that a library as complex as glibc shows this behavior only in a handful of functions (like, e.g., memmove()), for the sake of simplicity we have simply replaced these functions with less-optimized ones which are statically linked to the executable. Future work entails generalizing the approach, in order to specifically deal with this corner case with any third-party library.

To conclude, at the end of the instrumentation process, the organization of the memory map to execute a call to a library function is depicted in Figure 5.

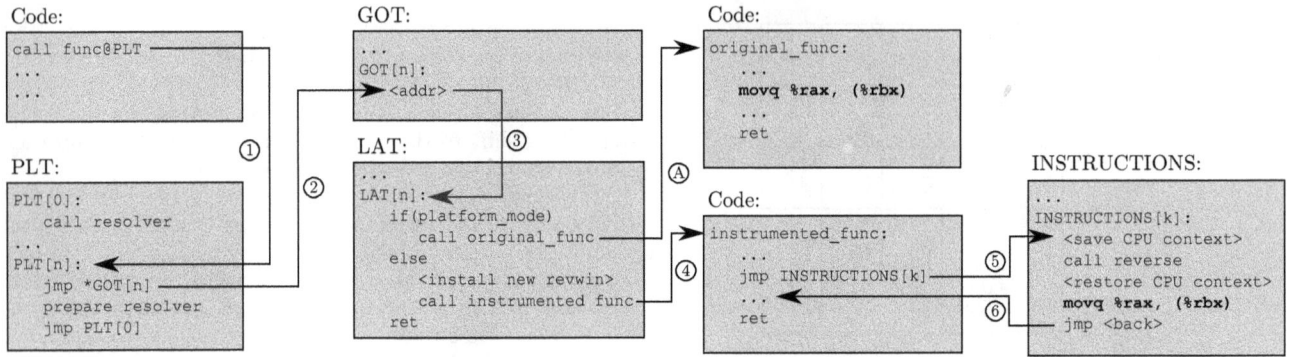

Figure 5: Organization of code, tables, and trampolines after instrumentation. ①: the application invokes the library function func, by calling into PLT[n]; ②: the program jumps to the corresponding LAT entry by dereferencing the n-th pointer in the GOT (③); Ⓐ: if in platform mode, the trampoline activates the original version of func, otherwise ④ the instrumented one; ⑤: instructions moved to the INSTRUCTIONS table are accessed via jumps; ⑥: the instrumented function regains control.

3.3 Generation and Management of Reverse Instructions

The instrumentation mechanism described so far allows, at runtime, to activate the reverse function just before any memory-update operation is performed. At this point, libreverse is notified of the application code's will to update the simulation model state, and therefore reverse instructions (to restore the state in case of a rollback operation) can be built on-the-fly.

If the activation of reverse is related to the execution (in the forward event) of a mov or a cmov instruction, the reverse instruction is built by accessing memory at the computed address and by reading the original value (i.e., the one before the write operation is executed). This value is placed within a data movement instruction as the source (immediate) operand, having as the destination address the same address. On the other hand, if the activation of reverse is due to a movs instruction, this can be easily determined by the size of the memory-write operation, as it is higher than the largest representable immediate[4]. The reverse instruction in this case can only be another movs instruction, having as the source operand a properly-allocated memory buffer where the original content has been copied upon reverse instruction generation.

The generation of reverse instructions is not a costly operation, except for the movs case where a memory buffer must be explicitly copied. Indeed, the set of instructions to be generated is very limited, and the opcodes are known beforehand. Therefore, we rely on a pre-compiled tables of instructions in which only the memory address and the old immediate should be packed within. With this approach, we pay an instrumentation overhead similar to that of incremental state saving solutions (see, e.g., [26]), but we are completely avoiding any generation of metadata, thus reducing the overhead for the installation of a previous snapshot during the execution of a rollback. In addition, differently from incremental state saving, our organization of reverse instructions has a direct positive impact on the re-

---

[4]We note that, by using this approach, a possible movs instruction involving few bytes of memory is negated using a standard mov instruction, which is nevertheless correct, and possibly more efficient.

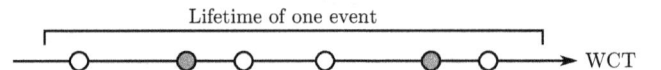

Figure 6: Interleaved memory updates within one event. White circles refer to memory updates directly made by the model's code. Grey circles refer to memory updates made through calls to shared library functions.

store operation. In fact, traditional incremental state saving approaches (see, e.g., [27]) require scanning the metadata table to determine which portions of the simulation state should be restored from a certain snapshot, and possibly require to generate temporary additional metadata during this operation. By relying on dynamically-generated reverse instructions, we do not incur into this cost.

In order to allow the PDES engine to correctly interact with the management of reversibility of library function calls, libreverse intrinsically works with the notion of *events* and *library call incarnation*. libreverse organizes reverse instructions in atomic blocks, on a per-thread fashion, in a way similar to the work presented in [8]. Every time that a new reverse instruction is generated, it is inserted in a stack of instructions, so that they appear in reverse order with respect to the forward execution. This is a fundamental prerequisite to undo the effects of library calls within an event, as they can be undone by simply issuing a call to the first instruction in the reverse window (i.e., the one pointed by pointer). Since the focus of this paper is on how to efficiently and effectively enable generic third-party libraries for reversibility, we will not describe in details reverse instructions are generated and managed. For a thorough description of this aspect, we refer the reader to the previous work in [8].

Nevertheless, packing together all the reverse instructions generated within the same event could lead to erroneous reconstructions of a previous state upon the execution of a rollback operation. In fact, if we look at the example in Figure 6, the same memory buffer could be updated in an interleaved fashion by calls to library functions and direct memory updates by the simulation model. Executing all reverse instructions generated by library functions as a whole, in fact, might not respect the ordering of updates executed in forward execution. To this end, `libreverse` uses a reverse window for each library call invocation, which is detected since the execution flow has to pass always through the corresponding LAT entry.

To let the simulation engine keep control of generated reverse windows on a per-event basis, `libreverse` exposes an API function named `finalize_event()` which, upon invocation, returns a list of all reverse windows generated since the last call to `finalize_event()` itself. The simulation engine can then link this set to any representation of the event in the just-descheduled LP's message queue. To facilitate the management of the operations, `libreverse` offers two additional API functions, namely `execute_revwin()` and `cleanup_revwin()`. The former allows to execute the reverse instructions kept by a reverse window by giving control to the instruction pointed by `pointer`. The latter can be used to release all memory buffers related to a set of reverse windows in case, e.g., an event is deemed committed or it is removed from the message queue due to the reception of an antimessage. To determine the proper execution order of reverse windows, each of them is stamped with a unique mark, based on the value of the Time Stamp Counter (TSC) x86 register. `libreverse` exposes the `get_mark()` API function (based on the `rdtsc` assembly instruction) to deliver values from TSC to the simulation engine. In this way, the engine can stamp as well portion of its data/metadata used to enforce reversibility of the model, determining in this way the proper execution order of reverse operations globally, for each event to be undone. By relying on this set of API functions, any Time Warp-based simulation engine can be easily integrated with `libreverse`.

As a last note, we should discuss how we deal with updates of *local variables* of library functions, which live in the stack of the instrumented function. In case a functions call is undone due to a rollback operation, we do not need to revert changes to these variables—they are ephemeral with respect to the scope of the function—and therefore we do not need to generate reverse instructions for these. To this end, we adopt the following approach to filter out stack updates, trying to reduce as well the overhead introduced at runtime. In particular, when disassembling an instruction, we check whether the addressing mode involves any displacement from the stack pointer or the base pointer, which are related to access to local variables. At the same time, we can easily check whether a memory-update operation involves the management of the stack (e.g., in case of `push` or `pop` instructions). In both cases, `libreverse` does not instrument these memory-access instructions, as they are related to data which is not necessary to reverse. Nevertheless, nothing prevents a program to pass as a reference a variable on stack. In this case, it is not possible to check the on-stack condition statically. Therefore, whenever the `reverse` function gains control, it checks whether the computed destination address of the memory write falls within the stack—this can be easily done by comparing with the current value of the stack pointer register. If it is so, `libreverse` simply returns, without generating any reverse instruction. We note that in this latter case we pay an additional overhead to compute the target address, but we keep consistency of the approach even under complex stack-usage patterns.

3.4 Dealing with Memory Allocations and Deallocations

The last aspect to be dealt with in order to support a correct restoration of a previous state is related to the management of allocation/deallocation operations. In particular, if during the execution of a forward event the model's code invokes a library function which allocates memory, this memory logically belongs to the LP which is currently scheduled. While designing `libreverse`, we have assumed that the simulation engine has a per-LP memory map manager, such as the one in [27], as providing a memory manager is out of the scope of our approach. Therefore, in order to correctly connect `libreverse` and the simulation engine, we must provide a means to map a forward memory allocation with the corresponding memory deallocation and vice versa.

To this end, `libreverse` offers two additional API functions, namely `register_alloc()` and `register_dealloc()`. These functions accept a function pointer each, which are defined as `void *(*allocate)(void *ptr)` for the former function, and `void (*deallocate)(void *ptr)` for the latter. These pointers allow to bridge the internals of `libreverse` with the simulation engine's memory manager, so that whenever a library allocates some memory a call to the `deallocate()` function is placed within the reverse window, while when a chunk of memory is deallocated, a call to `allocate()` is similarly stored. We emphasize that having the `allocate()` function accept a pointer is a strategic choice to allow piece-wise-deterministic replay of events upon a rollback operations, allowing to retrieve buffers at the same virtual addresses, and therefore support a memory map laid out in a generic way.

4. EXPERIMENTAL RESULTS

4.1 Test-bed Environment

We have integrated `libreverse` within the ROOT-Sim simulation platform[5] [25]. This is a C-based open source simulation package targeted at POSIX systems, which implements a general-purpose simulation environment based on the Time Warp synchronization paradigm. It offers a very simple programming model relying on the classical notion of simulation-event handlers (both for processing events and for accessing a committed and globally-consistent state image upon GVT calculations), to be implemented according to the ANSI-C standard, and transparently supports all the services required to parallelize the execution. It supports the execution of the rollback operation either via traditional checkpointing facilities [27], or via reverse code blocks [8].

Our experiments have been run on top of a 32-core HP ProLiant server equipped with 64GB of RAM and running Debian 6 on top of the 2.6.32-5-amd64 Linux kernel. This is a common setup for HPC applications, as this is a software configuration which offers a very good tradeoff between the services exposed to user space applications and performance. At the same time, our approach is so general that it can be used as well on more modern environments.

In order to integrate `libreverse` with ROOT-Sim, we have slightly touched two different aspects of the simulation engine: the models' compilation toolchain (which relies on the `rootsim-cc` custom compiler) and the reversibility facilities

---

[5]ROOT-Sim is available at http://github.com/HPDCS/ROOT-Sim.

already present in the engine [8]. As for the compilation toolchain, we have only statically linked the final executable against `libreverse`, allowing the program constructor described in Section 3 to take control before the actual simulation engine is started. This allows to setup the patched dynamic linker's resolver which will be activated whenever an invocation to a library function is issued.

On the other hand, ROOT-Sim's reversibility facilities presented in [8] rely on an instrumentation mechanism similar in spirit to the one used by `libreverse`. In particular, at compile time, ROOT-Sim performs a static binary instrumentation process, picking all the memory-update operations that are located in the simulation model's code. These instructions are intercepted by the memory map manager, which generate undo code blocks to reverse the effects of the execution of the event on memory. `libreverse`, on the other hand, keeps its reverse instructions in a separate buffer, as described in Section 3.3.

To ensure that the reverse execution is performed in the proper order, we rely on the `get_mark()` API exposed by `libreverse`, so that reverse code generated by ROOT-Sim can be tagged with data which allow to determine the total order of reverse actions to take. In this way, upon a rollback execution, ROOT-Sim is able to undo the effects on memory by the forward execution of events by either relying on its internal reversibility management, or invoking the `execute_revwin()` function.

4.2 Test-Bed Application Model

As a test-bed application, we rely on the Sensors Network Model (SNM), which simulate the behavior of wireless sensor networks (WSN). WSN are networks composed of small devices featuring power source, a microprocessor, a wireless interface, some memory and one or more sensors. They are used to gather information in a given location or region, yet due to the limited radio communication range, nodes can communicate using multi-hop routing protocols.

SNM implements the Collection Tree Protocol (CTP) [17] to collect data from wireless sensors networks. In particular, it relies on a variant of the library offered by TinyOS [9]. CTP is a distance vector routing protocol, which computes the routes from each node in the network to the root (specified destinations) in the network. Each node forwards packets to its parent, chosen among its neighbor nodes. In order to make a choice, each node must be aware of the state of its neighbors: that's why nodes continuously broadcast special packets, called *beacons*, describing their condition.

The metric adopted in CTP for the selection of the parent node is the *Expected Transmissions* (ETX). A node whose ETX is equal to n can deliver a data packet to the root node with an average of n transmissions. The ETX of any node is recursively defined as the ETX of its parent plus the ETX of its link to the parent; the root node represents the base case in this recursion, and its ETX is obviously equal to zero.

CTP uses these three mechanisms to overcome the challenges faced by distance vector routing protocol in a highly dynamic wireless network: i) the *link estimator*, which is in charge of computing incoming and outgoing quality of the links; ii) the *routing engine*, which is dedicated to the selection of the parent node, i.e. the neighbor with the lowest value of the multi-hop ETX, and iii) the *forwarding engine*, which forwards data packets, detects and tries to fix routing loops, and detects and drops duplicate packets.

It is interesting to note that the routing engine has to maintain a table, called routing table, where it stores the last ETX value read in the beacons from each neighbor. In this way, it is able to always choose the "best" neighbor (the one with the lowest multi-hop ETX) as parent. Therefore, it has to continuously update the table reading the information contained in the beacons received from the neighbors. In the simulation model, each LP represents a wireless sensor. The routing table managed by the routing engine (along with other data structures related to all three components of the CTP protocol) is kept within the LP's simulation state. Upon the reception of a simulation event representing a beacon, the simulation model passes the received information to the CTP library, which recomputes all parameters related to the network and then updates the routing table in the LP state, thus performing a set of memory updates. These memory updates are intercepted by `libreverse`, which therefore enables for reversibility the CTP library.

4.3 Experimental Data

In order to assess the overhead introduced by our proposal, we have relied on experiments using two variants of the model. In one variant, the CTP algorithm is dynamically linked to the simulation model, while in the other, the library's code is directly incorporated into the simulation model. In this latter configuration, the actions to correctly restore a previous checkpoint are completely demanded from ROOT-Sim. As mentioned, ROOT-Sim supports the rollback operation via both checkpointing facilities and reversibility facilities. Therefore, in the experiments we present data related to reversibility obtained when having the CTP library linked against the executable (LIB in the plots), by relying on the reversibility facilities offered by ROOT-Sim (REV in the plots), and by relying on traditional sparse state saving (CKPT in the plots), with the checkpointing interval optimized according to the results in [27].

We have run two sets of experiments. In one experiment, we have set the total number of sensors to 300, while in a second one, we have set it to 2000. At the same time, the area in which the sensors are deployed is kept fixed in both configuration, thus having a denser concentration of sensors in the second setup. In both configurations, the sensors are randomly placed within a square region. Since the CTP algorithm keeps a routing table within each LP's state, and since it is updated whenever a beacon message is received, the denser scenario has a twofold effect: i) the size of the state of each LP is larger, and ii) the frequency of state update by the CTP library is increased. Indeed, since when the number of sensors is increased to 2000, the average distance between two sensors decreases, so the number of beacons that can travel the transmission channel without being affected by fading effects is higher. All the experimental results are averaged over 10 different runs.

In Figure 7, we report experimental data when the model is run using 300 sensors. By the results, we can see that the configuration presenting the best performance profile is the one associated with reversible execution managed natively by ROOT-Sim. This is mainly due to the fact that the memory-update profile associated with this configuration does not entail a large number of memory updates. When using `libreverse`, there is an overhead around 7%,

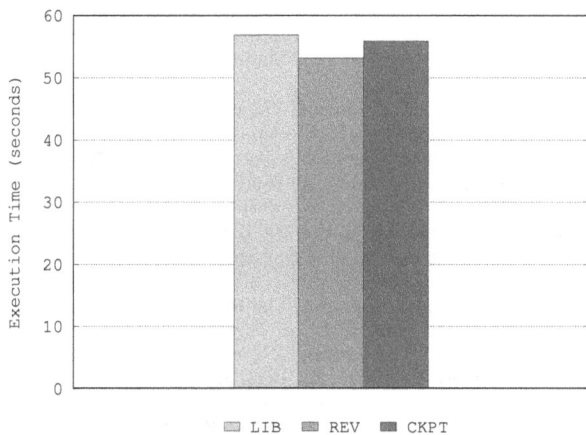

Figure 7: Results with 300 sensors.

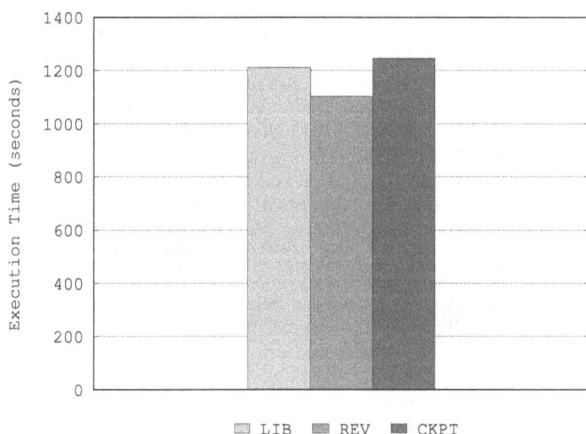

Figure 8: Results with 2000 sensors.

while when relying on checkpointing there is an overhead around 4%, which are both anyhow negligible.

The overhead introduced by `libreverse` is mostly related to the fact that the simulation model performs memory updates as well. Therefore, since the amount of data written by the CTP shared library is not very large, the time spent by the simulation engine to switch among the two reversibility approaches in order to guarantee the correct order of the actions is not paid off. At the same time, the overhead of `libreverse` is slightly higher than that of the checkpoint-based state restore exactly because both the size of the state and the amount of data updated in it is reduced, thus optimized checkpointing facilities (especially is realized according to autonomic facilities as in [27]) are able to fine tune themselves significantly. In addition to this, the rollback length is reduced—sensors are sparse, the communication is organized according to a tree, and therefore the probability of cascading rollbacks are small, and the number of LPs that can rollback each other is limited. In this scenario, plain reverse computation is not surprisingly delivering a better performance.

Figure 8 reports experimental data when running the configuration with 2000 sensors. In this configuration, the results slightly change: reverse computation managed by ROOT-

Sim still has the better performance result, checkpoint-based executions have the highest performance penalty (more than 12%), while `libreverse`-based reversibility has a overhead slightly smaller than 10%. The trend inversion among checkpoint based and reversibility based is due to the fact that, since the amount of state updates is non minimal, the checkpointing system has to restore a large amount of data, either in a full or incremental fashion. At the same time, the performance gain by the reversibility engine internal to ROOT-Sim is again related to the fact that in this case there is no need for the continuous switch to guarantee the correct order of the reversibility actions.

Overall, the overhead introduced by relying on `libreverse` is not extremely high (10% in the worst case), considering that much overhead is introduced by the fact that the simulation engine has the burden of ensuring the proper order of execution of reverse activities. What is most important, anyhow, is that the approach proposed allows to enable reversibility of generic third-party shared libraries in a completely transparent manner towards the application level code, closing the circle of automatic reversibility in the context of speculative Time Warp-based simulation.

5. CONCLUSIONS AND FUTURE WORK

In this paper we have discussed the design and implementation of `libreverse`, which allows to create on the fly instrumented versions of functions offered by any third-party library. By relying on this approach, it is possible to enable for reversibility any shared library, making them compliant with the Time Warp optimistic synchronization protocol. The experimental assessment has shown that it is possible to increase the programmability degree of PDES models, exactly relying on services offered by shared libraries, paying only a little overhead.

Future work entails the design of a reversible memory map manager, which can offer to the simulation engine (or, in general, to any program) a memory map on which effects of atomic actions (such as the execution of an event) can be reverted. This approach will drastically reduce the overhead due to repeatedly switching between reversibility actions. Additionally, it will be possible to rely on incremental checkpointing and reverse computing based both on binary instrumentation and source to source transformation, to any degree of integration. Similarly, a thorough experimental evaluation of the trade-offs between these approaches will be topic of future work.

Acknowledgements

This work was partially performed under the auspices of the U.S. Department of Energy by Lawrence Livermore National Laboratory under Contract DE-AC52-07NA27344, Lawrence Livermore National Security, LLC. IM release number LLNL-CONF-723277.

The authors warmly thank Davide Leoni for his implementation of SNM which has been used in this work for the experimental assessment.

6. REFERENCES

[1] GDB: The GNU Project Debugger.
[2] System V Application Binary Interface, Intel386 Architecture Processor Supplement, 1997.

[3] System V Application Binary Interface AMD64 Architecture Processor Supplement, 2007.

[4] V. Bala, E. Duesterwald, and S. Banerjia. Dynamo: a transparent dynamic optimization system. *SIGPLAN Notices*, 35(5):1–12, 2000.

[5] P. D. Barnes, C. D. Carothers, D. R. Jefferson, and J. M. LaPre. Warp speed: executing time warp on 1,966,080 cores. In *Proceedings of the 2013 ACM SIGSIM Conference on Principles of advanced discrete simulation*, PADS, pages 327–336, 2013. ACM Press.

[6] S. Bellenot. State skipping performance with the Time Warp operating system. In *Proceedings of the 6th Workshop on Parallel and Distributed Simulation*, PADS, pages 53–64, 1992. ACM Press.

[7] C. D. Carothers, K. S. Perumalla, and R. M. Fujimoto. Efficient optimistic parallel simulations using reverse computation. *ACM Transactions on Modeling and Computer Simulation*, 9(3):224–253, 1999.

[8] D. Cingolani, A. Pellegrini, and F. Quaglia. Transparently mixing undo logs and software reversibility for state recovery in optimistic PDES. In *Proceedings of the 2015 ACM SIGSIM Conference on Principles of Advanced Discrete Simulation*, PADS, 2015. ACM Press.

[9] U. Colesanti and S. Santini. The collection tree protocol for the castalia wireless sensor networks simulator. Technical report, ETH Zurich, 2011.

[10] D. Dechev, P. Pirkelbauer, and B. Stroustrup. Lock-Free Dynamically Resizable Arrays. In *Proceedings of the 10th International Conference on Principles of Distributed Systems*, pages 142–156. Springer-Verlag, 2006.

[11] J. Demmel. LAPACK: A portable linear algebra library for high-performance computers. *Concurrency: Practice and Experience*, 3(6):655–666, dec 1991.

[12] S. Economo, D. Cingolani, A. Pellegrini, and F. Quaglia. Configurable and Efficient Memory Access Tracing via Selective Expression-Based x86 Binary Instrumentation. In *Proceedings of the 24th International Symposium on Modeling, Analysis and Simulation of Computer and Telecommunication Systems*, MASCOTS, pages 261–270. IEEE Computer Society, 2016.

[13] J. Fleischmann and P. A. Wilsey. Comparative Analysis of Periodic State Saving Techniques in Time Warp Simulators. In *Proceedings of the 9th Workshop on Parallel and Distributed Simulation*, pages 50–58. IEEE Computer Society, 1995.

[14] M. Frigo and S. G. Johnson. FFTW: An adaptive software architecture for the FFT. In *Proceesings of the International Conference on Acoustics, Speech and Signal Processing*, ICASSP, pages 1381–1384, 1998.

[15] R. M. Fujimoto. Performance of Time Warp Under Synthetic Workloads. In *Proceedings of the Multiconference on Distributed Simulation*, pages 23–28. Society for Computer Simulation, 1990.

[16] M. Galassi, J. Davies, J. Theiler, B. Gough, G. Jungman, M. Booth, and F. Rossi. GNU Scientific Library Reference Manual. *Distribution*, 954161734:592, 2009.

[17] O. Gnawali, R. Fonseca, K. Jamieson, D. Moss, and P. Levis. Collection tree protocol. In *Proceedings of the 7th Conference on Embedded Networked Sensor Systems*, 2009.

[18] G. C. Hunt. Reversible load-time dynamic linking, 1998.

[19] D. R. Jefferson. Virtual Time. *ACM Transactions on Programming Languages and System*, 7(3):404–425, 1985.

[20] J. M. LaPre, E. J. Gonsiorowski, and C. D. Carothers. LORAIN: a step closer to the PDES 'holy grail'. In *Proceedings of the 2nd ACM SIGSIM Conference on Principles of Advanced Discrete Simulation*, PADS, pages 3–14, New York, USA, 2014. ACM Press.

[21] C. L. Lawson, R. J. Hanson, D. R. Kincaid, and F. T. Krogh. Basic Linear Algebra Subprograms for Fortran Usage. *ACM Transactions on Mathematical Software*, 5(3):308–323, 1979.

[22] Y.-B. Lin and E. D. Lazowska. *Reducing the saving overhead for Time Warp parallel simulation*. University of Washington Department of Computer Science and Engineering, 1990.

[23] N. Nethercote and J. Seward. Valgrind: A program supervision framework. In *Electronic Notes in Theoretical Computer Science*, volume 89, pages 47–69, 2003.

[24] A. C. Palaniswamy and P. A. Wilsey. An analytical comparison of periodic checkpointing and incremental state saving. In *Proceedings of the 7th Workshop on Parallel and Distributed Simulation*, PADS, pages 127–134. ACM Press, 1993.

[25] A. Pellegrini and F. Quaglia. The ROme OpTimistic Simulator: A tutorial. In D. an Mey, M. Alexander, P. Bientinesi, M. Cannataro, C. Clauss, A. Constan, G. Kecskemeti, C. Morin, L. Ricci, J. Sahuquillo, M. Schulz, V. Scarano, S. L. Scott, and J. Weidendorfer, editors, *Proceedings of the Euro-Par 2013: Parallel Processing Workshops*, PADABS, pages 501–512. LNCS, Springer-Verlag, 2014.

[26] A. Pellegrini, R. Vitali, and F. Quaglia. Di-DyMeLoR: Logging only dirty chunks for efficient management of dynamic memory based optimistic simulation objects. In *Proceedings - Workshop on Principles of Advanced and Distributed Simulation, PADS*, pages 45–53. IEEE, 2009.

[27] A. Pellegrini, R. Vitali, and F. Quaglia. Autonomic state management for optimistic simulation platforms. *IEEE Transactions on Parallel and Distributed Systems*, 26(6):1560–1569, 2015.

[28] F. Qin, C. Wang, Z. Li, H.-s. Kim, Y. Zhou, and Y. Wu. LIFT: A Low-Overhead Practical Information Flow Tracking System for Detecting Security Attacks. In *Proceedings of the Annual IEEE/ACM International Symposium on Microarchitecture*, pages 135–148, 2006.

[29] F. Quaglia. A Cost Model for Selecting Checkpoint Positions in Time Warp Parallel Simulation. *IEEE Transactions on Parallel and Distributed Systems*, 12(4):346–362, 2001.

[30] D. Quinlan, C. Liao, J. Too, R. Matzke, and M. Schordan. ROSE Compiler Infrastructure, 2013.

[31] R. Rönngren and R. Ayani. Adaptive Checkpointing in Time Warp. In *Proceedings of the 8th Workshop on Parallel and Distributed Simulation*, pages 110–117. Society for Computer Simulation, 1994.

[32] M. Schordan, D. Jefferson, P. Barnes, T. Oppelstrup, and D. Quinlan. Reverse Code Generation for Parallel Discrete Event Simulation. pages 95–110. 2015.

[33] M. Schordan, T. Oppelstrup, D. R. Jefferson, P. D. Barnes, and D. Quinlan. Automatic Generation of Reversible C++ Code and Its Performance in a Scalable Kinetic Monte-Carlo Application. In *Proceedings of the 2016 ACM SIGSIM Conference on Principles of Advanced Discrete Simulation*, PADS. ACM Press, 2016.

[34] J. M. Shearer and M. A. Wolfe. ALGLIB, a simple symbol-manipulation package. *Communications of the ACM*, 28(8):820–825, aug 1985.

[35] S. Skold and R. Rönngren. Event Sensitive State Saving in Time Warp Parallel Discrete Event Simulation. In *Proceedings of the 1996 Winter Simulation Conference*, pages 653–660. Society for Computer Simulation, 1996.

[36] D. West and K. Panesar. Automatic Incremental State Saving. In *Proceedings of the 10th Workshop on Parallel and Distributed Simulation*, PADS, pages 78–85. IEEE Computer Society, 1996.

[37] M. V. Zelkowitz. Reversible execution. *Communications of the ACM*, 16(9):566, 1973.

[38] Q. Zhao, R. Rabbah, S. Amarasinghe, L. Rudolph, and W. F. Wong. How to do a million watchpoints: Efficient Debugging using dynamic instrumentation. *Lecture Notes in Computer Science (including subseries Lecture Notes in Artificial Intelligence and Lecture Notes in Bioinformatics)*, 4959 LNCS:147–162, 2008.

Exposing Inter-Process Information for Efficient Parallel Discrete Event Simulation of Spatial Stochastic Systems

Jonatan Lindén, Pavol Bauer, Stefan Engblom and Bengt Jonsson
Dept. of Information Technology, Uppsala University
{jonatan.linden,pavol.bauer,stefane,bengt}@it.uu.se

ABSTRACT

We present a new efficient approach to the parallelization of discrete event simulators for multicore computers, which is based on exposing and disseminating essential information between processors. We aim specifically at simulation models with a spatial structure, where time intervals between successive events are highly variable and without lower bounds. In Parallel Discrete Event Simulation (PDES), the model is distributed onto parallel processes. A key challenge in PDES is that each process must continuously decide when to pause its local simulation in order to reduce the risk of expensive rollbacks caused by future "delayed" incoming events from other processes. A process could make such decisions optimally if it would know the timestamps of future incoming events. Unfortunately, this information is often not available in PDES algorithms. We present an approach to designing efficient PDES algorithms, in which an existing natural parallelization of PDES is restructured in order to expose and disseminate more precise information about future incoming events to each LP. We have implemented our approach in a parallel simulator for spatially extended Markovian processes, intended for simulating, e.g., chemical reactions, biological and epidemiological processes. On 32 cores, our implementation exhibits speedup that significantly outweighs the overhead incurred by the refinement. We also show that our resulting simulator is superior in performance to existing simulators for comparable models, achieving for 32 cores an average speedup of 20 relative to an efficient sequential implementation.

Keywords

Parallel Discrete-Event Simulation; PDES; Optimism control; Multicore; Spatial Stochastic Simulation

1. INTRODUCTION

Discrete Event Simulation (DES) is an important tool in a wide-ranging area of applications, such as integrated circuit design, modeling of biological systems, epidemics, network

SIGSIM-PADS 17, May 24 26, 2017, Singapore, Singapore

© 2017 ACM. ISBN 978-1-4503-4489-0/17/05. . . $15.00

DOI: http://dx.doi.org/10.1145/3064911.3064916

analysis, etc. To improve performance and accommodate for large scale models, a vast repertoire of techniques have been developed for Parallel DES (PDES) during the last 30 years [12, 17, 24, 26]. New synchronization techniques have been triggered by the advent of multicore processors (e.g., [4, 27, 34]). Still, achieving good performance and speedup for larger number of processing elements has proven to be very difficult in the general case.

In PDES, the simulation model is partitioned onto *logical processes* (LPs), each of which processes timestamped events to evolve its partition along a local simulation time axis. Events that affect the state of neighboring LPs are exchanged to incorporate inter-LP dependencies. A major challenge in PDES is to ensure that each LP's processing of incoming events from other LPs is correctly interleaved with its local events, to guarantee that causally dependent events are processed in the right order. If an LP could know the timestamps and causal dependencies of future incoming events, it would be able to optimally advance its local simulation as far as possible, without encountering incoming events that arrive "too late" (so called *stragglers*), thereby violating its local timestamp ordering. Unfortunately, LPs do not in general have this information e.g., since there is no shared state, and since incoming events may result from still unprocessed events in other LPs. To handle this lack of information, several approaches have been developed: *conservative* approaches introduce additional synchronization which guarantees that no stragglers will arrive [26], possibly causing significant performance loss by excessive synchronization and blocking of local LP execution; *optimistic* approaches allow stragglers by invoking suitable corrective action (rollback) [17, 24], possibly damaging performance by excessive checkpointing and processing of rollbacks. Many intermediate techniques have been proposed that allow stragglers, but control the optimism by various heuristic techniques (see for example the surveys [5, 16]).

In this paper, we show that availability of precise information about timestamps of future incoming inter-LP events is a crucial building block for the design of efficient PDES algorithms. We show this by parallelizing a widely used algorithm for simulation of spatial stochastic systems in two steps: we first design a natural parallelization, in which each LP has access to modestly precise information about future incoming inter-LP events. We thereafter refine this natural parallelization algorithm, by restructuring each LP's simulation algorithm in a way which exposes more precise information about future inter-LP events. Both algorithms include a synchronization mechanism for disseminating the available information about future inter-LP events. Our experimental evaluation shows that the refinement increases the parallel efficiency to an extent that significantly outweighs its overhead. The refinement also results in an efficient parallelization, which outperforms other existing parallelizations of the original simulation algorithm.

We consider stochastic spatial simulation of models governed by the mesoscopic Reaction-Diffusion Master Equation (RDME) [13]. The RDME describes a spatial Markov process, where the spatial domain is discretized into *subvolumes*, also known as voxels, each containing discrete numbers of entities (e.g., proteins) that evolve by performing reactions local to a subvolume or diffusions to neighboring subvolumes. In general, each subvolume can host several types of reactions and diffusions with different combinations of entities. The inter-event times between reactions and diffusions are stochastic, highly variable and without a lower bound. Chains of events may propagate fast over the spatial domain, making parallelization particularly challenging.

The most important algorithm for simulating this class of models is the Next Subvolume Method (NSM) [9]. In the NSM, the event queue contains the timestamp for the next event of each subvolume, but does not say *which* reaction or diffusion will happen. In other words, the reactions and diffusions in a subvolume are aggregated into one *subvolume event*. Only when processing a subvolume event, it is determined (by a weighted coin toss) whether it is a reaction (and of which type) or a diffusion to some neighboring subvolume. The advantage of the NSM is that the event queue contains as many entries as there are subvolumes, thereby adding modestly to the memory requirements. The NSM algorithm has been used to study, e.g., protein fluctuations taking part in cell division [10], regulatory processes relevant for differentiation of stem cells [32], or the polarization of yeast cells [20].

A natural parallelization of NSM, here called *Direct Parallel NSM* (Direct PNSM), has been proposed in, e.g., [7,18]. It partitions the subvolumes and event queue onto LPs. The event queue of each LP represents the timestamp of the next event in each of its subvolumes. However, since the event queue does not say which type of event will be processed, the timestamp of the next diffusion to a particular neighboring LP is not represented, making it hard to communicate precise information for optimism control.

In this paper, we therefore propose a refinement of Direct PNSM, called *Refined PNSM*, motivated by the need to disseminate accurate information about timestamps of future inter-LP diffusions. Refined PNSM differs from Direct PNSM in that each LP explicitly keeps the outgoing inter-LP diffusions to each neighboring LP separate. That is, outgoing inter-LP diffusions are *not* included in the aggregated subvolume event of their respective subvolume. Instead, each LP maintains, for each of its neighboring LPs, a separate event queue for outgoing diffusions to that neighbor, which explicitly represents the timestamp of the next occurrence of each outgoing diffusion. This allows the LP to disseminate precise information about timestamps of outgoing inter-LP diffusion events to neighboring LPs. For the dissemination of information from these diffusion queues, we use the *Dynamic Local Time Window Estimates* (DLTWE) technique developed in our previous work [2]. A disadvantage of Refined PNSM is that more memory is required for

representing the diffusion queues, and that effort is required to update the DLTWE estimates from these queues.

The DLTWE method for synchronization between LPs in our Refined PNSM is a further development of the method introduced in our previous work [2]. There it was used to parallelize the All Events Method (AEM) [1], which is an alternative to NSM for simulation of RDME models. The AEM does not aggregate reactions and diffusions in a subvolume, but maintains the next timestamp of all reactions and diffusions of the subvolumes in the event queue. The advantage of AEM is that it can be used for parameter sensitivity estimation, but its disadvantage is that the event queues require large amounts of memory and significant effort for maintaining them, causing sequential AEM to be significantly slower than sequential NSM. This disadvantage also applies to the parallelization of AEM. Therefore, parallel AEM achieves poor speedup relative to sequential NSM. However, its speedup over sequential AEM is quite good, due to the availability of precise information about timestamps of future inter-LP diffusions, as we showed in our previous work [2]. More details on the comparison with parallel AEM is found in Section 5.7.

We have implemented Refined PNSM with optimism control based on dissemination of information in its diffusion queues. We have also implemented Direct PNSM, both in a purely optimistic version without optimism control, as well as with optimism control based on the information available in its event queues: we have spent significant effort to investigate how to best use this information. The algorithms are compared on a representative set of benchmarks comprising unstructured and structured meshes. On 32 cores, Refined PNSM achieves an efficiency ranging between 50–103% for large models, and in average 35% for small models, compared to an efficient sequential simulation without any code for parallelization. In comparison to the Direct PNSM (with optimism control), the Refined PNSM shows an increase in efficiency between 24–84% for the large models. A detailed analysis of our optimism control in the Refined PNSM shows that rollbacks are almost eliminated, and that the amount of blocking is modest.

We also compare our resulting simulator, based on Refined PNSM, to other existing parallel simulators for the RDME that have been reported in the literature. We show that our simulator is superior in performance. E.g., in comparison to the simulator reported by Wang et.al. [33], we achieve a performance speedup on 32 cores which is approx. 63% better than theirs.

In summary, the contributions of this paper include:

- a methodology for parallelizing simulation algorithms based on the insight that availability and dissemination of precise information about future inter-LP events is crucial for efficiency,

- an efficient parallelization of the NSM simulation algorithm, which is superior in performance to other simulators reported in the literature, and

- experimental evidence that restructuring a simulation algorithm to expose precise information about future inter-LP events increases the parallel efficiency to an extent that significantly outweighs its overhead.

The work of this paper is to be integrated into the upcoming version 1.3 of the Unstructured RDME simulation framework (URDME) [8].

Organization of Paper The next section reviews previous related research. In Section 3, we describe the stochastic simulation framework at which our work is aimed, and the NSM algorithm. In Section 4, we describe the parallelization of the NSM by Direct and Refined PNSM, and their respective optimism control techniques. In Section 4.4, the algorithm is explained in detail. The experimental evaluation is found in Section 5. There we tune the optimism control parameters for the Direct and Refined PNSM algorithms, and compare their performance. The performance of the Refined PNSM algorithm is also compared to that of other comparable works. Section 6 contains the conclusions.

2. RELATED WORK

Numerous methods for parallelization of discrete event simulation (PDES) have been proposed. Here we will only review a selection and refer to the comprehensive surveys in [5, 12, 16].

Approaches to parallelization in PDES are coarsely classified into *conservative* [26] and *optimistic* [17, 24]. Optimistic approaches [17, 24] have the potential to achieve a higher degree of parallelism, but performance may be reduced by excessive rollbacks. To limit the frequency of rollbacks, various optimism control techniques have been developed.

While we only consider shared memory, we find it instructive to look at methods designed for distributed systems as well. Several techniques let LPs regulate their event processing rate in response to various statistics, such as the frequency of rollbacks [28], or the expected timestamps of future incoming events as estimated from statistics of past incoming events [11]. Another idea is to employ moving constant size *time windows*, often computed using model-specific knowledge, that bound how far each LP can advance its local time (e.g., [22, 29, 31]). We employ a similar concept in our optimism control. However, whereas the mentioned approaches use static information about minimum sizes of time windows, based on, e.g., known delays in communication channels, our time windows change dynamically and are based on dynamic and continuously updated information from neighboring LPs, enabling more accurate optimism control, even in situations where there are no minimum static time windows.

A further development of these approaches is the class of "near-perfect" state information (NPSI) protocols, including the *elastic time algorithm* [30]. Here, the time window is based on GVT and information about future messages to neighboring LPs, which is computed and communicated over a special high-speed network. Our optimism control can be seen as a refinement of this approach, where accurate information on future inter-LP messages is disseminated and used by neighboring LPs. We also realize this idea on a modern multicore without using a dedicated high-speed network.

PDES on multicores has gained increased attention lately. As an example, load balancing can be improved on multicores by allowing subdomains to be globally accessible by all cores (e.g., [4, 27]). This adds cost for synchronizing data accesses across cores. Marziale et al. [25] tries to remedy the cost of inter-core accesses by grouping domains of a certain granularity to one single LP. Lin et al. [21] employed a technique called Multi-Level Queuing, in order to minimize the communication latency among threads in a multicore RDME simulator. Wang et al. [34] present a NUMA-optimized version of the general optimistic simulator ROSS [3]. We believe that our simulator would also gain from additional memory optimizations, however such an improvement is orthogonal to what we present here.

Parallel simulation of RDME models using the Next Subvolume Method was previously addressed by [7, 18, 21, 33]. The simulators are implemented in MPI, where each LP simulates a subvolume [21, 33] or a subdomain [7, 18]. Dematté and Mazza [7] first proposed that optimistic PDES is favorable for solution of RDME models. Control of optimism was realized by a static time window [18] or Breathing Time Warp [33]. In Section 5.7, we compare our implementation to measurements reported by Wang et al. [33] and Lin et al. [21].

The synchronization method for optimism control of Refined PNSM is a further development of the method introduced in our previous work [2]. There it was used to parallelize the All Events Method (AEM) [1], which is an alternative to NSM for simulation of RDME models. The AEM does not aggregate reactions and diffusions in a subvolume, but maintains the next timestamp of all reactions and diffusions in the event queue. The advantage of AEM is that it can be used for parameter sensitivity estimation, but its disadvantage is that the event queues require large amounts of memory, causing sequential AEM to be significantly slower than NSM. For this reason, Parallel AEM achieves poor speedup relative sequential NSM. However, its speedup over sequential AEM is quite good, due to the availability of precise information about timestamps of future inter-LP events (see [2] and Section 5.7).

3. SPATIAL STOCHASTIC SIMULATION

The Reaction-Diffusion Master Equation (RDME) [13] describes systems where entities, called *species*, diffuse over a discretized space and may undergo transitions, or reactions, when in proximity to each other. The dynamics of the transitions are described by a spatially extended Markov process. The RDME is thus frequently used to model biological systems where the *copy number* (discrete count) of chemical species is low and discrete effects therefore play an important role.

The spatial domain is divided into subvolumes, each of which maintains the copy number of all participating species. The dynamics of the model is a continuous-time Markov chain over the state space, which consists of all copy numbers in all subvolumes. Two types of transitions are possible; *a*) in a *reaction* a combination of chemical species residing in a subvolume reacts and produces a new combination within the same subvolume, and *b*) in a *diffusion* a single entity of a chemical species moves to a neighboring subvolume. The next occurrence time for each transition is exponentially distributed with a rate that is proportional to the product of the copy numbers of the involved species, as given by the law of mass action.

Practically, the RDME is simulated using sampling methods, that produce single trajectories from the relevant probability space. Since the advent of the original algorithm, known as the Gillespie's Direct Method [15], numerous such sampling methods have been proposed. For spatial models, the most commonly used exact sampling method is the Next Subvolume Method [9] (NSM).

The NSM algorithm takes the form of standard DES, which proceeds by repeatedly a) selecting an event from the event queue, b) processing it by updating the simulation state, i.e., modifying the population in one or more subvolumes, and finally c) updating other scheduled events in the event queue. The last step consists of updating the next occurrence times of events whose rates depends on the copy numbers of the subvolumes modified in step b, and subsequently sorting the event queue. The new next occurrence times are obtained either by rescaling of the old occurrence time or by sampling [14].

An important property of the NSM is that the events in the event queue are *not* the next occurrence times of each reaction and diffusion within each subvolume. Instead, all reactions and diffusions within a subvolume are aggregated into a single subvolume event, whose rate is the sum of the individual rates of the aggregated reactions and diffusions. Thus, the event queue contains the next occurrence time of the next reaction or diffusion within each subvolume. Upon executing the aggregated subvolume event, a random draw decides *which* particular reaction or diffusion event occurred in that subvolume. This significantly reduces the size of the event queue and improves simulation efficiency.

4. PARALLELIZATION

In this section, we present our parallelization of the NSM. In Section 4.1, we first present a straightforward parallelization, called Direct PNSM. Thereafter, in Section 4.2, we present a refined version of the Direct PNSM, the Refined PNSM. Direct and Refined PNSM both have parameters that can be tuned to control the optimism, as described in Section 4.3. Both methods are exact parallelizations of the NSM, i.e., no additional error in the solution is introduced.

4.1 Direct PNSM

The Direct Parallel NSM (Direct PNSM) is a straightforward parallelization of the NSM algorithm to optimistic PDES based on Time Warp [17]. The subvolumes of the simulation model are partitioned into approximately equally sized subdomains, each of which is assigned to an LP. Each LP simulates the dynamics of the local subdomain while maintaining three main data structures: a) the *subdomain state*, i.e., for each subvolume, the copy number for each species, b) a time-sorted *event queue*, containing the occurrence time of future events in its subdomain, and c) a *rollback history*, which is a time-sorted sequence of events that have already been processed.

Each LP advances the simulation by finding the next event to process, either from the top of the event queue or from a message that has been received from another LP. In the NSM, a local event specifies the subvolume to be processed. A random draw then decides which individual transition occurs in the subvolume. Thereafter, the event is processed by a) updating the states of affected subvolumes, b) adding the event to the rollback history, and c) if the event was taken from the local event queue, determining a new next occurrence time for it.

If the event is a diffusion to another LP, a timestamped message is transmitted to the neighbor. In practice, the information is written into a bidirectional FIFO channel. Upon arrival, the message must be processed in the correct temporal order with respect to the local events of the receiving LP.

Whenever an LP receives a diffusion message that causes a causality violation (wrong temporal order of event updates), a so-called *straggler*, it must perform a rollback to a local time before the straggler's timestamp, using information from the rollback history. To do so, events are processed "backwards" until such a previous time is reached. In addition, all diffusion messages that have been sent by the LP during the rollback interval must be undone by sending *anti-messages* to the corresponding LPs. An anti-message cancels any event that was sent earlier with the same or a later timestamp. Anti-messages can cause cascading rollbacks that may involve several LPs, and are costly to resolve. In our implementations we use a refinement of the rollback technique, called *selective rollback* [2]. It is an adaptation of the breadth-first rollback mechanism [6], and prescribes that an LP that receives a straggler or an anti-message reverts only the events that are causally dependent on the received straggler or anti-message.

Rollbacks are undesirable, as the processing of rollbacks degrades performance. Hence, an LP should ideally not advance its local simulation time past the timestamp of a diffusion message that will be received in the future. For this purpose, we would like to design an optimism control strategy. Such a strategy involves the computation of *time window estimates*, which represent when the next diffusion message will be sent to a given neighbor, based on some available information in the inter-LP diffusion process. These estimates are then communicated to the respective neighbors via shared variables. The receiving neighbor is then able to use the estimates to derive a bound on its local simulation. If the timestamp of the next local event is larger than this bound, the neighbor blocks the execution, thereby causing waiting time, but reducing the risk of rollbacks.

However, it is not feasible to construct an accurate estimator of future inter-LP diffusion times in the Direct PNSM, since the method aggregates inter-LP diffusions into subvolume events. In a nutshell, the problem can be described as follows. Consider a subvolume on the boundary of an LP, which contains a number of intra-LP and a number of inter-LP diffusions, as well as a number of reactions. Since the NSM is used, the next occurrence time of the subvolume specifies solely when the next event in the subvolume occurs, without specifying which of the reaction or diffusion events it will be. Which event precisely occurs is determined only when the next occurrence time is reached, thus the simulator cannot know the time of a specific inter-LP diffusion event in advance.

As the model dynamics are stochastic and variable in time, the best alternative for deriving time window estimates in the Direct PNSM algorithm is to compute the expected time of the next diffusion event from the inter-LP diffusion rates and the current local simulation time. The estimates are communicated to neighbors and updated during each simulator loop execution. We refer to this best effort technique as *Time Window Estimates* (TWE) in the evaluation. The estimates can be tuned with a scaling parameter, as described in Section 4.3.

4.2 Refined PNSM

To alleviate the problem of limited information about future messages in the Direct PNSM, we have developed a refined approach, dubbed Refined PNSM. It is an extension to the Direct PNSM. We propose that outgoing inter-LP dif-

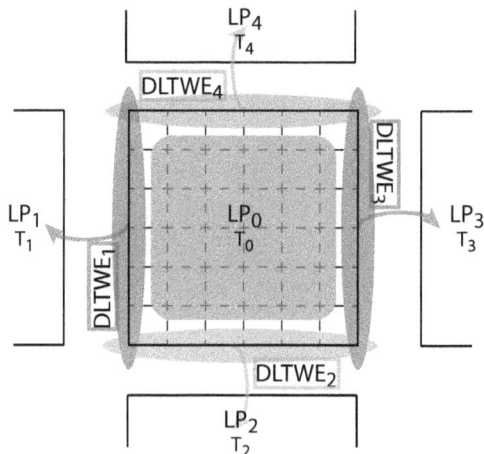

Figure 1: Schematic drawing of the Refined PNSM algorithm. The domain is divided into several LPs (solid lines), each operating at a local simulation time T_i. Each LP contains a number of subvolumes (dashed lines), within which a set of reactions and diffusions take place. We store the future scheduled events within the LP in different event queues. All reactions and internal diffusions (blue overlay) are stored in a local event queue. The local event queue contains aggregated next occurrence times for each subvolume. All outgoing inter-LP diffusions (red, green, cyan and yellow overlay) are stored in inter-LP queues, one per neighbor. The inter-LP event queues contain explicit next occurrence times and are used to compute DLTWEs. The DLTWEs are communicated to the LP's neighbors, which use them to derive a bound on their local simulation. A straightforward way to use the bounds are to advance the local simulation if the resulting local simulation time satisfies $T_i < \text{DLTWE}_i$, otherwise block the execution in order to minimize the risk of rollbacks.

fusions are not contained in aggregated subvolume events, but instead form separate events with an explicit next occurrence time. These timestamps are accurate predictors of inter-LP diffusion events and can be used for optimism control. LP-local events are still aggregated per subvolume, which is more memory efficient.

In practice, within each LP we create a) one event queue containing the aggregated subvolume events, representing reactions and intra-LP diffusions, and b) for each of its neighbors, an event queue containing all outgoing inter-LP diffusions to that neighbor (see Figure 1).

The prediction of future inter-LP messages in the Refined PNSM is straightforward. The next occurrence times of the outgoing inter-LP diffusions are extracted from the top of the inter-LP queues. Then, they are communicated to each neighbor as a time window estimate, and updated whenever the top entry of the queue changes. This is essentially the Dynamic Local Time Window Estimate (DLTWE) technique, introduced in our previous work [2].

The DLTWEs are accurate predictors of future inter-LP diffusions, which a receiver may use to significantly reduce

the amount of rollbacks. In contrast to the Direct PNSM, they accurately predict the times at which the inter-LP event will occur. However, rollbacks cannot be completely ruled out. The estimates are updated frequently due to state changes in the model, and may be updated to an earlier time as well. Thus, a neighbor may read an estimate, decide that it is safe to progress with local simulation, upon which the estimate is updated to an earlier time. The corresponding message from which the estimate was derived may then cause a rollback at arrival.

4.3 Tuning of Optimism Control

Typically, adaptive PDES can be tuned for optimal performance. In particular, the goal is to find the optimal trade-off between the cost of over-optimism ("too many rollbacks") against the cost of lost opportunity ("too much waiting time").

For the Direct PNSM and Refined PNSM, this tuning is given in terms of a parameter n, which defines how many of the received time window estimates should be used to compute a bound for the local simulation. Our experiments have shown that if all estimates are used, the result is an overly conservative simulation. By only considering a subset of the communicated estimates, the level of optimism can be increased. A further observation is that some neighbors may generate significantly more messages than others, thus provoking more rollbacks. The parameter n thus refers to the set of n neighbors, which have caused the highest amount of rollbacks on the LP during the simulation. An exception is made for LPs with a few number of neighbors, where the DLTWEs of all neighbors are used.

Furthermore, in the Direct PNSM, the expected next diffusion time is also scaled with a tunable parameter $k \geq 0$. The communicated time window estimate then equals $t + \sigma \cdot k$, where t is the local simulation time of the sending LP and σ is the expected inter-event time to the next inter-LP diffusion event. A small k implies a larger cost of lost opportunity, while a large k leads to a larger amount of rollbacks.

4.4 Detailed Algorithm Description of the Refined PNSM

Table 1: Structure of an LP.

1	**structure** LP_i:	
2	m	▷ *Number of neighbors*
3	n	▷ *Optimism control parameter*
4	$EventQueue[0\ldots m]$	▷ *Time-sorted queues*
		▷ *of events*
5	$SubvolumeState[1\ldots n_i]$	▷ *State of subdomain*
6	$History$	▷ *History of past events*
7	$Channel[1\ldots m]$	▷ *Channels of incoming messages*
8	$Dltwe[1\ldots m]$	▷ *Incoming DLTWEs*

Below we outline the structure of an LP_i with m neighbors. Each LP contains:

- $EventQueue[0\ldots m]$ is an array of priority queues, containing scheduled events sorted by timestamp. Here, $EventQueue[1\ldots m]$ are the inter-LP queues, each containing the diffusion events destined for a particular neighbor, and $EventQueue[0]$ is the intra-LP queue,

Algorithm 1: Main loop of the Refined PNSM algorithm, executed by each LP_i.

```
1  while true do
      ▷ First phase: find the next event to process
2     e_msg ← earliest message in { RETRIEVEMSG(Channel[j]) | 1 ≤ j ≤ m}   ▷ Peek at top of each message channel
3     e_local ← earliest event in {peek(EventQueue[j]) | 0 ≤ j ≤ m}
4     if e_msg.time ≤ e_local.time then                    ▷ If e_msg precedes any local event
5        e ← pop e_msg from its message channel  ▷ The event e to be processed is from the incoming channels
6     else
7        HotDltwe ← {indices of the n channels having caused the most rollbacks}
8        while ∃j ∈ HotDltwe s.t. Dltwe_j < e_local.time do  ▷ If next event is later than any selected DLTWE
9           if (Channel[j] has message) or (for some k ≠ j, ∃e_m ∈ Channel[k] s.t. e_m.time < Dltwe_j) then
10             restart main loop
11       e ← pop e_local from event queue       ▷ Otherwise the next event to be processed is local
      ▷ Second phase: process selected event
12    if e.time < SubvolumeState[e.dest].time or e is an anti-message then
13       SELECTIVEROLLBACK(e)               ▷ Revert state if e is a straggler (which may be local) or an anti-message
14       if e is an anti-message then restart main loop
15    add e to History
16    update SubvolumeState[e.subvol]
17    update timestamps of affected future reactions/diffusions in EventQueue[0 . . . m]
18    if e is a diffusion then
19       if e.dest is local then
20          update SubvolumeState[e.dest]
21       else
22          send diffusion message to LP_j where e.dest ∈ LP_j.SubvolumeState
23    for each neighbor LP_j do
24       LP_j.Dltwe_i ← time of peek (EventQueue[j])  ▷ Update the DLTWEs of neighbors
```

containing subvolume events that aggregate reactions and diffusions within the LP;

- *SubvolumeState* is an array representing the state of each subvolume in the subdomain, i.e., the number of entities of each species, and the timestamp of the last event affecting the subvolume (i.e., each subvolume has an individual timestamp),

- *History* is a time-sorted sequence of events already processed by the LP; old events are regularly removed from the history by fossil collection,

- *Channel*[$1 \ldots m$] is an array of incoming message channels, one for each neighbor, and

- *Dltwe*$_{1 \ldots m}$ is a set of incoming DLTWE estimates, one for each neighbor.

For an event e, we let e.time denote its timestamp; for a diffusion event e, we let e.dest denote its destination subvolume, which may reside in a different LP.

The main simulator loop consists of two phases, the selection of the next event to process, and the processing of the event. It has some similarities to the algorithm we previously presented in [2], where, in addition, the functions RETRIEVEMSG and SELECTIVEROLLBACK are explained in more detail.

The first phase (lines 2–11), selects the next event to be processed, as follows. First, for each incoming channel, the first message that is not canceled by a later anti-message in the channel, is retrieved by means of the function RETRIEVEMSG. Intuitively, the retrieved message is the first one in the channel that should be processed, after all anti-messages occurring in the channel have been processed. The

earliest message is assigned to e_{msg}. Second, the earliest local event e_{local} from all event queues is read. If e_{msg} is earlier than e_{local} (line 4), then e_{msg} is assigned to e for processing. Otherwise, the event e_{local} is assigned to e for processing, but only if none of the n selected DLTWE estimates is violated (line 8). If a DLTWE estimate would be violated, the LP blocks until a message from the corresponding neighbor, or an earlier message from another neighbor, is received, at which time the main loop is restarted, in order to process the message (line 10).

The second phase (lines 12–24) updates the subdomain state of the LP by processing the event e that was selected in the first phase. If e is an aggregated event, the type of transition and the destination are resolved by a random draw. It starts by checking whether e is a straggler or a local diffusion which violates causality in its destination subvolume, or if it is an anti-message; in all three cases a rollback is necessary. The rollback is performed by the function SELECTIVEROLLBACK(e) (line 13), which reverses the effect of all events, that are causally dependent on e. Thus, subvolumes may be rolled back to different times. The latter is also the reason why we might have rollbacks induced by other local events. In case the rollback performed was due to an anti-message, the main loop must restart (line 14), since the state of the subvolume of the currently selected event e may have changed. For a detailed description of the rollback function, we refer to our previous work [2].

After these checks, the selected event e is processed by adding it to the event history (line 15), updating the states of affected subvolumes, and updating the times of future events in the event queue that are affected by the state change(s) (lines 16 through 20). If e is a diffusion to another subdomain, a message is sent (line 22) to the appropriate LP. After that, the DLTWEs are updated (line 24) to inform the neighbors of the possibly new estimated times of the next diffusion events.

5. EVALUATION

In this section, we evaluate the efficiency and scalability of the Refined PNSM and the Direct PNSM algorithms. We look at the following five questions:

- *How do we tune the optimism control?* (Section 5.4)

- *How effective is the Refined PNSM algorithm?* (Section 5.5)

- *How big is the overhead of the Refined PNSM algorithm?* (Section 5.6)

- *How well does the Refined PNSM compare to other works?* (Section 5.7)

- *Which model parameters affect the performance of the Refined PNSM algorithm?* (Section 5.8)

5.1 Algorithms

To evaluate and compare the Direct PNSM and the Refined PNSM we implemented both algorithms. For both implementations, the baseline is the sequential implementation of the NSM method used in the URDME simulation framework [8], that has been shown to be efficient in comparison to other NSM implementations [8, Suppl. data]. Thus, all implementations share the same code for the sequential logic, but are extended for parallel execution in different ways. The optimism control, as described in Sections 4.1 and 4.2, was made optional and tunable in both implementations. In the following, we refer to the different configurations as follows.

NSM The original sequential NSM simulator.

D-PNSM The Direct PNSM algorithm, with optimism control turned off.

D-PNSM[TWE] Identical to D-PNSM, but with approximative adaptive optimism control turned on, as defined in Section 4.1.

R-PNSM The Refined PNSM algorithm, with optimism control turned off.

R-PNSM[DLTWE] Identical to R-PNSM, but with adaptive optimism control using DLTWEs turned on, as defined in Section 4.2.

The DLTWE technique requires detailed state information which is only available in the Refined PNSM algorithm, whereas the approximative TWE technique can directly use aggregated information, and therefore also works for the Direct PNSM algorithm.

To understand how the effort of the simulators is used, a fine-grained, low overhead (approx. 2%) instrumentation of the simulator was implemented, which records the time spent on different activities of interest. We categorize the activities of interest as follows (line numbers refer to Algorithm 1):

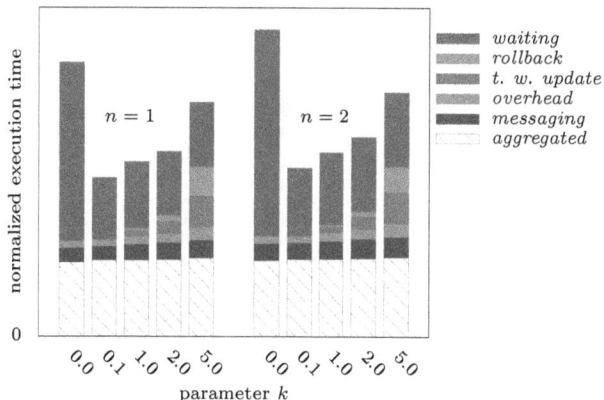

Figure 2: Instrumentation data for the D-PNSM[TWE] **algorithm for 32 cores on the sphere[L,d10] model. Time is normalized to the first bar of each group of the parameter** n.

aggregated Time spent on evaluating events from the queue with aggregated events. Corresponds to lines 15–24, if e is picked from the aggregated queue.

inter-LP Time spent on evaluating events from the inter-LP queues, lines 15–24, if e is picked from an inter-LP queue.

messaging Time spent on processing events from neighboring LPs, lines 15–24, if e is a received diffusion event.

overhead Time spent on updating the event history and fossil collection, that are directly related to the parallelization overhead. These are not detailed in Algorithm 1.

rollback Time spent in SELECTIVEROLLBACK, line 13, and time spent on re-simulating the time interval reverted by the rollback. The re-simulation cost is naively estimated to be equal to the cost of the rollback.

waiting Time spent on waiting for a neighboring LPs time window estimate, lines 8–10.

time window update Time spent on computing the time window estimates in the D-PNSM[TWE] algorithm, as described in Section 4.1.

Of the above mentioned categories, *aggregated*, *inter-LP* and *messaging* represent useful work. The *rollback* cost is caused by over-optimism, and *waiting* is the cost caused by too much conservatism.

5.2 Benchmarks

We now give a brief description of the benchmarks considered in the evaluation. The benchmarks are constructed to represent a variety of realistic RDME model properties. The topology is varied, which has an impact on the connectivity of LPs, and the reaction to diffusion event ratio (D:R ratio) is varied, which has an impact on the amount of communication between LPs. A more detailed description of the benchmarks is available in our previous study [2].

(1) The *reversible isomerization* benchmark consists of spatial models defined on three different geometries; *sphere*,

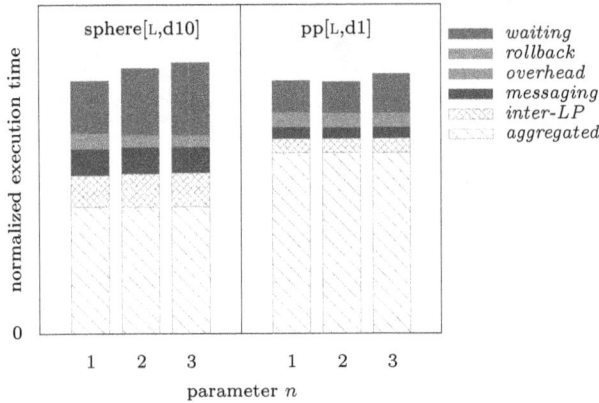

Figure 3: Instrumentation data for the R-PNSM[DLTWE] algorithm for 32 cores on the sphere[L,d10] and the pp[L,d1] models. Time is normalized to the first bar of each group per benchmark.

disc and *rod*. The geometries are discretized into three-dimensional unstructured meshes, leading to a high number of neighbors for each LP, except in the case of the rod model. For each shape, a model is generated in two different sizes of about 14.000 (*small*) and 140.000 (*large*) subvolumes. Each model contains two chemical species, A and B, which are allowed to freely diffuse within the domain with equal diffusion rates. The species may undergo the reversible reaction,

$$A \xrightarrow{c} B, \qquad B \xrightarrow{c} A,$$

with the tunable reaction intensity c. To arrive at a specific D:R ratio, we have determined the parameter in preceding test runs. For each model size, we set the D:R ratio to either 1:1, 10:1, or 100:1, which are the magnitudes found in realistic models, as in [10,32].

(2) The spatial *predator-prey* (denoted *pp* in the following) model was used as a benchmark in the study by Wang et al. [33]. In contrast to the previous models, the geometry is two-dimensional and the discretization is given by structured meshes, leading to a small number of neighbors for each LP. For the sake of comparison, we present the model at the same configurations as Wang et al., namely at a system size of 40.000 (*small*) and 160.000 (*large*) subvolumes and D:R ratios of 1:1 and 2:1.

We will denote specific model configurations as [*s*,d*y*], which means that the system size *s* is S (*small*) or L (*large*), and the D:R ratio is *y* : 1.

5.3 Experimental Setup

All experiments were run on a 4 socket Intel Sandy Bridge E5–4650 machine. Each processor has 8 cores and 20 MB L3-cache. Hyperthreading was not used, and threads were pinned to cores. The computer runs Linux 3.16.0, and the binaries were compiled using GCC 4.9.2. For the graphs, each data point is the average of three runs. The three-dimensional models were constructed using Comsol Multiphysics 4.3 and converted to computational models using the URDME framework. The two-dimensional structured meshes used in the spatial predator-prey model were constructed using custom Matlab scripts. All the meshes were then partitioned into subdomains using the multilevel k-

way partitioning method provided by the Metis library [19]. Metis optimizes the partitioning for minimal number of diffusions crossing subdomain boundaries, while maintaining an equal number of subvolumes in each subdomain.

5.4 Tuning the Optimism Control

In this section we tune the parameters of the D-PNSM[TWE] and R-PNSM[DLTWE] algorithms, as described in detail in Section 4.3. For both algorithms, we tune how many of an LP's received time window estimates are used, denoted as parameter n. For the D-PNSM[TWE], we additionally tune the parameter k in the time window estimate, as described in Section 4.3.

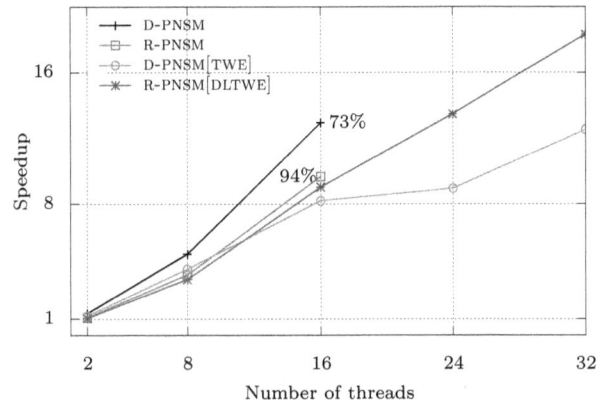

Figure 4: Speedup over NSM for the sphere[L,d10] model. The D-PNSM and R-PNSM did not complete for more than 16 cores due to rollback explosions. For 16 cores, the success rate of the D-PNSM is approx. 73%, and for the R-PNSM it is approx. 94%.

Figure 2 shows the time breakdown of the D-PNSM[TWE] algorithm, for different values of k and n in the sphere[L,d10] model. Each bar shows the time breakdown of a simulation with 32 cores and a combination of values of k and n. We find that the optimal values of k and n are at 0.1 and 1, respectively. The same values were found to be optimal for other benchmarks as well. In the figure, we also observe how the cost of rollbacks increases for bigger k, i.e., when communicating a bigger time window estimate.

The instrumentation data of the R-PNSM[DLTWE] algorithm is shown in figure 3, for different values of the parameter n, evaluated on the sphere[L,d10] and the pp[L,d1] models. We see that the best performance is achieved for $n = 1$, which we have also confirmed for several other benchmarks, not shown. Thus, in general, the best performance is achieved by observing the timestamps of future incoming diffusion events from only a single neighbor, viz., the one that has caused the most rollbacks.

The observation that the best performance is obtained when each LP waits on the DLTWE of only one other LP can, we believe, be explained as follows. An important goal of optimism control is to make each LP progress at approximately the same speed, i.e., no LP should advance its simulation time significantly further than the slowest LP. To achieve this, it should suffice that each LP wait for a single slower LP, thereby creating chains of waits-on dependencies, typically rooted at the slowest LP. It suffices that there is at least one dependency chain from the slowest LP to each

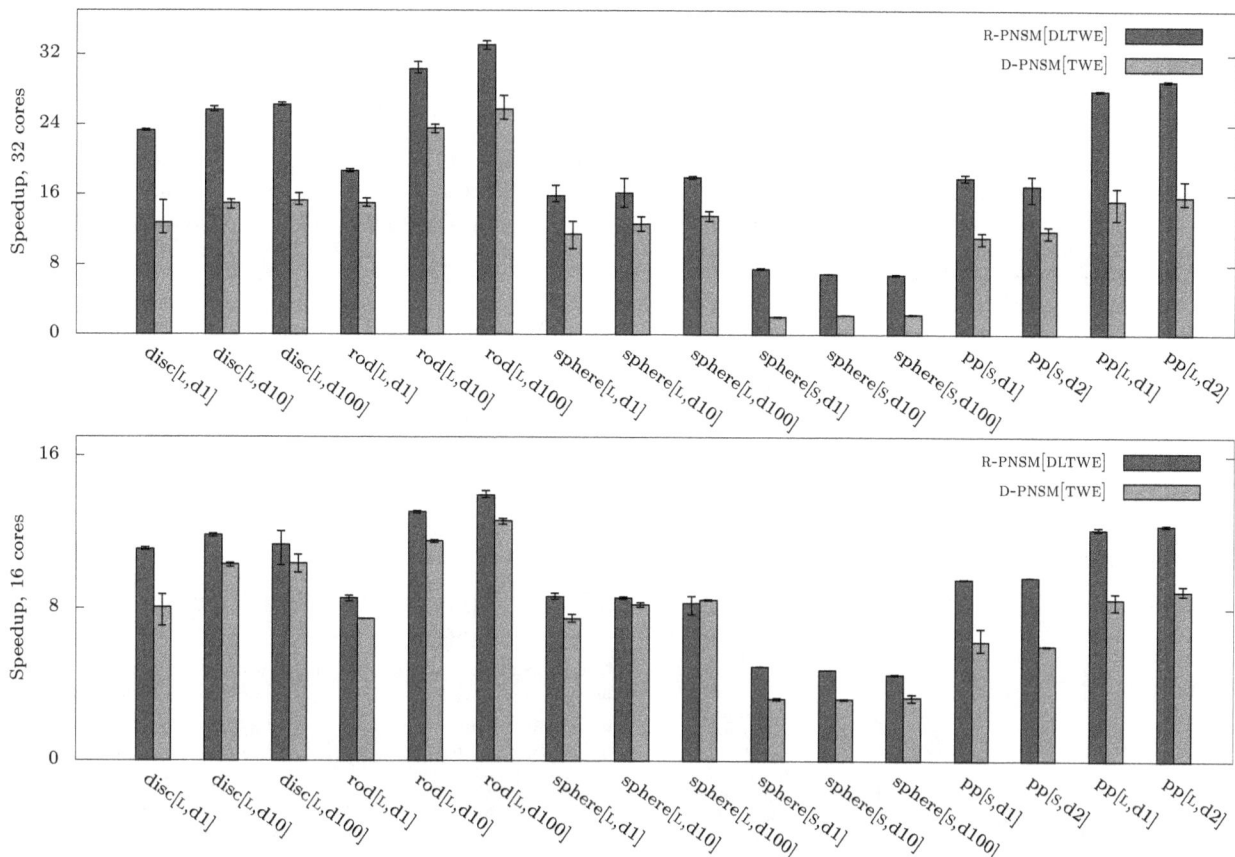

Figure 5: Speedup over NSM, 32 cores (top) and 16 cores (bottom), for all benchmarks. Error bars denote minimum and maximum speedup out of three runs.

other LP. Now, increasing n may add more waits-on relations than necessary, thereby increasing the overhead. Furthermore, increasing n can make the simulation more rigid than necessary by reducing the freedom that is necessary to accommodate modest temporary variations in simulation speed. It should be noted that with our selective rollback technique, a straggler need not cause a rollback; hence our simulator benefits from allowing modest differences in simulation time between LPs.

5.5 Scalability Comparison

In this section we compare the scaling of the two algorithms D-PNSM and R-PNSM, with and without optimism control.

In Figure 4, the speedup curves for the four parallel algorithms, evaluated on the sphere[L,d10] benchmark, are shown.

We would like to point out that the D-PNSM and the R-PNSM algorithms, i.e., the algorithms *without optimism control*, often suffer from rollback explosions, in which case the simulation does not finish within a reasonable amount of time (3 times the expected finishing time), or runs out of memory. In the cases the algorithms finish, the amount of rollbacks is relatively low. Similar behavior has previously been observed by others [23]. We have nevertheless chosen to include the data for the *successful runs only* for both the algorithms, as it is illustrative for the understanding of the

performance of the algorithms. For the sphere[L,d10] benchmark, 16 cores, the success probability of the D-PNSM algorithm is 73%, and of the R-PNSM algorithm it is 94%. For 32 cores it is 0% for both the algorithms, clearly showing the necessity of using a mechanism for optimism control.

Now, comparing the speedup for the D-PNSM and the R-PNSM algorithms in Figure 4, we see that the D-PNSM exhibits 34% better performance than the R-PNSM, for 2–16 cores, considering only successful runs. The performance cost of the optimism control for the two algorithms R-PNSM[DLTWE] and D-PNSM[TWE] is also illustrated in the figure. For the R-PNSM[DLTWE] algorithm, the performance loss over the R-PNSM is marginal. This is because the time window calculation, in this case maintaining the inter-LP queues, is already included in the R-PNSM algorithm. For the D-PNSM[TWE], the performance loss over D-PNSM is 25% for 16 cores.

Comparing both algorithms with optimism control on the same benchmark, the D-PNSM[TWE] algorithm has better performance than the R-PNSM[DLTWE] when only a small number of cores are being used. For 8 cores, it is 16% faster. However, for more than 16 cores, the opposite holds, and the R-PNSM[DLTWE] is up to 51% faster. The R-PNSM[DLTWE] algorithm clearly scales better than the D-PNSM[TWE].

The overall performance of the R-PNSM[DLTWE] and the D-PNSM[TWE] algorithms is illustrated in Figure 5. For 32 cores, the R-PNSM[DLTWE] achieves an efficiency ranging between 50–103% on the large models, compared to NSM. Compared to the D-PNSM[TWE], we see a performance improvement in the range of 24–84%. For the smallest model, under several different diffusion ratios, the performance of the R-PNSM[DLTWE] is up to about 4x better than the D-PNSM[TWE] algorithm. The average speedup of R-PNSM[DLTWE] over NSM for all benchmarks is 20.

On 16 cores, the performance improvement of the R-PNSM[DLTWE] over the D-PNSM[TWE] is in general smaller. The R-PNSM[DLTWE] algorithm has on average 23% better performance. We note that on the sphere[L,d100] benchmark, the D-PNSM[TWE] algorithm actually performs better.

We observe that for both algorithms, the unstructured models are in general more challenging than for example the *predator-prey* models, where the number of neighbors per LP is small. Likewise, the smaller models are more challenging, due to the limited amount of parallelism available. Especially for the smallest model, the performance difference of the D-PNSM[TWE] and the R-PNSM[DLTWE] is particularly accentuated. It also seems that the D-PNSM[TWE] algorithm performs better (in comparison to the R-PNSM[DLTWE]) in highly diffusive models.

5.6 Overhead of the Refined PNSM

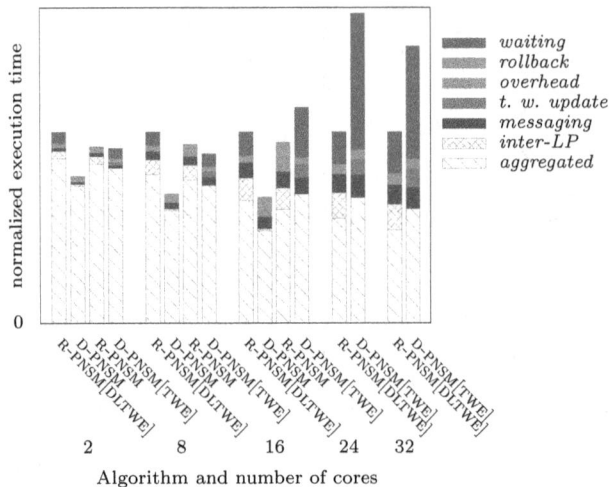

Figure 6: Instrumentation data for all algorithms on the sphere[L,d10] model. Time is normalized to the first bar of each group of cores. We recall from Figure 4, that the D-PNSM and R-PNSM did not complete for more than 16 cores due to rollback explosions. For 16 cores, the success rate of the D-PNSM is approx. 73%, and for the R-PNSM it is approx. 94%.

In this section we investigate the overhead of the R-PNSM algorithm over the sequential NSM and the D-PNSM algorithm, i.e., the cost of the parallelization and the cost of maintaining the inter-LP queues.

First, to estimate the parallelization overhead over NSM, we ran the D-PNSM sequentially (on a single LP) and compared it to the NSM, on the sphere[L,d10] benchmark. Note that, in the sequential case, the R-PNSM algorithm is identical to D-PNSM. The parallelization incurred an overhead of approx. 36%.

Next, in order to better understand the differences in Figure 4, we observe the instrumentation data of the same ex-

periment, shown in Figure 6. The total height of each bar in the figure corresponds to their execution time. The execution time is normalized to that of the R-PNSM[DLTWE] for each number of cores. To estimate the overhead of the R-PNSM algorithm over the D-PNSM, we calculate the difference in the amount of effort spent on all activities except *waiting* and *rollback* for each algorithm, as defined in Section 5.1. We see that the R-PNSM exhibits a significant amount of overhead over the D-PNSM: 38% at 8 cores, and 40% at 16 cores.

As we observed in Figure 4, the D-PNSM[TWE] algorithm is faster than the R-PNSM[DLTWE] for 2 and 8 cores, but the R-PNSM[DLTWE] is faster for more than 16 cores. An explanation is provided: For the R-PNSM[DLTWE] the relative amount of effort not spent on useful work increases by 63% when going from 8 to 16 cores, due to waiting. For the D-PNSM[TWE], the same effort more than doubles. Similar values are found for any increase in the number of cores. Thus, the initial cost of the R-PNSM[DLTWE] is higher, but the rate at which the overhead increases for the R-PNSM[DLTWE] is lower than for the D-PNSM[TWE], making it scale better.

5.7 Comparison to Other Works

In this section, we compare the performance of the Refined PNSM algorithm to that of similar algorithms of other works. We have looked at all to us known relevant papers for comparable experiments; the only two previously published RDME models for which experiments with more than 12 cores have been reported are [33] and [21].

Wang et al. [33] simulate a predator-prey model on a two-dimensional 200×200 structured grid, using their parallel Abstract NSM algorithm. Though it is unknown to us which sequential baseline they use for the comparison, they report a speedup of 11 on 32 cores. For the same benchmark, we achieve a speedup of 17.9. Lin et al. [21] simulate a three-dimensional calcium wave model using the NTW-MT simulator. They report a speedup of 9 on 32 cores. The parameters for the model were not available to us, thus we could not test our simulator on the benchmark.

In our previous work [2], we presented the PAEM algorithm, a parallelization of the AEM algorithm which does not aggregate reactions and diffusions in a subvolume, but maintains the next timestamp of all reactions and diffusions in the event queue. The sequential AEM is significantly slower than NSM, largely due to high memory requirements. Compared to sequential AEM, the PAEM achieved a speedup of 16.4 on 32 cores, for the above benchmark from [33]. The speedup for PAEM over the NSM, however, is only 5.2 on the same benchmark, largely due to its poor memory efficiency.

5.8 Performance Indicators: Inter-LP Diffusion Ratio and Degree

In this section, we investigate the relation between the parallel performance and the model parameters. We investigate the impact of two performance indicators, namely

Inter-LP Diffusion ratio The number of inter-LP diffusions over the total number of diffusions.

Degree The graph degree of the communication network between LPs.

In Figure 7 we compare the benchmark results of three models on 32 cores. Only one of the performance indicators

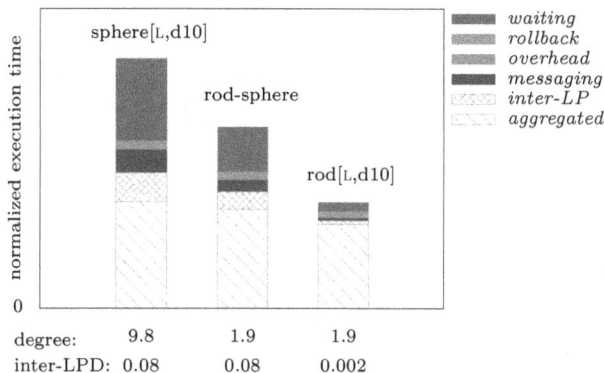

Figure 7: Instrumentation data of R-PNSM[DLTWE] **using all DLTWEs, on the sphere[L,d10], the rod-sphere, and the rod[L,d10] models, 32 cores.**

differ between each model. The *rod-sphere* benchmark is a modified version of the rod[L,d10] benchmark, with an inter-LP diffusion ratio that is equal to that of the sphere[L,d10] benchmark. All the three models have the same number of subvolumes, and the benchmarks take the same time to complete for the sequential simulator. We also want to ensure that the same number of inter-LP diffusions is used when deciding if an LP should block. Thus, we set the algorithm to use all the DLTWEs for this benchmark, and not only the n most important DLTWEs, as described in Section 5.4.

Comparing the sphere, with a degree of 9.8 to the rod-sphere, with degree 2, we see a performance difference of 38%. As expected, more time is spent on messaging and processing of inter-LP events for the sphere model. Additionally, the waiting time is increased. Comparing the rod-sphere, with an inter-LP diffusion ratio of 0.08, to the rod, with a ratio of 0.002, we see a performance difference of 71%. This gives some insight into the performance results in Section 5.5, where the large models in general had better performance than the small models, as they exhibit a smaller inter-LP diffusion ratio. Likewise it explains why the rod and the predator-prey benchmarks exhibited better performance than the other benchmarks, as they have a lower degree.

6. CONCLUSION

We have presented a new efficient approach to synchronization in optimistic PDES for spatial stochastic simulation of reaction-diffusion models, and used it to develop a parallel simulator, called Refined PNSM. A main contribution is to show that by refining the representation of the model state in order to expose explicit times for future diffusions between LPs, we can improve the accuracy of the optimism control, thereby significantly reducing the amount of rollbacks as well as maintaining the blocking at a modest level. Even though the refinement incurs a substantial overhead, experimental evaluation shows that the resulting parallel efficiency significantly outweighs the overhead.

We have also showed that our resulting simulator is superior in parallel performance to existing simulators for comparable models that have been reported in the literature, for cases where it has been possible to obtain data on simulated models.

We expect that the general strategy for the design of our parallelization also can be applied to simulators for other classes of models, where the partitions of different LPs exhibit tight and frequent interaction.

7. ACKNOWLEDGMENTS

This work was supported in part by the Swedish Research Council within the UPMARC Linnaeus centre of Excellence.

We would also like to thank the reviewers for their helpful comments.

8. REFERENCES

[1] P. Bauer and S. Engblom. Sensitivity estimation and inverse problems in spatial stochastic models of chemical kinetics. volume 103 of *LNCSE*, pages 519–527. Springer, 2015.

[2] P. Bauer, J. Lindén, S. Engblom, and B. Jonsson. Efficient inter-process synchronization for parallel discrete event simulation on multicores. In *Proc. SIGSIM-PADS*, pages 183–194. ACM, 2015.

[3] C. Carothers, D. Bauer, and S. Pearce. ROSS: a high-performance, low memory, modular time warp system. In *Proc. 14th Workshop on Parallel and Distributed Simulation*, pages 53–60. IEEE, 2000.

[4] L. Chen, Y. Lu, Y. Yao, S. Peng, and L. Wu. A well-balanced time warp system on multi-core environments. In *Proc. 25th Workshop on Parallel and Distributed Simulation*, pages 1–9. IEEE, 2011.

[5] S. R. Das. Adaptive protocols for parallel discrete event simulation. *J. Oper. Res. Soc.*, 51(4):385–394, 2000.

[6] E. Deelman and B. K. Szymanski. Breadth-first rollback in spatially explicit simulations. In *Proc. 11th Workshop on Parallel and Distributed Simulation*, pages 124–131. IEEE, 1997.

[7] L. Dematté and T. Mazza. On parallel stochastic simulation of diffusive systems. volume 5307 of *LNCS*, pages 191–210. Springer, 2008.

[8] B. Drawert, S. Engblom, and A. Hellander. URDME: a modular framework for stochastic simulation of reaction-transport processes in complex geometries. *BMC Syst. Biol.*, 6(1):76, 2012.

[9] J. Elf and M. Ehrenberg. Spontaneous separation of bi-stable biochemical systems into spatial domains of opposite phases. *Syst. biol.*, 1(2):230–236, 2004.

[10] D. Fange and J. Elf. Noise-Induced Min Phenotypes in E. coli. *PLoS Comput. Biol.*, 2(6):e80, 2006.

[11] A. Ferscha. Probabilistic adaptive direct optimism control in time warp. In *Proc. 9th Workshop on Parallel and Distributed Simulation*, pages 120–129. IEEE, 1995.

[12] R. M. Fujimoto. Parallel discrete event simulation. *Comm. of the ACM*, 33(10):30–53, 1990.

[13] C. W. Gardiner. *Handbook of stochastic methods for physics, chemistry, and the natural sciences*. Springer, 2007.

[14] M. A. Gibson and J. Bruck. Efficient exact stochastic simulation of chemical systems with many species and many channels. *J. Phys. Chem. A*, 104(9):1876–1889, 2000.

[15] D. T. Gillespie. Exact stochastic simulation of coupled chemical reactions. *J. Phys. Chem.*, 81(25):2340–2361, 1977.

[16] S. Jafer, Q. Liu, and G. A. Wainer. Synchronization methods in parallel and distributed discrete-event simulation. *Simul. Model. Pract. Th.*, 30:54–73, 2013.

[17] D. R. Jefferson. Virtual time. *ACM Trans. Program. Lang. Syst.*, 7(3):404–425, 1985.

[18] M. Jeschke, R. Ewald, A. Park, R. Fujimoto, and A. M. Uhrmacher. A parallel and distributed discrete event approach for spatial cell-biological simulations. *SIGMETRICS Perf. Eval. Rev.*, 35:22–31, 2008.

[19] G. Karypis and V. Kumar. A Fast and High Quality Multilevel Scheme for Partitioning Irregular Graphs. *SIAM J. Sci. Comput.*, 20(1):359–392, 1998.

[20] M. J. Lawson, B. Drawert, M. Khammash, L. Petzold, and T.-M. Yi. Spatial Stochastic Dynamics Enable Robust Cell Polarization. *PLoS Comp. Biol.*, 9(7), July 2013.

[21] Z. Lin, C. Tropper, M. N. Ishlam Patoary, R. A. McDougal, W. W. Lytton, and M. L. Hines. NTW-MT: A Multi-threaded Simulator for Reaction Diffusion Simulations in NEURON. In *Proc. SIGSIM-PADS*, pages 157–167. ACM, 2015.

[22] J. Liu and D. Nicol. Lookahead revisited in wireless network simulations. In *Proc. 16th Workshop on Parallel and Distributed Simulation*, pages 79–88. IEEE, 2002.

[23] B. Lubachevsky, A. Schwartz, and A. Weiss. An analysis of rollback-based simulation. *ACM Trans. Model. Comput. Simul.*, 1(2):154–193, 1991.

[24] B. D. Lubachevsky. Efficient parallel simulations of dynamic ising spin systems. *J. Comput. Phys.*, 75(1):103–122, 1988.

[25] N. Marziale, F. Nobilia, A. Pellegrini, and F. Quaglia. Granular time warp objects. In *Proc. SIGSIM-PADS*, pages 57–68. ACM, 2016.

[26] J. Misra. Distributed discrete-event simulation. *ACM Comput. Surv.*, 18(1):39–65, 1986.

[27] A. Pellegrini, R. Vitali, S. Peluso, and F. Quaglia. Transparent and efficient shared-state management for optimistic simulations on multi-core machines. In *Proc. MASCOTS*, pages 134–141. IEEE, 2012.

[28] P. L. Reiher, F. Wieland, and D. Jefferson. Limitation of optimism in the time warp operating system. In *Proc. 21st Winter Simulation Conference*, pages 765–770. ACM, 1989.

[29] L. M. Sokol, J. B. Weissman, and P. A. Mutchler. MTW: An Empirical Performance Study. In *Proc. 23rd Winter Simulation Conference*, pages 557–563. IEEE, 1991.

[30] S. Srinivasan and P. F. R. Jr. Elastic time. *ACM Trans. Model. Comput. Simul.*, 8(2):103–139, 1998.

[31] J. S. Steinman. Breathing time warp. In *Proc. 7th Workshop on Parallel and Distributed Simulation*, pages 109–118. ACM, 1993.

[32] M. Sturrock, A. Hellander, A. Matzavinos, and M. A. J. Chaplain. Spatial stochastic modelling of the Hes1 gene regulatory network: intrinsic noise can explain heterogeneity in embryonic stem cell differentiation. *J. R. Soc. Interface*, 10(80), 2013.

[33] B. Wang, B. Hou, F. Xing, and Y. Yao. Abstract next subvolume method: A logical process-based approach for spatial stochastic simulation of chemical reactions. *Comput. Biol. Chem.*, 35(3):193–198, 2011.

[34] J. Wang, D. Jagtap, N. B. Abu-Ghazaleh, and D. Ponomarev. Parallel discrete event simulation for multi-core systems: Analysis and optimization. *IEEE Trans. Par. Distr. Syst.*, 25(6):1574–1584, 2014.

Efficient Parallel Simulation over Social Contact Network with Skewed Degree Distribution

Yulin Wu[1], Xiangting Hou[1,2], Wen Jun Tan[1], Zengxiang Li[3], Wentong Cai[1]

[1]School of Computer Science and Engineering, Nanyang Technological University, Singapore
[2]Complexity Institute, Interdisciplinary Graduate School, Nanyang Technological University, Singapore
[3]Institute of High Performance Computing, Agency for Science, Technology and Research, Singapore

wuyulin@ntu.edu.sg, houx0009@e.ntu.edu.sg, wtan047@e.ntu.edu.sg
liz@ihpc.a-star.edu.sg, aswtcai@ntu.edu.sg

ABSTRACT

Social contact network (SCN) models the contacts between people by their daily activities. It can be formalized by an agent-to-location bipartite graph. The simulations over SCN are employed to study the complex social dynamics such as information propagation and disease spread among large-scale population. A challenge to the simulation is the skewed degree distribution of SCN, which contains a few hub locations with large numbers of visitors. The skewed degree distribution can cause load imbalance for parallel simulation and greatly degrade the execution performance. This paper proposes an approach which decomposes hub locations into small splits. Thus, SCN can be partitioned with better balanced workloads and multiple splits are able to run in parallel. Based on the pattern of information transmission between agents, we duplicate necessary data among splits to ensure the correctness of simulation. Furthermore, we enhance the parallel algorithm of SCN simulation to reduce the additional overhead from communication between splits. Finally, we build an experiment with epidemic simulation on an open dataset. The experimental results demonstrate that our approach achieves 14~35% performance improvement compared with the partitioning method without decomposition of hub locations.

CCS Concepts

•**Computing methodologies** → *Parallel algorithms; Modeling and simulation;*

Keywords

social contact network; parallel and distributed simulation; load balancing; skewed degree distribution; graph partitioning

SIGSIM-PADS 17, May 24-26, 2017, Singapore, Singapore

© 2017 ACM. ISBN 978-1-4503-4489-0/17/05. . . $15.00

DOI: http://dx.doi.org/10.1145/3064911.3064934

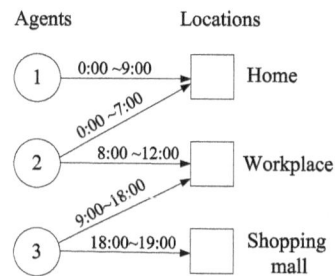

Figure 1: Social contact network modelled by agent-to-location (A2L) bipartite graph.

1. INTRODUCTION

A social contact network (SCN) is made up of a set of individuals and social relations between individuals. Compared with the online social network such as Facebook, SCN focuses on the contact relationship in real life [1]. For example, when persons travel to a location, there can be face-to-face interactions at that location. Simulation over SCN (which we call SCN simulation) is to simulate the social dynamics such as disease spread [2] and information diffusion [3] by modeling the behaviors of individuals who are members of SCN.

Following the work of Barrett et al. [4], the SCN model used in this paper is an agent-to-location (A2L) graph, as showed in Fig. 1. There are two distinguishing properties that make it different from the traditional social network based on agent-to-agent (A2A) graph [5]. The first is the bipartite structure, and the second is the temporal and spatial information in the network. Specifically, there are two types of nodes which represent agents and locations respectively. Each directed edge represents the visit activity from an agent to a location for a time period. The SCN simulation usually contains two kinds of agents. One example is the epidemic simulation involving infective and susceptible agents. Another example is the information propagation simulation involving active and inactive agents [6]. This paper uses the terms *Carrier* and *Receiver* to distinguish the two kinds of agents. The *contact* between agents refers to the information transmission from the carrier to the receiver. During simulation, the contact is computed by location for the agents with overlapped visit time.

A key feature of SCN is the skewed degree distribution [7], which means that most nodes in the network have relatively few connected neighbors while a few have large numbers of neighbors. For example, the popular locations such as metro stations and shopping malls may have a huge number of visitors. On the contrary, for large numbers of households, each usually contains only several members. The high-degree nodes in this kind of irregular network are called *hub nodes*. It has been observed that the irregular network structure has a strong impact on the social dynamics [8, 9]. For example, the hub nodes can accelerate disease spread due to the large number of neighbors [10]. This also implies that the simulation of hub nodes requires a large computational cost.

SCN simulation often runs at a large scale, which could contain up to billions of interacting individuals [11]. In order to gain insights from the simulation in a timely way, it is necessary to partition the SCN onto multiple processors to speed up the execution [12]. However, efficient parallel and distributed simulation over the irregular network has long been recognized as a challenge [13, 14]. Due to the hub nodes, the workloads among processors can be highly imbalanced. The load imbalance can cause performance degradation and scalability bottleneck for simulation.

Nguyen and Fujimoto [15] proposed a link partitioning method for simulation over irregular network. In their case of telecommunication network, each link between routers is mapped into a logic process (LP) to model the communication ports. The function of a router is partitioned among its ports. In this way, different ports of the same router can be simulated in parallel. As a result, the load imbalance caused by hub nodes is avoided. However, this approach is not suitable for SCN. The contact relationship in SCN is dynamic and is only maintained by the location. Therefore, it is difficult to decompose the functionality of the location using the approach. Yeom et al. [7] proposed an application-level approach to decompose the hub locations into small rooms for simulation on A2L graph, so that workloads can be distributed uniformly. In this study it is assumed that contact cannot be created between agents located in different small rooms. Hence, this approach cannot be applied to the scenario containing large public places where agents move around freely. For example, although the working place of a building can be divided into small offices, the metro station and shopping mall are difficult to decompose due to the dynamic crowd.

To address the load imbalance problem in large-scale SCN simulation, this paper proposes a new strategy which aims to decompose the hub location into splits. After the decomposition, all splits need to communicate with each other to maintain the original contact relationship between agents. We reduce the additional communication overhead due to the decomposition by overlapping the communication with computation. This paper uses an epidemic simulation on an open dataset to evaluate the performance. As a result, our approach shows 14~35% improvement of execution time when comparing with the partitioning method without decomposition of hub locations.

The remainder of this paper is organized as following. Section 2 introduces the SCN simulation and the challenge to SCN partitioning. Section 3 presents our approach of decomposing hub locations. Section 4 introduces the experimental model and evaluates the performance of our solution. Related works are described in Section 5. Section 6 concludes the paper with future work.

2. PROBLEM DEFINITION

2.1 Social Contact Network

SCN can be formalized by an edge-attributed bipartite graph $G_{PL} = (P, L, E)$, where $P = p_1, p_2, \ldots, p_m$ is the vertex set of agents, $L = l_1, l_2, \ldots, l_n$ is the vertex set of locations, and E is the set of attributed edges between P and L. An edge $e = (p, l, t)$ means that an agent p visits the location l with temporal information t, where $e \in E$, $p \in P$, $l \in L$ and $t = \{< t_a, t_d >\}$. For one visit, t_a is the arrival time and t_d is the departure time, $t_a < t_d$. An agent can visit the same location multiple times in one simulation cycle, so t is a collection of pair $< t_a, t_d >$.

The time attribute of edge indicates the contact is dynamic, because an agent can be at different locations at different time periods. The dynamics of the underlying network structure (i.e., adding or removing nodes and edges) is not considered in this paper.

For an agent p_i, we call the edge subset $E_{p_i} = \{e|e.p = p_i, e \in E\}$ as its *Activity List*. For a location l_i, we call the edge subset $E_{l_i} = \{e|e.l = l_i, e \in E\}$ as its *Visit List*. It can be proven that:

$$\sum |E_p| = \sum |E_l|, \text{where } p \in P, l \in L \qquad (1)$$

SCN data including both nodes and *Activity List* of each agent are simulation inputs. An agent's activity list defines its daily activities. Simulation runs periodically. In each simulation cycle (usually a simulated day), activities of each agent are scheduled using its activity list. The *Visit List* of location can be created from agents' activities during runtime.

2.2 Parallel SCN Simulation

Characterized by the bipartite graph, each simulation cycle in SCN simulation includes agent processing and location processing. The agent processing updates each agent's state and sends its *visit messages* to locations according to its activity list. The location processing computes contacts between agents and sends transmission results (which we call *contact results*) back to the agents. The actual contact result depends on specific application. For example, it refers to the newly infected state in the spread of disease.

Since agents are decoupled by the bipartite graph(i.e., there is no direct relationship between agents), they can be easily executed in parallel. It is the same for locations. Given this, a basic parallel method is to run agents and locations in turn, as shown in Algorithm 1 [4].

The algorithm runs in cycles, that is, in time-stepped manner. Δt is the step size (line 1). In each step, there are two sub-steps, corresponding to *agent processing* (line 2-6) and *location processing* (line 8-12). The computation includes: 1) agent updates status and computes visits (line 3 & 4); and 2) location computes contact results based on local visits with overlapped time (line 9 & 10). The visit messages are converted into arrival and departure events in time-order at line 9. Then the contacts between agents are processed upon the events at line 10.

The communication between P and L includes sending visit messages from agents (line 5) and returning contact

Algorithm 1 Synchronous SCN Simulation Algorithm

```
 1: for t = 0; t < MaxTime; t = t + Δt do
 2:     for each agent do
 3:         //Receive
                receives contact results and updates status;
 4:         //Compute
                computes visit messages for the period (t, t + Δt);
 5:         //Send
                sends the visit messages and status to locations;
 6:     end for
 7:     barrier synchronization;
 8:     for each location do
 9:         //Receive
                receives visit messages and converts them into
                arrival/departure events;
10:         //Compute
                computes contacts between agents;
11:         //Send
                sends contact results to agents;
12:     end for
13:     barrier synchronization;
14: end for
```

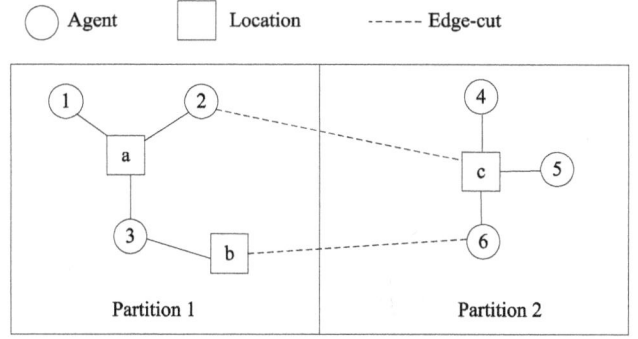

Figure 2: Example of SCN partitioning.

results from locations (line 11). When an agent p visits a location l in different computer, the communication over computer network is introduced. Synchronizations (line 7 & 13) are added at the end of each sub-step to ensure that all messages have arrived at receiver sides before progressing into the next sub-step.

Since an agent can visit multiple locations in one simulation step, its state can be changed at any location by contact. To enable concurrent execution of locations, the change should not influence other locations in the current step. The correctness is guaranteed by the *lookahead*, which refers to the delay period that contact result takes effect. For example, in disease transmission, there is an incubation period before signs and symptoms of the disease appear. During the period, the newly infected agent cannot infect others. Therefore, if one agent is infected at one location, it cannot infect the agents at other locations visited in the same simulation step. Formally, all locations can be computed in parallel only if $lookahead \geq \Delta t$.

2.3 Challenge of SCN Partitioning

For parallel execution, suppose G_{PL} is partitioned into k parts. Specifically, agent set P is partitioned into $P_1, P_2, \ldots, P_k$, and location set L is partitioned into $L_1, L_2, \ldots, L_k$. The logic process i is assigned with P_i and L_i, and then executes the agents $\{p | p \in P_i\}$ and locations $\{l | l \in L_i\}$. Fig. 2 shows an example of graph partitioning with edge-cut. A node is always allocated to a partition, while the edges between nodes can be split.

To achieve efficient parallel execution, the computational loads must be balanced among the processors. This is because the straggled processor with the heaviest workload will block the advancement of simulation, resulting other processors stay idle. To achieve load balancing, the accurate estimation of computational loads is required before graph partitioning.

The computational loads on the bipartite graph include two parts. First, the workloads of different agents do not show significant variance [7], and can be measured by the node degrees. Second, the workload of a location depends on the contact computing between visiting agents and is strongly correlated to the number of its visits. This is also

related to the node degree. Yeom et al. [7] approximated location workload by linear regression upon the number of visits and actual execution time of the location. This implies that the measurement of location workload depends on specific application. We use a function $f(|E_{l_j}|)$ to represent the workload, where E_{l_j} is the visit list of location l_j, and $|E_{l_j}|$ is its degree. The location workload of partition i is:

$$|L_i| = \sum_j f(|E_{l_j}|), \text{ where } l_j \in L_i \quad (2)$$

To keep load balanced, the following condition needs to be satisfied:

$$|L_i| \approx \frac{\sum f(|E_l|)}{k}, \text{ where } l \in L \quad (3)$$

Existing partitioning tools, such as METIS [16], use multi-constraint k-way partitioning algorithm to ensure load balancing of different computing phases on network. Hence, both the agent and location processing phases in Algorithm 1 can be balanced simultaneously. It also tries to minimize the number of cut edges (min-cut) so that the communication between partitions can be minimized. However, SCN poses a challenge to load balancing even if we employ such tools.

Firstly, different locations have variant workloads. The workload of a location is related to its degree and the skewed degree distribution means that the workloads of different locations vary widely. Fig. 3 shows the diversity of location workloads based on the experiment described in Section 4. We use the average execution time per node degree as the measurement. We can see that when the node degrees are high, the workloads are scattered across a wide range. The inaccurate estimation of workload by linear regression will cause imbalanced partitioning result.

Secondly, due to the social dynamics, the workload of a hub location can vary greatly during runtime. The node weight used for graph partitioning is based on the average workload, and the average value can only work well with large amounts of homogeneous nodes. For a few hub locations with highly varied workloads, the use of average value can also cause load imbalance.

Furthermore, the hub location has an impact on system scalability. The computational complexity of location l is $O(|E_l|^2)$ in the extreme case (e.g., each pair of visitors has a contact), and the hub locations will produce very large workloads. With the increase of computing resources, the average workload among partitions will decrease, but the partition with the largest hub location will be a performance bottleneck.

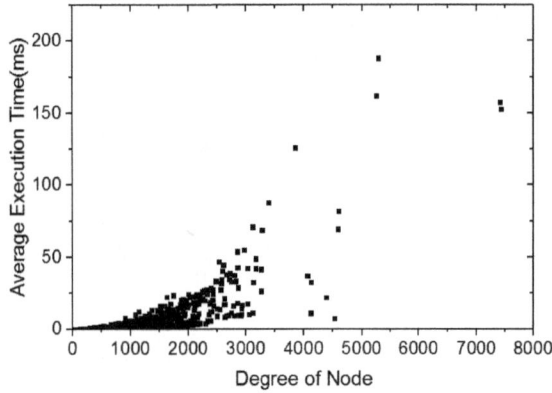

Figure 3: The workload distribution of location with degree.

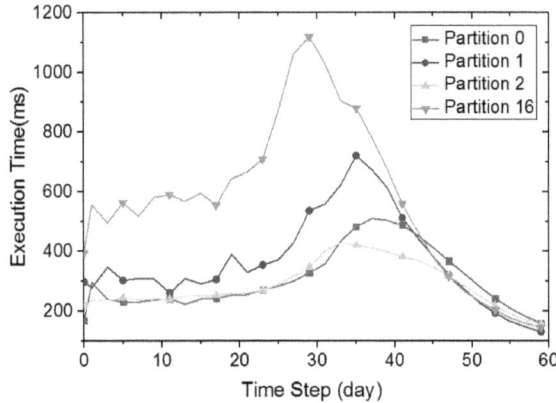

Figure 4: Load imbalance due to the hub location in *Partition 16*.

Fig. 4 shows an execution-time fragment of location processing with 60 partitions (only 4 partitions are plotted due to space constraints). METIS is used for network partitioning in the experiment. We can see that the *Partition 16* has much higher workload than other partitions, because the partitioning tool cannot handle the hub locations well.

3. HUB LOCATION DECOMPOSITION FOR SCN SIMULATION

3.1 Main Ideas

Since the agents can be partitioned easily due to their similar workloads, this paper focuses on the locations. The hub locations cause problems for load balancing. A straightforward idea is to decompose them into splits, so that the workloads of all locations will be more homogeneous and the bottleneck from the hub locations can be removed. We split hub locations at first, and then utilize METIS to partition the decomposed graph to achieve load balancing and mincut. During simulation, we replicate necessary data among splits for contact computing to enable parallel execution on the splits. Meanwhile, the additional overhead from communication between splits will be reduced by overlapping the communication with computation.

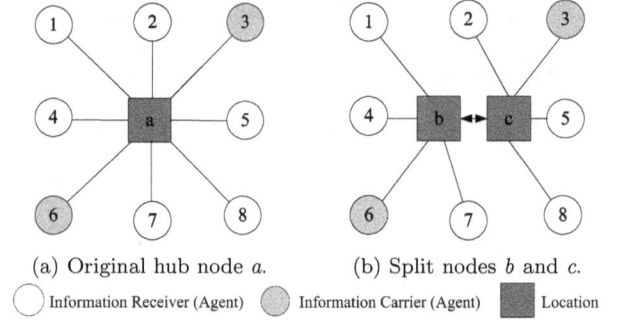

(a) Original hub node a. (b) Split nodes b and c.

○ Information Receiver (Agent) ● Information Carrier (Agent) ■ Location

Figure 5: Hub Location Decomposition.

3.2 Partitioning Based on Hub Location Decomposition

The partitioning of SCN is processed offline before simulation, which involves following steps:

1. Identify hub locations. A threshold of node degree D_T is used for the selection of locations to be split.

2. For each selected location l, its neighboring agents are split into groups with size $s = \frac{|E_l|}{D_T}$, where $|E_l|$ is the degree of l. The number of agents in each group is approximately equals to D_T. The agents for each group are selected according to ID sequence.

3. For each agent group, a new location split is created. The edges of agents in the group are rewired from the original hub location to the new split.

4. For each location split, the workload can be approximated by $\frac{f(|E_l|)}{s}$, where $f(|E_l|)$ is the workload of the original hub location.

5. Remove the original hub locations from network and partition the new network using METIS. The new network together with the partitioning result and the relational data among splits are used as simulation inputs.

In order to guarantee the correctness, the contact relationship within original location must be maintained after it is decomposed into multiple splits. For each pair of visitors, if one is carrier and another is receiver, then there is a possibility for the contact to be established. Hence, to maintain the original contact relationship, a solution is to make each split keep only a proportion of receivers but all carriers.

Fig. 5 shows the concept of hub location decomposition and the data exchange mechanism during simulation. For example, in Fig. 5a the degree of original hub location a is 8. After splitting the a into b and c (Fig. 5b), the degrees of both splits are 4. Suppose the agent 3 and 6 are carriers, their visit messages need to be exchanged between b and c. For example, message from agent 6 will be firstly delivered to split b, which will process the message locally for receivers 1, 4 and 7. At the same time the message is forwarded to split c by b, and then c will process the message locally for receivers 2, 5 and 8. Therefore, the workload at original hub location a is divided.

The approach has two advantages. First, the existing partitioning algorithms can be utilized to achieve min-cut and load balancing. Second, the number of splits can be controlled by the threshold D_T. The latter means that the extra

Table 1: Operation abstraction in SCN simulation

Operation	Node type	Description
Receive	Agent	Receives contact results and updates status
	Split and non-split locations	Receives visit messages and converts them into arrival/departure events
Compute	Agent	Generates visit messages
	Split and non-split locations	Computes the contact result according to arrival/departure events
Send	Agent	Sends visit messages to locations
	Split and non-split locations	Sends contact results to agents
Forward	Split	Forwards visit messages from carriers to the counterparts of the split

communication overhead between splits can be controlled. The communication overhead will be further discussed in the next subsection.

The decomposition enables the parallel execution of hub location because its splits can be assigned to different partitions. A remaining issue is how to assign the splits. Currently, we split hub locations into parts as many as possible by adjusting the D_T, and then rely on METIS to perform the assignment. Intuitively, if there are more splits, they are more likely to be distributed in different partitions. On the other hand, if two graph nodes have a link, they are possible to be assigned to the same partition due to the min-cut heuristics used by the METIS algorithm. To further increase the possibility of distributing splits to different partitions, links between splits are removed from the input graph to METIS. The relationship among splits is rebuilt at the initial phase of simulation.

3.3 Reduction of Additional Communication Overhead from Decomposition

To create contacts, visit messages of carriers need to be forwarded from one split to all other splits of the same location. This requires additional communication. The latency is linearly correlated to the number of visit messages of carriers per split. Moreover, the message forwarding introduces an extra phase which also requires synchronization. To ensure correctness, this phase should be placed between agent and location processing phases.

In order to reduce the overhead, we can overlap the message forwarding of splits with the processing of non-split locations. This requires the decomposition of message handling from the location processing. We abstract the processing of each node into *Receive*, *Compute* and *Send* operations, corresponding to the Algorithm 1. We also introduce a new operation *Forward* to represent the forwarding messages among splits of the same location. Table 1 summarizes all operations in our approach.

Algorithm 2 shows the modified algorithm to handle splits. At the first step of location processing phase, the framework

will call the *Receive* operation for splits (line 7). If there are carriers, their visit messages will be forwarded to the counterparts of the split by *Forward*. Then, the processing of non-split locations will be executed. Until the processing of non-split locations is done, the synchronization for forwarding phase will be called (line 12), and this will be followed by the *Update* and *Send* operations of the splits. In our implementation, we also utilized the idle time from agent synchronization (line 5) to forward messages that have been received by splits before the synchronization completes.

Suppose the cost F for message forwarding consists of Send (F_s), Transport (F_t) and Receive (F_r) parts, the overhead can be reduced from F to F_s by the interleaved execution. After sending the messages, the process needs not to wait for the completion of forwarding. The Receive part can be implemented by a background worker who receives messages but does not process them. When non-split locations are done, the forwarded messages should have arrived at receiver sides in most cases because the splits occupy only a small fraction of SCN. Hence, the latency from message forwarding can be hidden to a great extent by the processing of non-split locations.

Algorithm 2 Modified Synchronous Algorithm to Handle Location Splits

---

1: **for** $t = 0; t < MaxTime; t = t + \Delta t$ **do**
2:     **for** each agent **do**
3:         Call Receive() → Update() → Send();
4:     **end for**
5:     barrier synchronization;
6:     **for** each split **do**
7:         Call Receive() → Forward();
8:     **end for**
9:     **for** each non-split location **do**
10:         Call Receive() → Update() → Send();
11:     **end for**
12:     barrier synchronization (for Forwarding phase);
13:     **for** each split **do**
14:         Call Update() → Send();
15:     **end for**
16:     barrier synchronization;
17: **end for**

---

4. EXPERIMENT

In this section, we use an epidemic simulation to evaluate the performance of our approach. First, the experimental dataset and epidemic model are described. Then, the performance improvement is evaluated by comparing with the default partitioning method without splitting hub nodes. The impacts of experimental parameters on performance are also investigated.

4.1 SCN Dataset

We utilize an open dataset published by Network Dynamics and Simulation Science Laboratory (NDSSL) in our experiment. The dataset version in use is *Release 1*, which is a synthetic population of the city Portland of USA [17]. Table 2 lists the details of the network.

In Table 2, the *Edge* denotes the number of links between persons and locations. The *Visit Number* refers to the total number of the visits from persons to locations. Since one person may visit one location more than once, the *Visit Number* can be larger than the *Edge*. The value of the *Period of Activity* means the data set only covers activities within

Table 2: Dataset description

Property	Value
Population Source	Portland
Population	1,615,860
Location	243,423
Edge	6,108,721
Visit Number	8,922,359
Period of Activity	1 day

Table 3: Environment configuration

Cluster	6 machines
CPU	72 cores (6 cores per CPU, 2 × Intel Xeon E5-2620 v3 per node)
Memory	192GB (32GB per node)
Network	10G Ethernet
MPI	MPICH2 3.2
OS	CentOS 6.6
Graph Partitioner	METIS 5.1.0

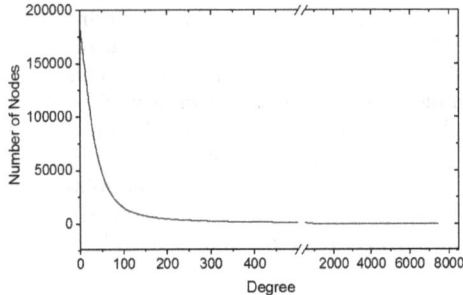

Figure 6: Degree distribution of locations.

1 day for each person. The activities will be repeated by agents in each simulation day.

Fig. 6 shows the degree distribution of location nodes. The location degree is calculated by the number of agents who visit that location. The distribution is skewed: most locations have a few visitors, while a few hub locations have large numbers of visitors.

4.2 Epidemic Model

The epidemic model has been widely studied [1, 5, 18]. It usually consists of two related parts: *Disease Progression Model* and *Disease Propagation Model*. The first one describes the disease progression within an infected person. The second describes the transmission probability between two contacting persons. This paper employs a basic epidemic model to simulate flu propagation among people without human autonomous behavior (e.g., making a decision to stay home or go to hospital when a person gets infected) and public healthy intervention (e.g., closing schools).

Disease Progression Model. The standard SEIR disease model [5, 18] is adopted to represent the disease progression. In the SEIR model, each person is in one of the four states at any time: *susceptible, exposed, infectious* and *recovery*. *Susceptible* denotes the state with no immunity to the disease and susceptible to the disease. *Exposed* is the state after being infected but without the ability to infect other *susceptible* individuals. *Infectious* stands for the state of being infected and being capable of spreading the diseases to other *susceptible* individuals. Finally, *recovery* denotes the state of being recovered from the disease. The *recovery* people will not be infected again in this experiment. In the initial phase of simulation, most people are *susceptible*, and only a small number of people are *infectious*. After a *susceptible* person v is infected, her/his health state becomes *exposed* immediately. She/he remains this *exposed* state for $t_E(v)$ days and then becomes *infectious* state. The agent will remain in the *infectious* state for $t_I(v)$ days. Finally,

she/he recovers from the disease and enters into *recovery* state. The recovered agent is removed from simulation to reduce computing cost.

Disease Propagation Model. If two persons stay in the same location l and have overlapped visit time, then a contact will be established. If person u's health state is *infectious* and she/he contacts with *susceptible* person v, the probability that the person v gets infected is calculated by Eqn. 4.

$$p(u, l, v) = \frac{1}{k} \times (1 - (1 - r)^{\Delta t(u,l,v)}), \qquad (4)$$

where r is the probability of disease transmission for contact per unit time. The larger value of r indicates higher chance that the infectious agent can infect the susceptible agent. $\Delta t(u, l, v)$ is the contact duration time between u and v in the location l. Specifically, it is the overlapped duration of arrivals and departures between u and v. The k is corrective coefficient for adjusting the disease transmission probability. During simulation, if the generated random number is smaller than the calculated probability, the susceptible agent v will be infected.

4.3 Experimental Setup

The experiments are executed on a cluster with 6 multi-core machines. The environment configurations are shown in Table 3. We implemented a common simulation framework supporting both our approach (denoted as *SplitGraph*) and the default approach using METIS without hub location decomposition (denoted as *SkewGraph*). In the framework, each partition is mapped to an LP, which is then executed by an MPI process. To reduce the overall communication overhead, small messages are aggregated in buckets before sending via MPI. When bucket is full or simulation synchronization is called, all messages in the bucket are flushed immediately.

The experimental parameters are shown in Table 4. Up to 60 cores are used to run LPs, and all LPs are evenly distributed among the machines. All experiments of performance evaluation are executed for 10 times and the mean value is used for analysis. The maximum coefficient of standard deviation is less than 2.8%. The initial infected people are selected from the whole population by even distribution of the population. The corrective coefficient k is adjusted so that the attack rate of the epidemic model (i.e., the ratio of total infected people to total population) is about 44%. The similar attack rates have been employed by the related epidemic models [5, 4, 19].

Table 4: Experiment settings

Parameter	Value
Number of LPs	6 to 60
Default Split Threshold (D_T)	500
Simulation Steps	120(Days)
Step Size	1(Day)
Initial Infected People	100
Disease Incubation Period $t_E(v)$	2(Days)
Disease Infectious Period $t_I(v)$	4(Days)
Transmission Probability r	0.3
Default Corrective Coefficient k	50

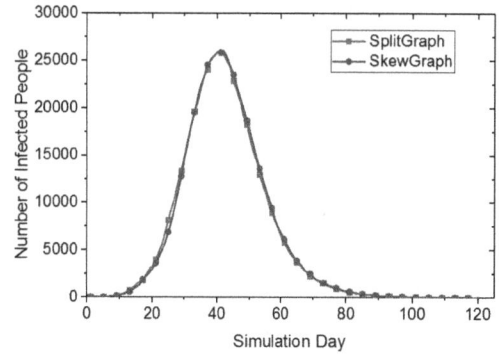

Figure 8: Number of newly infected people in each simulation step.

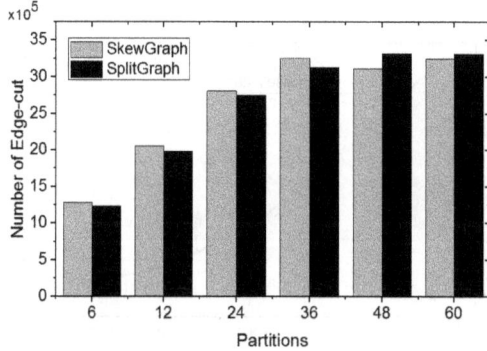

Figure 7: Number of edge-cuts of the two partitioning approaches.

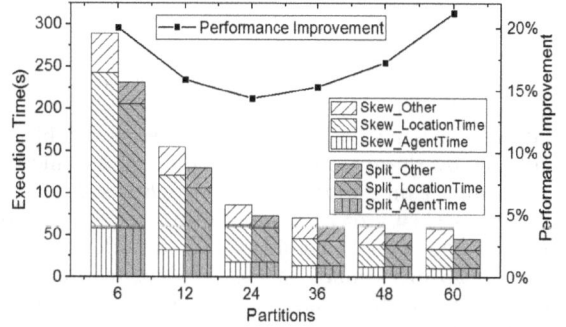

Figure 9: Simulation execution time of the two partitioning approaches.

4.4 Experimental Results and Analysis

4.4.1 Change of Edge-cut Number

Because in *SplitGraph* the network structure is changed before applying METIS tool, we need to understand the variation of the number of cut edges. Fig.7 shows the total cut edges of SCN by METIS. A lower value indicates the less communication overhead.

We can see that the number of edge-cuts do not show significant change after splitting hub locations. This is because the splitting with the default threshold D_T has a small influence on the overall network structure. The results also show the uncertainty of partitioning due to the network structure and partitioning algorithm. Generally, more partitions result in more edge-cuts, but it is not always true. For example, the number of edge-cuts in *SkewGraph* reduces when the number of partitions increases from 36 to 48.

4.4.2 Correctness of Hub Location Decomposition

To verify that the output of *SplitGraph* has the similar results with *SkewGraph* (considering the randomness in simulation, two instances cannot produce exactly the same results), we compare the numbers of the infected people produced by the two approaches. Both the average attack rates of the two approaches are about 44% with 10 runs. Fig. 8 shows the samples respectively with the numbers of infected people in each simulation step. The two curves are almost overlapped and it proves they produce the similar results.

4.4.3 Performance Improvement in the Base Scenario

Fig. 9 illustrates the total elapsed time of simulation with the two approaches. The time is decomposed into agent processing (*AgentTime*), location processing (*LocationTime*) and other overhead (*other*). The *AgentTime* and *LocationTime* are measured by the average time among partitions. They include the time of Receive, Compute and Send phases described in Algorithm 1 & 2, but do not include the transmission delay of messages. The *other* is the average system overhead which is mainly from the simulation synchronization. As is expected, the *AgentTimes* of the two approaches are similar since we only enhanced location processing.

Fig. 9 also illustrates the performance improvement of *SplitGraph* over *SkewGraph*. The results demonstrate *SplitGraph* always outperforms the *SkewGraph*, and gains about 14~21% performance improvement with the default settings. The use of 24 partitions obtains the lowest improvement, and the use of 60 partitions obtains the highest improvement. To investigate how much load imbalance is resolved from splitting hub locations, we recorded the execution time of each partition at each simulation step, and calculated load imbalance degree from the location computing, which is showed as Fig. 10. The imbalance degree is calculated by

$$L_{imb} = \sum_t \frac{L_{max}(t) - L_{avg}(t)}{L_{avg}(t)}, \quad (5)$$

where $L_{max}(t)$ is the maximum location processing time among partitions at each time step t and $L_{avg}(t)$ is the average time.

We can observe that the imbalance degree is small when the number of partitions is less than or equal to 24. This

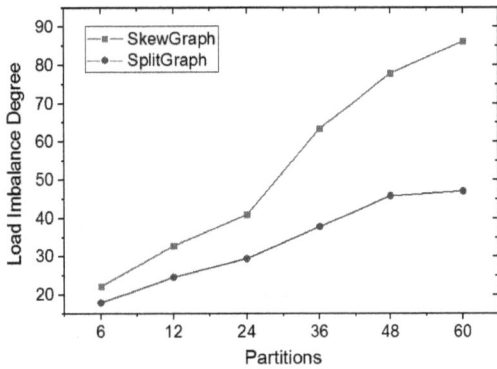

Figure 10: Accumulated load imbalance of simulation with the two partitioning approaches.

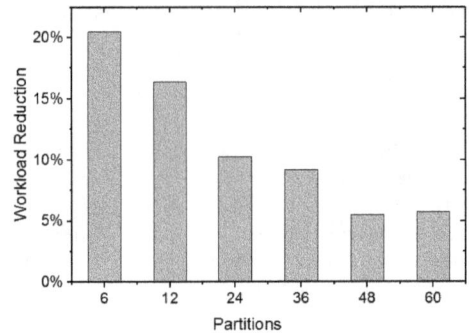

Figure 11: Reduction of location load due to the decomposition.

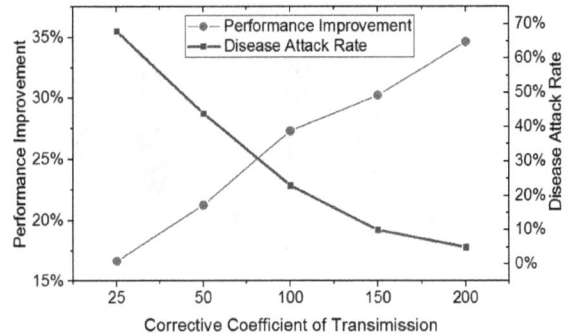

Figure 12: Performance improvement with different corrective coefficient of transimission (60 partitions).

is because there are only a few partitions and the load balancing can be achieved easily. With the increase of partitions, the influence from hub locations becomes apparent so that the imbalance in *SkewGraph* increases quickly. As a result, the overhead from the simulation synchronization has more impact on performance. The *SplitGraph*, by contrast, keeps a slow growth of imbalance degree. However, because this paper only considers the static load balancing, the *SplitGraph* cannot handle the dynamic imbalance at each simulation step, which also has a significant impact on performance.

According to Fig. 10, when there are 60 partitions the improvement of load balancing is significant. It accounts for the best performance improvement showed in Fig. 9. An interesting point in Fig. 9 is that the performance improvement is also significant when there are 6 partitions. In this case, the decomposition does not bring substantial benefit to load balancing because the degree of load imbalance is small according to Fig. 10. Furthermore, the performance improvement in Fig. 9 shows a trend that it drops at first and then increases. In addition to the improvement of load balancing, another important reason is the reduction of workloads due to the decomposition of hub locations.

First, location processing requires sorting arrival/departure events before computing contacts. The total sorting complexity of a hub location changes from $O((m+n)\log_2(m+n))$ to $O(\sum((m_i+n)\log_2(m_i+n)))$. Here m is the total number of information receivers and n is the total number of carriers in the hub location. The m is split into multiple m_i ($1 \leq i \leq s$, s is the number of splits). In our experiment, the n is small in most simulation steps. Under this condition, the decomposition can reduce the computational complexity of event sorting. Suppose $n \to 0$ and each split has equal number of visits, the total complexity changes from $O(m\log_2 m)$ to $O(m\log_2 \frac{m}{s})$. Second, location processing also involves the determination of contact pairs between agents. Suppose all agents have overlapped visit time at a location, the complexity of searching is $O((m+n)(m+n-1))$. After decomposition, the total complexity is $O((m+ns)(\frac{m}{s}+n-1))$. Since n is small and m is large, the complexity can be decreased significantly.

We measure the workload reduction by

$$W_r = \frac{L_{tot}(skew) - L_{tot}(split)}{L_{tot}(skew)}, \qquad (6)$$

where $L_{tot}(skew)$ is the total location processing time of all partitions using *SkewGraph*, and $L_{tot}(split)$ is the one using *SplitGraph*. The result is plotted as Fig. 11. For 6 partitions, the workload is reduced by about 20%. It accounts for the significant performance improvement in Fig. 9. With the increase of partitions, the ratio between extra overhead (e.g., system management and communication part of location processing) and useful computation (i.e., computing contacts) increases, and thus the workload reduction becomes less significant. In the case of 60 partitions, the workload reduction is only about 6%, and hence the overall performance improvement mainly comes from the improvement of load balancing.

Therefore, the trend of performance improvement in Fig. 9 is a combined result from load balancing and workload reduction, both of which are related to hub location decomposition.

4.4.4 Impact of Parameter Settings

The disease attack rate influences the workload of locations. When the rate is low, the workload is high in our experiments. This is because we removed the recovered agents from simulation to reduce the unnecessary contacts, and high attack rate means that a large number of agents can be removed. For the default experimental setting, the resulted attack rate (44%) is relatively high. We vary the corrective coefficient k to obtain a wide range of attack rate and investigate the performance improvements of *SplitGraph* over *SkewGraph*.

Fig. 12 shows the result upon 60 partitions. When k is 25,

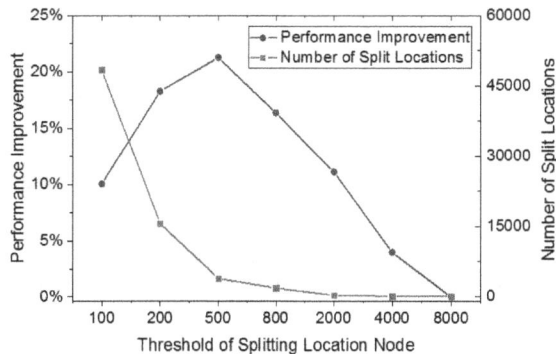

Figure 13: Performance improvement with different splitting threshold D_T (60 partitions).

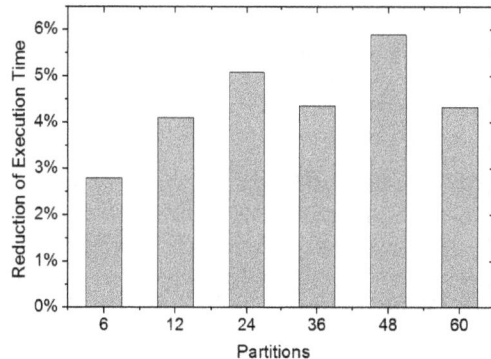

Figure 14: Reduction of execution time from interleaved processing.

the attack rate is 68%, and there is about 17% improvement of execution time. When k is 200, the attack rate is about 5%, and we get the most performance improvement (about 35%) in our experiment. According to Fig. 12, the higher workload of location, the more performance improvement can be achieved by *SplitGraph*.

We also investigate the impact of the number of splits on performance by varying the splitting threshold D_T. Fig. 13 shows the performance improvement results. This experiment is performed with 60 partitions. When the threshold is 8,000, no location is split because the maximum degree of location in this SCN is about 7,000. The thresholds are chosen unevenly due to the skewed degree distribution. Lower threshold results in more splits. In Fig. 13, the best threshold is 500, which achieves the highest performance improvement. When there are less splits, there is larger degradation of performance due to the load imbalance. When there are more splits, the overhead of communication between splits has a larger impact on performance. The result demonstrates that we should not excessively split a hub location.

4.4.5 Reduction of Communication Overhead among Splits

The reduced overhead of communication between splits is investigated by modifying the implementation of the message forwarding phase. Specifically, the forwarding phase is inserted between agent and location processing, without overlapping with non-split location processing, to measure the full overhead. Fig. 14 shows the reduction in execution time by overlapping message forwarding with non-split location processing. We can see that there is an average of 4% reduction in execution time. The reduction almost increases with the number of partitions, but this is not always true. This is because the splits introduce higher overhead when they are distributed in more partitions and the placement of splits depends on METIS.

5. RELATED WORK

5.1 SCN and SCN Simulation

Traditionally, SCN is abstracted using agent-to-agent (A2A) graph [5]. In the graph, there is only one kind of node which represents the agent, and the edge with time attribute represents the direct interaction between agents with a period of time. Compared with A2A graph, the A2L graph used in

this study contains the spatial locations where interactions happen.

With the development of artificial city [20] and synthetic population [21], several SCN datasets with spatial information are available to researchers nowadays [17, 22, 23]. A major application of SCN is to simulate disease spread among population. The performance of the simulation has attracted continuous attentions from researchers due to its very large scale. EpiSimdemics [4] is an epidemic simulation platform based on A2L graph. It supports population size over 100 million. In the early version, it partitioned SCN in a round-robin manner and obtained good performance only in small-scale simulation. In the later version, the scalability was extended to thousands of CPU cores. The communication overhead was reduced by message aggregation and synchronization latency was improved by advanced completion detection technology [7]. Especially, they addressed the hub locations at application level by splitting them into small sub-locations, as we discussed in the introduction section. By contrast, we use a system level decomposition which maintains the same semantic with the original network.

5.2 Simulation over Common Social Network

There are several studies about large-scale simulation over common social network without temporal or spatial information. Similar to A2L bipartite graph used in this paper, a social network is usually irregular. D'Angelo and Ferretti [24] proposed a general framework supporting simulation over irregular network. In this framework, the close relationship between agents can be discovered during run-time and these agents try to stick together by migrating between partitions. The load balancing is also achieved during this process. The method is suitable for dynamic system and light-weight agents with low cost of migration. In our study, we only consider the static network structure and focus on the hub nodes. CommPar is a community-based partitioning approach for social network simulation [25]. The network nodes are clustered before applying graph partitioning so that the community structure is exploited to reduce edge-cut and hence reduce computer communication overhead. However, it is limited to static network only. To address the dynamic network, Petkova et al. [26] used the label propagation algorithm (LPA) to detect community and re-partition network during simulation. The label is propagated together with agent's message and therefore it does not introduce significant overhead. On the other hand, they also illustrated that this approach encounters scalability issues in large-scale simulation. An important issue of community-based partitioning is that it may produce a few very large communities and many small communities for an irregular network, which can cause load imbalance among partitions.

5.3 Vertex-cut on Irregular Network

Vertex-cut is a novel method to partition irregular network. It is proposed by Gonzalez et al. [27] in the graph computing framework - PowerGraph. It has shown great performance improvement in machine learning applications due to the communication reduction and load balancing by vertex-cut. This idea is also adopted by other graph computing related work [28]. In their approaches, one edge is assigned to only one partition while one node can be split into parts as a result of the assignment. One split is selected as master and others are mirrors. The messages to mirrors can be combined by the commutative and associative operator locally before forwarding to master. However, it is not feasible for SCN to combine visit messages, and the messages from carriers need to be duplicated at each split. Nguyen and Fujimoto [15] proposed a vertex-cut based solution named link partitioning for simulation over irregular network. As we discussed in the introduction section, this approach is highly dependent on the characteristic of specific application. In their case of router network, the function of a router can be easily shared by ports so that all links modeling the ports can work in parallel. In our approach, we also split hub nodes, but we still employ vertex-oriented processing for simulation.

6. CONCLUSION

The skewed degree distribution of SCN causes the load imbalance problem for simulation over SCN. This paper proposed an approach to decompose the hub locations into multiple small splits to achieve better load balancing. Experimental results demonstrate that our approach can obtain 14~35% performance improvement compared with the graph partitioning without hub location decomposition. In addition, it is found that the decomposition can reduce the computational complexity of large locations.

As for future work, we will study larger scale and more complex scenarios to validate the effectiveness of our approach. In addition, we will extend the current work in the following directions. First, the graph partitioning algorithm will be enhanced to explore more parallelism among splits and reduce the communication between graph partitions. Second, dynamic network structure, i.e., adding and removing nodes and edges during runtime, will be taken into account to support more general applications. Third, a dynamic load-balancing mechanism will be investigated to improve SCN simulation performance further.

7. ACKNOWLEDGEMENTS

The research reported in this paper is financially supported by the Tier 1 Academic Research Fund (AcRF) under project Number RG23/14 (Ministry of Education, Singapore).

References

[1] Zhaoyang Zhang, Honggang Wang, Chonggang Wang, and Hua Fang. Modeling epidemics spreading on social contact networks. *IEEE Transactions on Emerging Topics in Computing*, 3(3):410–419, 2015.

[2] Stephen Eubank, Hasan Guclu, VS Anil Kumar, Madhav V Marathe, Aravind Srinivasan, Zoltan Toroczkai, and Nan Wang. Modelling disease outbreaks in realistic urban social networks. *Nature*, 429(6988):180–184, 2004.

[3] Andrea Apolloni, Karthik Channakeshava, Lisa Durbeck, Maleq Khan, Chris Kuhlman, Bryan Lewis, and Samarth Swarup. A study of information diffusion over a realistic social network model. In *International Conference on Computational Science and Engineering, 2009. CSE'09.*, volume 4, pages 675–682. IEEE, 2009.

[4] Christopher L Barrett, Keith R Bisset, Stephen G Eubank, Xizhou Feng, and Madhav V Marathe. Episimdemics: an efficient algorithm for simulating the spread of infectious disease over large realistic social networks. In *Proceedings of the 2008 ACM/IEEE conference on Supercomputing*, page 37. IEEE, IEEE, 2008.

[5] Keith R Bisset, Jiangzhuo Chen, Xizhou Feng, VS Kumar, and Madhav V Marathe. Epifast: a fast algorithm for large scale realistic epidemic simulations on distributed memory systems. In *Proceedings of the 23rd international conference on Supercomputing*, pages 430–439. ACM, ACM, 2009.

[6] Jiangming Jin, Stephen John Turner, Bu-Sung Lee, Jianlong Zhong, and Bingsheng He. Hpc simulations of information propagation over social networks. *Procedia Computer Science*, 9:292–301, 2012.

[7] Jae-Seung Yeom, Abhinav Bhatele, Keith Bisset, Eric Bohm, Abhishek Gupta, Laxmikant V Kale, Madhav Marathe, Dimitrios S Nikolopoulos, Martin Schulz, and Lukasz Wesolowski. Overcoming the scalability challenges of epidemic simulations on blue waters. In *2014 IEEE 28th International Parallel and Distributed Processing Symposium*, pages 755–764. IEEE, 2014.

[8] Youzhong Wang, Daniel Zeng, Zhidong Cao, Yong Wang, Hongbin Song, and Xiaolong Zheng. The impact of community structure of social contact network on epidemic outbreak and effectiveness of non-pharmaceutical interventions. In *Pacific-Asia Workshop on Intelligence and Security Informatics*, pages 108–120. Springer, 2011.

[9] Keith Bisset, Jiangzhuo Chen, Chris J Kuhlman, VS Kumar, and Madhav V Marathe. Interaction-based hpc modeling of social, biological, and economic contagions over large networks. In *Proceedings of the winter simulation conference*, pages 2938–2952. Winter Simulation Conference, 2011.

[10] Haifeng Zhang, Jie Zhang, Changsong Zhou, Michael Small, and Binghong Wang. Hub nodes inhibit the outbreak of epidemic under voluntary vaccination. *New Journal of Physics*, 12(2):023015, 2010.

[11] Joshua M Epstein. Modelling to contain pandemics. *Nature*, 460(7256):687–687, 2009.

[12] James M Brase and David L Brown. Modeling, simulation and analysis of complex networked systems: A program plan. *Lawrence Livermore National Laboratory*, 2009.

[13] Robert S Pienta and Richard M Fujimoto. On the parallel simulation of scale-free networks. In *Proceedings of the 1st ACM SIGSIM Conference on Principles of Advanced Discrete Simulation*, pages 179–188. ACM, 2013.

[14] Richard M Fujimoto. Research challenges in parallel and distributed simulation. *ACM Transactions on Modeling and Computer Simulation (TOMACS)*, 26 (4):22, 2016.

[15] Vy Thuy Nguyen and Richard Fujimoto. Link partitioning in parallel simulation of scale-free networks. In *2016 IEEE/ACM 20th International Symposium on Distributed Simulation and Real Time Applications (DS-RT)*, pages 77–84. IEEE, 2016.

[16] Amine Abou-Rjeili and George Karypis. Multilevel algorithms for partitioning power-law graphs. In *Proceedings 20th IEEE International Parallel & Distributed Processing Symposium*, pages 10–pp. IEEE, 2006.

[17] K Bisset, K Atkins, CL Barrett, R Beckman, S Eubank, A Marathe, M Marathe, HS Mortveit, P Stretz, and VA Kumar. Synthetic data products for societal infrastructures and proto-populations: Data set 1.0. Technical report, NDSSL Technical Report, 2006.

[18] Yu A Kuznetsov and C Piccardi. Bifurcation analysis of periodic seir and sir epidemic models. *Journal of mathematical biology*, 32(2):109–121, 1994.

[19] John J Grefenstette, Shawn T Brown, Roni Rosenfeld, Jay DePasse, Nathan TB Stone, Phillip C Cooley, William D Wheaton, Alona Fyshe, David D Galloway, Anuroop Sriram, et al. Fred (a framework for reconstructing epidemic dynamics): an open-source software system for modeling infectious diseases and control strategies using census-based populations. *BMC public health*, 13(1):1, 2013.

[20] Yuanzheng Ge, Rongqing Meng, Zhidong Cao, Xiaogang Qiu, and Kedi Huang. Virtual city: An individual-based digital environment for human mobility and interactive behavior. *Simulation*, 90(8): 917–935, 2014.

[21] Huadong Xia, Kalyani Nagaraj, Jiangzhuo Chen, and Madhav V Marathe. Synthesis of a high resolution social contact network for delhi with application to pandemic planning. *Artificial intelligence in medicine*, 65(2):113–130, 2015.

[22] Samarth Swarup, Stephen G Eubank, and Madhav V Marathe. Computational epidemiology as a challenge domain for multiagent systems. In *Proceedings of the 2014 international conference on Autonomous agents and multi-agent systems*, pages 1173–1176. International Foundation for Autonomous Agents and Multiagent Systems, 2014.

[23] Shannon Gallagher, Lee Richardson, Samuel L Ventura, and William F Eddy. Spew: Synthetic populations and ecosystems of the world. *arXiv preprint arXiv:1701.02383*, 2017.

[24] Gabriele D'Angelo and Stefano Ferretti. Simulation of scale-free networks. In *Proceedings of the 2nd International Conference on Simulation Tools and Techniques*, page 20. ICST (Institute for Computer Sciences, Social-Informatics and Telecommunications Engineering), 2009.

[25] Bonan Hou and Yiping Yao. Commpar: A community-based model partitioning approach for large-scale networked social dynamics simulation. In *2010 IEEE/ACM 14th International Symposium on Distributed Simulation and Real Time Applications (DS-RT)*, pages 7–13. IEEE, IEEE, 2010.

[26] A. Petkova, C. Hughes, N. Deo, and M. Dimitrov. Accelerating the distributed simulations of agent-based models using community detection. In *IEEE International Conference on Computing Communication Technologies, Research, Innovation, and Vision for the Future (RIVF)*, pages 25–30. IEEE, Nov 2016. .

[27] Joseph E. Gonzalez, Yucheng Low, Haijie Gu, Danny Bickson, and Carlos Guestrin. Powergraph: Distributed graph-parallel computation on natural graphs. In *Proceedings of the 10th USENIX Conference on Operating Systems Design and Implementation*, OSDI'12, pages 17–30, Berkeley, CA, USA, 2012. USENIX Association. ISBN 978-1-931971-96-6.

[28] Roger Pearce, Maya Gokhale, and Nancy M Amato. Scaling techniques for massive scale-free graphs in distributed (external) memory. In *2013 IEEE 27th International Symposium on Parallel & Distributed Processing (IPDPS)*, pages 825–836. IEEE, 2013.

Power Efficient Distributed Simulation

Richard M. Fujimoto[1], Michael Hunter[2], Aradhya Biswas[1], Mark Jackson[1], SaBra Neal[1]
[1]School of Computational Science & Engineering
[2]School of Civil and Environmental Engineering
Georgia Institute of Technology
Atlanta, GA 30332, USA
{fujimoto@cc.,michael.hunter@ce.,aradhya.biswas@,mjackson@,sneal6@}gatech.edu

ABSTRACT

Energy and power consumption have become important concerns for many computing systems ranging from embedded and mobile systems operating on battery-powered devices to high performance and cloud computing applications running on supercomputers and in data centers. To date, only a limited amount of work has considered power consumption in parallel and distributed simulations. A variety of options to analyze and explore power consumption in distributed simulations are discussed. These options range from design decisions in developing the simulation model to selection of algorithms in distributed simulation middleware to exploitation of hardware techniques. Work to characterize the power and energy consumed by different elements of parallel and distributed simulation systems are discussed and empirical measurements presented to quantify energy and power use, suggestive of directions for future research in this area.

1. INTRODUCTION

Energy and power consumption of computing applications has become a major concern. In mobile and embedded computing applications, power consumption has long been an area of interest due to its impact on battery size and battery life. Reduced energy consumption can lead to longer times between recharging or the ability to use smaller, lighter weight batteries. In high performance computing power consumption is a major impediment to achieving increased levels of performance due to limitations in dissipating heat from electronic circuits. Further, power consumption in data centers is a major expense for high performance and cloud computing applications. While traditional performance measures such as runtime and throughput remain important, energy and power consumption have become important additional concerns.

Energy is commonly defined as "the capacity for doing work" [3], and here refers to the energy expended by the computing system to execute a distributed simulation. A joule corresponds to the energy required to move one coulomb of electric charge through an electric potential of one volt. Power refers to the amount of

SIGSIM-PADS'17, May 24-26, 2017, Singapore, Singapore
Copyright is held by the owner/author(s). Publication rights licensed to ACM.
ACM 978-1-4503-4489-0/17/05...$15.00
DOI: http://dx.doi.org/10.1145/3064911.3069397

energy consumed per unit of time, with one watt referring to the expenditure of one joule of energy per second. As discussed below, energy and power are distinct quantities and one may be much more important than the other depending on the context in which the distributed simulation is executing. Here, we are concerned with both power and energy consumption, but use the term "power" whenever the distinction between the two is not important. Many of the techniques discussed here can be applied toward analyzing and reducing both power and energy consumption.

For mobile and embedded computing platforms operating on batteries, energy consumption is the principle concern. Batteries convert chemical energy from materials within the fuel cell into electricity. A battery has a fixed energy capacity that is defined as the amount of electrical charge the battery can deliver at its rated voltage, measured in amp-hours [4]. Thus, the amount of energy consumed by a computation directly impacts the battery's lifetime. Reducing the power consumed by the computation may not change or may even increase the energy used by the distributed simulation if the computation requires more time to complete. As such, reducing power consumption is not necessarily helpful in addressing battery lifetime or size concerns.

In high performance computing applications power is often the primary concern stemming from limitations in cooling the components making up the computing system, and the costs associated with operating data centers. The Thermal Design Power (TDP) is the amount of heat generated by a computer chip or component during normal operation for which the cooling system has been designed [5]. Power capping used in some systems places a maximum amount of power that can be consumed by a computer server. Thus, a typical goal for an HPC application might be to minimize execution time subject to a specified power cap constraint. The U.S. Department of Energy has set a goal of 20 megawatts as the maximum power consumed by an exascale supercomputer. Electricity is a major cost in operating data centers. It is estimated that in total, data centers consumed approximately 70 billion kW-hours or about 1.8% of the total electricity consumption in the U.S. in 2014 [6]. As such, reducing power consumption is increasing in importance for high performance and cloud computing applications.

Parallel simulation is concerned with executing a simulation on tightly coupled multiprocessor platforms while *distributed simulation* typically refers to execution on loosely couple distributed computing platforms. As such, power would appear to be of greater concern for parallel simulations, and energy for distributed simulations executing on mobile platforms. However, this is not always the case. For example, an area of increasing interest is micro-cluster servers composed of closely coupled

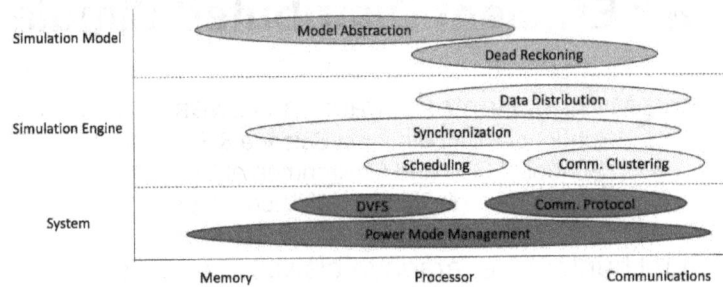

Figure 1. Framework of techniques for creating power efficient distributed simulations.

power-efficient processors operating in energy constrained mobile platforms. As such, energy consumption for parallel simulation codes executing on these platforms may be of greater interest than power consumption. Similarly, in distributed simulations where part or all of the simulation executes on back-end cloud computing platforms power consumption may be of great concern. Where the distinction between parallel and distributed is not important, we simply use the term "distributed simulation." Here, we are concerned with discrete event simulations.

The goal in any power efficient distributed simulation design is to reduce power consumption while meeting other performance goals such as execution time, throughput, model accuracy, and precision. While there is a substantial literature in power efficient computing, there has been only a limited amount of work focused specifically on parallel and distributed simulation. A principle objective of this paper is to focus attention on power consumption in distributed simulations, and to discuss various issues and methods that can be applied to analyzing and improving power efficiency.

The remainder of this paper is organized as follows. The next section describes a framework and taxonomy to characterize different power saving techniques in order to highlight their relationship with one another. A three-level hierarchy is described spanning the distributed simulation application, the distributed simulation engine or middleware, and the underlying hardware and software system. After a brief description of the experimental platform used for power measurements reported here, the sections that follow discuss specific techniques and empirical results within each of these three areas. The emphasis throughout this discussion concerns power efficiency issues that are specific to distributed simulations, or the application of more general techniques to distributed simulations.

2. FRAMEWORK FOR POWER EFFICIENT DISTRIBUTED SIMULATION

In order to characterize different approaches to realizing power-efficient distributed simulations, we use the framework depicted in Figure 1. This framework is not unlike that described in [7], but has been adapted to apply to distributed simulations. The framework has two dimensions. The vertical axis corresponds to a view of the hardware/software stack used to implement the distributed simulation system. Specifically, we differentiate between (1) the *simulation model layer* where the application-specific simulation program is defined, (2) the *simulation engine layer* that includes distributed simulation middleware, and (3) the *system layer* that includes the operating system and hardware upon which the simulation engine and simulation model execute. The second, horizontal axis differentiates between the power consumed for (1) computation, (2) memory and storage, and (3)

communications. Different techniques defined in the software stack will impact power consumption in different parts of the system.

The simulation model layer includes the representation of the state of the system under investigation and the code for transforming this state from one time instant to the next. It includes those portions of the distributed simulation that are specific to the simulation application. Several design decisions in creating the simulation model can have a large impact on power consumption. Perhaps most importantly, the degree of detail at which the system is modeled in space (e.g., the level of aggregation) and time (e.g., the time step size) will impact the amount of memory required and memory access patterns as well as the amount of computation required to update the system state. The model detail and abstractions will also impact the amount and frequency with which data must be communicated among the processes making up the distributed simulation. Decisions such as the precision at which data is represented and algorithms used to transform the state of the simulation model will similarly impact energy consumption. Techniques such as dead reckoning (DR) may be used to reduce the amount of communication required, and thus the amount of energy expended for communications, at the cost of increased computation to execute the DR models. Design of the distributed simulation model will require one to determine the minimal level of detail required to meet the accuracy and precision objectives of the simulation while simultaneously meeting runtime performance, memory, and power consumption constraints.

The simulation engine layer includes distributed simulation software that does not depend on the system being modeled. It includes the synchronization algorithm needed to ensure the distributed execution yields the same results as a sequential execution, as well as other functions such as event list processing and data distribution. This software is sometimes called the runtime infrastructure, e.g., the software responsible for implementing distributed simulation services such as those described in [8] for the High Level Architecture standard. Design decisions concerning the implementation of these services can have a significant impact on power consumption of the distributed simulation. For example, the synchronization algorithm, necessary to implement time management services described in [8], will have important ramifications on power consumption. The decision to use optimistic or conservative synchronization methods will similarly impact power consumption. Different approaches to implementing data distribution management services [8] and logical process scheduling will impact power. Clustering messages for inter-processor communications can also be used to reduce power consumption.

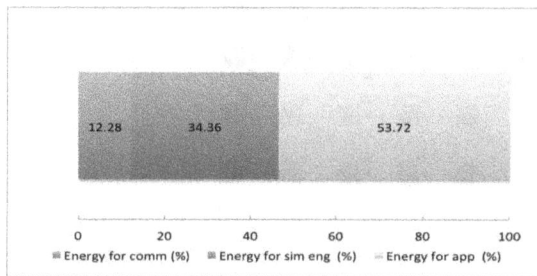

Figure 2. Energy profile for a typical distributed simulation [2].

The systems layer includes the underlying hardware and operating system over which the distributed simulation executes. Low power operating systems focus on techniques such as light-weight implementation of essential services to reduce power consumption while meeting performance requirements and/or task completion deadlines [9-11]. Many communication protocols are designed or optimized for low power operation. *Power mode management* techniques involve exploitation of different modes of operation for processors, memory, storage, and communication circuits [12-14]. For example, such components can often be disabled or switched to power saving states. The simulation computation can be mapped to a minimal number of processors necessary to meet delay and throughput needs, and the remaining cores can be powered down to reduce power consumption. Similarly, communications circuits can be powered down between communications. These techniques come at a cost, of course, e.g., in terms of increased execution time or longer communication latency. Many processors provide dynamic voltage and frequency scaling (DVFS) where the processor voltage or clock frequency can be reduced to trade off power consumption and performance [15-17].

Among these three layers – simulation application, simulation engine, and the system layer – the amount of energy consumed by each can be significant. Figure 2 shows an energy profile of a distributed simulation execution of a queueing network model using the Chandy/Misra.Bryant synchronization algorithm [2]. For this test case over half of the energy is consumed by the application, a third by the simulation engine, and the remainder by communications. In other applications, the portion used by communications can be much larger.

To date, there is a substantial literature in power aware design of embedded systems and a growing literature related to high performance computing. Most of this work focuses on the systems layer described above. Below we describe work specifically focused on power efficient distributed simulation in the context of the framework shown in Figure 1. This includes both aspects unique to distributed simulations such as synchronization algorithms, as well as methods involving the application of general techniques such as power mode management to distributed simulations.

3. EXPERIMENTAL CONFIGURATION
Two hardware configurations are utilized for the experimental results described here. The first is a distributed simulation system composed of simulations executing on cellular telephones that communicate with each other, or in some cases, with a laptop computer. The LG Nexus 5 cellular phone with a quad-core Qualcomm MSM8974 Snapdragon 800 processor, 2 GB memory, and 16 GB storage was used as the mobile computing platform.

While mobile systems may not necessarily use cellular telephones as their compute engine, they most likely will utilize the same or similar mobile processors. The phone runs the Android version 5.0.1 (Android Lollipop) operating system. The laptop is a Lenovo ThinkPad® running Ubuntu 14.04. All inter-processor communications used the device's 802.11n WiFi communications. A private wireless network was established among the devices to avoid interference resulting from Internet traffic. Energy and power consumption data were derived from direct measurement of the Android device using the "BatteryManager" class of the "android.os" API. The instantaneous power consumption was obtained and used to calculate energy consumption over time.

Parallel simulation experiments were performed on a micro-cluster platform designed for mobile, high performance computing. The hardware used were Jetson TK1 development boards with ARM A15 32-bit CPU with 4 cores operating at 2.3 GHz and 2 GB memory. The ARM includes an additional core providing low power computing. Energy and power measurements were performed using a PowerMon2 power measurement system [18].

4. SIMULATION MODEL
The simulation model layer includes all simulation model code. We first describe the use of task graphs to model the distributed simulation, followed by a case study considering the impact of modeling approaches and use of dead reckoning to reduce power.

4.1 Task Graphs
A distributed simulation is composed of a set of logical processes (LPs) that communicate by exchanging event messages. Each LP includes a set of state variables that represent the state of the system being modeled, i.e., the physical system. The computation within each LP is a sequence of timestamped event computations, where each computation may (1) modify one or more state variables, and/or (2) schedule new events. Events within each LP must be processed in timestamp order.

Task graphs are a natural approach to represent distributed simulations and have long been used for this purpose. Each event computation is referred to as a task, and is represented as a node in the graph. Let $E_{i,j}$ represent the jth event in LP i where events within an LP are ordered according to timestamp. Arcs represent precedence relationships between tasks, i.e., and arc from event $E_{i,r}$ to $E_{j,s}$ indicates that the computation for $E_{i,r}$ must be completed before the computation for $E_{j,s}$ can begin.

In a discrete event simulation, a precedence relationship exists if one of the following two rules applies:

- $E_{i,r} \rightarrow E_{i,r+1}$, i.e., a precedence relationship exists between successive events within the same LP, or

- $E_{i,r} \rightarrow E_{j,s}$ if event computation $E_{i,r}$ resulted in generating event $E_{j,s}$.

The precedence relationship is transitive. Figure 3(a) shows a task graph for a discrete event simulation with each box representing an event computation; its location on the horizontal and vertical axes indicate the event timestamp and the LP processing the event, respectively. For example, these events might correspond to arrivals of a vehicle at an intersection in a traffic simulation or a traffic signal change. Arcs between LPs indicate events scheduled by one LP to be processed by another. The values in each box indicate the event computation subscripts $E_{i,j}$ as defined above.

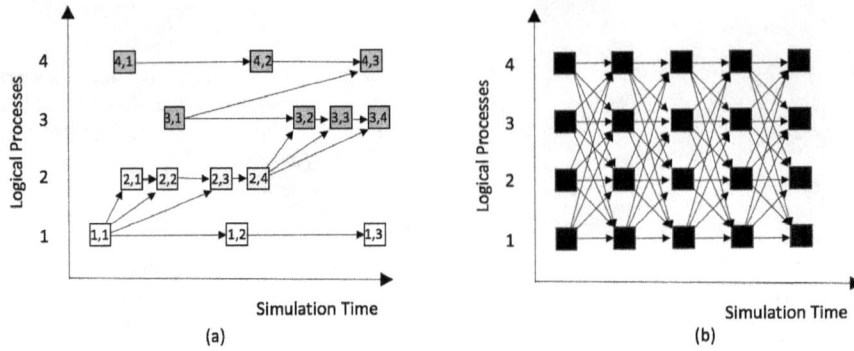

Figure 3. Task graphs for distributed simulations. (a) event-driven simulation. (b) time-driven simulation.

In a time-stepped simulation all of the event computations for one time step must be completed before the event computations in the next time step can begin. Figure 3(b) shows the precedence graph for a time-stepped simulation.

Precedence graphs can be used to determine the parallelism and minimum execution time of distributed simulations [19]. They have also been used extensively to estimate power consumption of embedded computations, e.g., see [20-22]. This is accomplished by mapping each task to the hardware responsible for completing the task and augmenting the task graph to specify the amount of energy required to complete the task. As such, task graphs are a useful way to model power consumption of distributed simulations.

For example, in Figure 3(a) if we assume each event computation requires one unit of time and one unit of energy, it is easy to see that this task graph will require at least 8 units of time and 14 units of energy. Later, we will show how the task graph model can be used to analyze power consumption.

Note that the above model does not consider the energy consumed for communications or other operations such as managing event lists or other data structures. These are accounted for in the simulation engine, as described later.

4.2 Model Abstraction

One of the principle means of controlling the amount of power consumed in the simulation model layer is the abstraction and level of detail used by the model. To illustrate, two approaches to modeling vehicle traffic are queueing network models using an event-driven simulation and a time-stepped cellular automata (CA) model. Further details of this study are described in [1].

The CA simulation models the micro level dynamics of traffic flow behavior. Each road segment is divided into cells. The state of each cell is either occupied or empty to indicate if a vehicle currently resides within the cell [23]. The simulation executes in a time-stepped fashion where the state of each cell is updated each time step in accordance with rules for vehicle movement. The CA used here is based on the two lane modeling approach described in [24]. The model consists of modules for cells, vehicles, and road segments. The simulation environment includes a two-dimensional array of 69 X 89 cells. Each cell was set to a size of 7.5 meters and can hold at most one vehicle. A cell can be in one of five states: empty, normal, source, sink, or a traffic light. A normal cell is one that is a part of a road segment. A source cell represents a location where vehicles enter the system. A sink cell represents the location within the model where vehicles leave the system. A traffic light cell represents a cell where a traffic light is

located. Vehicles are stopped based on the state of the traffic light and assigned a turn probability if applicable. An empty cell represents a cell that is currently not occupied by a vehicle. The state of each cell includes a row and column location, street id, the direction in which vehicles travel, and an array of turn probabilities for a vehicle that occupy that cell. Each vehicle has an id, vehicle arrival time, departure time, total time in the system, arrival street, and departure street. The vehicle's velocity specifies the number of cells the vehicle can advance each time step. The model was configured to simulate a road segment in midtown Atlanta, and driven by measurement data of the same area.

In the queuing model simulation traffic lanes are represented using queues that hold vehicles occupying a lane. The model state includes information concerning vehicles, intersections, and road segments. An event-driven execution paradigm is used with the event list implemented using a binary heap. Event handlers implement new vehicle arrivals and vehicle departures, as well as events modeling operations within each intersection. The latter includes events for vehicle arriving at, entering, crossing and departing from the intersection. Other events model traffic signal change events. Vehicle state variables include the vehicle's origin, destination, id, lane id, and velocity. A road segment corresponds to the section of road between intersections. The state of each segment includes information such as the number of vehicles in the section with a flag indicating congestion. Each lane of an intersection is represented by a queue that holds vehicles waiting to traverse the intersection.

The power consumed by the simulation model depends on the processor computations as well as the behavior of the memory system. It is not a priori clear which model requires more power. Precise power estimation requires detailed simulation of the processor and memory system or empirical measurement. The queueing network and cellular automata both require largely integer computations. The cellular automata model requires more event computations since the state of each cell must be updated each time step, however, it uses simple matrix data structures compared to the queues and heaps required in the queueing model. Memory footprint and access pattern impact the power consumed by the memory system. Both models require memory to hold state variables for vehicles and intersections, but the cellular automata model also requires memory for individual sections of roadway, something not required in the queueing model. On the other hand, the matrices in the cellular automata model can lead to greater reference locality compared to accesses to the irregular, dynamically allocated data structures used in the queueing model, offering the potential for reduced power consumption in the memory hierarchy.

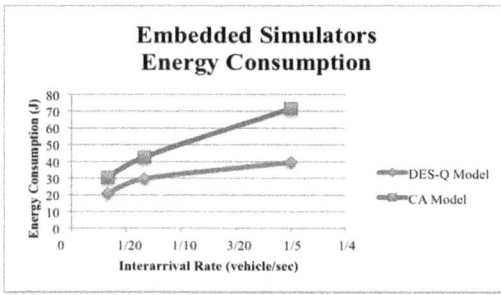

Figure 4. Energy consumption of cellular automata and queueing network traffic simulations [1].

The energy consumed by the two models as the rate of traffic is increased is shown in Figure 4. The cellular automata simulation requires more energy, mirroring its longer execution times. While these measurements pertain to a specific implementation of the simulation models, this example illustrates how the abstraction used in the model impacts power consumption and also highlights some of the issues one might consider during the development of power efficient simulation models.

4.3 Dead Reckoning

It is sometimes possible to reduce communication in a distributed simulation at the expense of increased computation. One example is the use of dead reckoning algorithms. Dead reckoning is a technique developed for real-time distributed simulations to reduce the amount of communications that are required [25-27]. A local dead reckoning model computes the estimated position of entities, typically vehicles, modeled on other computers based on information reported previously by the vehicle, e.g., its position, direction of travel, speed and acceleration. When the current position of the remote entity is required, the dead reckoning model is used to estimate its current position.

The dead reckoning model's prediction will become inaccurate if the vehicle's motion deviates from that last reported, e.g., if it turns to a new direction or begins to accelerate or decelerate. To limit the resulting error, the processor simulating the vehicle also monitors the dead reckoning model, and if the difference between the dead reckoned position deviates from the actual position by more than a defined threshold, an update message is sent to update the remote dead reckoning models.

Dead reckoning is an example of a technique that reduces inter-processor communications at the expense of increased computation. Because communication is relatively expensive in terms of power, it provides a technique to reduce power consumed by the distributed simulation. Further, if the amount of required communication can be reduced so that there is a significantly long delay between communications, the communications circuits can be switched off further reducing energy consumption. This approach is explored in [28] where an adaptive dead reckoning algorithm is proposed. More broadly, techniques such as dead reckoning provide a means for trading off computation and communications to reduce power consumption.

5. SIMULATION ENGINE

The simulation engine includes functionality such as LP scheduling, synchronization and data distribution algorithms to implement functionality required by the distributed simulation. We next highlight how LP scheduling can impact power consumption and discuss the power cost of conservative and optimistic synchronization as well as approaches to data distribution and communications.

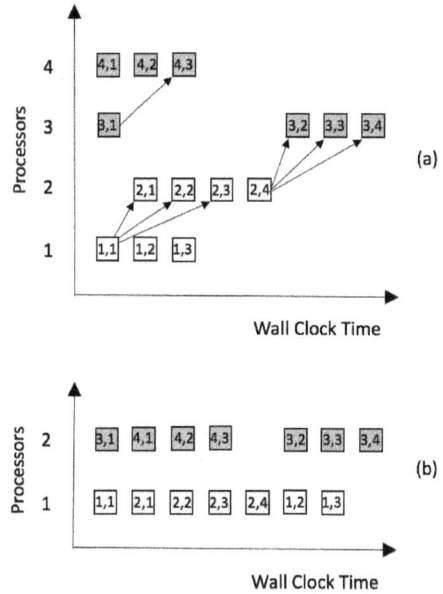

Figure 5. Energy and power consumption for two mappings of LPs to processors.

5.1 Logical Process Scheduling

The mapping of the distributed simulation computation to processors can have a significant impact on power consumption. To illustrate this point, consider a distributed simulation represented as a task graph, as discussed earlier. Specifically, consider the discrete event simulation shown in Figure 3(a). Assume each event consumes one unit of energy and requires one unit of time to complete.

Two executions of this task graph over time are shown in Figure 5. In Figure 5(a) each LP is mapped to a separate processor, and it is assumed that each event computation is performed as soon as its precedence constraints have been satisfied. For example, events $E_{1,1}$, $E_{3,1}$, and $E_{4,1}$ are processed in the first unit of wall clock time, $E_{1,2}$, $E_{2,1}$, and $E_{4,2}$ in the second, etc. The execution is completed in 8 time units, equal to the critical path execution time. An alternate execution of the same computation is shown in Figure 5(b) where LPs 1 and 2 are mapped to processor 1 and LPs 3 and 4 are mapped to processor 2. Arcs showing the scheduling of events are omitted to simplify the diagram. This execution also achieves the minimum, critical path execution time. Here, we assume an idealized conservative synchronization algorithm that can identify when each event can be processed without violating precedence constraints.

In a distributed simulation execution where battery life is the primary concern, we see that both executions consume a total of 14 units of energy, although it is noted that the two-processor execution requires less communication between processors, which will result in less energy consumption.

In a parallel execution where the maximum amount of power that can be utilized by the computation is capped, an analysis of the maximum power consumed by the computation may be useful. The maximum power using 4 processors is 3 because the maximum number of events that are processed concurrently is 3. The maximum power consumption in the two-processor case is 2, suggesting that this mapping can reduce power without sacrificing execution time. While this is clearly a simplified representation of the computation, this example does demonstrate that the approach to mapping LPs to processors can impact the maximum power consumption of the computation.

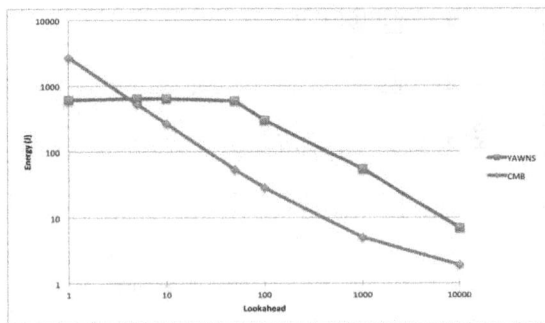

Figure 6. Energy consumed by Chandy/Misra/Bryant and YAWNS as lookahead is varied [2].

This simple analysis suggests that the mapping of processors to computing resources requires further consideration in evaluating power consumption for distributed simulations. This is an area that requires further research. Scheduling algorithms used in other areas, e.g., embedded systems, may be applicable here.

5.2 Conservative Synchronization

Distributed simulations require a synchronization algorithm to ensure the distributed execution yields the same results as a sequential execution. Because synchronization algorithms require a significant amount of inter-processor communication, one might expect a significant amount of energy will be required to ensure proper synchronization.

Synchronization algorithms are well studied in the distributed simulation literature [29]. Conservative algorithms require that LPs block until one can ensure that events are processed in timestamp order. Two well-known conservative synchronization algorithms are the Chandy/Misra/Bryant (CMB) null message algorithm [30, 31] and YAWNS [32]. CMB is asynchronous, with synchronization messages termed null messages sent between LPs in order to enable the receiving LP to identify the "safe" events that can be processed without violating the timestamp order constraint. By contrast, YAWNS is synchronous, and uses global barriers to identify safe events. The energy cost of these conservative synchronization algorithms has been studied in [2, 33, 34].

The results of one set of experiments comparing CMB and YAWNS is shown in Figure 6. This figure shows the energy consumed by these algorithms for a synthetic application with no event communications and only minimal event computation. As such, the energy consumed by the distributed simulation is largely to execute the synchronization algorithm. The amount of energy consumed as the lookahead is varied is shown in this figure. Note that the axes in this plot are on a logarithmic scale.

It is well known that the efficiency of conservative synchronization algorithms depends heavily on the lookahead present in the simulation application. Not surprisingly, this is reflected in the energy measurements as well. In these experiments the amount of energy consumed varied by two orders of magnitude across the lookahead values that were used.

CMB and YAWNS exhibit different behaviors with respect to energy consumption. In CMB the energy consumed steadily decreased as the lookahead was increased. CMB exhibits a behavior referred to as lookahead creep where null messages are

sent in cycles among the LPs, with each cycle advancing the simulation time of the LPs in the cycle by an amount equal to the lookahead. As the lookahead increases the advancement in each cycle increases in proportion. To a first order approximation this reduces the number of null messages that are sent in proportion to the lookahead, accounting for the reduced energy that was observed as lookahead increases. This observation was verified by measurements of the number of null messages that were sent, that decreased in proportion with the lookahead.

On the other hand, YAWNS demonstrated a different behavior. Energy consumption remains at a relatively constant level for small to moderate lookahead values, but then steadily decreased with increased lookahead at relatively high lookahead values. For lookahead values that are much less than the average amount of simulation time between successive events, each global synchronization operation in YAWNS will advance the simulation time of all LPs to essentially the time stamp of the next unprocessed event in the distributed simulation, largely independent of the exact lookahead value. When the lookahead is significantly larger than the simulation time between event, to a first order approximation YAWNS will behave more like a time stepped simulation, and process all events within a lookahead sized time step. In this mode of operation increasing the lookahead will result in a proportionate increase in the number of events that are processed before the next global synchronization operation.

Overall, these studies indicate that the synchronization algorithm can consume a significant amount of energy in executing the distributed simulation. Because the computations required to implement synchronization algorithms is usually minimal, energy consumption is driven largely by the amount of communication that is required. As such, the main challenge in creating power-efficient conservative synchronization algorithms is to minimize the number of messages without unnecessarily blocking LPs. Reducing the number of synchronization messages tends to also improve the performance of conservative synchronization algorithms, however, it remains to be seen if selecting the synchronization algorithm to minimize execution time also leads to one that minimizes energy.

5.3 Optimistic Synchronization

While conservative algorithms avoid synchronization errors, optimistic algorithms detect synchronization errors during the execution and use a rollback mechanism to recover. Time Warp is the most well-known optimistic synchronization algorithm [35]. If an LP receives an event with timestamp smaller than other events the LP has already processed, the computations for those events with timestamp larger than the newly received event must be rolled back. State saving techniques are typically used to restore the state of the LP. Messages sent by rolled back events are "unsent" by sending an antimessage for each message that must be canceled. When an antimessage is received, the corresponding positive message must be located, and if it has already been processed, another rollback is triggered, possibly resulting in additional antimessages. This process repeats recursively until the error is erased. Time Warp requires the computation of Global Virtual Time (GVT) to reclaim memory and commit I/O operations. These operations are performed by a computation termed fossil collection.

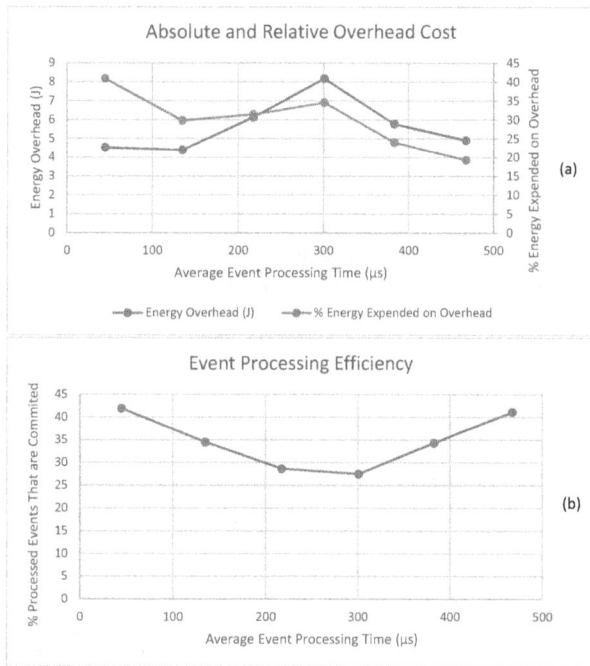

Figure 7. Power consumption and efficiency of Time Warp simulation.

The power overhead associated with conservative synchronization largely concerns the messages that must be sent to ensure proper synchronization. In optimistic algorithms, the power overhead takes on a different form. There are several sources of power consumption. These include the power expended to (1) perform state saving tasks, (2) perform rollback computations, (3) send, receive, and process antimessages, and (4) compute GVT and other operations associated with fossil collection that are not present in a sequential execution.

To measure the power used for optimistic synchronization an implementation of Time Warp was developed to run on the parallel simulation development boards. The experiments described here use PHOLD as the application program [36], and execute 4 logical processes, one for each logical process. The amount of computation per event was varied by adding a busy wait loop to each event.

The power overhead associated with optimistic processing was determined by running the PHOLD simulation with rollbacks turned off, capturing the power required to execute the distributed simulation application without synchronization overheads. The resulting value was subtracted from the power used by the Time Warp simulation to derive the power consumed for optimistic synchronization.

The measured power overhead for optimistic synchronization in processing a fixed number of committed events is shown in Figure 7(a) for different event granularities. This graph shows the absolute amount of energy used for optimistic synchronization as well as the percentage of the total expended energy used for synchronization. It is seen that the energy consumed for synchronization can be significant, as much as 40% in these experiments.

Efficiency, shown in Figure 7(b), is defined as the number of committed events divided by the total number of events processed. As can be seen energy overhead is correlated with

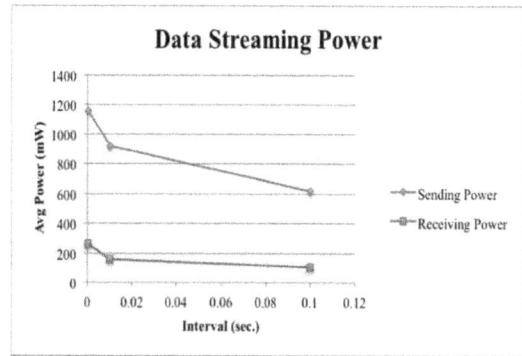

Figure 8. Power consumed to send and receive data.

efficiency, suggesting that rolled back events are a major contributor to energy overhead for synchronization in Time Warp. As the event granularity increases the amount of energy used for synchronization initially increases. Stated differently, the energy overhead for synchronization, which includes the overhead for rolled back event computations, increases with the event granularity. This is because increased event granularity results in more rolled back computation, as illustrated by the falling efficiency curve. As the granularity is increased further, the efficiency in this experiment increases, resulting in reduced energy overhead. Overall, the amount of energy used for the optimistic synchronization is correlated with the run time of the parallel simulator.

5.4 Power Consumption for Communications

As discussed earlier, communication is a significant source of power consumption in distributed simulations. Here, we describe results from some experiments to characterize this overhead.

Figure 8 shows the energy consumed in an online simulation application for communications of a stream of data from one source to a destination using the distributed simulation platform described earlier. The application sends a stream of data over the connection where the data are intended to represent vehicle position data in an online traffic simulation. The power required to send and receive this stream of messages is shown. It is also seen that the power required to send is approximately five times that required to receive the data stream.

One approach to reducing energy consumption is to aggregate messages in the data stream. If the simulation must send a stream of update messages, one could aggregate several messages into a single message, and send one larger message rather than a sequence of smaller messages. This approach, termed message aggregation, is commonly used in distributed systems in order to reduce communication overheads. Message aggregation comes at the cost of increasing latency as some messages must be held at the sender in a buffer while the data is being accumulated, rather than immediately sending the data to the receiver. A set of experiments was conducted to consider the impact of aggregation on energy consumption.

In each experimental run, the number of updates, and the size of the data in each update remain constant and the only variable is the number of updates aggregated to form a message. The application executed the cellular automata based traffic simulation described earlier. The amount of energy consumed per byte of transmitted data was measured. Figure 9 shows the results of this experiment. As expected, an initial reduction in the energy

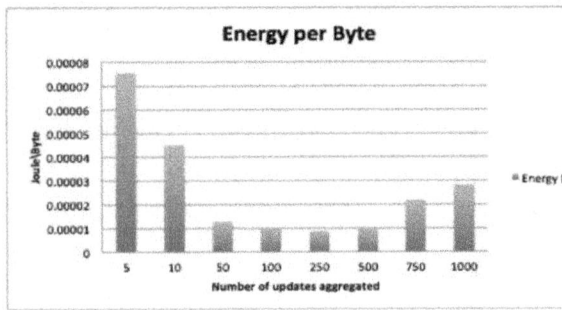

Figure 9. Energy reduction by clustering messages.

consumed is observed as message aggregation increases. This is because fewer messages are sent, thereby reducing the energy consumed to process the message and send overhead information such as message headers. However, an inflection point is reached and the energy consumed per byte of data starts increasing beyond a certain level of aggregation. This is because the operating system will automatically divide large messages into packets, and transmit each packet as a separate unit of data. Thus, from the standpoint of energy consumption, data aggregation is only effective up to the maximum data packet size used by the operating system.

5.5 Dynamic Data Distribution Management

Data Distribution Management (DDM) is a set of services defined in the High Level Architecture (HLA) standard [8]. DDM services are used to disseminate information among the simulators, termed federates, based on dynamically changing criteria such as a vehicle's location.

DDM is based on an abstraction called the routing space, which is simply an N-dimensional coordinate system. Each message that is sent is associated with a rectangular update region. Each federate specifies a rectangular subscription that indicates the portion of the routing space of interest to the federate. If the update region associated with a message overlaps with a federate's subscription region, that federate should receive a copy of the message.

Several approaches to implementing the DDM services have been proposed. Perhaps the most direct is the region-based approach. A multicast group is defined for each publication region. Each federate simply joins those groups that correspond to publication regions that overlap with its subscription regions [37]. A matching computation must be performed, often centrally, to determine overlaps between subscription and publication regions, in order to populate the multicast groups. This computation runtime is $O(N^2)$ where N is the total number of publication/subscription regions. Whenever a publication (subscription) region changes, the new region must be compared against all other subscription (publication) regions to determine overlaps with the new region.

The hybrid approach helps to reduce the computation overhead of the region based approach by defining a grid structure overlaid on the routing space [38]. Matching computations need only be performed on regions overlapping the grid cells of the modified region. Like the region-based approach, if the DDM mechanism is implemented centrally, communications with the central controller is necessary whenever regions change, necessitating additional power consumption. If the DDM implementation is distributed across a set of devices, communications among these devices is similarly required whenever regions change to coordinate management of the groups.

The grid-based approach avoids the need for matching computations to configure the multicast groups [37]. The routing space is divided into grid cells, not unlike the hybrid approach. A multicast group is defined for each grid cell. A federate must join all multicast groups that overlap with its subscription regions. When a message is sent, it is sent to all groups overlapping with the publication region associated with the message. The grid-based approach does require some computation to determine overlaps between regions and grid cells when a region changes, however, this computation is O(1). This will be significantly less than that required for the region-based approach. Further, the grid-based approach allows a fully distributed implementation without the need for coordination messages that are necessary in the region-based and hybrid approaches when regions change. However, the grid-based approach can result in duplicate and irrelevant messages, and thus incurs additional power consumption to send and receive these messages, something that is not required in the region-based and hybrid approaches.

To reduce the number of irrelevant and duplicate messages other DDM approaches have been proposed such as the dynamic grid approach [39]. This approach reduces the number of multicast groups that are utilized in the fixed grid approach by only assigning multicast groups to grids where at least one publication and at least one subscription region are located within the same grid cell. In contrast to the original grid-based scheme this prevents publishers from sending messages to groups where there are no subscribers, and reduces the number of required groups. This approach does not eliminate the irrelevant and duplicate message problem that occurs from utilizing a grid based approach but it does reduce it. The amount of additional communication will depend on factors such as the grid cell size, the number of federates, the size and location of publication and subscription regions, and the number of hops between communicating nodes in the network.

The tradeoffs among these factors are dependent on the distributed simulation scenario and specifics of the DDM design. In the following we empirically evaluate these questions through a combination of measurement and simulation. The scenario used in this work is based on a vehicle traffic network where individual vehicles travel past embedded traffic sensors that are responsible for monitoring the traffic volume within the traffic network. A two-dimensional routing space is used that corresponds to a traffic network measuring 50 by 50 kilometers. Sensor devices publish data such as measurements of traffic volume. Each publication region corresponds to an area surrounding the location of the sensor. Subscription regions represent areas of interest for a particular vehicle and are typically distant from the location of the subscriber federate.

Vehicles express interest in receiving data from sensors that are located 805 meters (0.5 miles) from their current location. The embedded sensors have a sensor range of 400 meters. Each moving vehicle is a federate that subscribes to receive updates and each embedded traffic sensor is a federate publishing data. The number of subscribing federates is varied from 100 to 1000. For grid-based approaches a grid cell size of 20 by 20 meters is used. The publication and subscription regions of every federate were chosen randomly within the routing space. The code for both implementations was written in Java using the Android Development Tool (ADT) plugin for Android Studio and a Java application for the server. The implementation was tested on the parallel simulation development board utilizing the powermon tool to measure current and power, as described earlier.

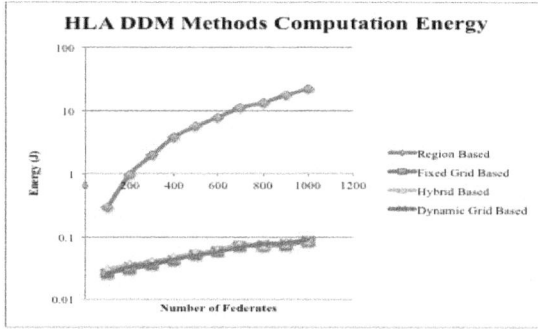
Figure 10. DDM energy for computation.

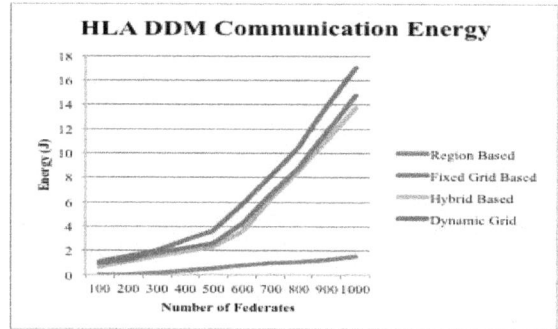
Figure 11. DDM energy for communication.

The energy consumed for matching computations in the four DDM implementations as the number of federates is increased is shown in Figure 10. Not surprisingly, the region-based approach requires the most energy, especially as the number of federates increases. The energy required for matching in all of the schemes using grids is insignificant compared to a purely region based approach. Even with a small number of federates the energy for computation is far less in the three approaches. The computation energy among the three other approaches are indistinguishable.

The energy consumed for communications is shown in Figure 11. The region-based approach uses far less energy than the three grid-based approaches. This is because the grid-based schemes all require much more energy for irrelevant and duplicate messages, especially as the number of federates increases. By contrast, the impact of increasing the number of federates in the region-based approach is much less. We note that these measurements include the energy consumption required by the RTI client using DDM services to communicate and gain information under the four different DDM approaches, e.g., to send information concerning its subscription and publication regions.

The results from these experiments highlight the trade-off between computation and communications in implementing DDM approaches. It is clear that utilizing a grid structure greatly reduces the energy needed for computation, but at a cost of increased energy for communications. Among the three schemes using grids, the hybrid and dynamic grid schemes use somewhat less energy for communications. One should caution, however, that different scenarios and different rates of region changes can result in very different quantitative results than those shown here.

6. SYSTEMS LAYER

At the hardware level, power consumption for CMOS circuits is broken down into three main components – power resulting from the current needed to charge capacitive loads as signals change, short circuit current that occurs momentarily when a CMOS circuit switches, and power due to leakage current as indicated by the three terms below [40]:

$$P = ACV^2f + \tau AVI_{short}f + VI_{leak}$$

Here A indicates the activity of the circuit (not all circuits switch on each clock), C is the total capacitive load on the circuit, V is the supply voltage, f is the clock frequency, τ indicates the time duration when the short circuit current flows, and I_{short} and I_{leak} are the short circuit and leakage current, respectively. The first two terms form the *dynamic* power consumption component and result from the operation and switching of active circuits. The third forms a *static* power consumption component that results from the circuit simply being powered on.

Dynamic Voltage and Frequency Scaling (DVFS) can be used to reduce dynamic power consumption. From the above discussion it is apparent that reducing the supply voltage V and/or the clock frequency f is a way to significantly reduce the dynamic power consumption of the circuit. These techniques will reduce performance, however, leading to slower running programs. Dynamic power consumption P as a function of processor speed s is generally assumed to be $P(s) = s^\alpha$ for some $\alpha > 1$; α is often assumed to equal 3 leading to the well-known cube-root rule, i.e., $P(s)=s^3$, or the power is proportional to the speed cubed [41]. In other words, doubling processor speed will result in an 8-fold increase in power consumption. These observations allow one to estimate the energy consumption for distributed simulation models by converting the weights specified in the task graph to energy values as a function of processor speed.

If the goal is to minimize power consumption with no additional constraints, then it is clear the best approach is to simply use the lowest frequency/voltage setting offered by the hardware, assuming static power consumption is negligible. A more interesting question is to select frequency/voltage settings to minimize power while meeting certain runtime performance constraints.

Another hardware approach to reducing power consumption is to use unconventional processing cores, e.g., GPUs, FPGA, or specialized hardware, which are generally more power efficient than general purpose cores. A third approach discussed in greater detail next is to use power management modes. This means powering down certain elements of the system to reduce power consumption, e.g., processing cores or communication circuits. This technique reduces both static and dynamic power consumption.

6.1 Power Mode Management: Processors

Power drawn by a processing unit and its components are very closely related to the performance of the system. Hence an understanding of the system behavior in terms of performance as the maximum allowed power is varied is indispensable for achieving the best possible performance with the given power constraints. Experimental results designed to provide an understanding of the effect of changes in power budget on performance of a parallel simulation are described next.

An MPI-based parallel telecommunication network simulation of the DARPA NMS Campus Network Model [42] was used as the benchmarking application in these experiments. NS3, a widely used discrete event network simulator was used to deploy the simulation application.

85

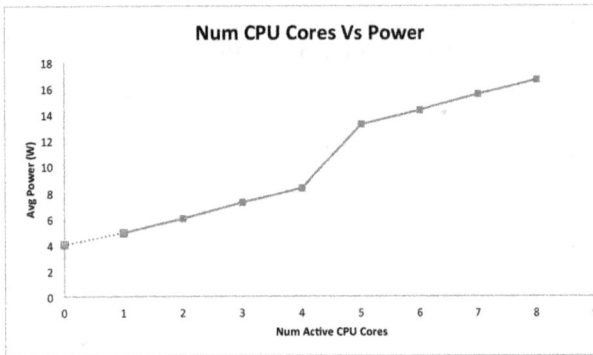

Figure 12. Average power consumed by the system with the increase in number of processes. The power depicted by 0 CPU core, depicts the power consumption of the Low power core.

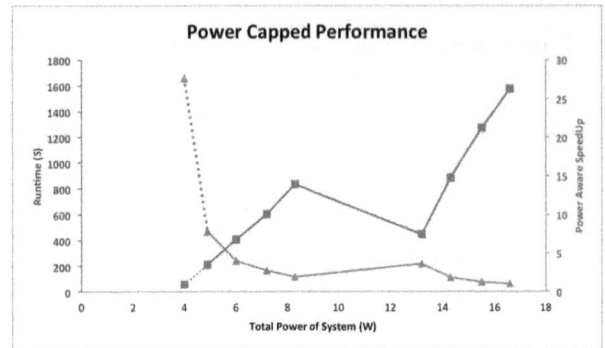

Figure 13. Strong scaling experiments showing the increase in the performance with the increase in the power cap of the system on the primary Y-axis. The Secondary Y-axis depicts corresponding power aware speedup.

The fundamental unit of the Campus Network Simulation is a campus network. For the current study, the simulation included 8 campus networks, connected in a ring topology. Each campus network consisted of 2 nodes per LAN.

The platform of experimentation was the micro-cluster described earlier. The Tegra K1 SOC of the Jetson TK1 boards includes a NVIDIA 4-Plus-1™ Quad-Core ARM® Cortex™-A15 CPU. The ARM CPU allows users to disable CPU cores as one way to control the power consumption on the boards. Another option provided by the board is the presence of a Low Power Core (in addition to 4 general CPU cores), intended to reduce the idle state energy consumption of the processor.

Two boards connected to a wired private LAN were used for the experiments. To vary the power consumption of the system of boards (referred to as the system), the number of active CPU cores was varied. The experiments consisted of a series of strong scaling runs with varying average power consumption of the system.

The power consumption monitoring system connected to one of the development boards was used to approximate the power consumption of the second board. For less than or equal to 4 active CPU cores, only one board is assumed active (in other words, the system until that points consists of only one board). Figure 12 shows the average power consumed by the system as the number of active CPU cores is increased. The dotted line signifies the movement from a low power core based system to a general CPU core. The bump in power drawn by the system, observed at the introduction of the 5th core can be explained by the introduction of the static power requirement of an additional board.

The results of strong scaling experiments are shown in Figure 13. These show the decrease in runtime of a constant workload as the average power consumption of the system is varied. The second metric depicted in the figure is power aware speed up [43]. For a power level p, power aware speed up is defined as the ratio of the execution time of the system at the specified power level divided by the execution time at the lowest possible power level. In this case, the latter is the system using one low power core. An application with higher power-aware speedup is more sensitive to change in the power levels.

As can be seen, the movement from the low power core to the general CPU core costs about a Watt (about 22%) in the power consumption of the system, but the performance improves by a factor of 3.5. Another point of interest is the addition of the 5th core to the system. The jump in the power consumption is not well reciprocated by the execution time of the system. So for this particular setup it would not be advisable to add 5th and 6th cores to the system if the power cap is 15 Watts. In other words, introduction of a second processor is efficient only if the introduction of a 7th core is possible.

6.2 Power Mode Management: Communication

Moving beyond the power consumption of just the processing elements, a system can conserve power and energy by restricting power consumed by other elements of the system. One such element of interest is the network [44]. Networks are generally over-provisioned both in terms of bandwidth and availability. In addition to the off-board power consumption of the network, the on board network/LAN card could also be powered down or turned off to conserve power and energy consumed by the system.

To test the nature of the possible gains due to the implementation of the proposed technique we conducted a benchmarking experiment. The experiment was conducted on the parallel simulation system discussed earlier. The experiment consisted of one board pinging another board over an Ethernet link. The boards as mentioned earlier, were connected over a private LAN network. Sets of ping requests, with lowest possible interval, were sent with intermittent low power periods. It should be noted that the low power period refers to the low power/turned off state of just the on-board network infrastructure. All other system components function as default.

The experiments were designed to crop out the energy savings achieved by turning off of the network card on-board. For this in one of the setups, the sleep time between the sets of ping requests was 16 seconds; this is called the *optimized setup*. For the second setup, the minimum sleep time was set to 20ms; this is called the *default setup*. It should be noted here that for the optimized setup, the on-board network card was turned off for 11 seconds. The buffer sleep period was to accommodate the transition of states. For the default setup, all the system components executed at their default configuration.

As mentioned the aim of this experiment was to determine the gain that can be achieved by varying the lengths of low power periods. Hence the total number of Ping messages sent out was fixed at 8000 and the interval between ping requests in a set was also constant. As the number of ping request was fixed the total message size sent out in both the setups is equal. Finally, the execution time of the experiments was fixed. This was achieved by varying the number of ping messages in a set. In the optimized setup, each set was comprised of 2000 ping requests, whereas in the default setup, each was comprised of 4 ping messages.

The energy consumed by the development board in the optimized setup added up to 156 Joules and for the default setup it added up to 273 Joules.

The proposed technique of alternating the power states of a network card generates a periodic communication pattern. The communication pattern of a system can be leveraged to support this alternation of the network state. This requirement imposes a constraint on the application development to either use a periodic communication pattern or be able to handle large message latency.

Another constraint introduced by the proposed technique is the minimum period between communications. This is introduced by the hardware and/or software requirements of transitioning from one state to another. The delay introduced by hardware switching to a different state was minimal for our test setup. The majority of the period/delay in the test system was contributed by the time required for the system to connect back to the LAN network. The total delay was in the orders of 5 seconds.

Finally, the system incurs an energy and power overhead while switching its states. Again, this will be influenced by both the hardware and software components of the system. Following from the time costs as mentioned in the previous paragraph, the most noticeable overhead was incurred while reconnecting to the network.

The gains of switching states can be increased by two major means. First by increasing the length of the low power period or in other words decreasing the frequency of communication. Second, decreasing the overhead of reconnecting to the network can increase the gain. The effect of the delay (and hence the energy and power overheads) incurred for connecting back to the network can be reduced by bringing down the network infrastructure of the system to a low power state where it stays connected to the network but does not incur full power draw of on-board network infrastructure.

7. CONCLUDING REMARKS

Power is now a very important issue in many areas of computing, but has seen only limited attention by the modeling and simulation research community. Analysis and development of new techniques to improve power efficiency in distributed simulations is an open field, with many unresolved questions and problems. The space of techniques can be viewed in the context of the software stack, encompassing the simulation application, simulation engine or middleware, and the underlying system. Approaches impact power consumption in the processor, memory and storage system, and communications network.

The first step in optimizing power in distributed simulations is to understand the relationship among modeling approaches, synchronization and data distribution algorithms, and hardware techniques with runtime and prediction accuracy and power consumption. Fundamental understandings will enable the development and evaluation of new techniques to reduce power, subject to traditional modeling objectives. In some cases, approaches can build upon other work in parallel and distributed computing in general. Other efforts will likely need to focus on aspects specific to distributed simulations.

ACKNOWLEDGMENTS

Funding provided by NSF/AFOSR Grant 1462503 and AFOSR grant FA9550-17-1-022 is gratefully acknowledged.

REFERENCES

[1]   S. Neal, R. M. Fujimoto, and M. Hunter, "Energy Consumption of Data Driven Traffic Simulations," presented at the Winter Simulation Conference, 2016.

[2]   A. Biswas and R. M. Fujimoto, "Energy Consumption of Synchronization Algorithms in Distributed Simulations," *Journal of Simulation,* 2016.

[3]   Encyclopedia Britanica. (2000, Accessed March 26, 2017). *Energy (Physics).* Available: https://www.britannica.com/science/energy

[4]   Wikipedia. (Accessed March 26, 2017). *Battery (Electricity).* Available: https://en.wikipedia.org/wiki/Battery_(electricity)

[5]   S. Huck, "Measuring Processor Power," Intel Corporation2011.

[6]   A. Shehabi, S. J. Smith, D. A. Sartor, R. E. Brown, M. Herrlin, J. G. Koomey, *et al.*, "United States Data Center Energy Usage Report," Lawrence Berkeley National Laboratory LBNL-1005775, June 2016.

[7]   L. Benini and G. De Michela, "System-Level Power Optimization: Techniques and Tools," *ACM Transactions on Design Automation of Electronic Systems,* vol. 5, pp. 115-192, 2000.

[8]   IEEE Std 1516.3-2010, *IEEE Standard for Modeling and Simulation (M&S) High Level Architecture (HLA) - - Interface Specification.* New York, NY: Institute of Electrical and Electronics Engineers, Inc., 2010.

[9]   S. Saewong and R. Rajkumar, "Practical voltage-scaling for fixed-priority rt-systems," presented at the IEEE Real- Time and Embedded Technology and Applications Symposium, 2003.

[10]   G. Quan and X. Hu, "Energy efficient fixed- priority scheduling for real-time systems on variable voltage processors," presented at the Design Automation Conference, 2001.

[11]   K.-M. Cho, C.-H. Liang, J.-Y. Huang, and C.-S. Yang, "Design and implementation of a general purpose power-saving scheduling algorithm for embedded systems," presented at the IEEE International Conference on Signal Processing, Communications and Computing, Xi'an, China, 2011.

[12]   A. Hoeller, L. Wanner, and A. Fröhlich, "A hierarchical approach for power management on mobile embedded systems," in *From Model-Driven Design to Resource Management for Distributed Embedded Systems,* ed, 2006, pp. 265–274.

[13]   K. Bhatti, C. Belleudy, and M. Auguin, "Power management in real time embedded systems through online and adaptive interplay of DPM and DVFS policies," presented at the International Conference on Embedded and Ubiquitous Computing, Hong Kong, China, 2010.

[14]   L. Niu and G. Quan, "Reducing both dynamic and leakage energy consumption for hard real- time systems," presented at the international conference on Compilers, architecture, and synthesis for embedded systems, 2004.

[15]   R. Ge, X. Feng, and K. W. Cameron, "Performance-constrained Distributed DVS Scheduling for Scientific

Applications on Power-aware Clusters," presented at the Proceedings of the 2005 ACM/IEEE conference on Supercomputing, Washington, DC, USA, 2005.

[16]   V. W. Freeh, D. K. Lowenthal, F. Pan, N. Kappiah, R. Springer, B. L. Rountree, *et al.*, "Analyzing the Energy-Time Trade-Off in High-Performance Computing Applications," *IEEE Trans. Parallel Distrib. Syst.,* vol. 18, pp. 835--848, June 2007.

[17]   S. Hua and G. Qu, "Approaching the Maximum Energy Saving on Embedded Systems with Multiple Voltages," presented at the IEEE/ACM International Conference on Computer-Aided Design, 2003.

[18]   D. Bedard, A. Porterfield, R. Fowler, and M. Y. Lim, "PowerMon 2: Fine-grained, Integrated Power Measurement,," RENCI, North Carolina, Technical Report TR-09-04, October 2009.

[19]   O. Berry and D. Jefferson, "Critical path analysis of distributed simulation," presented at the Proceedings of the SCS Conference on Distributed Simulation, 1985.

[20]   J. J. Brown, D. Z. Chen, G. W. Greenwood, X. Hu, and R. W. Taylor, "Scheduling for power reduction in a real-time system," presented at the Proceedings of the International Symposium on Low Power Electronics and Design, Monterey, CA, 1997.

[21]   D. Kirovski and M. Potkonjak, "System-level synthesis of low-power hard real-time systems," presented at the Proceedings of the Annual Conference on Design Automation, Anaheim, CA, 1997.

[22]   B. Dave, G. Lakshminarayana, and N. Jha, "COSYN: Hardware-software co-synthesis for heterogeneous distributed embedded systems," *IEEE Transactions on Very Large Scale Integration Systems* vol. 7, March 1999.

[23]   K. Nagel and M. Schreckenberg, "A Cellular Automata Model for Freeway Traffic," *J. Physique I,* vol. 2, pp. 2221-2229, 1992.

[24]   M. Rickert, K. Nagel, M. Schreckenberg, and A. Latour, "Two lane traffic simulations using cellular automata," *Physica A: Statistical Mechanics and its Applications,* vol. 231, pp. 534-550, 1996.

[25]   D. C. Miller and J. A. Thorpe, "SIMNET: The Advent of Simulator Networking," *Proceedings of the IEEE,* vol. 83, pp. 1114-1123, 1995.

[26]   K.-C. Lin and D. E. Schab, "The Performance Assessment of the Dead Reckoning Algorithms in DIS," *Simulation,* vol. 63, pp. 318-325, 1994.

[27]   R. Saunders, "Formal Expression of Dead Reckoning: Mathematical and Representation Recommendation," presented at the DIS Workshop, 1991.

[28]   W. Shi, K. S. Perumalla, and R. M. Fujimoto, "Power-aware State Dissemination in Mobile Distributed Virtual Environments," in *Workshop on Parallel and Distributed Simulation*, San Diego, 2003.

[29]   R. Fujimoto, *Parallel and Distributed Simulation Systems*: Wiley Interscience, 2000.

[30]   K. M. Chandy and J. Misra, "Distributed Simulation: A Case Study in Design and Verification of Distributed Programs," *IEEE Transactions on Software Engineering,* vol. SE-5, pp. 440-452, 1979.

[31]   R. E. Bryant, "Simulation of Packet Communication Architecture Computer Systems," M.S. thesis, MIT-LCS-TR-188, Computer Science Laboratory, Massachusetts Institute of Technology, Cambridge, Massachusetts, 1977.

[32]   D. M. Nicol, "The Cost of Conservative Synchronization in Parallel Discrete Event Simulations," *Journal of the Association for Computing Machinery,* vol. 40, pp. 304-333, June 1993.

[33]   R. M. Fujimoto and A. Biswas, "An Empirical Study of Energy Consumption in Distributed Simulations," presented at the IEEE/ACM International Symposium on Distributed Simulation and Real-Time Applications, 2015.

[34]   A. Biswas and R. M. Fujimoto, "Profiling Energy Consumption in Distributed Simulation," presented at the Principles of Advanced Discrete Simulation, 2016.

[35]   D. Jefferson, "Virtual Time," *ACM Transactions on Programming Languages and Systems,* vol. 7, pp. 404-425, 1985.

[36]   R. M. Fujimoto, "Performance of Time Warp Under Synthetic Workloads," in *Proceedings of the SCS Multiconference on Distributed Simulation.* vol. 22, ed, 1990, pp. 23-28.

[37]   A. Boukerche and C. Dzermajko, "Performance Comparison of Data Distribution Management Strategies," in *Proceedings of the 5th IEEE International Workshop on Distributed Simulation and Real-Time Applications*, Cincinnati, OH, 2001, pp. 67-75.

[38]   G. Tan, Y. Zhang, and R. Ayani, "A Hybrid Approach to Data Distribution Management," in *Proceedings of the 4th IEEE International Workshop on Distributed Simulation and Real-Time Applications*, San Francisco, CA, 2000, pp. 55-61.

[39]   A. Boucherche and A. J. Roy, "Dynamic Grid-Based Approach to Data Distribution Management," *Journal of Parallel and Distributed Computing,* vol. 62, pp. 366-392, 2002.

[40]   T. Mudge, "Power: A First-Class Architectural Design Constraint," *IEEE Computer,* vol. 34, pp. 52-58, 2001.

[41]   D. M. Brooks, P. Bose, S. E. Schuster, H. Jacobson, P. N. Kudva, A. Buyuktosunoglu, *et al.*, "Power-aware microarchitecture: Design and modeling challenges for next-generation microprocessors," *IEEE Micro,* vol. 20, pp. 26–44, 2000.

[42]   R. M. Fujimoto, K. S. Perumalla, A. Park, H. Wu, M. Ammar, and G. F. Riley, "Large-Scale Network Simulation -- How Big? How Fast?," in *Modeling, Analysis and Simulation of Computer and Telecommunication Systems*, 2003.

[43]   R. Ge and K. W. Cameron, "Power-Aware Speedup," presented at the IEEE International Parallel and Distributed Processing Symposium, 2007. IPDPS 2007., 2007.

[44]   V. Soteriou and L.-S. Peh, "Exploring the Design Space of Self-Regulating Power-Aware On/Off Interconnection Networks," presented at the IEEE Transactions Parallel and Distributed Systems.

A Performance Model of Composite Synchronization

David M. Nicol
Dept. of Electrical and Computer Engineering
University of Illinois at Urbana-Champaign
Urbana, Illinois, 61801
dmnicol@illinois.edu

ABSTRACT

Experience and intuition indicate that both synchronization and the mapping of workload to processors has significant impact on overall performance. However, the behavior of parallel simulations is quite complex, and the interrelationships between workload mapping and the synchronization overheads need mathematical explanation. This paper develops a performance model of a parallel simulation that is synchronized using composite synchronization. We use this model to help explain how mapping decisions and a synchronization tuning parameter impacts synchronization overhead, and hence performance. The observations we make should inform designers of algorithms to map conservatively synchronized parallel simulations to the available computing platform.

CCS Concepts

•Computing methodologies → Discrete-event simulation; Massively parallel and high-performance simulations; *Modeling methodologies;*

1. INTRODUCTION

The notion of using a distributed computing platform to execute a discrete-event simulation was introduced in 1979 in a classic paper by Chandy and Misra [5]. The motivation was to describe a model of an algorithm for time advancement, and prove the mechanism to be free from deadlock. Time increases monotonically at each "logical processor", and the proof requires in the model an ability to "look ahead" and occasionally provide a lower bound on the virtual time at which a message might next be sent from one logical processor to another. This foundational paper was followed by another, in 1985, by Jefferson [4], who describes algorithms for synchronizing discrete event simulations optimistically, now famously, "Time Warp". Here a logical process advances in simulation time without explicit coordination with others, and realigns in time and its state as needed when it receives messages with time-stamps in its temporal past.

SIGSIM-PADS 17, May 24 26, 2017, Singapore.

© 2017 ACM. ISBN 978-1-4503-4489-0/17/05. . . $15.00

DOI: http://dx.doi.org/10.1145/3064911.3069396

In the decades since a tremendous amount of research has been directed at parallel simulation. Intuition and experience suggest that the way that the simulation model is partitioned and laid out among processors has strong influence on the overheads of communication and of the synchronization method. There is an old literature considering issues in dynamic and static mapping of conservatively synchronized parallel simulations, e.g., [6, 1, 2, 7, 3]. The objective of this paper is to build a performance model that describes performance, and use implications of that model to understand how particular facets of conservative synchronization are influenced by the mapping.

In an optimistically synchronized system, if one processor tends to advance more slowly in virtual time than the others, it will rarely receive messages in its past, while messages it sends are more frequently received in the temporal past of the recipients, and rollbacks and anti-messages ensue. However, if the corrections are implemented fast relative to the rate at which the rollbacks are triggered, then their impact on overall execution time may be masked by the load imbalance caused by the processor advancing most slowly. On the other hand, in an optimistic simulation with good load balance the rollbacks and state restoration are more likely to lay on the critical path and so contribute more significantly to the overall advancement of virtual time. The mapping of model to processors also impacts performance through communication overhead. Spatial locality, if found and exploited can keep some communication on-processor and/or reduce the latency of off-processor communications.

Model characteristics and workload mapping have significant impact on performance of conservatively synchronized simulations. Three factors play significant roles. Like any parallel computation, the distribution of workload and the communication overhead between separated elements of the model influence performance. What is special though about conservatively synchronized parallelized discrete-event simulation is that communication overhead is significantly influenced by the synchronization technique and by the particulars of the workload mapping. Potential temporal dependencies are treated like data dependencies, which constrains the advancement of virtual time as a function of the workload mapping. The challenge we address in this paper is to develop a mathematical model that explains the interrelationships between model characteristics, workload mapping, and communication/synchronization overhead within the context of *composite synchronization.*

Mathematical models have utility as vehicles for exposing and explaining relationships, and (separately) as vehicles for prediction. The intent of this paper is to focus on explanation. Some concepts describe behavior in a way that is useful for explanation, but is not typically available for use by a mapping algorithm. A model to be used in a predictive way (such as for mapping) needs validation, which is beyond the intended scope of this paper.

What we do in this paper is to define a model that describes workload execution, communication, and synchronization overhead and captures how these overheads are influenced by the mapping of workload to processors. The model describes costs and logical precedences, and with this model a critical path analysis through a weighted graph computes the length of time needed to perform one "window" of a parallel simulation. We develop this model in the context of composite synchronization [8], which uses both asynchronous and synchronous techniques to maintain temporal fidelity. We then do a more qualitative analysis of how the precedence structure of the descriptive model gives insight into key considerations for mapping simulation workload. While we do not in this paper propose new mapping algorithms, the insights identified here may be helpful in designing such algorithms.

2. SIMULATION MODEL

We suppose the simulation model is decomposed into *entities* with state and a notion of virtual time, with associated *processes* that when executed modify the entity's state, and advance the entity's virtual time clock. A *channel* exists between two entities if it is possible for a process bound to an entity to communicate directly with a process bound to other using a *message*. A message has both a *send time* and a *receive time*, the former being the virtual time of the sending entity when it writes the message to the channel, the latter being the virtual time the message should be presented to the receiver. In this model the difference between these times is the message delay. Channels therefore ascribe delays to message transmission, and have attributes the modeler uses to describe precisely the desired delay. For example, a channel might model the point-to-point connection between two switches, and the message delay would be the point-to-point delay, plus the product of message size and link bandwidth. Figure 1 graphically illustrates these concepts. Entities have varying numbers of processes and channels, and following the SSF/S3F mode of expression [10, 9], it is possible for two entities to share more than one channel.

A channel $c_{i,j}$ between entities E_i and E_j is assumed to have a known *minimal delay* $\epsilon_{i,j}$. The delays imparted to messages that cross $c_{i,j}$ may have varying delays, but every one of them is at least as large as $\epsilon_{i,j}$.

An *event* in this model is a process execution, at a given instant of virtual time. Process executions may be triggered by the firing of an internally scheduled timer, or by the receipt of a message from a channel. In the former case the time of the event is the timer's firing time, in the latter case the time of the event is the message receive time.

A mapping algorithm assigns entities to *timelines*. A timeline manages the events associated with its entities using an ordinary event list, like any serial simulation. For instance, if a message is sent through a channel whose endpoints are co-aligned on a timeline, the event that sends the message just schedules through the event list an event to receive the message. An assumption of our model is that if channel $c_{i,j}$

has minimal delay 0, then E_i and E_j must be assigned to the same timeline. For the purposes of our discussion on synchronization, we assume that the software layer implementing the simulation at a timeline responds to the receipt of an off-timeline message with t by inserting an event into the timeline's event list with event time t.

Students of parallel simulation will recognize that what we refer to here as a timeline would classically be called a "logical process". Whatever the name, the important notion is that the timeline advances a virtual clock, communicates with other timelines, and synchronizes temporally with them. Given a mapping of entities to timelines, we classify each channel as internal or external, depending on whether the endpoint entities are assigned to the same timeline or not, respectively. Channels with 0 minimal delay are necessarily internal. Now if T_a and T_b are timelines, for the purposes of communication and synchronization it makes sense to aggregate all the channels which have one endpoint in an entity in T_a and the other endpoint in an entity in T_b. We call this aggregation an *xchannel*. While individual communications that pass through an xchannel will continue to have the latencies ascribed to them by the logic of the simulation, we know that the delay of any such message is no smaller than the smallest minimal delay among all channels in the aggregation.

A mapping function $\mathcal{M}$ assigns entities to timelines, so that $\mathcal{M}(E_i)$ is the timeline to which E_i is assigned. $\mathcal{E}(T)$ denotes the set of entities assigned to timeline T. For timelines T_a and T_b, we denote the xchannel between them by $xc_{a,b}$, denote the set of channels that pass through it as $\mathcal{C}(xc_{a,b})$ and define its minimal delay as

$$x\epsilon_{a,b} = \min_{c_{i,j} \in \mathcal{C}(xc_{a,b})} \{\epsilon_{i,j}\}. \quad (1)$$

Figure 2 illustrates the impact of an assignment on the model of Figure 1, showing each original channel as being implement through a timeline's event-list, or through the timeline's communication/synchronization logic and an xchannel.

3. COMPOSITE SYNCHRONIZATION

Classically, in a Chandy-Misra-Bryant (CMB) style algorithm, timelines exchange synchronization message through their xchannels sending "null messages" with minimal delays so that a timeline knows it is safe to execute the least-time event on its event list at time t when it has receive a message or null message from every one of these peers with a receive time of t or greater.

A well-known problem for CMB algorithms occurs when a timeline has xchannels with many others. One approach is to have the timeline send a null message across every xchannel, with every event execution. That will keep the peers up to date on the timeline's progress as quickly as possible. A less intensive approach is to have the timeline send a timestamped *appointment* across xchannel $xc_{i,j}$ every $x\epsilon_{i,j}$ units of virtual time (see equation 1.) A timeline can efficiently maintain and make decisions based on the last reported appointment time from each peer in a min-heap. This means the overhead of sending and receiving null messages is proportional to the log of the number of peers, times the sum of null message transmission frequencies.

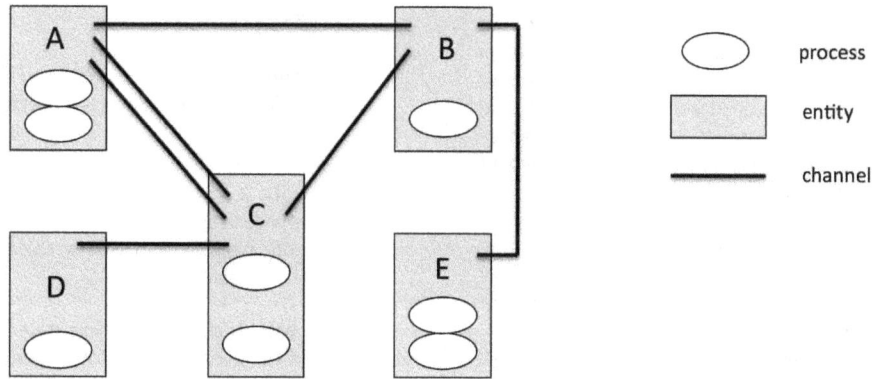

Figure 1: Simulation Model using Entities, Processes, and Channels

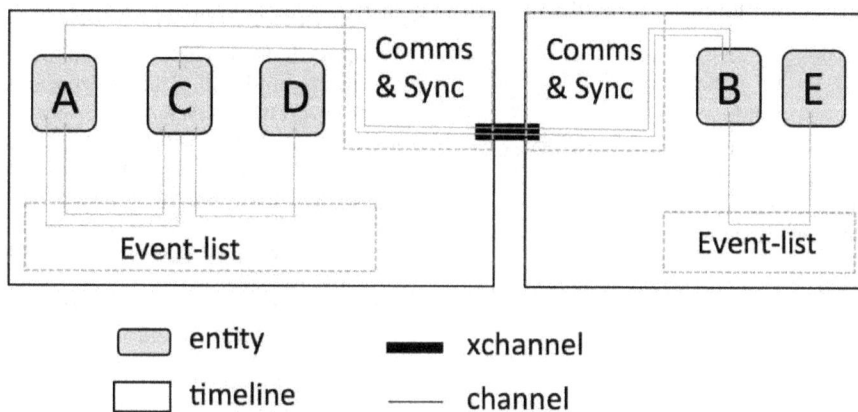

Figure 2: Timelines created by mapping of entities

A globally synchronous algorithm is completely insensitive to the number of peers a timeline has. The standard "YAWNS-style" [7] approach identifies the least minimal delay among all cross-timeline channels, say δ, and then requires timelines to synchronize globally every δ units of virtual time. If the last synchronization time was t_0, then timelines are free to execute all events with time-stamps strictly less than $t_0 + \delta$. Once the least-time event on a timeline's event list is at least as large as $t_0 + \delta$, it engages in the global barrier. Messages generated during the last window can be exchanged with corresponding receive events scheduled, and with a second global synchronization timelines know they are free to execute the next window of simulation time. Variations and optimizations on this description have been developed; the key idea is that global synchronization eliminates the overheads of null messages send across high peer counts, however, it forces all timelines to engage in a potentially expensive global synchronization frequently.

Composite synchronization [8] was invented to allow a middle ground between intensive local synchronization and frequent global synchronization, at least when model characteristics support it. The basic idea is to use both local

synchronization and global synchronization, as follows. A threshold τ is chosen; all xchannels with minimal delays less than τ are categorized as *asynchronous* xchannels, xchannels with minimal delays at least as large as τ are categorized as *synchronous*. A global synchronization window is applied every τ units of virtual time. Within such a window, any message that is written to a synchronous xchannel can be buffered up just as in the globally synchronous case. Timelines with asynchronous xchannels treat those as in the purely asynchronous case, and synchronize with those peers with whom they share asynchronous channels with null messages as described earlier.

Composite synchronization is most effective at performing better than either purely asynchronous or purely synchronous methods when the xchannels with small minimal delay tend to be connected to timelines with small numbers of peers, and/or timelines with many peers tend to have larger minimal delay. The use of a global window with τ smaller than the minimal delays on highly connected timelines frees them up from intensive local synchronization, but the asynchronous activity that needs to happen on the small minimal delay channels is not overwhelming.

4. WORKLOAD MODEL

The main idea behind our workload model is to describe the amount of wallclock time needed to advance simulation time. We do so with the notion of a *workload function*. We start with the assumption of some description of workload units, e.g., "instructions", with an assumption that these units are proportional to execution time, with the constant of proportionality depending on the processor actually used.

For any given execution of the simulation model, each entity E_i will execute events at discrete times $t_{i,0}, t_{i,1}, \ldots$. Allowing for the possibility of multiple events being executed at the same virtual time, we can associate the amount of workload associated with the events with timestamp $t_{i,j}$ by $w_i(t_{i,j})$. The total amount of workload associated with executing E_i's events over a virtual time interval $[s, t]$ is

$$W_i(s,t) = \sum_{t_{i,j} \in [s,t]} w_i(t_{i,j}). \qquad (2)$$

It follows that the total amount of workload associated with a timeline T_a over $[s, t]$ is the sum taken over all entities mapped to T_a:

$$TW_a(s,t) = \sum_{E_i \in \mathcal{E}(T_a)} W_i(s,t). \qquad (3)$$

Our model also includes the cost of communication. Event executions may send messages and induce communication overhead. As with computational workload, we can associate the volume of communication on an entity's channel with its send time. So we associate with event time $t_{i,j}$ a volume (e.g. in bytes) $v_{i,k}(t_{i,j})$ of communication by E_i, for each of its channels $c_{i,k}$. The total volume of communication written by E_i over channel $c_{i,k}$ in virtual time interval $[s, t]$ is

$$V_{i,k}(s,t) = \sum_{t_{i,j} \in [s,t]} v_{i,k}(t_{i,j}). \qquad (4)$$

It follows that the volume of communication written by entities assigned to timeline T_a for entities assigned to timeline T_b is the sum

$$TV_{a,b}(s,t) = \sum_{(E_i, E_k) \in \mathcal{E}(T_a) \times \mathcal{E}(T_b)} \sum_{t_{i,j} \in [s,t]} V_{i,k}(s,t). \qquad (5)$$

5. PERFORMANCE MODEL

5.1 Architecture Model

Performance depends obviously on the parallel architecture. We model a parallel machine comprised of multiprocessors. Each of P multiprocessors has n cores that run concurrently and share memory, multiprocessors can in addition communicate with each other over a communication infrastructure. We abstract key features used to transform the architecture-free units of work and communication into real time.

- μ is the real time required to execute one unit of computational work on one core of a multiprocessor. It is straightforward to allow each multiprocessor its own value of μ and would be necessary for an architecture where such differences exists and are significant, but is for our purposes an unnecessary complication for understanding how exposure of communication through mapping impacts performance.

- $1/\rho$ is the inter-multiprocessor channel bandwidth (in seconds/byte).

- γ is the point-to-point latency of a communication from one multiprocessor to another.

- α is the time required for a multiprocessor to communicate a short synchronization message to another multiprocessor. The time for synchronization among cores on a multiprocessor is taken to be so small it is effectively instantaneous.

This is a bare-bones model that does not include a number of things that a *predictive* performance model might need to include, e.g., message-size-independent overhead for communication, impacts on performance due to thread scheduling and shared caches. Our model is aimed at explaining how entities are mapped with the impact that has through communication and synchronization on overall performance.

5.2 Synchronization Model

Suppose that a timeline has synchronized globally at virtual time t_0, and will synchronize globally again at virtual time $t_0 + \tau$. Within this window the timeline T_a will advance from event to event, with pauses for synchronization with local cores and with asynchronous xchannels. Each synchronization appointment is implemented with two events assumed to have so little computation to allow them to be treated as having no computational load, at the appointment time t_x. The first event to be executed is the *pause* event, whose action is to cause the timeline to wait for a notification message from a timeline with which it synchronizes asynchronously. Once all notify events are satisfied, all *workload* events are processed with that same time stamp are executed, if any. Following this workload the timeline executes *notify* events, whose action is to have T_a send a message to T_b that it will not now send any messages with timestamps less than $t_x + x\epsilon_{a,b}$. Notice that the implementation must ensure that any communication generated for T_b by the the event processing must be received before the notify event is received. Standard networking methodology can assure this.

Now at the beginning of the window the timeline can schedule all of its synchronization events. For example if the $T_a - T_b$ xchannel has minimal delay $x\epsilon_{a,b} < \tau$, T_a can schedule appointment events at times $t_0 k * x\epsilon_{a,b}$ for all k such that $k * x\epsilon_{a,b} < \tau$. Of course, execution of workload events at any timeline sharing an asynchronous xchannel with T_a can separately cause the scheduling of new events for T_a that occur within the window but are not yet known at the beginning of the window.

Under our architectural assumptions of multiprocessor use, it is safe to assume that communication and computation may occur in parallel. We model this as follows. If t_w is the time of any workload event on timeline T_a, we have denoted already by $TW_a(t_w, t_w)$ the total volume (in workload units) of computation to be performed. This will take $TW_a(t_w, t_w)/mu$ time, recalling that μ is the real time needed to execute one unit of workload. Workload event execution may create communication, and we have denoted already the total volume of that communication directed toward T_b by $TV_{a,b}(t_w, t_w)$. This implies that the rate (in real time) that $T_a \to T_b$ communication demand is generated at T_a by executing events at t_w is

$$\lambda_{a,b}(t_w, t_w) = \mu * \frac{TV_{a,b}(t_w, t_w)}{TW_a(t_w, t_w)} \qquad (6)$$

Now if T_b is on the same multiprocessor as T_a, we will not ascribe any additional cost for the communication. The timelines share memory, with careful programming there is no need to copy the communication. However, if T_b is on a different multiprocessor, the time required for the message to be received in its entirety is a function of available bandwidth. Depending on the simulation model and the mapping, it is possible for multiple timelines on a multiprocessor to be trying to communicate through the same communication port to another multiprocessor. We need to notionally account for this common phenomena, but for the purposes of this paper not spend a great deal of time on the details. Under whatever assumptions one makes about communication scheduling we know there is a delay $d_{a,b}(t_w)$ between the time when the communication at T_a starts, and when it has completely finished.

With these definitions it is possible to describe processing costs, communication delays, and synchronization using a directed acyclic graph where nodes represent activities, weights on the nodes represent processing time, and arcs represent dependencies. A node cannot start its evaluation before each predecessor node as completed its evaluation. Viewed as a weighted graph where the cost of a path is the sum of the weights on the nodes of the path, the longest path through the graph gives the overall delay of performing the work it describes.

In our model there is a sequence of nodes associated with every timeline. There are dependency arcs in linear time order for nodes associated with a timeline, and there are dependency arcs between nodes on different timelines. Figure 3 illustrates a small portion of such a graph. Four node types differentiate between notify, pause, and workload events, and another node describes communication delay. The figure illustrates several points.

1. For a given virtual time t_x, if there are multiple nodes for a timeline with timestamp t_x, they are processed in the order of pause event nodes first, followed by workload event nodes if any, followed by notify event nodes.

2. Every notify node at time t_x sends an arc to a communication node, which sends an arc to a pause node with event time $t_x + x\epsilon_{a,b}$, where T_a and T_b are the timelines associated with the notify appointment. This combination reflects that the notify event promises to the recipient that any communication the sender has with a timestamp less than the pause node time has already been sent, and that there is a delay equal to the weight on the communication node before the recipient is aware of this message.

3. Every pause at time t_x receives an arc as described above.

4. A workload event node may, or may not generate communication. If it does at time t_w, there is a communication node labeled by $d_{a,b}(t_w)$, if the communication is passing from T_a to T_b and crosses between multiprocessors. A communication that stays on the same multiprocessor has weight 0. Like the workload node

on the T_a chain of events, the communication node receives an arc from the closest previous notify node. This allows both computation and communication to begin at the same time, and in parallel.

5. A communication node associated with a workload execution at time t_w has an arc to the recipient's pause node which has the smallest timestamp greater than or equal to t_w. This captures the requirement that the communication be completely received before the receiver crosses into a region of simulation time that might contain the message's receive time.

6. There are precedence arcs between adjacent nodes on a timeline's chain.

Point 1 is illustrated on Timeline A, which has appointments with Timeline B, but evidently also with some additional timelines not shown, which we infer from the presence of multiple pause and notify nodes at the same time stamp. An example of Points 2, 4 and 5 is the notify node at time 10 on Timeline A which communicates with Timeline B. One additional observation is that the workload node on Timeline B at time 18 might have been the result of the computation and communication on Timeline A at time 13. The precedence graph shows that all communication generated by Timeline A in the interval $[10, 15]$ for Timeline B has to be received by B before it passes through its pause node at time 15. The message received by that pause node is the promise that all such communication has already been generated.

Now consider the communication delays associated with execution of workload events at time 10 and 13 on Timeline A. In the first case the communication delay is just a touch larger than the computation delay. This reflects the assumption that communication is generated continuously throughout the execution burst and so is not finished until the burst is finished, but then there is an end-to-end delay (here 320-305 = 15) for the last bit to cross the wire and complete the communication. The placement of the communication node in parallel with the workload node, and with the same precedent constraints (so that it starts at the same time as the workload node) reflects an assumption that communication may occur in parallel with computation. The communication delay associated with the execution at time 13 of a burst with computation time 210 is significantly larger than 210, which implies either that the communication is generated at a rate faster than it can be transmitted, or that contention for the port slows this communication down.

The construction described above defines what we call an *appointment graph*. We can think of it as composed of a linear chain of nodes for each timeline, with communication nodes and dependencies arcs between them.

We are not yet done with modeling the real-time delay of completing a synchronization window. Composite synchronization uses global synchronization every τ units of virtual time. We assume that global synchronization uses a binary combining tree, which means that when a multiprocessor reaches the synchronization point, the synchronization message climbs the tree $\log P$ steps to establish when all multiprocessors have reached the barrier. As we have described, each timeline has a sequence of nodes describing notify, pause, and workload events, and dependency arcs between these nodes. We concatenate a standard combining tree graph describing implementation of the barrier to

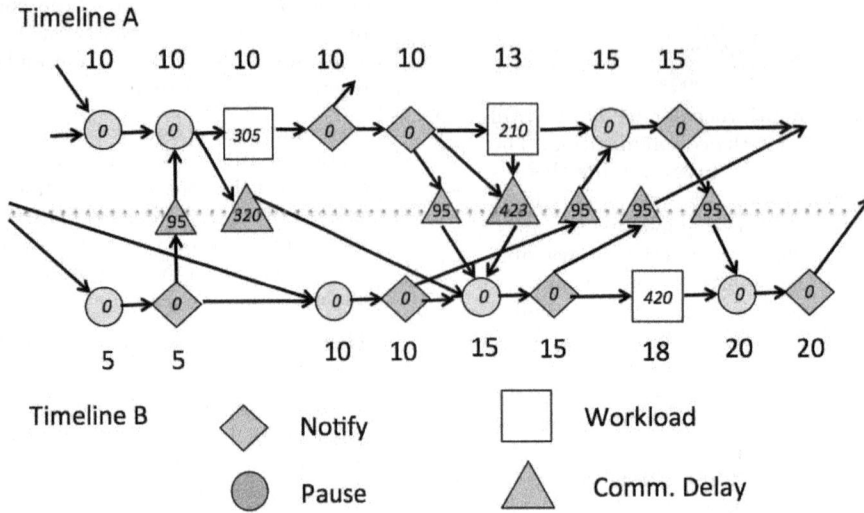

Figure 3: Illustration of directed acyclic graph used to describe processing costs and precedents

the graph used for appointments and workload events. The longest path to the last node in any timeline in the appointment/workload graph identifies the last timeline to enter the barrier, making the final length of time to complete the entire window that length, plus $\alpha * \log P$.

The model described here is explanatory. We don't know a priori what the workload events will be nor their execution times, nor do we necessarily know in advance what the communication load will be. However, the value in the description is that we can see that the longest path through the graph identifies the length of time needed to execute the window, and this attribute is something we can use to get more qualitative insight.

6. APPLICATION

The particular structure and weights of a graph will change from window to window. However if we consider a much more uniform structure we can get some important insights into how performance is impacted by mapping. Suppose that the workload generated by timeline T_a over a simulation interval $[s, t]$ is proportional to $t - s$, i.e.,

$$TW_a(s, t) = w_a * (t - s)$$

for some *workload constant* w_a. Suppose too that the volume of communication that T_a generates for each of the timelines it communicates with on different multiprocessors is proportional to $t-s$, and is identical for each such timeline. Finally, imagine that the workload nodes occur at the same virtual time as the various appointment times, and are weighted using the formula above, where t is the time of the event, and s is the time of the most recent prior appointment time before t. If the last appointment time for a timeline within a window is at t_z, then include a workload node at the very end of the synchronization window to reflect the work done between the last appointment and the engagement with the barrier, similarly weighted. Finally, imagine that the network bandwidth is large enough so that all communication

can be carried at the rate it is generated. We say that the graph has the *proportional workload* property.

These assumptions induce a particular structure to our performance graph. First, imagine the case where γ and α are very small relative to the workload costs, so small we may consider them to be zero. We then say that the graph has the *dominant workload* property. Now observe that we may partition timelines into connected components, considering only asynchronous xchannels. A timeline that does not communicate via appointments with any other is a singleton component. A critical observation is given below.

LEMMA 1. *Let an appointment graph have both the proportional workload and dominant workload properties. Suppose that a connected component of a proportional WB appointment graph is comprised of timelines $T_1, T_2, \ldots, T_k$. Without loss of generality, suppose that $w_1 \geq w_i$, for $i = 2, 3, \ldots, k$. Then the longest path through this connected component passes directly through every node of of T_1.*

PROOF. It is straightforward to construct an inductive argument which shows that T_1 never blocks at a pause event. □

This simply says that in graphs with the assumed properties the component's progress in virtual time is constrained by the rate of virtual time advancement of the slowest timeline. This implies that the time needed to compute the appointment synchronization portion of the window the maximum (over connected components) longest path. With the dominant workload property the individual communication costs of the barrier synchronization is so low that we can discount it. This means that this maximum is actually the time needed to complete the entire window.

The assumption of the graph having both the proportional workload and dominant workload properties, along with the assumption of perfectly parallel communication mitigates the impact of communication and synchronization overheads on the length of the longest path. The main observation of interest is that the progress of a connected component is limited by its slowest member. Another observation is that in this case, the parameter τ used to differentiate between asynchronous and synchronous xchannels is immaterial, every choice of τ leads to the same rate of simulation advance. This is interesting because changing τ changes the membership of the connected components.

LEMMA 2. *Consider a conjoined appointment and barrier synchronization graph which has the proportional workload and dominant workload properties. Without loss of generality suppose that among all timelines T_i, $w_1 \geq w_i$. Then the longest path through the conjoined appointment and barrier synchronization graphs has length $w_1 * \tau$. Therefore, the rate in real time at which the parallel simulation advances is $1/w_1$, independent of τ.*

PROOF. The longest path in the appointment graph through any connected component is $w_a * \tau$, where w_a is the advancement cost of the slowest timeline T_a in the component. The result follows from the observation that the barrier begins with the joining of the last timeline to do so, that this timeline will be the slowest, and that under the workload bound assumption the barrier synchronization has no cost. The rate (in real time) at which virtual time is advanced is thus $\tau/(w_1 * \tau) = 1/w_1$. $\square$

The latter result shows that while the proportional and dominant workload assumptions point out an interesting relationship related to connected components, graphs with these assumptions do not otherwise have enough complexity to highlight the impact of synchronization overhead on the overall rate of simulation time advance.

We can however still use these ideas. Imagine a graph that has proportional workload, but not dominant workload, so that α and γ are non-zero. We transform this graph into another as follows. Under the assumption of sufficient communication bandwidth, the difference in weight between a workload node and any communication node derived from it is just γ in the case of a communication between multiprocessors, and zero otherwise. Imagine now re-weighting the workload node by adding to it the weight $k * \gamma$, where k is the number of cross-multiprocessor communication nodes associated with the event. In like fashion, weight the notify nodes with α if the communication crosses multiprocessor boundaries. This transformation is equivalent to making the timeline wait to proceed until all of the communication it has generated has been fully delivered. Applying this transformation everywhere, call the result the *masked communication*. This is interesting because of the following obvious property.

LEMMA 3. *Consider a graph with proportional workload, and the corresponding masked communication graph. The longest path through the augmented workload graph is at least as long as the longest path through the proportional workload graph.*

PROOF. It is straightforward to show by induction on a partial ordering of the nodes that the longest path to a node predecessor is always at least as large in the masked communication graph as it is in the original graph. $\square$

We now appeal to the insight gained considering the proportional and dominant workload case. In the masked communication graph we have slowed timelines in accordance with their communication requirements so that net result is the same as if γ and α were zero. We are no longer working with proportional workload, however we can construct a graph that has proportional and dominant workload from the masked communication graph. Given τ, we can construct a proportional time advancement cost w_i for timeline T_i by summing the weights of T_i's nodes and dividing by τ. This gives an average computational cost per unit virtual time which depends on the frequency of appointments and numbers of timelines with which appointments are exchanged. We call this the *average proportional workload graph*, or APWG. By the masking of communication this graph has dominant workload, and by construction it has proportional workload. This gives us a vehicle now to consider the impact τ has on overall performance, and the key observations one might make in a mapping algorithm.

- as τ increases from the overall minimum non-zero channel delay, the larger connected components become, and the more appointments are managed per timeline. As the number of appointments increases, the node weights in the APWG become more weighty, and so the timeline average cost per unit simulation time increases. This implies that the time at which the last timeline in the corresponding APWG reaches the barrier increases with increasing τ.

- as τ increases the proportion of time spent in the simulation window computing the barrier synchronization decreases.

All of this modeling confirms the intuition that choice of τ balances tradeoffs between asynchronous and synchronous computation, but unlike before, provides some framework within which we might consider this tradeoff and the impact on mapping. Also, unlike before, it establishes an understanding of why, as τ increases, the time needed to complete the asynchronous portion of the synchronization window increases.

The cost of barrier synchronization is well-understood and easily modeled, the challenge has always been how to accrue the costs of asynchronous synchronization. Now we have a potential answer. Given a workload mapping, we know which entities are on the same timeline, and know which channels become xchannels. τ, we can classify each xchannel as being synchronous or asynchronous. Under the APWG assumptions we can then create workload, notify, and pause event nodes at known virtual times, and can identify the connected components in the appointment graph. Finally, given *some* sort of estimate of how much workload is created per unit virtual time and what the computational cost might be, we can weight the APWG nodes and compute an estimate of the time needed to complete the appointment portion of the performance graph.

7. CONCLUSION

The relationship between workload mapping and synchronization overhead in a conservatively synchronized parallel simulation is understood intuitively, but not quantitatively. This paper develops a model of these relationships in the context of composite synchronization. The model confirms intuition, but also provides a quantitative framework within which the impacts of mapping choice and synchronization tuning parameter can be considered. This is a necessary precursor for an algorithm to map workload to processors, which is future work.

8. REFERENCES

[1] A. Boukerche and S. K. Das. Dynamic load balancing strategies for conservative parallel simulations. In *Proceedings 11th Workshop on Parallel and Distributed Simulation*, pages 20–28, Jun 1997.

[2] E. Deelman and B. K. Szymanski. Dynamic load balancing in parallel discrete event simulation for spatially explicit problems. In *Parallel and Distributed Simulation, 1998. PADS 98. Proceedings. Twelfth Workshop on*, pages 46–53, May 1998.

[3] B. P. Gan, Y. H. Low, S. Jain, S. J. Turner, W. Cai, W. J. Hsu, and S. Y. Huang. Load balancing for conservative simulation on shared memory multiprocessor systems. In *Proceedings of the Fourteenth Workshop on Parallel and Distributed Simulation*, PADS '00, pages 139–146, Washington, DC, USA, 2000. IEEE Computer Society.

[4] D. R. Jefferson. Virtual time. *ACM Trans. Program. Lang. Syst.*, 7(3):404–425, July 1985.

[5] J. Misra and K. Chandy. Distributed simulation: A case study in design and verification of distributed programs. *IEEE Transactions on Software Engineering*, 5:440–452, 1979.

[6] B. Nandy and W. Loucks. An algorithm of partitioning and mapping conservative parallel simulations onto multiprocessors. In *Proceedings of the 6th Workshop on Parallel and Distribution Simulation*, volume 24, pages 139–146, January 1992.

[7] D. Nicol. The cost of conservative synchronization in parallel discrete-event simulations. *Journal of the ACM*, 40(2):304–333, April 1993.

[8] D. Nicol and J. Liu. Composite synchronization for parallel discrete event simulation. *IEEE Transactions on Parallel and Distributed Systems*, 13(5):433–446, May 2002.

[9] D. M. Nicol, D. K. Jin, and Y. Zheng. S3F: the scalable simulation framework revisited. In *Winter Simulation Conference 2011, WSC'11, Phoenix, AZ, USA, December 11-14, 2011*, pages 3288–3299, 2011.

[10] D. M. Nicol, J. Liu, and M. Liljenstam. Simulation of large-scale networks using SSF. In *Proceedings of the 2003 Winter Simulation Conference*, pages 650–657, New Orleans, LA, December 2003.

Durango: Scalable Synthetic Workload Generation for Extreme-Scale Application Performance Modeling and Simulation

Christopher D. Carothers
Rensselaer Polytechnic
Institute
110 8th Street
Troy, NY 12180
chrisc@cs.rpi.edu

Jeremy S. Meredith
Oak Ridge National
Laboratory
Oak Ridge, TN 37831
jsmeredith@gmail.com

Mark P. Blanco
Rensselaer Polytechnic
Institute
110 8th Street
Troy, NY 12180
mark.p.blanco@gmail.com

Jeffrey S. Vetter
Oak Ridge National
Laboratory
Oak Ridge, TN 37831
vetter@ornl.gov

Misbah Mubarak
Argonne National Laboratory
Lemont, IL 60439
mmubarak@anl.gov

Justin LaPre
Rensselaer Polytechnic
Institute
110 8th Street
Troy, NY 12180
laprej@cs.rpi.edu

Shirley Moore
Oak Ridge National
Laboratory
Oak Ridge, TN 37831
mooresv@ornl.gov

ABSTRACT

Performance modeling of extreme-scale applications on accurate representations of potential architectures is critical for designing next generation supercomputing systems because it is impractical to construct prototype systems at scale with new network hardware in order to explore designs and policies. However, these simulations often rely on static application traces that can be difficult to work with because of their size and lack of flexibility to extend or scale up without rerunning the original application. To address this problem, we have created a new technique for generating scalable, flexible workloads from real applications, we have implemented a prototype, called *Durango*, that combines a proven analytical performance modeling language, *Aspen*, with the massively parallel HPC network modeling capabilities of the CODES framework.

Our models are compact, parameterized and representative of real applications with computation events. They are not resource intensive to create and are portable across simulator environments. We demonstrate the utility of Durango by simulating the LULESH application in the CODES simulation environment on several topologies and show that Durango is practical to use for simulation without loss of fidelity, as quantified by simulation metrics. During our validation of Durango's generated communication model of LULESH, we found that the original LULESH miniapp code had a latent bug where the `MPI_Waitall` operation was used incorrectly. This finding underscores the potential need for a tool such as Durango, beyond its benefits for flexible workload generation and modeling.

Additionally, we demonstrate the efficacy of Durango's direct integration approach, which links *Aspen* into CODES as part of the running network simulation model. Here, Aspen generates the application-level computation timing events, which in turn drive the start of a network communication phase. Results show that Durango's performance scales well when executing both torus and dragonfly network models on up to 4K Blue Gene/Q nodes using 32K MPI ranks, Durango also avoids the overheads and complexities associated with extreme-scale trace files.

Keywords

Massively Parallel Simulation, HPC Networks Models, Structural Analytic Models

1. INTRODUCTION

Performance modeling of extreme-scale applications using accurate representations of potential architectures is critical for designing next generation supercomputing systems because it is impractical to construct prototype systems at scale with new network hardware in order to explore designs and policies. However, simulations often rely on static application traces that can be difficult to work with because of their size and lack of flexibility to extend or scale up without rerunning the original application. For example, the applica-

Publication rights licensed to ACM. ACM acknowledges that this contribution was authored or co-authored by an employee, contractor or affiliate of the United States government. As such, the Government retains a nonexclusive, royalty-free right to publish or reproduce this article, or to allow others to do so, for Government purposes only.

SIGSIM-PADS 17 May 24 26, 2017, Singapore, Singapore

© 2017 Copyright held by the owner/author(s). Publication rights licensed to ACM.

ACM ISBN 978-1-4503-4489-0/17/05...15.00

DOI: http://dx.doi.org/10.1145/3064911.3064923

tion traces available as part of the Design Forward program (see: http://www.exascaleinitiative.org/design-forward) can be hundreds of gigabytes. Moreover, once traces are created, they are fixed and cannot be changed Also, traces require a system and time where the trace can be created.

On the other hand, well-known patterns [10] coded in a simulator-specific language also have shortcomings. First, these patterns typically are synthetic and not often representative of real application behaviors, thus driving the need for real application traces. Second, these patterns often do not include any computation for the processors, so there is limited ability to inject realistic processor behaviors between communication events.

To address this problem, we have created a new technique for generating scalable workloads from real applications, and we have implemented a prototype, named Durango, that combines a proven analytical performance modeling language, *Aspen*, with the massively parallel HPC network modeling capabilities of the CODES framework. Our models are compact, parameterized and representative of real applications with computation events. They are not resource intensive to create and are portable across simulator environments. Specifically, we make the following two contributions in this paper:

- Comparison of the Aspen-generated network communication patterns for the LULESH miniapp with real LULESH application network communications via traces that are run through the CODES packet-level network simulation framework. Durango shows identical agreement with the real application trace data for key network performance statistics. During our validation of Durango's generated communication model of LULESH, we found that the original LULESH miniapp code had a latent bug where the `MPI_Waitall` operation was used incorrectly. This finding underscores the potential need for a tool such as Durango, beyond its benefits for flexible workload generation and modeling.

- A scaling study of Durango's direct integration approach, which links Aspen into CODES as part of the running network simulation model. Here, Aspen generates the application-level computation timing events as part of an overall discrete-event system model, which in turn drive the start of a network communication phase. Performance results show that Durango's performance scales well when executing both torus and dragonfly network models on upto 4K Blue Gene/Q nodes using 32K MPI ranks and avoids the overheads and complexities associated with extreme-scale trace files.

2. Durango OVERVIEW

To motivate Durango, we refer to Figure 1, which illustrates the multiple workflows for generating a simulation workload. In this paper, we consider four scenarios when capturing the characteristics of the application to be simulated. In the first scenario, we simply execute the application, capturing the communication events, and transferring execution control between the application and simulation as appropriate (path 1-2-3-9 in Figure 1). The application is built as it normally would be, but the communication events are intercepted by the simulator and then simulated on the theoretical network. This method is relatively straightforward and easy to perform, but it has the disadvantage that

it uses considerable resources in terms of execution time and memory.

In the second scenario, we use a tracing tool, such as DUMPI, to capture an event trace of all the communicating tasks and communication events in the application. This trace is digested by the simulator (path 1-4-5-3-9 in Figure 1) and the trace information is typically stored in a huge file. Moreover, all the parameters of the trace are fixed at capture time; that is, the architect cannot change the problem size or the number of processors after the trace has been created.

In the third scenario, we use synthetic communication patterns as a proxy for the application communication patterns (path 1-6-7-4-5-3-9 in Figure 1). In the fourth scenario, the proxy trace generator is glued directly into the simulator (path 1-6-8-2-3-9 in Figure 1). These last two approaches are the focus of this paper and are combined into a system we call *Durango*.

2.1 Aspen Overview

Aspen is a domain-specific language designed for analytical performance modeling [28, 31]. The models represented in Aspen comprise application models and abstract machine models. The machine models describe the hierarchy of a machine as well as speeds and feeds of its components for processing computation and communication. Application models contain descriptions of resource usage of an algorithm (such as the computation and communication requirements) and control flow (iteration, sequential and parallel dependencies, and kernel nesting).

The COMPASS framework described in [17] generates a parameterizable performance model from a target application's source code using OpenARC [18] for automated static analysis and then evaluates this model using various performance prediction techniques available in Aspen. Prior to using OpenARC, a small amount of manual annotation is required in order to specify regions of interest and declare parameters to be directly exposed in the generated Aspen application model. The Aspen control flow walker can dynamically instantiate values of parameters that cannot be determined statically. Generation of applications models for the LULESH proxy application and the matrix multiplication kernel used in the Durango research is described and validation of the Aspen resource usage and runtime predictions with measurements on a real system is given in [18]. Aspen currently combines a the throughput-based node performance model based on the Roofline model [32] with a simple latency plus bandwidth communication model, where computation and communication can be overlapped to a specified degree. Part of the motivation of the Durango research is to achieve more accurate communication modeling than is possible using Aspen's analytical methods.

Aspen, as an analytical tool, was initially designed to compute symbolic results for analysis queries, such as the number of floating-point operations at a given problem size or the performance of a kernel as a function of bus bandwidth. However, the expansion of Aspen's capabilities has allowed for more complex uses; while an Aspen model is not source code and cannot be executed per se, the representation of a control flow is sufficiently rich to allow Aspen-based tools to traverse an application model with the same control flow as with the original application. We build this new capability to provide synthetic communication trace generation along with direct integration in Durango.

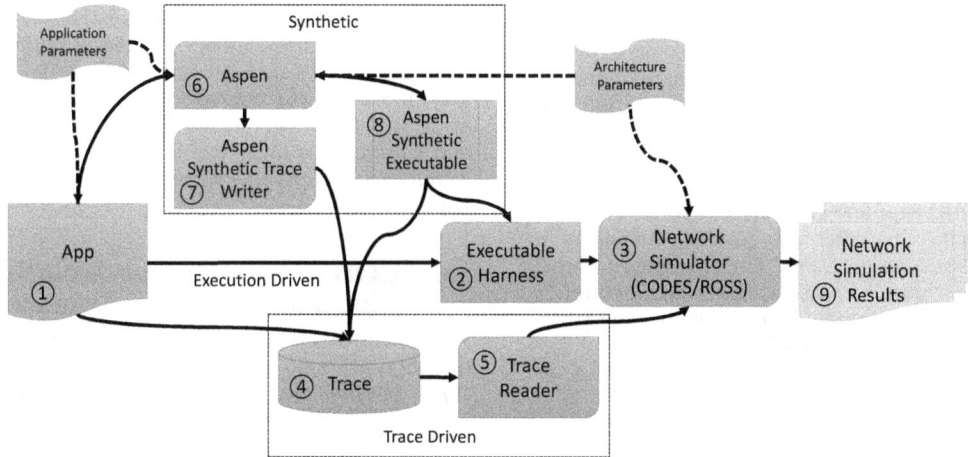

Figure 1: Durango overview.

2.2 Durango Approach

In contrast to the first two scenarios described above, our new approach allows the architect to create a parameterized model of an application, and then instantiate the application with specific parameters at simulation time. The potential benefit of this approach is multifaceted. First, the model is malleable: the user can easily change the application and architecture parameters. In our approach, a model can be instantiated for 16 MPI tasks as well as 1M MPI tasks. Second, the models are compact, typically being only a dozen lines for miniapplications and up to a few hundred lines for real applications. Third, the Durango models include computational and I/O events in addition to the communication events so that computation and I/O demands can change in concert with communication parameters. This approach has multiple benefits: the synthetic workload can be generated dynamically as necessary with the required architecture and application parameters; the description is compact; and the Aspen model can be as detailed or as sparse as required, including computation, communication, I/O, and other important events.

More specifically, Durango requires that the user create a parameterized Aspen model (6) of the application (1) and then use the Aspen model to create a synthetic workload, either by generating a compatible trace directly (7) or by generating a synthetic MPI application (8) that can then be traced (4-5-3-9 in Figure 1) or directly included in the simulation executable that avoids the need to perform expensive read operations of large trace datasets.

2.3 Representing Communication in Aspen

Resource descriptions in Aspen are user-defined. There are common conventions such as **flops**, **loads**, and **stores** for floating point operations and memory traffic, but these must merely match what is defined in the abstract machine model for Aspen to be able to return predictive costs such as runtimes and power consumption.

A commonly used resource for MPI communication is **messages**, but this results in a simplistic mapping. Extensions via traits enable more expressive message passing patterns. For example, a trait description such as "as positive_x" can direct an Aspen-based tool to generate MPI calls if given a regular processor decomposition. However, these trait descriptions are low-level, however, and require signifi-

cant effort from modelers to achieve communication patterns like 3D nearest-neighbor; for example, requiring up to 26 separate **message** resource calls to generate message traffic for each neighboring processor.

Listing 1: Example Aspen model with communication

```
1 model example
2 {
3    param nelem = 23
4    param wordsize = 8
5
6    kernel main
7    {
8        execute{flops [8*nelem^3] from Domain as
9               simd}
10       execute{comm [1] of size [word] as allreduce,
11              min}
12       execute{comm [nelem] of size [3*word] as nn3d,
13              face}
14   }
15 }
```

Instead, we created a new resource convention, **comm**, that represents communication patterns at a more semantic level. An abstract machine model can still easily interpret these in the same manner as the simpler **message** construct for the purposes of determining costs, but we are now free to interpret this new **comm** resource at a higher level in an Aspen tool in order to generate synthetic patterns for executables and traces.

Listing 1 shows an example Aspen application model using this new **comm** resource. Note how our new Aspen **comm** resource corresponds to popular synthetic communication patterns such as nearest-neighbor but can be customized for application kernels as well. In particular, the pattern is listed in the traits for the resource, and any options are listed as additional traits. For example, line 10 has the *allreduce* collective pattern with a *min* operation, and these are represented in the traits as **as allreduce, min**. Combined with the quantity and size, that resource description is sufficient to generate a synthetic MPI call. Line 12 has the nearest-neighbor 3D point-to-point pattern (**nn3d**) for a domain size of **nelelm** with three double-precision fields (**3*word**) and communication only along the six faces of each domain (**face**).

2.4 Synthetic Program Execution

Aspen models are not designed to be "executed" per se but have control flow such as iteration loops, parallel maps, and kernel invocations. This control flow information was sufficient for us to create a "walker" tool that uses the Aspen library to traverse application models in control flow order, as if they are executable programs.

The tool we created supports two major types of traversal: implicit and explicit. The difference typically manifests in control structures such as iteration. For example, if kernel K is called from within an iteration control with count 7, the explicit traversal will descend into the kernel call seven times, while the implicit traversal will descend into the kernel call only once but knows that it is executing with multiplicity seven with a sequential dependence.

Some types of analyses are amenable to implicit traversal. For counting floating-point operations, we can typically count how many operations are in kernel K in our example above and multiply by seven. This is not possible in all cases, however, for example, if floating point operation counts vary stochastically, we must use explicit traversal and sample values at each iteration. In the case of synthetic trace generation, both implicit and explicit traversal have their place.

In typical analyses, implicit traveral will be faster because it performs less analysis and accumulates results in bulk to provide the correct answer. In the context of generating a synthetic MPI executable, in the implicit mode we can output a C `for` loop containing the appropriate MPI calls, while the explicit mode would require generating many C copies of the same function calls. If Aspen were to hook up directly to a simulator, we would, by necessity, switch to explicit traversal because Aspen would need to feed the simulator every MPI call generated by the synthetic program.

Listing 2: Aspen model with control flow and communication.

```
1 model mpitest {
2   kernel main {
3     iterate [10] {
4       execute { comm [2] of size [word] as
5                 allreduce, min }
6     }
7   }
8 }
```

Listing 3: Source generated by model in Listing 2 using implicit traversal.

```
1 for (int loopctr=0; loopctr<10; loopctr++)
2 {
3   int nwords=2;
4   std::vector<float> sendvec(nwords, rank*1.0f);
5   std::vector<float> recvvec(nwords);
6   MPI_Allreduce(&(sendvec[0]), &(recvvec[0]),
7                 nwords, MPI_FLOAT,MPI_MIN,
8                 MPI_COMM_WORLD);
9 }
```

2.5 Durango-Instantiated Executable

Our first option for generating a synthetic workload is to instantiate an MPI-based source code file that captures the parameters and patterns of the application via the Aspen model. Listing 2 shows an example of a simple Aspen model with an iteration loop along with a single communication pattern — in this case, an Allreduce. Listing 3 shows the output code (minus boilerplate) for this small Aspen model. Note that this output was captured in implicit mode; in explicit mode we would get ten copies of the body of the `for` loop, instead of a `for` loop with a count of ten. After generating the source code instantiating the model's control flow and communication patterns, we can compile and execute it, optionally capturing a trace for study as output from the Durango tool.

2.6 CODES: An Extreme-Scale Systems Modeling and Simulation Framework

To demonstrate our new Durango's methodology and functionality, we have integrated Durango with a popular massively parallel simulation system for interconnection networks, CODES/ROSS.

CODES enables the design-space exploration of HPC networks and storage systems with the help of scalable discrete-event simulations of interconnection networks and storage systems. CODES uses ROSS as its underlying parallel discrete-event simulation framework, which enables efficient and scalable network models thanks to the optimistic event scheduling capability of ROSS [22]. The core object within a ROSS model is a *logical process (LP)*, which models some distinct component of a network such as a terminal or router. Simulation time is advanced by LPs exchanging time-stamped event messages. The optimistic parallel synchronization approach used by ROSS guarantees that events are processed in time stamp order.

CODES supports high-fidelity network models for dragonfly, torus, and SlimFly interconnect topologies. It uses an abstraction layer on top of the network models that allows users to conveniently plugin multiple network topologies while making minimal changes to their simulation code. The network topologies are simulated at a packet-level detail with congestion control being modeled through a credit-based flow control methodology on the virtual channels. The dragonfly network model in CODES is built on the high-radix, low-cost network configuration proposed by Kim et al. [15, 16]. It models four forms of routing algorithms: minimal, non-minimal, adaptive, and progressive adaptive routings. Multiple virtual channels are used for deadlock avoidance with different routing algorithms. The dragonfly model has been validated against the *Booksim* interconnect simulator using synthetic traffic patterns [21]. The torus network model is inspired by the Blue Gene architecture. It uses a bubble-escape virtual channel for deadlock avoidance with deterministic dimension-order routing. Validation of the torus model has been carried out against the Blue Gene/P and Blue Gene/Q architectures [20]. The SlimFly network model is based on another high-radix network topology proposed by Besta and Hoefler to reduce the network cost and diameter [6]. The CODES SlimFly simulation results were validated against the simulator by Besta and Hoefler.

The CODES network models report detailed statistics about network performance for each simulated network node and router. Using metrics such as the average number of hops traversed, average packet latency, data transmitted, and number of packets completed. Detailed statistics are reported at the network link level, including the amount of data transmitted at each network link and the time that the link gets saturated during the simulation. These metrics can be used to get detailed insight into the network performance with different workloads.

To replay the MPI operations on CODES network models, one needs a mechanism that avoids transmitting back to back MPI send messages on the network. Figure 2 shows how the MPI simulation layer interacts with the CODES network abstraction layer to replay the workload operations on top of the simulated networks. The MPI simulation layer in CODES digests the MPI operations from the workloads and simulates them on top of the network models. It tracks the queues of MPI sends and receives, matches sends with the receives, and simulates MPI wait and ait-all operations. This functionality is vital for maintaining the correct causality order of MPI operations coming from the traces.

2.7 Durango Direct Integration: Aspen with CODES

At the core of the Durango direct integration approach is a CODES discrete-event model that drives a network simulation component, coupled to an Aspen-based runtime estimator for parallel applications. The model defines Aspen Server Logical Processes (Aspen LPs), which are the entities in the simulation responsible for driving the creation of network traffic and for performing Aspen-related computations. Each Aspen LP is paired to a corresponding CODES network terminal LP to facilitate communication with the network layer within the CODES model. The CODES network LPs are generated and organized based on the network topology chosen for the current runtime estimation. When Aspen is called through the Aspen Server LPs, the estimation parameters are passed from the primary configuration file for Durango. In return, Aspen returns the runtime estimate based on the application and the machine details specified by the configuration file.

Listing 4: Aspen LP kickoff event handler.

```
1 static void handle_kickoff_event(
2     aspen_svr_state * ns,
3     tw_bf * b,
4     aspen_svr_msg * m,
5     tw_lp * lp)
6 {
7     int dest_id;
8     aspen_svr_msg m_local;
9     aspen_svr_msg m_remote;
10
11     m_local.aspen_svr_event_type = LOCAL;
12     m_local.src = lp->gid;
13     m_remote.aspen_svr_event_type = REQ;
14     m_remote.src = lp->gid;
15
16     /* record when transfers started
17     // on this server */
18     ns->start_ts = tw_now(lp);
19
20     dest_id = get_next_server(lp);
21
22     model_net_event(net_id, "test",
23         dest_id, payload_sz, 0,
24         sizeof(aspen_svr_msg),
25         (const void*)&m_remote,
26         sizeof(aspen_svr_msg),
27         (const void*)&m_local, lp);
28     ns->msg_sent_count++;
29 }
```

Under the current direct integration mode, Durango simulates a given application in two-step rounds of network simulation and computation runtime estimation, handled by the internal CODES model and Aspen respectively.

Figure 3 illustrates the runtime of a network-computation round in greater detail. First a CODES network simulation

is executed, and then the 0th Aspen Server LP, labeled "Aspen Master," reduces and processes all network data. Once the data have been reduced, the Master LP passes control of the simulation to the Aspen runtime in order to estimate the computation cost for the current round. Aspen returns a runtime estimate, and then returns control to the Master LP, which resumes subsequent simulator rounds by sending network restart events to all other Aspen LPs.

Listing 5: Aspen computation event handler.

```
1 static void handle_computation_event(
2     aspen_svr_state * ns,
3     tw_bf * b,
4     aspen_svr_msg * m,
5     tw_lp * lp)
6 {
7     // Compute overall network time elapsed:
8     delta += end_global - start_global;
9
10     /* Call ASPEN framework to estimate
11     // computation cost: */
12     delta += runtimeCalc(Aspen_App_Path[
13         roundsExecuted - computationRollbacks],
14         Aspen_Mach_Path,
15         Aspen_Socket[roundsExecuted -
16         computationRollbacks]);
17
18     // Save totalRuntime and then update it:
19     m->end_ts = totalRuntime;
20     totalRuntime += delta;
21
22     // Increment number of rounds executed:
23     roundsExecuted ++;
24     .
25     .
26     .
27 }
```

Each CODES network simulation phase begins with "kickoff" events sent by the Master LP to all Aspen Server LPs, itself included. The code for handling kickoff events is shown in Listing 4. In response to kickoff events, Aspen LPs record the current simulation time and use get_next_server(lp), a mapping function that uses the underlying CODES API for organizing the logical processes to retrieve the identity of the LP that they will communicate with for the duration of the network-computation round. Depending on the network traffic type specified in the configuration file, get_next_server(lp) returns a different ID. If nearest neighbor is specified, for example, then the next logical process ID that corresponds to an Aspen LP is returned. This is an important distinction, since some of the logical processes in the simulation serve other purposes, such as network terminals, rather than Aspen Servers. In the case of a random network traffic pattern, a random identity corresponding to any other Aspen LP is returned. This means that multiple Aspen LPs may communicate with one Aspen LP for the duration of the round, but it does not mean that they may communicate with themselves. The kickoff handler ends after the CODES API is used with model_net_event(...) to send a "ping" to the LP whose ID was returned by get_next_server(lp).

Upon receipt of a "ping" request, Aspen LPs respond with an acknowledgment event message to the sender. For every "ping" and "ack" event that an Aspen LP receives, counters are incremented and saved in the logical process state. The request-acknowledgment interchange continues until the Aspen LP that initiated the exchange has sent the configured number of requests and received the correct number of acknowledgments. The Aspen Server that initiated the ex-

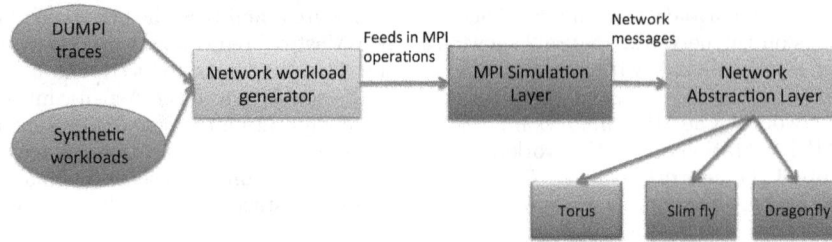

Figure 2: CODES network simulations.

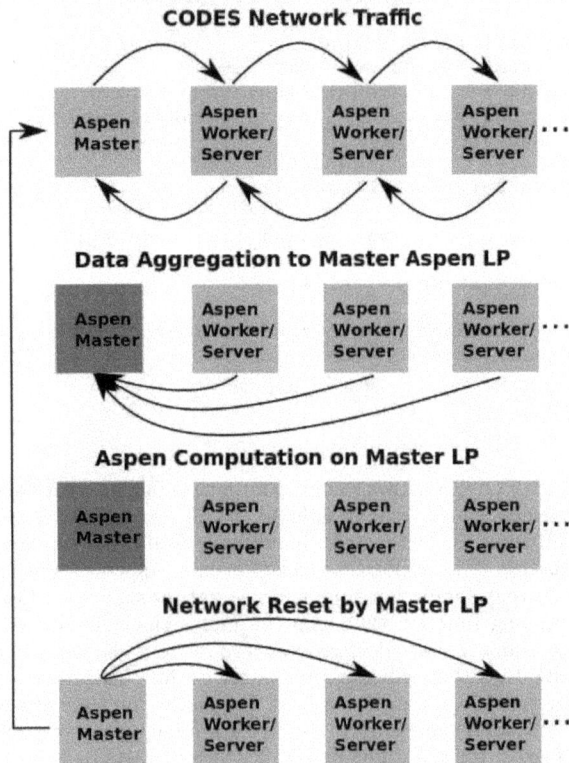

Figure 3: Durango hybrid runtime.

change records the simulation timestamp at which network communication ended with its counterpart.

With the first half of the network-computation round completed, the Aspen LPs cease driving network communications and send their start and end timestamps to the 0th Aspen LP. Note that the Aspen LPs could simply send their own total elapsed network communication time instead of the separate start and end values; however, then the overall longest communication time might not be accurately measured if the LP with the longest communication time begins simulation before some other LPs but also ends before other LPs that began their network conversations later. In all cases, the total network time elapsed is the difference between the globally earliest and globally latest start and

end timestamps, respectively. As a result, the 0th LP is responsible for finding the longest time spent in the network phase overall and therefore keeps track only of the earliest and latest values it receives from all of the Aspen LPs, itself included. This process is handled by the `handle_data_event(...)` handler. Once all timestamps have been received, the Master LP sends an "Aspen Computation" event to itself. The "Aspen Computation" event handler performs a function call to the Aspen simulation engine with paths to the application model and machine model sourced from the Durango configuration file. In Listing 5, an excerpt of the computation event handler, the total network runtime, is calculated. Then a call to Aspen is made, passing the parameters of the application and machine model as well as which compute socket to run on. The computation runtime is returned and added to the global running counter, marking the end of the network-computation round.

If only one round has been configured in the Durango configuration file, then the simulation will terminate with only one iteration of CODES network simulation and Aspen runtime computation estimation. Otherwise, the Master LP re-sends kickoff messages to each Aspen Server LP, signaling the start of a fresh network-computation round. Upon receiving the re-kickoff message, all Aspen Server LPs then find a new LP with which to communicate and start the next network simulation phase.

3. SYNTHETIC TRACE AND PERFORMANCE EVALUATION

In this paper, we describe two series of experiments. The first uses the LULESH miniapp and compares it with Durango's generated facsimile of its communication pattern. For these experiments, a 64-way multicore system is used with 64 GB of RAM and 2.2 TB of disk space. Here, the real LULESH DUMPI trace for a 4x4x4 grid (64 MPI ranks) configuration is compared with that of the Durango generator, which also runs and creates a DUMPI trace. For the comparison, both DUMPI traces are run through the CODES torus network simulator, which is configured with a torus network topology in a 4x4x4 configuration.

In the second series of experiments, we demonstrate the efficacy of our direct integration approach. Performance results are shown for Durango when a computational kernel implemented in Aspen is linked into a executable network model. For this series of experiments, both a torus and a dragonfly network are used. All simulations are run in parallel on the "AMOS" IBM Blue Gene/Q supercomputer located at the Center for Computational Innovations at Rensselaer.

3.1 Durango Generated vs. Real LULESH Results

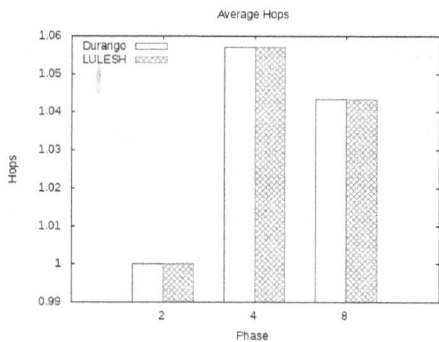

Figure 4: LULESH vs. Durango: Average torus network packet hop count as a function of the different LULESH phases.

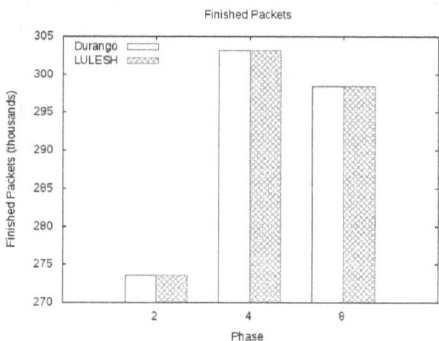

Figure 5: LULESH vs. Durango: Finished torus network packet count as a function of the different LULESH phases.

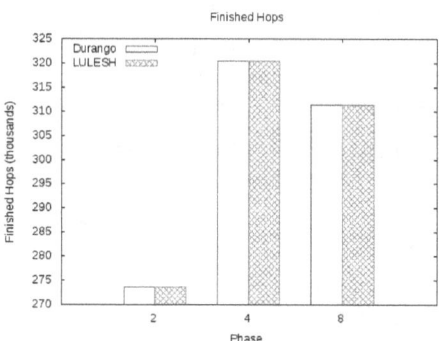

Figure 6: LULESH vs. Durango: Finished torus network packet hop count as a function of the different LULESH phases.

3.1.1 LULESH Proxy Application

LULESH [1, 13] is a scientific computing application that performs explicit shock hydrodynamics calculations on an

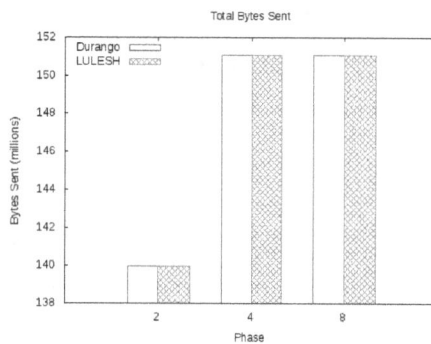

Figure 7: LULESH vs. Durango: Total torus network bytes sent as a function of the different LULESH phases.

unstructured grid. It has been ported to several programming models. To explore modeling of the communication behavior, we studied the parallel version of LULESH implemented by using MPI for interprocess communication.

LULESH has a processor decomposition that is regular. While the mesh elements are defined with explicit connectivity allowing for unstructured elements other than hexahedra, the implementation of communication between the problem domains has a logical structure that allows nearest neighbor communication along the three-dimensional mesh $i/j/k$ directions.

LULESH has three styles of communication:

(A) bidirectional nearest-neighbor communication across only faces;

(B) bidirectional nearest-neighbor communication across faces, edges, and corners and

(C) unidirectional communication across faces, edges, and corners, from a lower-rank task to a higher-rank task.

LULESH has four phases of communication, each conforming to one of these three styles. We label experiments using a bit pattern representing which phase is active: "1" for the first phase (style B), "2" for the second phase (style A), "4" for the third phase (style B), and "8" for the fourth phase (style C). This allows us to describe the behavior of the full application with multiple phases active by summing the bit patterns of every active phase. Because the first communication phase in LULESH is used only for problem initialization, we focused on the analysis of the other three phases, which occur every time step. The analysis results are labeled "2," "4" and "8" for their respective LULESH phases.

3.1.2 Experimental Results

In this first series of experiments, we compare the CODES network output statistics for the Durango generated and the real LULESH miniapp MPI communication traces. The key network statistics are as follows:

- **Average packet hop count:** the total number of hops traversals divided by the total number of packets sent into the network

- **Finished packets:** the total number of packets that reached their final destination

- **Finished packet hop count:** the total number of hop traversals divided by the total number of packets that reached their final destination

- **Total bytes sent:** total amount of data sent into the network

These statistics avoid any measure of time either absolute or relative such as an interarrival time. While such information is important, it largely depends on the amount of compute time between MPI messages and/or architectural features of the underlying machine model. The four statistics we use capture the communication behaviors that are independent from computation.

In validating Durango's generated LULESH communication patterns relative to the original LULESH miniapp code, we discovered an incorrect use of the `MPI_Waitall` operation by LULESH, whereas the Aspen-generated code was correct. Specifically, the number of wait requests sent is hard coded to 26 when only a small fraction (e.g., about 8) of the 26 available `MPI_Isend` and `MPI_Irecv` requests were used in this specific scenario. This error resulted in the CODES simulation prematurely terminating because of unmatched requests within the `MPI_Waitall`, which is a correct behavior for the simulator since it denotes a "bad" trace. Once provided the right number of active requests, the `MPI_Waitall` trace events were correct, and the CODES simulator completed without error. This finding underscores the potential need for a tool such as Durango beyond its benefits for flexible workload generation and modeling.

With regards to the network results, Figure 4 shows the average packet hop count as a function of different LULESH phases. The average ranges from 1.0 in phase 2 to nearly 1.06 in phase 4. Across all the phases, we observe identical results between the Durango generated and the real LULESH communication patterns.

Figures 5 and 6 show the number of finished packets and hops as a function of LULESH phases. In Figure 5 the number of finished packets ranges between 272K and 320K packets; similarly, the finished hop counts are in the same range because the hop count for the majority of LULESH packets is a single hop away in the 3D torus network. Across all the phases, we observe identical results the Durango finished packets/hop count and the real LULESH finished packets/hop count.

Figure 7 reports the total number of packets sent as a function of LULESH phases. As before, we observe no difference between the Durango generator and the real LULESH miniapp. The range in packets is 140MB for phase 2 up to 151MB for phases 4 and 8.

3.2 Evaluation of Durango Direct Integration

The Durango direct integration approach was executed on *AMOS*, an IBM Blue Gene/Q supercomputer located at the Rensselaer Polytechnic Institute Center for Computational Innovation. *AMOS* has 5 racks, each with 1,024 nodes. Each node contains 16 GB of DDR3 RAM and one IBM A2 processor, clocked at 1.6 GHz with 16 compute cores and 64 hardware threads.

Across all tests, Durango was run using BG/Q node counts ranging from 4 to 4096 nodes and 32 to 32,768 MPI ranks. For the network simulation component, torus and dragonfly network models were configured with a nearest-neighbor traffic pattern, and a custom Aspen machine model based on the AMD processors was written for calculating runtimes with a matrix multiplication kernel model. The torus network is a 5D (8^5) topology yielding 32K nodes with each link having 2 GB/sec bandwidth. The dragonfly network's configuration is taken from [20] and has 1.3M terminal nodes.

Unlike the previous test, Aspen is driving the compute time between phases of nearest-neighbor communications. The purpose of this performance study is to demonstrate that the Aspen compute model does impede the parallel network simulation. Future work on Durango will enable the Aspen system model to drive both compute node timing activity and network patterns at the same time.

3.2.1 Runtime Configuration

Configuration of Aspen when executed in this direct integration mode with the CODES parallel simulation framework is accomplished through a primary and secondary configuration file. The primary configuration file is used to specify the Aspen compute kernel and machine models that will be utilized during each network-computation round. This configuration file also allows per-round selection of the socket on each node of the Aspen machine to be used to "run" the compute kernel, as well as the number of rounds to be simulated. The number and size of the "ping" requests sent between Aspen Server logical processes are configured as well. A sample primary configuration file is shown in part in Listing 6, where Durango has been configured to simulate two rounds of matrix multiplication on an AMD-based cluster using the CPU in the first round and the GPU in the second round over the CODES-provided "SimpleNet" testing topology. Note that in the primary configuration file, the level of debug information can be adjusted as follows:

- Level 0: supresses all debug output

- Level 1: allows configuration details to be printed

- Level 2: allows runtime progress messages to be printed

Listing 6: Aspen parameter configuration excerpt.

```
1 ASPEN_PARAMS
2 {
3     debug_output="1";
4     network_conf_file="simplenet.conf";
5     network_traffic_pattern="random";
6     num_rounds="2";
7     aspen_mach_path="./models/
8                    machine/BigTestRig.aspen";
9     socket_choice000="amd_830";
10    socket_choice001="amd_HD5770";
11    aspen_app_path000="./models/matmul/
12                    matmul.aspen";
13    aspen_app_path001="./models/matmul/
14                    matmul.aspen";
15 }
16
17 server_pings
18 {
19     num_reqs="128";
20     payload_sz="1024";
21 }
```

The second configuration file used by Durango is included in the simulator runtime by a parameter in the primary configuration file, called `network_conf_file`. The parameters in the network configuration file are directly passed on to the underlying CODES-Net framework, and allow for network topology and size settings to be adjusted. The network configuration file also controls how logical processes are organized in the simulator. Durango contributes the Aspen Server LP. Required by the CODES framework are the network-level "server" LPs and the chosen network topology's routing LPs. Listing 7 shows the basic network configuration file for the SimpleNet network topology.

LPGROUPS contains the *ASPEN_SERVERS* subcategory, and lists the classes and organization of the LPs in the simulation. For the SimpleNet topology the only two LP types needed are the CODES-level "modelnet_simplenet" LPs and the "server" LPs, which drive the overall Aspen-CODES simulation layer. The other two supported topologies, torus and dragonfly, also require two CODES-level LPs to function.

Listing 7: Aspen SimpleNet network configuration.

```
 1 LPGROUPS
 2 {
 3     # simplenet has a set of servers, each with
 4     # point-to-point access to each other
 5     ASPEN_SERVERS
 6     {
 7         # required: number of times to repeat
 8         the following key-value pairs
 9         repetitions="4096";
10         # LP types
11         server="1";
12         modelnet_simplenet="1";
13     }
14 }
15 # Network Params:
16 PARAMS
17 {
18     # ROSS-specific parmeters:
19     # - message_size:
20     message_size="340";
21     pe_mem_factor="512";
22     # model-net-specific parameters:
23     # - individual packet sizes for network
24     #       operations where each "packet" is
25     #       represented by an event
26     # - independent of underlying network being
27     #       used
28     packet_size="512";
29     # - order that network types will be presented
30     #       to the user in
31     #       model_net_set_params. In this example,
32     #       we're only using a single
33     #       network topology
34     modelnet_order=( "simplenet" );
35     # - packet scheduling algorithm
36     modelnet_scheduler="fcfs";
37     # - simplenet-specific parameters
38     net_startup_ns="1.5";
39     net_bw_mbps="20000";
40 }
```

PARAMS includes topology-specific configuration details; for the excerpt shown here include the packet size, network bandwidth, latency, and packet scheduling algorithm. The dragonfly network topology adds to this list the number of routers in each subgroup, the global and local channel bandwidths, and several other topology-specific parameters. The torus topology also adds several unique parameters to this section, including the torus dimensionality (and corresponding dimension sizes).

3.2.2 Performance Results

Figure 8 shows strong-scaling results for Durango when configured with a 32K node torus network and executed using 32 to 2048 MPI ranks across a varing number of ranks per compute node on the Blue Gene/Q supercomputer. Here, the execution time ranges from 24,000 seconds down to just over 1,000 seconds. This implies an overall worst-case to

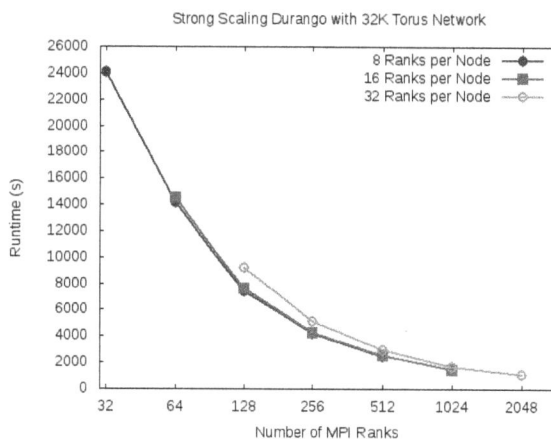

Figure 8: Durango in direct integration mode with 32K node torus network and Aspen compute node generator for 32 to 2,048 MPI ranks.

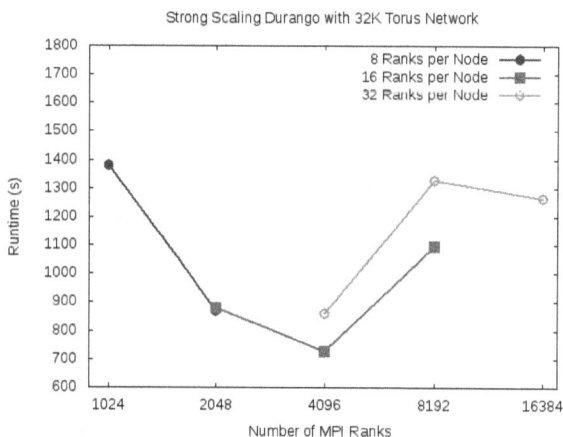

Figure 9: Durango in direct integration mode with 32K node torus network and Aspen compute node generator for 1K to 16K MPI ranks.

best case speedup of 24x using just 16x the hardware (e.g., 4 nodes to 64 nodes). This superlinear performance is attributed to performance gains because of a smaller memory "working set" which yields higher cache hit rates as the core counts increase. Similar performance gains were reported by Barnes et al. [5]. Parallel simulation efficiency ranges from a peak of 92% on 4 nodes with 32 ranks to a low of 61% on 64 nodes using 2048 ranks. This is to be expected because of the likelihood of out-of-order event computations grows as the number of nodes increase.

The out-of-order event computations become more problematic at larger MPI rank counts, as shown Figure 9. Here, the same 32K node torus network configured with an Aspen LP for determining the compute phase timing for the matrix-multiplication kernel is being scaled from 1K to 16K MPI ranks and 128 to 512 Blue Gene/Q compute nodes. The worst-case efficiency of -314% is report when using 512 nodes and 16K MPI ranks. This implies that nearly three events are being rolled back for each forward event per the efficiency definition used in [5]. Clearly, the simulation has

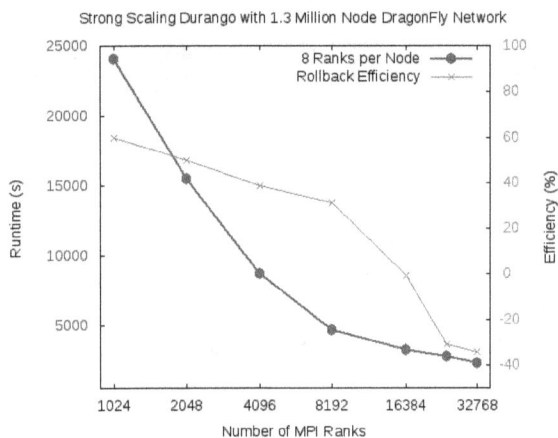

Figure 10: Durango in direct integration mode with 1.3M node dragonfly network and Aspen compute node generator for 1K to 32K MPI ranks.

become overly speculative. The fastest execution case is with 256 nodes and 4,096 MPI ranks and completes in 726 seconds.

If we increase the network simulation workload by using a much larger network, we observe much better Durango performance, as shown in Figure 10. Here, a 1.3M node dragonfly network is configured with the Aspen computation timing event generation. The parallel simulation run with 128 nodes and 1K MPI ranks completes in 24,000 seconds while the run with 4,096 node and 32K MPI ranks completes in just 2200 seconds. The observed performance is nearly a 11x speedup for 32x the hardware, which is in line with results reported in previous dragonfly network simulation studies [22].

Overall, the integration of Aspen's code timing event generation does not impact the overall Durango performance. Also, we avoid the performance penalty of reading in large, memory-intensive traces datasets.

4. RELATED WORK

Durango touches on many research areas but especially tracing tools and systems simulators.

Tracing Tools: Tracing is an important and traditional technique for capturing communication, memory [29], and instruction events. Relevant here are tracing tools that capture communication events in large scale systems including DUMPI [25], which is part of the Structural Simulation Toolkit (SST). DUMPI has been used to create a trace database for the key miniapps used in performance benchmarking of network design for the DOE Design Forward and Fast Forward programs. In addition to DUMPI traces, Tracer [2] provides an alternative approach to replaying trace-based communication workloads within the CODES network modeling and simulation framework.

ScalaTrace is an MPI tracing toolset that uses intra- and internode lossless compression techniques to produce near-constant-size communication traces regardless of the number of nodes while, preserving communication structure information [23]. Recent enhancements include MPI-IO and POSIX I/O tracing and improved extrapolation of MPI, MPI-IO, and POSIX I/O traces. Synthetic benchmarks that reflect application behavior can be generated from the compressed

tracefiles in different ways: (1) by generating from the tracefile a high-level abstract conceptual pseudocode from which a specific implementation (e.g,. C+MPI) can be generated [34] or (2) by directly generating the C+MPI synthetic benchmark from the trace using ScalaBenchGen [33].

Compiler-Based Approaches: A compiler framework that can identify communication patterns for MPI-based parallel applications is described in [27]. The compiler uses a communication pattern representation scheme that captures the properties of communication patterns and allows manipulations of these patterns. Communication phases can be detected and logically separated within the application. The predicted LBMHD, CG and MG communication patterns were verified by comparing with application trace data.

HPC System Simulators: Dimemas [24, 26], a performance analysis tool for MPI applications, is used in conjunction with Venus, an Omnest-based network simulator [30] to perform trace-driven simulations [19, 8]. Initial results are shown at a scale of up to 512 cores on the Blue Gene/P platform.

BigSim [35] is a parallel discrete-event simulation framework built on the POSE PDES engine [2]. It has been used to explore intelligent topology-aware job mappings for the PERSC architecture [35, 7]. BigSim also can generate traces by emulating application behavior on architectures that do not yet exist. The generated application traces can then be replayed on network simulations for performance prediction. However, the POSE PDES engine imposes performance penalties, which makes it difficult to scale the simulation to large core counts. A recent study by the BigSim and CODES team demonstrates that CODES is an order of magnitude faster than BigSim [2].

Booksim [9] is a serial, cycle-accurate interconnection network simulation framework that supports multiple network topologies such as torus, fat tree, and dragonfly. Kim et al. used *Booksim* to propose the dragonfly network topology on a scale of 1,056 network nodes [15, 16]. *Booksim* supports a detailed router model for the networks along with detailed routing algorithms for each topology. A modified version of *Booksim* was also used to simulate the performance of a Slim Fly network topology [6, 14].

The WARwick Performance Prediction Toolkit (WARPP) [11] uses the following modeling approach: (1) manual or automated source code analysis to identify basic blocks and MPI calls, (2) machine benchmarking on the target machine to measure runtime for basic blocks and to do MPI benchmarking, and (3) input of the application model and the benchmarking results to a discrete event simulator. Currently, only the 2008 version of the simulation engine, which is written in Java with its accompanying documentation, is available.

POEMS [3] is an end-to-end performance analysis framework for HPC applications. This includes the modeling of the application software, runtime and operating software, and hardware architecture. Central to this framework is the POEMS Specification Language compiler that generates an end-to-end system automatically from a system specification. Unlike POEMS, Durango enables the prediction of an application's computational and network performance on future or hypothetical hardware configurations. This feature of Durango is attributed to structural analytic modeling approach of Aspen on the application calculation side, and packet-level modeling approach of CODES on the network side. In contrast, POEMS relies on a simple latency/bandwidth hardware network model that is unable to track the detailed congestion events that can happen across different network topologies.

The Structural Simulation Toolkit (SST) is a parallel discrete-event simulation framework that uses a conservative synchronization approach to model a number of components such as network, processors and memory [12, 25]. Detailed SST models can run at small scale with a few network nodes. Large-scale network simulations use a low fidelity model buit in the SST macro layer. Here, the DUMPI trace library is used to capture the communication behavior of MPI applications.

The most recent related results are in [4]. Here, a new Python-based HPC network modeling framework that is built on the Simian parallel discrete-event engine demonstrates accurate performance predication of a Cray 3D torus network across a number of MPI application traces. A network model using 156K MPI rank trace as input is shown to efficently run in parallel on up to 3K AMD Opteron cores. Unlike Durango, this approach currently does not appear to include models for predicting the computational overhead associated with the scientific applications.

5. CONCLUSIONS

In this paper, we introduce a new performance analysis tool called *Durango* that integrates the analytical performance modeling capabilities of the Aspen domain specific language with the efficient, massively parallel network simulation capabilities of CODES. Aspen has been extended to enable communication pattern specification. The efficacy of Durango is demonstrated as a new approach to the performance modeling of extreme-scale systems in two ways:

- Comparing the Aspen generated communication patterns with real application network communications via traces that are run through the CODES packet-level network simulation framework. Durango shows strong agreement with the real application trace data for key network performance statistics.

- Performing a scaling study of Durango's direct integration approach that links Aspen with CODES as part of the running network simulation model. Here, Aspen generates the application-level computation timing events, which in turn drive the start of a network communication phase. Results show that Durango's performance scales well when executing both torus and dragonfly network models on up to 4K Blue Gene/Q nodes using 32K MPI ranks.

We plan to extend Durango's capabilities by enabling Aspen to drive both the compute kernel timing and the network communication patterns for key supercomputing applications. This extension will enable end-to-end performance prediction capabilities for current and future extreme-scale systems.

6. ACKNOWLEDGMENTS

The CODES project is supported by the U.S. Department of Energy, Office of Science, Office of Advanced Scientific Computer Research (ASCR), under contract DE-AC02-06CH11357 managed by Lucy Nowell. The Aspen/Durango work is supported by the U.S. Department of Energy, Office of Science, Office of Advanced Scientific Computer Research (ASCR), under contract number DE-SC0012636 managed by Richard Carlson. Additional support is provided by the Air Force Research Laboratory under contract number FA8750-15-2-0078 managed by Mark Barnell. Computational resources for this work are provided by the Center for Computational Innovations at Rensselaer Polytechnic Institute.

7. REFERENCES

[1] Hydrodynamics Challenge Problem, Lawrence Livermore National Laboratory. Technical Report LLNL-TR-490254.

[2] B. Acun, N. Jain, A. Bhatele, M. Mubarak, C. D. Carothers, and L. V. Kale. Preliminary evaluation of a parallel trace replay tool for hpc network simulations. In *Workshop on Parallel and Distributed Agent-Based Simulations*, 2015.

[3] V. S. Adve, R. Bagrodia, J. C. Browne, E. Deelman, A. Dube, E. N. Houstis, J. R. Rice, R. Sakellariou, D. J. Sundaram-Stukel, P. J. Teller, and M. K. Vernon. POEMS: End-to-end performance design of large parallel adaptive computational systems. *IEEE Trans. Software Engineering*, 26(11):1027–1048, 2000.

[4] K. Ahmed, M. Obaida, J. Liu, S. Eidenbenz, N. Santhi, and G. Chapuis. An integrated interconnection network model for large-scale performance prediction. In *Proceedings of the 2016 Annual ACM Conference on SIGSIM Principles of Advanced Discrete Simulation*, SIGSIM-PADS '16, pages 177–187, New York, NY, USA, 2016. ACM.

[5] P. D. Barnes, C. D. Carothers, D. R. Jefferson, and J. M. LaPre. Warp speed: executing time warp on 1,966,080 cores. In *Proc. of the 2013 ACM SIGSIM Conf. on Principles of Advanced Discrete Simulation (PADS)*, pages 327–336, May 2013.

[6] M. Besta and T. Hoefler. Slim fly: A cost effective low-diameter network topology. In *Proc. of the Int. Conf. for High Performance Comput., Networking, Storage and Anal. (SC)*, pages 348–359, 2014.

[7] A. Bhatele, N. Jain, W. Gropp, and L. V. Kale. Avoiding hot-spots on two-level direct networks. In *Int. Conf. for High Performance Comput., Networking, Storage and Anal. (SC).*, pages 1–11, 2011.

[8] R. Birke, G. Rodriguez, and C. Minkenberg. Towards massively parallel simulations of massively parallel high-performance computing systems. In *Proc. of the 5th Int. ICST Conf. on Simulation Tools and Techn.*, pages 291–298, 2012.

[9] W. J. Dally and B. Towles. *Principles and practices of interconnection networks*. Morgan Kaufmann Publishers, San Francisco, 2003.

[10] W. J. Dally and B. P. Towles. *Principles and Practices of Interconnection Networks*. Burlington, MA, USA: Morgan Kaufmann, 2004.

[11] S. Hammond, G. Mudalige, J. Smith, S. Jarvis, J. Herdman, and A. Vadgama. WARPP: A toolkit for simulating high performance parallel scientific codes. In *2nd International Conference on Simulation Tools and Techniques*, Rome, Italy, Mar. 2009. ACM SIGSIM.

[12] C. L. Janssen, H. Adalsteinsson, S. Cranford, J. P. Kenny, A. Pinar, D. A. Evensky, and J. Mayo. A simulator for large-scale parallel computer architectures. *Technology Integration Advancements in Distributed Systems and Computing*, 179, 2012.

[13] I. Karlin, A. Bhatele, J. Keasler, B. L. Chamberlain,

J. Cohen, Z. DeVito, R. Haque, D. Laney, E. Luke, F. Wang, D. Richards, M. Schulz, and C. Still. Exploring traditional and emerging parallel programming models using a proxy application. In *27th IEEE International Parallel & Distributed Processing Symposium (IEEE IPDPS 2013)*, Boston, USA, May 2013.

[14] G. Kathareios, C. Minkenberg, B. Prisacari, G. Rodriguez, and T. Hoefler. Cost-effective diameter-two topologies: analysis and evaluation. In *Proceedings of the International Conference for High Performance Computing, Networking, Storage and Analysis*, page 36. ACM, 2015.

[15] J. Kim, W. Dally, S. Scott, and D. Abts. Cost-efficient dragonfly topology for large-scale systems. *Micro, IEEE*, 29(1):33–40, Feb. 2009.

[16] J. Kim, W. J. Dally, S. Scott, and D. Abts. Technology-driven, highly-scalable dragonfly topology. *ACM SIGARCH Comput. Architecture News*, 36(3):77–88, June 2008.

[17] S. Lee, J. S. Meredith, and J. S. Vetter. COMPASS: A framework for automated performance modeling and prediction. In *Proceedings of the 29th ACM on International Conference on Supercomputing*, pages 405–414, Newport Beach, California, USA, 2015. ACM.

[18] S. Lee and J. S. Vetter. OpenARC: extensible openACC compiler framework for directive-based accelerator programming study. In *Proceedings of the First Workshop on Accelerator Programming using Directives (with SC14)*, pages 1–11, New Orleans, 2014. IEEE Press.

[19] C. Minkenberg and G. Rodriguez. Trace-driven co-simulation of high-performance computing systems using OMNeT++. In *Proc. of the 2nd Int. Conf. on Simulation Tools and Techn.*, pages 65–72, 2009.

[20] M. Mubarak, C. Carothers, et al. A case study in using massively parallel simulation for extreme-scale torus network codesign. In *Proc. of the 2nd ACM SIGSIM/PADS Conf. on Principles of Advanced Discrete Simulation*, pages 27–38, 2014.

[21] M. Mubarak, C. D. Carothers, R. B. Ross, and P. Carns. Modeling a million-node dragonfly network using massively parallel discrete-event simulation. In *High Performance Comput., Networking, Storage and Anal. (SCC) SC Companion*, pages 366–376, 2012.

[22] M. Mubarak, C. D. Carothers, R. B. Ross, and P. Carns. Enabling parallel simulation of large-scale hpc network systems. *IEEE Trans. Parallel Distrib. Syst.*, 28(1):87–100, Jan. 2017.

[23] M. Noeth, P. Ratn, F. Mueller, M. Schulz, and B. R. de Supinski. Scalatrace: Scalable compression and replay of communication traces for high-performance computing. *J. Parallel Distrib. Comput.*, 69(8):696–710, 2009.

[24] V. Pillet, J. Labarta, T. Cortes, and S. Girona. Paraver: A tool to visualize and analyze parallel code. In *Proceedings of WoTUG-18: Transputer and occam Developments*, volume 44, pages 17–31. March, 1995.

[25] A. F. Rodrigues et al. The structural simulation toolkit. *ACM SIGMETRICS Performance Evaluation Rev.*, 38(4):37–42, Mar. 2011.

[26] G. Rodriguez, R. M. Badia, and J. Labarta. Generation of simple analytical models for message

passing applications. In *Euro-Par 2004 Parallel Processing*, pages 183–188. Springer, 2004.

[27] S. Shao, A. K. Jones, and R. Melhem. A compiler-based communication analysis approach for multiprocessor systems. In *Proceedings of the 20th International Conference on Parallel and Distributed Processing*, IPDPS'06, pages 85–85, Washington, DC, USA, 2006. IEEE Computer Society.

[28] K. L. Spafford and J. S. Vetter. Aspen: A domain specific language for performance modeling. In *SC12: International Conference for High Performance Computing, Networking, Storage and Analysis*, pages 1–11, Salt Lake City, 2012.

[29] R. A. Uhlig and T. N. Mudge. Trace-driven memory simulation: A survey. *Acm Computing Surveys*, 29(2):128–170, 1997.

[30] A. Varga. The OMNeT++ discrete event simulation system. In *Proceedings of the European simulation multiconference (ESMâĂŹ2001)*, volume 9, page 65. sn, 2001.

[31] J. S. Vetter and J. S. Meredith. Synthetic program analysis with aspen. In *Proceedings of the 3rd International Conference on Exascale Applications and Software*, pages 1–6. University of Edinburgh, 2015.

[32] S. Williams, A. Waterman, and D. Patterson. Roofline: an insightful visual performance model for multicore architectures. *Communications of the ACM*, 52(4):65–76, 2009.

[33] X. Wu, V. Deshpande, and F. Mueller. ScalaBenchGen: Auto-generation of communication benchmarks traces. In *Proceedings of the 2012 IEEE 26th International Parallel and Distributed Processing Symposium*, IPDPS '12, pages 1250–1260, Washington, DC, USA, 2012. IEEE Computer Society.

[34] X. Wu, F. Mueller, and S. Pakin. A methodology for automatic generation of executable communication specifications from parallel mpi applications. *ACM Trans. Parallel Comput.*, 1(1):6:1–6:30, Oct. 2014.

[35] G. Zheng, G. Kakulapati, and L. V. Kalé. Bigsim: A parallel simulator for performance prediction of extremely large parallel machines. In *Proc. of 18th IEEE Int. Parallel and Distributed Process. Symp.*, pages 78–87, 2004.

Time Warp on the GPU: Design and Assessment

Xinhu Liu and Philipp Andelfinger
Institute of Telematics
Karlsruhe Institute of Technology
76131 Karlsruhe
xinhu.liu90@gmail.com,
philipp.andelfinger@kit.edu

ABSTRACT

The parallel execution of discrete-event simulations on commodity GPUs has been shown to achieve high event rates. Most previous proposals have focused on conservative synchronization, which typically extracts only limited parallelism in cases of low event density in simulated time. We present the design and implementation of an optimistic fully GPU-based parallel discrete-event simulator based on the Time Warp synchronization algorithm. The optimistic simulator implementation is compared with an otherwise identical implementation using conservative synchronization. Our evaluation shows that in most cases, the increase in parallelism when using optimistic synchronization significantly outweighs the increased overhead for state keeping and rollbacks. To reduce the cost of state keeping, we show how XORWOW, the default pseudo-random number generator in CUDA, can be reversed based solely on its current state. Since the optimal configuration of multiple performance-critical simulator parameters depends on the behavior of the simulation model, these parameters are adapted dynamically based on performance measurements and heuristic optimization at runtime. We evaluate the simulator using the PHOLD benchmark model and a simplified model of peer-to-peer networks using the Kademlia protocol. On a commodity GPU, the optimistic simulator achieves event rates of up to 81.4 million events per second and a speedup of up to 3.6 compared with conservative synchronization.

1. INTRODUCTION

In the past years, heterogeneous GPU-accelerated simulation approaches have begun to complement traditional CPU-based parallel and distributed simulations to satisfy the computational demands created by the increasing scale and complexity of discrete-event models. Even inexpensive commodity many-core GPUs can provide substantial speedup compared with a purely CPU-based execution.

Since large-scale simulations using CPU-based clusters frequently occupy substantial amounts of computing resources,

such approaches must be justified by the gains in productivity. Recent work has also begun to take the energy consumption of distributed simulations into consideration [5]. Further, since researchers typically rely on shared computational resources, the delays between submission of a simulation task and its execution can be substantial. In such cases, a commodity GPU in a researcher's workstation can enable swift feedback at comparatively low resource and energy consumption.

GPU-based discrete-event simulation approaches fall into two main categories: *Hybrid* CPU-GPU-based simulation [2, 4, 11, 23] maintains a CPU-based simulator core, while executing some or all parts of the simulation model on the GPU. Hybrid simulation performs well in case individual simulation events are associated with significant computation. In *fully* GPU-based simulation [1, 13, 21, 22, 28, 32], the simulator core is executed on the GPU as well. Since significant data transfers between the CPU and GPU context are required only during initialization and termination, fully GPU-based simulation can efficiently execute models with fine-grained events as well.

In parallel simulations, the choice of synchronization algorithm has a strong impact on performance. Most previous works on fully GPU-based simulation focused on conservative synchronization, where the simulation correctness is maintained at all times. These works already demonstrated the large event rates achievable on commodity GPUs.

Optimistic synchronization allows for temporary violations of correctness, but restores a previous simulation state in case such a violation occurs. Hence, larger parallelism may be extracted at the cost of occasional rollbacks. On the one hand, optimistic synchronization seems to be an attractive approach to fully GPU-based simulation, since the massively parallel computational resources of a GPU may be utilized more fully. On the other hand, the rollback mechanism tends to increase the frequency of memory accesses, which are associated with particularly large costs on the GPU.

In this paper, we aim to clarify whether the benefits of optimistic synchronization outweigh its drawbacks in the context of fully GPU-based discrete-event simulation and make the following main contributions:

1. Time Warp on the GPU: We propose a design and implementation of optimistic synchronization for parallel discrete-event simulation on a GPU. We identify key simulator parameters and apply heuristic optimization to select suitable parameter combinations at runtime. The simulator and model code is made available to the community[1].

---

[1]http://github.com/GPUTW

2. Reverse Computation for CUDA RNG: We show how XORWOW, the default random number generator in CUDA, can be reversed to reduce the cost of rollbacks.

3. Comparison with Conservative Synchronization: The overall performance is evaluated in comparison with a synchronous conservative scheme on the example of the PHOLD benchmark model and a simplified model of peer-to-peer networks based on the Kademlia protocol.

The remainder of the paper is organized as follows: Section 2 discusses required background and related work in parallel discrete-event simulation and general-purpose computation on GPUs. Section 3 describes our simulator design and implementation. Section 4 analyzes performance-critical parameters and describes the autotuning approach. Section 5 presents a reversal of the XORWOW random number generator. Section 6 evaluates the performance of the simulator. Section 7 discusses limitations and open research issues. Section 8 summarizes and concludes the paper.

2. BACKGROUND AND RELATED WORK

2.1 Parallel Discrete-Event Simulation

Parallel discrete-event simulation is a method to decrease the wall-clock runtime of a discrete-event simulation by distributing the system state to a number of *logical processes* (LPs), each of which maintains its own simulation time and executes events in non-decreasing timestamp order. Newly created events may be sent to other LPs. To maintain the causal correctness of the simulation, two main classes of synchronization algorithms have been proposed: in conservative synchronization, LPs execute events only in case future causality violations can be ruled out, i.e., no event with smaller timestamp may be received from a remote LP. Optimistic synchronization allows for temporary causality violations and subsequently restores a previous correct simulation state using a rollback mechanism. An introduction to parallel and distributed simulation is given in [8].

YAWNS [19] is a well-known conservative synchronization algorithm that executes the simulation by considering a sequence of intervals in simulated time spanning the current minimum timestamp of any event in the simulation up to a limit determined using the lookahead, i.e., the lowest possible delta between a new event's timestamp and its creation. Valid lookahead values are determined according to simulation model characteristics and may vary over time and between different pairs of simulated entities. In simulations of computer networks, a lookahead value that is valid over the course of the entire simulation is given by the lowest possible link latency between any two nodes in the network. Events are processed in multiple *executions*, wherein each LP either executes one event or is idle. Assuming identical per-event processing times, if events within a window are not evenly distributed to LPs, an increasing number of LPs becomes idle before a new window is determined.

Time Warp [10] is an optimistic synchronization algorithm that can scale to millions of cores [3]. Rollbacks in Time Warp are bounded by global virtual time (GVT), which is a point in simulated time at which the correctness of the simulation state is guaranteed. If none of the LPs has executed any events out of timestamp order yet, the GVT can be calculated as the lowest timestamp of any LP's next event, if any. If a causality violation occurs, the simulation must be rolled back at most to the GVT.

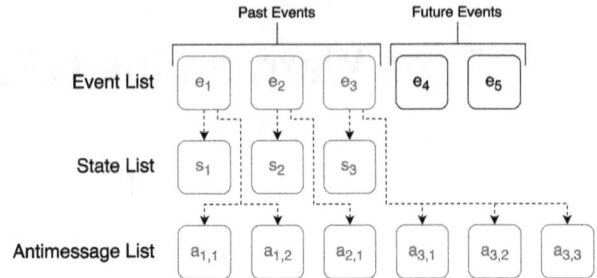

Figure 1: The three lists used in the Time Warp protocol.

Contrary to the single future event list per LP in conservative algorithms, Time Warp requires three lists per LP: The **event list** is similar to the future event list in conservative synchronization, but may temporarily hold past events as well. During a rollback, past events may be undone and subsequently re-executed. The **state list** stores snapshots of an LP's state that are used during rollbacks to restore a correct simulation state. The **antimessage list** contains a copy ("antimessage") of each event sent to a remote LP. Antimessages are sent to remote LPs to cancel previously sent events. The remote LP removes the event from its event list. If the event in question has already been handled, the LP rolls back to an earlier point in simulated time.

Figure 1 illustrates the three lists. The event list contains past and future events. For each past event, there is one state in the state list and as many entries in the antimessage list as there are newly scheduled events.

Depending on the operations performed in event handlers, using *reverse computation* [6] can be applied to arrive at a previous state. While some operations such as incrementation of an integer are non-destructive and can be reversed without any state saving, typically a combination of reverse combination and state saving is applied. The benefits of reverse computation are a decreased memory consumption and – depending on the cost of memory accesses in relation to computation – a potential decrease in simulation runtime.

2.2 GPGPU Basics

While GPUs were originally designed to handle the data-parallel workloads involved in rendering three-dimensional scenes, general-purpose computation on GPUs (GPGPU) enables the use of the hundreds of arithmetic units of modern graphics cards to solve computational problems in a variety of domains such as signal processing or machine learning. Here, we briefly discuss key GPGPU concepts, focusing on the GPGPU platform NVIDIA CUDA [20].

CUDA code is formulated in so-called kernels, which can be called from CPU code. GPU threads execute in groups of 32 called warps. Threads in a warp execute a shared sequence of instructions in lock-step. In case of divergent branching (e.g., through *if-else*), the branches are serialized. Threads are further organized into blocks of configurable size, which are assigned a small region of low-latency memory shared within the block. An important restriction is that the visibility of writes to memory among threads *within* a block can be guaranteed during execution of a kernel without significant overhead, whereas guaranteeing the visibility across blocks is more expensive and typically achieved by terminating the currently running kernel. CUDA provides a number of atomic operations for memory accesses. Since the graphics memory is designed for high throughput instead of low latency, cache misses can incur up to 600 clock cycles of latency. Given a sufficient number of concurrent warps, a hardware scheduler can hide memory access latencies by dynamically exchanging control between warps.

2.3 GPU-Based Simulation

We differentiate between two classes of approaches that make use of GPUs for acceleration of discrete-event simulations: in *hybrid* GPU-based simulation, event management – i.e., the selection of events for execution and the scheduling of new events – remains on the CPU, while the execution of events is performed in parallel on the GPU (e.g., [2, 11, 23, 4]). A benefit of the hybrid approach is that multiple GPUs can be utilized easily. On the other hand, events must be sufficiently computationally expensive so that the parallel execution on the GPU amortizes the cost of data transfers between host and graphics memory.

In *fully* GPU-based simulation, event management is performed on the GPU as well. Hence, fully GPU-based simulation largely avoids the costs of data transfers between host and graphics memory and can efficiently support models where individual events are associated with only small amounts of computation. Here, we focus on fully GPU-based discrete-event simulation, omitting time-stepped approaches and works that focus on specific model domains (e.g., [17]).

In 2006, Perumalla explored various fully GPU-based simulator designs [22]. Although a traditional discrete-event execution process was not feasible due to hardware limitations at the time, substantial speedup was achieved by exploiting the concurrency of events with identical timestamps.

In 2010, Park et al. proposed a fully GPU-based simulator that uses a tolerance interval in simulated time to increase the number of events that can be executed in parallel [21].

In 2013, Tang et al. presented a fully GPU-based simulator that processes events similarly to the YAWNS algorithm [32]. Instead of strictly limiting execution to events within the current window, parallelism is increased by identifying candidate events that may become safe to execute before a new window is calculated. When limiting the set of receivers of each simulated entity, the authors report an event rate of up to about 13 million events per second.

In 2014, Andelfinger et al. proposed a fully GPU-based conservative simulator implementation that adapts the LP size at runtime to balance parallelism and event management overheads [1]. Similarly, our proposed optimistic simulator adapts the LP size as one of the autotuned parameters.

In 2015, Swenson proposed a number of fully GPU-based simulator designs [28]. An event rate of up to 120 million events per second is achieved under the assumption that each event creates exactly one new event.

The previously discussed approaches are all based on conservative synchronization. A fully GPU-based simulator design using an optimistic synchronization approach was presented in 2013 by Li et al. [13]. The approach requires all events to be created before any events are executed. During the execution phase, all of the events are executed in parallel. Now, events are iteratively canceled and re-executed until a correct final simulation state is reached.

Contrary to some of the discussed works, our proposed simulator poses no restrictions on event creation beyond limits given by the available graphics memory. The core logic

of our design is quite similar to CPU-based Time Warp systems in shared memory settings [7]. Differences arise from the fine-grained parallelism of the GPU, which enables us to maintain low list management overheads by forming small LPs of only a few simulated entities each.

2.4 Considered Simulation Models

2.4.1 PHOLD

PHOLD (parallel hold) [9] is a generalization of the sequential hold benchmark model [31] that, in addition to simulated time, also considers a configurable number of simulated entities to which events are assigned. We apply the PHOLD model as follows: a constant number of events (the *population*) is initially created and assigned to simulated entities in a round-robin fashion. The execution of an event creates a new event targeting a random entity after a random delta in simulated time. Target entities are drawn from a uniform distribution and deltas in simulated time are drawn from an exponential distribution. We configure an arbitrary lookahead of 10 by adding this value to each drawn time delta. The PHOLD model accepts three parameters: the number of simulated entities, the population size and the parameter λ of the exponential distribution. Since the performance of the simulation is strongly affected by the relation between λ and the chosen lookahead, we vary λ over multiple orders of magnitude. We refer to the simulated entities as nodes. However, the proposed simulator is not confined to simulations of networks.

Since executing an event involves only a low amount of computation, hold and PHOLD emphasize the event management performance of the simulator (e.g., [25]). As all events are handled in the same manner, there are no divergent branches across parallel event executions. Thus, event execution on the GPU must be expected to be more efficient than with models of real-world systems.

2.4.2 Peer-to-Peer Network

To show the effects of larger event complexity and more significant branching across events, we additionally evaluate the simulator using a model of networks based on Kademlia [16]. Kademlia is a protocol used to form distributed hash tables (DHTs) for key-value storage and retrieval in a peer-to-peer network and is the basis of the BitTorrent Mainline DHT, currently comprised of around 10 million nodes[2]. The value associated with a key is retrieved in a *lookup* by iteratively querying nodes on the path to the key.

After initialization, events of three types occur: 1. Creation of initial requests to immediate neighbors of the initiating node. 2. Reception of a request: on reception, the current node looks up the nearest known nodes to the desired identifier and transmits a response message to the node that initiated the lookup. 3. Reception of a response: a reception event updates a list of the closest nodes to the desired key known to the initiating node and transmits further requests to maintain a configured number of in-flight requests. Link latencies between nodes are drawn from a uniform distribution on $\{10, 11, \ldots, 200\}$. Once a response contains no closer nodes and all nodes in the list have responded, the lookup terminates and a new lookup is scheduled after a random delay drawn from a uniform distribution on $\{10, 11, \ldots, D_{\max}\}$, $D_{\max}$ being a model parameter. Smaller $D_{\max}$ increases the

---

[2]http://dsn.tm.kit.edu/misc_2917.php

event density in simulated time. Due to the fixed lower bound on the link latency and lookup delay distributions, we use a fixed lookahead value of 10.

Execution of an event involves memory accesses to look up routing table entries, the creation of up to 8 new events, and atomic operations to access global statistics such as the number and duration of key-value lookups.

3. SIMULATOR DESIGN

In the following, we describe the simulation loop executed by the GPU-based simulator, as well as the chosen memory layout. A number of performance-critical simulator parameters arise – the number of simulated nodes that form an LP, the degree of optimism when executing events, and the threshold of inactive LPs before synchronization is performed. These parameters are further analyzed in Section 4.

The user implements a new model by providing the following core functions: `set_model_params()` and `init_node()` initialize the model, `get_lookahead()` returns the lookahead of the model, `handle_event()` and `roll_back_event()` perform forward and backward execution of an event described by a pointer to an event structure (cf. Section 5.2). State saving is performed during event handling by calling `append_state_to_queue()` and `append_antimsg_to_queue()`.

3.1 Simulation Loop

Our goal is to map the steps of a discrete-event simulation loop – selection of events for execution, handling of events, and creation of new events – to the GPU. Since the GPU's threads have shared access to graphics memory, the simulation can act on global knowledge of the simulation state. The single-program, multiple-data paradigm of the GPU suggests a synchronous simulation process, i.e., all threads perform the same simulation step at the same time.

The simulation proceeds as a sequence of *iterations* consisting of multiple steps (cf. Figure 2), the core step being the parallel *execution* of up to one event per LP by each GPU thread. The remaining steps are required for synchronization between LPs and for event management. As a consequence of separating the execution of events from the insertion into event lists, newly created events are not visible to LPs before a new iteration begins. Thus, a challenge lies in balancing synchronization and event management overheads with parallelism: multiple executions can be performed within a single iteration, while still maintaining strict correctness and deterministic results. However, as illustrated in Figure 3, when increasing the number of executions per iteration, more and more LPs become idle, either due to a lack of further events, or due to event lists being at capacity. Due to an increase of the deviation of simulation times between LPs, in the optimistic case, the probability of rollbacks may increase as well. Once a new iteration begins, newly created events are considered for execution, increasing the opportunities to execute events in parallel.

In the following, we contrast the simulation steps per iteration for the conservative and optimistic case:

Conservative synchronization first determines the earliest timestamp $t_{\min}$ in the simulation. Events within $[t_{\min}, t_{\min} + $ lookahead$)$ can be executed safely. This is done in one or more executions, each LP processing its earliest event, if any. During each execution, new events may be created, which are appended in an unsorted fashion to the target LP's future event lists (FEL) using atomic operations. Since events

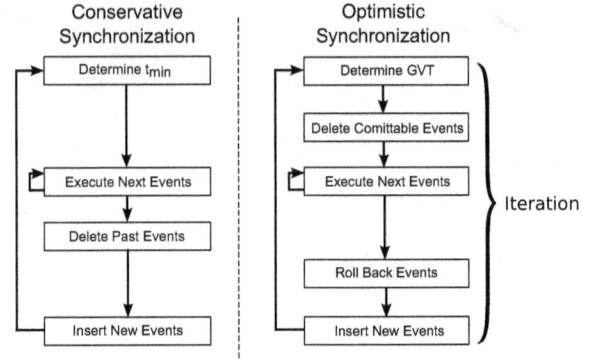

Figure 2: Comparison of the simulation steps during an iteration with conservative and optimistic synchronization.

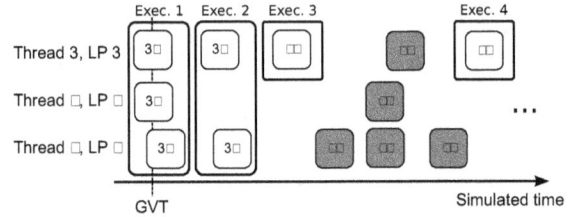

Figure 3: An example of performing multiple executions in one iteration to reduce synchronization overhead. Events grouped in a rectangle are processed in one execution. Since newly created events (gray) are not considered before the next iteration begins, the number of executions per iteration affects both the parallelism and the probability of rollbacks.

are extracted by one thread per queue, atomic operations are not required during extraction. After a number of executions, processed events are deleted from the LPs' FELs. Finally, in preparation for the next iteration, each FEL is sorted, including newly created events.

Optimistic synchronization first calculates the global virtual time (GVT) as a lower bound for future rollbacks. Entries in the event list, state list, and antimessage list with earlier timestamp than the GVT will not be required in any future rollback and are deleted. Now, as in conservative synchronization, LPs process their respective earliest event in parallel. Contrary to conservative synchronization, it is not necessary to limit the consideration of events to a certain range in simulated time. However, we will see in Section 4.1.2 that artificially limiting the optimism can increase performance. As with conservative synchronization, new events are initially appended in an unsorted fashion to the target LPs' event lists. Due to the memory requirements of storing three lists per LP and of storing uncommitted events, there is a need to handle cases where newly created events exceed the capacity of the receiving LP. In such cases, the LP that created the event rolls back its current event and is inactive for the remainder of the iteration.

During the executions within an iteration, the minimum timestamp of any newly received event of each LP is stored. After a number of executions, previously executed events with timestamps larger than or equal to this minimum are rolled back to restore the correctness of the simulation. Finally, the event lists are sorted before a new iteration begins.

To enable a fair comparison between conservative and optimistic synchronization on the GPU, we implemented both mechanisms as part of the same simulator engine, using a shared implementation of event lists, event insertion, earliest timestamp calculation, and so forth. Both t_{min} and GVT are determined by a parallel reduction in logarithmic time. Event handling and list operations are performed by a single thread per LP. Thus, in case threads within a warp perform the same operation, e.g., executing an event of the same type or moving an event, the single-instruction, multiple-data (SIMD) architecture of the GPU is exploited.

3.2 Memory Layout

Due to the substantial cost of dynamic memory allocation on the GPU, all memory is allocated statically during initialization. For each list type (event list, antimessage list, state list), a single array in graphic memory is allocated that holds all LPs' lists. We implemented the LPs' lists as circular buffers (cf. Figure 4). For each LP, we store the offset o_{head} of the first entry, the offset o_{future} of the first entry in the simulated future, the offset $o_{unsorted}$ of the first entry that has not yet been inserted into the sorted part of the list, and the offset o_{next} of the next new entry. The offsets separate the list into past, future, and unsorted entries.

List operations are performed by one GPU thread per list. Removal of the earliest entry from a list can be performed in constant time. Inserting a new entry requires linear time, since all entries with larger timestamps are moved one position towards the end of the list. The large cost for insertion can be tolerated in case each list contains only a relatively small number of entries, which we can strive for by using the massive core counts of the GPU to form extremely small LPs, e.g., of only 1-32 simulated nodes in the case of a network simulation. We investigate the impact of different overall numbers of list entries on the simulation performance in Section 6. An assessment of alternative list implementations is part of our future work.

The simulator design poses no limitations of the memory layout used by models. However, to achieve high performance, dynamic memory allocation should be minimized.

The number of nodes that are aggregated to form an LP (*LP size*) can be adapted by adjusting the LP boundaries in memory and merging or separating events according to the new boundaries. In Figure 5, events are represented by their

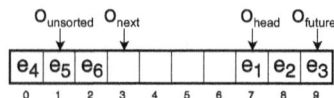

Figure 4: Example of an event list for a single LP. Stored offsets separate past, future and unsorted entries.

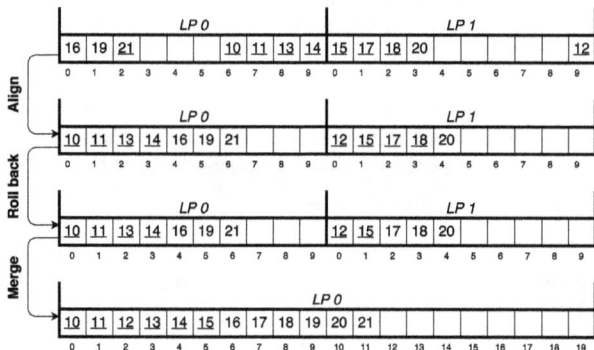

Figure 5: Steps during merging to double the LP size.

timestamps and underlined in case they have already been executed. First, to create space for the merged list, each LP's events are aligned to the beginning of the LP's segment. The events in the merged list must be sorted according to whether they have already been executed, and in timestamp order. To ensure these properties, some LPs may need to perform rollbacks (cf. Appendix A).

The LP size incurs a tradeoff between event insertion overhead and parallelism: a small LP size, e.g., 1 node per LP, leads to small event lists and low overhead for event insertion. At the same time, the probability increases that an LP has no safe event and thus remains idle during an execution.

While with conservative synchronization, the only required list operations are removal of the earliest event and insertion of new events, optimistic synchronization requires event deletion as well: if an LP initiates a rollback, events up to a previous point in simulated time are removed. In case events have been sent since then, antimessages are sent to the receivers of the events. Each antimessage may trigger the deletion of an event. In our implementation, such events are identified using linear search in reverse order during the rollback step and deleted in the insertion step.

4. PARAMETER ANALYSIS AND AUTOTUNING

The GPU-based simulator provides a number of tuning parameters that enable a tradeoff between parallelism and overhead for synchronization and event management. In this section, we study the impact of these parameters on the simulation performance and describe the autotuning approach used to determine a suitable configuration at runtime.

Our measurements system is equipped with 4 12-core Intel Xeon E5-2660 processors (base clock rate: 2.1 GHz, turbo clock rate: 3.3 GHz), 64 GiB of RAM and an NVIDIA GeForce GTX 980 Ti with 6 GiB of RAM and 2816 CUDA cores clocked at up to 1392 MHz. Plotted event rates are averages of 3 runs. 95% confidence intervals are plotted but frequently small enough to be nearly invisible.

4.1 Impact of Parameters

4.1.1 LP Size

On a GPU, typically a much larger number of threads is scheduled than there are physical cores, enabling the GPU's hardware scheduler to perform memory access latency hiding. This has two consequences: first, the large number of threads enables the use of small LPs, e.g., of 1-32 simulated nodes in a network simulation. Second, since the thread count is decoupled from the core count, a suitable LP size cannot be deduced directly from hardware properties.

Figure 6 shows the event rate achieved for the PHOLD model with a network size of 1 048 576 nodes and a population equal to the network size with different LP sizes and conservative synchronization. Initially, events are evenly distributed to the nodes, with timestamps according to the index in each node's queue, i.e., all zero in the cases where the population equals the network size. We can see that with small λ, the LP size has a substantial impact on performance. As discussed in Section 3.1, with lower event density in simulated time, the average number of LPs that have a safe event during an execution decreases. An increase in LP size tends to increase the number of LPs with a safe event at the cost of the increased overheads of larger FELs.

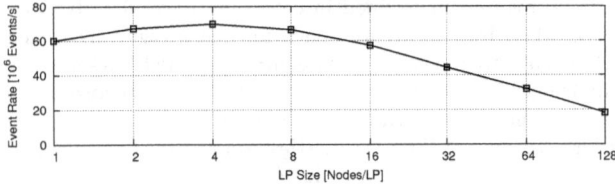

(a) $\lambda = 10^{-2}$

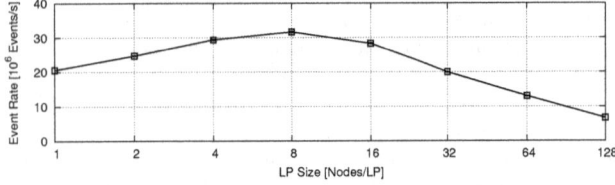

(b) $\lambda = 10^{-4}$

Figure 6: Event rate with different LP sizes for PHOLD using conservative synchronization.

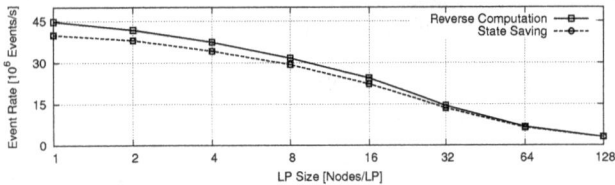

Figure 7: Event rate with different LP sizes for PHOLD with $\lambda = 10^{-2}$ using optimistic synchronization.

With optimistic synchronization, we observed that with these parameters, a one-to-one mapping of nodes to LPs achieves highest performance (cf. Figure 7 for $\lambda = 10^{-2}$). However, when varying the remaining simulator parameters, the optimal LP size varies with the model parameters as well.

4.1.2 Optimism Bound

In its purest form, optimistic synchronization allows for execution of events that lie arbitrarily far in the simulated future. However, with an increasing deviation of current simulation times between LPs, the probability of causality violations increases as well. Hence, as already proposed in early works in the field [27, 24, 30], it can be beneficial to limit the execution of events to timestamps below a certain delta from the GVT. We refer to this delta as the *optimism bound*. Since executing events within [GVT, GVT + lookahead) cannot cause causality violations, suitable optimism bounds are equal to or larger than the lookahead. Figure 8 illustrates the use of an optimism bound.

Figure 9 shows the event rates achieved with different optimism bounds for the PHOLD model with a network size of 1 048 576 nodes and a population of 1 048 576. The optimal optimism bound depends strongly on λ, being around 2 200 units of simulated time with $\lambda = 10^{-2}$ and around 12 000 units with $\lambda = 10^{-4}$. Event rates decline substantially if an exceedingly small or large optimism bound is selected.

4.1.3 Inactivity Threshold

As described in Section 3.1, the simulation proceeds in a sequence of iterations, each of which includes one or more executions of events. If only one execution is performed per iteration, the simulator may perform calculation of GVT or

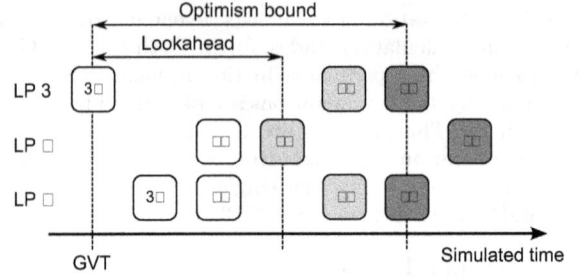

Figure 8: Bounding the optimism in Time Warp. White events cannot cause causality violations and are safe to be processed; light gray events may cause violations; dark gray events are not considered for execution yet.

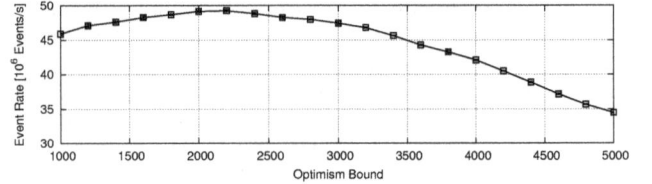

(a) $\lambda = 10^{-2}$

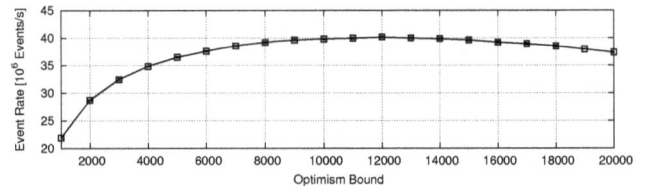

(b) $\lambda = 10^{-4}$

Figure 9: Event rate with different optimism bounds for PHOLD using optimistic synchronization with state saving.

$t_{\min}$, deletion of committable events, roll backs and insertion of new events into lists more frequently than necessary, potentially incurring substantial overhead. However, with increasing numbers of executions in a single iteration, more and more LPs will become inactive due to a lack of events in the current window or within the optimism bound, or due to lists being at capacity. Figure 10 shows the event rates achieved for the PHOLD model with a network size of 1 048 576 nodes and a population of 1 048 576, varying the percentage of inactive LPs (*inactivity threshold*) at which executions for the current iteration are terminated. The LP size was set to 4 nodes per LP. Again, there is a strong dependence on the PHOLD parameter λ. With the relatively large event density in simulated time given by $\lambda = 10^{-2}$, the optimal threshold is around 95%, while with $\lambda = 10^{-4}$, values around 45 60% are optimal. With $\lambda = 10^{-2}$, the average number of executions per iteration increases monotonously from approximately 1 to 9 for thresholds of 0% to 95% and peaks at about 18 for a threshold of 100%.

4.1.4 Block Size

The configured number of CUDA threads per block influences the allocation of the GPUs resources to the scheduled threads. The selection of a suitable block size without prior performance measurements can be nontrivial [29]. Figure 11 shows measurement results for the PHOLD model with a network size of 1 048 576, a population of 1 048 576,

(a) $\lambda = 10^{-2}$

(b) $\lambda = 10^{-4}$

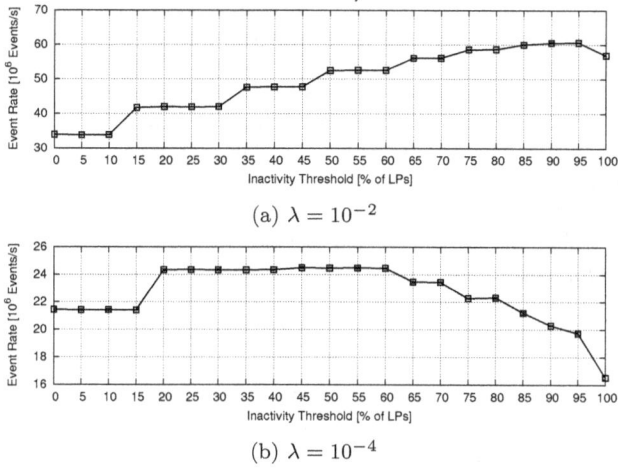

Figure 10: Event rate with different inactivity thresholds for PHOLD using optimistic synchronization with state saving.

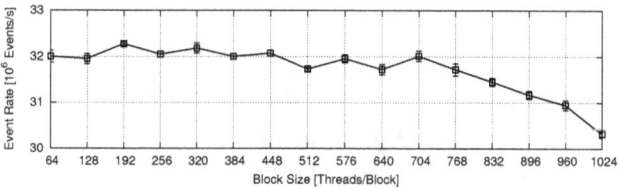

Figure 11: Event rate with different block sizes for PHOLD with $\lambda = 10^{-2}$, optimistic synchronization with state saving.

and $\lambda = 10^{-2}$. Since the event rates for block sizes between 64 and 704 did not vary substantially and since the results for other model parametrizations were similar in shape, we selected a block size of 256 threads for all our experiments.

4.2 Autotuning Procedure

We have identified the LP size, the optimism bound and the number of executions per iteration as three simulator parameters with a strong impact on performance. Optimal values for these parameters depend on the simulation model behavior and thus cannot be determined easily prior to a simulation run. The selection of suitable values is further complicated by the dependence across parameters. Figure 12 shows examples of the effect of two of the considered parameters on the event rate when executing the PHOLD model with a network size and population of 1 048 576.

To determine suitable parameter combinations for different models and model parametrizations, we perform measurements and adaptation at runtime. We apply the Nelder-Mead optimization algorithm [18], which searches heuristically for an extremum of a non-linear function without the need for calculating derivatives. The algorithm considers $(n + 1)$ points of an n-dimensional objective function and iteratively replaces the point with the worst function value with a new point with a better function value.

For each new point, the simulator parameters are adapted and the resulting simulator performance is measured. The duration of each measurement is a model-dependent tradeoff between the measurement accuracy and the cost of executing at suboptimal parameter combinations. At each parameter combination, after a warm up time of 200ms of wall-clock time, we measured event rates averaging over 300ms.

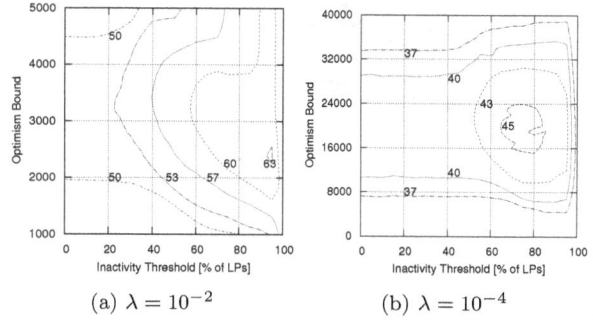

(a) $\lambda = 10^{-2}$ (b) $\lambda = 10^{-4}$

Figure 12: Contour graph of event rates for PHOLD, optimistic synchronization with state saving. The dependency between optimal parameter settings and the variation across model configurations illustrates the need for autotuning.

5. REVERSE COMPUTATION

A major concern in optimistic synchronization is the cost of rollbacks. In this section, we describe how XORWOW, the default random number generator in NVIDIA CUDA, can be reversed, i.e., how a previous generator state can be derived solely from the current state.

Although XORWOW has been shown to fail several of the statistical tests of the TESTU01 suite [12, 26], it is used as the default random number generator in CUDA. Some previous works applied reverse computation to combined linear congruential generators [6]. Reversal of the Mersenne Twister RNG [15] has also been described previously[3].

5.1 Reversal of CUDA RNG

As proposed by Marsaglia [14], a pseudo-random number generated by XORWOW is the sum of a number generated by an Xorshift generator and a number generated by a Weyl sequence. Xorshift generates the next random number by calculating the exclusive OR of bit-shifted versions of previously generated numbers according to:

$$X_n = X_{n-1} \quad (X_{n-1} << 4) \quad X_{n-4} \quad (X_{n-4} >> 2)$$
$$(X_{n-4} << 1) \quad ((X_{n-4} >> 2) << 1).$$

The Weyl sequence used in XORWOW is defined by the equation
$$Y_n = Y_{n-1} + 362437 \bmod 2^{32}.$$

In CUDA, the mutable part of the RNG state for XORWOW is defined by an unsigned 32 bit integer d and an array v of 5 unsigned 32 bit integers, i.e., 24 bytes in total.

CUDA provides a function `curand_init()` to skip an arbitrary offset in the generated sequence. The number of clock cycles required to execute this function for XORWOW depends logarithmically on the offset. On an NVIDIA GeForce GTX 980 Ti, setting the offset to 2^{18} and 2^{62} required 1.12×10^7 and 1.33×10^8 clock cycles, respectively. At the graphics card's maximum clock rate of 1392 MHz, this translates to 8.1ms and 96ms. Since the target offset in the random number sequence required by rollbacks increases over the course of a simulation, `curand_init()` is too expensive to be a viable alternative to reverse computation.

Figure 13 illustrates the logical operations and state variables of XORWOW. Here, we sketch the basic idea of the reversal process on the basis of the values t and r marked in

---

[3]https://jazzy.id.au/2010/09/22/cracking_random_number_generators_part_3.html

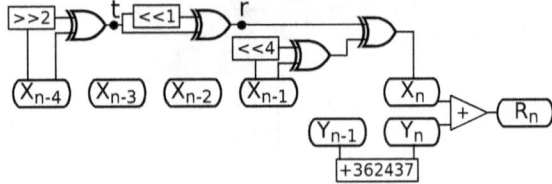

Figure 13: Logical operations and state variables of the XORWOW random number generator.

the figure. The description of the overall reversal procedure is included in the appendix. The goal is to calculate all bits t_i of t using only the bits r_i of r. To simplify the example, we treat t and r as 4 bit values. During forward generation, the relationship between r and t is $r = t \oplus (t << 1)$. On the bit level, we have:

$$\begin{array}{cccc} t_1 & t_2 & t_3 & t_4 \\ t_2 & t_3 & t_4 & 0 \\ \hline r_1 & r_2 & r_3 & r_4 \end{array}$$

During reversal, the goal is to determine t from r. First, obviously, $t_4 = r_4$. The remaining bits can be determined in an iterative fashion: $t_i = r_i \oplus t_{i+1}, i \in \{1, 2, 3\}$. The same idea is applied to reverse all other Xorshift operations of XORWOW. Since the Weyl sequence used in XORWOW involves only a simple addition, its reversal is trivial. The resulting full reversal procedure is described in Appendix B.

Figure 14 compares the time required by forward generation and reversal of $1\,048\,576$ random numbers per thread, varying the number of parallel threads (at least 10 repetitions, 95% confidence intervals). On our test system, reversal of a random number generation is around a factor of 12 to 16 slower than forward generation, independently of the number of parallel threads. Using 1 thread, our test system performed about 5.95×10^7 generations or about 3.70×10^6 reversals per second, while with $1\,048\,576$ threads, 3.84×10^{11} generations or 2.61×10^{10} reversals per second were achieved.

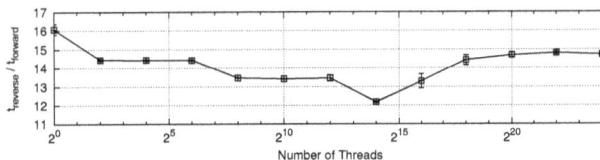

Figure 14: Comparison of time required for $1\,048\,576$ forward random number generations (t_{forward}) or reversals (t_{reverse}) per thread using the XORWOW generator.

5.2 Memory Savings

The state of the XORWOW generator in CUDA is comprised of 24 bytes of mutable state and 24 bytes holding parameters for generating numbers following the normal or Poisson distribution. In the PHOLD model, an event requires 16 bytes of memory. Since the system state of the PHOLD model is defined solely by the RNG states of all nodes, reverse computation enables us to eliminate the state list and the antimessage list entirely. However, past events must still be stored until the GVT is updated.

In the peer-to-peer network model, a node's state is defined by its RNG state, the state of any current lookup, i.e., the number of in-flight messages and the list of closest nodes to the desired key, as well as statistics such as the number of executed lookups. Overall, each state comprises 144 bytes. Events hold data associated with requests and responses and comprise 52 bytes. With reverse computation, each state can be reduced to 76 bytes. The remaining state variables can be determined computationally, e.g., the number of executed lookups is decremented in case an event representing a final response message is rolled back.

6. PERFORMANCE EVALUATION

Our performance measurements of the simulator implementation focus on the following questions:

- Does the autotuning mechanism determine parameter combinations close to the optimum?
- To what degree does the simulation performance benefit from reverse computation?
- How does the overall performance of the optimistic simulator compare to its conservative counterpart?

The measurements were performed on an NVIDIA GeForce GTX 980 Ti of the system specified in Section 4. The host memory usage was below 100 MiB. One CPU core was fully utilized for performing CUDA API calls. The CPU usage can be reduced at some cost in performance by using interrupts instead of polling to interact with the GPU.

6.1 Parameter Autotuning

To study the effectiveness of the parameter autotuning, we compare event rates achieved using parameter autotuning to the results of optimal parameter settings. We first performed a parameter sweep to determine the combination of LP size, optimism bound, and number of executions per iteration that achieved the highest event rate. The results from these runs are compared to runs using autotuning. This process was repeated for different values of λ and for the three considered synchronization schemes during brief simulation runs spanning 10^9 events, or between approximately 10s and 30s of wall-clock time. Table 1 compares the results of the runs with the highest average event rate ("Optimal Param. Rate") with the results using autotuning when considering the highest event rate during any measurement interval of 300ms ("Adaptive Peak Rate") and the average over a simulation run of 10^9 events ("Adaptive Avg. Rate").

We can see that the autotuning process succeeds in selecting suitable parameter combinations. Due to fluctuations in event rates, the adaptive peak rate occasionally even exceeds the average rate at the optimal parameter combination. Since during the autotuning process, some time is spent in non-optimal parameter combinations, the average rate is significantly lower than the peak rate. This effect diminishes when increasing the simulation duration. Averaged over 10^9 events, autotuning attained 78.29% or more of the event rate of the optimal parameter combination.

6.2 Synchronization Approaches

The overall event rate using the different simulator variants was evaluated for the PHOLD and peer-to-peer network models in simulations spanning 5×10^9 and 1×10^9 events, respectively. Runs with very low event density in simulated time ($\lambda = 10^{-4}$ with $16\,384$ nodes for PHOLD and $D_{\max} = 10$min for the peer-to-peer network model) were limited to 2×10^9 and 2×10^8 events. For PHOLD, the population was chosen equal to the network size. The measurement results are shown in Figure 15. With $\lambda = 1$

	$\lambda = 1$	$\lambda = 10^{-2}$	$\lambda = 10^{-4}$
Optimal Param. Rate	93.00	85.96	35.95
Adaptive Peak Rate	90.84	82.78	34.74
Adaptive Avg. Rate	75.16	74.73	31.98
Percentage of Opt.	80.82%	86.94%	88.96%

(a) Conservative synchronization.

	$\lambda = 1$	$\lambda = 10^{-2}$	$\lambda = 10^{-4}$
Optimal Param. Rate	63.47	63.16	45.45
Adaptive Peak Rate	65.07	63.86	46.60
Adaptive Avg. Rate	55.66	56.87	37.11
Percentage of Opt.	87.69%	90.04%	81.65%

(b) Optimistic synchronization with state saving.

	$\lambda = 1$	$\lambda = 10^{-2}$	$\lambda = 10^{-4}$
Optimal Param. Rate	84.24	85.35	58.46
Adaptive Peak Rate	84.17	84.47	57.33
Adaptive Avg. Rate	70.92	68.91	45.77
Percentage of Opt.	84.19%	80.74%	78.29%

(c) Optimistic synchronization with reverse computation.

Table 1: Comparison of event rates [10^6 events/s] using the optimal parameter configuration or autotuning for PHOLD with a network size and population of $1\,048\,576$.

and $\lambda = 10^{-2}$, for most parameter combinations, a modest increase in event rate up to a factor of 1.3 is achieved using reverse computation compared with conservative synchronization. With network sizes of $524\,288$ nodes and above, conservative synchronization outperforms reverse computation. In these cases of high event density, the overhead for maintaining additional lists and performing rollbacks in optimistic synchronization outweighs any gain in parallelism. In contrast, with $\lambda = 10^{-4}$, the event density is low enough so that optimistic synchronization with reverse computation substantially outperforms conservative synchronization for all considered network sizes, by a factor of up to 3.0. Reverse computation consistently achieved higher event rates than state saving, by a factor of up to 1.3. State saving still significantly outperformed conservative synchronization for low event densities or small networks, by a factor of up to 2.9. Figure 16 shows the comparison for the peer-to-peer network model, varying the maximum delay between key-value lookups by the individual nodes. LPs were formed by merging neighboring queues in memory without consideration of the network topology. Optimistic synchronization with reverse computation consistently outperformed conservative synchronization, by a factor of up to 3.6. For nearly all parameter combinations, reverse computation achieved higher event rates than state saving, by a factor of up to 1.2. Again, state saving still consistently outperformed conservative synchronization, by a factor of up to 3.4.

As expected, due to the larger complexity of the model compared to PHOLD, the overall event rates with the peer-to-peer network model are lower. In fact, for all three synchronization approaches, the event rates achieved for $D_{\max} = 10\text{min}$ and small network sizes seem to be within the range achievable by sequential CPU-based simulators. However, optimistic synchronization reduces the event density required to efficiently execute models on the GPU. The size of the confidence intervals depends chiefly on the selection of simulator parameters through autotuning, which varies to different degrees depending on the model parametrization.

Table 2 lists an example of the runtime spent on the five core simulation steps with the different synchronization approaches for runs spanning 10^{10} events each. Conservative

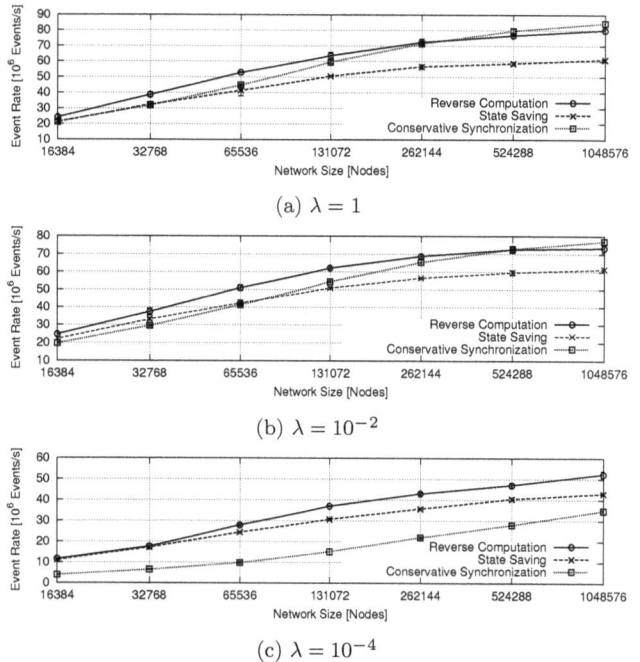

(a) $\lambda = 1$

(b) $\lambda = 10^{-2}$

(c) $\lambda = 10^{-4}$

Figure 15: Overall performance comparison for PHOLD.

	Conserv.	State Saving	Rev. Comp.
$t_{\min}$ or GVT	2.99 ± 0.03s	2.38 ± 0.19s	2.45 ± 0.26s
Delete Events	7.18 ± 0.02s	10.08 ± 0.62s	9.96 ± 0.92s
Handle Events	84.69 ± 0.25s	116.12 ± 0.86s	76.77 ± 0.78s
Rollbacks	N/A	2.17 ± 0.37s	2.73 ± 0.64s
Insert Events	15.25 ± 0.03s	15.98 ± 0.40s	16.38 ± 0.61s
Other	2.03 ± 0.04s	1.66 ± 0.13s	1.53 ± 0.13s
Total	112.14 ± 0.33s	148.39 ± 1.56s	109.82 ± 1.53s

Table 2: Composition of runtime for PHOLD with a network size and population of $1\,048\,576$ and $\lambda = 10^{-2}$.

synchronization and reverse computation spend less time on deleting events than state saving, since only one list must be managed and past events can be deleted immediately. Further, handling events is substantially less expensive than with state saving, since no state information must be stored. As in most above results, reverse computation achieves the lowest runtime overall, since the cost of rollbacks is amortized through higher parallelism during event handling. The average number of events processed per execution for conservative synchronization, state saving and reverse computation was about 1.17×10^5, 1.28×10^5 and 1.69×10^5.

Figure 17 shows the effect of varying the population at a fixed network size of $131\,072$ with $\lambda = 10^{-2}$. The results show the tradeoff between parallelism and costs of list operations: the event rate increases with larger event density, since more events tend to be processed per execution. However, around a population of $1\,048\,576$, the costs for list operations begin to outweigh further increases in parallelism. With the given combination of model parameters, conservative synchronization achieves higher event rates than reverse computation at populations of $1\,048\,576$ and above.

To summarize our measurements, we make two main observations: first, reverse computation outperformed state saving in nearly all cases. Second, optimistic synchronization outperformed conservative synchronization in nearly all cases. Particular benefits are seen at low event densities.

(a) $D_{\max} = 10\text{s}$

(b) $D_{\max} = 1\text{min}$

(c) $D_{\max} = 10\text{min}$

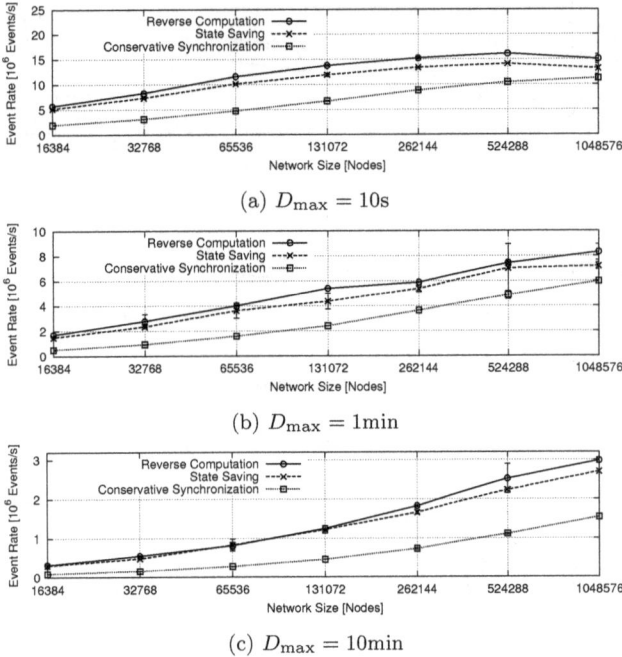

Figure 16: Overall performance comparison of the simulator variants for the peer-to-peer network model.

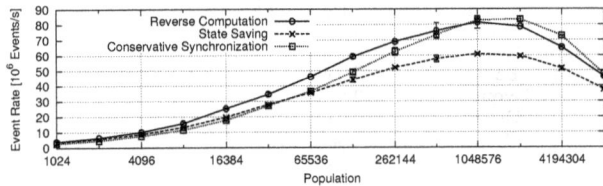

Figure 17: Event rate when varying the population for the PHOLD model with a network size of $131\,072$ and $\lambda = 10^{-2}$.

7. DISCUSSION

A number of avenues in the design of fully GPU-based simulators remain to be explored:

Asynchronous execution: Similarly to most previous GPU-based approaches, the LPs in our simulator execute synchronously. Zhu et al. have previously shown that an asynchronous approach is feasible in a conservative context when exploiting properties of logic simulation models [33]. Since synchronous simulations may frequently force LPs to wait for other LPs to progress, an asynchronous approach may unlock further parallelism in the optimistic case as well.

Memory distribution: We assumed that each LP is assigned the same overall amount of memory for its lists. Further, the memory allocated for each of the three lists was the same across all LP. Since the list size affects blocking of LPs and thus the required frequency of GVT calculation, a dynamic adaptation of list sizes may increase performance.

List implementation: One of the focal points of existing works on fully GPU-based simulation has been the FEL or event list implementation. Here, we use simple per-LP circular buffers with constant-time removal and linear-time insertion of events. In our evaluation, we have seen the resulting significant dependence of the simulation performance on the lists' loads. Insertion overhead and parallelism is balanced by dynamically resizing LPs. We observed a substantial de-

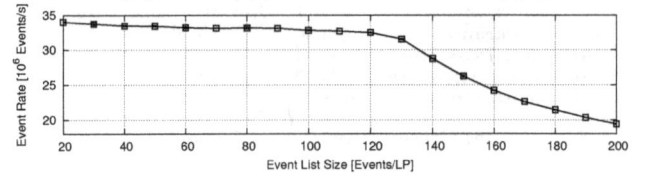

Figure 18: PHOLD event rate with different per-LP event list allocation sizes with a network size and population of $1\,048\,576$, $\lambda = 10^{-2}$, 1 node per LP using state saving. Event rates decline strongly when allocating space for more than 128 events per LP, or 2 GiB of memory for all event lists.

crease in performance when increasing the combined size for the FELs or event lists beyond around 2 GiB, e.g., from an event rate of about 3.2×10^7 events per second at 2 GiB to fewer than 2.0×10^7 events per second at 3.2 GiB (cf. Figure 18). The substantial drop-off in performance beyond specific overall allocation sizes given highly scattered memory accesses seems to be due to details of the translation lookaside buffer implementation of current NVIDIA cards[4]. Potentially, an alternative list implementation may reduce this effect. Our future work includes a systematic comparison of FEL or event list implementations on the GPU.

Inter-GPU communication: Since our focus is on models associated with fine-grained events, we minimize data transfers between host and graphics memory by executing the simulation on a single GPU, achieving PHOLD event rates of up to 8.14×10^7 events per second. The highest PHOLD event rates events rates we are aware of have been reported by Barnes et al. [3]. For similar PHOLD parametrizations to our experiments, event rates were between one and two magnitudes larger than those reported by us. However, these results were achieved on a system with $32\,768$ CPU cores, in contrast to the single GPU used in our experiments. For larger PHOLD instances and when parametrizing PHOLD so that communication is reduced, up to 5.04×10^{11} events per second were reported by Barnes et al. on a system using about 2 million CPU cores. To enable GPU-based simulations at larger scale, future work could explore whether some of the benefits of fully GPU-based simulation can be maintained while applying multiple GPUs using direct inter-GPU communication and synchronization.

Real-world models: Finally, a general open issue in fully GPU-based simulation is the viability of the approach to execute models of the complexity found in widely used CPU-based simulators. Although the considered peer-to-peer network model goes beyond the simplistic assumptions in the PHOLD model, many realistic models may be comprised of events whose costs due to branching and memory accesses dwarf the gains through parallelization in the GPU context. Hence, feasibility studies are required before more comprehensive porting efforts are undertaken.

8. CONCLUSION

The proposed fully GPU-based implementation of Time Warp achieves average event rates of up to 81.4 million events per second on a commodity GPU. Our evaluation shows that the optimistic synchronization substantially outperforms conservative synchronization in nearly all consid-

---

[4]https://devtalk.nvidia.com/default/topic/
878455/cuda-programming-and-performance/
gtx750ti-and-buffers-gt-1gb-on-win7/1

ered scenarios, by a maximum factor of 3.6. In particular, optimistic synchronization improves the viability of GPU-based simulation for models with comparatively low event density. Due to a reduction in costly accesses to graphics memory, reverse computation outperformed rollbacks based on state saving by a factor of up to 1.3. Further, autotuning at runtime successfully approximates the performance achieved with optimal simulator parameter combinations.

We consider evaluations of the suitability of different realistic model types for execution using a fully GPU-based simulator the most pressing issue for future work. We hope that the publicly available simulator code will be used by the community to further explore the possibilities and limitations of fully GPU-based discrete-event simulation.

9. REFERENCES

[1] P. Andelfinger and H. Hartenstein. Exploiting the Parallelism of Large-Scale Application-Layer Networks by Adaptive GPU-Based Simulation. In *Proc. of the Winter Simul. Conf.*, pages 3471–3482. IEEE, 2014.

[2] P. Andelfinger, J. Mittag, and H. Hartenstein. GPU-Based Architectures and Their Benefit for Accurate and Efficient Wireless Network Simulations. In *Proc. of the Int'l Symposium on Modeling, Analysis and Simulation of Computer and Telecommunication Systems*, pages 421–424. IEEE, 2011.

[3] P. D. Barnes, Jr., C. D. Carothers, D. R. Jefferson, and J. M. LaPre. Warp Speed: Executing Time Warp on 1,966,080 Cores. In *Conf. on Principles of Advanced Discrete Simulation*, pages 327–336. ACM, 2013.

[4] B. Ben Romdhanne. *Large-Scale Network Simulation over Heterogeneous Computing Architecture.* Dissertation, EURECOM, 2013.

[5] A. Biswas and R. Fujimoto. Profiling Energy Consumption in Distributed Simulations. In *Proceedings of the Conf. on Principles of Advanced Discrete Simulation*, pages 201–209. ACM, 2016.

[6] C. Carothers, K. Perumalla, and R. Fujimoto. Efficient Optimistic Parallel Simulations Using Reverse Computation. *ACM Transactions on Modeling and Computer Simulation*, pages 224–253, 1999.

[7] S. Das, R. Fujimoto, K. Panesar, D. Allison, and M. Hybinette. GTW: a Time Warp System for Shared Memory Multiprocessors. In *Proc. of the Winter Simulation Conference*, pages 1332–1339. Society for Computer Simulation International, 1994.

[8] R. Fujimoto. Parallel and Distributed Simulation. In *Proceedings of the Winter Simulation Conference*, pages 45–59. IEEE Press, 2015.

[9] R. M. Fujimoto. Performance Measurements of Distributed Simulation Strategies. Technical report, DTIC Document, 1987.

[10] D. R. Jefferson. Virtual Time. *ACM Transactions on Programming Lang. and Systems*, 7(3):404–425, 1985.

[11] G. Kunz, D. Schemmel, J. Gross, and K. Wehrle. Multi-Level Parallelism for Time- and Cost-Efficient Parallel Discrete Event Simulation on GPUs. In *Proceedings of the Workshop on Principles of Advanced and Distributed Simulation*, pages 23–32. IEEE Computer Society, 2012.

[12] P. L'Ecuyer and R. Simard. TestU01: A C Library for Empirical Testing of Random Number Generators.

[13] X. Li, W. Cai, and S. J. Turner. GPU Accelerated Three-Stage Execution Model for Event-Parallel Simulation. In *Conf. on Principles of Advanced Discrete Simulation*, pages 57–66. ACM, 2013.

[14] G. Marsaglia. Xorshift RNGs. *Journal of Statistical Software*, 8(14):1–6, 2003.

[15] M. Matsumoto and T. Nishimura. Mersenne Twister: a 623-Dimensionally Equidistributed Uniform Pseudo-Random Number Generator. *ACM Transactions on Modeling and Computer Simulation (TOMACS)*, 8(1):3–30, 1998.

[16] P. Maymounkov and D. Mazieres. Kademlia: A Peer-to-Peer Information System Based on the XOR Metric. *Peer-to-Peer Systems*, pages 53–65, 2002.

[17] M. Nanjundappa, A. Kaushik, H. D. Patel, and S. K. Shukla. Accelerating SystemC Simulations Using GPUs. In *International High Level Design Validation and Test Workshop*, pages 132–139. IEEE, 2012.

[18] J. A. Nelder and R. Mead. A Simplex Method for Function Minimization. *The Computer Journal*, 7(4):308–313, 1965.

[19] D. M. Nicol. The Cost of Conservative Synchronization in Parallel Discrete Event Simulations. *Journal of the ACM*, 40(2):304–333, 1993.

[20] NVIDIA Corporation. *NVIDIA CUDA C Programming Guide.* Version 7.0, NVIDIA Corporation, 2015.

[21] H. Park and P. A. Fishwick. A GPU-Based Application Framework Supporting Fast Discrete-Event Simulation. *Simulation*, 86(10):613–628, 2010.

[22] K. S. Perumalla. Discrete-Event Execution Alternatives on General Purpose Graphical Processing Units (GPGPUs). In *Proceedings of the Workshop on Principles of Advanced and Distributed Simulation*, pages 74–81. IEEE Computer Society, 2006.

[23] S. Raghav, M. Ruggiero, A. Marongiu, C. Pinto, D. Atienza, and L. Benini. GPU Acceleration for Simulating Massively Parallel Many-Core Platforms. *IEEE Transactions on Parallel and Distributed Systems*, 26(5):1336–1349, 2015.

[24] P. L. Reiher, F. Wieland, and D. Jefferson. Limitation of Optimism in the Time Warp Operating System. In *Proceedings of the Winter Simulation Conference*, pages 765–770. ACM, 1989.

[25] R. Rönngren and R. Ayani. A Comparative Study of Parallel and Sequential Priority Queue Algorithms. *ACM Transactions on Modeling and Computer Simulation*, 7(2):157–209, 1997.

[26] M. Saito and M. Matsumoto. A Deviation of CURAND: Standard Pseudorandom Number Generator in CUDA for GPGPU. In *Proceedings of 10th Int'l Conf. on Monte Carlo and Quasi-Monte Carlo Methods in Scientific Computing*, 2012.

[27] L. M. Sokol, D. P. Briscoe, and A. P. Wieland. MTW: A Strategy for Scheduling Discrete Simulation Events for Concurrent Execution. In *SCS Multiconference on Distributed Simulation*, pages 34–44, 1988.

[28] B. P. Swenson. *Techniques to Improve the Performance of Large-Scale Discrete-Event*

ACM Trans. on Math. Software, 33(4):22, 2007.

Simulation. Dissertation, Georgia Institute of Technology, 2015.

[29] Y. Torres, A. Gonzalez-Escribano, and D. R. Llanos. uBench: Exposing the Impact of CUDA Block Geometry in Terms of Performance. *Journal of Supercomputing*, 65(3):1150–1163, 2013.

[30] S. J. Turner and M. Q. Xu. *Performance Evaluation of the Bounded Time Warp Algorithm*. University of Exeter, Department of Computer Science, 1990.

[31] J. G. Vaucher and P. Duval. A Comparison of Simulation Event List Algorithms. *Communications of the ACM*, 18(4):223–230, 1975.

[32] T. Wenjie, Y. Yiping, and Z. Feng. An Expansion-Aided Synchronous Conservative Time Management Algorithm on GPU. In *Proceedings of the Conference on Principles of Advanced Discrete Simulation*, pages 367–372. ACM, 2013.

[33] Y. Zhu, B. Wang, and Y. Deng. Massively Parallel Logic Simulation with GPUs. *ACM Trans. on Design Automation of Electronic Systems*, 16(3):29, 2011.

APPENDIX

A. ROLLBACKS WHEN MERGING LPS

Figure 19 illustrates a situation where merging without a prior rollback leads to an incorrect result: since the earliest future event of LP 0 has a timestamp of 16 and LP 1 has already executed an event at timestamp 18, two past events with timestamps 17 and 18 are placed before the future event at timestamp 16. Such violations can be avoided by a rollback that ensures that no LP has past events with timestamps greater than or equal to the next future event of the respective other LP. The above describes the minimum requirement for rollbacks before merging. In our implementation, since the LP size is only changed infrequently, all LPs are simply rolled back to the GVT before merging. Finally, two lists are merged by iteratively selecting the event with the earliest timestamp and lowest originating LP from the two lists. Since all past events in the event lists are rolled back, the state lists and antimessage lists are empty and can be merged simply by adjusting their offsets in memory.

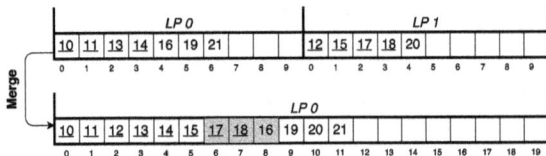

Figure 19: Invalid ordering of list entries when omitting rollback before merging.

B. REVERSAL OF XORWOW IN CUDA

Listing 1 shows the forward random number generator code for XORWOW in CUDA 7.5.

Reversing d is straightforward: d is simply decremented by the constant 362437. Reversal of $v[1]$ through $v[4]$ is achieved by assigning the current value with the next smaller index, i.e., $v'[i] = v[i-1]$ with $i \in \{1,2,3,4\}$. To reverse $v[0]$, we start with the last occurrence of t in Listing 1:

$$v[4] = v'[4] \oplus (v'[4] << 4) \oplus t \oplus (t << 1)$$

where $v'[4]$ denotes the old value of $v[4]$ and $\oplus$ denotes the XOR operation. Since the old value of $v[4]$ is the new value

Listing 1: Implementation of XORWOW in the NVIDIA CUDA Toolkit 7.5 (`curand_kernel.h`).

```
unsigned int
curand(curandStateXORWOW_t *state) {
    unsigned int t = (state->v[0] ^
                     (state->v[0] >> 2));
    state->v[0] = state->v[1];
    state->v[1] = state->v[2];
    state->v[2] = state->v[3];
    state->v[3] = state->v[4];
    state->v[4] = (state->v[4] ^
                  (state->v[4] << 4)) ^
                  (t ^ (t << 1));
    state->d += 362437;
    return state->v[4] + state->d; }
```

of $v[3]$, we replace $v'[4]$ with $v[3]$:

$$v[4] = v[3] \oplus (v[3] << 4) \oplus t \oplus (t << 1)$$

Thus, we have:

$$t \oplus (t << 1) = v[4] \oplus v[3] \oplus (v[3] << 4)$$

We define $r := t \oplus (t << 1)$ and let r_i denote the i-th bit of r and let t_i denote the i-th bit of t. Then, we have:

$$r_i = t_i \oplus t_{i+1}, i \in \{1,2,\ldots,31\}$$
$$r_{32} = t_{32} \oplus 0 = t_{32}$$

The bits of t can be calculated as follows:

$$t_{32} = r_{32}$$
$$t_{31} = r_{31} \oplus t_{32} = r_{31} \oplus r_{32}$$
$$t_{30} = r_{30} \oplus t_{31} = r_{30} \oplus r_{31} \oplus r_{32}$$
$$\ldots$$
$$t_1 = r_1 \oplus t_2 = r_1 \oplus r_2 \oplus r_3 \oplus \ldots \oplus r_{32}$$

Let v_i denote the i-th bit of v'[0], the old value of v[0]. We have:

$$t_1 = v_1 \oplus 0 = v_1; t_2 = v_2 \oplus 0 = v_2$$
$$t_i = v_i \oplus v_{i-2}; i \in \{3,4,\ldots,32\}$$

Finally, the bits of $v'[0]$ can be calculated as follows:

$$v_1 = t_1; v_2 = t_2$$
$$v_3 = v_1 \oplus t_3 = t_1 \oplus t_3$$
$$v_4 = v_2 \oplus t_4 = t_2 \oplus t_4$$
$$v_5 = v_3 \oplus t_5 = t_1 \oplus t_3 \oplus t_5$$
$$v_6 = v_4 \oplus t_6 = t_2 \oplus t_4 \oplus t_6$$
$$\ldots$$
$$v_{31} = v_{29} \oplus t_{31} = t_1 \oplus t_3 \oplus t_5 \oplus \ldots \oplus t_{31}$$
$$v_{32} = v_{30} \oplus t_{32} = t_2 \oplus t_4 \oplus t_6 \oplus \ldots \oplus t_{32}$$

Listing 2 shows our CUDA implementation of the reversal.

Listing 2: CUDA implementation of the reversal function for XORWOW.

```
__device__ void
curand_reverse(curandStateXORWOW_t *state) {
    unsigned int r = state->v[4] ^
        state->v[3] ^ (state->v[3] << 4);
    unsigned int t = 0;
    for (int i = 0; i < 32; i++) {
        t = t ^ r; r = r << 1;
    }
    unsigned int v0 = 0;
    for (int i = 0; i < 32; i += 2) {
        v0 = v0 ^ t; t = t >> 2;
    }
    state->v[4] = state->v[3];
    state->v[3] = state->v[2];
    state->v[2] = state->v[1];
    state->v[1] = state->v[0];
    state->v[0] = v0;
    state->d -= 362437; }
```

Performance Characterization of Parallel Discrete Event Simulation on Knights Landing Processor

Barry Williams
Binghamton University
barry@cs.binghamton.edu

Dmitry Ponomarev
Binghamton University
dima@cs.binghamton.edu

Nael Abu-Ghazaleh
UC Riverside
naelag@ucr.edu

Philip Wilsey
University of Cincinnati
philip.wilsey@uc.edu

ABSTRACT

Performance and scalability of Parallel Discrete Event Simulation (PDES) is often limited by fine-grain communication, especially in execution environments with high communication cost. However, the low cost of on-chip communication in emerging many-core processors offers a promise to substantially alleviate conventional PDES bottlenecks. In this paper, we present a detailed evaluation and characterization of multi-threaded ROSS simulator on Intel's Knights Landing (KNL) processor. KNL is the second generation of the Intel Xeon Phi family of processors offering significant architecture improvements including 64 out-of-order multithreaded cores, sharing of some levels of the cache hierarchy among the cores, fast 2D mesh interconnect network and the ability to reconfigure the processor to support various clustering modes.

We analyze the performance and scalability of ROSS simulator on KNL processor under different thread counts, communication patterns, event processing granularities, synchronization periods, thread placement policies, and workload partitioning schemes. We conclude that within a single KNL processor, up to 2X performance improvement can be achieved compared to commodity Xeon multicore processors. We show that in most cases the performance of ROSS scales well with the best results achieved when thread affinity is assigned, CPU cores are evenly loaded, cache sharing is exploited and communication is limited to small clusters of cores.

Keywords

Parallel Discrete Event Simulation, Intel Xeon Phi, Knights Landing, Manycore Architectures, Performance

1. INTRODUCTION

Parallel Discrete Event Simulation (PDES) is a fine-grain communication-dominated application that has been diffi-

SIGSIM-PADS 17, May 24 26, 2017, Singapore.

© 2017 ACM. ISBN 978-1-4503-4489-0/17/05. . . $15.00

DOI: http://dx.doi.org/10.1145/3064911.3064929

cult to scale beyond a modest number of computing nodes, despite the presence of abundant parallelism in many models. Earlier efforts to scale PDES were limited by high communication latencies in traditional cluster computing environments [1, 2, 3]. The advent of multi-core and many-core processors and systems that use these processors as building blocks led to several more recent research efforts to accelerate PDES on these emerging platforms. For example, Bauer et al. demonstrated scalable PDES on IBM Blue-Gene's supercomputer [4]. Recent work also investigated PDES performance and scalability on multi-core systems such as Intel's Core i7, AMD Magny-cours [5, 6], and the Tilera architecture [7].

A recent trend in computer architecture is the emergence of many-core processors that feature several tens of simple cores integrated on the same chip. A prominent example of such architecture is the Intel Xeon Phi family of processors [8]. Unlike other specialized accelerators, such as the Tilera processor [9] or General Purpose Graphical Processing Units (GPGPUs), the Xeon Phi is similar in the core architecture to standard x86 processors, allowing the use of the rich tool chains and programming environments developed for x86 ecosystem, thus facilitating faster design and deployment of applications.

The first generation of Xeon Phi, called the Knights Corner (KC) microarchitecture, was implemented as an accelerator card interfaced to the rest of the system using PCIe interconnect. To run applications on KC, they have to be explicitly moved to the accelerator and the amount of available memory is limited to what is provisioned on the card - typically 8 or 16GB. The study of [10] investigated performance and scalability of PDES (using multi-threaded ROSS simulator as a vehicle) on KC-based platform. Given the limitations of the KC architecture, the results reported in [10] showed comparable performance to commodity systems. This is true for most simulation scenarios including the ones with a small percentage of events generated remotely. The performance advantage of KC was demonstrated only when the vector units were fully utilized. The reasons for the lack of scalability are the memory limitations, slow in-order individual cores, and the absence of shared caches, requiring memory access for every cross-core communication.

At the end of 2016, Intel released the second generation of the Xeon Phi family, called Knights Landing (KNL). The

KNL microarchitecture and organization are significantly different and more advanced than the KC microarchitecture. First, the KNL processor is implemented as the main CPU in the system and programs executing on it have access to the entire system memory, including the disk. Second, the out-of-order execution capability with branch prediction was added to individual cores, thus alleviating the computational bottleneck of slow in-order cores of KC. Third, neighboring cores in KNL share their L2 cache (which acts as the last-level cache in this system), thus allowing threads executing on these "buddy cores" to access their shared data through the L2 cache and avoid expensive memory accesses.

These important new features of KNL make it imperative to investigate, characterize and understand PDES performance and behavior on this architecture and contrast it with the earlier results obtained for KC processors. Our goal in this paper is to understand how the new features of KNL impact PDES performance under different conditions, execution scenarios and parameter settings.

We pursue these investigations via experiments running ROSS parallel discrete event simulation kernel [11] on KNL processor. For our experiments, we use a multithreaded version of ROSS [5], where the simulation processes have been replaced with threads communicating directly through shared memory without relying on MPI-based communication. Previous studies demonstrated that this variant of ROSS is more efficient compared to the MPI-based version as it reduced the amount of data copying in the course of communication and takes more direct advantages of available shared cache hierarchy (the L2 caches shared by the buddy cores in the case of KNL). Our goal in this paper is to determine conditions under which PDES performance can scale up with the number of cores on a single KNL node, which is capable of executing up to 256 threads in total - 4 threads on each of the 64 cores. We also aim to understand performance bottlenecks and consider possible approaches for future work that can address these bottlenecks.

The main contributions and the key conclusions of this paper are:

- **KNL offers significant performance gains for PDES**: Our study represents only the first look at using KNL architecture for executing PDES applications, yet we demonstrated promising results. If the issues of core loading, model partitioning and thread placement are carefully considered in concert with the architecture details, significant performance advantages can be realized compared to an unoptimized simulation, and also compared to simulation running on commodity Xeon multicore systems. We note that it is not just the sheer power of the cores, but also the new architecture design features that make simulations on KNL substantially faster and more scalable compared to commodity Xeon processors. We expect that the results of our work will motivate future research into more architecture-specific optimizations to further boost PDES performance on KNL systems. Future research needs to also consider expanding this work across multiple KNL nodes.

- **Affinity should be controlled**: We show that in most scenarios, the best results in terms of committed

event rate of simulation are achieved when affinity is used to pin threads to CPU cores.

- **Balanced core loading matters**: We show that in most scenarios, the best results in terms of committed event rate of simulation are achieved when each CPU core is evenly loaded with modest number of threads - typically 1 or 2 threads per core provides the best performance. Filling the chip to capacity by executing 4 threads per core often results in core oversaturation, worse cache performance and overall slowdown. Furthermore, balanced loading results in better performance over round-robin core assignment scheme even if some cores remain completely unused - this is because synchronous progress of simulation threads promoted by even loading is critical for PDES.

- **Communication patterns matter**: We demonstrate that specific thread-to-core placement for the same number of threads per core and the same amount of remote communication significantly impact performance in many cases. In addition, we demonstrate that the *message flow* needs to be considered as it also has a noticeable impact on simulation performance.

- **Communication-aware partitioning is critical**: We demonstrate that it is critical to properly partition the simulation model to minimize the number of different cores with which a thread communicates. Several-fold performance improvement can be realized if most communications are limited to only a cluster of cores.

- **Detailed performance characterization**: We perform a detailed evaluation of multithreaded ROSS on an Intel KNL processor. We investigate the performance sensitivity to a number of simulator parameters, including percentage of remote events, synchronization period, event processing granularity, thread placement and workload distribution policies. We also compare simulation on KNL against KC and commodity Xeon processors and show that KNL significantly outperforms them.

The rest of the paper is organized as follows. Section 2 provides the background on Intel's Knights Landing architecture and describes our evaluation and experimentation methodology. The results of our experiments are presented and discussed in Section 3. Section 4 reviews the related work and we offer our concluding remarks in Section 5.

2. BACKGROUND AND EXPERIMENTAL SETUP

In this section, we overview ROSS simulator, review the Intel Knights Landing architecture and describe our experimental setup.

2.1 Overview of ROSS Simulator

PDES is a parallel implementation of DES [12], extending the performance and capacity advantages of parallel processing to this important application. The key idea behind PDES is to break the simulation model into multiple Logical Processes (LPs) and allow these LPs to execute in parallel on multiple processing cores. The LPs communicate with each other by exchanging time-stamped event messages [12,

13]. The LPs have their own local event queues and process the events from these queues in time-stamped order. Some events are generated locally within the LP, while other events are generated remotely and the timing of the event arrival to a destination LP depends on the physical delays that the message encounters while traversing the on-chip interconnects (for core-to-core communication within a chip) or network links (for cluster-level communication).

Due to the event dependencies between the LPs and physical delays in the system, a PDES simulation engine needs to use synchronization mechanism to ensure that events are executed at different LPs in correct time-stamped order. Two types of synchronization algorithms are used in PDES systems: conservative and optimistic. To support recovery to a safe state upon a rollback in an optimistic simulator, state checkpoints during simulation run have to be created. These event histories can grow large over time and the ones that are no longer needed must be garbage collected. To achieve this, the Global Virtual Time (GVT) is periodically computed to compute the global progress of the simulation.

For the experiments in this paper, we use ROSS [11] optimistic PDES simulator. To effectively exploit the shared memory available on Knights Landing processors, we use multi-threaded implementation of ROSS [5], where the simulation processes are implemented as threads, as opposed to processes, requiring no expensive MPI-based communications and directly exploiting shared memory hierarchy.

PDES simulations have to be driven by benchmarks. The most popular and versatile benchmark for evaluating PDES is the classical *Phold* model. *Phold* is a synthetic, but versatile benchmark that allows characterization of the performance of applications under different scenarios. For example, it allows control of the percentage of events generated locally to the same core and the percentage of events generated for the other cores (thus, requiring inter-core communication and delays). One can also alter the event processing granularity (EPC) to control how much CPU processing is required for each event. As a result, this allows us to evaluate systems with different computation/communication balance (by varying the EPC) and with different execution locality patterns (by varying the percentage of remote events).

2.2 Overview of the Intel Knights Landing Architecture

The Intel Knights Landing [8, 14] is the second generation of the Many Integrated Core (MIC) architecture designed to be used as both a standalone processor and a co-processor for High Performance Computing (HPC) applications.

Knights Landing processors [15] feature up to 72 cores, each capable of executing 4 simultaneous threads. The cores run at a maximum frequency of 1.3 GHz and can achieve better than 6000 Gflops/s single precision and 3000 Gflops/s double precision when the vector processing units are utilized fully.

A major upgrade to the Knights Corner architecture, Knights Landing adds branch prediction and out-of-order execution logic to each core. Vector Processing Units (VPU) have been increased to 2 per core. Also, a 1 Mbyte L2 cache is now shared between every core pair, forming a tile. Finally, KNL systems are augmented with 16 GB on-package MCDRAM memory module. In its default mode, it acts

as the L3 cache to the DDR4 memory. Our version of the Knights Landing processor has 64 cores and 96 GB of DDR4 memory. The high-level diagram of the Knights Landing architecture used for this study (not including the DDR4 memory) is shown in Figure 1.

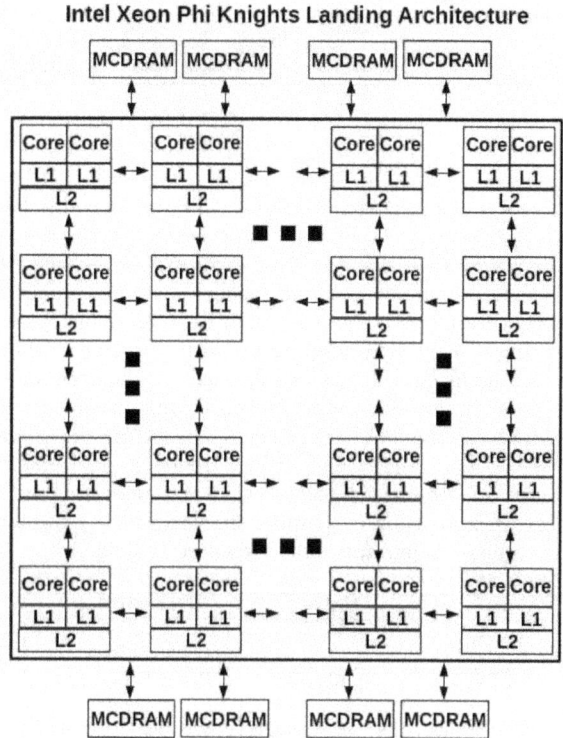

Figure 1: Intel Knights Landing Architecture

KNL processor is commonly socketed and utilized as a standalone CPU as is the case in our experimental system. KNL runs standard Linux distributions as a full host computer thus eliminating the idiosyncrasies of accelerator interfacing.

2.3 Experimental Setup and Metrics

Table 1 summarizes the configurations and hardware details of the host Xeon processor and the Xeon Phi Knights Corner (KC) and Knights Landing (KL) processors. Note that Xeon and Knights Corner systems are only used for comparison purposes in the results presented in Section 3.8.

For all presented experiments, we execute the multi-threaded version of ROSS simulator driven by the Phold benchmark. In the Phold benchmark, we vary the thread count, the percentage of remotely generated events, the GVT interval, the event processing granularity (EPC), and the thread placement and assignment policies. Our goal is to understand the behavior and scaling trends of the ROSS simulator while executing on a single Knights Landing node. We also directly compare performance against a 12-core Xeon processor and a Knights Corner system (the previous generation of Xeon Phi).

Platform	Xeon	KC	KL
Model	E5-2620	5110p	7230
Frequency	2.40GHz	1.053GHz	1.3GHz
# of Cores	12	60	64
Memory Type	DDR4 2133	GDDR5	DDR4 2400
Memory Size	60G	8G	96GB + 16GB
OS	CentOS 6.6	uOS	CentOS 7.2
Compiler	Intel Parallel Studio Cluster V 2017	Intel Parallel Studio Cluster V 2017	Intel Parallel Studio Cluster V 2017

Table 1: Details of Experimental Platforms

We report the performance results in terms of committed events per second. As we increase the number of processing nodes, we maintain the number of starting events per node, thus proportionately increasing the total number of events generated by the simulator. If the underlying system is capable of efficiently keeping up with this load without incurring additional delays, we can expect the committed event rate to also show improvements commensurate with the increase in the number of nodes. This is known as *weak scaling* [4]. Our results and scaling trends clearly indicate the potential for using Knights Landing processors as efficient engines for running parallel simulations. A summary of the simulation parameters is shown in Table 2.

Variable	Value	Description
Remote %	0 - 100	Proportion of Events Local vs Remote
EPC	0, 100, 500	Event Processing Time
Initial Events	128 * # Threads	Number of events to start simulation
GVT Period	32, 128, 512	Synchronization frequency

Table 2: Simulation Parameters

3. EXPERIMENTAL RESULTS AND DISCUSSION

We present our analysis along multiple dimensions. First, we analyze in detail the scaling trends and the impact of multiple simulation parameters (such as the percentage of remote events, the event processing granularity, and the GVT period) on the performance of ROSS simulator on KNL. We first perform these studies assuming the round-robin assignment of threads to cores, and then study different thread assignment and placement policies. We first consider simple scaling where at most one thread is placed on a core, and then we investigate the impact of multithreading support by executing multiple threads per core, up to 256 threads total.

3.1 Performance under Round-Robin Scheduling

We first analyze ROSS performance under the Round-robin assignment of threads to cores. While this assignment scheme is the most natural, it can create uneven loading of the individual cores at large thread counts in situations where multiple threads are placed on some cores. We quan-

tify the performance problems arising from that effect in this section. The issue of uneven core loading on the same chip becomes especially important in many-core architectures where both the likelihood of such scenario and its impact on performance increase. We also analyze the impact of thread affinity on the performance.

3.1.1 Single Thread per Core: Impact of Thread Affinity

In our first experiment, we analyze the committed event rate of ROSS executed on KNL for different percentages of events that are generated remotely. For this experiment, we assume a fairly large GVT interval of 512 (a parameter in ROSS) and the event processing granularity (EPC) of zero. A large GVT interval reduces the overhead of GVT computation (which is significant on many-core architecture such as KNL, as we demonstrate later), but increases the rollback cost. The low EPC value implies that event processing does not consume any CPU time, other than generating a new event and sending it to a random destination LP. This represents an extreme case of a communication-dominated model. In our experiments, we used a *weak scaling* model, where the number of simulation events increases proportionately with the number of threads. The metric of interest in this case is the total number of committed events per second. In a scalable execution scenario, the addition of extra cores/threads will translate into commensurate increases in this metric.

We present the results for two cases. In the first case, we scale the simulation up to the available number of cores by placing at most one simulation thread on each core. In the second case, we exploit the presence of simultaneous multithreading support within each core and scale simulation upto the maximum number of threads supported by the core (up to 4 threads per core). Since the trends and observations from these experiments are quite different, we present these results using separate figures and analyze them separately.

The results for simulations upto 64 threads are presented in Figure 2. The total committed event rate is depicted as a function of the number of threads for different remote percentages. In this experiment, we used the model with zero percent remote events (that is, all events are generated locally and the cross-core communication is only needed for computing GVT), and another model with 5% remote events to gauge the impact of remote communication. The results are presented for each case with and without thread affinity setting. When thread affinity is set, each simulation thread is pinned to a particular core throughout its execution, thus promoting the exploitation of caches and locality of references. When thread affinity is not set, threads can bounce across different cores following context switches and CPU yielding events.

For executions up to 64 cores, the simulation performance scales well for both 0% and even 5% remote events, although better scaling and substantially higher performance is observed for 0% remote events, as expected. Specifically, for models with affinity set, we observed a 34X speedup compared to sequential simulation for 0% remote event case, and only 20X speedup for 5% case. In terms of direct comparison, the case with 0% remote is roughly twice as fast as the case with 5% remote for 64-way simulations. It is

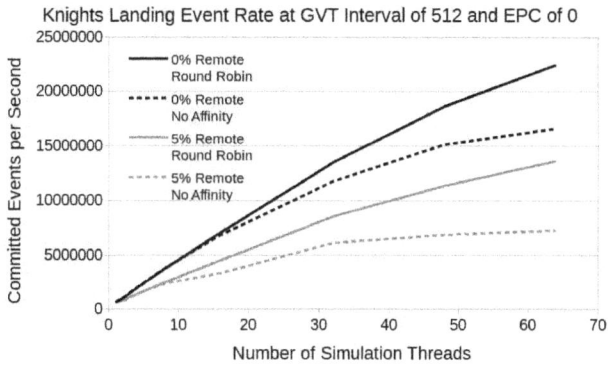

Figure 2: Committed Event Rate with and without affinity, 0% & 5% Remote

still impressive to observe that even simulations with 5% remote events enjoy solid scaling on KNL architecture up to 64 cores, which is in sharp contrast to the results obtained for similar scale on multi-chip systems [1].

Another important observation from the results presented in Figure 2 is that thread affinity matters and it significantly improves performance for simulation models with and without remote events at larger thread counts. For the case with no remote events, there is virtually no performance difference between the runs with and without affinity for thread count below 16. As the simulation thread count increases above 16, the system with thread affinity starts to outperform the one without it, and the performance gap widens as the number of simulation threads increases. For 64-way simulation, we observed 35% performance benefits of affinity. The reason behind such behavior is that the increase in the number of simulation threads and utilized cores leaves fewer cores idle and increases the likelihood that a particular thread will be reassigned to a different core upon a context switch or a CPU yielding event. We observe similar trends for the simulation model with 5% remote events, but this time the divergence starts at a lower point (about 8 cores), performance with no affinity flattens much earlier, and the relative advantage of affinity is even higher at large core counts (for example, the difference is 88% for 64-way simulations). Therefore, in the rest of the paper we assume fixed thread affinity, unless indicated otherwise.

3.1.2 Single Thread per Core: Impact of Remote Communication

Figure 3 compares the scaling of fixed-affinity models for different values of remote percentages when the number of threads is varied from 2 to 64, with at most one simulation thread per physical core. The simulation performance scales linearly all the way to 64 cores for the fraction of remote communications up to 10% - this is quite an impressive result showing better scalability than on multi-chip systems of similar scale. Of course, as seen from the figure, the slope of the performance graphs decreases with higher remote percentages, because cross-core communication starts to become a more dominant factor. At 25% remote events, the simulation scales to about 32 cores, at which point the performance curve flattens. For the models with 50% remote communications and above, there is no scalability and

adding more cores/threads does not result in higher performance. In summary, results presented in Figures 2 and 3 lead to the following key observations:

Observation 1: If a simulation model can be properly partitioned so that the percentage of remotely generated events is kept at 10% or below (for the parameters used in this study), almost linear performance increases of as much as 34X can be realized on a KNL system as the simulation scales to 64 threads when at most one thread is placed per core. As the simulation scales to 128 threads, performance continues to increase to as much as 44X as shown in the following section. If partitioning can not achieve this level of locality, then performance tapers off earlier or the model does not scale at all.

Observation 2: Thread affinity is an important feature for achieving higher performance of ROSS on a KNL system. Specifically, when threads are pinned to the individual cores, performance improvements in the range of 35% to 88% are realized for 64-way simulation. Furthermore, the advantages of set affinity increase with larger thread counts and larger fraction of remote communication.

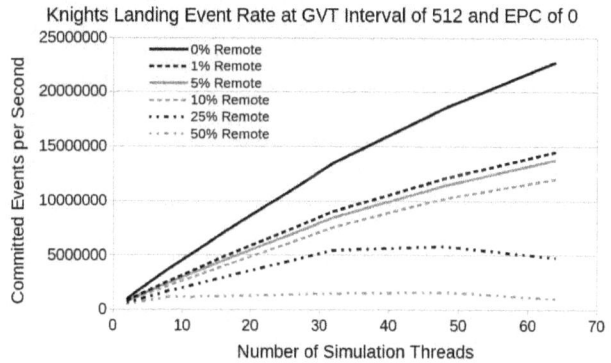

Figure 3: Committed Event Rate For Different Remote Percentages

3.1.3 Scaling with Multiple Threads per Core

The results presented above demonstrate scaling trends for up to the number of available cores. Next, we investigate the opportunities to extract further performance from a KNL chip by increasing the number of threads placed on each core, thus exploiting SMT support available within each core. Figure 4 extends the results of Figure 2 by increasing the number of simulation threads to 256 (four threads for each core) in a round-robin assignment of threads to cores.

As seen from the results, even a small remote percentage has a dramatic impact on the simulation event rate. With zero percent remote events (i.e. all generated events are targeting the same LP), the simulation event rate first grows linearly with the number of cores up to the point where the number of simulation threads exceeds the number of cores (which happens at 64 cores). For simulations with no remote events, as the number of threads exceeds the number of physical cores, the simulation commit event rate drops because of the imbalanced core loading, and the simulation progress is limited by slow threads. Eventually, performance

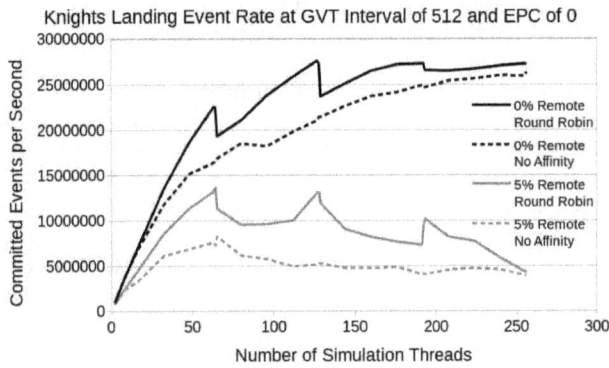

Figure 4: Committed Event Rate with and without affinity, 0% & 5% Remote

recovers as more threads are added, but the nature of this recovery depends on weather or not thread affinity is used.

With thread affinity control, the simulation threads that are pinned in a way that they share physical cores become slower. As a result, they consistently lag in performance and impede the simulation progress, because all threads have to be periodically synchronized to compute GVT. As can be observed from the graph with thread affinity, as we move from 64-way to 65-way simulation, performance drops by 14%, which roughly matches the performance drop that a single thread experiences when it simultaneously executes on a core with another thread. As we add more simulation threads, less cores are being wasted waiting at GVT interval for slower threads and the overall simulation performance gradually improves. It takes 24 more cores to match performance of a 64-thread simulation, and the performance peak is reached at 128 threads (two threads per physical core). After that, performance again drops sharply due to further core imbalance and slowly recovers. Performance never reaches the level recorded at 128 threads due to over utilization of cores beyond that point.

It is also interesting to compare this case with simulation results where thread affinity is not set and threads can migrate among the physical cores across context switches. In this case, performance grows more gradually and there is only a very small drop from 64 to 65 cores that is quickly recovered. This is because no single simulation thread becomes a constant bottleneck and threads are not tied up by slower cores. However, due to poorer exploitation of caches in simulation with no thread affinity, the absolute performance is always below the case where affinity is used. Similar trends can be observed for the case with 5% remote events, although unbalanced execution creates additional rollbacks in this case, which degrades performance further and makes recovery from performance dips more challenging. In this case, the best performance is observed with 64 threads, the case with 128 threads almost matches it.

For simulation models with non-zero remote percentage, the additional problem due to uneven progress of the simulation threads is the increased probability of straggler events and rollbacks. Despite much lower values of committed event rates at non-zero remote percentages, those simula-

tions also show slower performance increases with the increase in thread count.

3.2 Impact of Balanced Loading

To address performance problems of round-robin thread assignment, we studied alternative thread placement schemes that preserve balanced core loading when the number of threads exceeds the number of available physical cores. Figure 5 and Figure 6 show the impact of these schemes on performance. Specifically, we implemented two such schemes, called *linear* and *balanced*. *Linear* assignment assigns threads to cores in a way that consecutively saturates individual cores. For example, the first four threads are placed on core 0, the next four threads are placed on core 1 and so on. *Balanced* assignment scheme evenly distributes all simulation threads across all cores, such that the number of threads per core depends on the total number of threads in simulation. For example, for a 96-way simulation, 48 cores (cores numbered 0 through 47) will execute two threads each, and the other 16 cores will remain idle.

We present the results for the scenario with no remote events (Figure 5) and 10% remote events (Figure 6). In the case of no remote events, the performance dip due to imbalanced core loading is encountered only because of GVT computation cycle. The impact is modest, only about 10% of performance is lost with round-robin assignment when we start exceeding the number of cores. Note that balanced and round-robin assignments perform about the same, but linear assignment exhibits smoother growth with lower performance at smaller thread counts. This is because at smaller thread counts, a few CPU cores remain over utilized (executing 4 threads each) while others remain idle. For the execution scenario with 10% remote events (Figure 6), the performance drop after 64 cores is much more significant - about 50% of performance is lost with round-robin after we reach 64 and then 128 simulation threads. This is because a non-trivial amount of remote communications causes straggler events, increases the number of rollbacks due to asynchrony in simulation progress, and decreases the simulation efficiency. Balanced execution matches the round-robin performance peaks at multiples of 64 threads, but provides better performance at all intermediate points. As in the case with no remote communication, performance of linear scheme lags behind the other two, but the graph is more smooth without rigid peaks and valleys. At very large thread counts, all three schemes converge to the same values. From these results, we make the following observation:

Observation 3: To avoid potential performance problems, it is important to balance the core usage and assign each core the same number of threads. While the performance peaks at discrete points match the performance of a round-robin scheme, balanced loading provides significantly better performance for the intermediate points, and the performance difference increases with higher percentage of remote events.

From all performance results presented up to this point, the following observation can be made in terms of optimal core loading for the models considered so far:

Observation 4: When the percentage of remote events is significant (e.g. above 10%), it is counter-productive to place more than one thread to a physical core. With lower

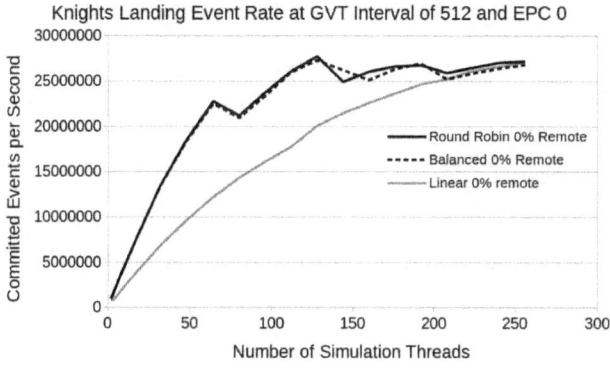

Figure 5: Committed Event Rate for KNL for Different Placement Schemes, 0% Remote

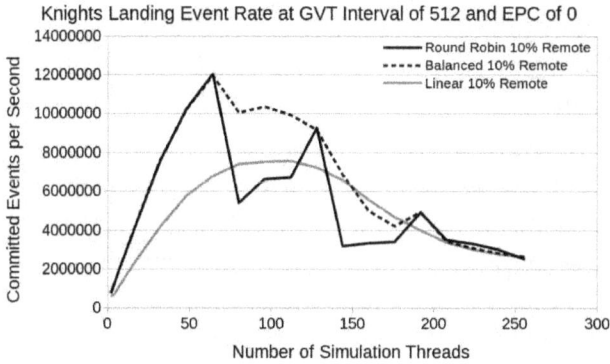

Figure 6: Committed Event Rate for KNL for Different Placement Schemes, 10% Remote

remote percentage, a higher performance can be achieved with two threads per core, but the thread-to-core assignment has to be balanced. No model with small event processing granularity (EPC of 0) features performance improvements beyond two threads per core.

3.3 Impact of Event Processing Granularity

Figure 7 shows the impact of the event processing granularity (EPC) on the simulation commit event rate for different number of threads with no remote events. The results are shown for the large GVT value of 512. Three different EPC values are compared - 0, 100 and 500. Larger EPC values add longer processing loops inside each event. In all three cases, we used balanced assignment of threads to cores, as described previously.

As expected, the event processing rate decreases as the EPC increases and the simulation becomes more computationally-bound. However, the performance scalability curves exhibit quite different behavior depending on the EPC value. For the EPC value of zero, the maximum performance is achieved with 2 threads per core and further increase in the number of threads does not increase the event commit rate. In contrast, as the EPC value increases and simulation becomes more computationally bound, placing additional threads on the cores results in further per-

formance gains - the highest performance is observed for 256-way simulation for both 100 and 500 EPC values.

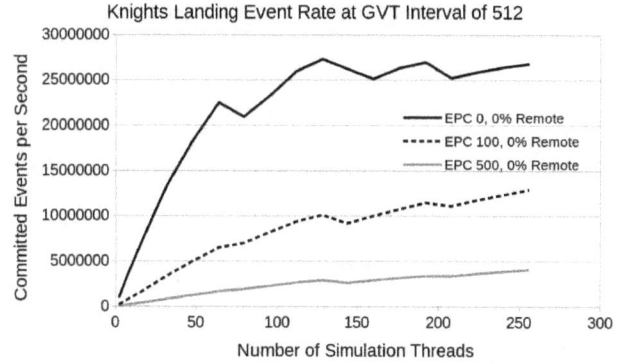

Figure 7: Committed Event Rate for EPC values of 0, 100 & 500 with no Remote Communication

Figure 8 shows the event commit rate for different EPC values (0, 100 and 500) for the situation where 10% of events are generated remotely. In this case of 10% remote events, the balance between computation and communication is tilted towards communication for the EPC of 0. Consequently, as seen from the results of Figure 8, the scenario with EPC of 0 and 10% remote events produces more rollbacks, lower efficiency and lower event commit rate at larger thread counts; the performance is highest at 64 threads in this case and drops continuously after that. In contrast, even with 10% remote events, simulations with 100 and 500 EPC continue to scale up to the maximum number of threads, although the performance increases at larger thread counts are lower than in the case with no remote communication. A somewhat counterintuitive result demonstrating the complex nature and the inter-dependencies of simulation parameters is that after about 150 threads the absolute performance of simulation with EPC of 100 exceeds that of simulation with EPC of 0, despite the former requiring 100 times longer processing time for each event compared to the latter. The reason is that longer processing delays provide more opportunities for the remote events to be generated on time, thus decreasing rollbacks and increasing simulation efficiency — the execution progresses more predictably and steady in this case.

In summary, our experiments with various EPC values and remote communication frequencies lead to the following observation:

Observation 5: As event processing time increases and simulation becomes more computation-bound, the commit event rate scales with the number of threads all the way to the maximum number of threads that can be executed on a KNL chip (256). More surprisingly, the absolute performance of simulations with higher EPC can be higher than simulation with lower EPC at large thread counts for models with substantial remote communication.

3.4 Impact of GVT Period

Next, we analyze the impact of the GVT period on the simulation performance. Figures 9 and 10 depict the simulation event rate for three different GVT intervals: 512, 128 and 32. Results are presented for the remote percentages

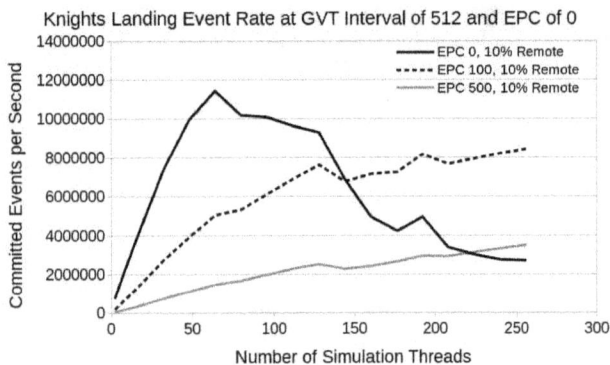

Figure 8: Committed Event Rate for KNL for EPC values of 0, 100 & 500 for the Remote Percentage of 10%

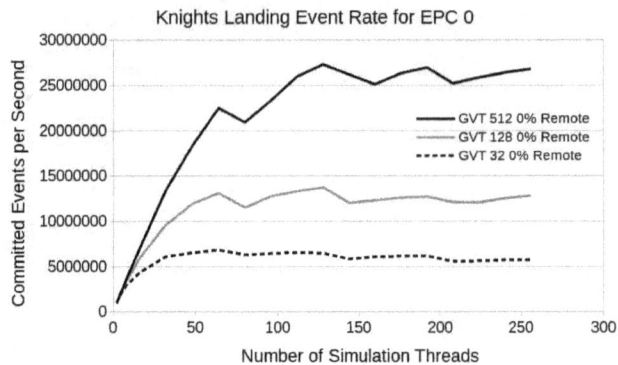

Figure 9: Committed Event Rate for Different GVT Periods, no Remote Events

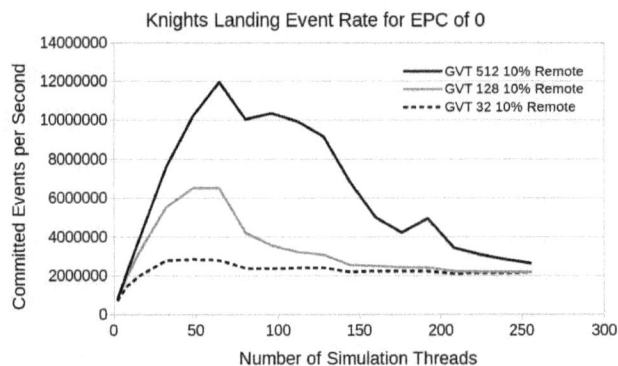

Figure 10: Committed Event Rate for Different GVT Periods, 10% Remote Events

of 0% and 10% and the EPC value of 0. Larger GVT values reduce the frequency of checkpoint creation and GVT update cycles, but increase the memory pressure (because larger amount of state needs to be maintained between consecutive checkpoints) and make individual rollbacks more expensive. On the other hand, smaller GVT intervals require less state information to be maintained for rollback recovery, but increase the overhead of GVT maintenance because GVT iterations are needed more frequently.

As seen from the presented results, in all cases that we evaluated, larger GVT periods resulted in significantly better performance, indicating that GVT maintenance is an expensive operation. For example, according to Figure 9, there is almost 5X performance improvement between the GVT periods of 32 and 512 for 256-way simulation. There is also about 2X performance difference between the GVT periods of 128 and 256. The reason for such drastic impact is that GVT updates in ROSS rely on expensive all-reduce operations that involves full group communication and synchronization across simulation threads to agree on the minimal value of their local virtual times. At the low level, this involves chip-wide cache coherence traffic and OS intervention, leading to significant slowdowns. While more efficient asynchronous implementations of the GVT algorithm are possible [16, 17], their exploration and adaptation for ROSS framework running on KNL is left for future work. The results shown in Figures 9 and 10 lead to the following observation.

Observation 6: Synchronous GVT updates on the KNL architecture are relatively expensive. At the same time, memory capacity is not a limitation since the KNL processor has access to the entire system memory. Therefore, larger GVT intervals provide better performance.

3.5 Impact of Cache Sharing

Next, we investigate the impact on cache sharing between threads on performance. The Knights Landing processor has a two-level cache hierarchy. Each core has its own private Level 1 (L1) cache but shares its Level 2 (L2) cache with a neighboring core as part of a tile. To investigate the performance impact of this cache architecture, we evaluated three communication schemes that we call *same node*, *same tile* and *tile pairs*. In *same node* mode, each thread communicates with another thread running on the same core — this

model maximizes the exploitation of the L1 cache. In *same tile* pattern, each thread communicates with a thread running on an adjacent (buddy) core — in this case the data can come from the shared L2 cache. With *tile Pairs*, each thread communicates with a thread running on a core in the next tile, requiring communication beyond the local L1 and L2 caches. We note that to realize *same node* pattern, multiple threads have to be placed on the same core. For example, for a 64-way simulation, 32 cores will have two threads each and the other 32 cores will be unused. Therefore, the positive effect of L1 cache sharing is offset by overutilization of cores and reduced processing throughout in general.

Figure 11 shows the performance of our three communication schemes scaling with at most one thread per core up to 64 cores. All events are generated remotely in this model. As one would expect, communication in *tile pairs* mode is slower than communication that exploits the L1 or L2 cache. However, there is negligible difference between communication utilizing the L1 cache (*same node*) and the L2 cache (*same tile*) — in this case exploitation of L1 caches for faster communication is offset by the extra processing load on the cores. At the same time, the *same tile* model allows for the low-latency communication through L2 caches without core overloading.

Figure 12 extends the data to 256 simulation threads introducing additional core loading. The trends seen above are

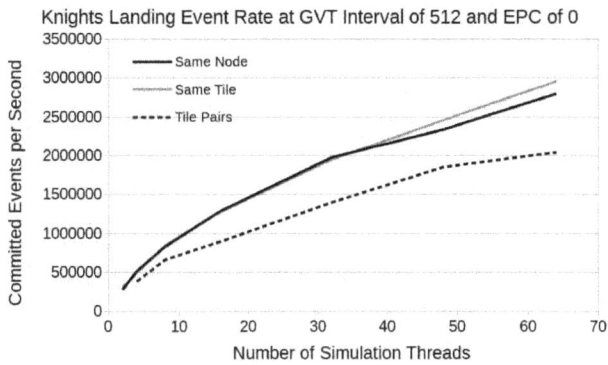

Figure 11: Committed Event Rate for Communication Patterns Using *Same Node, Same Tile and Tile Pairs* Policies at 100% Remote Percentage and EPC of 0 up to 64 Threads

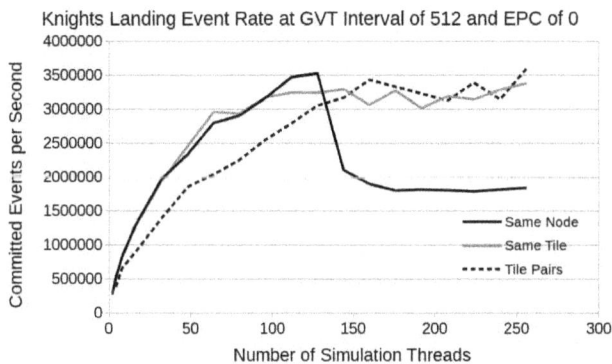

Figure 12: Committed Event Rate for Communication using *Same Node, Same Tile, Tile Pairs and Next Tile* Policies upto 256 Threads

preserved until thread count reaches 128, after that point a different behavior is observed. First, there is a precipitous drop in performance of *same node* pattern (Figure 12). The reason for the drop is that the pressure on a small L1 cache further increases with more co-located threads, resulting in more cache misses and less advantages due to cache sharing. Furthermore, we observe that *same tile* and *tile pairs* converge in performance as the number of threads increases. The following observation summarizes our cache-related experiments.

Observation 7: For simulations up to 64 threads, attempting to exploit L1 cache for low-latency communication by collocating communicating threads on the same core does not result in performance gains due to the extra core loading. However, limiting communication to the same tile without increasing core loading (thus exploiting the L2 cache) improves the performance by almost 50% compared to the case when communications cross the tile boundary. As the thread count further increases and L2 cache capacity is exceeded, the advantages of tile-level communication are lost.

3.6 Impact of Partitioning, Clustering and Message Flow

As demonstrated in previous sections, remote communication can have a significant impact on performance. One of the approaches to minimize amount of remote communications is model partitioning that localizes communication to small cluster of nodes [18]. In this section, we evaluate the impact of such partitioning on performance. We varied our simulated configurations from 128 2-node clusters to a single 256-node cluster, the latter being equivalent to non-clustered operation considered in previous sections. We evaluated three message flow algorithms within these clusters - a directional flow pattern, a random message flow pattern, and a bidirectional flow pattern.

The directional pattern sends all message traffic to the next node in the cluster with the final node in the cluster wrapping messages back to the first. In the phold model, after a message is sent at initialization, messages are only sent after being received. Thus, this represents a very balanced and uniform message flow pattern.

Conversely, the random message flow pattern has an equal chance of the message destination being any node within the cluster. Should the destination end up being the source node, a different node in the cluster is picked using the direction pattern outlined above. This is done to ensure message traffic is to a different core and is thus exercising the same communication path.

The bidirectional pattern alternates message traffic between previous and subsequent nodes in the cluster with the destinations decrementing and incrementing respectively. The destinations are wrapped around to remain within the cluster. Similar to directional flow, this represents a very balanced and uniform message flow pattern, but also utilizes more communication channels.

As seen from the results of Figure 13, clustering offers as much as 3.5X speedup when compared with random non-clustered communication. We also observe that message flow has an impact on communication performance, although less than the effects of cluster size. At the point of 2 nodes per cluster, the destination is the same regardless of the algorithm as there is only one valid destination. Interestingly, directional flow is the slowest of the three at this cluster size due again to increased GVT all reduce processing. However, as the node size increases beyond 4 nodes per cluster, directional communication provides a performance advantage over random and bidirectional communication, resulting in a 25% gain even at 256 node cluster size (this point represents non-clustered communication). In summary, these results lead to the following observation:

Observation 8: Simulation model partitioning and limiting communication to a small number of adjacent cores can lead to significant improvement in simulation performance, especially for small cluster sizes, upto 3.5X in some scenarios. This is achieved by only limiting the size of communicating clusters, and not reducing the remote percentage (which still remains at 100% for these results).

3.7 Impact of Communication Distance with at Most One Thread per Core

Additionally, for the scenarios with at most one thread per core, we implemented two policies for placing threads

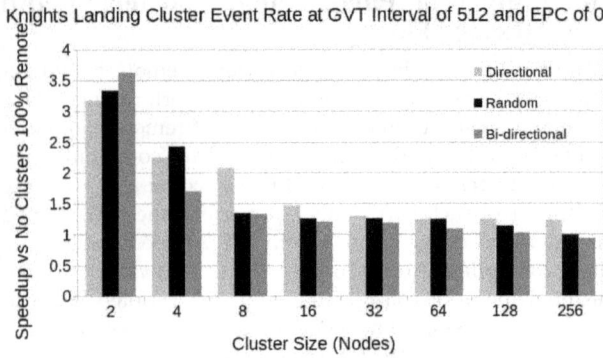

Figure 13: Committed Event Rate for KNL for Different Message Traffic Patterns Within Clusters of Varying Sizes

among the cores: *distant* placement and *nearby* placement. In the distant policy, the communicating threads are placed as far from each other as possible thus requiring the longest number of links to be traversed on the mesh interconnect for communication. Conversely, in the nearby policy, the threads are placed as close as possible to each other to minimize the number of link traversals in the mesh. The intent of these experiments is to gauge the impact of thread placement on the interconnect performance.

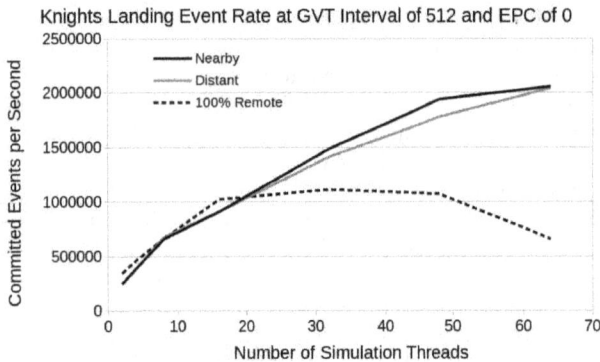

Figure 14: Committed Event Rate for KNL for *Nearby and Distant* Placement at 100% Remote Communication and EPC of 0

We compared the performance of two placement policies at 100% remote events, as this provides the highest communication intensity between threads and stress-tests our scenarios. As seen from the results of Figure 14, thread placement has little effect on the committed event rate. We observe that even when communication between threads has to traverse the entire length of the interconnect, there is no change in performance. This alludes to the high performance nature of the Knights Landing interconnect design. Similar conclusions were made in the study of [7] for the Tilera processor.

Observation 9: The mesh interconnect is not the limiting factor in performance and is not saturated during PDES execution even under stress-testing experiments with distant placement described above. This also corroborates previously reported conclusions for Tilera many-core chip [7].

3.8 Performance Comparison with Knights Corner and 12-core Xeon

Intel Xeon Phi architectures provide interesting opportunities to partition, map, and execute PDES simulations on many cores within the same chip. However, while demonstrating impressive speedups against own sequential execution, some previous manycore architectures failed to match the raw performance achieved on a commodity Xeon processor. In this section, we directly compare the performance of PDES on a Xeon dual socket 12-core system with Knights Corner and Knights Landing Xeon Phi architectures.

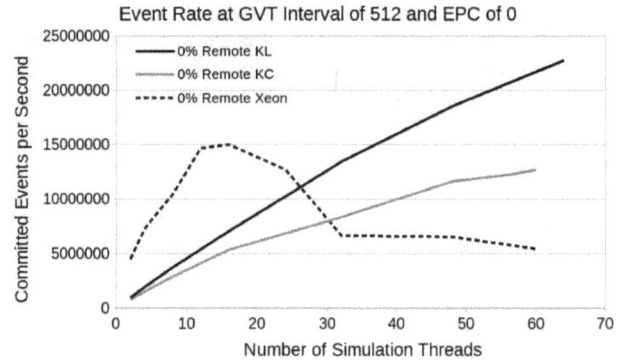

Figure 15: Performance Comparison of KNL, KC and 12-core Xeon for 0% Remote Events

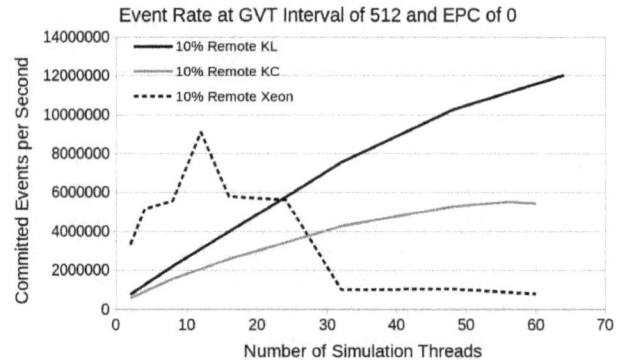

Figure 16: Performance Comparison of KNL, KC and 12-core Xeon for 10% Remote Events

Figures 15 and 16 show the performance of PDES on the three processors for 0% and 10% remote communication respectively. These results are shown for up to 64 threads, we expand to more threads later. As expected, the Xeon peaks at 12 nodes and begins a steeper decline at 24 threads when its hardware thread count is exceeded (Xeon supports 2-way hyperthreading). KNL, as reported earlier in this paper, scales almost linearly to 64 threads. KC, though linear, fails to achieve the peak event rate of Xeon resulting in 40% lower performance for the 10% remote case. Conversely, KNL achieves a 32% performance increase over Xeon for the 10% remote communication case and 51% increase for simulations with no remote events.

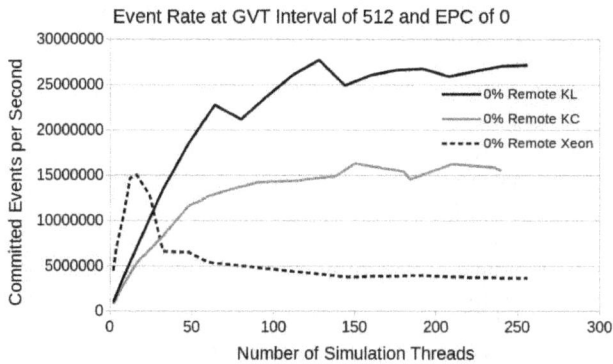

Figure 17: Performance Comparison of KNL, KC and 12-core Xeon

As we scale past 64 nodes, shown in Figure 17, KC and KNL continue to provide performance increases up to 128 threads. It is only at this point that KC matches the performance of the 12-core Xeon. At 128 threads, KNL expands its performance gain over the Xeon to 84%, and the performance of KNL stays about the same as the number of threads grows beyond 128. These results are summarized by the following observation.

Observation 10: Xeon Phi architectures are well suited to PDES simulation. Though Knights Corner processor exhibits at best equal performance to commodity Xeon processors, Knights Landing provides almost a 2X performance increase and retains scalability to high number of threads.

4. RELATED WORK

The works of [5, 6] investigated several optimizations within multithreaded PDES simulator to achieve scalability on relatively smaller-scale platforms such as Intel's Core-i7 and AMD's Magny-cours. The work of [7] investigated PDES performance on the Tilera processor, whose architecture is close in spirit to the KNL design studied in this paper. While the results of [7] demonstrate excellent scalability of the simulation and the capability of the interconnection network to sustain high throughput even under heavy pressure, no comparison against the simulation results on a traditional high-frequency multicore processor were provided. Therefore, it is difficult to gauge the practicality of using the Tilera system for running PDES based on these results and relatively low performance of Tilera cores. Our study corroborated some of the results achieved on Tilera, specifically that longer communication distance on the interconnect do not impact ROSS performance.

In the supercomputing domain, Bauer et al. designed scalable PDES for IBM's Blue Gene supercomputer [4]. To achieve almost linear speed-up, they rely on reverse computation - a mechanism that replaces state saving that is built into ROSS simulator. Reverse computation essentially undoes the computations that need to be rolled back by performing reverse operations (for example, to roll back addition, subtraction is performed). If the rollbacks are infrequent (as in the case of the models considered in [4]), reverse computation is more efficient than state saving, because the overhead of computing GVTs and creating checkpoints is

eliminated. In this paper we evaluate a range of models, including the ones with high remote percentage rate, high rollbacks and low efficiency. Consequently, we do not use reverse computation, but rely on traditional state saving mechanism which is implemented in ROSS.

The work of [19] is the follow-up to [4], reporting impressive event processing rates on Sequoia BlueGene/Q supercomputer. The recent effort of [10] evaluated PDES performance on Knights Corner processor. The main conclusion of [10] is that Knights Corner does not outperform the host Xeon processor in terms of event rate unless vector units are fully utilized, and increasing the number of threads does not alter that trend - this is corroborated by our comparison results shown in Section 3.8. The reasons behind such subpar performance are slower in-order cores and limited amount of physical memory on the accelerator card.

Several other studies investigated the performance of various parallel applications on Xeon Phi (Knights Corner) platforms [20, 21, 22, 23, 24, 25]. However, all of these applications are very different from PDES and in general offer more parallelization opportunities. Evaluating PDES on KNL provides an insight of how similar fine-grain communication-dominated applications will be expected to perform on these platforms.

5. CONCLUDING REMARKS

In this paper, we performed a comprehensive characterization of PDES performance on the Intel Knights Landing processor in an effort to understand whether this architecture is an attractive hardware platform for running distributed simulations. Specifically, we studied performance sensitivity of PDES to many key simulation parameters, including percentage of remote events, event processing granularity, GVT period, thread placement strategies and communication patterns. In general, the results of our evaluations are very promising demonstrating significant speedup compared to sequential execution (up to 44X) and also performance improvements compared to both Knights Corner and commodity Xeon processors (up to 2X).

Our results indicate that the best performance on KNL processors is achieved when thread affinity control is used, at most two threads are placed on each core and physical cores are evenly balanced. We showed that simulation scales well even in the presence of significant fraction of events that are generated remotely and that scaling continues for larger thread counts with increased event processing granularity. We quantified the benefits of localizing communication to smaller clusters of cores and showed that a performance improvement of up to 3.5X can be achieved compared to all-to-all communication models. We also demonstrated that GVT computation on a KNL system is expensive thus favoring simulation setups with larger GVT periods.

Our future work will consider extension of this study to clusters of KNL processors and exploitation of the specifics of memory organization and clustering modes.

6. ACKNOWLEDGMENTS

This material is based upon work supported by the AFOSR under Award No. FA9550-15-1-0384 and DURIP award FA9550-15-1-0376.

7. REFERENCES

[1] S. Das, R. Fujimoto, K. Panesar, D. Allison, and M. Hybinette, "GTW: a Time Warp system for shared memory multiprocessors," in *Proceedings of the 1994 Winter Simulation Conference* (J. D. Tew, S. Manivannan, D. A. Sadowski, and A. F. Seila, eds.), pp. 1332–1339, Dec. 1994.

[2] R. M. Fujimoto and M. Hybinette, "Computing global virtual time in shared-memory multiprocessors," *ACM Transactions on Modeling and Computer Simulation*, vol. 7, no. 4, pp. 425–446, 1997.

[3] R. Fujimoto and K. Panesar, "Buffer management in shared-memory Time Warp system," in *Proceedings of the 9th Workshop on Parallel and Distributed Simulation (PADS 95)*, pp. 149–156, June 1995.

[4] D. Bauer, C. Carothers, and A. Holder, "Scalable time warp on bluegene supercomputer," in *Proc. of the ACM/IEEE/SCS Workshop on Principles of Advanced and Distributed Simulation (PADS)*, 2009.

[5] D. Jagtap, N.Abu-Ghazaleh, and D.Ponomarev, "Optimization of parallel discrete event simulator for multi-core systems," in *International Parallel and Distributed Processing Symposium*, May 2012.

[6] J. Wang, D. Jagtap, N. Abu-Ghazaleh, and D. Ponomarev, "Parallel discrete event simulation for multi-core systems: Analysis and optimization," *IEEE Transactions on Parallel and Distributed Systems*, vol. 25, no. 6, pp. 1574–1584, 2014.

[7] D. Jagtap, K. Bahulkar, D. Ponomarev, and N. Abu-Ghazaleh, "Characterizing and understanding pdes behavior on tilera architecture," in *Workshop on Principles of Advanced and Distributed Simulation (PADS 12)*, July 2012.

[8] G.Chrysos, "Intel xeon phi x100 family coprocessor - the architecture," in *Intel white paper*, 2012.

[9] "Tilera TILE64 processor," 2008. Documentation from Tilera Website http://www.tilera.com.

[10] H. Chen, Y.Yao, and W. Tang, "Can mic find its place in the world of pdes?," in *Proceedings of International Symposium on Distributed Simulation and Real Time Systems (DS-RT)*, 2015.

[11] C. Carothers, D. Bauer, and S. Pearce, "ROSS: A high-performance, low memory, modular time warp system," in *Proc of the 11th Workshop on Parallel and Distributed Simulation (PADS)*, 2000.

[12] R. Fujimoto, "Parallel discrete event simulation," *Communications of the ACM*, vol. 33, pp. 30–53, Oct. 1990.

[13] D. Jefferson, "Virtual time," *ACM Transactions on Programming Languages and Systems*, vol. 7, pp. 405–425, July 1985.

[14] A. S. amd R. Gramunt, J. Corbal, H. Kim, K. Vinod, S. Chinthamani, S. HUtsell, R. Agarwal, and Y. Liu, "Knights landing: Second-generation intel xeon phi product," in *IEEE Micro*, 2016.

[15] A. Sodani, R. Gramunt, J. Corbal, H.-S. Kim, K. Vinod, S. Chinthamani, S. Hutsell, R. Agarwal, and Y.-C. Liu, "Knights landing: Second-generation intel xeon phi product," *IEEE Micro*, vol. 36, no. 2, pp. 34–46, 2016.

[16] S. Srinivasan and P. F. Reynolds Jr, "Non-interfering gvt computation via asynchronous global reductions," in *Proceedings of the 25th conference on Winter simulation*, pp. 740–749, ACM, 1993.

[17] G. Chen and B. K. Szymanski, "Dsim: scaling time warp to 1,033 processors," in *Proceedings of the 37th conference on Winter simulation*, pp. 346–355, Winter Simulation Conference, 2005.

[18] K. Bahulkar, J. Wang, N. Abu-Ghazaleh, and D. Ponomarev, "Partitioning on dynamic bahavior for parallel discrete event simulation," in *26th IEEE/ACM/SCS Workshop on Principles of Advanced and Distributed Simulations (PADS)*, July 2012.

[19] P. D. Barnes Jr, C. D. Carothers, D. R. Jefferson, and J. M. LaPre, "Warp speed: executing time warp on 1,966,080 cores," in *Proceedings of the 1st ACM SIGSIM Conference on Principles of Advanced Discrete Simulation*, pp. 327–336, ACM, 2013.

[20] A. Ramachandran, J. Vienne, R. Wijmgaart, L. Koesterke, and I. Sharapov, "Performance evaluation of nas parallel benchmarks on intel xeon phi," in *Proceedings of International Conference on Parallel Processing (ICPP)*, 2013.

[21] G. Misra, N. Kurkure, A. Das, M.Valmiki, S. Das, and A. Gupta, "Evaluation of rodinia codes on intel xeon phi," in *Proceedings of the 4th International Conference on Intelligent Systems, Modelling and Simulation*, 2013.

[22] A. Heinecke, K. Vaidanathan, M. Smelianskiy, A. Kobutov, R. Dubtsov, G. Henri, A. Shet, G. Chrysos, and P. Dubey, "Design and implementation of the linpack benchmark for single and multi-node systems based on intel xeon phi coprocessor," in *Proceedings of International Parallel and Distributed Processing Symposium (IPDPS)*, 2013.

[23] S. Pennycook, C. Hughes, M. Smelianskiy, and S. Jarvis, "Exploring simd for molecular dynamics using intel xeon processor and intel xeon phi coprocessors," in *Proceedings of International Parallel and Distributed Processing Symposium (IPDPS)*, 2013.

[24] M. Lu, L. Zhang, H. Hyunh, Z. Ong, Y. Liang, B. He, R. Goh, and R. Huynh, "Optimizing the mapreduce framework on intel xeon phi coprocessor," in *Proceedings of International Conference on Big Data*, 2013.

[25] B. Xie, X. Liu, J. Zhan, Z. Jia, Y. Zhu, L. Wang, and L. Zhang, "Characterizing data analytics workloads on intel xeon phi," in *Workload Characterization (IISWC), 2015 IEEE International Symposium on*, pp. 114–115, IEEE, 2015.

PDES-A: a Parallel Discrete Event Simulation Accelerator for FPGAs

Shafiur Rahman
University of California
Riverside
mrahm008@ucr.edu

Nael Abu-Ghazaleh
University of California
Riverside
nael@cs.ucr.edu

Walid Najjar
University of California
Riverside
najjar@cs.ucr.edu

ABSTRACT

In this paper, we present initial experiences implementing a general Parallel Discrete Event Simulation (PDES) accelerator on a Field Programmable Gate Array (FPGA). The accelerator can be specialized to any particular simulation model by defining the object states and the event handling logic, which are then synthesized into a custom accelerator for the given model. The accelerator consists of several event processors that can process events in parallel while maintaining the dependencies between them. Events are automatically sorted by a self-sorting event queue. The accelerator supports optimistic simulation by automatically keeping track of event history and supporting rollbacks. The architecture is limited in scalability locally by the communication and port bandwidth of the different structures. However, it is designed to allow multiple accelerators to be connected together to scale up the simulation. We evaluate the design and explore several design tradeoffs and optimizations. We show the accelerator can scale to 64 concurrent event processors relative to the performance of a single event processor.

Keywords

PDES, FPGA, accelerator, coprocessor, parallel simulation

1. INTRODUCTION

Discrete event simulation (DES) is an important application used in the design and evaluation of systems and phenomena where the change of state is discrete. It is heavily used in a number of scientific, engineering, medical and industrial applications. Parallel Discrete Event Simulation (PDES) leverages parallel processing to increase the performance and capacity of DES, enabling the simulation of larger, more detailed models, for more scenarios and in a shorter period of time. PDES is a fine-grained application with irregular communication patterns and frequent synchronization making it challenging to parallelize.

In this paper, we present an initial exploration of a general Parallel Discrete Event Simulation (PDES) accelerator im-

plemented on an FPGA. In recent years, many researchers have developed and analyzed PDES simulators for a variety of parallel and distributed hardware platforms as these platforms have continued to evolve. The widespread use of both shared and distributed memory cluster environments has motivated development of PDES kernels optimized for these environments such as GTW [7], ROSS [3] and WarpIV [29]. The recent emergence of multi-core and many-core processors has attracted considerable interest among the high-performance computing communities to explore PDES in these emerging platforms. Typically, these simulators [32, 10, 26] use multi-threading and develop synchronization friendly data structures to take advantage of the low communication latency and tight memory integration among cores on same chip. Using similar insights, PDES has been shown to scale well on many-core architectures such as the Tilera Tile64, the Intel Xeon Phi (also known as Many Integrated Cores or MIC) as well as GPGPUs. Several researchers have explored the use of GPGPUs to accelerated PDES [19, 31, 20]. Similarly, Jagtap et al. explored the performance of PDES on the Tilera Tile64 [15], while Chen et al. studied its performance on the Intel Xeon Phi coprocessor [4, 34].

In contrast to these effort, relatively fewer works have considered acceleration of PDES using non-conventional architectures such as FPGAs, motivating our study. In particular, our interest in FPGAs stems from the fact that they do not limit the datapath organization of the accelerator, allowing us to experiment with how the computation should ideally be supported. In addition, the end of Dennard scaling and the expected arrival of dark silicon makes the use of custom accelerators for important applications one promising area of future progress. Many types of accelerators have already been proposed for a large number of important applications such as deep learning [28] and graph processing [35]. Thus, the exploration of accelerator organization for PDES informs possible design of custom accelerators for important simulation applications.

An FPGA implementation of PDES offers several possible advantages.

- Fast and high-bandwidth, on-chip communication: An FPGA can support fast and high bandwidth on-chip communication, substantially alleviating the communication bottleneck that often limits the performance of PDES [33]. On the other hand, often the memory latency experienced by FPGAs is high (but the available bandwidth is also high), necessitating approaches to hide the memory access latency.

- Specialized, high-bandwidth datapaths: General pur-

SIGSIM-PADS '17, May 24–26, 2017, Singapore.

© 2017 ACM. ISBN 978-1-4503-4489-0/17/05...$15.00

DOI: http://dx.doi.org/10.1145/3064911.3064930

pose processing provides high flexibility but at the price of high overhead and a fixed datapath. A specialized accelerator in contrast, can more efficiently implement a required task without unnecessary overheads of fetching instructions and moving data around a general datapath. These advantages have been estimated to yield over 500x improvement in performance for video encoding, with 90% reduction in energy [11]. Moreover, an FPGA can allow high parallelism limited only by the number of processing units and the communication bandwidth available between them, as well as the memory bandwidth available to the FPGA chip.

We believe that PDES is potentially an excellent fit for these strengths of FPGAs. PDES exhibits *ordered irregular parallelism* (OIP) with the following three characteristics: (1) total or partial order between tasks; (2) dynamic and unpredictable data dependencies; and (3) dynamic generation of tasks that are not known beforehand [21]. OIP applications have inherent parallelism that is difficult to exploit in a traditional multiprocessor architecture without careful implementation. To preserve order among the tasks and maintain causality, hardware based speculative implementations such as thread-level speculation (TLS) often introduce false data dependencies, for example, in the form of a priority queue [17]. Run-time overheads such as those of communication limit the scalability of PDES [12]; these overheads may be both lower and more easily maskable in the context of an FPGA[33]. For models where event process is computationally expensive, FPGA implementations are likely to yield to more streamlined customized processors. On the other hand, if the event processing is simple, FPGAs can accommodate a larger number of event processors, increasing the raw available hardware parallelism. Finally, for many reasons, FPGAs have exceptional energy properties compared to GPGPUs and many-cores.

We present our initial design of a PDES accelerator (PDES-A). We show that PDES-A can provide excellent scalability for Phold up to 64 concurrent event processors. Our initial prototype outperforms a similar simulation on a 12-core 3.5GHz Intel Core i7 CPU by 2.5x. We show that there remains several opportunities to optimize our design further. Moreover, we show that multiple PDES-A accelerators can fit within the same FPGA chip, allowing us to further scale the performance.

FPGA based accelerator development platforms have recently progressed rapidly to make FPGA based accelerators available to all programmers. Microsoft's Catapult [22] and the Convey Wolverine [5] are examples of recent systems that offer integrated FPGAs with programmability, tight integration, advanced communication and memory sharing with CPU in industry standard HPC clusters. After the acquisition of Altera last year, Intel has already started shipping versions of its Xeon processors with integrated FPGA support [2]. Modern memory technologies such as Micron's Hybrid Memory Cube [14] can offer up to 320GB/s effective bandwidth providing excellent bandwidth to applications requiring high memory demand such as PDES. However, specialized hardware support is required to take advantage of this bandwidth. The recent take over of Convey Computing by Micron paved the way to have Hybrid Memory Cube in FPGA based coprocessors. Potentially, an FPGA implementation can yield high performance and low-power PDES

accelerators as well as inform the design of custom accelerators for PDES.

Our work is in the vein of prior studies that explored customized or programmable hardware support for PDES. Fujimoto et al. propose the Rollback chip, a special purpose processor to accelerate state saving and rollbacks in Time Warp[9]. In the area of logic simulation and computer simulation, the use of FPGA offers opportunities for performance since the design being simulated can simply be emulated on the FPGA [30]. Noronha and Abu-Ghazaleh explore the use of a programmable network interface card to accelerate GVT computation and direct message cancellation [18]. Similarly, Santoro and Quaglia use a programmable network interface card to accelerate checkpointing for optimistic simulation [27]. Our work differs in the emphasis on support of complete general optimistic PDES. Most similar to our work, Herbrodt et al. [13] explore FPGA implementation of a specific PDES model for molecular dynamics, but the design is specialized to this one application rather than supporting general simulation.

The remainder of this paper is organized as follows. We use section 2 to present some background information related to PDES and introduce the Convey Wolverine FPGA system we use in our experiments. Section 3 introduces the design of our PDES-A accelerator and its various components. Section 4 overviews some implementation details and the verification of PDES-A. Section 5 presents a detailed performance evaluation of the design. In section 6 we explore the overhead of PDES-A and project the potential performance if we integrate multiple PDES-A accelerators on the same FPGA chip. Finally, Section 7 presents some concluding remarks.

2. BACKGROUND

In this section, we provide some background information necessary for understanding our proposed design. First, we discuss PDES and then present the Convey Wolverine FPGA application accelerator we use in our experiments.

2.1 Parallel Discrete Event Simulation

A discrete event simulation (DES) models the behavior of a system that has discrete changes in state. This is in contrast to the more typical time-stepped simulations where the complete state of the system is computed at regular intervals in time. DES has applications in many domains such as computer and telecommunication simulations, war gaming/military simulations, operations research, epidemic simulations, and many more. PDES leverages the additional computational power and memory capacity of multiple processors to increase the performance and capacity of PDES, allowing the simulation of larger, more detailed models, and the consideration of more scenarios, in a shorter amount of time [8].

In a PDES simulation, the simulation objects are partitioned across a number of *logical processes* (LPs) that are distributed to different Processing Elements (PEs). Each PE executes its events in simulation time order (similar to DES). Each processed event can update the state of its object, and possibly generate future events. Maintaining correct execution requires preserving time stamp order among dependent events on different LPs. If a PE receives an event from another PE, this event must be processed in time-stamped order for correct simulation.

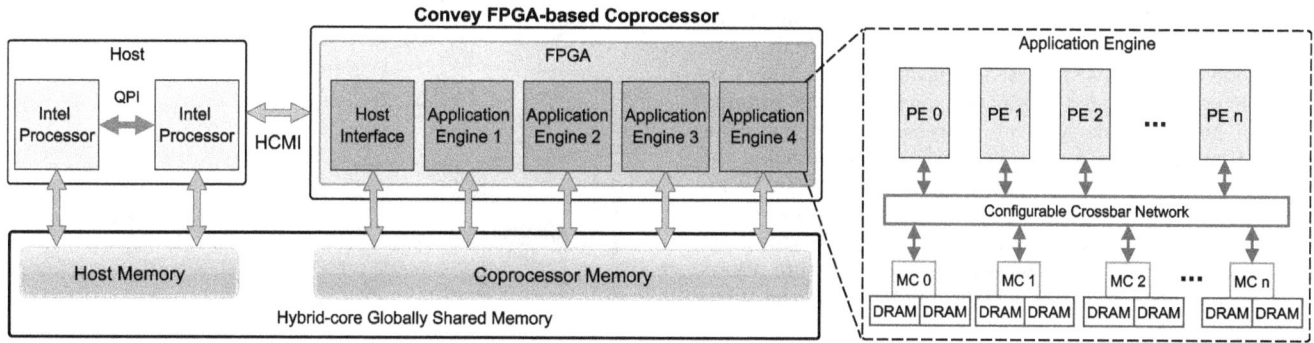

Figure 1: Overview of the Convey Hybrid-Core architecture

To ensure correct simulation, two synchronization algorithms are commonly used: conservative and optimistic synchronization. In conservative simulation, PEs coordinate with each other to agree on a *lookahead* window in time where events can be safely executed without compromising causality; in other words, the model property determines a time window in which events cannot be generated due to the simulation time delay between processing an event and any future events it schedules. This synchronization imposes a overhead on the PEs to continue to advance. In contrast, optimistic simulation algorithms such as Time Warp [16] allow PEs to process events without synchronization. As a result, it is possible for an LP to receive a *straggler* event with a time stamp earlier than their current simulation time. To preserve causality, optimistic simulators maintain checkpoints of the simulation, and rollback to a state in the past earlier than the time of the straggler event. The rollback may require the LP to cancel out any event messages it generated erroneously using *anti-messages*. This approach uses more memory for keeping checkpoint information, which need to be garbage collected when they are no longer needed to bound the dynamic memory size. A *Global Virtual Time* (GVT) algorithm is used to identify the minimum simulation time that all LPs have reached: checkpoints with a time lower than GVT can be garbage collected, and events earlier than GVT may be safely committed.

2.2 Convey Wolverine FPGA Accelerator

The Convey Wolverine FPGA Accelerator is an FPGA based coprocessor that augments a commodity processor with processing elements optimized for key algorithms that are inefficient to run in a conventional processors. The coprocessor contains standard FPGAs coupled with a standard x86 host interface to communicate with the host processor. The system also includes a standard Xeon based CPU integrated with the Convey Wolverine WX2000 coprocessor.

The Wolverine WX2000 integrates three major subsystems: Application Engine Hub (AEH), Application Engines (AEs), and the Memory Subsystem (MCs) [5]. Figure 1 shows an abstracted view of the system architecture. AEs are the core of the system and implement the specialized functionality of the coprocessor. There are four AEs in the system implemented inside a Xilinx Virtex-7 XC7V2000T FPGAs. The AEs are connected to memory controllers via 10GB/s point-to-point network links. In an optimized implementation, up to 40GB/s of bandwidth is available to the system. The clock rate of the FPGAs is much lower than that of the CPU (150MHz), but they can implement many specialized functional units in parallel. When utilizing the memory bandwidth properly, the throughput can be many times that of a single processor. This is why the system is ideal for applications benefiting from high computation capability and large high-bandwidth memory. Each of the Application Engines are dedicated FPGAs that can be programmed with same or different application. Number of processing elements in an AE is limited by the resources available in the FPGA chip used. The processing elements can connect to the memory subsystem through a crossbar network which allows any processing element to access any of the physical memory.

The AEH acts as the control and management interface to the coprocessor. The Hybrid Core Memory Interconnect (HCMI), implemented in the AEH, connects the coprocessor to the processor to fetch instructions and to process and route memory requests to the MCs. It also initializes the AEs, programs them, and conveys execution instructions from the processor. The memory subsystem includes 4 memory controllers supporting 8 DDR2 memory channels providing a high bandwidth, but also high-latency, connection between memory and application engines [6]. The memory subsystem provides simplified logical memory interface ports that connects to a crossbar network which in turn connects to the physical memory controller. Programmers can use the memory interface ports in any implementation.

Another important part of the memory system is the Hybrid Core Globally Shared Memory architecture. It creates a unified memory address space where all physical memory is addressable by both the processor and the coprocessor using virtual address. The memory subsystem implements the address translation, crossbar routing, and configuration circuits. Both the memory subsystem and the application engines hub are provided by the vendor and their implementation remains the same in all designs. Note that there is a substantial difference in the latency and bandwidth between accesses to local memory and accesses to remote (CPU) memory.

The architecture of the Convey system can present some advantages in the design of a PDES system. The event processing logic in PDES are simple for many models. Memory access latency and communication overhead usually prevent the system from achieving high throughput. The high bandwidth parallel data access capability in the Convey system can be exploited to bypass the bottleneck by employing a large number of event processors. In this way, while one event processor waits for memory, others can be active, enabling the system to effectively use the high memory bandwidth. Also, the reconfigurable fabric allows us to implement optimized datapaths, including the communication network among event processors to reduce communication and synchronization overheads. Leveraging the standard x86 interface, multiple Convey servers can be interconnected, which opens up the possibilities to scale up the PDES system to a large cluster based implementation. And finally, the global shared memory architecture allows the host processor to easily initialize and observe the simulator.

3. PDES-A DESIGN OVERVIEW

In this section, we present an overview of the unit PDES accelerator (PDES-A). Each PDES-A accelerator is a tightly coupled high-performance PDES simulator in its own right. However, hardware limitations such as contention for shared event and state queue ports, local interconnection network complexity, and bandwidth limit restrict the scalability of this tightly coupled design approach. These scalability constraints invite a design where multiple interconnected PDES-A accelerators together work on a large simulation model, and exploiting the full available FPGA resources. In this paper, we explore and analyze only PDES-A, and not the full architecture consisting of many PDES-A accelerators. In the design of PDES-A, we are careful to modularize it to facilitate integration with other PDES-A accelerators or any PDES execution engines that are compatible with its event API.

In an FPGA implementation, event processing, communication, synchronization, and memory access operations occur in a way different from how these operations occur on general purpose processors. Therefore, both performance bottlenecks and optimization opportunities differ from those in conventional software implementations of PDES. We developed a baseline implementation of PDES-A and used it to identify performance bottlenecks. We then used these insights to develop improved versions of the accelerator. We describe our design and optimizations in this section.

3.1 Design Goals

The goal of the design is to provide a general PDES accelerator, rather than an accelerator for a specific model or class of models. We expect that knowledge of the model can be exploited to fine tune the performance of PDES-A, but we did not pursue such opportunities. To support this generality, PDES-A provides a modular framework where various components can be adjusted independently to attain the most effective data path flow control across different PDES models. Since the time to process events in different models will vary, we designed an event-driven execution model that does not make assumption about event execution time. We decided to implement an optimistically synchronized simulator to allow the system to operate around the large memory access latencies. However, the tight coupling within the system should allow us to control the progress of the simulation and naturally bound optimism.

3.2 General Overview

The overall design of PDES-A is shown in Figure 2. The simulator is organized into four major components: (1) Event Queue, which stores the pending events; (2) Event Proces-

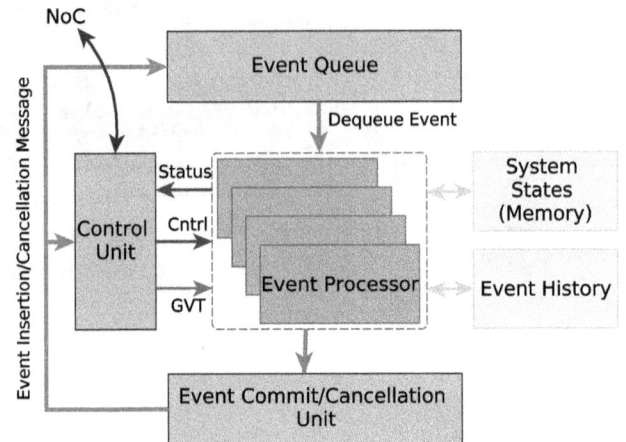

Figure 2: PDES-A overall system organization

sors: custom datapaths for processing the event types in the model; (3) System State Memory: holds relevant system state, including checkpointing information; (4) and the Controller: which coordinates all aspects of operation. The first three components correspond to the same functionality in traditional PDES engines in any discrete event simulator, and the last one oversees the event processors to ensure correct parallel operation and communication. We will look into how these components fit together in a PDES system first, and then into their implementation.

Communication between different components uses message passing. We currently support three message types: Event messages, anti-messages, and GVT messages. These three message types are the minimum required for an optimistic simulator to operate, but additional message types could be supported in the future to implement optimization, or to coordinate between multiple PDES-A units. Please note that the architecture can be modified to support conservative simulation while preserving most of its structure because of the decision to support general message passing. A conservative version of PDES-A requires changes to message types and the controller (different dispatch logic, and replacing GVT with synchronization), while eliminating the checkpointing information; we did not build a conservative version of PDES-A.

Figure 2 shows the major components of PDES-A and their interactions. The event queue contains a sorted list of all the unprocessed events. Event processors receive event messages from the queue. After processing events, additional events that may be generated are sent and inserted into the event queue for scheduling. The system needs to keep track of all the processed events and the changes made by them until it is guaranteed that the events will not be rolled back. When an event is received for processing, the event processor checks for any conflicting events from the event history. Anti-messages are generated when the event processor discovers that erroneous events have been generated by an event processed earlier. Since the state memory is shared, a controller unit is necessary to monitor the event processors for possible resource conflict and manage their correct operation. Another integral function of the control unit is the generation of GVT which is used to identify the events and state changes that can be safely committed. The

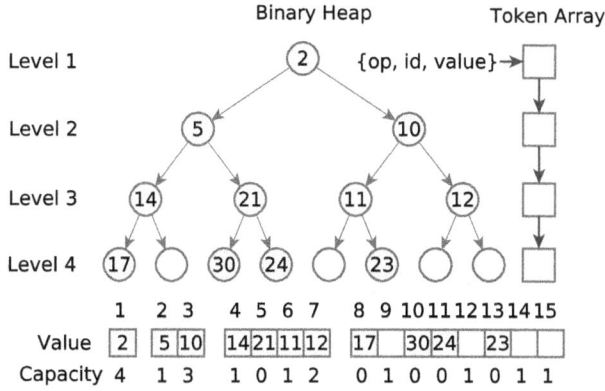

Figure 3: The P-heap data structure[23]

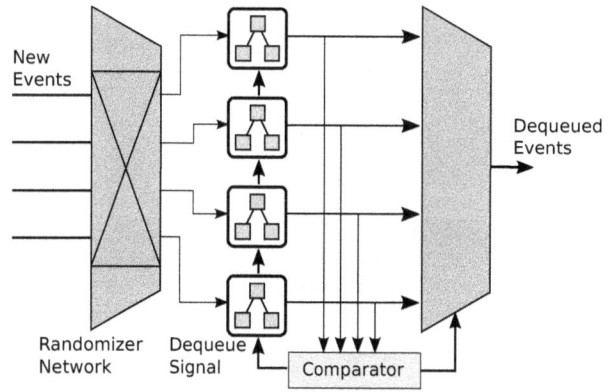

Figure 4: Multiple event issue priority queue

control unit computes GVT continuously and forwards updated estimates to the commit logic. These messages should have low latency to limit the occurrence of rollbacks and to control the size of the event and message history. In the remainder of this section, we describe the primary components in more detail.

3.3 Event Queue

The event queue maintains a time-ordered list of events to be processed by the event processors. It needs to support two basic operations - *insert* and *dequeue*. An *invalidate* operation can be included to make early cancellation possible for straggler events that have not been processed yet and still reside in the queue.

The event queue structure and its impact on PDES performance has been studied in the context of software implementations [25]; however, it's important to understand suitable queue organizations implemented in hardware. Prior work has studied hardware queue structures supporting different features. Priority queues offer attractive properties for PDES such as constant time operation, scalability, low area overhead, and simple hardware routing structures. Simple binary heap based priority queues are commonly used in hardware based implementations, but requires $O(log(n))$ time for enqueue and dequeue operations. Other options have other drawbacks; for example, Calendar Queues [1] support $O(1)$ access time but are difficult and expensive to scale in a hardware implementation. QuickQ [24] uses multiple dual-ported RAM in a pipelined structure which provides easy scalability and to support constant time access. However, the access time is proportional to the size of each stage of RAM. Configuring these stages to achieve a small access time necessitates a large number of stages, which leads to high hardware complexity. For these reasons, we selected a *pipelined heap* (P-heap in short) structure as the basic organization in our implementation [23], except for a few modifications which we describe later. P-heap uses a pipelined binary heap to provide two cycles constant access time (to initiate an enqueue or dequeue operation), while having a hardware complexity similar to binary heaps.

The P-heap structure uses a conventional binary heap with each node storing a few additional bits to represent the number of vacancies in the sub-tree rooted at the node (Figure 3). The capacity values are used by *insert* operations to find the path in the heap that it should percolate

through. P-heap also keeps a *token* variable for each stage which contains the current operation, target node identifier and value that is percolating down to that stage. During an insertion operation, the value in token variable is compared with the target node: the smaller value replaces the target node value and the larger value passes down to the token variable of the following stage. The *id* value of the next stage is determined by checking the capacity associated with the nodes.

For the dequeue operation, the value of the root node is dequeued and replaced by the smaller of its child nodes. The same operation continues to recurse through the branch, promoting the smallest child at every step. During any operation any two of the consecutive stages are accessed; one read access and the other write access. As a result, a stage can handle a new operation every two cycles, since the operation of the heap is pipelined with different insert and/or dequeue operations at different stages in their operation [23].

P-heap can be efficiently implemented in hardware on an FPGA. Every stage requires *a Dual Ported RAM*, which is a memory element having one write port and two read port. Depending on the size of that stage, it can be synthesized with registers, distributed RAM, or block RAM elements to maximize resource utilization. An arbitrary number of stages can be added (limited by block RAM resource availability) as the performance is not hurt by the number of stages in the heap due to pipelining, making it straightforward to scale.

In an optimistic PDES system, it is possible that ordering can be relaxed to improve performance, while maintaining simulation correctness via rollbacks to recover from occasional ordering violations. This relaxation opens up possibilities for optimization of the queue structure. For example, multiple heaps may be used in parallel to service more than one request in a single cycle. In an approach similar to that used by Herbordt et al.[13], we can use a randomizer network to direct multiple requests to multiple available heap (Figure 4). There is a chance that two of the highest priority events may reside in the same heap and ordering violation will occur at the queue during multiple dequeue. However, when the number of LPs and PEs are large, such occurrence which is handled by the rollback mechanism would be rare resulting in a net performance gain. Although we have a version of this queue implemented, we report our results without using it. Other structures that sacrifice full order-

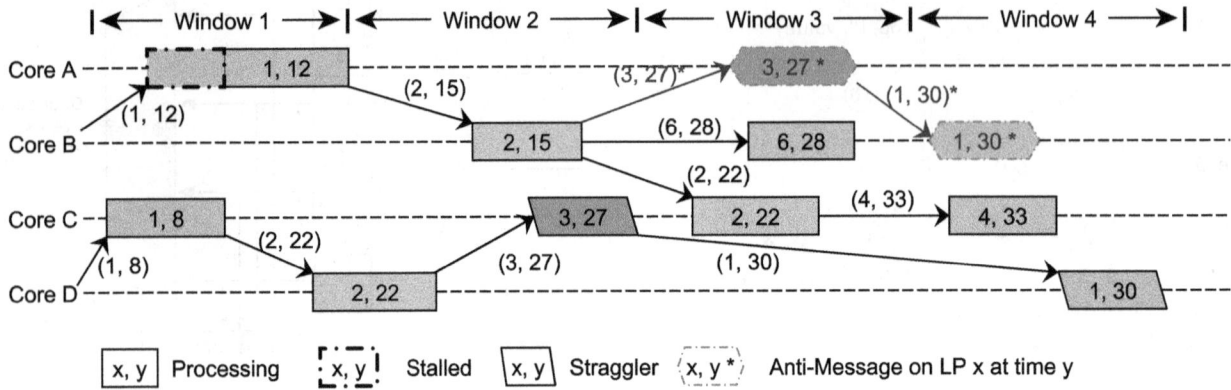

Figure 5: Simplified timeline representation showing scheduling of events in the system.

ing but admit higher parallelism such as Gupta and Wilsey's lock-free queue may also be explored [10].

The queue stores a key-value pair. We use 64 bit entries with event time-stamp acting as the key. The value contains the id of the target LP and a payload message. In cases where the payload message is too large, we store a pointer to a payload message in memory. For the Phold model we use in our evaluation, all messages fit in the default value field.

3.4 Event Processor

The event processor is at the core of PDES-A. The front-end of the processor is common to all simulation models. It is responsible for the following general operations: (1) to check the event history for conflicts; (2) to store and clean up state snapshots by checking GVT; (3) to support event exchange with the event queue; and (4) to respond to control signals to avoid conflicting event processing. In addition, the event processors execute the actual event handlers which are specialized to each simulation model to generate the next events and compute state transitions.

The task processing logic is designed to be replaceable and easily customizable to the events in different models. It appears as a black box to the event processor system. All communications are done through the pre-configured interface. The event processor passes event message and relevant data to the core logic by populating FIFO buffers. Once the events are processed, the core logic uses output buffers to store any generated events. The core logic has interfaces to request state memory by supplying addresses and sizes. The fetched memory is placed into a FIFO buffer to be read from the core. The interface to the memory port is standard and provided in the core to be easily accessible by the task processing logic.

The model we use in our evaluation (Phold) has only one type of event handler, simplifying the mapping of events to handlers. However, in models where multiple event handlers exist, interesting design decisions arise about whether to specialize the event processors to each event type, or to create more general, but perhaps less efficient event handling engines. If a reasonable approximation of the distribution of the task frequency in knows, the numbers of different kind of event processors may be tuned to the requirement of the model to maximize resource utilization. It is also possible to create a mix of specialized handlers for common events, and more general handlers to handle rare events. We will consider such issues in our future work.

3.5 Event scheduling and processing

Figure 5 shows a representative event execution timeline in the system. Events are assigned to the event processors in order of their timestamps; on the figure, the event is represented by a tuple (x, y) where x is the LP number and y is the simulation time. Event $(1, 8)$ is scheduled to core C. A second event $(1, 12)$ belonging to the same LP is scheduled to core A while event $(1, 8)$ is still being processed. Because of the dependency, core A is stalled by the controller unit until the first event completes. At the completion of an event, the controller allows the earliest timestamp among the waiting (stalled) events for that core to proceed as shown in window 1. Each event may generate one or more new events when it terminates. These events are scheduled at some time in the future when a core is available. Occasionally, an event is processed after another event with a later timestamp has already executed (i.e., *a straggler event*). When discovering this causality error, the erroneously processed events need to be rolled back to restore causality. Window 2 in Figure 5 shows one such event $(2,22)$ which executes before event $(2,15)$. We use a lazy cancellation and roll-back approach. Event processing logic detects the conflict by checking the event history table and initiates the roll-back. The new event will restore the states and generate events it would have normally scheduled $(6, 28)$ along with anti-messages (anti-message $(3, 27^*)$ in this example) for all events generated by the straggler event, and new event $(2, 22)$ that reschedules the cancelled event.

The anti-messages may get processed before or after its target event is done. An anti-message $(3, 27^*)$ checks the event history and if the target event has already been processed, it rolls back the states and generates other necessary anti-messages $(1, 30^*)$ to *chase* the erroneous message chain (i.e., cascading rollbacks) much like a regular events as shown in window 3 of Figure 5. If the target message is yet to arrive, the anti-message is stored in the event history table. The target message $(1,30)$ cancels itself upon discovery of the anti-message in the history and no new event is generated as shown in window 4.

4. IMPLEMENTATION OVERVIEW

We used a full RTL implementation on Convey WX-2000 accelerator for prototyping the simulator. The current prototype fits in one of the four available Virtex-7 XC7v2000T FPGAs (Figure 13). The event history table and queue were implemented in the BRAM memory available in the FPGAs. The on-board 32GB DDR3 memory was used for state memory implementation, although very little memory was necessary for the Phold model prototype. The system uses a 150MHz clock rate. The host server was used to initialize the memory and events at the beginning of the simulation. The accelerator communicated through the host interface to report results as well as other measurements we collected to characterize the operation of the design. For any values that we want to measure during run time, we instrument the design with hardware counters that keep track of these events. We complemented these results with others such as queue and core occupancy that we obtained from functional simulator of the RTL implementation using Modelsim.

Our goal in this paper is to present a general characterization of this initial prototype of PDES-A. We used the Phold model for our experiments because it is widely used to provide general characterization of PDES execution that is sensitive to the system. On the Convey, the memory system provides high bandwidth but also high latency (a few hundred cycles). This latency could dominate event execution time for fine-grained models where event handling is simple. To emulate event-processing overhead we let each event increment a counter to a value picked randomly between 10 and 75 cycles. The model generates memory accesses by reading from the memory when the event starts and writing back to it again when it ends.

Since our design is modular, we can scale the number of event processors. However, as the number of processors increases, we can expect contention to arise on the fixed components of the design such as the event queue and the interconnection network. We experiment with cluster sizes from 8 to 64 in order to analyze the design trade-offs and scalability bottlenecks. The performance of the system under variable number of LPs and event distribution gives us insight about the most effective design parameters for a system. We sized our queues to support up to 512 initial events in the system. The queue is flexible and can be expanded in capacity, or even be made to dynamically grow.

Design Validation: Verification of hardware design is complex since it is difficult to peek into the hardware as it executes. However, the hardware design flow supports a logic level simulator of the design that we used to validate that the model correctly executes the simulation. In particular, the Modelsim simulator was used to study the complete model including the memory controllers, crossbar network, and the PDES-A logic. Since the design admits many legal execution paths, and many components of the system introduce additional variability, we decided to validate the model by checking a number of invariants that are not model specific. In particular, we verified that no causality constraints are violated in the full event execution trace of the simulation under a number of PDES-A and application configurations.

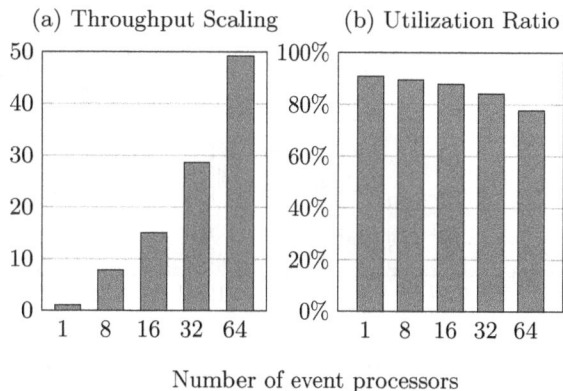

Figure 6: Effect of variation of number of cores on (a) throughput and (b) percentage of core utilization for 256 LP and 512 initial events.

5. PERFORMANCE EVALUATION

In this section, we evaluate the design under a number of conditions to study its performance and scalability. In addition, we analyze the hardware complexity of the design in terms of the percentage of the FPGA area it consumes. Finally, we compare the performance to PDES on a multi-core machine and use the area estimates to project the performance of the full system with multiple PDES-A accelerators.

5.1 Performance and Scalability

In this first experiment, we scale the number of event processors from 1 to 64 while executing a Phold model. Figure 6-a shows the scalability of the throughput normalized to the throughput of a configuration with a single event handler. The scalability is almost linear up to 8 event handlers and continues to scale with the number of processors up to 64 where it reaches a little bit above 49x. As the number of cores increases contention for the bandwidth of the different components in the simulation starts to increase leading to very good but sub-linear improvement in performance. Figure 6-b shows the event processor occupancy, which is generally high, but starts dropping as we increase the number of event processors reflecting that the additional contention is preventing the issue of the events to the handlers in time.

Figure 7 shows the throughput of the accelerator as a function of the number of LPs and the density of events in the system for 64 event processors. The throughput increases significantly with the number of available LPs in the system. As the events get distributed across a larger number of LPs, the probability of events belonging to the same LP and therefore blocking due to dependencies goes down. In our implementation, we stall all but one event when multiple cores are processing events belonging to the same LP to protect state memory consistency. Thus, having a higher number of LPs reduces the average number of stalled processors and increases utilization. In contrast, the event density in the system influences throughput to a lesser degree. Even though having a sufficient number of events is important to keeping the cores processing, once we have a large enough number of events increasing the event population further does not improve throughput appreciably.

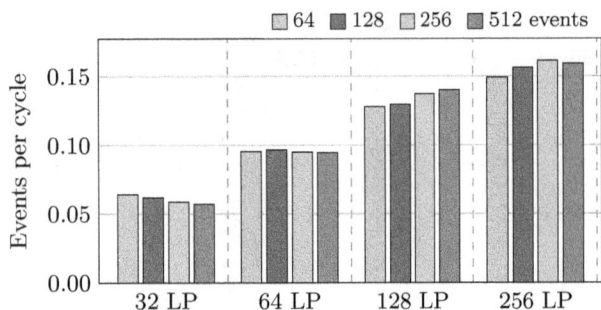

Figure 7: Event processing throughput using 64 event processors for different number of initial events and LPs.

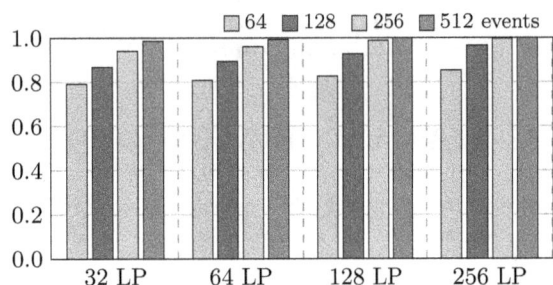

Figure 8: Ratio of number of committed events to total processed events using 64 event processors.

5.2 Rollbacks and Simulation Efficiency

The efficiency of the simulation, measured as the ratio of the number of committed events to processed events, is an important indicator of the performance of optimistic PDES simulators. Figure 8 shows the efficiency of a 64-processor PDES-A as we vary the number of events and the number of LPs. The fraction of events that are rolled-back depends on the number of events in the system but is not strongly correlated to the number of LPs. With a large population of initial events, we observe virtually no rollbacks since there are many events that are likely to be independent at any given point in the simulation. Newly scheduled events will tend to be in the future relative to currently existing events, reducing the potential for rollbacks. However, keeping all other parameters same, reducing the number of initial events can cause the simulation efficiency to drop to around 80% (reflecting around 20x increase in the percentage of rolled back events). For similar reasons, the number of rolled-back events decreases slightly with a greater number of LPs in the simulation. Most causality concerns arise when events associated with same LP are processed in the wrong order. When events are more distributed when number of LPs is higher, thus reducing the occurrence of stalled cores. However, this effect is relatively small.

5.3 Breakdown of event processing time

Figure 9 shows how the average event processing time varies with the number of LPs and the initial number of events, along with the breakdown of the time taken for different tasks, for systems with 32 and 64 processors. The primary source of delay in event processing is the large memory

access latency on the Convey system. Another other major delay source is the delay of processors stalling to wait for potentially conflicting events. These two factors are the primary delays in the system and dominate other overheads in the event processors such as task logic delays and maintaining event history, which also increase as we go from 32 to 64 cores.

The average event processing time is highest when the number of LPs or number of initial events are low. The average number of cycles goes down as more events are issued to the system or the number of LPs is increased (which reduces the probability of a stall). The reason for this behavior is apparent when we consider the breakdown of the event cycles. We notice that about the same number of cycles are consumed for memory access regardless of the configuration of the system because the memory bandwidth of the system is very large. However, the average stall time for the processors is significantly higher with fewer LPs and constitutes the major portion of the event processing delay. For example, with 64 cores, and 32 LPs, we can have no more than 32 cores active; any additional cores would hold an event for an LP that has another active event at the moment. A system of 64 LPs has over 150 stall cycles on average, with 64 processors. The stall times drop substantially as we increase the number of LPs and events in the model. These dependencies result in a high number of stall cycles to prevent conflicts in LP specific memory and event history. At the same time, a small number of LPs increases the chance of a causality violation. The probability that an event will become a straggler goes up with a smaller number of LPs This effect is most severe when the number of LPs is close to the number of event processors. As the number of LPs is increased the events are distributed to more LP, and can be safely processed in parallel.

Figure 10 shows a visualization fo the PDES-A's core operation by showing how the processors are behaving over time for a simulation with 256 LPs and 512 events. The black color shows the cycles when the processors are idle before receiving a new event. Yellow streaks represt the times a processor is stalled. Since an event processor has to stall until all other events associated with the same LP finish, the stall time can sometimes be long if more than two events belonging to the same LP are dispatched. Fortunately, scenarios like this are rare when there are sufficiently large number of LPs and for models that achieve uniform event distribution over the LPs.

The memory access time remains mostly unaffected by the parameters in the system. The state memory is distributed in multiple memory banks and accesses depend on the LPs being processed. The appearance of different LPs in the event processor are not correlated in Phold and therefore poor locality results without any special hardware support. However, the higher number of events may increase the probability of repeating accesses in the same memory area and therefore occasionally decrease the memory access time as these accesses are coalesced by the memory controller or cached by the DRAM row buffers. This effect reduces the average memory access delay slightly.

We note that the actual event handler processing time is a minor component of the event execution time consuming less than 10% of the overall event processing time even in the worst case. We believe that this observation motivates our future work to optimize PDES. In particular, the mem-

140

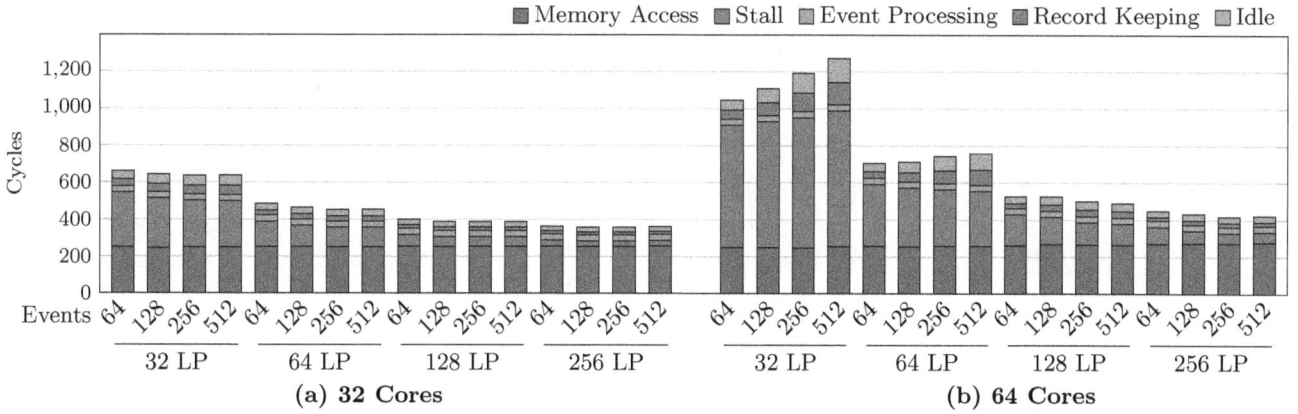

Figure 9: Breakdown of time spent by the event processors on different tasks to process an event using (a) 32 event processors and (b) 64 event processors with respects to different number of LPs and initial event counts.

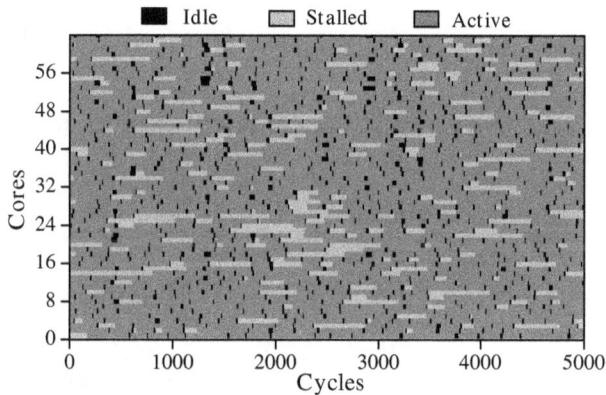

Figure 10: Timeline demonstrating different states of the cores for during a 5000 cycles frame of the simulation.

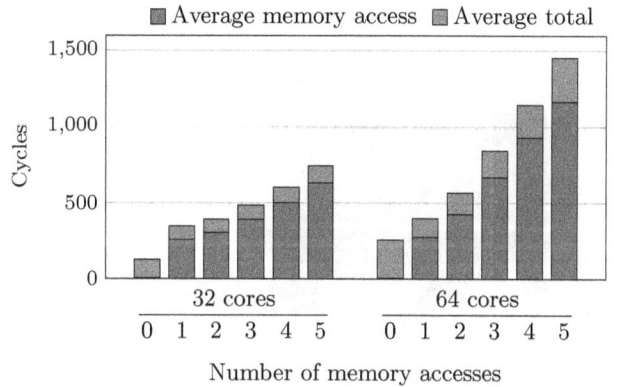

Figure 11: Effect of number/size of state memory access on event processing time

ory access time can be hidden behind event processing if we allow multiple event executions to be handled concurrently by each handler: when one event accesses memory, others can continue execution. This and other optimization opportunities are a topic of our future research.

5.4 Memory Access

Memory access latency is a dominant part of the time required to process an event. Figure 11 shows the effect of variation of the memory access pattern on average execution time. The number of memory accesses can also be thought of as the size of the state memory read and updated in the course of event processing. The leftmost column in the plot shows the execution time without any memory access, which is small compared to the execution time with memory accesses. About 300 cycles are needed for the first memory access. Each additional memory access adds about 50 cycles to the execution time. The changes in the average execution time are almost completely the result of changes in memory access latency. It is apparent that the memory access latency does not scale linearly with the number or size of memory requested. Even if stalls are less frequent, each can take a long time to resolve. Thus, we believe the

memory system can issue multiple independent memory operations concurrently leading to overlap in their access time. We have made the memory accessed by any event a contiguous region in the memory address space, which may also lead to DRAM side row-buffer hits and/or request coalescing at the memory controller.

5.5 Effect of event processing granularity

Figure 12 shows the effect of processing time granularity on the system performance. Since memory access latency is a major source of delay that is currently not being hidden (and therefore adds a constant time to event processing), we configure a model that does not access memory in this experiment. We also allow the event processing to be configured to a controllable delay by controlling the number of iterations the event handler increments a counter. The results of this study are shown in Figure 12-a. As the granularity increases, we simulate models that have increasingly computationally intensive event processing. Initially, the additional processing per event does not affect the system throughput since the system overheads lead to low utilization of the event handling cores when the granularity is small. As the utilization rises (Figure 12-b), additional increases in the event gran-

141

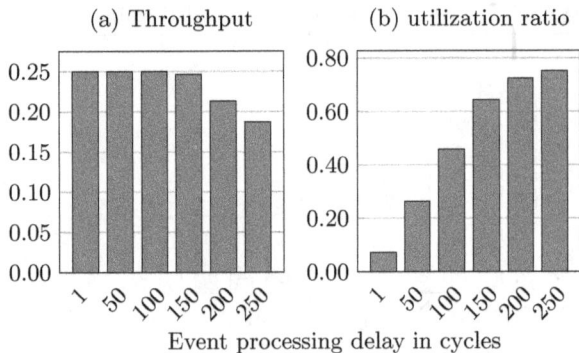

| (a) Throughput | (b) utilization ratio |

Event processing delay in cycles

Figure 12: Effect of variation of processing delays (in cycles) on (a) throughput, (b) ratio of core utilization for 64 event processors with 256 LP and 512 initial events.

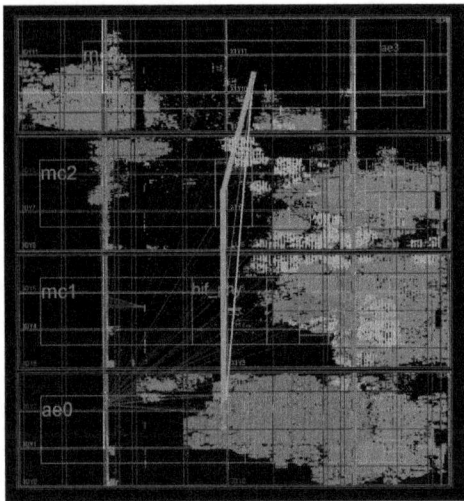

Figure 13: Implementation of the synthesized design on a Virtex-7 XC7V2000T FPGA. Red highlight marks the core simulator, green shows crossbar network, and memory interface logic is highlighted purple.

ularity start to lower the average rate of committed events per cycle since each event is more computationally demanding. Throughput does not improve after reaching 150 cycles event processing time.

5.6 Comparison With ROSS

To provide an idea of the performance of PDES-A relative to a CPU-based PDES simulator, we compared the performance of PDES-A with MPI based PDES simulator ROSS[3]. Although the modeling flow for the two environments is quite different, we configured ROSS to run the Phold model with similar parameters to the PDES-A simulation. The FPGA implementation has the advantage of having access to customized data paths to provide functions such as a single cycle hardware implemented Pseudo Random Number Generator (PNRG), which would require significantly longer time to implement on the CPU in software. On the other hand, the CPU can handle irregular tasks well,

Table 1: Comparative analysis of PDES simulation of Phold model ROSS and PDES-A

Parameters	ROSS	PDES-A
System		
Device	Intel Xeon E5-1650 12 MB L2	Xilinx Virtex-7 XC7V2000T
Frequency	3.50GHz	150MHz
Memory	32 GB	32 GB
Simulation		
PE	72 (12 cores×6 KP)	64
LP	252	256
Event Density	504	512
Remote Event	5%	100%
Performance		
Events/second	9.2 million	23.85 million
Efficiency	80%	~100%
Power	130 Watt	<25 Watt

and execute multiple instructions per cycle at a much higher clock rates.

We changed the Phold model in ROSS to resemble our system by replacing the exponential timestamp distribution with a uniform distribution. We set the number of processing elements, LPs and number of events to match our system closely. One particular difference is in the way remote events are generated and handled in ROSS. In our system, all cores are connected to a shared set of LPs, so there is no difference between local and remote events. In ROSS, remote events have to suffer the extra overhead of message passing in MPI, although MPI uses shared memory on a single machine. We set the remote event threshold in ROSS to 5% to allow marginal communication between cores.

Table 1 shows the parameters for both the systems and their performance. At this configuration, PDES-A can processes events 2.5x faster than a 12-core CPU version of ROSS. When the remote percentage drops to 0% (all events are generated to local LPs), the PDES-A advantage drops to 2x that of ROSS. At higher remote percentages, the advantage increases, up to 10x at 100% remote messages. We believe that as we continue to optimize PDES-A this advantage will be even larger. Moreover, as we see in the next section, there is room on the device to integrate multiple PDES-A cores, further improving the performance.

6. FPGA RESOURCE UTILIZATION AND SCALING ESTIMATES

In this section, we first present an analysis of the area requirements and resource utilization of PDES-A. The FPGA resources utilization by the cores is presented in table 2. A picture of the layout of the design with a single PDES-A core is shown in Figure 13. The overall system takes over about 20% of the available LUTs in the FPGA. The larger portion of this is consumed by the memory interface and other static coprocessor circuitry which will remain constant when the simulator size scales. The core simulator logic utilizes 3.3% of the device logics. Each individual Phold event processor contributes to less than 0.03% resource usage. Register usage is less than 2% in the simulator. We can reasonably expect to replicate the simulation cluster more than 16 times in

Table 2: FPGA resource utilization

Component	LUT (1221600)		FF (2443200)		BRAM (1203)	
	Utilization	% Util.	Utilization	% Util.	Utilization	% Util.
Simulator	40412	3.31%	46715	1.91%	4	0.33%
Event Processor (1x)	391	0.03%	393	0.02%	0	0%
Controller	3610	0.30%	5557	0.23%	0	0%
Event Queue	6795	0.56%	5278	0.22%	0	0%
Memory Interface	143945	11.78%	132857	5.44%	206	17.12%
Crossbar Network	22051	1.81%	38713	1.58%	0	0%
Overall	236673	19.37%	261567	10.71%	223.5	18.58%

an FPGA, even when a more complex PDES model is considered and networking overheads are taken into account. Thus, there is significant potential to improve the performance of PDES-A as we use more of the available FPGA real-estate.

Finally, an inherent advantage of FPGAs is their low power usage. The estimated power of PDES-A was less than 25 Watts in contrast to the rated 130 Watts TDP of the Intel Xeon CPU. We believe that this result shows that PDES-A holds promise to uncover significant boost in PDES simulation performance.

7. CONCLUDING REMARKS

In this paper, we presented and analyzed the design of a PDES accelerator on an FPGA. PDES-A is designed to allow supporting arbitrary PDES models although we studied our initial design only with Phold. The design shows excellent scalability up to 64 concurrent event handlers, outperforming a 12-core CPU PDES simulator by 2.5x for this model. We identified major opportunities to further improve the performance of PDES-A targeted around hiding the very high memory latency on the system. We also analyzed the resource utilization of PDES-A: we believe that we can fit up to 16 PDES-A processors with 64 event processing cores on the same FPGA chip, further improving performance, at a fraction of the power consumed by CPUs.

Our future work spans at least three different directions. First, we will continue to optimize PDES-A to reduce the impact of memory access time and resource contention. Next our goal is to study a full chip (or even multi-chip) design consisting of multiple PDES-A accelerators working on larger models. Finally, we hope to provide programming environments that allow rapid prototyping of PDES-A cores specialized to different simulation models.

Acknowledgements

This material is based upon work supported by the Air Force Office of Scientific Research (AFOSR) under Award No. FA9550-15-1-0384 and a DURIP award FA9550-15-1-0376.

8. REFERENCES

[1] R. Brown. Calendar queues: A fast 0 (1) priority queue implementation for the simulation event set problem. 31(10):1220–1227.

[2] J. Burt. Intel begins shipping xeon chips with fpga accelerators, June 2016. Downloaded Feb. 2017 from eWeek: http://www.eweek.com/servers/ intel-begins-shipping-xeon-chips-with-fpga-accelerators. html.

[3] C. D. Carothers, D. Bauer, and S. Pearce. Ross: A high-performance, low memory, modular time warp system. In *Proceedings of the Fourteenth Workshop on Parallel and Distributed Simulation*, PADS '00, pages 53–60, Washington, DC, USA, 2000. IEEE Computer Society.

[4] H. Chen, Y. Yao, W. Tang, D. Meng, F. Zhu, and Y. Fu. Can mic find its place in the field of pdes? an early performance evaluation of pdes simulator on intel many integrated cores coprocessor. In *2015 IEEE/ACM 19th International Symposium on Distributed Simulation and Real Time Applications (DS-RT)*, pages 41–49, Oct 2015.

[5] Convey Computers™ Corporation. *The Convey WX Series*, conv-13-045.5 edition, 2013.

[6] Convey Computers™ Corporation. *Convey PDK2 Reference Manual*, 2.0 edition, jul 2014.

[7] S. Das, R. Fujimoto, K. Panesar, D. Allison, and M. Hybinette. Gtw: A time warp system for shared memory multiprocessors. In *Proceedings of the 26th Conference on Winter Simulation*, WSC '94, pages 1332–1339, San Diego, CA, USA, 1994. Society for Computer Simulation International.

[8] R. Fujimoto. Parallel and distributed simulation. In *Proceedings of the 2015 Winter Simulation Conference*, WSC '15, pages 45–59, Piscataway, NJ, USA, 2015. IEEE Press.

[9] R. M. Fujimoto, J.-J. Tsai, and G. C. Gopalakrishnan. Design and evaluation of the rollback chip: Special purpose hardware for time warp. *IEEE Transactions on Computers*, 41(1):68–82, 1992.

[10] S. Gupta and P. A. Wilsey. Lock-free pending event set management in time warp. In *Proceedings of the 2nd ACM SIGSIM Conference on Principles of Advanced Discrete Simulation*, pages 15–26, 2014.

[11] R. Hameed, W. Qadeer, M. Wachs, O. Azizi, A. Solomatnikov, B. C. Lee, S. Richardson, C. Kozyrakis, and M. Horowitz. Understanding sources of inefficiency in general-purpose chips. In *Proceedings of the 37th Annual International Symposium on Computer Architecture (ISCA)*, pages 37–47, 2010.

[12] M. A. Hassaan, M. Burtscher, and K. Pingali. Ordered vs. unordered: A comparison of parallelism and work-efficiency in irregular algorithms. In *Proceedings of the 16th ACM Symposium on Principles and*

Practice of Parallel Programming, PPoPP '11, pages 3–12, New York, NY, USA, 2011. ACM.

[13] M. C. Herbordt, F. Kosie, and J. Model. An Efficient O(1) Priority Queue for Large FPGA-Based Discrete Event Simulations of Molecular Dynamics. pages 248–257. IEEE.

[14] Hybrid Memory Cube Consortium. *Hybrid Memory Cube Specification 2.1*, 2.1 edition, 2014.

[15] D. Jagtap, K. Bahulkar, D. Ponomarev, and N. Abu-Ghazaleh. Characterizing and understanding pdes behavior on tilera architecture. In *Proceedings of the 2012 ACM/IEEE/SCS 26th Workshop on Principles of Advanced and Distributed Simulation*, PADS '12, pages 53–62, Washington, DC, USA, 2012. IEEE Computer Society.

[16] D. R. Jefferson. Virtual time. *ACM Trans. Program. Lang. Syst.*, 7(3):404–425, July 1985.

[17] M. C. Jeffrey, S. Subramanian, C. Yan, J. Emer, and D. Sanchez. A scalable architecture for ordered parallelism. In *Proceedings of the 48th International Symposium on Microarchitecture*, MICRO-48, pages 228–241, New York, NY, USA, 2015. ACM.

[18] R. Noronha and N. B. Abu-Ghazaleh. Early cancellation: an active nic optimization for time-warp. In *Proceedings of the sixteenth workshop on Parallel and distributed simulation*, pages 43–50. IEEE Computer Society, 2002.

[19] H. Park and P. A. Fishwick. A gpu-based application framework supporting fast discrete-event simulation. *Simulation*, 86(10):613–628, Oct. 2010.

[20] K. S. Perumalla. Discrete-event execution alternatives on general purpose graphical processing units (gpgpus). In *20th Workshop on Principles of Advanced and Distributed Simulation (PADS'06)*, pages 74–81, 2006.

[21] K. Pingali, D. Nguyen, M. Kulkarni, M. Burtscher, M. A. Hassaan, R. Kaleem, T.-H. Lee, A. Lenharth, R. Manevich, M. Méndez-Lojo, D. Prountzos, and X. Sui. The tao of parallelism in algorithms. *SIGPLAN Not.*, 46(6):12–25, June 2011.

[22] A. Putnam, A. M. Caulfield, E. S. Chung, D. Chiou, K. Constantinides, J. Demme, H. Esmaeilzadeh, J. Fowers, G. P. Gopal, J. Gray, M. Haselman, S. Hauck, S. Heil, A. Hormati, J.-Y. Kim, S. Lanka, J. Larus, E. Peterson, S. Pope, A. Smith, J. Thong, P. Y. Xiao, and D. Burger. A reconfigurable fabric for accelerating large-scale datacenter services. In *Proceeding of the 41st Annual International Symposium on Computer Architecuture*, ISCA '14, pages 13–24, Piscataway, NJ, USA, 2014. IEEE Press.

[23] B. L. Ranjita Bhagwan. Fast and Scalable Priority Queue Architecture for High-Speed Network Switches. In *In Proceedings of Infocom 2000*. IEEE Communications Society.

[24] J. Rios. An efficient FPGA priority queue implementation with application to the routing problem. Technical Report UCSC-CRL-07-01, University of California, Santa Cruz, 2007. Downloaded March 2017 from https://www.soe.ucsc.edu/research/technical-reports/UCSC-CRL-07-01.

[25] R. Rönngren and R. Ayani. A comparative study of parallel and sequential priority queue algorithms. *ACM Transactions on Modeling and Computer Simulation (TOMACS)*, 7(2):157–209, 1997.

[26] A. Santoro and F. Quaglia. Multiprogrammed non-blocking checkpoints in support of optimistic simulation on myrinet clusters. *Journal of Systems Architecture*, 53(9):659 – 676, 2007.

[27] A. Santoro and F. Quaglia. Multiprogrammed non-blocking checkpoints in support of optimistic simulation on myrinet clusters. *Journal of Systems Architecture*, 53(9):659–676, 2007.

[28] H. Sharma, J. Park, D. Mahajan, E. Amaro, J. K. Kim, C. Shao, A. Mishra, and H. Esmaeilzadeh. From high-level deep neural models to fpgas. In *2016 49th Annual IEEE/ACM International Symposium on Microarchitecture (MICRO)*, pages 1–12, Oct 2016.

[29] J. S. Steinman. The warpiv simulation kernel. In *Proceedings of the 19th Workshop on Principles of Advanced and Distributed Simulation*, PADS '05, pages 161–170, Washington, DC, USA, 2005. IEEE Computer Society.

[30] Z. Tan, A. Waterman, R. Avizienis, Y. Lee, H. Cook, D. Patterson, and K. Asanovic. Ramp gold: an fpga-based architecture simulator for multiprocessors. In *Design Automation Conference (DAC), 2010 47th ACM/IEEE*, pages 463–468. IEEE, 2010.

[31] W. Tang and Y. Yao. A gpu-based discrete event simulation kernel. *Simulation*, 89(11):1335–1354, Nov. 2013.

[32] J. Wang, D. Jagtap, N. Abu-Ghazaleh, and D. Ponomarev. Parallel discrete event simulation for multi-core systems: Analysis and optimization. *IEEE Transactions on Parallel and Distributed Systems*, 25(6):1574–1584, 2014.

[33] J. Wang, D. Ponomarev, and N. Abu-Ghazaleh. Performance analysis of a multithreaded pdes simulator on multicore clusters. In *2012 ACM/IEEE/SCS 26th Workshop on Principles of Advanced and Distributed Simulation*, pages 93–95, July 2012.

[34] B. Williams, D. Ponomarev, N. Abu-Ghazaleh, and P. Wilsey. Performance characterization of parallel discrete event simulation on knights landing processor. In *Proc. ACM SIGSIM International Conference on Principles of Advanced Discrete Simulation*, 2017.

[35] S. Zhou, C. Chelmis, and V. K. Prasanna. High-throughput and energy-efficient graph processing on fpga. In *International Symposium on Field-Programmable Custom Computing Machines (FCCM)*, pages 103–110, May 2016.

Towards Simulating the Communication Behavior of Real-Time Interactive Applications

Tim Humernbrum
University of Münster,
Germany
humernbrum@wwu.de

Christian Ahlbrand
University of Münster,
Germany
ahlbrand@wwu.de

Sergei Gorlatch
University of Münster,
Germany
gorlatch@wwu.de

ABSTRACT

Real-Time Online Interactive Applications, e. g., multiplayer online games, connect a high number of users who interact with the application and with each other in real time, i. e., a response to a user's input should happen virtually immediately. We address the problem of reproducing the communication behavior of such applications in order to study the effect of various design decisions (application logic, underlying infrastructure, network protocols, etc.) at early stages of application development. We develop a flexible, lightweight simulator as an alternative to the state-of-the-art simulation approaches that rely on the recorded communication traffic of real applications. The advantage of our approach is that we can easily adapt to a particular application design and its underlying infrastructure and we can measure various communication metrics, without relying on existing application prototypes and real users. Our experiments demonstrate that the simulator realistically reproduces communication behavior for high numbers of users and that simulation results are very near to the communication patterns of recorded communication traffic, e. g., for the commercially successful multiplayer game *Counter Strike*.

Keywords

Real-Time Interactive Applications; Simulation; QoS

1. MOTIVATION AND RELATED WORK

Real-Time Online Interactive Applications (ROIA) are distributed applications connecting a high number of users who interact with the application and with each other in real time, i. e., a response to a user's input should happen virtually immediately. Typical representatives of ROIA are multiplayer games, simulation-based e-learning, etc. Due to the high number of users with intensive interactions, ROIA often have a complex communication behavior that poses challenging requirements on the application design. If the communication is delayed, e. g., due to a poor network *Quality of Service (QoS)* or limited computational resources, this

SIGSIM-PADS '17, May 24–26, 2017, Singapore.

© 2017 ACM. ISBN 978-1-4503-4489-0/17/05...$15.00

DOI: http://dx.doi.org/10.1145/3064911.3064931

may have a negative effect on the users' experience, which in turn is tightly coupled to the commercial success, especially of multiplayer games. Hence, it is crucial for ROIA developers to determine the impact of certain design decisions on the user experience, e. g., how the chosen transport protocol affects a game's response time and thereby the ability of players to act in real time. Furthermore, it is important to obtain such feedback already in an early development phase, because changing fundamental architectural aspects in later phases is complicated and time consuming.

A common approach to evaluating the effects of communication behavior is to perform tests with early prototypes. However, the immature nature of prototypes often leads to unrealistic results which do not reflect the final application's behavior. Tests with the final application contradict the aim of gaining information in an early development phase, they need a high number of simultaneously acting users, and the requirements on the underlying hardware are high, e. g., for the graphical representation of the game world. Therefore, attempts are made to reproduce the application's communication behavior in terms of packet-size distribution and inter-packet arrival time as exactly as possible.

The state-of-the-art approach to simulating multiplayer game communication introduced in [4] and formalized in [3] is based on reproducing communication patterns which are identified by analyzing the packet-by-packet network traffic of recorded game sessions [6, 9]. However, this approach has several drawbacks. For recording game sessions, the actual game client and server applications have to be available. Also real interacting users are required, as well as the hardware for running the game client of each user. Human users can sometimes be replaced by AI-controlled bots, but this requires a great development effort for the adaptation of the game. Therefore, it only makes sense to use this approach if the number of users is limited or the test is performed with a small user number and the results of the analysis can be extrapolated to higher user numbers [5].

This paper presents a flexible simulator for reproducing ROIA communication behavior. In contrast to the state-of-the-art techniques based on statistical analysis of network traffic recorded in advance, our simulator is a lightweight application that takes into account major parts of the application logic and network features responsible for the arising communication. The simulation is controlled by the developer using configuration parameters which can be derived easily from the early design of a specific ROIA: there is no more need for previously recorded network traffic of the actual application.

2. THE SIMULATOR: DESIGN AND USE

A typical ROIA application is conceptually separated into a static and dynamic part. The static part includes, e. g., landscape, buildings, and other non-changeable objects. The dynamic part includes entities like avatars, non-playing characters (NPCs) controlled by the computer and, generally, objects that can change their state.

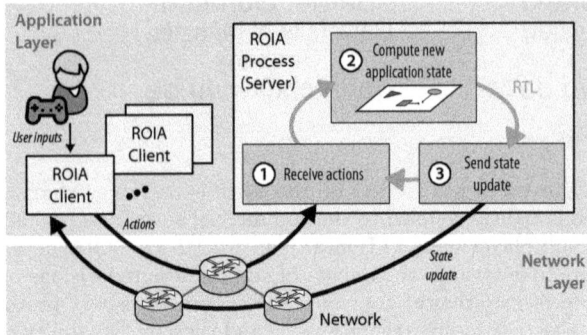

Figure 1: Structure of a ROIA.

Figure 1 shows the structure of a ROIA with a single *ROIA Process* on the server which serves the connected *ROIA Clients*; the typical scenario includes a group of ROIA Processes distributed across several server machines. In a continuously progressing ROIA, the application state is repeatedly updated on the server in real time in an infinite loop, called *real-time loop*. A loop iteration (also known as a *tick*) consists of three major steps as follows. At first, the clients process the users' inputs and transmit them as actions via the network to the ROIA Process (step ① in Figure 1). The process calculates a new application state by applying the received user actions and the application logic to the current application state (step ②). As the result of this calculation, the states of several dynamic entities may change. The final step ③ of the loop transfers the new, updated application state to the clients.

Our simulator is designed as a lightweight client/single-server application with the same structure as in Figure 1: every simulation client controls one avatar on a virtual map and is operated either by a real or simulated user (bot). When avatars are moved on the map, their movement actions are sent to the simulation server which applies these actions to the application state and sends state updates back to the clients. An important goal when developing our simulator has been to be able to simulate high user numbers even on low-cost hardware. Therefore, the application logic has been limited to the parts that influence the communication behavior of ROIA. On the server side, this includes the processing of the client actions and interest management: the so called *Area of Interest (AoI)* of a client defines up to what distance other avatars can be seen. An important simplification is that we ignore collision detection between avatars, as well as interpolations and predictions, e. g., of avatar positions, as used by many actual multiplayer games to compensate for high response times. The application logic is further simplified by using a two-dimensional map with the restriction of only horizontal and vertical movements of avatars. As a result, in its basic configuration our simulator corresponds to a very simple multiplayer game with only minimal requirements on network QoS.

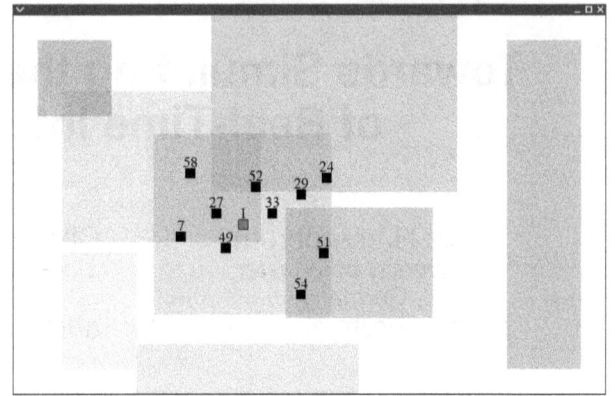

Figure 2: Graphical representation of the application state as seen by client 1. The client's avatar is colored red and its AoI is visualized by a gray rectangle. The other rectangles represent map areas which trigger different communication behavior.

Figure 2 shows how the user of the simulator (e. g., ROIA developer) can significantly enrich this basic case and thus the behavior of the simulator in order to reproduce dynamic changes of the communication behavior. To trigger specific actions based on the current position of avatars, the user defines rectangular areas on the map as in Figure 2 and associates them with various so-called *Position-Dependent Actions (PDAs)*. PDAs modify specific communication parameters for each client whose avatar is located inside the corresponding area. When an avatar leaves this area, all modifications of the area's PDAs are undone. Areas may overlap or be limited to a specific communication direction (i. e., client-server or server-client) to specify even more complex communication behavior.

```
1  {"width": 850, "height": 500,
2   "areas":
3   [{"lowerLeft" : [50,150],
4     "upperRight": [150,50],
5     "actions": {"tick rate": 20,
6                 "state update payload": 64,
7                 "view distance": 100}},
8   ... ]}
```

Listing 1: Example map configuration.

Listing 1 shows an excerpt of the JSON configuration for the map shown in Figure 2. In line 1, the map size of 850x500 is specified, followed by the definition of the upper left red area (lines 3–7). The area is defined by its lower left and upper right coordinates and comprises three PDAs which set the tick rate of the client to 20 ms and enlarge the state updates for this client sent by the server by 64 bytes. Also a new size of 100 units is set for the client's AoI.

There are currently 10 predefined PDAs that can be used to modify the network communication of our simulator dynamically, depending on the position of avatars. For instance, many commercial games provide voice chat to gamers or send single data chunks in a running game in order to dynamically reload content (so-called content distribution). This is simulated by additional data streams started by a PDA, which are independent from other communication. These streams can be limited in transmission rate and overall data size that has to be sent. If some functionality is not provided by a predefined PDA, the developer can easily implement custom PDAs in C++: they are registered at the simulator and executed via a callback mechanism.

In addition to the fine-grained manipulation of the application logic by modifying the virtual map like in Figure 2, the user can specify general parameters of the simulator's server and client part in separate configuration files, including: the IP version, transport protocol, number of threads used by the server, client and server tick rates, maximum message size and client count, configuration of additional NPCs simulated by the server, etc. Currently, there are 75 different parameters for configuration.

After the simulator is configured, it is run by starting the simulation server and clients, e.g., on separate machines in a large-scale network. During runtime, the simulator records a wide set of monitoring data regarding the simulated application's communication behavior. This allows for studying the effect of different design decisions on the communication behavior and, eventually, on the user's experience. Also consequences of external influences like different network topologies, transport protocols, server-side tick and transmission rates, background content streaming, and the use of Software-Defined Networking (SDN) for improving network QoS [8] can be evaluated.

Among the recorded data, there are two sets of metrics: 1) network-related metrics like throughput, inter-packet arrival times, packet sizes, and packet loss; 2) performance metrics, e.g., CPU load of the server, the duration of a tick, and the waiting time of ready-to-send messages in the send queue. The user determines which metrics should be recorded both on server and client side. To simplify the subsequent evaluation, all clients transmit their recorded data to the server which stores it in a file for further processing.

The history of a simulation session can be recorded and reproduced later. This allows to compare different configurations of the simulator in separate runs, e.g., to compare the effect of different transport protocols (UDP vs. TCP) on the response time. For this purpose, the routes of all avatars as well as the client inputs are recorded. Thus, a recorded session can be reproduced, even if important configuration parameters like tick and transmission rates are changed.

3. EXPERIMENTAL EVALUATION

We evaluate our simulator in several experiments using five quad-core Intel Xeon E3-1240v2 machines with Intel I350 Gigabit server NICs, connected via a Netgear JGS524F small-business switch. In all experiments, the simulation server is executed on one machine, while each of the remaining four machines runs several clients.

In the first experiment, we demonstrate that the simulator can realistically study the communication behavior of ROIA even for high numbers of users. For this purpose, we configure the simulator with parameters typical for multiplayer games like Counter Strike [2]: the server is configured with a tick rate of 20 ticks/s, sending one state update to every client at each tick using UDP. The clients are limited to send 15 actions/s to the server. We repeat the experiment with an increasing number of simulation clients and with 1, 2, 4, and 8 threads used by the server. In each experiment run, we add 256 clients and measure their response time as well as the update rate of the server. During the experiment, we observe a packet loss starting at 1,024 connected clients which

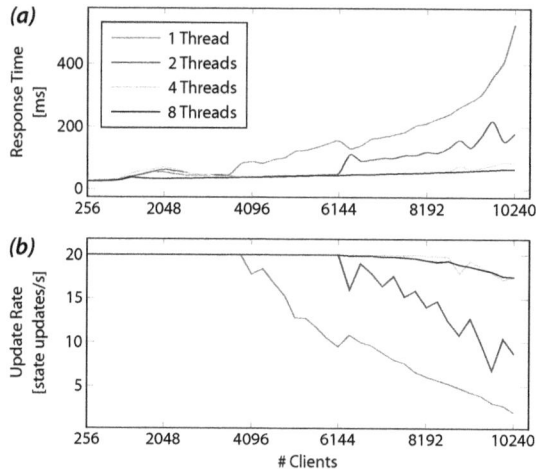

Figure 3: Average response time of the clients and update rate of the server with increasing number of connected clients.

increases up to 5 % in case of 10,240 clients. The packet loss is caused by the high network load that could not be handled by the used switch without dropping packets.

Figure 3 (a) shows the average response time of the clients and the corresponding update rate of the server depicted in Figure 3 (b). The more clients are connected to the server, the harder it becomes for the server to hold the specified update rate. In turn, this leads to an increased response time measured on the clients. We observe that our simulator scales well with the number of threads used in the server: when using 8 threads, up to 10,240 clients can be handled by the server with only moderate increase in the clients' response time up to 50 ms which usually cannot be noticed by the human player. We repeated the experiment with TCP instead of UDP and observed similar results with slightly higher response times due to managing the mentioned above packet loss by TCP.

In order to study how precisely our simulator can reproduce the communication behavior of existing ROIA, in the following we compare simulated communication with recorded game sessions' network traffic for the multiplayer game Counter Strike (CS). We monitor and analyze the two most important metrics for ROIA's communication behavior: inter-packet arrival time, i.e., the delay between receiving two successive packets, and packet sizes. For packet sizes, we focus on the actual payload, i.e., we do not consider packet headers or other network-related overhead. We visualize our measurements and the real traffic metrics using cumulative distribution functions (CDFs) [7].

In Figure 4, we compare our simulated communication for the popular first-person shooter Counter Strike (CS), with recordings from Armitage et al. available in the SONG database [1]. We use three different recordings of game sessions with 2, 4, and 8 players. These show that packet sizes vary between 20 and 180 bytes. With our simulator, we are able to reproduce the server-to-client packet size distribution by adding NPCs simulated by the server on a 1000x1000 virtual map and a client AoI of 215. These NPCs behave similarly to the bot players of the simulation clients, but no additional messages have to be exchanged via the network. However, the positions of the NPCs are taken into account

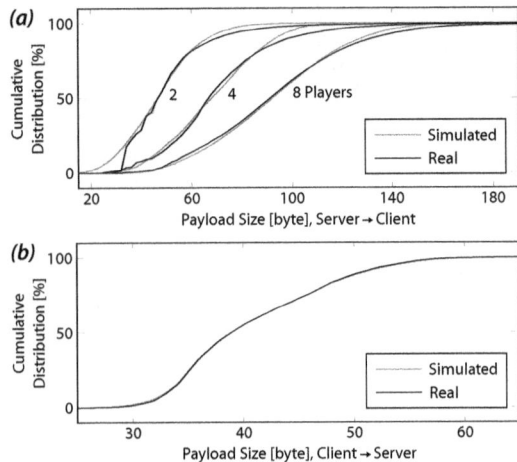

Figure 4: Counter Strike packet size distribution.

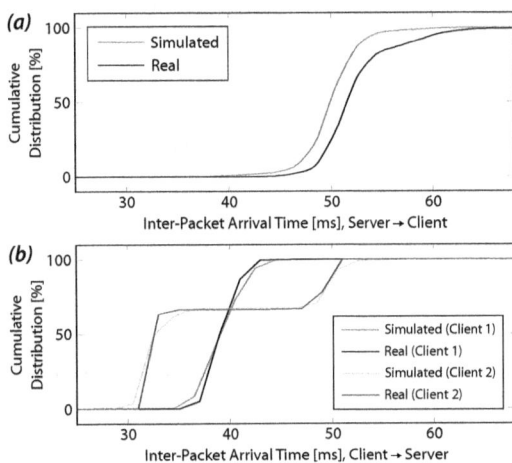

Figure 5: Counter Strike inter-packet arrival time.

in the state updates that are sent to the clients. We observe empirically that the number of required NPCs depends almost linearly on the number of players ($40 + 10n$, where n is the number of players).

Figure 4 (a) shows the CDF of the simulated and real packet size. The maximum absolute deviation is only 2.9 % in the case of 8 players. In the case of 2 and 4 players, the maximum deviations are slightly higher with 8.2 % and 5.5 %, respectively. The average absolute deviation is 0.8 % in the case of 2 and 4 players, and 0.5 % in the case of 8 players, i. e., the packet sizes of a CS server are reproduced with good accuracy. The size of CS client packets is independent from the number of players which is typical for ROIA. However, their reproduction with our simulator is more tricky compared to server packets: to manage it, we added 20 different PDAs to an area which covers the whole virtual map. These PDAs modify the size of client actions that are sent to the server. Using this configuration, the distribution of client packet sizes can be reproduces with high accuracy, as shown in Figure 4 (b). The maximum absolute deviation is 0.8 %, the average absolute deviation is 0.2 %.

Figure 5 depicts client-side (a) and server-side (b) inter-packet arrival times for an 8-player Counter Strike session. We take this number of players because the recorded real

communication shows only minimal differences between 2, 4, and 8 players in the packet arrivals. With a maximum absolute deviation of 29.2 %, our simulator seems to be unable to reproduce the client-size arrivals very accurately with the chosen configuration. We found that this is due to the real server's update rate: the server sends 18.6 state updates/s instead of the default rate (20 updates/s), possibly caused by hardware limitations. When adapting the simulation server to this update rate, the maximum absolute deviation decreases to 7.1 % with an average of 1.1 %. Also the recordings of the real clients differ from default values. Moreover, different clients may have significantly different communication behavior as shown in Figure 5 (b) for two out of the eight clients. After we adapted the tick rate of each simulation client, we were able to reproduce the server-side inter-packet arrival times with a maximum absolute deviation of 12.3 % and an average deviation of 1.7 %.

4. CONCLUSION

Our contribution is a lightweight and highly flexible simulator that allows for reproducing the communication behavior of Real-Time Online Interactive Applications (ROIA). In contrast to the state-of-the-art simulation approaches that rely on the recorded communication traffic of real applications, our simulator can be easily adapted to a particular application design for measuring various communication metrics without relying on application prototypes and real users. We experimentally confirm the feasibility of simulating ROIA with high numbers of users (more than 10,000) on low-cost hardware. We show that the communication behavior of existing applications can be accurately reproduced on the example of the commercial game Counter Strike.

5. REFERENCES

[1] G. Armitage, P. Branch, J. But, and T. Cricenti. Simulating Online Networked Games Database (SONG). http://caia.swin.edu.au/sitcrc/song/, 2006.

[2] G. Armitage, M. Claypool, and P. Branch. *Networking and Online Games: Understanding and Engineering Multiplayer Internet Games*. Wiley, 2006.

[3] R. A. Bangun and E. Dutkiewicz. Modelling Multi-Player Ggames Traffic. In *Proceedings International Conference on Information Technology: Coding and Computing*, pages 228–233, 2000.

[4] M. S. Borella. Source Models of Network Game Traffic. *Computer Communications*, 23:403–410, 2000.

[5] A. L. Cricenti and P. A. Branch. A Generalised Prediction Model of First Person Shooter Game Traffic. In *IEEE 34th Conference on Local Computer Networks*, pages 213–216, Oct 2009.

[6] J. Färber. Traffic Modelling for Fast Action Network Games. *Multimedia Tools Appl.*, 23(1):31–46, 2004.

[7] J. E. Gentle. *Computational Statistics*. Springer, 2009.

[8] S. Gorlatch and T. Humernbrum. Enabling High-Level QoS Metrics for Interactive Online Applications Using SDN. In *International Conference on Computing, Networking and Communications 2015 (ICNC)*, pages 707–711, Feb 2015.

[9] T. Lang, P. Branch, and G. Armitage. A Synthetic Traffic Model for Quake3. In *ACM SIGCHI International Conference on Advances in Computer Entertainment Technology*, pages 233–238, 2004.

Simulation of a Software-Defined Network as One Big Switch

Jiaqi Yan
Illinois Institute of Technology
10 West 31st Street
Chicago, Illinois, 60616
jyan31@hawk.iit.edu

Xin Liu
Illinois Institute of Technology
10 West 31st Street
Chicago, Illinois, 60616
xliu125@hawk.iit.edu

Dong Jin
Illinois Institute of Technology
10 West 31st Street
Chicago, Illinois, 60616
dong.jin@iit.edu

ABSTRACT

Software-defined networking (SDN) technology promises centralized and rapid network provisioning, holistic management, low operational cost, and improved network visibility. Researchers have developed multiple SDN simulation and emulation platforms to expedite the adoption of many emerging SDN-based applications to production systems. However, the scalability of those platforms is often limited by the underlying physical hardware resources, which inevitably affects the simulation fidelity in large-scale network settings. In this paper, we present a model abstraction technique that effectively transforms the network devices in an SDN-based network to one virtualized switch model. While significantly reducing the model execution time and enabling the real-time simulation capability, our abstracted model also preserves the end-to-end forwarding behavior of the original network. To achieve this, we first classify packets with the same forwarding behavior into smaller and disjoint Equivalence Classes (ECs) by analyzing the OpenFlow rules installed on the SDN devices. We then create a graph model representing the forwarding behavior of each EC. By traversing those graphs, we finally construct the rules of the big-switch model to effectively preserve the original network's end-to-end forwarding behavior. Experimental results demonstrate that the network forwarding logic equivalence is well preserved between the abstracted model and the original SDN network. The model abstraction process is fast, e.g., 3.15 seconds to transform a medium-scale tree network consisting of 53,260 rules. The big-switch model is able to speed up the simulation by 4.3 times in average and up to 6.69 times among our evaluation experiments.

Keywords

Network Simulation; Model Abstraction; Software-Defined Networking;

SIGSIM-PADS 17, May 24-26, 2017, Singapore, Singapore

© 2017 ACM. ISBN 978-1-4503-4489-0/17/05. . . $15.00

DOI: http://dx.doi.org/10.1145/3064911.3064918

1. INTRODUCTION

Software defined networking (SDN) centralizes and simplifies control of network management, and has been increasingly adopted in data centers and internet exchange points [8, 11, 15]. Similar to traditional computer network systems, it is crucial to perform appropriate testing and evaluation of SDN-based applications before deploying on a real system. Researchers in the simulation community have extended various existing network simulators to support SDN capability [3, 4, 21]. To improve experimental fidelity, researchers have also developed network emulation testbeds (e.g., Mininet [13]) that utilize Linux containers over shared hardware resources and real network stack to run high-fidelity SDN experiments. However, container-based emulators cannot reproduce the correct behavior of a real network with a large network topology and high traffic load because of the limited underlying physical resources. For example, on a commodity machine with 2.98 GHz CPU, 4 GB RAM, and 3 Gbps internal bandwidth, Mininet can only emulate a network up to 30 hosts, each with a 100 MHz CPU, 100 MB RAM and connected by 100 Mbps links [14]. Therefore, increasing SDN testbed scalability and speed without losing the desired fidelity is essential.

In this paper, we present a model abstraction technique to transform an SDN-based network model to a "one-big-switch" network model. The idea was inspired by the work on rule placement optimization in [17]. With the highly abstracted network, SDN application developers now only need to consider simple end-to-end policy when programming a network, and are shielded from the details on routing policy, switch memory limits, and distributing rules across switches. Our work applies the idea of one-big-switch abstraction for enhancing the scalability of network simulation and emulation, while preserving the end-to-end forwarding logic.

This technique is useful if users only care about the end-to-end behavior rather than the details within the network, such as hop-by-hop routing, or table lookup on each single switch.

For example, users may want to simulate a large-scale complex network of networks consisting of traditional TCP/IP networks, SDN networks, industry control communication networks, etc. The SDN components in this scenario may not be the focus, and thus maintaining only the end-to-end behavior is sufficient for running the hybrid experiment. Our technique is also useful for real-time network simulation, in which models must be executed no slower than the wall-clock time in order to interact with real implementations of network protocols and applications. Failing to do so may result

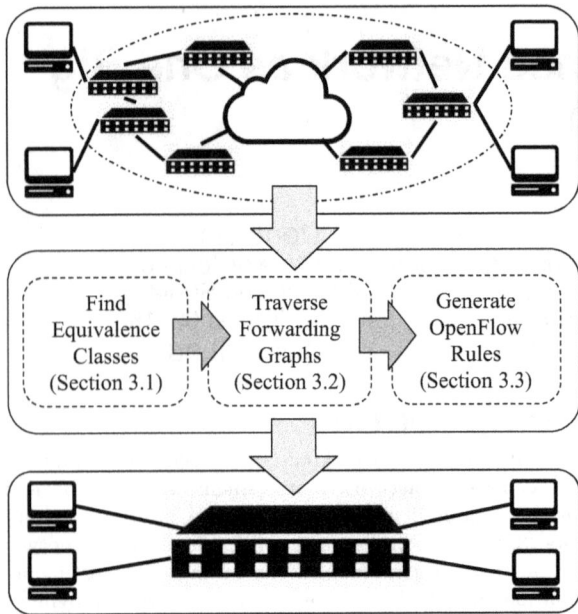

Figure 1: Transforming an SDN network to a big OpenFlow switch based network while preserving the network forwarding logic equivalence.

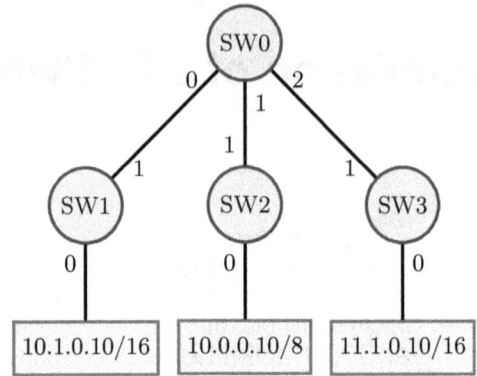

Figure 2: A Tree-Topology SDN Network

in temporal faults, i.e., the simulation fails to process events before the designated deadlines required by the emulation or physical components. In addition, industrial collaborators may not want to disclose the details of their production network (e.g., topology, routing, middle-box location and functionality) to modelers for privacy and security concerns. They can use our model abstraction techniques on the target network and share the resulting "one-big-switch" model. We develop a three-step approach to transform an SDN network to a big OpenFlow switch based network, while still preserving the network forwarding logic equivalence. The high-level idea is illustrated in Figure 1, and the details are discussed in Section 3. We first group all packets into equivalence classes by analyzing the matching fields (e.g., source/destination MAC address/IP address/port, VLAN id, etc.) of the OpenFlow rules installed on the switches. An equivalence class represents a set of packets of the same network forwarding behavior. We then create a graph-based model for each equivalence class to model its packet forwarding behavior. Finally, we traverse all the forwarding graph models to generate rules for the big switch, and the number of rules is largely reduced. This way, we reduce the SDN network to a big-switch-based network to improve the scalability of SDN simulation or emulation.

The reduction in the number of switches and the number of rules significantly enhances the testbed scalability and reduces the experiment running time. For example, after abstracting a tree-topology network of depth 4 and fanout 3, the total number of switches required to simulate is reduced from 40 to 1, and the number of rules existed in the SDN network is reduced by 89%. The big-switch based network model can save about 75% to 85% simulation execution time as compared to simulating the original network. We can also reuse the abstracted network model. For example, after one complete experimental run of a complex network, users can abstract (possibly part of) the network, and reproduce the simulation results with a much simpler configuration, including link connectivity and flow tables. We can partition a large-scale network model, and abstract each partition in parallel. By combining those abstracted network models, a testing platform with limited hardware resources now can afford such network simulation/emulation experiments. As the network state evolves, the abstracted big-switch model may also need to be frequently updated. Our approach is lightweight. For example, we can reduce 50,000+ rules in a large tree-topology network to 5,000+ rules in a big-switch-based network in three seconds, while still preserving the network forwarding rule equivalence. In addition, our approach allows incrementally updating the big-switch model, i.e., modifying the rules that are only affected by the current network changes.

In this work, we present a model abstraction technique to reduce networked SDN switches to a one-big-switch model. We mainly focus on preserving the end-to-end network forwarding logic. Our long term goal is to investigate systematic model abstraction approaches that preserve end-to-end performance equivalence as well, such as latency and packet drop, to further enhance the model fidelity.

The remainder of this paper is organized as follows. Section 2 illustrates the problem and the approach using a simple motivating example. Section 3 describes the details of the three-step model abstraction design. Section 4 presents the evaluation results in terms of forwarding logic equivalence, simulation time, reduction in flow rules, and model abstraction execution time. Section 5 summarizes the related works, and Section 6 concludes the paper with future works.

2. MOTIVATING EXAMPLE

In this section, we describe our model abstraction technique to transform an SDN network model to a big-switch model with a concrete network example. Let us consider a tree-topology network connected by four OpenFlow switches, as shown in Figure 2. The centralized SDN controller (not shown in the figure for simplicity) installs the forwarding rules on each switch to establish connections for all three subnets. All the switch rules are shown in Table 1. We assume that during the process of model abstraction, the rules have been installed on each OpenFlow switch, and there is no link down or rule modification. OpenFlow switch 0 (i.e., SW0) works as an **aggregation switch** that provides con-

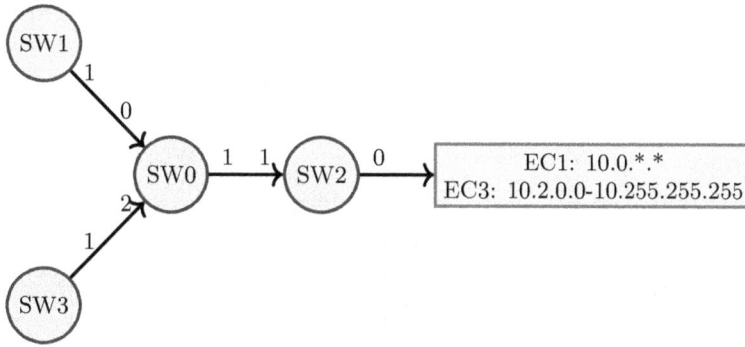

(a) Forwarding Graph for EC1 and EC3

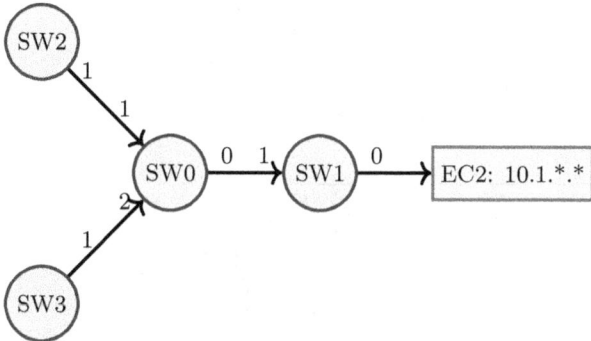

(b) Forwarding Graph for EC2

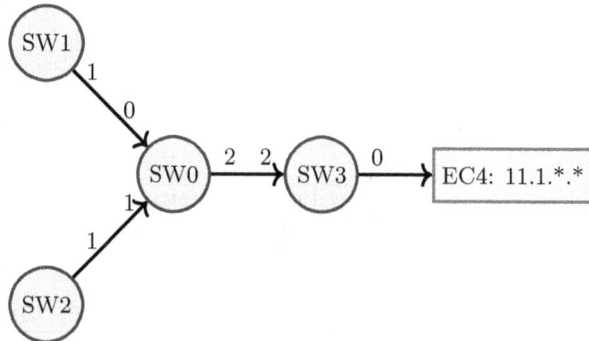

(c) Forwarding Graph for EC4

Figure 3: Forward Graph for Each EC

nectivity for other switches. SW1, SW2 and SW3 work as **edge switches** that provide connectivity for each subnet, and each edge switch connects to one end-host.

Our approach abstracts the network to one big switch that has logically equivalent forwarding behavior.

The first step in the abstraction process is to extract *equivalence classes* through the OpenFlow rules installed on network devices, i.e., aggregation and edge switches. Equivalence class (EC) is the set of packets that experience identical forwarding action at **all** network devices. We utilize EC to merge all the rules on a set of switches. For example, the flow rules shown in Table 1 can be sliced into four **disjoint** ECs based on the NW_DST field as follows. Note that the matching field IN_PORT cannot be used in identifying ECs, since it is not a packet-dependent, but topology-dependent field.

- Packets in EC1 are destined to the network address 10.0.*.*.

- Packets in EC2 are destined to hosts with address 10.1.*.*.

- Packets in EC3 are destined to the address range from 10.2.0.0 to 10.255.255.255

- Packets in EC4 are destined to the subnet 11.1.*.*.

After identifying all the ECs from the rule set, we generate *forwarding graph* for each EC, which models how packets within an EC are forwarded through the network [19]. The node in a forwarding graph represents a network device, and the directed edge represents how the network device

forwards the packets. The sink nodes, i.e., the red rectangle nodes in Figure 3, indentifies the EC that this forwarding graph belongs to. Each equivalence class will have exactly one forwarding graph, as shown in Figure 3. Note that {EC1, EC2, EC3, EC4} is not yet the minimal set of ECs in the network. In fact, EC1 and EC3 can be merged because the forwarding behaviors of both ECs are identical at any device in the network, as depicted in Figure 3a that EC1 and EC3 share the same forwarding graph.

We finish the model abstraction by generating a new set of forwarding rules that are to be installed on the big switch. To make the process more efficient, we only have to consider those ECs whose packets traverse edge switches in the network.

Table 2 shows the resulting rules that will be installed in the big switch (see Figure 4). The resulting one-big-switch network has the identical forwarding functions to the original tree network from the end-to-end communication perspective. The number of switches we need to simulate or emulate is now reduced from four to one, and the number of rules in the network is reduced from twelve to four. If we only consider OpenFlow rules that match the NW_DST field and the action is always forwarding, then the total number of rules in the big switch is proportional to the number of ECs, whereas in the original SDN network, the total number of rules is $O(S \times P)$, where S is the number of switches and P is the number of address prefixes.

3. SDN MODEL ABSTRACTION

Our objective is to effectively transform a static SDN data plane configuration (i.e., a snapshot of the network state) to

Table 1: Forwarding Rules on Each OpenFlow Switch in the 3-ary Tree Network

Switch	Priority	Match Field	Action
SW0	10	NW_DST=10.1.*.*	FWD: OUT_PORT=0
	1	NW_DST=10.*.*.*	FWD: OUT_PORT=1
	1	NW_DST=11.1.*.*	FWD: OUT_PORT=2
SW1	10	IN_PORT=1, NW_DST=10.1.*.*	FWD: OUT_PORT=0
	1	IN_PORT=0, NW_DST=10.*.*.*	FWD: OUT_PORT=1
	1	IN_PORT=0, NW_DST=11.1.*.*	FWD: OUT_PORT=1
SW2	10	IN_PORT=0, NW_DST=10.1.*.*	FWD: OUT_PORT=1
	1	IN_PORT=1, NW_DST=10.*.*.*	FWD: OUT_PORT=0
	1	IN_PORT=0, NW_DST=11.1.*.*	FWD: OUT_PORT=1
SW3	10	IN_PORT=1, NW_DST=11.1.*.*	FWD: OUT_PORT=0
	1	IN_PORT=0, NW_DST=10.*.*.*	FWD: OUT_PORT=1
	1	IN_PORT=0, NW_DST=10.1.*.*	FWD: OUT_PORT=1

Table 2: Forwarding Rules on the "Big OpenFlow Switch"

Switch	Priority	Match Field	Action
SW	10	NW_DST=10.0.*.*	FWD OUT_PORT=1
	10	NW_DST=10.1.*.*	FWD OUT_PORT=0
	10	NW_DST=11.1.*.*	FWD OUT_PORT=2
	10	NW_DST=10.2.0.0-10.255.255.255	FWD OUT_PORT=1

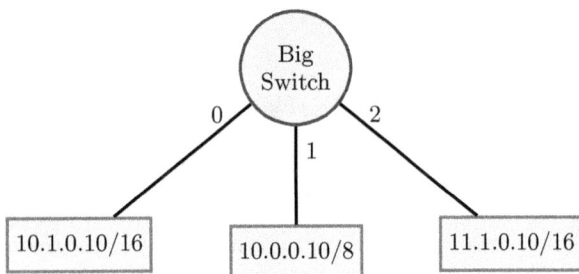

Figure 4: Compressed SDN Network for Scalable Simulation

"one-big-switch" model, which preserves the same end-to-end forwarding behavior. To achieve this objective, we need to identify how every packet is processed in the snapshot, and how to correctly configure the big-switch model to reflect the identical forwarding logic. In this paper, we develop a three-step model abstraction method, which is summarized as follows.

- **Identifying Equivalence Classes.** We partition all possible packets in the network into mutually exclusive sets (i.e., equivalence class, as formally defined in Section 3.1), and the packets belongs to the same set are processed in the same way. Those sets are identified according to the matching field of **all** the OpenFlow rules on **all** the SDN switches in the original network.

- **Creating Forwarding Graphs.** We model the forwarding behavior of each packet set using the topology information as well as the local information stored on SDN switches (e.g., port mapping, rule priorities, etc), and generate a graph-based model to represent the forwarding behavior.

- **Generating OpenFlow Rules of the Big Switch.** We generate the OpenFlow rules for the big switch in order to preserve the end-to-end forwarding logic. This step includes (1) constructing the port-to-host mapping, (2) generating the rules by matching the packet header of each set, and (3) forwarding the packet to the correct output port, which is determined by traversing the forwarding graph acquired in step 2.

Our three-step approach has two assumptions. First, the controller can dynamically change the configuration of each network device, but we assume that the frequency of issuing such control messages is far less than the rate of the incoming packets. Between two configuration updates, the data plane remains unchanged. Therefore, we can exclude the SDN controller from the abstracted network model. Second, we do not consider packet header modification actions on the network device. We describe each step in details in the remainder of the section.

3.1 Identifying Equivalence Classes

We first give the definition of equivalence class (EC), and then present the data structure and algorithms to partition the packets into ECs.

Definition 1. An equivalence class is a set of packets that experience identical forwarding action at **any** network device in the network.

Each packet is uniquely identified by its header field values, which are matched against the forwarding rules in the OpenFlow switches to determine the appropriate action. Since the matching fields of the OpenFlow rules typically contain the wildcard suffix (e.g., longest prefix match of IP source/destination addresses), a group of packets with consecutive header values are often processed by the same rule.

We use a trie structure, originally proposed by VeriFlow [19], to maintain the matching fields of all the OpenFlow rules in the network. The trie is composed of several sub-tries, and each sub-trie stands for a matching field (e.g., source/destination MAC address/IP address/port, etc.). Each node in sub-trie presents one bit in the corresponding matching field, and each node has three edges to the next node (i.e., next bit in the matching field). The edges represent three possible bit-to-bit rule matching conditions: zero, one, or wildcard (i.e., don't care). The rule metadata are stored in the corresponding leaf node, including the rule's location (i.e., switch index), action (e.g., forwarding to an out port or dropping the packet), priority, etc.

Having all the OpenFlow rules inserted in the aforementioned trie structure, we perform the following three steps to identify the equivalence classes in the network. (1) We traverse the trie to obtain the consecutive header values for each rule. (2) After having a collection of header value intervals, which are denoted by the starting and end values, we develop an algorithm to split the existing intervals into smaller and non-overlapping intervals. Each non-overlapping interval identifies the packets belonging to an equivalence class. (3) We merge certain equivalence classes in order to reduce the time and space complexity for the forwarding graph generation (Section 3.2) and the big-switch rule generation (Section 3.3). The details of the second and third steps for EC identification are presented as follows.

3.1.1 Splitting Overlapping Intervals

By traversing from the root node to all leaf nodes, we obtain a set of packet header intervals that match all the rules along the traversal. Each interval is represented by a pair of starting and ending values as A, B and C as shown in Figure 5. We split this set of intervals, I, to a list of non-overlapping intervals, each of which forms an EC. We develop Algorithm 1 to generate a set of disjoint intervals, and show that the generation can be accomplished in $O(N \times M \log M)$ time, where M is the number of intervals in I, and N is the number of header bits.

First, we place I into an array A of $2M$ elements. Each element is either a beginning value or an ending value of an interval. We denote the set of beginning values as S and the set of ending values as E. We visit each value x in a sorted order, and maintain the difference d between the number of visited starting points and the number of visited end points.

- If the current element $x \in S$ and $d > 0$, we finish processing the previous interval with the ending value $x - 1$ and create the next interval with a starting value x (line 8-10).

- If the current element $x \in E$, we end the previous interval with the ending value x. (line 14).

- In either case, we update the potential new interval's starting value *prev* (line 11 and 15).

Updating the network forwarding rules will change the EC set. By maintaining the rules in a trie, we can efficiently update ECs in an incremental way. An insertion of a new rule requires us to do a depth first traversal. This process automatically narrows down the set of affected rules by ignoring those non-overlapping branches with the new rule. The output is the set of affected intervals, and we can run Algorithm 1 to update only those affected ECs.

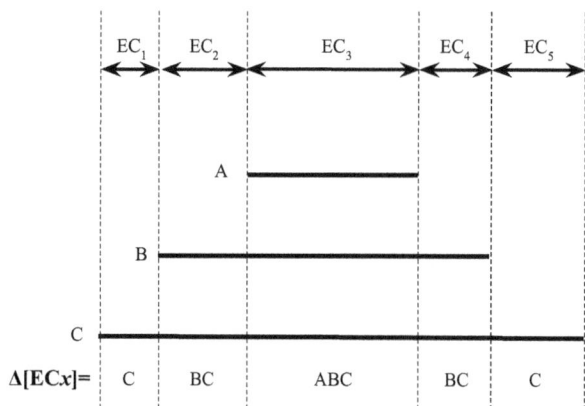

Figure 5: A set of packets are identified by an interval of packet header values. Five equivalence classes, EC_1 to EC_5, can be obtained via splitting three intervals A, B and C. Finding $\Delta[EC_x]$ (i.e., the rules that intersect with EC_x) is instrumental for merging ECs, as shown in the bottom of the figure.

3.1.2 Combining Equivalence Classes

We can further union certain ECs obtained from Algorithm 1, if they essentially represent identical packet forwarding behavior (see the definition of ECs). For example, EC_2 and EC_4 in Figure 5 can be combined as one EC, since the packets in both ECs experience the same set of forwarding rules in the network.

LEMMA 1. *If packets in EC α and EC β experience the same forwarding actions on all network devices, then $\alpha \cup \beta$ is also an EC.*

Combining two EC into a single one reduces the running time in the next two phases, i.e., generating the forwarding graph and populating the final OpenFlow rules. The number of the resulting forwarding rules in the big switch can also be reduced. We present the following lemma to identify whether two ECs can be unioned.

LEMMA 2. *EC α and EC β can be unioned into one EC, if both packet header values are covered by the same set of rules in the network.*

For example, both EC_2 and EC_4 are covered by interval B and C in Figure 5, and therefore, we can treat them as one EC. The explanation is illustrated below.

First, we define a function $\Delta(x)$ that maps an EC x to a set of forwarding rules, whose matching fields cover the header values of all the packets in x. Assume $\Delta(\alpha) = \Delta(\beta)$, and let $\delta \in \Delta(\alpha)$ be the rule on a network device d with the highest priority. If no such δ exists, packets from both α and β are dropped on d. Otherwise, packets in both α and β match the rule δ and are processed with the same action specified in δ. Note that in another device d', the highest priority rule that covers both α and β may be different, i.e., $\delta' \neq \delta$. However, as long as δ is unique at a given d, the forwarding behavior at d for both α and β are always identical.

Given an EC, we can efficiently calculate $\Delta(\alpha)$ using two data structures: an array of pointers and a central interval

ALGORITHM 1: Splitting Overlapping Intervals

Data: I = a set of packet header intervals from the leaves of the trie

Result: D = a set of disjoint intervals as equivalence classes

```
1   cnt ← 0
2   S = {beginning values of ∀i ∈ I}
3   E = {ending values of ∀i ∈ I}
4   A ← Sort(S ⋃ E) in a non-decreasing order
5   D ← ∅
6   foreach x ∈ A do
7       if x ∈ S then
8           if cnt ≠ 0 then
9               D ← D ⋃ [prev, x − 1]
10          end
11          prev ← x
12          cnt ← cnt + 1
13      else
14          D ← D ⋃ [prev, x]
15          prev ← x + 1
16          cnt ← cnt − 1
17      end
18  end
```

ALGORITHM 2: Generating a Forwarding Graph for EC x

Input: $nodes$ = Switches containing rules for EC x
$topo$ = Network topology

Result: Forwarding graph $FG(x)$ for EC x

```
1   Function traverse(curr, src, snk)
2       if curr is NOT visited then
3           r ← highest-priority rule on curr that processes EC x
4           if r is NULL or r.action is DROP then
5               snk ← (curr, NULL)
6               generate_rules(x, src, snk)
7               return
8           end
9           next ← topo[curr][r.action.outport]
10          if next ∉ nodes then
11              snk ← (curr, r.action.outport)
12              generate_rules(x, curr, src, snk)
13              return
14          end
15          mark curr as visited
16          traverse(next, src, snk)
17      else
18          report forwarding loop
19      end
20  return
21
22  foreach n ∈ neighbors of SRCˣ do
23      if n is NOT visited then
24          inport ← input port number from SRCˣ to n
25          traverse(n, src =(n, inport), snk =NULL)
26      end
27  end
```

tree. Each of them is responsible for one of the two cases specified in [2].

- Case 1: A rule δ overlaps with an EC α with its beginning and/or ending value in α. We can reuse the sorted array A in Algorithm 1. We augment each value, either a beginning value or an ending value of an interval in A with a pointer to the corresponding rule. By doing a binary search, we can find the minimum and maximum values in A, which bound the interval of α. Therefore, we can ignore two types of rules: the ones with ending values smaller than the minima and the ones with beginning values larger than the maxima. We then perform a linear search in the new set of rules, and check one-by-one whether the interval overlaps with α. The total time complexity for both the linear search and the binary search are $O(\log M + K)$, where K is the number of reported intervals in $\Delta(\alpha)$.

- Case 2: Rule δ covers α entirely. We can build a central interval tree [10] with all the available intervals. We pick a random value $x \in \alpha$ and query the central interval tree for all the ranges that intersect with x, which can be done in $O(\log M + K)$ time. It takes $O(M \log M)$ time to build the central interval tree. Since the central interval tree supports efficient incremental operations (i.e., insertion and deletion), our design also supports dynamic changes of the rule set.

Using the interval tree and the ordered list, for each EC α, we calculate $\Delta(\alpha)$ by mapping each rule $\delta \in \Delta(\alpha)$ to a unique binary ID c_δ of length $\log_2 M$. We can encode $\Delta(\alpha)$ to a string of c_δs, starting with small IDs. This string of unique IDs, named C_α, has a $M \log_2 M$ upper bound in length. We then use a hash table H to combined the ECs by hashing each EC x to C_x. The minimal size of ECs is the number of unique keys in H. Note that in the subsequent algorithmic designs, iterating through all ECs refers to iterating through the first ECs in each set $H[key]$.

3.2 Generating Forwarding Graphs

In the second step, we compute a forwarding graph for each EC, and then effectively reduce the size of the forwarding graph to improve efficiency for the third step.

First, we define a function $FG(\alpha)$ that maps an EC α to a corresponding forwarding graph. A forwarding graph is a directed graph that represents how packets belonging to the same EC are processed by the network. A node u in the forwarding graph is a networking device, and an edge (u, v) in the graph means that device u forwards the packets to device v in the network. A forwarding graph not only concatenates the forwarding behavior for each EC, but also visualizes the data flow of the EC in the network. Since our objective is to abstract the network forwarding logic into a big switch, our end-to-end modeling focuses on the sources and sinks of the graph. Figure 6 depicts the generalized forwarding graph $FG(x)$ for EC x.

3.2.1 Network Traversal for Forwarding Graph Generation

We develop a forwarding graph generation algorithm as shown in Algorithm 2. The notations are defined as follows. $FG(x)$ denotes the forwarding graph for a particular equivalence class x. A *edge switch* is defined as a switch that has at least one link to a node located outside of the original network. A *non-edge switch* is defined as a switch with all connected nodes that are inside of the oritinal network. The forwarding behavior of the non-edge switches are not considered in the big-switch model abstraction. Let src and snk denote the source and sink nodes of the forwarding path for an EC. Note that all src in $FG(x)$ are edge switches, and snk in $FG(x)$ can be either edge switches or non-edge switches. Let $curr$ denote the current traversed node in the network.

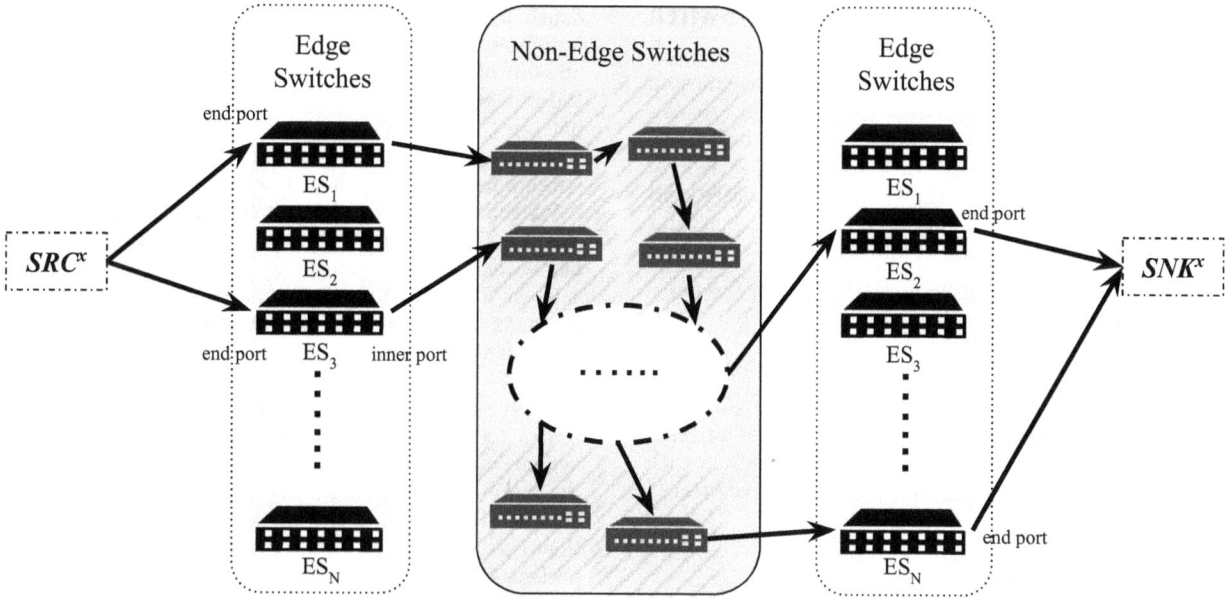

Figure 6: Modeling a Forwarding Graph of an Equivalence Class

ALGORITHM 3: Generating Forwarding Rules for EC x on the Big-Switch Model

Data: $PortMap$, which maps a $port$ on sw to a $port$ on the big switch

$global\_port$, for port number assignment, and is initialized to 0

Result: A new rule r to install on the big switch

```
1  Function generate_rules(x, src, dst)
2      r.match ← x
3      if src.port ∉ PortMap[src.sw] then
4          PortMap[src.sw][src.port] ← global_port + +
5      end
6      r.inport = PortMap[src.sw][src.port]
7      if dst.port is NULL then
8          r.action ← drop_action
9      else
10         if dst.port ∉ PortMap[dst.sw] then
11             PortMap[dst.sw][dst.port] ← global_port + +
12         end
13         r.action ← forward_action
14         r.action.outport ← PortMap[dst.sw][dst.port]
15     end
16 return
```

We add a super-source node, SRC^x, and a super-sink node, SNK^x, as the boundaries of $FG(x)$.

Algorithm 2 is designed to generate $FG(x)$. We start the process from each src that connects to SRC^x, and then traverse EC x's forwarding graph using a depth-first-based search and follow the action specified in the forwarding rule with the highest priority for EC x at each node along the traversal.

We distinguish two kinds of port on an edge switch:

- *end port* that connects to a node that is either the forwarding end point or outside the target network;

- *inner port* that connects to a node inside the target network.

We add an edge from SRC^x to a src, if the source node has a forwarding rule r that matches EC x, or the IN_PORT field of rule r on the source node is an end port. Otherwise, we do not initiate a traverse (see line 22 to 27 in Algorithm 2). Correspondingly, we add an edge from a snk to the super sink SNK^x, if the following two conditions are satisfied:

1. the sink node is an edge switch in the network;

2. the OUT_PORT field determined by the rule's action on the sink node is an end port.

3.2.2 Network Traversal Outcomes

After running Algorithm 2, we can discover three kinds of "paths" in $FG(x)$ that are useful for the forwarding rule generation process for the big-switch model, i.e., the third step of our model abstraction process (see Section 3.3).

- **Forwarding path** (line 10-14). The path from the super source node to the super sink node. This is a normal forwarding path for packets in EC x.

- **Dropping packets in the network** (line 4-8). The path ends at a device inside the network, and fails to reach the super sink node. This indicates that the packets in EC x are dropped inside the network.

- **Forwarding loop** (line 18). There is a directed cycle in the graph. One can simulate a forwarding loop in the network by (1) adding a rule in the big switch to drop the looping packets; or (2) dynamically monitoring the volume of the looping packets and adjusting the delay of looping packets and other packets sharing the communication path. We choose the first method since the model abstraction in the paper is focus on the forwarding logic equivalence, and will leave the second method as future work when investigating end-to-end performance equivalence.

3.3 Populating Flow Tables on the Big-Switch Model

We develop an algorithm to generate OpenFlow rules on the big switch to abstract the forwarding behavior (see Algorithm 3). We maintain a hash table $PortMap$ to map the end ports of the edge switches to the ports of the big switch. This table is configured using the $global\_port$ variable during the rule generation procedure. Algorithm 3 generates the mandatory fields in an OpenFlow rule:

- The $MATCH$ field is given by the EC x, i.e., the range of matching packets header (line 2);

- The IN_PORT field is the mapped port number of $src.port$ (line 6);

- Depending on the dst port, we generate either a packet drop action (line 8) or a packet forwarding action with the appropriate mapped port number of $dst.port$ (line 10-14).

4. EVALUATION

4.1 Network Forwarding Logic Equivalence

We perform experimental evaluation of our network model abstraction technique that transforms an SDN-based network to one-big-switch model. The evaluation results show that our approach significantly saves simulation/emulation resources (e.g., number of forwarding rules) and simulation execution time, while still preserving the forwarding behavior of the original network.

Our experiments simulate and emulate networks of type tree topology. The tree network is described by two topological parameters: depth d and fanout f. Such network $tree(d, f)$ can connect f^d hosts with $\frac{f^d-1}{f-1}$ switches in total. All end-hosts in a tree network are fully-connected with at most $2d$ hops.

We first demonstrate that the forwarding logic of the original software-defined network is exactly preserved by the abstracted big-switch model. We created a tree-topology network net_1 in Mininet [13], and connected all the switches to an SDN controller running a layer-two learning switch application [5]. After performing the ping tests between randomly selected pairs of end-hosts, the controller application generated all the network forwarding rules and installed them on the switches. We then took a snapshot of the network, including (1) the host-to-switch and switch-to-switch connections, and (2) the rules on all the switches using the ovs-ofctl dump-flows command. The snapshot was used to generate the rules for the big-switch model as well as the port mapping according to the algorithms presented in Section 3.

We then created another emulated network net_2 in Mininet, consisting of one OpenFlow switch and the same number of hosts as net_1. The switch was connected to f^d hosts with the port numbers derived from both the $PortMap$ (Algorithm 3) and the link information (net_1's topology). The rules generated by Algorithm 3 were installed on the switch using the ovs-ofctl add-flow command.

To validate that the big-switch-network preserved the network forwarding logic of the original network, we recorded the connectivity between *every* host pair in both net_1 and net_2, and compared the results. Specially, the original network net_1 is a tree network with f^d hosts, where d is the

depth and f is the fanout of a tree network. Each host sent a number of ping packets to every other host in net_1, and the amount of packet was randomly selected between 1 and 10. We repeated the experiments in net_2 with the same traffic pattern. The result was represented in a matrix $\mathcal{R}$, where $\mathcal{R}[i][j]$ denotes the numbers of successfully received ping packets from host i to host j, where $i = j$, and $i, j \in [1, f^d]$.

We repeated the experiment for different combinations of d and f, i.e., $(d, f) \in \{(2, 3), (2, 4), (3, 3), (3, 4), (4, 3)\}$. For each network scenario, we saved the experimental results in $\mathcal{R}_1$ and $\mathcal{R}_2$, and compared the two matrices using the diff command. We found that $\mathcal{R}_1 = \mathcal{R}_2$ holds true for all five network scenarios. We visualized $\mathcal{R}_1$ and $\mathcal{R}_2$ for the $(d = 2, f = 3)$ and $(d = 4, f = 3)$ cases in Figure 7. We can see that the original SDN-based network and the abstracted one-big-switch-based network have the identical network forwarding logic, measured by the connectivity and the number of receiving packets for each connection. Note that the brightness of the element in the matrix is proportional to $\mathcal{R}[i][j]$, i.e., the number of successfully delivered packets from host i to host j.

4.2 Performance Gain

Number of OpenFlow Rules. We compare the total number of rules installed on the switches in both net_1 and net_2 with the same experimental settings in Section 4.1. The results are plotted in Figure 8 for networks with various topological parameter settings. The number of rules needed to preserve the forwarding logic is significantly less in the one-big-switch-based network as compared with the original SDN-based network for all scenarios in the range of 71.93% to 89.05% reduction. For example, in the case of a network with depth = 4, and fanout = 3, 52,660 rules in the original network were reduced to 5,766 rules in the big-switch-based network.

Simulation Time. Our approach significantly reduces network simulation model complexity in terms of the number of switches and the number of rules. A key benefit is to reduce the time to run simulation experiments.

We performed the same set of experiments on a network simulator, S3FNet [21]. We simulated two SDN-based networks: one models a tree-topology network $net_1(d, f)$, and the other models the corresponding big-switch-based network net_2. We set half of the hosts as TCP clients and the other half as TCP servers, and conducted one-to-one communication among them. We sent each traffic flow for 100 seconds in simulation time. We repeated each experiment ten times and recorded the simulation execution time for both net_1 and net_2 in Figure 9 for comparison. The error bars indicate the standard deviations of the running time for all ten independent simulation runs. We can see that simulating the big-switch-based network is 3.42 to 6.68 times faster than simulating the original SDN-based network.

4.3 Model Abstraction Execution Time

We discussed the asymptotic time complexity of our model abstraction technique in Section 3. We now evaluate the execution time for transforming an SDN-based network to a big-switch-based network. We recorded the running time for converting various tree networks, i.e., $(d, f) \in \{(2, 3), (2, 4), (3, 3), (3, 4), (4, 3)\}$ in Figure 10. We can see that the model abstraction process is lightweight. For example, it took about 40 milliseconds to abstract a small tree net-

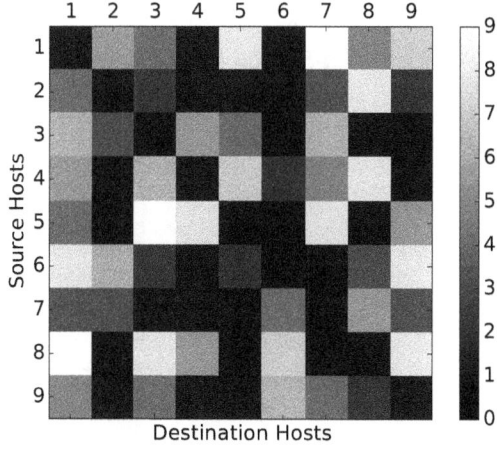

(a) $\mathcal{R}_1$, packets received per host in $net_1(d=2, f=3)$

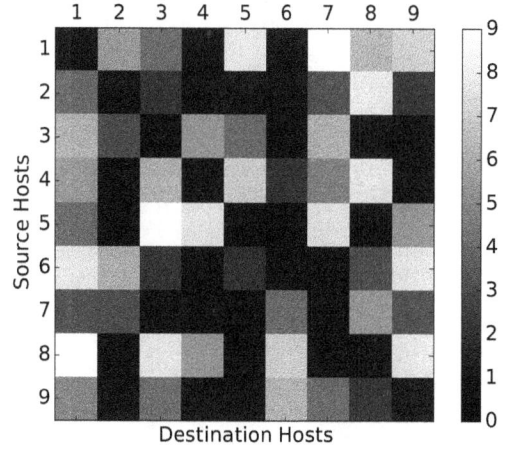

(b) $\mathcal{R}_2$, Packets received in $net_2(d=2, f=3)$

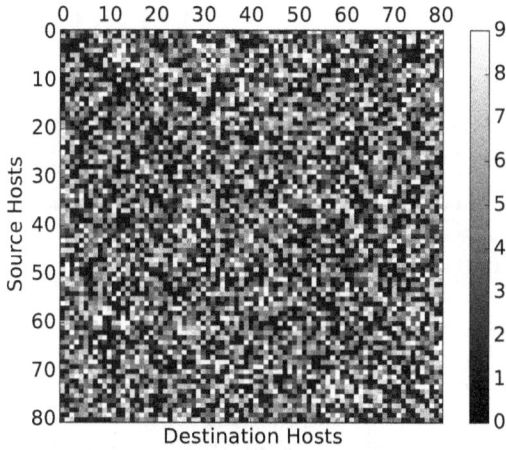

(c) $\mathcal{R}_1$, Packets received in $net_1(d=4, f=3)$

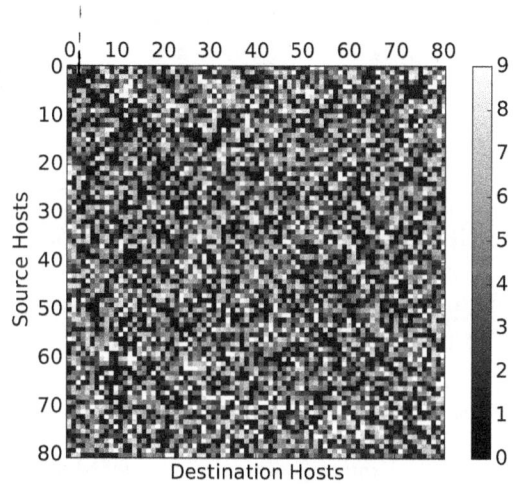

(d) $\mathcal{R}_2$, Packets received in $net_2(d=4, f=3)$

Figure 7: Matrix $\mathcal{R}$ represents the number of packets received at each host. net_1 is the original SDN network with a tree topology (d, f), where d is depth and f is fanout. net_2 is the corresponding one-big-switch-based network. The gradient legend visualizes the number of received packets. $\mathcal{R}_1$ and $\mathcal{R}_2$ are identical, which indicate that our model abstraction technique preserves the network forwarding logic.

work $(d=4, f=2)$; for a medium-scale medium-scale tree network (depth 4 and fanout 3), it took about 3.15 seconds to process 52,660 rules. The fast model abstraction execution time is useful. As the network state keeps evolving, it is essential to constantly update the abstracted big-switch model to reflect the changes, preferably in an online fashion. In fact, the three-step approach allows us to incrementally update the big-switch model and requires far less execution time, i.e., we only need to update a small set of rules that are different in the new network snapshot.

5. RELATED WORK

5.1 SDN Forwarding Rules Abstraction

The idea of "one big switch" is originated from [17] for a different purpose. In their work, the one-big-switch network abstraction is used to reduce conflicting rules generated by various high-level SDN applications that simultaneously run on one or even multiple controllers. Their system takes an optimization-based approach to solve the rule placement problem with the objective of minimizing the number of rules that need to be installed in forwarding devices. Application developers are now shielded from the rules distributed across switches, and only need to specify the end-to-end policies on the big switch model. The objective of our work on the other hand is to reduce the model execution time and to enhance the scalability of network simulation and emulation. We take a different technical approach based on statically analyzing snapshots of the network state to generate rules in the big switch abstraction model. There exists a line of research on network fault detection by analyzing software, configuration and network-wide data-plane state [6, 7, 20, 22]. Those approaches typically operate offline on timescales of seconds to hours. Real time network

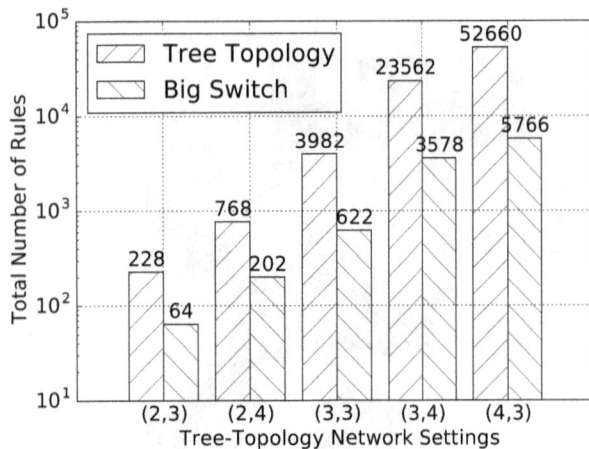

Figure 8: Number of rules needed to preserve the network forwarding logic. The number of rules on the big switch is about 72% to 89% less than the number of rules in the original tree-topology network. The x-axis label (d, f) represents the depth and fanout parameters in a tree topology network.

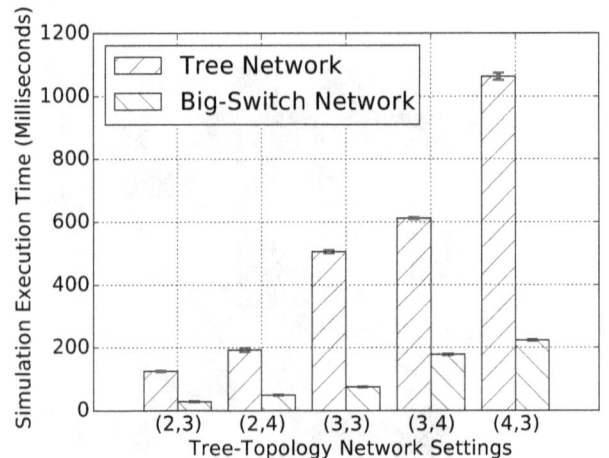

Figure 9: Comparison of simulation execution time. The big-switch-based network model saves about 75% to 85% running time as compared to simulating the corresponding SDN-based network. The x-axis label (d, f) represents the depth and fanout parameters in a tree topology network.

verification tools are developed to enforce correctness in connectivity [18, 19]. Our work leverages the idea of slicing the entire network into equivalence classes in [19] to reduce the problem space, which enables fast model abstraction execution speed.

5.2 SDN Emulation and Simulation

There are a number of SDN emulation and simulation testbeds based on the OpenFlow protocol. Examples include Mininet [13], EstiNet [1], ns-3 [3], S3FNet [16], fs-sdn [12] and OpenNet [9]. Mininet [13] applies container-based virtualization technique and cgroup based resource isolation to provide a lightweight and high fidelity emulation platform. Its functional fidelity is guaranteed by executing real SDN switch/controller software. ns-3 [3] offers simulation models of SDN networks and emulation of SDN controllers via the direct code execution (DCE) technique. S3FNet [16] is a hybrid OpenFlow-based SDN testing platform that integrates a parallel network simulator with an OpenVZ-based network emulator. fs-sdn [12] extends fs, a flow-level discrete event network simulator, with the SDN capability. We develop a model abstraction method in this paper to transform a large scale and complicated SDN network to a one-big-switch-based network. We can use the resulting abstracted network model in all the aforementioned simulation and emulation environment for performance gain while still preserving the network forwarding logic.

6. CONCLUSION AND FUTURE WORK

We present a three-step model abstraction technique to transform an SDN-based network to an "one-big-switch" based network without losing the forwarding behavior as defined by the OpenFlow rules in the network devices. Experimental results demonstrate that the big-switch abstraction correctly models the end-to-end forwarding logic of the original SDN network, and the abstracted model significantly saves the experiment running time and system resources. The ultimate

goal of the one-big-switch abstraction is to enhance simulation and emulation scalability while preserving packet-level fidelity. This paper mainly focuses on the end-to-end forwarding logic equivalence, and we will investigate end-to-end performance equivalence, such as latency and packet drop in the future.

7. ACKNOWLEDGMENTS

The author would like to thank the authors of [19] share the Veriflow codebase for research purpose . This paper is partly sponsored by the Maryland Procurement Office under Contract No. H98230-14-C-0141, and the Air Force Office of Scientific Research (AFOSR) under grant FA9550-15-1-0190. Any opinions, findings and conclusions or recommendations expressed in this material are those of the author(s) and do not necessarily reflect the views of the Maryland Procurement Office and AFOSR.

8. REFERENCES

[1] Estinet. http://www.estinet.com/. Accessed: 2016-12-31.

[2] Interval tree. https://en.wikipedia.org/wiki/Interval_tree#With_an_interval. Accessed: 2016-12-20.

[3] ns-3. https://www.nsnam.org. Accessed: 2016-12-29.

[4] Software defined network OPNET simulation SDN. https://www.youtube.com/watch?v=MPpu8blePfc. Accessed: 2016-12-29.

[5] The POX controller. https://github.com/noxrepo/pox. Accessed: 2016-12-31.

[6] E. Al-Shaer and S. Al-Haj. FlowChecker: Configuration analysis and verification of federated OpenFlow infrastructures. In *Proceedings of the 3rd ACM Workshop on Assurable and Usable Security Configuration (SafeConfig)*, pages 37–44, 2010.

[7] E. Al-Shaer, W. Marrero, A. El-Atawy, and K. ElBadawi. Network configuration in a box: Towards end-to-end verification of network

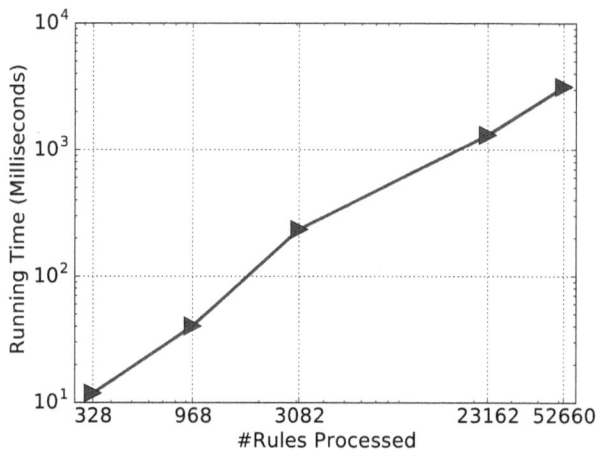

Figure 10: Execution time to transform an SDN-based network to a big-switch-based network.

reachability and security. In *Proceedings of the 17th IEEE International Conference on Network Protocols (ICNP)*, pages 123–132, 2009.

[8] M. Banikazemi, D. Olshefski, A. Shaikh, J. Tracey, and G. Wang. Meridian: an SDN platform for cloud network services. *IEEE Communications Magazine*, 51(2):120–127, February 2013.

[9] M. C. Chan, C. Chen, J. X. Huang, T. Kuo, L. H. Yen, and C. C. Tseng. OpenNet: A simulator for software-defined wireless local area network. In *Proceedings of the 2014 IEEE Wireless Communications and Networking Conference (WCNC)*, pages 3332–3336, April 2014.

[10] M. de Berg, O. Cheong, M. van Kreveld, and M. Overmars. Interval tree. *Computational Geometry*, pages 220–226, 2008.

[11] A. Gupta, L. Vanbever, M. Shahbaz, S. P. Donovan, B. Schlinker, N. Feamster, J. Rexford, S. Shenker, R. Clark, and E. Katz-Bassett. SDX: A software defined internet exchange. In *Proceedings of ACM SIGCOMM*, pages 551–562, 2014.

[12] M. Gupta, J. Sommers, and P. Barford. Fast, accurate simulation for sdn prototyping. In *Proceedings of the Second ACM SIGCOMM Workshop on Hot Topics in Software Defined Networking*, HotSDN '13, pages 31–36, New York, NY, USA, 2013. ACM.

[13] N. Handigol, B. Heller, V. Jeyakumar, B. Lantz, and N. McKeown. Reproducible network experiments using container-based emulation. In *Proceedings of the 8th International Conference on Emerging Networking Experiments and Technologies*, CoNEXT '12, pages 253–264, New York, NY, USA, 2012. ACM.

[14] N. Handigol, B. Heller, V. Jeyakumar, B. Lantz, and N. McKeown. Reproducible network experiments using container-based emulation. In *Proceedings of the 8th International Conference on Emerging Networking Experiments and Technologies*, pages 253–264, New York, NY, USA, December 2012. ACM.

[15] S. Jain, A. Kumar, S. Mandal, J. Ong, L. Poutievski, A. Singh, S. Venkata, J. Wanderer, J. Zhou, M. Zhu, J. Zolla, U. Hölzle, S. Stuart, and A. Vahdat. B4: Experience with a globally-deployed software defined wan. In *Proceedings of ACM SIGCOMM*, pages 3–14, 2013.

[16] D. Jin, Y. Zheng, and D. Nicol. S3F/S3FNet: Simpler scalable simulation framework. University of Illinois at Urbana-Champaign. https://s3f.iti.illinois.edu/, 2013.

[17] N. Kang, Z. Liu, J. Rexford, and D. Walker. Optimizing the "one big switch" abstraction in software-defined networks. In *Proceedings of the Ninth ACM Conference on Emerging Networking Experiments and Technologies*, CoNEXT '13, pages 13–24, New York, NY, USA, 2013. ACM.

[18] P. Kazemian, M. Chang, H. Zeng, G. Varghese, N. McKeown, and S. Whyte. Real time network policy checking using header space analysis. In *Proceedings of the 10th USENIX Conference on Networked Systems Design and Implementation*, NSDI'13, pages 99–112, Berkeley, CA, USA, 2013. USENIX Association.

[19] A. Khurshid, X. Zou, W. Zhou, M. Caesar, and P. B. Godfrey. Veriflow: Verifying network-wide invariants in real time. In *Proceedings of the 10th USENIX Symposium on Networked Systems Design and Implementation*, NSDI'13, pages 15–27, Lombard, IL, 2013.

[20] H. Mai, A. Khurshid, R. Agarwal, M. Caesar, P. B. Godfrey, and S. T. King. Debugging the data plane with anteater. In *Proceedings of ACM SIGCOMM Computer Communication Review*, SIGCOMM'11, pages 290–301, New York, NY, USA, 2011. ACM.

[21] D. M. Nicol, D. Jin, and Y. Zheng. S3F: The scalable simulation framework revisited. In *Proceedings of the Winter Simulation Conference (WSC)*, pages 3288–3299, 2011.

[22] G. G. Xie, J. Zhan, D. A. Maltz, H. Zhang, A. Greenberg, G. Hjalmtysson, and J. Rexford. On static reachability analysis of IP networks. In *Proceedings of the 24th Annual Joint Conference of the IEEE Computer and Communications Societies (INFOCOM)*, volume 3, pages 2170–2183. IEEE, March 2005.

Code-transparent Discrete Event Simulation for Time-accurate Wireless Prototyping

Martin Serror‡, Jörg Christian Kirchhof‡, Mirko Stoffers‡, Klaus Wehrle‡, James Gross§
‡Communication and Distributed Systems, RWTH Aachen University, Germany
§School of Electrical Engineering, KTH Royal Institute of Technology, Sweden
{serror, kirchhof, stoffers, wehrle}@comsys.rwth-aachen.de, james.gross@ee.kth.se

ABSTRACT

Exhaustive testing of wireless communication protocols on pro-totypical hardware is costly and time-consuming. An alternative approach is network simulation, which, however, often strongly abstracts from the actual hardware. Especially in the wireless domain, such abstractions often lead to inaccurate simulation results. Therefore, we propose a code-transparent discrete event simulator that enables a direct simulation of existing code for wireless prototypes. With a focus on lower layers of the communication stack, we enable a parametrization of the simulation timings based on real-world measurements to increase the simulation accuracy. Our evaluation shows that we achieve close results for throughput (deviation below 3 % for UDP) and latency (corrected deviation about 13 %) compared to real-world setups, while providing the benefits of code-transparent simulation, i.e., to flexibly simulate large topologies with existing prototype code. Moreover, we demonstrate that our approach finds implementation defects in existing hardware prototype software, which are otherwise difficult to track down in real deployments.

CCS Concepts

•**Networks** → *Network simulations;* •**Hardware** → *Wireless devices; Testing with distributed and parallel systems;*

Keywords

Wireless Communications; Discrete Event Simulation; Hardware Prototypes; Testing Methods

1. INTRODUCTION

For testing and development of wireless communication protocols, a combined methodology of computer simulation and prototypical hardware deployments, which facilitates the transition from one domain into the other, is highly beneficial. Regarding prototypical hardware, so-called Software Defined Radio (SDR) platforms emerged [25] offering an open and flexible way to modify hard- and software, while enabling testing under realistic conditions. Such a platforms typically consist of a Field Programmable Gate Array (FPGA), a radio interface, and several I/O ports. Thus, they

SIGSIM-PADS'17, May 24 - 26, 2017, Singapore, Singapore

© 2017 Copyright held by the owner/author(s). Publication rights licensed to ACM.
ISBN 978-1-4503-4489-0/17/05. . . $15.00

DOI: http://dx.doi.org/10.1145/3064911.3064913

enable a flexible implementation of custom-made physical and data link layer protocols and are particularly suited for the development and testing of new wireless protocols. It is, however, costly to deploy and maintain complex topologies of such devices, which often impedes developers and researchers to exhaustively test their protocols in larger distributed setups.

In contrast, a relatively cheap and powerful method to test and evaluate new communication protocols is by means of simulation. Computer simulation allows to perfectly control a simulated environment and thus to ensure reproducibility [5], which enables testing of specific aspects of a newly proposed protocol. Moreover, it facilitates the discovery of implementation defects, which is especially useful in distributed settings, offering a global view on the current protocol state of each simulated instance. Advanced simulation tools using the Discrete Event Simulation (DES) paradigm ensure scalability and flexibility of the simulated communication scenarios. Prominent examples for such tools are ns-3 [24] and OMNeT++ [1, 26]. Nevertheless, at a certain point, the simulation abstracts from the real world, which might, depending on the use-case, lead to inaccurate behavior in the simulation.

In general, the development of a communication protocol benefits from both simulation and prototypical implementation, as the advantages of both methods nicely complement each other: Simulation enables the evaluation of large-scale scenarios and facilitates debugging, while prototypical implementation offers a realistic view on possible side effects. In practice, however, this implies that two models of the protocol specification are needed, i.e., one for the prototypical hardware and one for the simulation. As each model typically follows its own paradigm, the models can not be easily translated into each other. This leads to two different models, where, in general, it is hard to show that the models are equivalent to each other and thus impedes a direct comparison of both.

For ns-3, Lacage proposed Direct Code Execution (DCE) [14] to execute existing user space as well as kernel space protocol implementations in the simulator. This extension enables a seamless transition from real network deployments to computer simulation and further improves the comparability to the real world. However, DCE operates independently of soft- and hardware processing times, and therefore only offers limited performance insights, especially when considering prototypical hardware deployments.

In this paper, we propose *Code-transparent Wireless Prototype Simulation (CoWS)*, a DES approach built upon ns-3 and DCE to comprehensively develop and test communication protocols both on real wireless prototyping hardware and in simulations. In this context, we refer to code-transparency as executing the same, unmodified user code on hardware boards and in simulations. This eliminates the risk of errors that might occur when translating from hardware implementation to simulation model and thereby enables a seamless cyclic development process including prototypical deployment and simulation. The code-transparent approach thus allows to establish a direct relation between real world and simulation and is, therefore, an important step towards achieving realistic and reproducible simulation of wireless communication protocols and network applications. Furthermore, when carefully calibrating the DES, based on measurements obtained from an SDR platform, accurate results can be achieved in both domains. Finally, we show that CoWS, through its inherent debug capabilities, eases the process of finding implementation defects compared to debugging in distributed hardware deployments. Our approach thus contributes to short development cycles for new wireless protocols enabling reliable and well-tested software for researchers and developers.

In particular, our contributions are as follows.

- A thorough analysis of the necessary steps to enable code-transparent simulation (see Sec. 2);

- A detailed design description of Code-transparent Wireless Prototype Simulation (CoWS) to show the feasibility of our code-transparent DES approach (see Sec. 3);

- A validation of our methodology (see Sec. 4) and a performance evaluation of CoWS showing its applicability in scalable scenarios (see Sec. 5); and

- A case study illustrating new debug possibilities (see Sec. 6).

The paper concludes with a related work discussion (see Sec. 7) and some final remarks.

2. ANALYSIS

The goal of this paper is to propose a *code-transparent* approach to combine the advantages of experimentation on real-world SDRs with experimentation in scalable DES. We define code-transparency as the property that the same user code, which runs on hardware devices, also runs in the simulation. In this section, we describe the preliminary steps that are needed to integrate a hardware design into a simulator, following a DES paradigm.

In general, prototypical hardware boards, such as SDRs, consist of *hardware components*, e.g., a microprocessor, and a *software library* that allows accessing the hardware components. On top resides the *user code*, which implements certain functionality based on the underlying hardware. The library thus allows the *user code* to easily access existing hardware, e.g., sending a packet over the radio, without having to deal with low-level hardware details.

One of the most challenging tasks in simulation is to find the right level of abstraction, trading accuracy for complexity [29]. Although most analytic considerations in this section are not limited to a specific SDR design, we base our analysis on the 802.11 Reference Design for Wireless Open Access Research Platform (WARP) v3 [17] to provide a concrete example. WARP is widely used in wireless communications research and is part of many scientific publications in this area, e.g., [2, 6, 30]. In this section, after providing a short introduction to the general architecture of the 802.11 Reference Design, we analyze the different aspects that need to be considered in a code-transparent DES. Afterward, in Sec. 3, we describe the design of Code-transparent Wireless Prototype Simulation (CoWS), which is based on the analysis.

2.1 The WARP 802.11 Reference Design

The 802.11 Reference Design provides an implementation of the IEEE 802.11-2012 standard [10], where parts of the standard are realized in hardware, i.e., with the help of an FPGA, while other

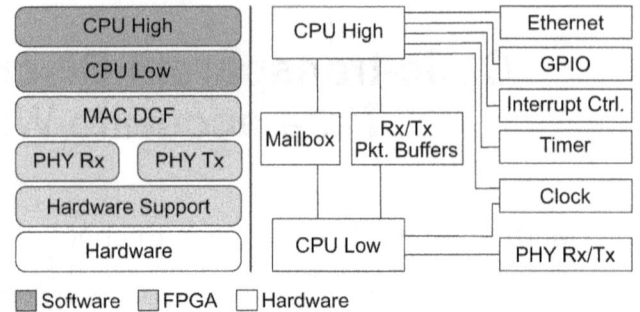

Figure 1: Simplified architecture of the WARP v3 Reference Design (adapted from [20]). On the left, the different layers of the architecture are shown. On the right, the access to hardware components from the user code, i.e., CPU High and CPU Low, is illustrated.

parts are realized in software, i.e., running on two Xilinx MicroBlaze Central Processing Units (CPUs). The basic architecture of the 802.11 Reference Design is depicted in Fig. 1.

The architecture consists of WARP v3 hardware, custom FPGA cores, and two Xilinx MicroBlaze CPUs, i.e., CPU High and CPU Low. The user code, running on the Xilinx MicroBlaze CPUs, implements major functionalities of the Medium Access Control (MAC) protocol. It further parameterizes the FPGA core, where parts of the MAC and Physical (PHY) protocol are realized, and thus allows to flexibly configure its components. The interface between hardware and software is a library offering a set of functions to the user code, which, depending on their task, set certain registers or manipulate the hardware in another way.

For our code-transparent simulation, this library offers a straightforward abstraction layer from real world to simulation. Instead of manipulating real hardware, we change the library functions to translate their functionality into DES. At the same time, the function prototypes remain unchanged to enable code-transparent simulation of the user code. In the following, we analyze the different components of embedded system designs and explain the required adaption to match DES.

2.2 Interrupts and Polling

Basically, there are two different ways for a processor to notice changes in attached hardware components: Either by interrupting the current execution with the help of an interrupt controller or by continuously polling the components for changes. Both methods should be supported by the simulation engine.

Interrupts nicely match the DES paradigm, as an interrupt simply implies adding a new event into the future event set. The event handler can process this event like any other event, i.e., with no additional overhead. However, a polling approach requires a bit more logic: When the user code actively polls for changes in the hardware, the state of the simulation instance does not change until there is an actual change in the hardware. Following the DES paradigm, this implies that the mere act of polling might be neglected to reduce the simulation overhead.

Therefore, we propose that at the beginning of a polling phase the user code transfers control to the simulator until a change in the (simulated) hardware occurs. Such a hardware change is, analog to simulated interrupts, represented by an event in the future event set. When the event handler processes this event, the simulation time is updated and the control is handed back to the user code, which may then react depending on the hardware change. The control flow of

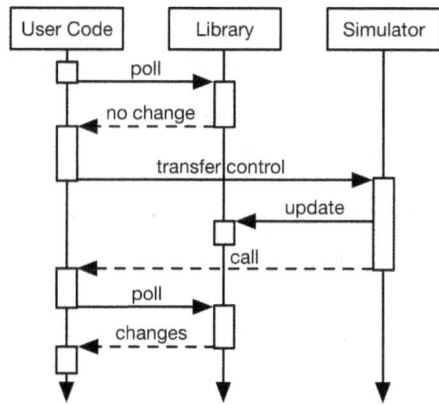

Figure 2: Control flow of polling in the simulator. When a polling phase begins, the user code transfers control to the simulator until a hardware change occurs. Then, the control is handed back to the user code to react upon the change.

(a) Scheduled timers on real hardware.

(b) Proposed model for scheduled timer in DES.

Figure 3: While on real boards timers periodically fire to check whether a function is scheduled for execution (a), the proposed model for simulated timers only fires at the time of the scheduled execution (b).

the simulated polling process is depicted in Fig. 2. It includes a user code, a library, and a simulator instance. The user code instance polls the library instance once for hardware changes, then it transfers control to the simulator instance until a hardware change occurs and the control is handed back to the user code. This allows gaining the same advantages as when simulating interrupts, while still modeling the polling process through the simulation time.

2.3 Timers and Schedulers

Another important component of embedded systems are timers. Timers allow the user code to schedule a certain function at a specific point in time. Moreover, timers are also used to periodically execute a certain functionality, e.g., sending a Beacon message every 100 ms. In the 802.11 Reference Design, for example, a coarse (200 ms accuracy) and a fine (64 μs accuracy) grain timer are provided. The accuracy defines the time interval, i.e., when the timer is fired to check whether a scheduled function should be executed or not. This process is conceptually illustrated in Fig. 3 (a). A direct modeling of this approach into DES would imply the creation of a new event each time the timer fires. To avoid this large and unnecessary overhead, we propose to create a single event for the scheduled time of the respective function, thus skipping void interrupts for the timers. Fig. 3 (b) depicts the proposed behavior of a timer in the simulation. Note that the simulation time only needs to be updated when the event handler processes the timer event leading to the execution of the scheduled function.

Additionally, hardware boards typically also provide a system time. The 802.11 Reference Design, for example, offers a `system time` and a `MAC time`, where the user code can adjust the `MAC time` while the `system time` is read-only. These times are realized each by a 64-bit register, which is incremented every microsecond. To simulate the progression of time in DES, it suffices to update such time registers only when they are accessed by the user code, by adding the simulated time between the previous access and the current access to the according register. This again considerably reduces the number of generated events, without constraining the simulation of the user code.

2.4 Memory Management

Memory is a trade-off between size, access times, and persistence. Especially in the design of embedded systems, different types of memory, e.g., Random Access Memory (RAM), Electrically

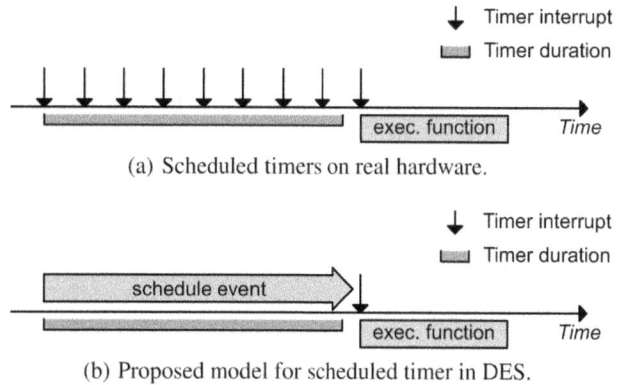

Erasable Programmable Read-Only Memory (EEPROM), and flash, are used for different purposes. Depending on the simulation model, the characteristics of a specific memory type should be considered. For a code-transparent simulation, it is indispensable to map the memory address space from the embedded device to a simulated storage location.

In SDRs, mainly hardware registers and RAM are used for memory. The available EEPROM is used for contents that should persist on the boards even when the power is turned off, e.g., the board MAC address. To achieve a similar behavior in the simulation, we propose to write the content of the EEPROM to a file on the host computer in order to persist various simulation runs.

Regarding the RAM, an essential feature of the simulator is to only provide those parts of the memory that are currently needed in the simulation. To be more specific, the simulation engine shall dynamically allocate and initialize only the needed memory parts. During our analysis of the WARP library code, for example, we found that the large parts of the available RAM are initialized, although these parts of the RAM are never used for write and read operations. Thus, such memory parts do not need to be allocated and initialized in the simulator. In this way, the overall used memory of all simulated instances can be kept low, which, in turn, ensures efficient memory usage on the host system.

Similarly, typically not all hardware registers are used during the execution of the user code. Consequently, only those registers that are accessed by software or by (simulated) hardware components need to be allocated in the simulation. For code-transparency, such simulated registers can be realized in a map, where each entry consists of the register's address and the corresponding value.

2.5 FPGA Cores

FPGAs are increasingly integrated into SDRs, as they provide a flexible way in realizing certain tasks, e.g., signal processing, in the hardware [25]. While some of these tasks might be abstracted in the simulation, such as the radio transceivers, other functionality needs to be considered by the simulator.

As shown in Fig. 1, for example, essential parts of MAC protocol are realized in the FPGA of the 802.11 Reference Design. In particular, the Distributed Coordination Function (DCF) of IEEE 802.11-2012 [10] relies on a MAC support core in the WARP v3 FPGA. This core is essential for the correct protocol behavior of the board and must be therefore modeled in the simulation.

A typical approach for specifying a hardware design is by using Finite State Machines (FSMs) [22]. The advantage of such an approach is that it can be easily translated into an imperative programming language, such as C, and nicely fits the DES paradigm. For the code-transparent simulation of an SDR platform, the different hardware FSMs, depending on the SDR design, can thus be directly modeled into the simulator. With this approach, the user code is still able to parameterize the simulated hardware support cores, but design changes in the FPGA consequently require changes in the simulation framework.

2.6 Processor

The main component of an SDR platform is the processor, enabling the execution of programmable user code. For a code-transparent simulation, the processor of the SDR board needs to be represented in the simulator. The speed of a processor mainly depends on its clock rate and on its architecture, e.g., whether it supports floating point operations or not. One way to accurately model the processor behavior is by Instruction Set Simulation (ISS) [4]. However, such fine-grained models create a large overhead for the simulation engine, especially when simulating a large distributed topology. Consequently, we opt for not modeling the execution of every processor instruction, but instead to measure the execution time for time-consuming tasks, e.g., copying data from one memory location to another, and to calibrate our DES engine accordingly. Further details regarding the calibration process are provided in Sec. 4.1.

2.7 Hardware I/O

Finally, an SDR platform consists of various hardware I/O components, which enable the board to interact with its environment. Such components typically include, for example, General-Purpose Input/Output (GPIO) pins, a Liquid Crystal Display (LCD), Universal Asynchronous Receiver / Transmitter (UART), Ethernet ports, and an antenna. For each component, the input and output characteristics must be analyzed to allow for an adequate modeling in the simulator. Output that is only meant for logging purposes, e.g., GPIO pins, LCD, and UART, might be simply written to text files in the simulation for a subsequent evaluation. For input, e.g., a user pressing a button, the simulation might include a user model pressing the button when a certain condition applies.

3. DESIGN

In this section, we present our design for *Code-transparent Wireless Prototype Simulation (CoWS)*, which builds upon the analysis in Sec. 2. Although the proposed design mostly offers general approaches for the simulation of wireless prototypes, we show its feasibility by describing the integration of the existing 802.11 Reference Design for WARP v3 into the popular DES framework ns-3. In the following, we first provide a short overview of the main design components. Then, we describe each component more detailed in individual sections.

3.1 Overview

The main architecture of CoWS consists of three layers, which are depicted in Fig. 4, namely SDR code, DCE, and ns-3. On the SDR code layer, we further differentiate between *user code* and *library*. The user code is by design *code-transparent*, i.e., the same code runs on SDR hardware as in the simulation. In the library code, in turn, the function prototypes are unchanged while the implementations might be adapted to call the simulation engine instead of real hardware components. The clear separation between user code and library thus facilitates the code-transparent simulation of any user code that is also based on the SDR design. For the code-

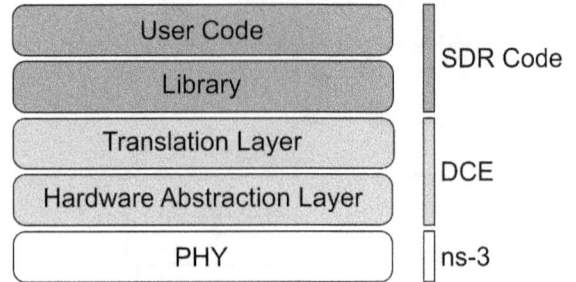

Figure 4: Proposed architecture of CoWS. The design consists of three main layers: ns-3, DCE, and the SDR Code.

transparent simulation of different SDR platforms, the respective library code and hardware functions need to be analyzed (cf. Sec. 2) and similarly interfaced to the DCE layer.

The DCE layer includes an adaptation of the ns-3 extension DCE by Lacage [14] to enable the code-transparent simulation. It is structured into a *translation* and a *hardware abstraction layer*. The translation layer maps function calls from the SDR code layer to their counterpart in the simulation, while the hardware abstraction layer models the behavior of hardware components using DES.

Finally, the ns-3 layer provides the simulation engine, which is used to model all network-related functions, e.g., the physical topology of the network or the respective transmission channels. As the modifications on this layer are only marginal, it may be easily replaced by another network simulation engine, e.g., OMNeT++ [1], given that a similar extension like DCE is available to the simulator. A more detailed description of the three layers is provided in the remainder of this section.

3.2 SDR Code Layer

To integrate the SDR source code into ns-3, the code needs to be analyzed in order to identify those code fragments that access different hardware components. In general, the user code accesses such components through a library that implements different functions. In the WARP v3 design, this library is divided into a library for CPU High, and a library for CPU Low, as the design implements two CPUs. Apart from such hardware accesses, there are other factors in the code execution that prevent the user code to be directly simulated with DES. In the following, we shortly describe different aspects of the user and library code that need to be addressed in code-transparent DES.

C Libraries.

The user code as well as the library code might both use C libraries, most prominently the C standard library. As such libraries are typically not specific to certain hardware, they can be directly integrated into the simulation. In the 802.11 Reference Design, for example, the user code frequently accesses the C library function `malloc` to allocate memory. In the simulation, such functions are typically also available on the host system. However, some library functions need to be modified to match the DES paradigm. Yet, to simulate an SDR platform in ns-3, there is typically no need to adapt the libraries, as DCE already provides the necessary adaptions.

In this context, it is important to note that the system architecture of the host system might be different from the simulated SDR platform. This might have an effect on the sizes of certain data types, e.g., the SDR platform might have a 32-bit architecture, while modern computer systems typically provide a 64-bit architecture. To avoid unexpected behavior when switching from embedded device to simulation, data types should have a specified size, e.g., by using `int32_t` instead of `int`.

Polling in Infinite Loops.

To simulate the user code with a DES paradigm, a major problem occurs when the code is indefinitely polling for hardware changes, which we already described in Sec. 2.2. According to the DCE manual [7], infinite loops need to be modified in a way that the user code periodically hands over control to the simulator engine in order to let the event handler process the next event. Otherwise, a deadlock situation occurs where the user code polls for hardware changes, which can not happen because future events are not processed as long as the current event, i.e., indefinite polling, does not complete.

There are several ways in how to hand over control to the simulation engine. One possibility is let each polling function in the library code call the simulation engine. This would also preserve the code-transparency of the user code. However, this might result in many unnecessary simulation engine calls and eventually slow down the simulation execution time. Therefore, we opt for slightly modifying the user code in a way that each infinite loop, e.g., the polling loop in the `main` function, calls the simulation engine after one iteration, which typically consists of polling different hardware components. The control is then only handed over to the user code when the next event is processed. As such loops are intended by the developer to poll indefinitely for hardware changes, they can be easily identified manually. Moreover, there are also ways in automatically detecting such loops, e.g., with static code analysis [3].

Random Numbers.

Randomness is an important aspect of real-world communication protocols, which is difficult to adequately address in computer simulation. Indeed, in many cases it is even useful that real-world stochastic processes are controllable in the simulation, as this enables reproducibility of simulation results.

In CoWS, the user code may get random numbers, which are internally provided by a pseudo-random number generator. For most specifications, e.g., the IEEE 802.11 standard [10], such a pseudo-random number generator suffices. Additionally, this allows to set a specific seed and thereby to reproduce simulation runs. Otherwise, each simulated SDR node is seeded with another random number to ensure a different behavior when relying on the pseudo-random number generator.

3.3 DCE Layer

The main purpose of DCE is to enable the simulation of existing user and kernel space implementations in ns-3 [14]. Thereby, a core feature of DCE is to map Portable Operating System Interface (POSIX) API calls to ns-3. This enables the code-transparent simulation of Linux applications, e.g., iperf, in ns-3. For CoWS, we make use of DCE to enable code-transparent simulation of SDR user code. In order to do so, DCE needs to support the functionality of the respective SDR library and, where necessary, provide abstractions from the actual hardware.

Following the DCE architecture, POSIX functions are provided through shared libraries. To simulate WARP nodes, we extend DCE with an additional shared library, which we name `libwarp`. In general, DCE allows to add a system call either by using the implementation provided by the host operating system, a so-called `NATIVE` symbol, or by replacing the implementation in the library with an own implementation, a so-called `DCE` symbol [7]. The latter is applied for symbols where the behavior needs to be adapted for DES. The `libwarp` thus acts as an interface between modified WARP library and DCE layer to hand over control to the simulator.

All `libwarp` symbols are of the kind `DCE`, as they do not exist in the host operating system. Their respective implementations are provided on the DCE layer. For each SDR design, a corresponding shared library needs to be implemented in DCE in order to enable the simulation of the respective SDR platform. In the following, we describe how the library and hardware abstraction of the most important functions is realized.

Processors and Shared Memory.

SDR platforms might include more than one CPU to parallelize the execution of tasks. As described in Sec. 2.1, the 802.11 Reference Design, for example, implements two Xilinx MicroBlaze CPUs, namely CPU High and CPU Low, where the latter is responsible for time-critical tasks such as sending acknowledgement packets and the former is responsible for high-level management tasks such as the association of new stations. The communication between the two CPUs is enabled through shared memory, e.g., the CPUs may both access the transmit and the receive buffers, and via message passing. For the latter, the 802.11 Reference Design implements a `Mailbox`, which manages the messages for the respective CPUs in first in, first out (FIFO) queues. To receive a new message, CPU High may register for an interrupt or use polling, while CPU Low exclusively uses polling.

In CoWS, the simulation of multiple CPUs is supported by letting the code for each CPU run each in its own thread, which CoWS manages on its DCE layer. The DCE layer also centrally manages the communication via shared memory and message passing, e.g., the FIFO queue of the `Mailbox` can be easily achieved with `std::queue`. Moreover, the message interrupts and polling mechanisms nicely fit into DES, when modeled as described in Sec. 2.2.

Radio Communication.

Most parts of the radio communication are directly handled by ns-3, and can thus be configured as one would usually configure such communication in ns-3. However, when handing over a packet from the user code to ns-3, and vice versa, translation steps are necessary. We address these changes on the DCE layer, which acts as a translation layer between the user code and ns-3.

Moreover, the simulation engine, similar to a real SDR board, needs certain information to be able to transmit a radio packet. This metadata, e.g., the total packet length, the employed Modulation and Coding Scheme (MCS), the transmission power, etc., is thus used to configure the transceiver. On the DCE layer, such parameters need to be passed from the user code to the simulated PHY.

Similarly, for each received packet the PHY captures certain metadata, e.g., the measured Received Signal Strength Indicator (RSSI) during the reception. In the simulation, such information needs to be conveyed from the simulated PHY to the simulated SDR user code, besides the actual data packet. The 802.11 Reference Design defines two C structs, i.e., `tx_frame_info` and `rx_frame_info`, which are stored in the transmit and accordingly in the receive buffer along with the data packet for information exchange between PHY and user code.

FPGA Support Cores.

Given that the SDR design includes FPGA support cores for the user code, these support cores need also to be considered for code-transparent simulation, as already mentioned in Sec. 2.5. The FPGA of the 802.11 Reference Design, for example, includes a MAC Support Core, which handles sending of radio packets according to the IEEE 802.11-2012 standard [10]. More specifically, it implements low-level MAC mechanisms of DCF, i.e., the access to the shared medium according to the protocol. The implementation into the

FPGA fabric guarantees a deterministic timing, which is essential for respecting the Inter-Frame Spaces (IFSs). The MAC Support Core is composed of three controllers, where each consists of an FSM handling the transmission of different packet types.

The simulation of an FPGA configuration, which is specified in Hardware Description Language (HDL) or Verilog, is not supported in a code-transparent way in CoWS. Remember that the code-transparent simulation of an FPGA is not the focus of this work, but rather the code-transparent simulation of the user code. FPGA support cores are therefore considered as another (static) hardware component that needs to be modeled in the simulator. A convenient way to do so is to use an automatic tool that converts HDL or Verilog into C/C++. Based on the translated code, we implement the support cores in the DCE layer. Each simulated SDR node then relies on an own instance of the simulated cores.

Ethernet Communication.

SDR platforms often provide one or more Ethernet ports, which are primarily used to transparently forward Ethernet packets via the radio and to exchange configuration / measurement data with a desktop computer. In the 802.11 Reference Design (cf. Fig. 1), CPU High is responsible for receiving and sending packets via the Ethernet ports. For receiving, interrupts may be enabled through the user code, which CoWS realizes as described in Sec. 2.2.

As ns-3 supports the simulation of Ethernet hosts using the Tap Bridge Model, this part can be reused for CoWS. Again ns-3 separates the Ethernet header from the payload, which requires a small translation step from standard-compliant Ethernet packets (as expected by the user code) to the ns-3 representation of Ethernet packets. Apart from this minor modification, Ethernet communication with simulated SDR nodes seamlessly integrates into ns-3, as further explained in Sec. 3.4.

3.4 ns-3 Layer

The ns-3 layer contains the DES core and is further responsible for the simulation of the communication network. This includes the different network components, e.g., an SDR instance, a physical topology of the simulated network, and the respective channel models. As mentioned before, ns-3 already provides flexible configurations for these components, which we can directly integrate into CoWS. It is, for example, possible to include simulated SDR and ns-3 Wifi nodes in the same topology. In the following, we describe the integration of SDR nodes into ns-3 network topologies and furthermore provide details on the simulated PHY and possible channel model configurations.

Simulation of a Network Component.

In ns-3, simulated nodes use the `NetDevice` class for communication with other nodes. Therefore, an ns-3 node includes for each communication channel an instance of `NetDevice`. For standard Wifi communication, for example, a node may include an instance of `WifiNetDevice`, which is derived from `NetDevice`. When simulating a specific SDR design, it might be necessary to provide a custom derivation of `NetDevice` for the respective radio interface.

The architecture of a simulated WARP node in CoWS is depicted in Fig. 5. It consists of the user code, the WARP library code, DCE hardware abstractions, and instances of `NetDevice` for communication to other nodes. For the radio communication, we created the `WarpNetDevice` class, which is similar to `WifiNetDevice` but uses the MAC implementation and PHY configuration defined in the WARP user code and on the DCE layer. For the 802.11 Reference Design this corresponds to the IEEE 802.11-2012 standard [10], but as the user code and the FPGA can be modified, this might

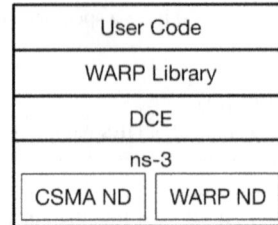

Figure 5: Architecture of a simulated WARP node in CoWS.

follow any custom-made MAC protocol and PHY configuration. Moreover, simulated WARP nodes include a `CsmaNetDevice`, an ns-3 module for an Ethernet connection to other nodes.

PHY and Channel Models.

To model a wireless channel in ns-3, the user may either implement its own channel model or rely on already existing ones. When considering IEEE 802.11, ns-3 provides `YansWifiPhy` for the corresponding simulation of the PHY and `YansWifiChannel` for the simulation of a wireless propagation model [15]. These classes offer a wide range of configuration options, which allow representing a similar setup in the simulation to the setup of the real prototyping boards. In the next section, we provide more details on the configuration of `YansWifiPhy` and `YansWifiChannel`, which we use for the validation of CoWS.

4. VALIDATION

The aim of this section is to validate CoWS in real-world deployments, i.e., we use different performance metrics to assess the validity of the results obtained by CoWS in comparison to the real world. Before describing our validation results in more detail, we first discuss the applied validation methodology.

4.1 Methodology

As explained in Sec. 3, major parts of the hardware design functionalities are modeled in CoWS to enable code-transparent simulation of the user code. Regarding their timings, we differentiate between four distinct cases: (i) *inherent timings*, e.g., a hardware timer of $100\,\mu s$, (ii) *standard-defined timings*, e.g., a DCF Inter-Frame Space (DIFS) in IEEE 802.11, (iii) *nature-defined timings*, e.g., wireless propagation speed, and (iv) *hardware-dependent timings*, e.g., a channel switch on the transceiver. While (i) to (iii) can be directly configured in the DES engine, (iv) requires measurements on the target platform to calibrate the simulation accordingly. Such measurements strongly depend on the selected hardware and therefore need to be performed for each platform prior to its accurate simulation. As an example, we provide details on the calibration of the 802.11 Reference Design (v1.5.2) on WARP v3 hardware, followed by the considered scenarios and metrics. Note that it is also possible to calibrate simulation code that is purely based on ns-3. However, we will show that with calibration, our code-transparent approach performs at least as well as a pure ns-3 solution.

Calibration.

For the calibration of CoWS, we first analyze which WARP design functionalities might have an impact on the execution time. Where necessary, we measure the actual execution time of the selected functionality in the real hardware. We repeat each measurement 1000 times to compute an average value; the variance is for all measurements negligibly small. Table 1 summarizes our findings.

Design component	Timing $[\mu s]$
Read/write mailbox	≈ 1
Channel switch	93.6
Radio transmissions	time modeled by ns-3
Ethernet transmissions	time modeled by ns-3
Print text via UART	$86.999x + 0.013$
Direct Memory Access	$1.240; \quad x < 1\,\mathrm{MB}$
	$2.862; \quad x \geq 1\,\mathrm{MB}$
memcpy	$0.007x + 0.012; \quad x < 100\,\mathrm{Byte}$
	$0.05x - 0.073; \quad x \geq 100\,\mathrm{Byte}$

Table 1: Measured timings in μs of different 802.11 Reference Design components on WARP v3, where x denotes the number of Bytes used in the respective operation.

Note that the timing of some functionalities also depends on the size of the input, e.g., printing text via UART depends on the number of Bytes x. The timings are then used to calibrate the simulation time of respective events in ns-3. However, not all design aspects that require execution time are considered in Table 1. It is known, for example, that floating point operations need a relatively long computation time on WARP nodes due to the missing hardware support for floating point operations. Nevertheless, this issue is not considered in CoWS, as our DES model abstracts from the CPU instruction level as already explained in Sec. 2.6.

Validation Scenario.

We base our validation on an existing real-world installation, namely the *wireless bridge* scenario [1], which is depicted in Fig. 6(a). In this scenario, two WARP nodes are each connected to a computer via Ethernet. This allows to run any application on the computers, e.g., iperf, to test or benchmark the radio communication between the WARP nodes. Therefore, Ethernet packets from one computer to a WARP node are transparently forwarded via the radio to the other WARP node. This other board then forwards the packets via Ethernet to the application on its connected computer. From the application layer perspective, the replacement of the Ethernet connection by this wireless WARP bridge does not require any changes in the application code, as the 802.11 Reference Design includes encapsulation and decapsulation functions to covert Ethernet to WiFi packets and vice versa. To compare the results obtained in the real-world scenario with a simulated scenario, we additionally simulate this scenario in CoWS. The architecture of the simulated nodes and their topology is depicted in Fig. 6(b).

Both scenarios of Fig. 6 consist of an AP and a STA. The STA is wirelessly associated to the AP at a distance of 1 m. We selected these idealized conditions, as the aim of this paper is not to model a specific propagation environment in ns-3, but to validate the behavior of the simulator in a scenario comparable to the real-world scenario. We perform our measurements in the 2.4 GHz and in the 5 GHz band to validate our approach under various influences on the wireless propagation. The Operating System (OS) on each computer is an Ubuntu Linux with kernel version 2.6.35, as this is the closest match to the default Linux kernel version of DCE kernel mode (version 2.6.36) [7]. In total, we differentiate between four configurations of the mentioned scenario:

WARP Antenna. The real-world wireless bridge scenario, where the WARP nodes use their antennas for Single Input and Single Output (SISO) communication. The antennas are placed

[1] https://warpproject.org/trac/wiki/OFDMReferenceDesign/Applications/Bridge

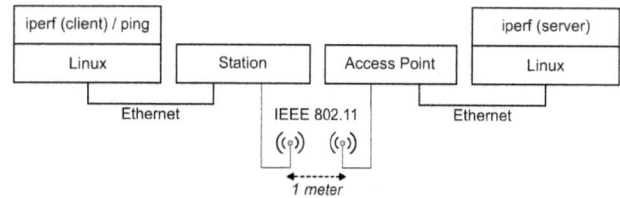

(a) Real-world wireless bridge scenario.

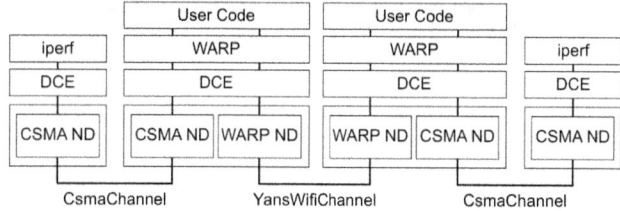

(b) Simulated wireless birdge scenario.

Figure 6: Validation scenario: A STA is wirelessly connected to an AP. For performance measurements, e.g., with iperf or ping, both devices are connected to a computer via Ethernet.

at a distance of 1 m to each other. Additionally, each WARP node is connected via Ethernet to a computer with Linux kernel version 2.6.35.

WARP Cable. This configuration equals to the WARP Antenna configuration, except that the antennas are replaced by a coaxial cable to shield the radio communication from external interference. Moreover, an attenuator of 42 dB is included in the cable connection to avoid damage to the radio controllers.

CoWS. A simulation of the wireless bridge scenario in CoWS, as shown in Fig. 6(b). As wireless channel model, we use `YansWifiChannel` with log distance propagation model and constant speed propagation delay for communication at a simulated distance of 1 m. Each WARP node is connected to a simulated node via an ns-3 `CsmaChannel`. The simulated hosts run with kernel version 2.6.36.

ns-3 WiFi. This configuration equals to the CoWS configuration, with the difference that the simulated WARP nodes are replaced by ns-3 `WifiNetDevices`. Consequently, they do not run the 802.11 Reference Design, but they are, however, also simulating IEEE 802.11 and configured to use the same MCS, transmit power and wireless channel as the WARP nodes. We use this configuration to investigate how close the provided ns-3 models match real-world scenarios.

Metrics.

Based on the previously described calibration and validation scenarios, we are mainly interested in two performance metrics to validate the behavior of CoWS compared to real-world deployments. The first one is the achieved *throughput*, or more specifically, the *goodput* we achieve in real-world configurations compared to simulations. Secondly, we are interested in how well the latency is modeled in CoWS compared to the real-world and to the ns-3 WiFi simulation. In the four validation configurations, we measure goodput and latency using the tools iperf and ping, respectively. In the following, we present the measured results of the tools, each in an individual section.

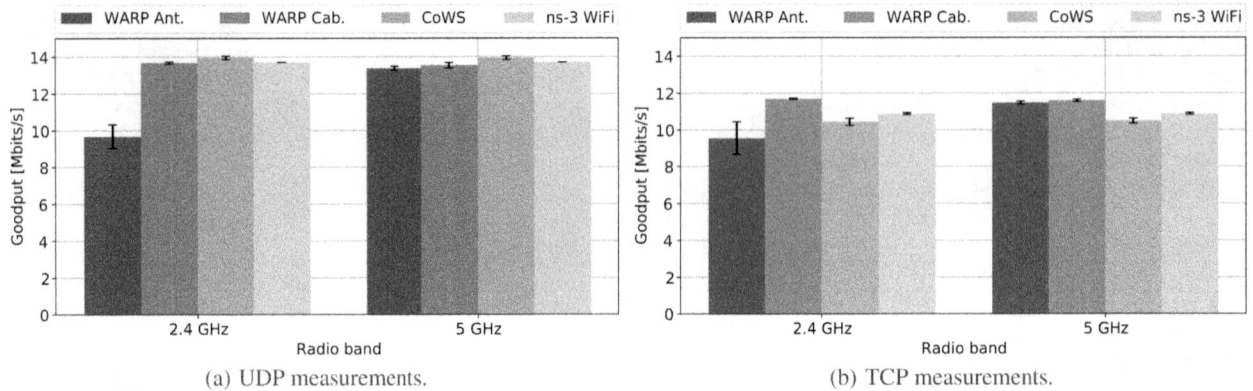

(a) UDP measurements. (b) TCP measurements.

Figure 7: Mean UDP / TCP goodput for each of the four scenario configurations in the 2.4 GHz and the 5 GHz band.

4.2 Goodput

For each of the four configurations that we described in the previous section, we measure the achieved *goodput*, i.e., the rate of successful data delivery on the application layer. The measurements are performed with iperf, where the iperf server runs on the computer / simulated host that is connected to the AP. The iperf client, in turn, runs on the computer / simulated host that is connected to the STA. Following the default configuration of the 802.11 Reference Design, we set the MCS to Quadrature Phase Shift Keying (QPSK) and with 3/4 coding, which achieves a theoretical PHY throughput of 18 Mbit/s. We repeat the measurements for a single configuration 30 times to compute an average and a standard deviation; the goodput results are extracted from the iperf server report.

UDP Measurements.

The results of the User Datagram Protocol (UDP) goodput are shown in Fig. 7(a). When comparing the WARP Antenna results for the 2.4 GHz and 5 GHz band, we note that the achieved goodput is about 3 Mbit/s lower than in the 5 GHz band. We attribute this observation to the increased interference in the 2.4 GHz band due to co-existing radios. The results in the 5 GHz band, which is much less crowded by other technologies, are almost the same as for WARP Cable, where no interference occurs. As interference is currently not considered in the channel model of our simulation, the channel of the WARP Cable configuration actually closely matches the channel model in CoWS and ns-3 WiFi. Still, we observe a slightly higher goodput with CoWS compared to WARP Cable, on average about 0.28 Mbit/s higher with 2.4 GHz, and on average about 0.4 Mbit/s higher with 5 GHz, as the additional attenuation of 42 dB in the cable setup is not modeled in the simulation, which results in slightly better propagation conditions in the simulation.

In comparison, the goodput of the ns-3 WiFi configuration is on average 0.25 Mbit/s lower than with CoWS, as we are considering two independent implementations of IEEE 802.11 with slight differences. These results show that CoWS achieves a close match in the UDP goodput compared to the real world, simulating the calibrated 802.11 Reference Design with a deviation below 3 %.

TCP Measurements.

Compared to UDP, which is a stateless transport protocol with low overhead, the main features of Transmission Control Protocol (TCP) are retransmissions, and flow / congestion control to provide reliable, in-order data streams between a client and a server. However, these mechanisms might come at the price of a reduced goodput compared

UDP, as observed in the results of Fig. 7(b). There, in the WARP Antenna configuration, the goodput is at 9.55 Mbit/s in the 2.4 GHz band, and at 11.48 Mbit/s in the 5 GHz band. Even the WARP Cable configuration only achieves about 11.65 Mbit/s in both bands. In comparison to WARP Cable, the results of CoWS and ns-3 are lower with about 10.45 Mbit/s and 10.87 Mbit/s, respectively. Tazaki et al. also observed in [23] that simulating TCP in DCE kernel mode yields a lower goodput than the corresponding real-world setup, although both use the same kernel version. This indicates that the DCE kernel mode needs to be further revised to obtain better-aligned goodput results.

In conclusion, the results show that CoWS achieves comparable goodput results to a real-world scenario, although we detected slight differences due to the model abstractions. The ns-3 WiFi approach also achieves comparable results to the WARP Cable configuration, but it lacks code-transparency whereas in CoWS we can support any protocol that was developed for the hardware platform. Nevertheless, the communication latency needs to be further investigated, especially regarding the simulation of the Linux communication stack, which we do in the following section.

4.3 Latency

For the communication latency measurements, or more precisely the RTT, we consider again the four configurations presented in Sec. 4.1. In these configurations, we measure the RTT between the STA and the AP using ping. Apart from this modification, the four configurations remain unchanged. We repeat the measurements for each configuration in the 2.4 GHz and in the 5 GHz band 100 times. The results are plotted in Fig. 8(a) and Fig. 8(b), respectively.

The WARP Antenna results in Fig. 8(a) and Fig. 8(b) once again show the effects of a crowded transmission band, i.e., at 2.4 GHz, in combination with a random back-off scheme on the MAC layer. The average latency of the WARP Antenna configuration in the 5 GHz band, which is less affected by wireless interference, is almost identical to the latency of the WARP Cable configuration, i.e., about 750 μs. However, in comparison, the latency for CoWS is significantly lower at about 430 μs and the latency for ns-3 WiFi reaches an average of 340 μs. We attribute this time difference to the fact that CoWS models more exactly different (hardware) design functionalities due to the calibration process. Nevertheless, there remains a time difference of about 320 μs between CoWS and WARP Cable, which we further investigate in the following.

We suspect that in DCE kernel model, the processing time in the Linux kernel is not accurately modeled in ns-3. To confirm this hypothesis, we conduct an additional experiment that focuses

(a) 2.4 GHz band.

(b) 5 GHz band.

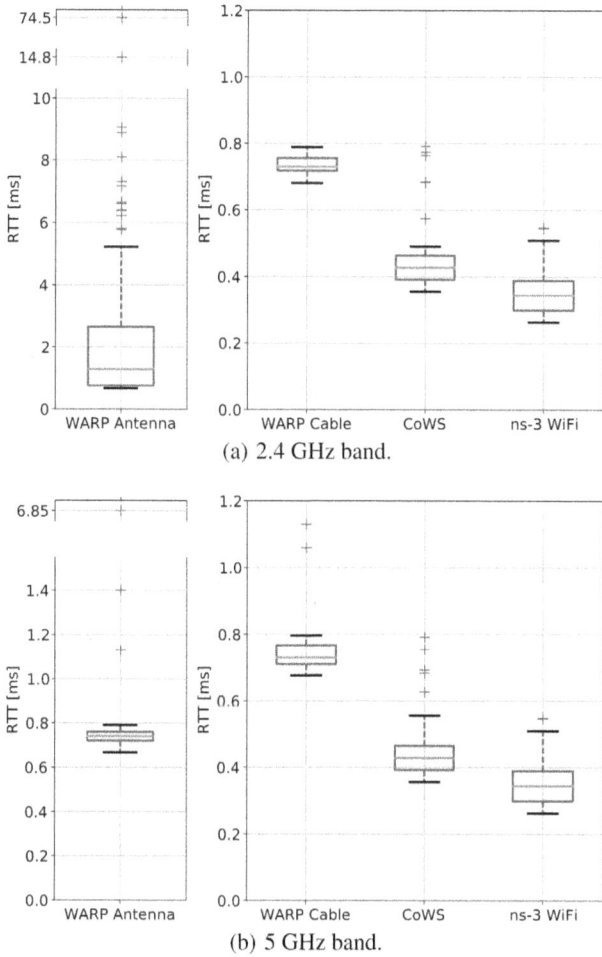

Figure 8: RTTs of the four configurations in the 2.4 GHz and in the 5 GHz band. The measurements are based on using ping.

(a) Real hardware setup.

(b) ns-3 CSMA setup.

(c) Linux / Ethernet latencies.

Figure 9: RTTs between two Ethernet-connected computers in real world and in ns-3 (c). The real hardware and the ns-3 CSMA setups are shown in (a) and (b), respectively.

on the processing times in the Linux communication stack. The measurement setup is shown in Fig. 9(a). It consists of two hosts that are directly connected via Ethernet. We implement this setup with real hardware and, for comparison, with DCE kernel mode, again with Linux kernel version 2.6.35 for both setups. The measurement setup in the simulation is depicted in Fig. 9(b). We measure the RTT between the two hosts with ping, where we repeat the measurements 100 times for both the real and the simulated setup. The obtained results are shown in Fig. 9(c).

In the real hardware setup, the average RTT is 237 μs whereas, in the ns-3 setup, we measure a constant RTT of 30 μs. The time difference between the two setting is thus about 207 μs. We attribute this time difference mainly to processing within the Linux communication stack and on the network cards, as the propagation time over a 1 m twisted pair cable is below 10 ns and can thus be neglected. This indicates that such processing times are not considered in ns-3, thus leading to shorter RTTs.

When we thus add the processing time difference of 207 μs to the measured RTT of CoWS (cf. Fig. 8), there still remains a time difference of 100 μs to the average RTT of the WARP Cable configuration. We account this difference to the CPU processing on the WARP nodes, which is limited to a certain speed on real world hardware, but is, however, not modeled in CoWS, as we abstract from CPU instruction level in the DES.

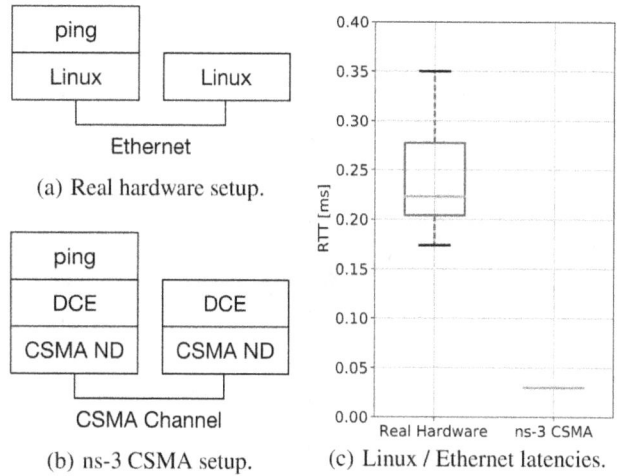

In total, the latency measurements show that with CoWS we can accomplish a similar timing behavior as in a hardware setup, with a corrected deviation of about 13 %. To achieve a closer match between simulation and real hardware timings, the involved setup components, e.g., the Linux network stack, need to be carefully analyzed and calibrated in ns-3.

5. EVALUATION

After the validation of CoWS with real-world setups in the previous section, we are further interested in the efficiency of our implementation. Remember that a central benefit of network simulation is the ability to flexibly scale the simulation scenario to a required (large) network size. Especially when working with prototyping platforms, such as WARP, medium-size networks, i.e., already with more than ten nodes, are expensive and difficult to maintain. Therefore, an important performance indicator for CoWS is the scalability, i.e., how does our code-transparent approach affect memory consumption and computation time depending on the network size? In the following, we first describe the chosen evaluation setup. Then, we discuss the measured results for the memory consumption and the computation time.

5.1 Setup

The evaluation setup consists of a simulated 5 m × 5 m area in which n simulated nodes are randomly placed. We consider various configurations of the network size, in the range of $1 \leq n \leq 1000$. In each configuration, we have one AP and the remaining nodes are STAs. The AP and STA user codes are simulated with CoWS as described in Sec. 3, based on version 1.5.2 of the 802.11 Reference Design, DCE version 1.8, and ns-3.25. For comparison, we simulate this scenario also through ns-3 WiFi, using `WifiNetDevices` for AP and STAs. The simulation runs on a Ubuntu Desktop 14.04 machine with an Intel i7 3.1 GHz CPU and 16 GB RAM. We repeat the measurements for each configuration 30 times.

5.2 Memory Usage

We measure the peak memory consumption of the ns-3 process that is responsible for simulating the WARP nodes. In the considered time frame, CoWS has initialized the needed data structures for each simulated WARP node and the user code is in its `main` function

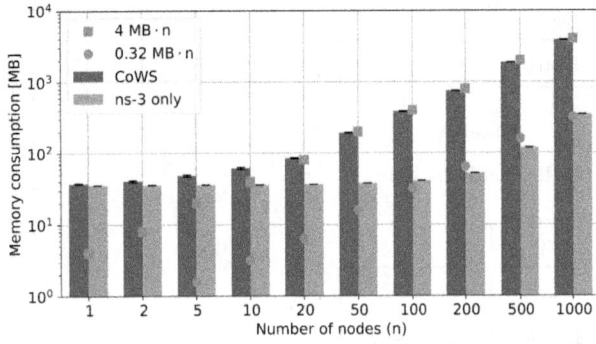

Figure 10: Total memory consumption for simulated networks of different sizes.

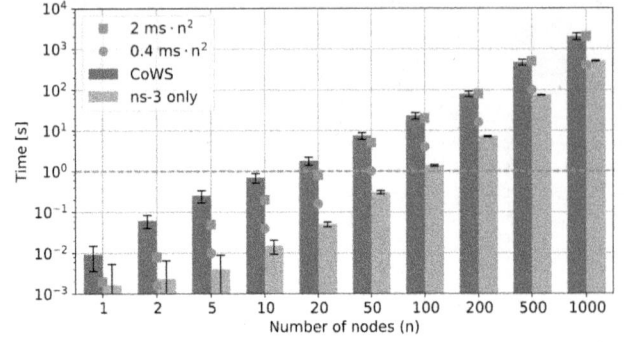

Figure 11: Total computation time for the simulation of 1 s (dashed line) in networks of different sizes.

polling for inputs or accordingly waiting for interrupts. Similarly, we also measure the peak memory consumption of the ns-3 WiFi scenario. The results for both simulation scenarios, depending on the number of nodes, are depicted in Fig. 10.

In both scenarios, we see that for small network sizes (up to 10 nodes), the memory consumption is dominated by a constant amount of required memory for the ns-3 process. Then, a linear growth of the occupied memory with each additional node can be observed. For CoWS, it can be approximated by the linear function

$$f(n) = 4\,\mathrm{MB} \cdot n \quad, \tag{1}$$

where n denotes the number of simulated nodes. Hence, each simulated WARP node occupies about 4 MB of memory, although the real WARP v3 boards have a RAM of 2 GB at their disposal. However, as described in Sec. 2, CoWS only allocates the amount of memory that a simulated WARP node currently needs. Thus, we are able to reduce the memory allocation per WARP node to about 4 MB. In the ns-3 WiFi scenario, we observe that each simulated node requires roughly 300 kB memory, as its growth depending on n can be approximated by

$$g(n) = 0.32\,\mathrm{MB} \cdot n \quad. \tag{2}$$

These results show that, as expected, both scenarios have a linear growth in their memory consumption, where for code-transparent simulation the amount of needed memory per board can be kept low when analyzing the library code accordingly (cf. Sec. 2.4).

5.3 Computation Time

Besides the memory usage, an important factor for the scalability of our approach is the required computation time, as, in DES, the simulation time does not necessarily match the actual time to execute the simulation, which is influenced by many factors. Thus, we measure the computation time for a simulation of 1 s in networks of different sizes. During this time, each simulated node periodically broadcasts messages to the other nodes, as all nodes are in wireless reception range of each other. The obtained results for CoWS and ns-3 WiFi are shown in Fig. 11.

For larger network sizes (above 20 nodes), the computation time for both scenarios grows quadratically with n. At this topology size, the simulation time corresponds to the computation time, which, however, strongly depends on the underlying scenario, as further discussed in the remainder of this section. The computation time of CoWS can then be approximated by the following function:

$$f(n) = 2\,\mathrm{ms} \cdot n^2 \quad. \tag{3}$$

For configurations below 20 nodes, the computation time is relatively higher, as other ns-3 tasks, which are independent of n, dominate the

measurements. In the ns-3 WiFi scenario we also have a quadratic growth, with a lower constant factor than in CoWS, which can be roughly approximated to

$$g(n) = 0.4\,\mathrm{ms} \cdot n^2 \quad, \tag{4}$$

as in simulation approaches that are not code-transparent, typically less DES events are required due to the higher abstraction level.

The quadratic growth of the computation time in both scenarios is caused by the communication complexity: As each of the n nodes broadcasts messages to $n-1$ nodes, the total communication complexity is $\mathcal{O}(n^2)$, where we need at least one event per message. These results show that even computationally expensive scenarios with a quadratic communication complexity can be simulated in CoWS in an acceptable time on commodity hardware for typical wireless network sizes, i.e., below 100 nodes. For larger networks, however, more advanced simulation techniques should be considered in CoWS as well as in ns-3 WiFi, e.g., parallel DES [19].

6. DEBUG FUNCTIONALITY

Besides scalability, a further advantage of simulation compared to prototypical deployments is the enhanced ability to find implementation defects. For distributed systems, it is difficult to concurrently inspect the state of interacting entities, while simulation of such systems, in turn, offers a global view on the current state of the network due to implicit synchronization, which significantly facilitates the analysis. Furthermore, when pursuing a *code-transparent* approach as in CoWS, the simulation may also be used to find *implementation* defects to improve the common code basis for simulation and prototypes. On the host computer, which is used for the simulation, already advanced debugging tools are provided through the OS, while direct debugging of embedded systems is typically a rather cumbersome process. In the following, we describe our preliminary results of searching for implementation defects with CoWS.

As an example to test the debug functionality enabled by CoWS, we analyze the 802.11 Reference Design with GNU Project Debugger (GDB) [8]. Therefore, we configure a simple scenario consisting of a STA and an AP, which we run with CoWS on a Ubuntu Desktop 14.04 machine with an Intel i7 3.1 GHz CPU and 16 GB RAM. During the execution of the simulation, we attach GDB to the STA and to the AP to inspect the program state during run-time. We found several implementation defects in the user code as well as in the WARP library. In general, each detected defect should be analyzed regarding its impact on the hardware board and reproduced on the board to rule out defects introduced by the simulation.

These defects were mainly caused by access to uninitialized pointers or by dereferenciation of `null` pointers. For embedded devices, in contrast to systems that are managed by an OS, it is typically possible to write to any addressable part of the memory. However, writing to arbitrary parts of the memory may lead to unexpected and erroneous behavior of the device, which is, in addition, difficult to track down. In particular, we found, in the 802.11 Reference Design code (version 1.5.2), dereferencing of an uninitialized pointer[2], wrong usage of a memory comparison function[3], and an erroneous register access[4]. All reported code defects were acknowledged and fixed by the WARP project in code version 1.5.3[5].

Although the focus of this work was not to thoroughly test a specific protocol implementation, our small case study already shows the potential of CoWS. We expect that the integration of more systematic testing approaches, e.g., symbolic execution [12], will enable CoWS to exhaustively test code of prototyping hardware regarding implementation defects and ultimately improve the reliability of such deployments.

7. RELATED WORK

CoWS enables code-transparent simulation of wireless prototypes to better analyze and to flexibly scale existing hardware deployments. Therefore, we compare our approach to advanced analysis tools for wireless prototype networks as well as code-transparent simulation techniques in this context, which we present in the following.

The Power Aware Wireless Sensors (PAWiS) simulation framework [28] allows simulating various aspects of Wireless Sensor Networks (WSNs) based on OMNeT++. The focus of this simulation framework is to optimize WSN deployments regarding power efficiency and reliability. Therefore, a model of each WSN node, including its function, timing, and power consumption needs to specified, where the detail granularity of the model can be adapted depending on the simulation aspect that the user is interested in. Moreover, data post processing tools allow to analyze the output of a simulation run, and subsequently to optimize the WSN based on the results. Nonetheless, the specification of an adequate simulation model is a cumbersome and error-prone process, which we avoid by our code-transparent approach.

In a similar regard, Dustminer [11] provides a debug tool that analyzes logs from deployed nodes to discover events that lead to errors in the interaction patterns. The output logs need to be fed to Dustminer, which allows a post factum search for irregular behavior patterns. With CoWS, however, we envision that such analysis tools find implementation defects during run-time due to the easy access of node logs in simulation. For validation, found implementation defects in simulation may be then recreated in a real-world setup using the same code basis.

The authors of [9] propose *Wireless MAC Processor*, a framework that abstracts from a specific Network Interface Card (NIC) by providing a set of elementary actions and signals, which programmers use to define FSMs for the MAC protocol behavior. Such programs may then be ported to different NIC with no additional programming effort and even during run-time. Although not directly envisioned by the authors of the original paper, this also enables the simulation of such MAC models and thus facilitates the transition from real hardware to simulation.

Hybrid Simulation framework (HySim) [13] allows simulating the execution of code on microprocessors on instruction-level, which is referred to as ISS. This allows for a very precise simulation but also significantly slows down the simulation process, especially

in distributed settings with a large number of nodes. The authors of [18], in turn, tackle this trade-off between scalability and accuracy with a cross-level simulator for the Contiki OS (COOJA), which allows for simultaneous simulation at different abstraction levels. COOJA enables simulation of a small subset of the network at a very high precision, i.e., at OS level or even ISS, while the remaining part of the network is simulated at the application level. This constitutes an interesting feature, which could be considered for the further development of CoWS.

A TinyOS Simulator (TOSSIM) was introduced in [16]. It enables a code-transparent simulation of TinyOS applications in WSNs with a DES. Therefore, it replaces low-level TinyOS components with TOSSIM components to translate hardware interrupts into simulation events. Similarly to CoWS, the authors were able to discover several bugs in TinyOS with the help of simulation. The main difference to our approach is the lack of an accurate timing behavior and that TOSSIM uses own, simplified channel models instead of a state-of-the-art network simulator.

In [21], the authors propose *WARPsim*, which, similar to CoWS, also provides a code-transparent simulation of WARP. Therefore, WARPsim offers a subset of the OFDM Ref. Design for WARP v1/2, which enables an execution of WARP code on standard desktop computers. The execution of WARP instances in different processes, which are coordinated via Inter-Process Communication (IPC), allows the simulation of small networks. However, this approach does not scale well for larger typologies as each additional WARP node requires its own process. Moreover, hardware timings are not considered in WARPsim, which leads to a limited comparability with real-world setups. Lastly, a major drawback of WARPsim is that is does not rely on an advanced network simulator, such as ns-3 or OMNeT++, which strongly limits its application.

Finally, a simulation framework for multicore systems, named Manifold, is proposed in [27]. This framework enables a full system simulation of a multicore architecture by flexibly integrating user-defined component models. The simulation takes place at CPU instruction-level and may be conducted in a parallel or in a sequential way. While Manifold offers a precise simulation of complex multicore architectures, it is unclear whether this approach is suited for simulating large network topologies due to the fine grain simulation steps that are involved. However, with CoWS we follow a similar modular approach to facilitate the adaptation and extension of our simulation framework.

8. CONCLUSION

In this paper, we propose a code-transparent simulation framework of wireless prototypes. We first analyze the needed steps to achieve code-transparent simulation and then present our design, which is embedded into ns-3 / DCE and enables the simulation of SDR nodes. The validation of our approach is based on WARP and real-world scenarios and shows that, after calibration, we are able to achieve a similar behavior in the simulation compared to the real-world. The UDP goodput revealed a deviation below 3 % and the corrected latency results deviate about 13 %, where, for the latter, we identified further potential for improvement. Furthermore, it would be interesting to validate our approach in more complex scenarios including more stations.

The memory and computation overhead of our framework is in the same complexity class as a corresponding simulation that is realized purely by ns-3. With our approach, however, we have the benefits of code-transparency, i.e., a common code-base for prototypes and simulation, and a strong correlation between both domains. In a small case study, we show the ability of our framework to find implementation defects in the wireless prototype code by

---

[2]http://warpproject.org/forums/viewtopic.php?id=3201

[3]http://warpproject.org/forums/viewtopic.php?id=3206

[4]http://warpproject.org/forums/viewtopic.php?id=3217

[5]http://warpproject.org/trac/wiki/802.11/Changelog

detecting bugs in the 802.11 Reference Design. We expect that with more systematic approaches, e.g., with symbolic execution, we will find further defects, which will strongly increase the reliability and correctness of prototypical deployments.

To summarize, our framework will not replace the development and testing of wireless communication protocols on SDR platforms, as the quality of its results depends on a strong correlation to the real world. However, it is a powerful tool to seamlessly switch from the real-world deployment to the simulation domain and vice versa. It thus complements results from a real-world deployment by enabling scenarios that were previously not possible due to time and cost constraints and, finally, it eases the verification process for wireless communication protocols.

Acknowledgments

The research leading to these results has received funding from the German Research Foundation (DFG) under Agreement n. 625799 (MemoSim) and from the European Research Council under the EU's Horizon2020 Framework Programme / ERC Grant Agreement n. 647295 (SYMBIOSYS).

9. REFERENCES

[1] A. Varga. OMNeT++ Discrete Event Simulator. [Online] https://www.omnetpp.org.

[2] N. Anand, J. Lee, S. J. Lee, and E. W. Knightly. Mode and User Selection for Multi-user MIMO WLANs Without CSI. In *IEEE Conf. on Computer Communications (INFOCOM)*, pages 451–459, Apr. 2015.

[3] N. Ayewah, D. Hovemeyer, J. D. Morgenthaler, J. Penix, and W. Pugh. Using Static Analysis to Find Bugs. *IEEE Software*, 25(5):22–29, Sept. 2008.

[4] G. Braun, A. Nohl, A. Hoffmann, O. Schliebusch, R. Leupers, and H. Meyr. A Universal Technique for Fast and Flexible Instruction-Set Architecture Simulation. *IEEE Trans. on Computer-Aided Design of Integrated Circuits and Systems*, 23(12):1625–1639, Dec. 2004.

[5] L. Breslau, D. Estrin, K. Fall, S. Floyd, J. Heidemann, A. Helmy, P. Huang, S. McCanne, K. Varadhan, Y. Xu, and H. Yu. Advances in Network Simulation. *IEEE Computer*, 33(5):59–67, June 2000.

[6] W. Choi, H. Lim, and A. Sabharwal. Power-Controlled Medium Access Control Protocol for Full-Duplex WiFi Networks. *IEEE Trans. on Wireless Communications*, 14(7):3601–3613, July 2015.

[7] Direct Code Execution Project. ns-3 Direct Code Execution (DCE) Manual, Release 1.8. Technical report, Mar. 2016.

[8] Free Software Foundation. The GNU Project Debugger. https://www.gnu.org/software/gdb/.

[9] P. Gallo, D. Garlisi, F. Giuliano, F. Gringoli, I. Tinnirello, and G. Bianchi. Wireless MAC Processor Networking: A Control Architecture for Expressing and Implementing High-Level Adaptation Policies in WLANs. *IEEE Vehicular Technology Magazine*, 8(4):81–89, Dec. 2013.

[10] IEEE. Standard for Information Technology–Telecommunications and Information Exchange Between Systems Local and Metropolitan Area Networks–Specific Requirements Part 11. *IEEE Std 802.11-2012*, pages 1–2793, Mar. 2012.

[11] M. M. H. Khan, H. K. Le, H. Ahmadi, T. F. Abdelzaher, and J. Han. Dustminer: Troubleshooting Interactive Complexity Bugs in Sensor Networks. In *Proc. of the 6th ACM Conf. on Embedded Netw. Sensor Systems*, pages 99–112, Nov. 2008.

[12] J. C. King. Symbolic Execution and Program Testing. *Communications of the ACM*, 19(7):385–394, July 1976.

[13] S. Kraemer, L. Gao, J. Weinstock, R. Leupers, G. Ascheid, and H. Meyr. HySim: A Fast Simulation Framework for Embedded Software Development. In *5th IEEE/ACM/IFIP International Conference on Hardware/Software Codesign and System Synthesis*, pages 75–80, Sept. 2007.

[14] M. Lacage. *Experimentation Tools for Networking Research*. PhD thesis, Université de Nice-Sophia Antipolis, 2010.

[15] M. Lacage and T. R. Henderson. Yet Another Network Simulator. In *Proceeding from the Workshop on ns-2: The IP Network Simulator*. ACM, Oct. 2006.

[16] P. Levis, N. Lee, M. Welsh, and D. Culler. TOSSIM: Accurate and Scalable Simulation of Entire TinyOS Applications. In *Proc. of the 1st Int'l Conf. on Embedded Networked Sensor Systems*, pages 126–137. ACM, 2003.

[17] Mango Communications. 802.11 Reference Design. [Online] http://mangocomm.com/802.11.

[18] F. Osterlind, A. Dunkels, J. Eriksson, N. Finne, and T. Voigt. Cross-Level Sensor Network Simulation with COOJA. In *Proceedings of the 31st IEEE Conference on Local Computer Networks*, pages 641–648, Nov. 2006.

[19] J. Pelkey and G. Riley. Distributed Simulation with MPI in Ns-3. In *Proc. of the 4th Int'l ICST Conf. on Sim. Tools and Techn.*, SIMUTools '11, pages 410–414. ICST, Mar. 2011.

[20] Rice University and Mango Communications. The WARP Project. [Online] https://www.warpproject.org/trac.

[21] A. Schumacher, M. Serror, C. Dombrowski, and J. Gross. WARPsim: A Code-Transparent Network Simulator for WARP Devices. In *IEEE 16th Int'l Symp. on a World of Wireless, Mobile and Multimedia Networks*, June 2015.

[22] V. Sklyarov. Reconfigurable Models of Finite State Machines and Their Implementation in FPGAs. *Journal of Systems Architecture*, 47(14-15):1043–1064, Aug. 2002.

[23] H. Tazaki, F. Urbani, and T. Turletti. DCE Cradle: Simulate Network Protocols with Real Stacks for Better Realism. In *Proc. of the 6th Int'l ICST Conf. on Simulation Tools and Techniques*, pages 153–158, Mar. 2013.

[24] The ns-3 Consortium. ns-3 Discrete Event Network Simulator. [Online] https://www.nsnam.org.

[25] T. Ulversoy. Software Defined Radio: Challenges and Opportunities. *IEEE Communications Surveys Tutorials*, 12(4):531–550, Apr. 2010.

[26] A. Varga. The OMNeT++ Discrete Event Simulation System. *Proc. of the Europ. Sim. Multiconference (ESM)*, 2001.

[27] J. Wang, J. Beu, R. Bheda, T. Conte, Z. Dong, C. Kersey, M. Rasquinha, G. Riley, W. Song, H. Xiao, P. Xu, and S. Yalamanchili. Manifold: A Parallel Simulation Framework for Multicore Systems. In *IEEE Int'l Symp. on Perf. Analysis of Systems and Softw. (ISPASS)*, pages 106–115, Mar. 2014.

[28] D. Weber, J. Glaser, and S. Mahlknecht. Discrete Event Simulation Framework for Power Aware Wireless Sensor Networks. In *5th IEEE International Conference on Industrial Informatics*, volume 1, pages 335–340, June 2007.

[29] K. Wehrle, M. Güneş, and J. Gross, editors. *Modeling and Tools for Netw. Simulation*. Springer Berlin Heidelberg, 2010.

[30] H. Yu, O. Bejarano, and L. Zhong. Combating Inter-cell Interference in 802.11ac-based Multi-user MIMO Networks. In *Proc. of the 20th Int'l Conf. on Mobile Computing and Networking (MobiCom)*, pages 141–152. ACM, Sept. 2014.

Efficient Simulation of Nested Hollow Sphere Intersections

for Dynamically Nested Compartmental Models in Cell Biology

Till Köster
University of Rostock
Institut für Informatik
Albert-Einstein-Straße 22
Rostock, Germany 18059
till.koester@uni-
rostock.de

Kalyan Perumalla
Oak Ridge National
Laboratory
One Bethel Valley Rd
Oak Ridge, Tennessee,
37831-6085, USA
perumallaks@ornl.gov

Adelinde Uhrmacher
University of Rostock
Institut für Informatik
Albert-Einstein-Straße 22
Rostock, Germany 18059
adelinde.uhrmacher@uni-
rostock.de

ABSTRACT

In the particle-based simulation of cell-biological systems in continuous space, a key performance bottleneck is the computation of all possible intersections between particles. These typically rely for collision detection on solid sphere approaches. The behavior of cell biological systems is influenced by dynamic hierarchical nesting, such as the forming of, the transport within, and the merging of vesicles. Existing collision detection algorithms are found not to be designed for these types of spatial cell-biological models, because nearly all existing high performance parallel algorithms are focusing on solid sphere interactions. The known algorithms for solid sphere intersections return more intersections than actually occur with nested hollow spheres. Here we define a new problem of computing the intersections among arbitrarily nested hollow spheres of possibly different sizes, thicknesses, positions, and nesting levels. We describe a new algorithm designed to solve this nested hollow sphere intersection problem and implement it for parallel execution on graphical processing units (GPUs). We present first results about the runtime performance and scaling to hundreds of thousands of spheres, and compare the performance with that from a leading solid object intersection package also running on GPUs.

Keywords

Neighbor Lists, Nearest Neighbors, Cellular Biology, Compartmental Models, Nested Shells, Smooth Particles, GPU, CUDA, Prefix Sum

1. INTRODUCTION

1.1 Background and Motivation

Particle-based reaction-diffusion models in continuous space are computationally very expensive. One possibility to speed

SIGSIM-PADS 17 May 24-26, 2017, Singapore, Singapore

© 2017 ACM. ISBN 978-1-4503-4489-0/17/05...15.00

DOI: http://dx.doi.org/10.1145/3064911.3064920

up simulation is parallelization [9]. Over the past decade, general purpose graphical processing units (GPU)-based computation has been effectively exploited for simulation [28, 22, 25], and for simulating cell biological systems in particular [5]. Models that are executed on the GPU are typically composed of many individual entities with similar behavior patterns, where the simulation proceeds stepwise and the calculations per simulation step are quite similar [24]. Thus, individual particles moving stepwise [8, 4, 26] or stochastic reaction-diffusion algorithms based on operator-splitting, lend themselves very well to GPU-based execution [10].

To take excluded volumes and crowding into account in particle-based reaction-diffusion models [30], sub-cellular components may be abstracted as spherical in shape of different radii, with a diffusion-excluded interior [32]. The core computational problem concerns the proximity-based interaction of many sub-cellular components [30]. If a particle attempts a move, it is checked whether the particle will as a result of the move overlap with another particle and, if so, the move will be rejected. Other tools rely on energy landscapes to model the interaction of particles. Independently, whether the particles' interactions are modeled by move rejection [14, 27] or by potentials (energy landscape) [29], typically they are assumed to be *solid* (hard-core or soft-core) spheres.

However, abstracting them as solid spheres ignores the dynamic nesting of cell-biological systems that plays a key role in the functioning of the cell. In addition to static compartments, such as the nucleus in eucaryotes, we find dynamic compartments and vesicles, like mitochondria and lysosomes, whose number, volume, content, and interconnectivity changes over time. This is illustrated in Figure 1 [23], which shows the process of receptor recycling in the cell schematically. Vesicles form at the membrane and engulf protein receptor complexes, those are transported to a lysosome. The vesicle merges with the lysosome. Part of the receptor complex is freed and returns to the membrane (being recycled) whereas the other part of the receptor complex is degraded within the lysosome.

The forming, merging, and destruction of vesicles lead to dynamically and arbitrarily nested compartmental structures. These require the models to treat cells, compartments, and vesicles as *hollow* spheres that allow an arbitrary dynamic nesting of spheres within each other [3]. In cell biological systems of interest to us, the nesting is such that there are a small number of large-sized compartments

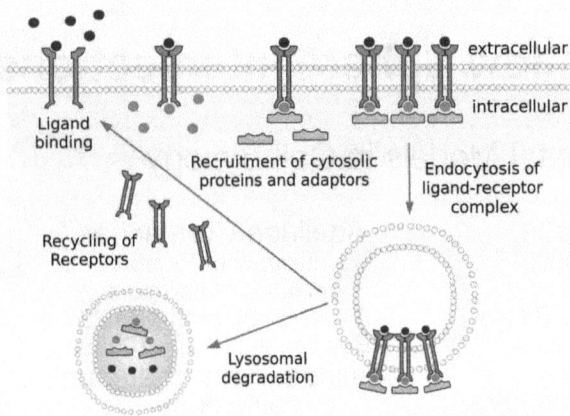

(a) Biological view

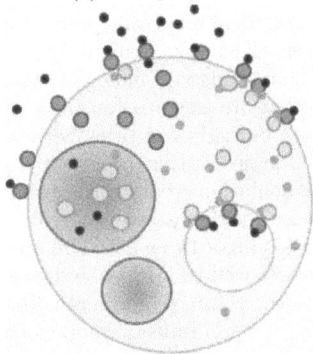

(b) Hollow spheres view

Figure 1: Illustration of a cellular subsystem model whose components can be specified as nested arrangements of objects within objects that interact at intersection points and can be approximated to spherical objects/shells of various sizes and thicknesses moving within and through each other

such as nucleus, cytosol, or membrane, and a larger number of smaller-sized compartments, such as mitochondria or lysosomes interacting with many small objects like proteins.

Additional applications in which nested containment in hollow spheres is used include simulations of friction-based contacts among many objects ("intersection" of a range) for estimating the dissipated energy in rotating containers [31]. To meet desired configurations containing 200,000 particles, parallel simulation is warranted. Other peripherally related applications include simulation of foams and foam-packed materials.

1.2 Contributions

In this paper, we identify core computational problem in such cellular simulations in terms of a new, formally-defined and generalized problem of arbitrarily nested configurations of hollow spheres or shells. The determination of intersections is a crucial step in such simulations to model the interactions. The determination of interaction activity due to intersections forms a major, time-intensive part of cellular simulations.

We analyze the nested sphere problem in detail with the range of possible scenarios of nesting levels, sphere densities, sphere radii, thicknesses, and position distributions. Based

on this problem specification, we propose a new, efficient solution for fully arbitrary nested configurations. We present a novel algorithm that is efficient and scalable to large numbers of nested hollow spheres with widely varying radii and thicknesses. We have completed an efficient implementation of the algorithm on the GPU (implemented in CUDA and run on a NVIDIA K80 card) and have tested correctness. The implementation addresses multiple GPU-specific issues, the most challenging of them being the variable loading per GPU thread. We present runtime performance data of the new algorithm on multiple benchmarks exercising a range of scenarios with varying sizes and positions of large numbers of spheres.

The algorithm and results presented here are among the first in the literature on the definition of the novel problem in nested spherical body intersections, along with algorithm, implementation, and performance data tested in a experimental design with variation of many scenario parameters. The algorithm and implementation have also been integrated into a cell biological simulator that has been sped up with our algorithm to simulate scenarios with higher scale. A separate experimental study is underway in analyzing the runtime gains of the overall application, which are planned for a subsequent publication. In this paper, we focus on the computation of the underlying general problem of computing nested hollow sphere intersections.

1.3 Related Work

The problem of collision detection (also called intersection detection) is well explored in the literature [15, 19, 7], predominantly studied in the context of solid, non-nested bodies. When interested in the collisions of n objects, the naïve approach would be to simply perform a brute force pass over all the objects, checking each object for potential intersection with all other objects. However, this leads to an execution time of $O(n^2)$, which is impractical for large systems. At this point, we can exploit the fact that all potential object-object intersections exist only at the scales of the particle sizes rather than at the full domain length scales. As identified by Hubbard [12], most state of the art collision detection algorithms consist of two phases, a broad phase and a narrow phase, as follows.

Broad Phase In this phase, a rough measure is used to separate *potential* collisions (of objects that are in some vicinity of one another) from *non-potential* collisions (of object pairs that are too far from one another to intersect).

Narrow Phase In this phase, the *potential* pairs of objects identified in the Broad Phase are more closely investigated. In computer graphics, this phase often involves computationally intensive mesh calculations, as the objects tend to have complex three dimensional geometrical structures defined by triangle meshes.

In this paper, we focus on the broad phase due to the simplicity of geometries typically assumed in our immediate application of interest, namely, particle-based reaction-diffusion simulation. We are interested in a rough pruning of the n^2 set of pairs for large number of objects. After the broad phase, the pruning of this set during the narrow phase can be rather easily done with our type of objects (see Section 2.1), compared to the sometimes very complex triangle meshes as found in other applications such as visualization, computer gaming, and computer graphics. Consequently, we describe different broad phase algorithms here. Specifically, we will be examining algorithms that are suited for execution on the GPU, which is a power efficient parallel processing hardware architecture for simulating systems with large numbers of particles.

Fixed radius on grid

There exists a very fast and refined solution for a particular sub-problem, that of equal-sized (or very similarly-sized) spheres. This fixed radius collision problem has been investigated and well understood, because a consistent spherical cutoff is commonly encountered in many simulation contexts, such as smooth particle hydrodynamics and molecular dynamics simulations [6].

In the state of the art algorithm [11] called *fast Fixed Radius Nearest Neighbor* (fFRNN), the system is organized into bins such that each particle, after being assigned to its own bin, only needs to check the bins in its Moore neighborhood in order to find all possible neighbors. This works only when the interaction cutoff between two particles is ensured to be smaller than the bin width. Moreover, solidity of objects is implicit.

Grids for variable sizes

One way to approach the problem of finding intersections among a number of complex shaped particles is to allow one particle to span across multiple bins in the grid. This is achieved in some approaches [20] by approximating all particles as boxes spanning over multiple bins (easy to calculate for the axis aligned boundary box (AABBs)). AABB means a rectangle or cuboid whose edges are aligned with the x, y and z axis of the underlying coordinate system. Object identifiers are added to all the bins. For each bin, all possible collisions are calculated. Finally, the redundantly counted collisions need to be removed.

Sweep and prune

The sweep-and-prune (SAP), also called sort-and-sweep, algorithm originates in works by Baraff [2]. The idea is to project the objects onto one linear axis. All objects then calculate the starting and the ending points of their projection onto that axis. The objects are then sorted by both these values. If one object's starting point or ending point lies within the starting and ending interval of another object, these two objects potentially have a collision. Projection is then repeated for all axes (for example, the three axes for 3D space). If two objects have overlapping intervals for all tested projections, they are considered a possible collision pair.

An advantage of this algorithm is that the axis projections do not completely change, if the system is only minutely altered. Specific sorting algorithms are employed, which are efficient for sorted lists (such as insertion sort). Numerous optimizations exist, such as using Principal Component Analysis (PCA) for determining the axes. The SAP method cannot immediately be ported to the GPU, as there are some naturally sequential parts (mostly contained in the sweep phase). After some modifications, an efficient GPU variant has been developed [18]. This however only works for small ($< 64K$) system sizes, as SAP does not cope well with very large systems. Scaling for large systems has been achieved

in their implementation by introducing coarse bins for the system that are independently "swept and pruned."

Bounding volume hierarchy trees

A more complex approach to the collision problem is that of a bounding volume hierarchy. The underlying data structure of this approach is a tree (usually a binary tree), whose leaves are the objects of the system. Every other node of the system contains a volume. The tree is built in such a manner that all child node's volume is contained in their parent node's volume. These trees can be built with varying quality (e.g. how balanced they are). For applications in which the system is static and the tree is frequently traversed, such as in ray tracing, higher quality trees are used. For our application, we need to frequently rebuild the tree. This can be done efficiently using the algorithm proposed by Karras [13] which is based on the M-Code [16]. Lauterbach also presents an efficient way to traverse the tree on the GPU [17].

1.4 Organization

The rest of the paper is organized as follows. We describe the hollow sphere/shell intersection problem in Section 2, followed by a presentation of our new hollow sphere/shell intersection algorithm in Section 3. Section 4 describes the parallel version of the algorithm and presents the details of its implementation on GPUs. A detailed performance study is presented in Section 5. Finally, Section 6 concludes the paper with a summary of the results and findings, and outlines future work.

2. HOLLOW SPHERE INTERSECTION

In what follows, we will refer to the solid sphere intersection problem as SSX and the nested hollow sphere intersection problem as HSX. Also, in the context of HSX, we will use the terms spheres and shells interchangeably.

2.1 Definition and Description

The HSX problem is concerned with finding all pairs of spheres that are overlapping and can be formally defined as follows (vectors are denoted in bold font).

A single hollow sphere object h_i is defined by its position $\boldsymbol{x}_i$, its radius r_i, and its shell thickness q_i ($q_i = 0$ is a valid choice). Note, that an sphere's radius marks the outer perimeter, while a sphere around $\boldsymbol{x}_i$ with radius r_i q_i marks the inner perimeter of the hollow sphere.

This allows for the definition of the following three relations.

- Non-commutative *contains* relation $C(j,i)$ that specifies whether shell h_j is completely contained within shell h_i:

$$C(j,i) = \begin{cases} true & \text{if } |\boldsymbol{x}_i \quad \boldsymbol{x}_j| < r_j \quad q_j \quad r_i \\ false & \text{otherwise} \end{cases} \quad (1)$$

- Commutative *contains* relation $\hat{C}(j,i)$ that specifies whether one of the shells h_j and h_i completely contains the other:

$$\hat{C}(j,i) = C(j,i) \quad C(i,j), \text{ and} \quad (2)$$

- Commutative *intersection* relation $I_{\text{HSX}}(j,i) = I(j,i)$

that specifies if shells h_i and h_j intersect:

$$I(j,i) = \begin{cases} true & \text{if } \neg \hat{C}(j,i) \wedge |\boldsymbol{x}_i - \boldsymbol{x}_j| \le r_j + r_i \\ false & \text{otherwise} \end{cases}. \tag{3}$$

The HSX problem can now be defined as: given a set of n hollow spheres, compute the set of unique pairs of intersecting spheres $\{ \langle j,i \rangle \,|\, I(j,i) = true\}$.

2.2 HSX versus SSX

The SSX problem only differs from HSX in the definition of the intersection relation. In SSX, the commutative intersection relation $I_{\text{SSX}}(j,i)$ is defined as

$$I_{\text{SSX}}(j,i) = \begin{cases} true & \text{if } |\boldsymbol{x}_i - \boldsymbol{x}_j| \le r_j + r_i \\ false & \text{otherwise} \end{cases}. \tag{4}$$

Since the HSX intersection criterion is stricter than that of SSX, it follows that an HSX intersection implies an SSX intersection, that is,

$$I_{\text{HSX}}(j,i) \Rightarrow I_{\text{SSX}}(j,i) , \tag{5}$$

but not the other way around. This means that any result of SSX can be converted to an HSX result by means of a linear pass over the results to cull spurious pairs that do not intersect in the hollow sense. However, such an approach of generate-and-cull-pairs can be prohibitively expensive. Consider a simple scenario in which all n spheres share the same center, but have varying radii and zero thickness. Any SSX algorithm would return $\frac{n(n-1)}{2} = \mathcal{O}(n^2)$ pairs, however the correct HSX result would be 0 pairs. The difference is further illustrated in Figure 2.

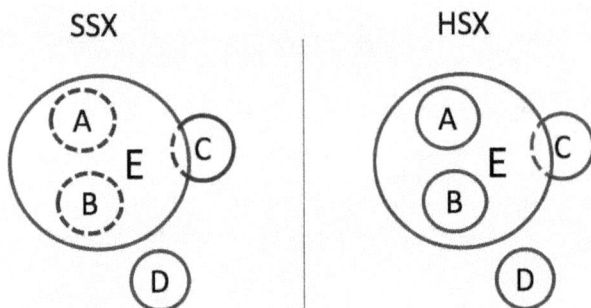

Figure 2: Here the difference between HSX and SSX is illustrated. Collisions are indicated by dashed lines. On the right, the HSX case illustrates a collision occurring between E and C. On the left, in the SSX case, the inclusion of A and B in E is also counted as a collision, which are not valid collisions in HSX

2.3 Computational Problem

The computation of the list of pairs of intersecting pairs is a major computational burden in the simulation of cell biology systems [3]. Hence, efficiency improvements in the computation of intersections directly will improve the simulator speed and the size and number of models that can be simulated.

Efficient intersection algorithms exist for calculating collisions of solid spheres, which could be applied to hollow

sphere models as a rough approximation. However, for dynamically nested models as in cell biological systems, the use of solid sphere intersection algorithms is fundamentally mismatched. The computationally intensive core problem is in fact an HSX problem, rather than SSX.

Although it is possible to apply SSX algorithms for solving the HSX problem, (a) the number of pairs generated by SSX algorithms is potentially much larger than what HSX defines, and (b) more computational work/runtime may be wasted by SSX algorithms when applied to the HSX problem.

In many systems spheres only move very little between steps. Instead of recalculating all intersections every step, it could be useful to calculate all neighbors in some vicinity and update that data only occasionally. This can easily be done by enlarging the radius and thickness of the spheres during the neighbor calculation. A simple upper bound for the size/thickness increase may be computed by considering the maximum velocity in the system and then calculating the maximal distance covered by any object within a given time step.

3. NEW HSX ALGORITHM

In this section, we present our new algorithmic approach to solve HSX problems. An overview of the algorithm is provided, followed by the details of the algorithmic steps, and a description of how large and small spheres are handled in the algorithm.

3.1 Algorithm Description

The algorithmic framework for HSX we propose here is inspired by the fast Fixed Radius Nearest Neighbor (fast FRNN, or fFRNN) algorithm proposed by Hoetzlein [11]. The FRNN problem can be seen as a special case of SSX in which all spheres have the same radius. The fFRNN algorithm provides a very efficient way to solve such problems on the GPU, by binning all spheres into a grid and then iterating over that grid. In fFRNN, each sphere is associated with exactly one bin, and the bins are large enough such that each sphere needs to only consider the neighboring bins for possible collisions.

Input: Set M of shells (hollow spheres)
Data: The initial grid size d_0
Result: Set R of possible HSX collisions
1   $d \leftarrow d_0$ // typically, $d_0 = \min_i(r_i)$
2   while $M \neq \emptyset$ do
3     $S \leftarrow \{s_i | s_i \in M \wedge r_i \cdot 2 < d\}$
4     $L \leftarrow \{s_i | s_i \in M \wedge r_i \cdot 2 \ge d\}$
5     $G_{\text{FRNN}} \leftarrow grid(S,d)$
6     $R_S \leftarrow \{ \langle s_j,s_i \rangle \,|\, \text{inMoore}(G, s_j, s_i)\}$
7     $B_{l_i} \leftarrow$ $\{b | b \in G \wedge \exists s_k \{b = \text{Bin}(s_k, G) \wedge I(s_k, l_i) = true\}\}$
8     $R_L \leftarrow \{ \langle s_j,l_i \rangle \,|\, s_j \in S \wedge s_j \in b \wedge b \in B_{l_i}\}$
9     $R \leftarrow R \cup R_S \cup R_L$
10    $M \leftarrow M \setminus S$
11    $d \leftarrow d \cdot 2$
12 end
13 return R

Algorithm 1: The new HSX algorithmic framework

Our algorithm builds on the concept of grid-based binning,

but introduces different phases for different sizes of shells. This will be covered in the following step-by-step description of Algorithm 1.

Initially, a grid size d is chosen that is able to handle the smallest sphere in an fFRNN fashion. Grid size here refers to the width of the spatial bins. Thus, as a reasonable choice, d needs to be larger than the diameter of the smallest sphere. Furthermore, at the beginning, all the spheres are considered to be *unprocessed* and are therefore part of the set M of spheres that have not yet been fully processed.

In the main loop (**while** starting on line 2), the number of unprocessed spheres M is iteratively decreased until all spheres are fully processed and the problem is completely solved.

First, spheres are partitioned into two sets: L being those spheres with a diameter larger than d, and S being those with a diameter less than or equal to d. Next, these two sets are processed in relation to each other.

3.2 Processing Small Spheres

The grid G_{FRNN} is used to determine, in constant time, all small spheres in a certain area of space. This is shown in Algorithm 1 on line 5. Each sphere in S is assigned to a grid cell in G_{FRNN} as determined by the position of its center. Efficient creation of the grid and its associated look-up structure is discussed in Section 4.1.

On line 3, all collisions among the spheres within S are determined, that is, one small sphere overlapping with another small sphere. The notion of "small" is relative to the current value of d: at any given iteration, all spheres in S are of size no larger than d. Since all spheres in S are smaller than the grid width in terms of diameter, it is sufficient to examine the 9 cells (in 2D models) or 27 cells (in 3D models) within the Moore neighborhood of each sphere s_i (including itself). This is accomplished in line 6, where inMoore(G, s_j, s_i) denotes that the spheres s_j and s_i are contained in the Moore neighborhood of each other within the grid G.

It is also useful to make sure that redundancies are avoided, such as in the pairs a, b and b, a. This can be easily achieved by imposing an ordering criteria (for example, using the sphere identifiers).

3.3 Processing Large Spheres

The goal when processing the large spheres is to find all grid cells for each large sphere that contain smaller spheres potentially colliding with the larger spheres. In other words, for each large sphere, this part of the processing considers all smaller spheres whose centers are located in any of the grid cells spanned by the large sphere.

This is accomplished in two steps. First, in line 7, for each large sphere l_i, a list B_{l_i} is created that contains all the grid cells that could possibly contain a small sphere s with a potential collision with l_i. This list of grid cells is designed to only consider the rim of the large sphere and avoid the potentially empty space in the middle of the sphere where no intersections can occur with that sphere. This computation would take into account the discretization of the sphere into d-sized grid cells enclosing the shell walls. In line 8, the grid cells B_{l_i} of each l_i are consulted to determine each small sphere s_j that actually lies in those grid cells and, thereby, mark s_j, l_i as a colliding pair.

In the next step, in line 9, all the cells that were found to contain potentially colliding small spheres are added to the

resulting list R. This is the combination of R_S, which contains small-small sphere collisions, and R_L, which contains small-large sphere collisions.

All the small spheres of this level (corresponding to grid size d) can now be removed from the M, as they no longer need to be processed. This is done in line 10. The loop is then repeated with an increased value of grid size d, as shown in line 11.

4. PARALLEL EXECUTION ON GPU

The HSX algorithm in Algorithm 1 has been designed with the objective of applying it to parallel computing hardware such as GPUs. Therefore, each step of the algorithm has been designed to allow implementation as parallel computing operations.

Note that, as a general rule, all spheres are stored in contiguous memory arrays to enable efficient memory access throughout the algorithm. To implement line 3 and line 4 of Algorithm 1, the array containing the sphere data is partitioned such that all smaller spheres are in front and all larger spheres are behind a certain indexed position. This is parallelized on the GPU using techniques such as indicator sequences and prefix sums [21].

4.1 Creating the Grid

To implement line 5 of Algorithm 1, the process of creating the grid for fast look-up via counting sort on the GPU (similar to the method used by fFRNN) is as follows.

1. Generate a vector V of integers initialized to zero, with each entry in the vector corresponding to one grid cell.

2. Iterate (in parallel) over all spheres, calculating their grid cell identifier to which they belong, (atomically) incrementing the corresponding counter (of that grid cell) in V by 1, storing the old value of V at that position with each sphere. This value will indicate for each sphere its rank within a grid cell. The global atomic operations on modern GPUs permit this step to be accomplished very efficiently.

3. Compute the prefix sums[1] of V. This is a well studied operation that is efficiently parallelized on the GPU.

4. Create a new vector K storing all spheres in a different order – the new position of each element is computed as the index i, where i is equal to the value of its grid cell in the prefix-summed V plus its rank stored from the earlier access to V. This guarantees that each sphere has a different position in K, and all spheres can be moved to K independently, which allows this operation to be performed in parallel.

5. As a result of the previous steps, the data structures V and K are created that, when used together, allow constant-time access to all spheres in a certain grid cell. For example, queries to all spheres in any given i-th cell can be found in constant time. These are conveniently stored as contiguous elements from $K[V[i]]$ to $K[V[i+1]]$.

---

[1] An exclusive prefix sum is an operation on a list of numbers in which each element is the sum of all its preceding elements

4.2 Assembling to the Result Set

In principle, it is possible to parallelize the operation of looping over all data in order to implement line 9 of Algorithm 1. However, parallel execution of operations on data structures such as R might lead to race conditions. After all the pairs are determined, the pairs are scattered in multiple segments across the memory. Therefore, they need to be collected into a single contiguous array before they are returned as the result. This is done in the following way in our implementation when processing the small-small sphere interaction.

1. Create an array with an integer entry for each grid cell.

2. Iterate in parallel over each grid cell to determine the maximum number of collisions found by looking at the number of spheres in the *Moore Neighborhood* of that grid cell and store that count in the array.

3. Perform a prefix sum on the array and allocate sufficient storage for R such that all possible collisions would fit.

4. Using the array as an index structure, iterate in parallel over each grid cell and write all possible collisions to R.

5. Prune the list R under the criterion of redundancy ($a, b \quad b, a$). Since the previous steps iterate through the result anyway, the precise intersection condition Equation 3 can also compute and remove the pairs that were erroneously added due to the grid being too coarse (that is, they were incorrectly flagged as intersecting).

6. Removing spheres from an array A in parallel is a simple, four-step process, outlined here for illustration, similar to the array partitioning operation previously indicated.

   (a) Create a second array C that has an integer corresponding to each entry in the array.

   (b) In parallel, set each entry to 0 if the corresponding entry in A is to be removed, or set it to 1 if the entry should stay.

   (c) Perform a prefix sum on C.

   (d) Re-position all entries to be kept in A to their new position as given by C.

The same process of creation followed by removal can also be used for adding the small-large collisions to R. However, pruning is not necessary for R as there cannot be redundant entries.

4.3 Finding Grid Cells for Large Spheres

In implementing line 7 of Algorithm 1, the task of finding the grid cells that enclose each large sphere's shell walls is not an easy operation to accomplish on a GPU. This is because different sphere sizes lead to different workloads per sphere. To address this problem, we have chosen the following approach.

1. For each sphere, using a rectangular bounding box, estimate the maximum number of grid cells that it overlaps.

2. Instantiate each of these grid cells in an array B and check if the cells actually overlap the sphere, or, if the cell is surrounded by l_i, but, due to its finite thickness, there is no possibility of collision. If not, mark them and remove them from the array.

3. Now, for each of these grid cells b in B, find the corresponding grid cell g_{FRNN} in G_{FRNN}.

4. For all b, determine the collisions of all small spheres in g_{FRNN} with the large sphere that spans the grid cell b. Add these collision pairs to the result set R.

4.4 Implementation Details

We have implemented our algorithm using NVIDIA CUDA v8.0 and the `thrust` package. The `thrust` package is a library that provides numerous standard algorithms, such as the aforementioned *partition* or *prefix sum* operations, with a consistent iterator interface that is inspired by the C++ standard template libraries. This offers us several advantages. First, the implementation effort is simplified because basic algorithms such as prefix sums do not need to be reimplemented in CUDA. Secondly, the code remains resilient to hardware changes as the `thrust` library is continuously updated and optimized to fit the latest parallel hardware. The benefits of the approach are evident from the fact that it was not necessary to specify low-level CUDA configuration such as block and thread counts to obtain optimal performance in our current hardware setup. Our HSX algorithm required several complex functions or CUDA-specific expressions such as atomics, but even those were utilized via the `thrust` interface (such as *for each*) available in the form of C++11 lambda functions. In the form of zip iterators, `thrust` also provides a convenient and consistent way to use the structure-of-arrays idiom, that is preferred for performance considerations over the, array-of-structures idiom, that is commonly used in object oriented programming. Finally, `thrust` also provides a back-end for CPU parallelism. This would allow us to create a parallel CPU version of the code with little extra work.

Our prototype can handle both two-dimensional (2D) and three-dimensional (3D) scenarios. Our code supports both single and double precision floating point arithmetic, but performance results presented here are with single precision.

5. PERFORMANCE STUDY

In order to empirically understand the performance of the algorithm and its implementation (called GHSX), we undertake a scalability study and run time evaluation of the system operating on a range of scenarios.

5.1 Experimental Setup

For each number of spheres investigated, we generated multiple system configurations, with different random initialization. Each of the generated scenarios was processed using different intersection algorithms. For each system-algorithm pair, the average run time is recorded from ten runs (five runs in the case of less sensitive configurations). In order to compare our algorithm to some baseline, we chose the `chrono::collide` package from the *Project Chrono* suite of physical simulation tools [33]. The source code for `chrono::collide` was published and documented under BSD-3 licence on github [1]. The `chrono::collide` package is a CUDA-based GPU implementation of a uniform grid collision detection algorithm. The experimental study executed all scenarios with each intersection algorithm. Note that our algorithm as well as the `chrono::collide` package return a set of pairs that are *potential* collisions rather than *actual* collisions. This is because generally broad phase collision detection algorithms don't return a *perfect* result containing only the actual collisions.

Hence, for a fair comparison, we prune the returned results from all algorithms the same way (to determine *actual* collisions from the computed *potential* collisions set). This pruned (tighter) set is the final result transferred back from the GPU. Operationally, this is achieved by means of a `thrust::remove_if` call. Note that `chrono` takes the initial grid size as a parameter, just as our algorithm (d_0 in Algorithm 1 line 1). For both algorithms we always chose the optimal grid size.

For simplicity and scenario-independence, we increase the grid size d by a factor of 2 in each iteration (Algorithm 1 line 11). In future work, we plan to investigate the impact of this growth function of grid size on the overall performance of our algorithm depending on the type of system.

In order to make a reasonable comparison, the tool should run on the GPU and be able to handle arbitrary sphere sizes. Many current tools that originate in the areas of molecular dynamics or fluid dynamics are unsuitable, because they do not support the combination of GPU-based execution and arbitrary sphere sizes. The gSAP system for simulating collisions among many rigid bodies [18] (available on-line) is an exception, but it does not offer documentation and is restricted to Windows platform (communication with the authors also was not fruitful).

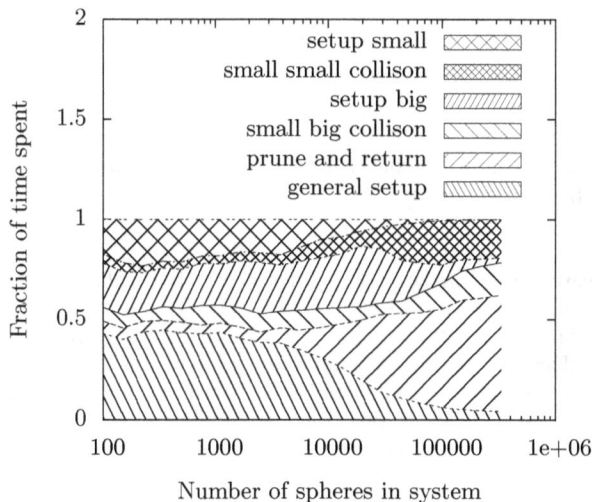

Figure 3: Run time spent in different parts of the algorithm, as a function of the number of spheres

5.2 Benchmarks

The generalized HSX problem can be instantiated in a variety of system configurations. To exercise the algorithm and its implementation, multiple parameters are varied: the total number of spheres in the system, the distribution of the spheres' radii, the density of the system measured in

spheres per unit volume, and the thickness of the shell walls. All systems are investigated in 3D, except where explicitly mentioned otherwise.

Generally, in cell biological systems of interest to us, there are a relatively smaller number of large-sized compartments such as nucleus, cytosol, or membrane, and a larger number of smaller-sized compartments, such as mitochondria or lysosomes interacting with many small objects like proteins. In our test cases we model this variance by means of an exponential distribution

$$\mathcal{P}(r) = e^{-r} \ , \tag{6}$$

as it offers a representative distribution of sizes.

In order to avoid system boundary overlap (or periodic boundary conditions), that are supported by GHSX, but not by `chrono`, the systems are initialized as follows.

1. Generate an sphere with uniform random position inside the volume and a radius from the exponential distribution (Equation 6)

2. If the sphere does not overlap with the systems border, add it to the system. Otherwise, discard it.

3. Repeat the preceding steps until the system has the desired density for the scenario.

When applied to systems with a small number of spheres, this process results in a slight bias towards smaller spheres, as they are less likely to intersect with the outline of the volume, when placed randomly. For larger systems, this bias asymptotically approaches zero.

For specific sections of the performance evaluation we also study other special cases, such as uniform sphere size. Some of the system scenarios are illustrated in 2D in Figure 4.

5.3 Software and Hardware Enviroment

All the experiments were executed on a headless server, DELL PowerEdge R730, containing two Intel Xeon Processor E5-2683v4 (40M Cache, 2.10 GHz), 256GB RDIMM Memory (2400MT/s) and running CentOS version 7. GPU acceleration was provided by an Nvidia Tesla K80 card using a driver version 367.48 under the CUDA toolkit version 8.0.44.

5.4 Performance Results

Our first key result (as observed from Figure 5) is that for a dense large (10000) system the performance of our algorithm performs well, running faster than `chrono` by about 50%. However, for sparse systems, it does not perform as well, as shown in Figure 6. This is expected because our algorithm is specially designed to handle nesting, while sparse systems exhibit limited nesting. All these runs used the same exponential distribution for the sphere sizes. The density was varied between 10 and 0.1 spheres per unit volume.

The density relation can also be seen in Figure 7. Clearly our implementation benefits from having a more tightly packed system. The denser a system is, the higher the number of collisions between large and small spheres, and, more importantly, the more likely it is that non-HSX tools will spend extra work detecting spurious collisions that do not exist when nesting is considered.

The observation that large spheres make the difference can be made from Figure 8. In highly dense scenarios containing

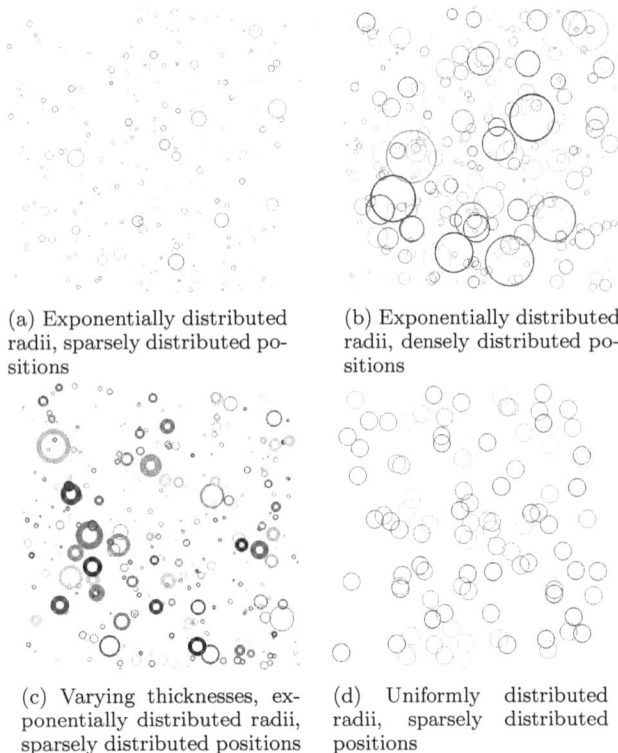

(a) Exponentially distributed radii, sparsely distributed positions

(b) Exponentially distributed radii, densely distributed positions

(c) Varying thicknesses, exponentially distributed radii, sparsely distributed positions

(d) Uniformly distributed radii, sparsely distributed positions

Figure 4: Illustrations of some of the benchmark cases

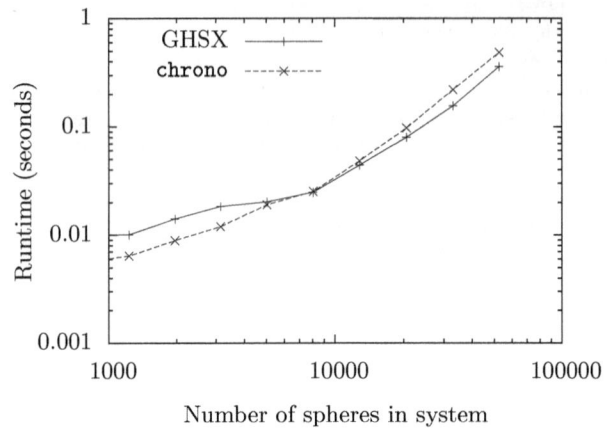

Figure 5: Run time for very dense system with exponentially distributed radii. At large system sizes, the performance gain of GHSX is about 50%

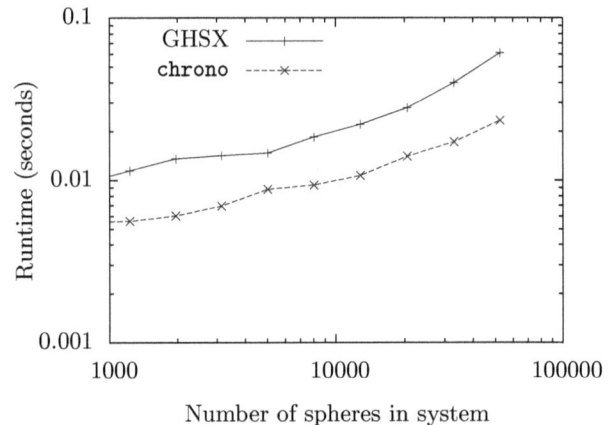

Figure 6: Run time for sparse system with exponentially distributed radii. chrono is significantly faster than GHSX for this sparse scenario

large spheres, both tools perform fairly similarly. This is because both of them perform roughly the same steps.

When the system contains spheres of only one size, there is no need for our algorithm to iterate through multiple phases, as there are only small spheres. The small-small intersection is already handled in an optimal way. Nonetheless, it can be seen that chrono performs better, at least at a large number of spheres. This is due to differences in implementation between the two software tools, to be able to account for nesting or not. Interestingly, chrono performs poorly at 5000 spheres (actually slower than with 10000 spheres). In this case, our implementation was 20% faster. This performance persists even when the positional configuration of the spheres is changed; also, it appears in sparse systems as in Figure 6, although not as pronounced. We hypothesize it as attributable to some thread allocation or buffer size which is perhaps sub-optimally set.

5.5 Number of Collisions

Further motivation for our multiphase algorithm can be found by looking at the theoretical number of HSX collisions present in the system compared to what other variants find. Here we focus on the theoretical minimum that could possibly be found by an ideal algorithm. In reality, most algorithms (including ours) return a larger set. In Figure 10, the difference between, the collisions found by using HSX, SSX and axis aligned boundary boxes (AABBs), as used by chrono is laid out. It is clear that in this test case the difference between HSX and SSX in marginal. This can be further seen in Figure 9, where varying the thickness of the spheres only very slightly changed the number of collisions. The run time was also hardly influenced by the thickness.

However, what makes a big difference in both plots is the difference between AABB and HSX/SSX. This is also where the performance difference seen in Figure 5 stems from. Not only does our algorithm handle nesting well, but also, as a byproduct, offers an efficient, generalized way of handling large spheres in close proximity to smaller ones. This is due to the finer grid used to sample the surroundings of big spheres, whereas chrono uses an AABB approach.

5.6 Scaling with System Size

In Figure 11, we investigate the scaling characteristics of the algorithm in 2D and 3D. It is seen that, with fewer than 10000 spheres, the resources are not used very well, as time per sphere or collision is seen to increase. The 2D version is observed to be relatively less efficient than the 3D simulations. This is possibly because the program, designed for 3D, has unused memory when only doing 2D. It could be customized to perform well specifically for 2D. *Unlike ours, few other tools offer the useful capability to handle both 2D and 3D scenarios in the same implementation.*

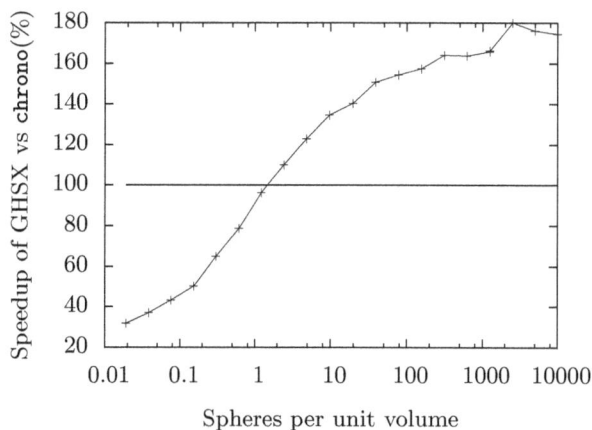

Figure 7: Performance when density is varied in a system of 30000 spheres. GHSX is significantly faster at higher densities

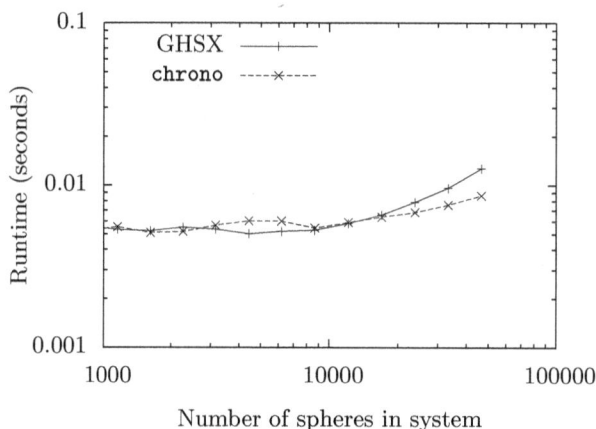

Figure 8: Run time for a system with uniformly distributed radii, corresponding to the configuration illustrated in Figure 4d

5.7 Highly Nested Case

The preceding experiments using random initial positions offer only a low degree of nesting. In physically-based structures, as in cell biology, the degree of nesting is higher. Spheres are more likely to be fully nested than to be intersecting. Therefore, to experiment with an extreme case, a scenario is created in which all spheres are perfectly nested within one another (concentric spheres).

As expected, Figure 12 shows that increased amount of nesting leads to a significant speedup of our implementation over chrono, because chrono, by design, only handles non-nested (solid) spheres, and hence does not account for the nesting.

5.8 Performance Improvements

There are a few aspects of the implementation that remain to be improved. Figure 3, shows that *pruning and returning* takes up a significant fraction of time towards the end of the execution. This is mainly due to design choices made for ease of implementation. In some places, in order to sim-

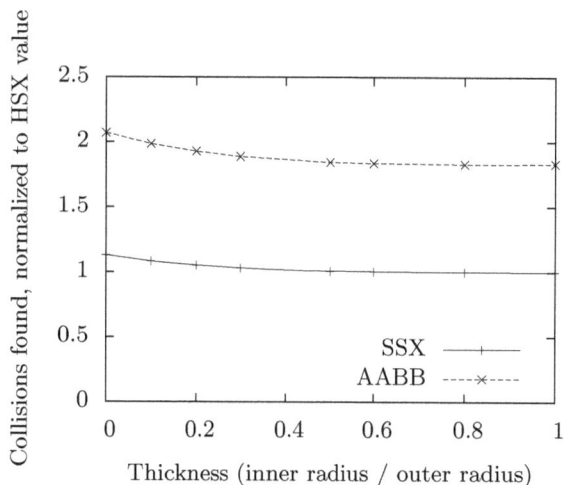

Figure 9: Variation of the number of estimated collisions with the thickness of the spheres in the case of exponentially distributed radii. Thickness is observed to have little bearing for a given algorithm, but the difference between the AABB and SSX algorithms is observed to persist even with increased thicknesses

plify memory access, the used amount of memory needs to be overestimated, leading to data structures that turn out to be smaller than estimate and hence need to be pruned. Furthermore, data layout could be improved after pruning which makes most memory access not coalesced.

Another potential improvement is in the work balance among the computational threads. When threads are assigned per spheres, large spheres induce higher work loads, leaving threads with smaller spheres idle.

The current implementation is also limited in the size of the problem due to memory concerns. The current data structures limit the number of spheres to 50000-200000, depending on problem structure. This is planned to be fixed in the future by partitioning larger problems into manageable sizes. Sometimes in the later iterations of the algorithm, only a small number of large spheres remain. At this stage, a simple brute force approach of checking all pairs for potential intersection would be faster, compared to the cost of building up a complex grid data structure as is done currently.

Additionally, there are potentially *algorithmic* improvements. The first concerns the determination of the initial grid size and, related to that, the growth factor of the grid size, or, more generally, a non-linear growth function. At the moment, in each iteration we simply double the grid width, but other more efficient ways can be imagined, dependent on the properties of the system.

6. SUMMARY AND FUTURE WORK

Motivated by the problem to introduce dynamic nesting into particle-based reaction diffusion simulation in continuous space, we identified a core computational problem, namely, the efficient determination of all pairs of spatial intersections of the spheres.

Detecting whether or not two spheres intersect (and thus collide) is a crucial step in such simulations, as it forms the basis for determining various types of biochemical reactions. Most collision detection algorithms focus on solid

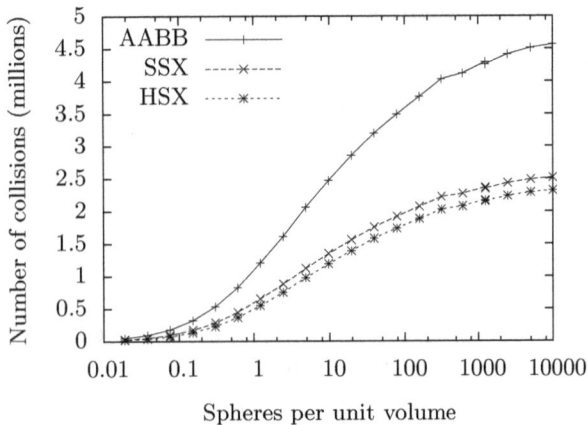

Figure 10: Variation of the number of estimated collisions in a system with exponentially distributed radii, counted using HSX, SSX, and AABB

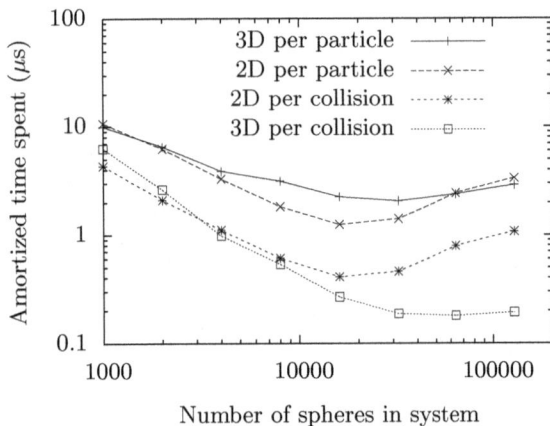

Figure 11: Scaling for 2D/3D variants of semi-dense system with exponentially distributed sphere radii. The number of collisions was kept similar for both 2D and 3D

sphere interactions (SSX) and thus tend to identify spurious collisions.

As a new and more suitable formalization, we defined the problem of hollow sphere intersections (HSX), which is an elegant generalization of dynamically nested compartmental structures. The abstraction is based on spherical bounding boxes for the spheres and inter-sphere interactions at multiple levels of nesting. We addressed the computational problem in determining all pairs of intersecting spheres under the special considerations of nested containment.

We designed a novel algorithm for the problem and implemented the algorithm on the GPU platform. We executed experiments with several scenarios of hollow spheres of different sizes, thicknesses, positions and nesting levels in systems of varying density. A comparison with another GPU-based algorithm from a leading solid sphere intersection package demonstrated the value of our new approach, not only with regard to handling highly nested systems but also for handling systems with spheres of varying sizes, whether they are solid or hollow.

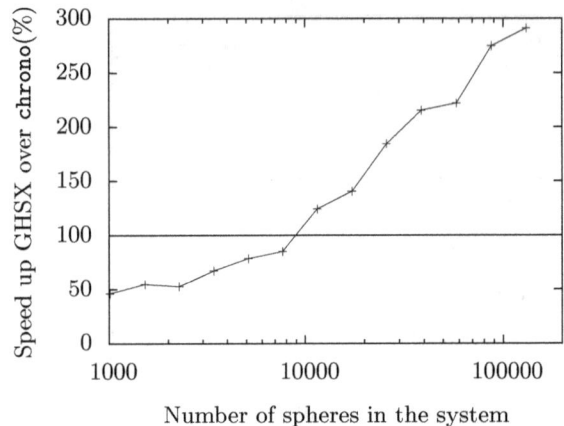

Figure 12: Speed up observed in a highly nested case

The quality of collision detection results and the run time performance of the algorithm are very encouraging. Our implementation presents a proof of concept with many possibilities for additional improvement. The algorithm and implementation have also been integrated into a cell biological simulator to simulate scenarios at larger scale and higher speed. A separate study is underway in analyzing the performance of the overall application with cell-biology configurations.

Acknowledgements

This work was partly supported by a fellowship of the German Academic Exchange Service (DAAD) and the German Research Foundation (DFG) via the research grant ES-CEMMO (UH66-14).

This manuscript has been authored by UT-Battelle, LLC under Contract No. DE-AC05-00OR22725 with the U.S. Department of Energy. The United States Government retains and the publisher, by accepting the article for publication, acknowledges that the United States Government retains a non-exclusive, paid-up, irrevocable, worldwide license to publish or reproduce the published form of this manuscript, or allow others to do so, for United States Government purposes. The Department of Energy will provide public access to these results of federally sponsored research in accordance with the DOE Public Access Plan (http://energy.gov/downloads/doe-public-access-plan).

7. REFERENCES

[1] https://github.com/uwsbel/collision-detection, 2014.
[2] D. Baraff. *Dynamic Simulation of Non-Penetrating Rigid Bodies*. Ph. D thesis, Computer Science Department, Cornell University, 1992.
[3] A. Bittig and A. M. Uhrmacher. ML-Space: Hybrid spatial gillespie and particle simulation of multi-level rule-based models in cell biology. *IEEE/ACM Transactions on Computational Biology and Bioinformatics*, online first: August, 2016.
[4] L. Dematte. Smoldyn on Graphics Processing Units: Massively Parallel Brownian Dynamics Simulations. *IEEE/ACM Transactions on Computational Biology and Bioinformatics*, 9(3):655–667, May 2012.

[5] L. Dematté and D. Prandi. GPU computing for systems biology. *Briefings in Bioinformatics*, 11(3):323–333, May 2010.

[6] P. Eastman, M. S. Friedrichs, J. D. Chodera, R. J. Radmer, C. M. Bruns, J. P. Ku, K. A. Beauchamp, T. J. Lane, L.-P. Wang, D. Shukla, T. Tye, M. Houston, T. Stich, C. Klein, M. R. Shirts, and V. S. Pande. OpenMM 4: A Reusable, Extensible, Hardware Independent Library for High Performance Molecular Simulation. *Journal of Chemical Theory and Computation*, 9(1):461–469, Jan. 2013.

[7] C. Ericson. *Real-time collision detection*. Morgan Kaufmann series in interactive 3D technology. Elsevier, Morgan Kaufmann, Amsterdam, nachdr. edition, 2008. OCLC: 551935024.

[8] M. Falk, M. Ott, T. Ertl, M. Klann, and H. Koeppl. Parallelized agent-based simulation on CPU and graphics hardware for spatial and stochastic models in biology. In *Proceedings of the 9th International Conference on Computational Methods in Systems Biology*, pages 73–82. ACM, 2011.

[9] R. M. Fujimoto. Research challenges in parallel and distributed simulation. *ACM Trans. Model. Comput. Simul.*, 26(4):22:1–22:29, May 2016.

[10] M. J. Hallock, J. E. Stone, E. Roberts, C. Fry, and Z. Luthey-Schulten. Simulation of reaction diffusion processes over biologically relevant size and time scales using multi-GPU workstations. *Parallel Computing*, 40(5-6):86–99, May 2014.

[11] R. C. Hoetzlein. Fast Fixed-Radius Nearest Neighbors: Interactive Million-Particle Fluids, 2014.

[12] P. M. Hubbard. Interactive collision detection. In *Virtual Reality, Proceedings., IEEE Symposium on Research Frontiers in*, pages 24–31, 1993.

[13] T. Karras. Maximizing parallelism in the construction of BVHs, octrees, and k-d trees. In *Proceedings of the Fourth ACM SIGGRAPH/Eurographics conference on High-Performance Graphics*, pages 33–37. Eurographics Association, 2012.

[14] M. T. Klann, A. Lapin, and M. Reuss. Agent-based simulation of reactions in crowded and structured intracellular environment: Influence of mobility and location of reactants. *BMC systems biology*, 5(1), 2011.

[15] S. Kockara, T. Halic, K. Iqbal, C. Bayrak, and R. Rowe. Collision detection: A survey. In *2007 IEEE International Conference on Systems, Man and Cybernetics*, pages 4046–4051, Oct. 2007.

[16] C. Lauterbach, M. Garland, S. Sengupta, D. Luebke, and D. Manocha. Fast BVH Construction on GPUs. *Computer Graphics Forum*, 28(2):375–384, Apr. 2009.

[17] C. Lauterbach, Q. Mo, and D. Manocha. gProximity: hierarchical GPU-based operations for collision and distance queries. In *Computer Graphics Forum*, volume 29, pages 419–428. Wiley Online Library, 2010.

[18] F. Liu, T. Harada, Y. Lee, and Y. J. Kim. Real-time collision culling of a million bodies on graphics processing units. In *ACM Transactions on Graphics (TOG)*, volume 29, page 154. ACM, 2010.

[19] L. Loi. Fast gpu-based collision detection. 2010.

[20] H. Mazhar, T. Heyn, and D. Negrut. A scalable parallel method for large collision detection problems. *Multibody System Dynamics*, 26(1):37–55, June 2011.

[21] H. Nguyen. *GPU Gems 3*. Addison-Wesley Professional, 1 edition edition, Aug. 2007.

[22] A. J. Park and K. S. Perumalla. Efficient heterogeneous execution on large multicore and accelerator platforms: Case study using a block tridiagonal solver. *Journal of Parallel and Distributed Computing*, 73(12):1578–1591, Dec. 2013.

[23] D. Peng, T. Warnke, F. Haack, and A. M. Uhrmacher. Reusing simulation experiment specifications to support developing models by successive extension. *Simulation Modelling Practice and Theory*, 68:33–53, 2016.

[24] K. S. Perumalla and B. G. Aaby. Data parallel execution challenges and runtime performance of agent simulations on gpus. In *Proceedings of the 2008 Spring simulation multiconference*, pages 116–123. Society for Computer Simulation International, 2008.

[25] K. S. Perumalla, B. G. Aaby, S. B. Yoginath, and S. K. Seal. Interactive, graphical processing unitbased evaluation of evacuation scenarios at the state scale. *SIMULATION*, page 0037549711425236, Oct. 2011.

[26] K. S. Perumalla and V. A. Protopopescu. Reversible simulations of elastic collisions. *ACM Transactions on Modeling and Computer Simulation*, 23(2):12, 2013.

[27] D. Ridgway, G. Broderick, A. Lopez-Campistrous, M. Ru'aini, P. Winter, M. Hamilton, P. Boulanger, A. Kovalenko, and M. J. Ellison. Coarse-grained molecular simulation of diffusion and reaction kinetics in a crowded virtual cytoplasm. *Biophysical journal*, 94(10):3748–3759, 2008.

[28] S. Rybacki, J. Himmelspach, and A. M. Uhrmacher. Experiments with Single Core, Multi-core, and GPU Based Computation of Cellular Automata. In *International Conference on Advances in System Simulation. SIMUL '09*, pages 62–67, Sept. 2009.

[29] J. Schöneberg and F. Noé. Readdy-a software for particle-based reaction-diffusion dynamics in crowded cellular environments. *PLoS One*, 8(9):e74261, 2013.

[30] J. Schöneberg, A. Ullrich, and F. Noé. Simulation tools for particle-based reaction-diffusion dynamics in continuous space. *BMC Biophysics*, 7(1):1–10, 2014.

[31] T. Steinle, J. Vrabec, and A. Walther. Dynamic simulation of particle-filled hollow spheres. *Proceedings of the Applied and Mathematical Mechanics (PAMM)*, 11:881–882, 2011.

[32] K. Takahashi, S. Tănase-Nicola, and P. R. ten Wolde. Spatio-temporal correlations can drastically change the response of a mapk pathway. *Proc. of the National Academy of Sciences*, 107(6):2473–2478, 2010.

[33] A. Tasora, R. Serban, H. Mazhar, A. Pazouki, D. Melanz, J. Fleischmann, M. Taylor, H. Sugiyama, and D. Negrut. Chrono: An open source multi-physics dynamics engine. In *International Conference on High Performance Computing in Science and Engineering*, pages 19–49. Springer International Publishing, 2015.

GDS: Gradient Based Density Spline Surfaces for Multiobjective Optimization in Arbitrary Simulations

Patrick Lange, Rene Weller, Gabriel Zachmann
University of Bremen, Germany
{lange,weller,zach}@cs.uni-bremen.de

ABSTRACT

We present a novel approach for approximating objective functions in arbitrary deterministic and stochastic multi-objective blackbox simulations. Usually, simulated-based optimization approaches require pre-defined objective functions for optimization techniques in order to find a local or global minimum of the specified simulation objectives and multi-objective constraints. Due to the increasing complexity of state-of-the-art simulations, such objective functions are not always available, leading to so-called blackbox simulations.

In contrast to existing approaches, we approximate the objective functions and design space for deterministic and stochastic blackbox simulations, even for convex and concave Pareto fronts, thus enabling optimization for arbitrary simulations. Additionally, Pareto gradient information can be obtained from our design space approximation. Our approach gains its efficiency from a novel gradient-based sampling of the parameter space in combination with a density-based clustering of sampled objective function values, resulting in a B-spline surface approximation of the feasible design space.

We have applied our new method to several benchmarks and the results show that our approach is able to efficiently approximate arbitrary objective functions. Additionally, the computed multi-objective solutions in our evaluation studies are close to the Pareto front.

Keywords

Objective function approximation; Knowledge discovery in simulation; multi-objective optimization; Spline interpolation; Simulation based optimization; Data mining; B-Spline surface

1. INTRODUCTION

Traditional simulation-based optimization approaches [17, 12] usually require pre-defined objective functions which directly describe the influence of all simulation input parameters on the specified simulation objectives (denoted as model

behavior). An optimization toolset (e.g. [6]) uses these objective functions (e.g. ordinary differential equations) in order to find a local or global minimum which satisfies given constraints. As a consequence of the increasing complexity of state-of-the-art simulations, such objective functions are not always available. Even more, there are many technical complex systems whose long-term behavior can not be described by a set of equations (e.g. long-term behavior of autonomous systems in changing environments). This kind of simulation-based optimization problem is called blackbox simulation problem because the objective functions are unknown to both: the simulation engineer and optimization toolset.

Therefore, the model behavior analysis in these blackbox simulations and the determination of the valid design space, is either done manually by simulation experts or by an automated process. The goal in both approaches is to approximate the behavior of the objective functions in order to interpolate and extrapolate the model behavior. The manual analysis method is widely used [8], although it yields many disadvantages because it is based on subjective judgements from the simulation engineer [21]: the simulation expert usually takes an educated guess, based on his experience, which parameters might be influential on the simulation scope and varies these cleverly in multiple simulation runs in order to do both: approximate the feasible design and reduce the process complexity [19]. The resulting simulation results are later manually analyzed with respect to the given simulation constraints. This workflow can be partly supported (e.g. visualization of parameter sets, clustering analysis of results) by different tools [6, 19, 16] that can be introduced by the simulation expert. However, state-of-the-art blackbox simulation problems are further dominated by a multi-objective optimization problem (MOP) in which multiple and conflicting criteria have to be satisfied, which usually can not be determined by manual analysis [9]. Therefore, [8] refers to this as the error-prone "trial-and-error approach".

Consequently, recent approaches avoid a manual analysis and automatically analyze such multi-objective blackbox simulations via a knowledge discovery process which can compute suitable input configurations for a given simulation model without the need of an expert guiding this process. By definition, they incorporate some kind of data mining process which samples the simulation input parameter space with respect to known [19][16] or unknown [21] objective functions.

SIGSIM-PADS 17, May 24-26, 2017, Singapore.

© 2017 Copyright held by the owner/author(s). Publication rights licensed to ACM.
ISBN 978-1-4503-4489-0/17/05. . . $15.00

DOI: http://dx.doi.org/10.1145/3064911.3064917

Unlike traditional approaches for solving MOP in black-box simulations, these knowledge discovery processes in simulations are not limited to a static, pre-determined input dataset for model behavior and optimization. Instead, the simulation is used as a generator for new data by a simulation sampling process. This enables a knowledge discovery process to investigate the simulated model behavior in more detail and larger bandwidth [21] via its data mining scheme. This data mining scheme directly determines the efficiency and quality of the resulting objective function approximation because it defines the simulation sampling process.

However, state-of-the-art approaches do not support stochastic simulation behavior and are therefore restricted to deterministic simulations. Nevertheless, sophisticated simulations involve real-world scenarios which incorporate stochastic processes or properties. Approximating objective functions in stochastic simulations is more difficult and complex because the underlying noise of the stochastic process involves variations in the simulation and consequently in the data farming process. State-of-the-art studies model stochastic processes as deterministic ones which leads not only to inferior approximation of the objective functions but also to inferior solutions of the multi-objective optimization toolset as we will show in our evaluation. In this paper, we present a novel data mining approach which is directly based on above observations and the idea of knowledge discovery processes in simulations.

In detail, our approach is able to

- approximate objective functions (resp. the feasible design space) in arbitrary deterministic and stochastic blackbox simulations as B-spline surfaces,
- compute a Pareto gradient from the feasible design space approximation for concave, convex or interrupted Pareto fronts, which can be used with different optimization strategies,
- compute a Pareto solution from the feasible design space approximation via a hierarchical multi-agent system approach.

Another main advantage of our approach is that our B-spline surface based feasible design space approximation evaluation is computationally very fast and replaces costly simulation evaluations which are usually required. Consequently, our approach also delivers a performance boost when computing a solution for the given multi-objective optimization problem. Furthermore, our approach is very generic. It can be easily incorporated into existing simulation-based optimization approaches which use a knowledge discovery process (e.g. [21]). Even more, the computed Pareto solutions are close to the Pareto front for deterministic and stochastic simulations. Additionally, of our approach provides optimization strategies. These strategies can be used by state-of-the-art multi-objective optimization solvers in order to investigate a larger bandwidth of the simulated model behavior.

Our presented approach is immensely important for simulation applications because simulation technology in general bases its core competence on the usage of simulation results. Our work is designed to extract as much valuable information as possible from a simulation system and its results, thus, increasing the usefulness of sophisticated simulations.

2. RELATED WORK

Approximating objective functions in simulation-based optimization scenarios has attracted increasing interest in the last decade. Mostly, such approximations are implemented as a sophisticated data mining approach within a complex knowledge discovery (KD) process.

The research can be classified into two groups: KD approaches aiming at single or multi-objective optimization problems. All presented KD approaches have in common, that they only support deterministic simulations. Current KD approaches for single-objective optimization problems reduce the optimization problem, e.g. to a single function f which updates the simulation state x with parameter set θ via $x_{k+1} = f(x_k, \theta)$ [16]. This approach reduces the complexity of the optimization process by finding a suitable set of points θ in which a pre-defined simulation state is achieved. Likewise, other approaches, such as [18], neglected multi-objective simulation properties. The approach applied a linear regression to all input parameters $x_i, ... x_n$ for a specific simulation objective state y. This results in a linear model which was used to describe the input configuration space. This model was further used in a clustering approach in order to find the most influencing parameters. The above studies can not be applied to multi-objective based simulations in which the simulation model is governed by a set of (possible) contradicting functions because they do not concern such structures within the simulation. Similar approaches, are either restricted to a small number of simulation input parameters due their quadratic runtime [2] or are highly depending on the simulation expert supervising the KD process [19].

In summary, all above mentioned studies focused on building passive models between simulation input and objective-related simulation output while minimizing the simulation parameter scope or by focusing on single-objective linear simulation models in deterministic simulations. These passive models describe the simulation without enabling interpolation or extrapolation of the simulated model behavior for simulation-based optimization purposes. They deliver coarse granularity parameter relationship information which can not be used to approximate the feasible design space nor to compute a Pareto gradient information (e.g. gradient information of the analyzed data with respect to the Pareto front), especially for stochastic simulations.

In contrast to the above studies, [21] introduced a KD process which builds an active model between simulation input and simulation output. It is able to uncover hidden relationships between simulation input and unknown objective functions. It approximates the feasible design space which is suitable for solving multi-objective optimization problems. Other KD approaches based on multi-objective simulations [25, 11, 15, 5] focussed on extracting additional information from pre-determined concave Pareto sets or analzying these sets within the simulation. Consequently, they can not be used to approximate the feasible design space nor to compute a Pareto solution itself. Concluding, all above studies are restricted to deterministic simulations which leads to several disadvantages as stated before.

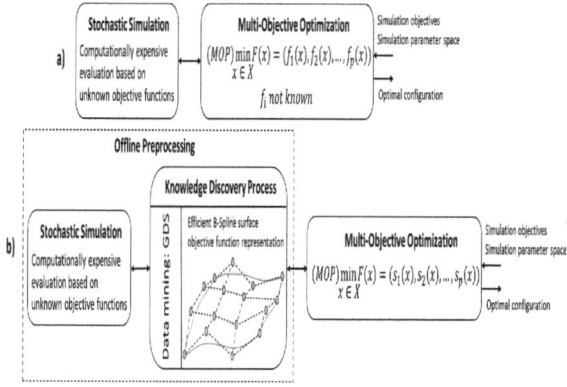

Figure 1: Our approach introduces an efficient objective function approximation within a knowledge discovery process via novel B-spline surface representations.

3. OUR APPROACH

In this work, we present our gradient based density spline surface (GDS) algorithm (see Figure 1). GDS is able to approximate arbitrary unknown objective functions in deterministic and stochastic blackbox simulations, for convex and concave as well as interrupted Pareto fronts. GDS consists of three main concepts:

- B-spline surface representation of the relationship space (see Section 3.1),
- density based clustering of objective function samples which determines the noise behavior of the stochastic simulation (see Section 3.2),
- gradient based sampling of the parameter space which reduces the required amount of samples (see Section 3.3).

The result of GDS is an efficient approximation of the objective functions as a set of B-spline surfaces which can be used in various simulation based optimization scenarios, such as complex multi-objective optimization problems. This efficient approximation is computationally very inexpensive compared to usually very costly simulation evaluations. It can be further effectively utilized in optimizaton toolsets. We present the application in our multi-agent system optimization approach as a use-case study (see Section 3.4).

3.1 Relationship Definition

We assume that every relationship between a parameter $C = c_0, ..., c_k$ with parameter space k and objective value $O = o_0, ..., o_k$ with objective space k can be formally represented as a continuous function $f : C, T \rightarrow O = f(c, t) \rightarrow o_\mathcal{O}$ which maps the parameter space to a given simulation objective $\mathcal{O}$ with its objective function space at a given time step $t \in T$ of the simulation. It would be possible to perfectly determine the behavior of f with respect to C by brute-force sampling the whole parameter space k with $s \geq k$ samples. However, in real world applications k can be arbitrary large or continuous and the simulation evaluation computationally very expensive. Therefore, a brute-force sampling of the parameter space is infeasible. Consequently, it is necessary to reduce the amount of needed samples: $s \ll k$.

Overall, the relationship constitutes a large three- dimensional cartesian space $\mathbb{R}^3$ (spanned by C, O and T), which we denote as relationship space (see Figure 2).

The general idea of cubic splines is to represent a function by a different cubic function on each interval between data points. For n data points, the spline $S(x)$ is the function

$$S(x) = \begin{cases} F_1(x), x_0 \leq x \leq x_1 \\ F_i(x), x_{i-1} \leq x \leq x_i \\ F_n(x), x_{n-1} \leq x \leq x_n \end{cases} \quad (1)$$

where each F_i is a cubic function.

The most general cubic function has the form

$$F_i(x) = a_i + b_i x + c_i x^2 + d_i x^3 \quad (2)$$

In sophisticated simulations, the same parameter configuration will contribute to different objective values at different time steps in the simulation (e.g. a fuel state/configuration in a car simulation which changes over time). Because of configurations like this, we prefer to define a spline of the objective function for each simulation time step individually. This results in a list of splines: $S_{t_o}(C), ..., S_{t_n}(C) = O_{t_0}, ..., O_{t_n}$ for n simulation time steps with:

$$S_{t_i}(C) = O_{t_i} \quad (3)$$

where

t_i : simulation time

C : parameter space

O : objective values of the corresponding objective function

We use these splines to formulate a cubic B-spline surface:

$$C(u) = \sum_{i=0}^{n} p_i N_{i,3}(u), 0 \leq u \leq 1 \quad (4)$$

$$s(u,v) = \sum_{i=0}^{m} \sum_{j=0}^{n} P_{ij} N_{i,3}(u) N_{j,3}(v), 0 \leq u,v \leq 1 \quad (5)$$

where $P_{ij}(i = 0, 1, ..., m; j = 0, 1, ..., n)$ are the control points of the surface which are determined by $S_{t_o}(C), ..., S_{t_n}(C) = O_{t_0}, ..., O_{t_n}$ via a uniform coverage of the splines. u, v are the knot vectors in the direction of u or v and $N_{i,3}(u), N_{j,3}(v)$ is the B-spline basis (see Figure 2).

This B-spline approximation replaces the unknown objective function $f : C, T \rightarrow O = f(c, t) \rightarrow o_\mathcal{O} = s(c, t) \rightarrow o_\mathcal{O}$ and is efficiently used to define the required gradient information (see Section 3.4) for optimization purposes.

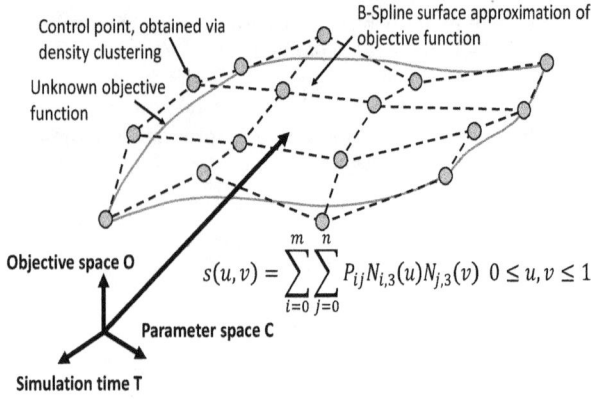

Figure 2: B-Spline surface representation of the three-dimensional space constructed by simulation input parameter C, simulation time T and objective function space O.

3.2 Density Splines

In order to enable a precise B-spline surface approximation of the relationship space, the splines which define $s(u, v)$ must be very close to the unknown objective function. However, as stated above, stochastic simulations are governed by diverse noise behavior which makes it hard to approximate these unknown objective function. Therefore, we define every spline sampling point (c, o) via a density clustering from n simulation samples.outliers and therefore enables our splines to approximate the unknown objective function more precisely.

In order to incorporate this density clustering for the unknown noise distribution of the objective function, we extend the general spline definition (see Equation 1). Every spline is defined with a triple, consisting of the cubic function F_i, variance of the computed density cluster θ and certainty of measurement p.

In detail, every F_i is constructed with the centre point of the most dense cluster of every simulation sample set per sampling configuration of the simulation. In order to incorporate the simulation noise behavior, every centre point is associated with the variance θ of the corresponding cluster. Our spline definition will interpolate some of the objective values due to the gradient-based sampling of the parameter space (see Section 3.3) because we sample only a small subset of the parameter space. This means that, by definition, some approximated objective values are more likely precise (based on simulation samples) than others (based on the spline interpolation). Therefore, p indicates whether or not the resulting approximated objective value is interpolated resp. close (in parameter space) to a drawn simulation sample.

Therefore, for n sampling points, the spline $S_{t_i}(c)$ is the function:

$$S_{t_i}(c) = \begin{cases} (F_1(c), \Theta(\psi), p(c, \theta)), c_0 \leq c \leq c_1 \\ (F_i(c), \Theta(\psi), p(c, \theta)), c_{i-1} \leq c \leq c_i \\ (F_n(c), \Theta(\psi), p(c, \theta)), c_{n-1} \leq c \leq c_n \end{cases} \quad (6)$$

where

$\Theta(\psi)$: variance $\frac{1}{k-1} \cdot \sum_{i=0}^{k} (o_i - \bar{o})^2$

$p(c, \theta)$: certainty of measurement

$$\begin{cases} 1, \text{ if } c \leq \theta \\ 1 - \frac{|c - c_j|}{k}, \text{ otherwise} \end{cases}$$

Ω : Dbscan core cluster of ψ
ψ : n samples of c $\{(c, o_i), ..., (c, o_n)\}$ with c $\leq \theta$
θ : sampling configurations
$F_i(x)$: cubic function based on θ: $a_i + b_i x + c_i x^2 + d_i x^3$
c_j : closest previous sample point $\leq \theta$ to c

The sampled objective values are clustered with the Dbscan (density-based spatial clustering of applications with noise) data clustering algorithm [14] (see Figure 3). Dbscan has several advantages with respect to other clustering approaches (such as [7, 3, 13]) because

- it does not require a specification on the expected cluster amount,
- it can find arbitrarily shaped clusters,
- it has a notion of noise which makes it robust to outliers.

This density clustering is important because it enables a more accurate approximation of the unknown objective function via its detection of noise outliers. Therefore, just averaging ψ is insufficient. Even more, the computed Dbscan clusters can be used to retrieve the standard deviation and variance of the measurement. We further utilize this information in our optimization process in order to investigate arbitrary multi-objective problems from different optimization perspectives (see Section 3.4).

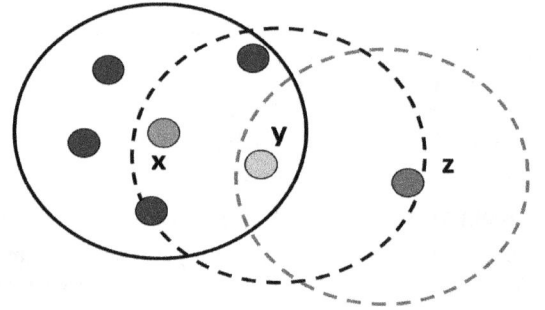

Figure 3: Illustration of the Dbscan algorithm: A data point is inside a dense region (core point, x), on the edge of the region (boundary point, y) or in a spare region (noise point, z). The example is given for at least six neighbours. Adapted from [14].

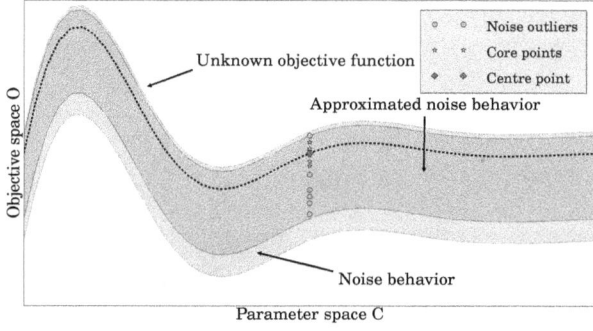

Figure 4: Approximating an unknown objective function with our density spline: Noise outliers are detected and the cluster centre point is used to construct the spline. Subsequently, the variance Θ of the clustering is propagated through the spline.

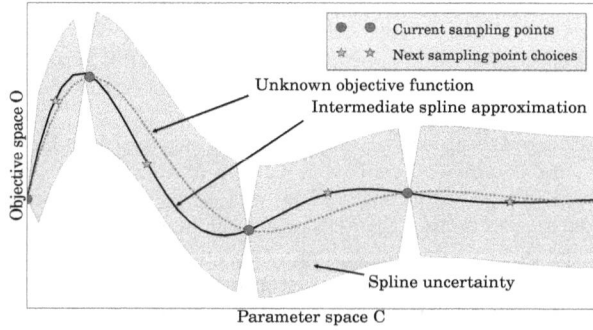

Figure 5: Spline approximation of an unknown objective function f: The spline is iteratively updated until it approximates the unknown objective function within a certain error degree. The spline uncertainty p is propagated through the spline.

3.3 Gradient-based Sampling

The main idea of our gradient-based simulation data sampling is to minimize the amount of samples s (see Section 3.1) which are required approximate the original behavior of f. In order to do so, we iteratively approximate the unknown objective function f with our spline definition for a certain simulation time t. This spline is iteratively updated with more sampled data until the spline approximates f within a specified error degree.

In order to minimize the amount of required samples, we utilize a property of spline-based interpolation. When interpolating with splines, the spline can change drastically when updated with new sample points at interpolated gradient minima and maxima. This is due to the fact that splines ensure that the first and second derivative of the spline will match at the knot points. Therefore, it is desirable to determine the spline gradient while approximating the unknown objective function in order to find large spline gradient changes. These gradient changes are used to draw a new sample from the parameter space which will more likely change the adjacent spline knots and therefore reduce the amount of required samples due to the aforementioned inherent behavior of spline interpolation (see Algorithms 1,2 and Figure 5). After successfully approximating the un-

known objective function, we combine the variances of all clusters for each spline in order gain an accurate approximation for the noise distribution of the relationships. Given two clusters, C_1 and C_2, with their respective mean and variance of their largest cluster, $\bar{X}_1, \bar{X}_2$ and $S_1{}^2, S_1{}^2$ with n_1, n_2 observations, we compute the combined variance (see Equation 7). We iteratively apply this formula on all clusters of each spline and retrieve the overall variance of the spline approximation.

Algorithm 1 Objective function approximation via density splines splineApprox(amount of samples n, parameter $\mathscr{C}$ with space $\mathscr{k}$, spline error threshold ϵ, simulation time t)

$\mathscr{D} = c_0, c_{\frac{k}{2}}, c_k \quad \mathscr{C}$, sampling configurations
$\mathscr{F} =$ simulation results of $\mathscr{D}$ with n samples
$\mathscr{K} =$ Dbscan clusters of $\mathscr{F}$
$\mathscr{S} =$ spline based on $\mathscr{D}, \mathscr{K}$
$\mathscr{R} =$ amount of remaining samples: $\mathscr{k} \quad 3$
$\mathscr{E} =$ empty list of rejections
while $\mathscr{R} > 0$ **and** $\mathscr{E} < \epsilon_{rejections}$ **do**
    $d = $ gradientConfiguration($\mathscr{S}, \mathscr{D}$)
    $\mathscr{D}\ += d$
    $\mathcal{O} =$ empty list of simulation results
    for n samples **do**
        $\mathcal{O}\ +=$ simulation result of d at t
    end for
    $o_{spline} = \mathscr{S}(d)$
    $\mathscr{T} =$ largest Dbscan cluster of $\mathcal{O}$
    $o_{sim} =$ centre of $\mathscr{T}$
    $o_\Theta =$ variance of $\mathscr{T}$
    $o_p = 1$
    if $| o_{sim} - o_{spline} | < \epsilon_{deviation}$ **then**
        $\mathscr{E}\ += d$
    end if
    $\mathscr{S} =$ rebuild spline based on $\mathscr{D}, \mathcal{O}$
    $\mathscr{R} = \mathscr{R} - 1$
end while
return $\mathscr{S}$

Algorithm 2 Sampling of the parameter space based on gradient information: gradientConfiguration(current spline definition $\mathscr{S}$, sampled configuration $\mathscr{D}$)

$c =$ return configuration
$t =$ maximum threshold: 0
for $d_1, d_2, \quad \mathscr{D}$ **do**
    $d_1 = \dot{\mathscr{K}}(d_1)$
    $d_2 = \dot{\mathscr{K}}(d_2)$
    if $| \quad d_1 \quad d_2| > t$ **then**
        $c = \frac{d_1 + d_2}{2}$
        $t = | \quad d_1 \quad d_2|$
    end if
end for
return c

$$S_c{}^2 = \frac{n_1 S_1{}^2 + n_2 S_2{}^2 + n_1(\bar{X}_1 \quad \bar{X}_c)^2 + n_2(\bar{X}_2 \quad \bar{X}_c)^2}{n_1 + n_2}$$
$$= \frac{n_1[S_1{}^2 + (\bar{X}_1 \quad \bar{X}_c)^2] + n_2[S_2{}^2 + (\bar{X}_2 \quad \bar{X}_c)^2]}{n_1 + n_2}$$

$$(7)$$

where

$$X_c{}^2 = \frac{n_1 \bar{X}_1 + n_2 \bar{X}_2}{n_1 + n_2} \qquad (8)$$

189

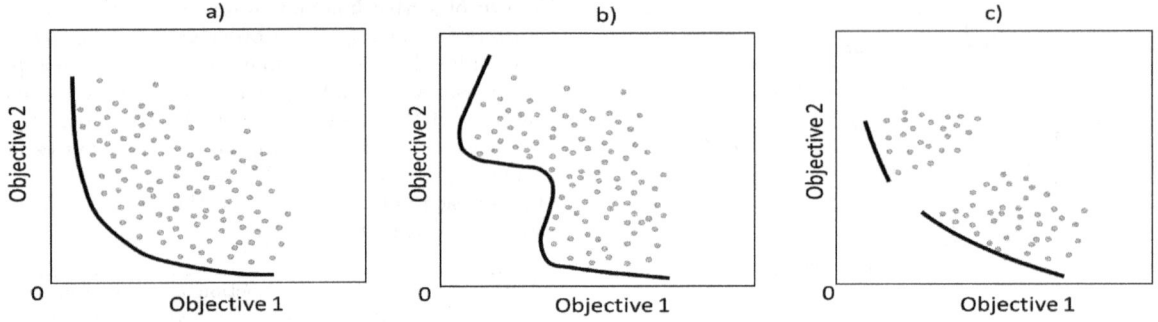

Figure 6: Pareto optimal solutions of multi-objective dominate every other possible solution: Concave (a), convex (b) or interrupted Pareto fronts (c) can occur. Our approach efficiently approximates all possible frontiers.

3.4 Multi-Objective Optimization

Today, simulation models are dominated by a multi-objective optimization problem (MOP) because many real world problems involve decisions based on multiple and conflicting criteria [9, 21]. The goal of multi-objective optimization is to determine best trade-off solutions (so-called Pareto solutions) among these criteria. These multi-objective optimization problems can be found in many situations, for example, in product design where several criteria must be simultaneously satisfied [4, 23, 24]. We define MOP according to [9, 21]: Given a subset X of $\mathbb{R}^n$ and p functions $f_j : X \rightarrow \mathbb{R}$ for $j = 1, 2, ..., p$, MOP is defined as:

$$(MOP) \max_{x \in X} F(x) = (f_1(x), f_2(x), ..., f_p(x)) \qquad (9)$$

where $F : X \rightarrow \mathbb{R}^p$ is the objective function vector. We assume that X is of the form $X = \{x = (x_1, x_2, ..., x_n) \in \mathbb{R}^n : a_i \leq x_i \leq b_i, i = 1, 2, ..., n\}$, where a_i and b_i are the lower and upper bound of the ith component of variable x, respectively. When the objective functions conflict with each other, no single solution can simultaneously minimize all scalar objective functions $f_j(x), j = 1, ..., p$. In these scenarios, the goal of MOP is to identify a subset of the Pareto optimal points ($\mathscr{P}$) which is able to represent the Pareto front or to compute a single trade-off solution $x \in \mathscr{P}$ (see Figure 6) [21]. The definition of Pareto optimality can be provided by using Pareto dominance relation [1]:

- Let $x_u, x_v \in X$ be two decision vectors. $F(x_u)$ dominates $F(x_v)$ (denoted $F(x_u) \succ F(x_v)$) if and only if $f_i(x_u) \geq f_i(x_v) \forall i \in \{1, 2, ..., p\}$ and $f_j(x_u) < f_j(x_v) \exists j \in \{1, 2, ..., p\}$
- A point $x^* \in X$ is globally Pareto optimal if and only if there is no $x \in X$ such that $F(x) \succ F(x^*)$. Then, $F(x^*)$ is called globally efficient. The image of the set of globally efficient points is called the Pareto front. In general, computational methods cannot guarantee global Pareto optimality [10], but at best local Pareto optimality that is defined as:
- A point $x^* \in X$ is locally Pareto optimal if and only if there exists an open neighborhood of x^*, $B(X)$, such that there is no $x \in B(x^*) \cap X$ satisfying $F(x) \succ F(x^*)$. $F(x^*)$ is then called locally efficient. The image of the set of locally efficient points is called the local Pareto front.

In general, identifying the set of all Pareto optimality points is not a tractable problem and mostly impossible, particularly when the knowledge on the structure of the problem is very minimal or not available [9].

Within simulation-based multi-objective optimization problems, engineers are interested in several different optimal solutions, e.g. which are reliable in many scenarios or which maximize the objective function for certain aspects. Therefore, our approach enables a Pareto solution of a multi-objective optimization problem with three different optimization strategies which determine different feasible design spaces while maintaining Pareto efficiency:

- Compliance strategy: Determination of the parameter space which maximizes or minimizes the objective function.
- Reliability strategy: Determination of the parameter space which maximizes the sampling probability.
- Closeness strategy: Determination of the parameter space which minimizes the clustering variance.

Due to our relationship definition, we can substitute the unknown objective functions $f_j(x), j = 1, ..., p$ from Equation 9 with our B-spline surface approximation:

$$(MOP) \max_{x \in X} F(x) = (f_1(x), f_2(x), ..., f_p(x))$$

$$(10)$$

$$(MOP) \max_{c,t \in C,T} F(c,t) = (s_1(c,t), s_2(c,t), ..., s_p(c,t))$$

Our strategies determines a different feasible design space within above definition, namely a sub-set $\{\{c_i, ..., c_j\}, ..., \{c_n, ..., c_m\}\} = C_{Strategy} \subseteq \{c_o, ..., c_k\} = C_k$ with $0 \leq i, i < j, n < m, j < n, m \leq k$. In detail, the compliance strategy (see Equation 11) maximizes objective function above a given minimum threshold, m, for all $t \in T$. In contrast to this, the reliability strategy (see Equation 12) and closeness strategy (see Equation 13) either maximize the probability p or minimize the variance Θ of each measurement.

190

$$C_{compliance} = \{c_i | \quad s_q(c_i, T).F \quad m\} \qquad (11)$$

$$(c_i, \overline{p_i}) = (c_i, \frac{\sum_{q=0}^{q=k} \sum_{n=0}^{t} s_q(c_i, t_n).p_i}{k}) \qquad (12)$$

$$C_{reliability} = max_p\{(o_0, p_0), ..., (o_k, p_k)\}$$

$$(c_i, \overline{\Theta_i}) = (c_i, \frac{\sum_{q=0}^{q=k} \sum_{n=0}^{t} s_q(c_i, t_n).\Theta_i}{k}) \qquad (13)$$

$$C_{closeness} = min_\Theta\{(o_0, \Theta_0), ..., (o_k, \Theta_k)\}$$

Depending on the strategy, different sub-sets are determined. Each sub-set is transformed into a feasible design space ω, depending on the multi-objective constraints of the specific configuration parameter, namely the set of objective functions which are influenced by the paramter:

$$\omega_i(c, t) = \frac{\sum_{p=0}^{p=k} (\Theta_p(|\frac{o}{n} \quad s_p(c, t) \sum_{q=0}^{q=k} (\frac{o}{t_q - s_q(c, t)})|))}{k} \qquad (14)$$

where

$1 \quad o \quad 1$: simulation weighting factor
k : the number of related objective functions of i
t : the objective threshold
Θ : the Pareto weighting factor
c : configuration from corresponding strategy

Consequently, our approach is able to find either a qualitative solution (see Equation 11), a reliable solution (see Equation 12) or the most dense solution (see Equation 13) that can be directly used in order to investigate the multi-objective problem from different perspectives.

The Pareto gradient ω is defined with unit vectors i, j, k which span the feasible design space:

$$\omega_{pareto} = \frac{\partial \omega}{\partial c}i + \frac{\partial \omega}{\partial t}j + \frac{\partial \omega}{\partial o}k \qquad (15)$$

Figure 7 illustrates this concept for the compliance strategy in a simple two-dimensional example.

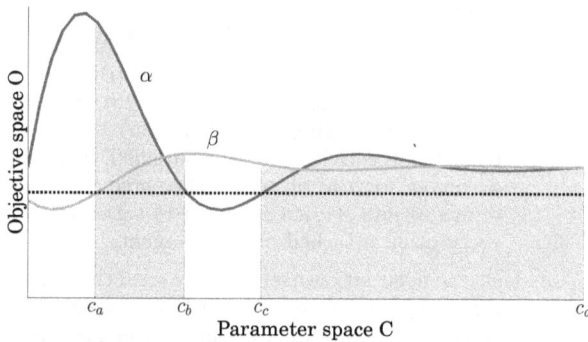

Figure 7: Approximation of the feasible design space for a parameter space, simulation objectives (α, β) and given minimum objective value (dotted line): $(c_a, c_b), (c_c, c_d)$ determines the feasible parameter configurations with $\Theta_\alpha = \Theta_\beta = 1$.

4. MAS BASED OPTIMIZATION

We present in this section how our feasible design space approximation and optimization strategies can be incorporated into a powerful optimization toolset for finding a Pareto solution. The optimization system proposed here is based on a hierarchical multi-agent system (MAS) which aims at dynamically tuning all given input configuration parameters with respect to the approximated feasible design space. Such hierarchical MAS have already proven their feasibility for solving multi-objective optimization problems such as [6, 20]. Our main idea is that every agent introduces a part-wise modelling (single and multi-objective constraints per input parameter) of the problem and its behavior and communication to other agents is used to solve the global (multi-objective optimization) problem.

In the following, we describe at first the required MAS infrastructure with its modular agent organizations and their relationships to the feasible design space approximation. Following this, we explain the input and output data as well as communication structure of the agents. At last, we outline the adaptation solving process with its negotiation mechanisms and how multi-objective problems can be solved.

Our MAS is composed of several agent organizations. Each of these organizations aims at optimizing a subset of configuration parameters to one or more simulation objectives, each one represented by our feasible design space approximation.

These agent organizations are defined per specified simulation objective and consist of a hierarchy of two agent types: objective- and negotiation-agents. For each identified input parameter, one objective-agent is defined. Therefore, one objective-agent can belong to several agent organizations. The goal of every defined objective-agent is to maximize or minimize every attached simulation objective under Pareto constraints. Several optimization constraints arise because of the underlying multi-objective optimization problem. Therefore, a negotiation-agent is defined for every specified objective. The goal of every negotiation agent is to manage requests between the objective-agents in order to satisfy the existing multi-objective constraints between the objective-agents.

Figure 8 illustrates this agent organization concept with respect to the overall proposed approach. The input and output data as well as communication structure of these agents is described in the next section.

4.1 Parameters, Objectives and Utilities

Given a multi-objective optimization problem, as defined in Equation 10, we can uniquely identify every adjustable input configuration parameter C with its valid range. These configuration parameters and the corresponding B-spline surface based feasible design space approximation constitute the input of our multi agent system. Additionally, we define the objectives and utilities of our MAS based control system.

Each objective-agent strives for maximizing or minimizing each single-objective optimization problem of its attached input parameter under multi-objective constraints. Therefore, each objective-agents computes several objective values, one for each attached objective.

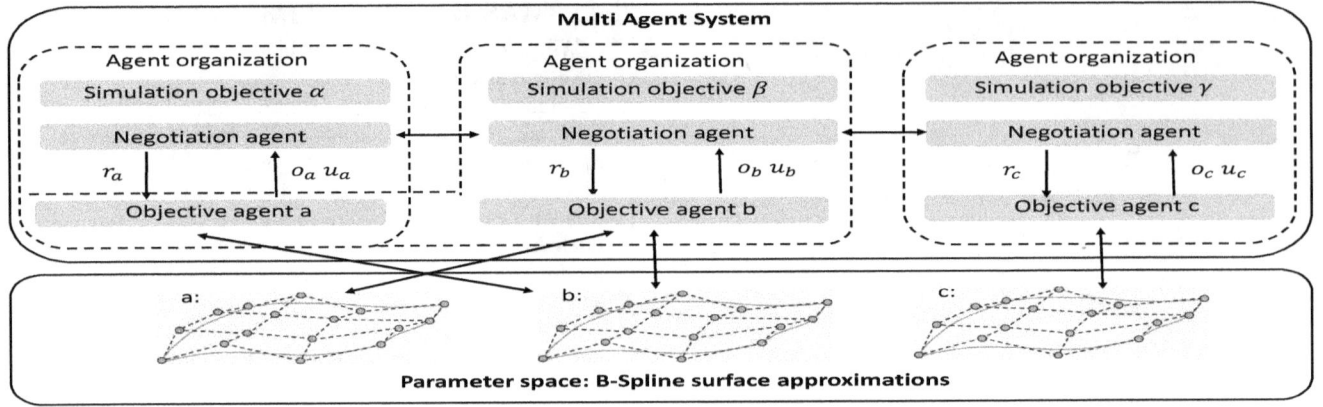

Figure 8: Our MAS based optimization approach for a mixed objective problem statement (one multi-objective objective (β) and two single-objective problems (α, γ) with three input parameters): Each agent organization optimizes the parameter set for one objective. Negotiation agents handle requests between the objective-agents in order to effectively find the optimal parameter configuration.

The set of all agent objectives OBJ is defined as follows:

$$OBJ = \{o_1...o_n\} \quad \{0,1\}$$
$$o_i = \omega(c,t) \tag{16}$$

where

ω : corresponding approximated feasible design space

In addition to the objectives to be satisfied, our MAS also considers the possible utility when changing the given parameter with respect to the current negotiation state among the agents. Consequently, we introduce a utility function. It is used to calculate the difference between current Pareto solution and highest achievable single-objective solution. This utility value is then later used by the negotiation-agent to select the most appropriate action.

The set of all utility values is defined as follows:

$$UTL = \{u_1...u_n\} \quad \{0,1\}$$
$$u_i = s_i(c,t) \quad \omega(c,t) \tag{17}$$

where
s_i : corresponding approximated objective function
ω_i : corresponding approximated feasible design space

Therefore, the aim of our MAS based optimization system is to minimize UTL while maximizing OBJ. In other words, it is to tune all the parameters so all the constraints and objectives are satisfied.

In order to implement this efficiently in an agent-based organization, we define requests which are shared between the agents. These requests are used to lower or higher the Pareto weight or objective value threshold from Equation 14 if any agent has partially solved one objective:

$$REQ = \{(\Theta_o, t_o), ...(\Theta_n, t_n)\}$$
$$\Theta_i \quad \{0,1\} \tag{18}$$
$$t_i \quad \{0,1\}$$

where
Θ_i : corresponding Pareto weight for the associated objective
m_i : corresponding objective value threshold for the associated objective

4.2 Solving Process Principle

When designing a multi-agent system based optimization process, the focus is set on agent behaviors and communications in order to cover the isolated parts of the global problem which each agent models. Each of our objective-agent tackles an isolated sub-problem (finding a solution to its attached single or multi-objective constraints) and emergence is used to solve the overall (multi-objective optimization) problem. Therefore, the solving process is distributed among all objective-agents via negotiation-agents. Consequently, the definition of objective- and negotiation-agent behaviours is also one of the key aspects of our multi-agent system and is described hereafter.

- Negotiation-agents monitor the objectives and utilities of all corresponding objective-agents of their agent organization and distribute requests between objective-agents: In the first step, they update (see below) the attached objective-agents if they have open requests. In this step, each objective-agent may achieve a new Pareto solution. In the second step, they collect new requests from each objective-agent and group them according to the multi-objective Pareto satisfaction:

  - a) if the objective is completely satisfied, it requests a change for the Pareto weight $\Theta = 0$ for every other attached objective-agent.
  - b) if the objective is partially satisfied, it requests a change for the objective threshold t in order of magnitude of current objective satisfaction for every other attached objective-agent.

  At last, the negotiation-agent will forward the requests (change in objective threshold t or Pareto weight Θ) of those objective-agents with the highest utility value.

- An objective-agent has a rather simple behaviour: it computes the objective and utility value for every attached objective for the current Pareto configuration (objective thresholds, Pareto weights and parameter configuration) based on our feasible design space approximation. It updates these values every time a request for change in Pareto weighting or objective threshold is received from an negotiation-agent.

5. EVALUATION

We implemented our GDS algorithm in C++. We performed our experiments on a machine with Intel Core i7 quad-core processor with Hyperthreading enabled and 8GB of memory.

We applied different experiments to measure the performance and quality of our approach within several synthetic benchmark scenarios. These synthetic benchmarks are based on generated blackbox simulations. Consequently, the objective functions of the simulation are unknown to all evaluated algorithms. The synthetic benchmarks compared the performance of our GDS algorithm to the approximation approach from [21] and different clustering (Dbscan, k-means) and sampling approaches (uniform, random, gradient). In order to perform this evaluation, we generated two different types of random objective functions based on polynomials (f_p) and Gaussian functions (f_g). Furthermore, we added noise terms (N) for ten different noise distributions in order to obtain a stochastic simulation behavior. a, b, c, p, q are the known scalar values for each corresponding function:

$$f_p(c, t) = \sum_{i=0}^{n} a_i(c \quad p)^i + \sum_{j=0}^{m} b_j(t \quad q)^j + N \qquad (19)$$

$$f_g(c, t) = \sum_{i=0}^{n} a_i e^{-\frac{(c-b_i)^2}{2c_i^2}} + \sum_{j=0}^{m} b_j e^{\frac{(t-b_j)^2}{2c_j^2}} + N \qquad (20)$$

Based on above equations, we have evaluated our approach with more than 100 different versions of f_p and f_g in order to obtain a profound evaluation. These synthetic benchmarks have been supplemented by a qualitative evaluation in order to evaluate whether or not our B-spline surfaces can be used for optimization purposes.

We compared the mean approximation error for approximating an unknown polynomial objective function with a 30% noise variance (see Figure 9) and a relationship space of 10,000. Our GDS approach is able to outperform all its competitors up to a factor of four. This performance boost also increases with the noise variance of the unknown object function (see Figure 10). This evaluation shows that the non-clustering approaches perform worse than any clustering-based approach. Even more, the error variance of our GDS approach is the smallest, especially when comparing to the uniform sampling approach without clustering [21] as well as for the random sampling. Therefore, it can be observed that a clustering is inevitable in order to approximate the unknown objective function accurately.

In addition to the mean error evaluation, Figure 10 shows the mean average approximation error for an increasing noise behavior of the unknown objective function. It can be clearly observed that the clustering approaches adapt very well to an increased noise behavior of the unknown objective function while all other approaches clearly decrease in their performance.

Furthermore, all non-clustering based approaches need more samples than the clustering based competitors, when comparing their performance for the same required approximation error threshold (see Figure 11).

In this context, Figure 12 shows the impact of the sampling amount with respect to the clustering analysis. It can be observed that only a few samples (12) per simulation configuration are required in order to precisely (10%) approximate the given unknown polynomial objective

function. Overall, these evaluations strongly emphasize the quality improvement of our GDS approach with respect to its competitors.

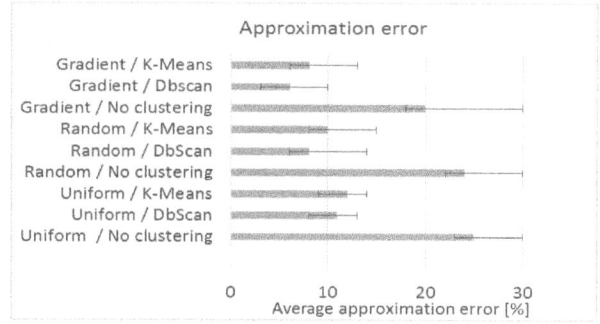

Figure 9: Our approach (gradient/Dbscan) outperforms its competitors: It approximates unknown objective functions with less error and smaller error variance.

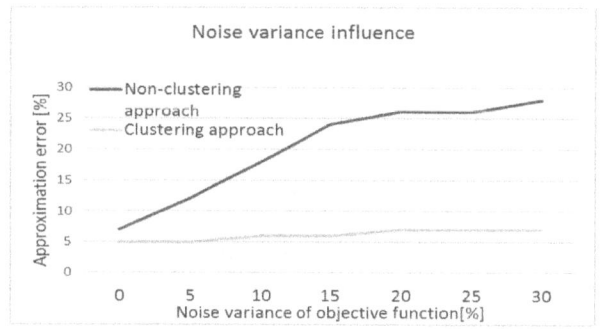

Figure 10: Clustering based approaches do not suffer as much as non-clustering approach from the objective function noise behavior.

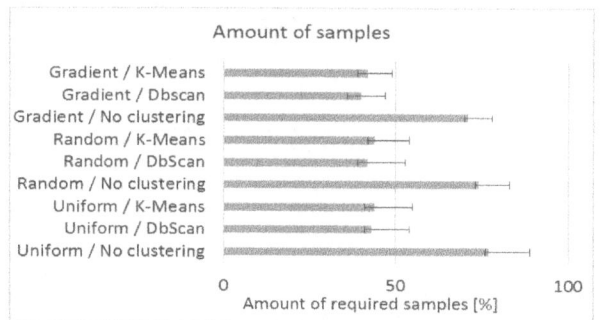

Figure 11: Our approach (gradient/Dbscan) requires less samples than its non-clustering based competitors. It further delivers both, best sampling variance and best approximation error.

Furthermore, Figure 13 depicts the relationship between polynomial degree of the objective function and the GDS mean error of the objective function approximation. Surprisingly, our GDS approach is almost not affected by the polynomial degree of the objective function. Therefore, even complex objective functions can be precisely approximated by our GDS approach.

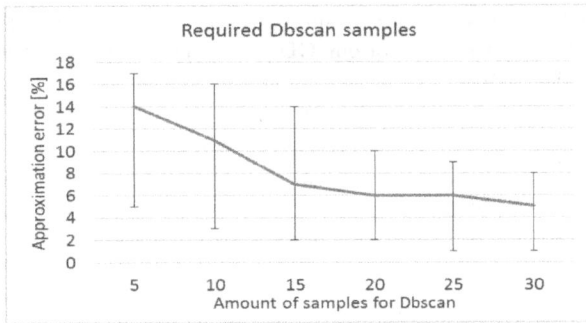

Figure 12: Only a few samples (≤ 12) are required in order to efficiently (≤ 10 % error) approximate the noise distribution of the stochastic simulation.

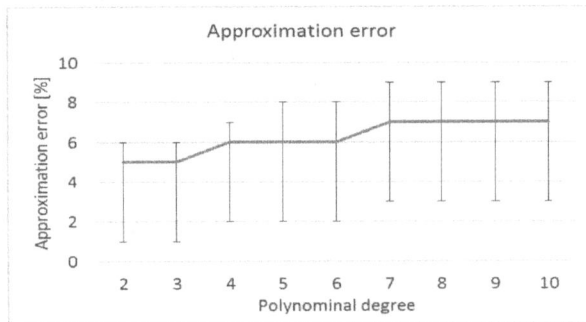

Figure 13: Effect of the polynomial degree of the unknown objective function on the mean error of our approach: The degree has almost no influence as the mean error varies around 6%.

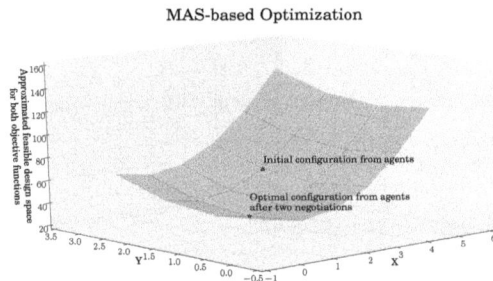

Figure 14: Evaluation of our use case study: Our agents are directly initialized at the single-objective solution and converge fast to the multi-objective solution.

For deterministic simulations, all presented approaches perform very similar and obtain approximation errors less than 1% for arbitrary polynomial objective functions.

Finally, Figure 14 depicts the results from our proposed MAS-based optimization. For this evaluation, we considered the following standardized test function for multi-objective optimization problems from Binh and Korn [26] as a use case study. We further added noise terms to the functions in order to obtain a stochastic behavior:

$$f_1(x, y) = 4x^2 + 4y^2 + N$$
$$f_2(x, y) = (x - 5)^2 + (y - 5)^2 + N$$
$$s.t. \tag{21}$$
$$g_1(x, y) = (x - 5)^2 + y^2 - 25$$
$$g_2(x, y) = (x - 8)^2 + (y + 3)^2 - 7.7$$

In this use case study, we approximate f_1, f_2 with our GDS algorithm and deliver the B-splines as input to our MAS. Two advantages from our approach can be observed in this use case study (see Figure 14): First, the initial guess from the agents is directly the single-objective solution of the problem, indicating that the approximated feasible design space is close to the Pareto front. This enables a much faster optimization process because our MAS requires less negotiations for converging to the correct solution. This reduces the probability of converging to a local instead of a global minimum. Second, already after a few negotiations (in this use case study: two negotiations) the objective-agents reached the Pareto front and returned one optimal configuration.

In summary, Table 1 shows a detailed overview of our synthetic benchmarks for both test functions f_p and f_g. It can be seen that our GDS algorithm outperforms its competitors for all given noise distributions in mean error.

6. CONCLUSION

We presented our novel GDS approach for approximating unknown objective functions in arbitrary deterministic and stochastic blackbox simulations which are governed by a multi-objective optimization problem.

Our approach is capable of

- approximating objective functions (resp. the feasible design space) in arbitrary deterministic and stochastic blackbox simulations,
- computing Pareto gradient from the feasible design space approximation for concave, convex or interrupted Pareto fronts, which can be used with different optimization strategies,
- computing a Pareto solution from the feasible design space approximation via a hierarchical multi-agent system approach.

Even more, our approach can be easily integrated into existing knowledge discovery processes.

The results from our benchmarks show that our approach is able to analyze stochastic simulations with large parameter spaces while precisely approximating arbitrary unknown objective functions. Furthermore, the resulting optimization solutions are close to the Pareto front. Due to its generality, our approach is applicable to a wide variety of simulation domains such as engineering design problems, including layout, design, and process optimization.

In the future, we would like to further evaluate our approach with standard optimization via simulation problems using the SimOpt library [22]. Additionally, we would like to extend our approach with other interpolation approaches: we could analyze the unknown objective function with several approximations (linear, polynomial, spline) in parallel. This would lead to specific approximation types per simulation objective which could further minimize the approximation error. Another interesting idea would be to replace our B-spline surface concept with a high dimensional input space. Here, we would need to extend our B-spline surface concept to B-spline volumes. These B-spline volumes could be directly used for high-dimensional optimization. At last, we would like to incorporate GPGPU programming into our data mining approach. We believe that such massively parallel implementation can be efficiently used to analyze large-scale simulations.

7. ACKNOWLEDGMENTS

This research is based upon the project KaNaRiA, supported by German Aerospace Center (DLR) with funds of the German Federal Ministry of Economics and Technology (BMWi) under grant 50NA1318.

8. REFERENCES

[1] Ajith Abraham, Lakhmi C. Jain, Robert Goldberg. Evolutionary Multiobjective Optimization: Theoretical Advances and Applications. *Springer Verlag*, 2005.

[2] Andreas Lattner, Joerg Dallmeyer, Ingo Timm. Learning Dynamic Adaptation Strategies in Agent-Based Traffic Simulation Experiments. *Ninth German Conference on Multi-Agent System Technologies (MATES)*, pages 77–88, 2011.

[3] A.P. Dempster, N.M. Laird, D.B. Rubin. Maximum Likelihood from Incomplete Data via the EM algorithm. *Journal of the Royal Statistical Society*, 39:1–38, 1977.

[4] Benjamin Wilson, David Cappelleri, Timothy W. Simpson, Mary Frecker. Efficient Pareto frontier exploration using surrogate approximations. *Optimization and Engineering*, pages 31–50, 2001.

[5] Catarina Dudas, Amos H. C. Ng, Henrik Bostroem. Post-Analysis of Multi-Objective Optimization Solutions Using Decision Trees. *Intelligent Data Analysis*, 19:259–278, 2015.

[6] Dario Izzo. PYGMO and PYKEP: Open Source Tools for Massively Parallel Optimization in Astrodynamics. *International Conference on Astrodynamics Tools and Techniques (ICATT)*, 2012.

[7] David Arthur, Sergei Vassilvitskii. k-means++: The Advantages of Careful Seeding. *SODA '07 at 8th ACM-SIAM symposium on Discrete algorithms*, 1027-1035, 2007.

[8] Jack P. C. Kleijnen, Susan M. Sanchez, Thomas M. Cioppa. A User's Guide to the Brave New World of Designing Simulation Experiments. *INFORMS Journal on Computing (Summer 2005)*, 17:263–289, 2005.

[9] Jong-Hyun Ryu, Sujin Kim, Hong Wan. Pareto Front Approximation With Adaptive Weighted Sum Method in Multiobjective Simulation Optimization. *Winter Simulation Conference*, pages 623–633, 2009.

[10] Jorge Nocedal, Stephen J. Wright. Numerical Optimization. *Springer Verlag*, 1999.

[11] Kazuyuki Sugimura, Shigeru Obayashi, Shinkyu Jeong. Multi-Objective Design Exploration of a Centrifugal Impeller Accompanied With a Vaned Diffuser. *ASME/JSME Joint Fluids Engineering Conference*, 2007.

[12] L. Jeff Hong, Barry L. Nelson. A Brief Introduction to Optimization via Simulation. *Winter Simulation Conference*, 2009.

[13] Linli Xu, James Neufeld, Bryce Larson, Dale Schuurmans. Maximum Margin Clustering. *Advances in Neural Information Processing Systems*, 17:1537–1544, 2005.

[14] Martin Ester, Hans-Peter Kriegel, Joerg Sander, Xiaowei Xu. A Density-Based Algorithm for Discovering Clusters in Large Spatial Databases with Noise. *AAAI Press*, pages 226–231, 1996.

[15] Martin Liebscher, Katharina Witowski, Tushar Goel. Decision Making in Multi-Objective Optimization for Industrial Applications - Data Mining and Visualization of Pareto Data. *8th World Congress on Structural and Multidisciplinary Optimization*, 2009.

[16] M.C. Burl, D. DeCoste, B.L. Enke, D. Mazzoni, W.J. Merline, L. Scharenbroich. Automated Knowledge Discovery from Simulators. *6th SIAM International International Conference on Data Mining*, pages 82–93, 2006.

[17] Michael C. Fu. Optimization via Simulation: A Review. *Annals of Operations Research*, 53:199–248, 1994.

[18] Michael Painter, Madhav Erraguntla, Gary Hogg, Brian Beachkofski. Using Simulation, Data Mining, And Knowledge Discovery Techniques For Optimized Aircraft Enginee Fleet Management. *Winter Simulation Conference*, pages 1253–1260, 2006.

[19] Niclas Feldkamp, Soeren Bergmann, Steffen Strassburger. Knowledge Discovery in Manufacturing Simulations. *ACM SIGSIM PADS*, pages 3–12, 2015.

[20] Patrick Lange, Rene Weller, Gabriel Zachmann. Multi Agent System Optimization in Virtual Vehicle Testbeds. *EAI SIMUtools*, 2015.

[21] Patrick Lange, Rene Weller, Gabriel Zachmann. Knowledge Discovery for Pareto based Multiobjective Optimization in Simulation. *ACM SIGSIM PADS*, 2016.

[22] Raghu Pasupathy. SimOpt: A Library of Simulation Optimization Problems. *Winter Simulation Conference*, pages 4075–4085, 2011.

[23] Ravindra V. Tappeta, John E. Renaud. An Interactive Multiobjective Optimization Design Strategy for Decision Based Multidisciplinary Design. *40th AIAA/ASME/ASCE/AHS/ASC Structures, Structural Dynamics, and Materials Conference and Exhibit*, pages 78–87, 1999.

[24] Songqing Shan, Gary G. Wang. An Efficient Pareto Set Identification Approach for Multiobjective Pptimization on Black-box Functions. *Journal of Mechanical Design 127*, 5:866–874, 2004.

[25] Sunith Bandaru, Kevin Deb. Automated discovery of vital knowledge from Pareto-optimal solutions: First results from engineering design. *IEEE Congress on Evolutionary Computation (CEC)*, pages 1–8, 2010.

[26] Thanh Binh, Ulrich Korn. An Evolution Strategy for the Multiobjective Optimization. *2nd International Conference on Genetic Algorithms*, pages 23–28, 1996.

Table 1: Synthetic performance comparison overview: Our GDS approach (grey) outperforms its competitors for all noise distributions (mean error $\bar{e}$ in %)

Sampling:	Uniform						Random						Gradient					
	Det.		Dbscan		K-Means		Dbscan		Det.		K-Means		Dbscan		Det.		K-Means	
Clustering:	$\bar{e}_p$	$\bar{e}_g$	$\bar{e}_p$	$\bar{e}_g$	$\bar{e}_p$	$\bar{e}_g$	$\bar{e}_p$	$\bar{e}_g$	$\bar{e}_p$	$\bar{e}_g$	$\bar{e}_p$	$\bar{e}_g$	$\bar{e}_p$	$\bar{e}_g$	$\bar{e}_p$	$\bar{e}_g$	$\bar{e}_p$	$\bar{e}_g$
Probability mass functions																		
Binomial, $t = 9.0, p = 0.5$ $\quad P(i\|t,p) = \binom{t}{i} \cdot p^i \cdot (1-p)^{t-i}$	15.8	15.9	10.71	10.8	13.86	13.96	10.55	10.59	16.68	16.71	13.42	13.56	8.67	8.71	15.65	15.72	11.34	11.41
Geometric, $k = 0.3$ $\quad p(i\|k) = k \cdot (1-k)^i$	15.66	15.71	10.61	10.67	13.34	13.58	10.33	10.4	16.54	16.68	13.23	13.32	8.62	8.69	15.52	15.76	11.56	11.63
Pascal, $k = 3.0, p = 0.5$ $\quad p(i\|k,p) = \binom{k+i-1}{i} \cdot p^k \cdot (1-p)^i$	15.6	15.72	10.58	10.61	12.26	13.37	10.32	10.4	16.27	16.32	13.67	13.7	8.53	8.6	15.65	15.86	11.23	11.38
Uniform, $a = 0.1, b = 9.0$ $\quad p(x\|a,b) = \frac{1}{b-a}$	15.33	15.56	10.29	10.41	13.44	13.49	10.07	10.12	16.02	16.1	13.72	13.79	8.32	8.45	15.3	15.53	11.67	11.75
Poisson, $\mu = 0.1$ $\quad p(x\|\mu) = \frac{\mu^i}{i!} e^{-\mu}$	15.59	15.81	10.54	10.61	12.19	12.55	10.3	10.38	16.42	16.51	13.21	13.32	8.56	8.61	15.56	15.62	11.85	11.93
Probability density functions																		
Cauchy, $a = 5.0, b = 1.0$ $\quad p(x\|a,b) = \frac{1}{\pi \cdot b \cdot [1+(\frac{x-a}{b})^2]}$	15.1	15.3	10.44	10.48	12.42	12.56	10.25	10.3	16.24	16.28	13.33	13.42	8.47	8.52	15.15	15.25	11.24	11.4
Chi-squared, $n = 3.0$ $\quad p(x\|n) = \frac{1}{\Gamma(\frac{n}{2}) \cdot 2^{\frac{n}{2}}} \cdot x^{\frac{n}{2}-1} \cdot e^{-\frac{x}{2}}$	15.7	15.9	10.61	10.63	12.11	12.46	10.4	10.48	16.28	16.43	13.56	13.61	8.62	8.7	15.7	15.78	10.87	10.96
Fisher-F, $m = 2.0, n = 2.0$ $\quad p(x\|m,n) = \frac{\Gamma(\frac{m+n}{2})}{\Gamma(\frac{m}{2}) \cdot \Gamma(\frac{n}{2})} \cdot \frac{(\frac{mx}{n})^{\frac{m}{2}}}{x \cdot (1+\frac{mx}{n})^{\frac{m+n}{2}}}$	15.35	15.51	10.84	10.88	12.71	12.83	10.73	10.79	16.35	16.48	13.56	13.6	8.75	8.81	15.13	15.31	11.74	11.83
Normal, $\mu = 5.0, \sigma = 2.0$ $\quad p(x\|\mu,\sigma) = \frac{1}{\sigma\sqrt{2\pi}} \cdot e^{-\frac{(x-\mu)^2}{2\sigma^2}}$	15.56	15.62	10.55	10.63	11.98	12.68	10.39	10.44	16.4	16.53	13.67	13.72	8.48	8.54	15.52	15.59	11.52	11.6
Exponential, $\lambda = 3.5$ $\quad p(x\|\lambda) = \lambda e^{-\lambda x}$	15.65	15.7	10.62	10.67	13.46	13.66	10.34	10.41	16.36	16.48	13.73	13.78	8.63	8.78	15.6	15.72	11.64	11.67

A Framework for Validation of Network-based Simulation Models: an Application to Modeling Interventions of Pandemics

Sichao Wu
Biocomplexity Institute
Virginia Tech
Blacksburg, Virginia 24060
sichao@bi.vt.edu

Henning S. Mortveit
Biocomplexity Institute
Virginia Tech
Blacksburg, Virginia 24060
hmortvei@bi.vt.edu

Sandeep Gupta
Biocomplexity Institute
Virginia Tech
Blacksburg, Virginia 24060
sandeep@bi.vt.edu

ABSTRACT

Network-based computer simulation models are powerful tools for analyzing and guiding policy formation related to the actual systems being modeled. However, the inherent data and computationally intensive nature of this model class gives rise to fundamental challenges when it comes to executing typical experimental designs. In particular this applies to model validation. Manual management of the complex simulation work-flows along with the associated data will often require a broad combination of skills and expertise. Examples of skills include domain expertise, mathematical modeling, programming, high-performance computing, statistical designs, data management as well as the tracking all assets and instances involved. This is a complex and error-prone process for the best of practices, and even small slips may compromise model validation and reduce human productivity in significant ways.

In this paper, we present a novel framework that addresses the challenges of model validation just mentioned. The components of our framework form an ecosystem consisting of (*i*) model unification through a standardized model configuration format, (*ii*) simulation data management, (*iii*) support for experimental designs, and (*iv*) methods for uncertainty quantification, and sensitivity analysis, all ultimately supporting the process of model validation. (Note that our view of validation is much more comprehensive than simply ensuring that the computational model can reproduce instance of historical data.) This is an extensible design where domain experts from e.g. experimental design can contribute to the collection of available algorithms and methods. Additionally, our solution directly supports reproducible computational experiments and analysis, which in turn facilitates independent model verification and validation.

Finally, to showcase our design concept, we provide a sensitivity analysis for examining the consequences of different intervention strategies for an influenza pandemic.

SIGSIM-PADS 17, May 24 26, 2017, Singapore.

© 2017 ACM. ISBN 978-1-4503-4489-0/17/05... $15.00

DOI: http://dx.doi.org/10.1145/3064911.3064922

Keywords

Network-based epidemic simulation; model validation; simulation management; computer experimental design; sensitivity analysis.

1. INTRODUCTION

In network-based simulation models, which includes agent-based simulation models, the interactions of the modeled systems are represented by a graph where agents are captured as nodes and their possible interactions are given by edges. This model class provide insight into how local interactions and behaviors assemble to generate the global system dynamics. Examples of network-based simulation models include epidemic modeling [18], transportation modeling [3], and modeling of coupled infrastructure systems in the case of resilience studies for natural disasters or an improvised nuclear device [2]. In order to guarantee the quality of models, it is essential to understand how well the real system is captured, what are the influential parameters, how uncertainties propagate trough the model and how model discrepancies can be reduced. These understandings can be gained from model *verification and validation* (V & V) which involves the assessment of the fact that the model implemented is actually what one intended to implement (verification) and assessment that the model adequately represents the system it was intended to capture (validation). Verification and validation are broad concepts that connect tightly with uncertainty quantification, sensitivity analysis and experimental design [14].

By nature, network-based simulation models often require large data sets as well as a large variety of data sets, elements placing heavy demands on both data management and computation. As an example, an infectious disease simulation experiment for the United States uses a synthetic population network with 280 million nodes [41]. Naturally, the data volume will continue to increase as infrastructure systems such as transportation and power grid models are integrated for more comprehensive analyses. Experiments involving data sets of this scale will bring even greater challenges to data management and computing infrastructures.

When performing model validation, the challenges will be intensified since the model validation process is usually accompanied by experimental designs involving a large number of cells, each with multiple replicates. Management of a large number of experiment instances along with the associated input/output/configurations is nontrivial. Moreover, it is often desirable that model validation can be done by a third-party in addition to or rather than by the modelers themselves to guarantee the credibility, a process sometimes referred to as independent verification and validation (IV&V) [14]. For this, it is highly desirable to make sure the experiment results are reproducible. However, the involved process of conducting such analyses complicates matters. There is a lack of standardized model configurations as well as ways to actually invoke the simulation models, which makes it challenging to even execute the work-flows, not even considering the possible statistical designs involved. The challenge is compounded by the need to integrate domain experts (who typically lack modeling and computing skills), and the needs for advanced expertise covering programming, high performance computing, statistical analysis, and data management.

Contributions. Here we present a novel approach to address the above challenges for model validation of network-based simulation models in an integrated manner. This is a continuation of our previous work presented in [40]. Our design is a framework that provides a comprehensive environment supporting simulation model execution, experimental designs, data management, uncertainty quantification and sensitivity analysis for a variety of network-based simulation models. This framework can streamline the simulation experiment work-flow in a scientifically repeatable manner and can handle the data registration automatically. High-level methods including experimental design, model configuration, data access, experiment instance registration, and analysis are supported through a collection of services. Model validation will benefit from this framework in the sense that domain experts will mainly need to focus on the experimental design and analysis itself rather than the sophisticated computing, data management, and model-specific issues.

To demonstrate the framework, we have included a sensitivity analysis for a network-based epidemic simulation model applied to containment of an influenza pandemic in the urban areas of Chicago, Miami and Seattle. Sensitivity analysis is an integral component of model validation. Here we examined effects of key model parameters such as disease transmissibility, intervention initiating threshold, and effects of various intervention strategies. This case study is an extension of the work in [18]. The experiment results show that one of the intervention options (school closure) is more effective than the other two options (work closure and general social distancing). Not only can this model validation framework accelerate studies like this and facilitate new knowledge discovery, but can also greatly improve productivity by eliminating error-prone manual procedures.

The remainder of this paper is organized as follows. In the next section, we briefly review related existing work. Following that, we provide a detailed introduction to framework and its design in Section 3. In Section 4 we present the sensitivity analysis case study for the influenza pandemic and possible intervention strategies. Finally, we conclude with a discussion of current limitations and future work.

2. BACKGROUND AND RELATED WORK

To the best of our knowledge, there is no system that covers all the functionalities of the framework proposed in this paper. However, there are systems that cover subsets of features. Example subsets include (*i*) methods for model validation, uncertainty quantification, sensitivity analysis and

experimental design of computer simulation models (*ii*) standardized simulation initialization and management, and (*iii*) scientific data registry system. In the following, we review central tools and methods from each of these categories.

Verification and validation (V & V) of simulation models are broad concepts combining uncertainty quantification (UQ), sensitivity analysis (SA), design of experiment (DOE), model calibration, optimization, and so on [14]. There is a multitude of software platforms supporting different aspects of these tasks. For example, DAKOTA [1], which is developed by the Sandia National Laboratories, provides comprehensive parameter studies, uncertainty quantification, and optimization algorithms running on supercomputer platforms. PSUADE [38] is a C++ based open-source software package. It runs on Linux-like systems only through command line interfaces. UQ-PyL [39] is a Python UQ tool-kit with a graphical user interface that improves the user experience. All of the above mentioned systems incorporate comprehensive UQ/SA/DOE methods and solutions. We believe each individual software or a combination of them can facilitate the model validation life cycle. Unfortunately, most of them lack a standardized model invocation mechanism, a data management scheme for handing large amount data sets in diverse formats, and support for repeatable experiments.

As indicated in [16], scientific data and work-flow management is a major challenge in simulation science, especially for those using network-based models with complex structures and vast data throughput. System like Kepler [5] provides comprehensive solution for scientific work-flow and data management. Other systems including SAFE [29] and JAMES II [15] focus on simulation experiment automation. However, they are either domain-specific or not related to model validation.

As a matter of fact, this lack of a system combining both UQ/SA/DOE methods and simulation experiment management is a key motivation of our design.

Terminology. Throughout this paper, we will use following terms: a *Network-based simulation model* is a class of agent-based simulation models where the agents (or entities) of the system are represented through a network. For experimental designs, a *factor* is a selected parameter (or more generally, a parameter complex) to be varied and investigated; a *level* is a particular value or instance of that factor; a *cell* of is a particular combination of levels for all the factors in the experimental design. Finally, a cell may have multiple *replicate*, that is, simulation model invocations for that particular combination of levels. Replicates are typically used with any simulation model containing stochastic elements or random number aspects.

3. MODEL VALIDATION FRAMEWORK

3.1 General Model Validation Work- ow

Model validation evaluates the discrepancy between the simulation model and the actual system or phenomenon being modeled as well as sensitivity elements and uncertainties in the simulation model. This procedure often involves examining the model hypotheses, quantitatively assessing the uncertainties, conducting sensitivity analysis, and evaluating model reliability. One part of model validation is data validation, that is, comparing the simulation output data sets and the actual data sets. The aims can include evaluating model credibility, reducing discrepancy with modeled system, calibrating model parameters and achieving a particular optimization goal.

More broadly, model validation requires one to examine a broad combination of model parameter configurations and replicates thereof, and, as a result, efficient experimental design is essential since exhaustively exploring the parameter space is often computationally prohibitive. Traditional experimental design methods such as factorial design consider a small number of parameters and levels, which is not adequate for modern computer experiments with large parameter space. Sparse, space-filling design techniques such as Latin Hypercube Sampling (LHS), and orthogonal arrays [24, 36] were developed and have become widely adopted in recent decades because they are able to more uniformly cover and represent the parameter space with limited sample points. They can thereby save considerable computational time and resources compared to traditional experimental designs or Monte-Carlo methods.

Figure 1 shows a typical model validation work-flow. First, one specifies model parameters and quality of interests (QoIs), then designs experiments to explore the model parameter space and runs the simulation model accordingly. Based on the simulation outcome, uncertainties are investigated quantitatively, parameter sensitivities are evaluated and model parameters can be calibrated if realistic data is available. The model validation, in turn, can guide the experimental design and model development itself.

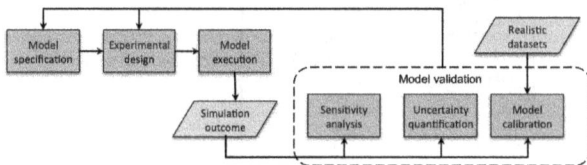

Figure 1: Typical model validation work-flow.

This procedure is data-intensive for large-scale simulation experiments since it involves frequent inspection of existing data sets and generation of new data sets. Even with advanced space-filling experimental design techniques, hundreds or thousands of simulation runs may be required to achieve a desirable accuracy for UQ/SA analysis. Our proposed framework is designed to handle this complex model validation work-flow, and will be elaborated in the next section.

3.2 Framework Design

A general model validation framework is expected to have the following features: (i) a uniform model invocation mechanism, (ii) capability to accommodate a variety of simulation models, (iii) systematic data management, (iv) efficient experimental design and SA/UQ analysis, and (v) repeatable computational results. Addressing these issues, we designed our framework through several core components illustrated in Figure 2. First, a *standardized configuration module* generalizes configuration formats for a variety of simulation models, a key factor allowing for uniform model invocation. This module consists of a suite of XML/XSD grammars with associated service code. With the standardized simulation model configuration format, it is possible to conduct experimental designs in a uniform manner because reading and writing configuration files can be handled through the standardized interfaces and through model-

specific constraints processed transparently by a *model wrapper* code, which is the second important component. A model wrapper processes model-native requirements, in particular, it translates standardized configuration files into model-compatible formats and handles model execution requests. Third, we designed an internal *central registry* system built upon a relational database, in which study and experiment instances, associated configurations and data sets are indexed. Operations related to simulation data management are done through a collection of registry APIs. Finally, an *algorithm library* contains a large number of methods for uncertainty quantification, sensitivity analysis and experimental designs. The design is such that each method can be implemented as a plug-in to ensure that the library is extensible. It is worth noting that we have a loosely-coupled design, in other words, all of the core components are standalone, and are not aware of other components. In this way, each single component can provide services for external applications, and the system as a whole can also function in concert. We will elaborate on the details of each core component in the following subsections.

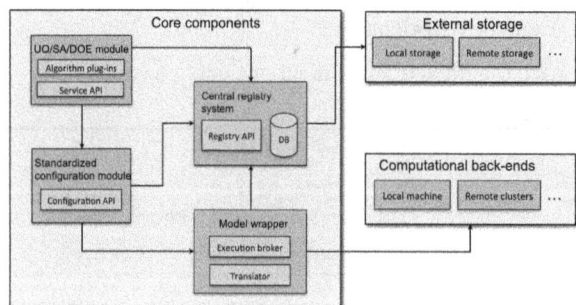

Figure 2: An overall system architecture.

In addition to the core components, we assume several supporting infrastructures. First, a physical data storage portion will handle the actual data storage. It will deal with arbitrary combinations of hardware and storage methods (e.g., flat files, DBMS, and RDF) and will interact with the registry system via generic APIs. Second, platforms such as Simfrastructure [10] support a general environment for high performance computing (HPC). It is worth noting that although the supporting components are necessary, we do not assume any particular form of them, thus ensuring that our framework remains independent and generic.

3.2.1 Standardized Model Con guration

A simulation work-flow is a collection of methods (e.g., programs and scripts) with matching invocation configurations applied to existing data sets (inputs). These will, in turn, gives rise to new data sets which are the simulation outcomes. A challenge linked to computational experiments with simulation models is dealing with the complex model configurations and the large variety of such formats. Moreover, when considering experimental design, it is difficult to identify and specify statistical factors from configuration parameters in a generic manner. This is especially so for models with heterogeneous configuration formats involving multiple files, sub-configuration sections, and command line parameters.

We have designed a generic XML-based configuration format that generalizes model configuration specifications that follow a tree structure. For this format, we classify configuration elements (also called keys or parameters) into two types. A *simple configuration element* is an atomic configuration entry represented by a leaf node; a *complex configuration element* is captured by a tree branch and is composed by a collection of related elements, both simple and complex, contained in this branch. The formal XSD grammar of a configuration element is given in Figure 3. Note that a parameter element can contain an arbitrary number of sub-parameters. If a parameter has no sub-parameters, it is a simple element, otherwise, it is a complex element. Each parameter element has associated the following attributes:

key: the unique identifier of the given parameter;

type: the parameter data type. Permissible values are: `int`, `float`, `string`, and `Boolean`;

exposed: a Boolean value encoding whether or not the given parameter is exposed as a factor for experimental designs;

optional: a Boolean value encoding whether or not the parameter is optional;

default: the default value of an optional parameter.

```
<xsd:complexType name="parameterType">
  <xsd:sequence>
    <xsd:element name="value" type="xsd:string"/>
    <xsd:element name="registry_id" type="xsd:string"
     minOccurs="0" maxOccurs="1"/>
    <xsd:element name="parameter"  type="parameterType"
     minOccurs="0" maxOccurs="unbounded"/>
  </xsd:sequence>
  <xsd:attribute name="key" type="xsd:string" use="required"/>
  <xsd:attribute name="type" type="xsd:string" use="required"/>
  <xsd:attribute name="exposed" type="xsd:boolean" use="required"/>
  <xsd:attribute name="optional" type="xsd:boolean" use="required"/>
  <xsd:attribute name="default" type="xsd:string" use="optional"/>
</xsd:complexType>
```

Figure 3: The formal XSD definition of parameter type.

As a concrete example, Figure 4 gives a parameter element conformant with this grammar used in the case study of Section 4. In this example, "InterventionFile" is a complex parameter type that contains a collection of sub-parameters; we only list the sub-parameter "school_closure_compliance" here for conciseness.

```
<parameter key=âĂĲInterventionFile" type='string"
 exposed="false" optional="false" default="Intervention">
  <value>Intervention</value>
  <registry_id>data_set_114</registry_id>
  <parameter key="school_closure_compliance" type="float"
   exposed="true" optional="false" default=0.3>
    <value>0.5</value>
  </parameter>
  ...
</parameter>
```

Figure 4: An example complex parameter element.

This is a modular design that allows one to assemble arbitrarily complex configuration elements as needed. Each complex configuration element is registered in a central registry system (see Section 3.2.2), in this way, it can be easily accessed and reused for other application instances. For each simulation model, there will be a base configuration file complying with this standardized structure and account for model-specific requirements or constraints. This base configuration file serves as a template representing the model/domain-specific knowledge.

It is worth noting that this standardized configuration format is designed for a variety of simulation models and not for a particular one. There will be a model wrapper code that handles model-native format translation, all in a transparent and automatic manner. Figure 5 shows how to use the standardized configuration format to initialize experiments. Domain experts will specify parameter specifications (parameter range, distribution for continuous parameters and levels for discrete parameters), experimental design type though the user interface, all at the standardized level. Model initialization, data preparation, model translation and execution are handled at a model-native level. If one needs to integrate new simulation models, model wrappers must be provided by the user.

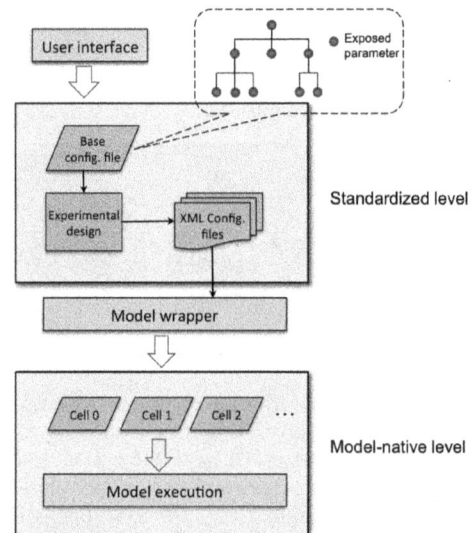

Figure 5: Using standardized configuration format to initialize experiments.

3.2.2 Central Registry System

Data type, data class and data set are fundamental concepts for data management. At a specification level, using the notion of *data types*, one can specify templates or definition for *data sets*. These definitions are called *data classes*. A data class is comparable to the C++ notions of a "struct" or "class", and a data set is an instance of a particular data class.

Generally, with this data architecture, the complex data objects mentioned in this paper, (e.g., input/output data sets, model configuration files, simulation work-flow specifications, and experiment instances) can be regarded as data sets with respect to specific data class definitions. They are managed through a central registry system.

The purpose of the *registry* is to serve as a central place containing full information about the exact structure of the data sets. The registry may be compared to a library index providing central access to all data sets and their full specification along with metadata. The registry itself does not provide ways to perform high-level browsing and searching. Instead, it provides low-level APIs to allow such services to be built for specific uses, see Figure 6 as an illustration of the overall registry system design.

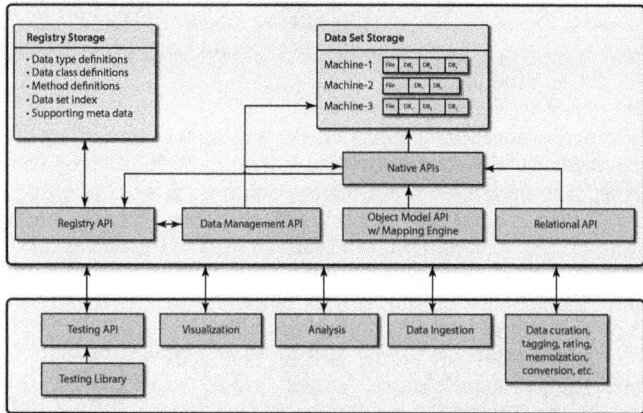

Figure 6: Overall architecture of the central registry system. The upper portion of the diagram is referred to as the system side while the lower portion is referred to as the application side.

The storage portion of the architecture will handle the actual data. It handles arbitrary combinations of hardware (single machine, distributed systems, etc.) and storage methods (files, rational databases, RDF, etc.), and will provide a generic API for data access and maintenance.

This central registry serves two major functions within our framework: providing data access and registration for heterogeneous data formats, and recording data flow and simulation work-flow for repeatable experiments.

3.2.3 Experimental Design Module and UQ/SA Analysis Methods

We have integrated several experimental design methods in a plug-in manner. The experimental design module generates sample points according to the user-specified design type. Next, a model wrapper creates actual copies of cells for model execution, see Figure 5. After all jobs are completed, the simulation outcomes are registered in the central registry and one can perform analysis over the results. We also maintain an analysis algorithm library that provides common data analysis methods such as data visualization, surrogate modeling, sensitivity index calculations, and so on. Table 1 gives a partial list of currently integrated UQ/SA/DOE methods; this list is still expanding.

4. CASE STUDY

4.1 Scenario

4.1.1 Modeling Pandemic Outbreak

Infectious diseases constitute a major public health challenge all over the world. The 2014 Ebola outbreak in Western Africa and the more recent Zika virus have caused hundreds of thousands of deaths and brought significant threat

Table 1: Partial list of integrated UQ/SA/DOE methods.

Category	Method
Experimental design	Full-factorial design [26]
	Fractional-factorial design [26]
	Plackett-Bruman design [30]
	Box-Behnken design [12]
	Central-composite design [26]
	Monte-Carlo method [33]
	Latin hypercube sampling (LHS) [24]
	Orthogonal array design (OA) [19]
	OA-based Latin hypercube design [36]
Sensitivity analysis	Fourier amplitude sensitivity test (FAST) [32]
	Morris one at a time(MOAT) [27]
	Sobol sensitivity analysis [35]
	Surrogate model-based sensitivity analysis [28]
	Analysis of variance (ANOVA) [26]
Surrogate modeling	Gaussian process [31]
	Generalized linear model [33]
	Random forest [13]
	Support vector machine (SVM) [34]
Calibration & parameter optimization	Bayesian parameter calibration [21]
	Genetic algorithm [25]
	Simulated annealing [22]
	Surrogate model-based optimization [21]

to human lives and society [23]. New infectious diseases are emerging and there is still no cure for many of them. According to a World Health Organization (WHO) report [20], every year transmissible influenza result in an estimated three to five million cases of severe illness and 250,000 to 500,000 deaths. Planning a response to an outbreak of a pandemic is a high public health priority. Due to ethical and practical reasons, controlled experiments are often impossible in epidemiology. Fortunately, computational models allow us to identify the spatial-temporal dynamics of epidemics and can therefore help policy makers forecast the epidemic propagation pattern, plan medical facility placements, and prepare response strategies.

Social contact network-based simulations has been widely used for modeling pandemic outbreaks [7, 23]. Often, this type of simulation models incorporates highly resolved synthetic representations of the person-to-person contact patterns of people in a specific geographical region, which is central to modeling disease transmission. Computational epidemiologists have conducted simulations to test the effectiveness of a set of potentially feasible intervention strategies [18, 4], and made considerable contributions to combating infectious diseases.

4.2 Simulation Method

4.2.1 Modeling Disease Transmission Over Contact Networks

Many simulation tools for modeling infectious disease have been developed [6, 8, 9]. In this paper, we use EpiFast [8] for our illustration experiments. EpiFast is a stochastic simulation model for disease propagation over large contact networks. It has been used in many studies with sophisticated settings to evaluate various dynamic interventions like vaccination and to provide decision support for public health policy makers. For model execution, we used Espresso [17], which is an experimentation middleware built upon EpiFast.

In EpiFast, the person-to-person contacts are formally represented by a network $G(V, E, W)$, where V is the node set, E is the edge set, and W is the edge weight set. In this network, nodes correspond to individuals and edges represent contacts between two end nodes. An edge $e = (u, v)$ with weight $w(e)$ denotes that node u has contact with node v for a duration $w(u, v)$ throughout the day, and during which the disease may transmit from u to v with probability $p(w(e))$. The function p typically depends on specific disease infectivity.

Many stochastic simulations adopt the standard SEIR disease model which is widely used in epidemiology [8]. Each person is in one of the four health states at any time: susceptible (S), exposed (E), infectious (I) and removed (R). A person is in the susceptible state until she/he becomes exposed. The person will remain exposed for an incubation period, during which she/he is not infectious. Then the person becomes infectious and remains so for an infectious period. Finally, she/he becomes removed (or recovered) and remains so permanently. With the SEIR model, the disease spreads in a population in the following way: it can only be transmitted from an infectious node to a susceptible node. On any day, if node u is infectious and v is susceptible, disease transmission from u to v occurs with probability

$$ p(w(u, v)) = 1 \quad (1 \quad r)^{w(u,v)}, \tag{1} $$

where r is the disease transmissibility, the probability of disease transmission for a contact of one unit time. Infections from multiple infectious individuals to a susceptible individual are treated as independent events. Thus, the disease propagates probabilistically along the edges of the contact network.

4.2.2 Targeted Layered Containment Strategies of Influenza Pandemic

In [18], Halloran et al. developed targeted layered containment strategies of an influenza pandemic happening in the Chicago area by using stochastic, spatially structured, network-based simulation models. To control the pandemic spread, a set of interventions were considered. They combined antiviral treatment and household isolation of identified cased, prophylaxis and quarantine of their household contacts, closure of schools, social distancing in the workplace. Because these interventions include both targeted and general strategies, they are called targeted-layered containment (TLC) approaches. In [18], the researchers examined different levels of ascertainment of symptomatic influenza cases, and compliance with the interventions and cumulative illness *attack rate* (total number of infected people – past and present) threshold for initiating interventions.

In this case study, we revisit the TLC simulation experiment and use our framework to streamline the study pipeline.

4.3 Experiment Description

One uncertain factor of the model is the transmissibility of a disease. This uncertainty also poses challenges for estimating how transmissible a future pandemic will be. Typically, the transmissibility is measured by using the reproductive number, that is, the number of secondary cases for each primary case. In our study, it is characterized by the probability of transmission per unit of contact time between two persons (r in Equation 1), which is a real number. As a matter of fact, transmissibility is a dominant factor that affects the cumulative attack rate significantly, and this will be shown in the experiment results.

Interventions for an ascertained case include antiviral treatment for the infected individual, targeted antiviral prophylaxis of household contact, home isolation (ill person is isolated in the home but not isolated from housemates), and quarantine of household contacts (household contacts are all quarantined within the home). General population-wide interventions are summarized as follows:

School closure. All schools, including primary, middle and high schools are closed at a particular threshold cumulative illness attack rate. Students are expected to stay at home with certain compliance levels.

Work closure. At a particular threshold cumulative illness attack rate, workplaces are closed and contacts are reduced by a certain percentage and also by a certain compliance level.

Social distancing. Community social distancing results in fewer public activities. Examples include closing shopping centers, and reducing visits to restaurants and other public locations. After a particular threshold attack rate, people are encouraged to stay at home with a certain compliance.

These interventions are triggered when a threshold fraction of the population become infected. In [18], several scenarios were considered based on different levels of the threshold values which varied from 1% to 0.01%. Different combinations of intervention compliance levels were also examined, but in a coarse manner (such as 30%, 60%, 90%). An advantage of our experimental design module and automated model configuration method, is that one is able to run hundreds and even thousands of simulations to explore the parameter space more extensively, something that was effectively impossible in the original study.

4.4 Experiment Setup

4.4.1 Model Configuration

Figure 7 shows an example EpiFast main configuration file, which contains references to a collection of sub-configuration files. Typically, experiment parameters can be in either the main configuration file or any sub-configuration file. Sub-configuration files are organized in a rather arbitrary manner, they can be located in different working directories or even on different machines. In practice, it is generally hard to perform experimental designs with such unstructured configuration format. In this particular study, model parameters such as school closure compliance rate, work closure compliance rate and social distancing compliance rate are located in a sub-configuration file called intervention file. Manually configuring the model is tedious and can easily introduce errors.

To facilitate generalized experimental design and uniform model invocation, we devised a standardized configuration

```
ConfigVersion = 2009
ContactGraphFile = LBR_430-socnet.efi
Transmissibility = 3.07537688442e-05
InfectiousPeriodFormat = DISTRIBUTION
InfectiousPeriodFile = Infectious.Period.Distribution
IncubationPeriodFormat = DISTRIBUTION
IncubationPeriodFile = Incubation.Period.Distribution
EpidemicSeedType = RANDOM_SEEDS_FIRST_DAY
EpidemicSeedNumber = 5
EpidemicSeedFile = subpop_all.txt
SimulationRandomSeed = 7654321
InterventionFile = Intervention
IterationNumber = 10
OutputFile = out/EFO
SimulationDuration = 200
```

Figure 7: An example of the main EpiFast configuration file. Here red boxes denote references to sub-configuration files.

format for EpiFast using the tree architecture discussed earlier, where the main configuration file is the trunk and sub-configuration files are treated as branches, see Figure 8 for an example. With the associated parameter navigation API, fast parameter locating is possible. In addition, we support saving and loading of parameter tree branches to and from external files which enables customized configuration assembly. The entire configuration specification and all tree branches are also indexed by the central registry system. This has a lot of practical applications, for example, a particular intervention file usually corresponds to a specific intervention strategy and is devised by domain experts. With the standardized configuration format along with the central registry system, complex intervention strategies can be easily archived and reused when necessary without duplication of efforts.

```
<epifast_cfg>
  <parameter key="ConfigureVersion" type="int"
   exposed="false" optional="false">
    <value>2009</value>
  </parameter>
  <parameter key="ContactGraphFile" type="string"
   exposed="false" optional="false">
    <value>LBR_430-socnet.efi</value>
  </parameter>
  ...
  <parameter key="InfectiousPeriodFile" type="string"
   exposed="false" optional="false">
    <value>Infectious.Period.Distribution</value>
    <registry_id>data_set_112</registry_id>
    ...
  </parameter>
  ...
  <parameter key="InterventionFile" type="string"
   exposed="false" optional="false">
    <value>Intervention</value>
    <registry_id>data_set_114</registry_id>
    <parameter key="school_closure_compliance" type="float"
      exposed="true" optional="false">
      <value>0.5</value>
    </parameter>
    ...
  </parameter>
  ...
</epifast_cfg>
```

Figure 8: Standardized XML configuration file for EpiFast shown in Figure 7. Some configuration entries are omitted for clarity.

4.4.2 Experimental design

By using the standardized model configuration format, experimental parameters are automatically exposed, along with the user specified parameter space, and it is sufficient for the experimental design module to take samples in a uniform manner. We utilized the Latin hypercube sampling (LHS) plug-in in the algorithm library for parameter sensitivity analysis. The reason we use LHS instead of traditional DOE methods such as factorial design is that exhaustively exploring parameter space for studies of this scale is not practically feasible. For instance, running one TLC study can take fifteen to twenty minutes over the Miami and the Seattle networks; thirty to forty minutes over the Chicago network on a high-performance computing cluster. Clearly, it is not possible to run all combinations of the parameter settings, and therefore, a sparse space-filling experimental design with economic run size is essential for conducting the sensitivity analysis.

After the generation of the experiment configurations, the EpiFast model wrapper prepares the model execution environment and automatically submits job execution requests to the computational back-end. Meanwhile, the registry records the information of the experiment instance such as working directory, input and output data sets, computing platform, execution log and so on. This is useful when the finished experiment instances need to be repeated.

4.4.3 Sensitivity Analysis

When all the model execution jobs are finished, the model wrapper will process the simulation outcome and extract quality of interests from the raw output data. The processed data are used to perform parameter sensitivity analysis. Sensitivity analysis is concerned with how changes in the model inputs influence the outputs. Generally speaking, there are two types of sensitivity analyses: local sensitivity analysis examining individual parameter effects (also known as main effects), and global sensitivity analyses which also consider interactive effects among two or more parameters. Both of them can enhance the understanding of a complex model, find aberrant model behavior, identify which inputs have significant effect on a particular output and so on. In this study, we first investigated individual parameter effects one at a time and then used two global sensitivity metrics for assessing the parameter effects: Sobol's method [35] which partitions the output variance in terms of input parameters and their increasing order of interactions as

$$V(X) = \sum_i V_i(x_i) + \sum_{i<j} V_{i,j}(x_i, x_j) + \cdots + V_{1\ldots s}(x_1, \ldots, x_s) ,$$
(2)

and the delta sensitivity indicator [11] which examines the influence of input uncertainty on the entire output distribution without reference to a specific moment of the output. We will give the sensitivity analysis results with respect to both measurements in the next section.

4.5 Results

4.5.1 Experiment #1: Transmissibility and Intervention Threshold

In this experiment, we used synthetic contact networks of the three US cities Miami, Seattle and Chicago. Miami and Seattle have similar population sizes but distinct demographics, see Table 2, whereas Chicago area has much larger population size (9,038,163 nodes) and mixed demographic properties as compared to the other two cities. Thus, we use the simulation over the Chicago network as a control experiment.

Table 2: Age and household size composition of the Miami and Seattle populations [37].

	Miami region	Seattle region
Population size	2,092,076	3,206,897
Age group		
Preschool (0-4 years)	6.74%	6.78%
School aged (5-18 years)	15.03%	20.33%
Adults (19-64 years)	65.04%	63.08%
Seniors (65 years)	13.18%	9.80%
Household size		
Small (1 person)	7.96%	10.90%
Medium (2-3 persons)	38.21%	45.76%
Large (3 persons)	53.83%	43.34%

Intuitively, cumulative illness attack rate will increase with greater disease transmissibility, and reductions in the attack rate are expected when TLC interventions are installed. The initiating threshold fraction of illness is also an important factor to consider since it determines how stringent the intervention strategy will have to be. We considered three scenarios in this experiment: the baseline scenario without intervention, interventions initiated after 1% and 0.1% of the population has developed symptomatic influenza for the other scenarios, in which, compliance rate for school closure, work closure and social distancing interventions were fixed at 30%, 50% and 50%, respectively.

The results of the experiment are shown in Figure 9. It can be observed that TLC interventions can effectively contain the influenza spread. Scenario 3 with a more stringent intervention initiating threshold achieves a lower illness attack rate comparing with Scenario 2. When comparing the results across cities, Seattle has a higher attack rate than Miami if no intervention is applied. However, when TLC interventions were implemented, Seattle achieves a lower attack rate. This inversion results from the fact that Seattle has a larger portion of schoolage people and the fact that school closure intervention is the most significant factor for controlling the disease spread, see Table 2. This is demonstrated in the next set of experiments. Chicago always has a higher attack rate because this area has a larger population size and the cascade effect can result in a pandemic expanding.

4.5.2 *Experiment #2: Sensitivity Analysis of Intervention Compliances*

In the TLC study, we mainly considered three types of interventions: school closure, work closure, and general social distancing. The compliance level of these interventions is a major factor that influences the overall attack rate. We conducted both local and global sensitivity analyses to assess their effects.

In this study, we fixed the disease transmissibility at 5.8×10^{-5}, intervention initiating threshold value at 1%, and we used the Miami network. First, we varied the intervention compliance levels one at a time for 30 different values to evaluate their local sensitivities. Each experiment had 5 replicates. Figure 10 gives the OFAT sensitivity analysis result. It is shown that all these three interventions have apparent effects on the overall illness attack rate, but that school closure intervention is more effective than the other two in decreasing the illness attack rate.

For global sensitivity, we varied the three intervention compliance levels simultaneously for 1000 runs by using the Latin hypercube sampling method. Figure 11 is the scatter plot for each dimension of the parameter space. One can observe that school closure intervention shows a stronger pattern whereas the other two are more random, which again indicates that school closure intervention dominates the intervention efficacy.

Quantitatively, we calculated the sensitivity indices for the three intervention strategies, see Table 3. Both the Delta measurement and Sobol's measurement show that school closure is the most effective intervention option. Our experiment results suggest that the combination of various intervention strategies can reduce the illness attack rate significantly.

Table 3: Parameter ranking with two sensitivity importance measures.

parameter	Delta measurement	Sobol's measurement
School closure compliance	0.534339	0.836894
Work closure compliance	0.082681	0.055476
Social distancing compliance	0.082046	0.047361

4.6 Discussion

In this paper, we have presented a general computational framework for the network-based simulation model validation. In addition to developing and deploying the system, we have undertaken simulation experiments to illustrate how this system fits in a model validation pipeline and the significant benefits compared to manual approaches. Handling simulation work-flows and the big data issues is challenging: the original TLC study in [18] was conducted in cooperation with technical experts and domain experts, and only a small number of levels for each parameter were considered (for example, three levels for transmissibility). This is not sufficient for uncertainty quantification and sensitivity analysis which usually require a large number of samples. In contrast, we performed 1000 runs for global sensitivity analysis by using Latin hypercube sampling, and the resulted data set reached 954 GB when the Chicago contact network was used, thus illustrating that our framework is able to handle complex simulation work-flows with large data volume as needed to support model validation.

However, there are currently some limitations of our framework: integration of a new simulation models still requires extra efforts. Specifically, the model wrapper module needs to be provided by the user. Moreover, the execution and computational efficiency of this framework depends largely on the simulation model itself and in most cases, overshad-

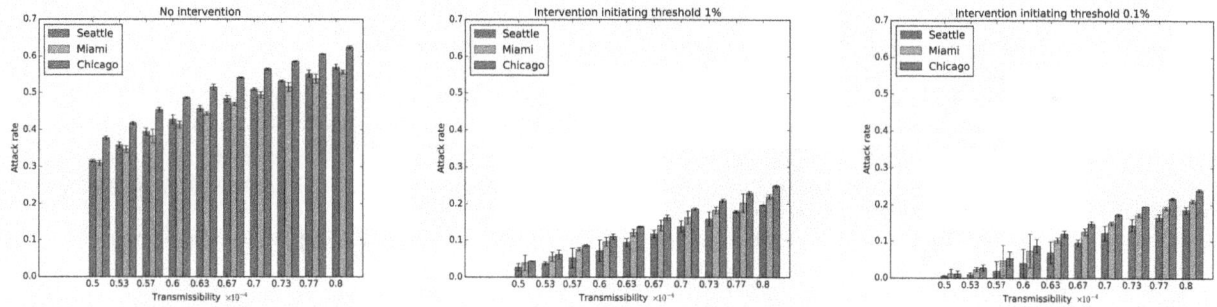

Figure 9: Illness attack rates for three US cities Seattle, Miami and Chicago without intervention and with TLC interventions for 1% and 0.1% initiating threshold values. Each experiment ran with 5 replicates. Error bars denote standard deviation.

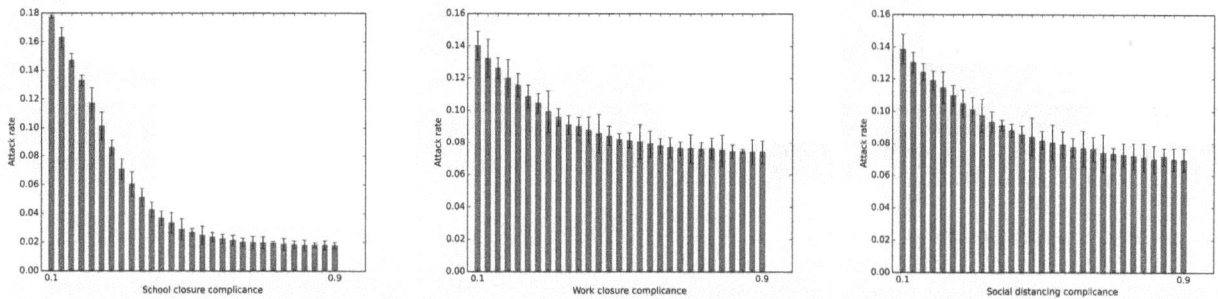

Figure 10: Local sensitivity analysis of intervention compliance parameter. Each parameter is examined for 30 different values with 5 replicates. Error bars denote standard deviation.

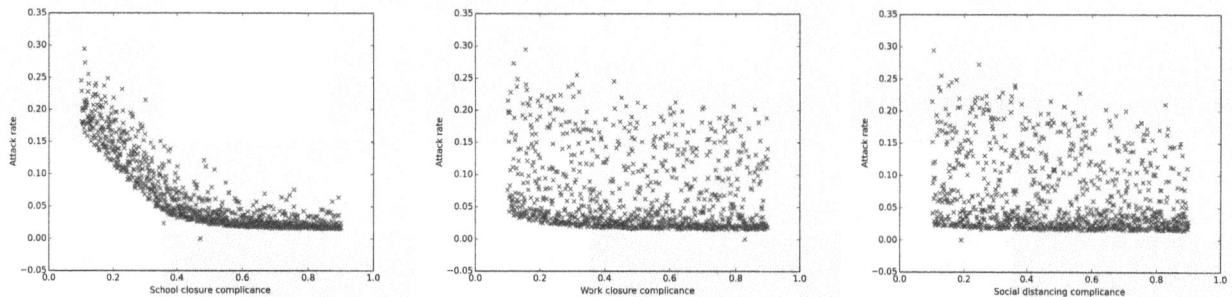

Figure 11: Scatter plot of the global sensitivity analysis. Here 1000 sample points were evaluated using the Latin hypercube Sampling method.

ows the overall running time. However, the increase in human productivity and reduction in inadvertent errors is expected to be significant. We have not yet had the time to conduct a formal study or survey to quantify this, but from our own hands-on experience with this class of simulation models, this saving is tremendous. Moreover, the standardized format has several additional advantages waiting to be addressed. For example, it supports automated and instant GUI construction (through the standardized configuration file) which in turn provides domain experts immediate ways to specify model configurations and conduct studies.

To summarize, our framework provides a novel solution for supporting model validation of large-scale network-based simulations. Any individual modeler, research group, or third party can benefit from using this system to conduct the model validation studies as well as other analyses.

5. ACKNOWLEDGMENTS

We thank our external collaborators and members of the Network Dynamics and Simulation Science Laboratory (NDSSL) for their suggestions and comments. This work has been partially supported by DTRA CNIMS Contract HDTRA1-11-D-0016-0001, USAID Cooperative Agreement No. AID-OAA-L-15-00001 and DTRA Grant HDTRA1-11-1-0016. The authors thank Dr. Madhav Marathe, Dr. Bryan Lewis, Dr. Stephen Eubank, Dr. Achla Marathe, Dr. Xinwei Deng and Dr. Srini Venkatramanan for many helpful discussions.

6. REFERENCES

[1] B. Adams, M. Ebeida, M. Eldred, J. Jakeman, L. Swiler, A. Stephens, D. Vigil, and T. Wildey. DAKOTA, a multilevel parallel object-oriented framework for design optimization, parameter estimation, uncertainty quantification, and sensitivity analysis: Version 6.0 userâĂŹs manual. Technical report, Sandia National Laboratory, 2014. Sandia Technical Report SAND2014-4633.

[2] A. Adiga, M. V. Marathe, H. S. Mortveit, S. Wu, and S. Swarup. Modeling urban transportation in the aftermath of a nuclear disaster: The role of human behavioral responses. In *Transportation Research: Part C (International Journal of Transportation)*. 2013.

[3] A. Adiga, H. S. Mortveit, and S. Wu. Route stability in large-scale transportation models. In *Workshop on Multiagent Interaction Networks, AAMAS*, volume 13, 2012.

[4] A. Adiga and A. Vullikanti. Temporal vaccination games under resource constraints. In *AAAI*, pages 2438–2444, 2016.

[5] I. Altintas, C. Berkley, E. Jaeger, M. Jones, B. Ludascher, and S. Mock. Kepler: an extensible system for design and execution of scientific workflows. In *Scientific and Statistical Database Management, 2004. Proceedings. 16th International Conference on*, pages 423–424. IEEE, 2004.

[6] C. L. Barrett, K. R. Bisset, S. G. Eubank, X. Feng, and M. V. Marathe. Episimdemics: an efficient algorithm for simulating the spread of infectious disease over large realistic social networks. In *Proceedings of the 2008 ACM/IEEE conference on Supercomputing*, page 37. IEEE Press, 2008.

[7] K. R. Bisset, J. Cadena, M. Khan, C. J. Kuhlman, B. L. Lewis, and P. Telionis. An integrated agent-based approach for modeling disease spread in large populations to support health informatics. In *IEEE International Conference on Biomedical and Health Informatics*, Las Vegas, NV, February 24-27, 2016, 2016.

[8] K. R. Bisset, J. Chen, X. Feng, V. Kumar, and M. V. Marathe. Epifast: a fast algorithm for large scale realistic epidemic simulations on distributed memory systems. In *Proceedings of the 23rd international conference on Supercomputing*, pages 430–439. ACM, 2009.

[9] K. R. Bisset, J. Chen, X. Feng, Y. Ma, and M. V. Marathe. Indemics: an interactive data intensive framework for high performance epidemic simulation. In *Proceedings of the 24th ACM International Conference on Supercomputing*, pages 233–242. ACM, 2010.

[10] K. R. Bisset, S. Deodhar, H. Makkapati, M. V. Marathe, P. Stretz, and C. L. Barrett. Simfrastructure: A flexible and adaptable middleware platform for modeling and analysis of socially coupled systems. In *Cluster, Cloud and Grid Computing (CCGrid), 2013 13th IEEE/ACM International Symposium on*, pages 506–513. IEEE, 2013.

[11] E. Borgonovo. A new uncertainty importance measure. *Reliability Engineering & System Safety*, 92(6):771–784, 2007.

[12] G. E. Box and D. W. Behnken. Some new three level designs for the study of quantitative variables. *Technometrics*, 2(4):455–475, 1960.

[13] L. Breiman. Random forests. *Machine learning*, 45(1):5–32, 2001.

[14] Committee on Mathematical Foundations of Verification, Validation and Uncertainty Quantification, Board on Mathematical Sciences and Their Applications, and Division on Engineering and Physical Sciences. *Assessing the Reliability of Complex Models: Mathematical and Statistical Foundations of Verification, Validation, and Uncertainty Quantification*. The National Academies Press, Washington, D.C., 2012.

[15] R. Ewald, J. Himmelspach, M. Jeschke, S. Leye, and A. M. Uhrmacher. Flexible experimentation in the modeling and simulation framework james ii-implications for computational systems biology. *Briefings in bioinformatics*, 11(3):290–300, 2010.

[16] J. Gray, D. Liu, M. Nieto-Santistevan, A. Szalay, D. DeWitt, and G. Heber. Scientific data management in the coming decade. *ACM SIGMOD Record*, 34(4):34–41, 2005.

[17] S. Gupta and V. Cedeno. Espresso (lite) 1.0beta user manual. Technical report, NDSSL, 2017.

[18] E. Halloran, N. Ferguson, S. Eubank, I. Longini, D. Cummings, B. Lewis, S. Xu, C. Fraser, A. Vullikanti, and T. Germann. Modeling targeted layered containment of an influenza pandemic in the united states. *Proceedings of the National Academy of Sciences*, 105(12):4639–4644, 2008.

[19] S. Hedayat, N. J. A. Sloane, and J. Stufken.

Orthogonal arrays: theory and applications. Springer, 1999.

[20] D. Heymann, T. Prentice, and L. T. Reinders. *The world health report 2007: a safer future: global public health security in the 21st century.* World Health Organization, 2007.

[21] D. Higdon, J. Gattiker, B. Williams, and M. Rightley. Computer model calibration using high-dimensional output. *Journal of the American Statistical Association,* 2012.

[22] C.-R. Hwang. Simulated annealing: theory and applications. *Acta Applicandae Mathematicae,* 12(1):108–111, 1988.

[23] S. Kurahashi. A health policy simulation model of ebola haemorrhagic fever and zika fever. In *Agent and Multi-Agent Systems: Technology and Applications,* pages 319–329. Springer, 2016.

[24] M. McKay, R. Beckman, and W. Conover. Comparison of three methods for selecting values of input variables in the analysis of output from a computer code. *Technometrics,* 21(2):239–245, 1979.

[25] M. Mitchell. *An introduction to genetic algorithms.* MIT press, 1998.

[26] D. Montgomery. *Design and analysis of experiments,* volume 7. Wiley New York, 1984.

[27] M. D. Morris. Factorial sampling plans for preliminary computational experiments. *Technometrics,* 33(2):161–174, 1991.

[28] J. Oakley and A. O'Hagan. Probabilistic sensitivity analysis of complex models: a bayesian approach. *Journal of the Royal Statistical Society: Series B (Statistical Methodology),* 66(3):751–769, 2004.

[29] F. Perrone, C. Main, and B. Ward. Safe: simulation automation framework for experiments. In *Proceedings of the Winter Simulation Conference,* page 249. Winter Simulation Conference, 2012.

[30] R. L. Plackett and J. P. Burman. The design of optimum multifactorial experiments. *Biometrika,* 33(4):305–325, 1946.

[31] C. E. Rasmussen. Gaussian processes for machine learning. 2006.

[32] A. Saltelli, S. Tarantola, and K.-S. Chan. A quantitative model-independent method for global sensitivity analysis of model output. *Technometrics,* 41(1):39–56, 1999.

[33] T. J. Santner, B. J. Williams, and W. Notz. *The design and analysis of computer experiments.* Springer, 2003.

[34] A. J. Smola and B. Schölkopf. A tutorial on support vector regression. *Statistics and computing,* 14(3):199–222, 2004.

[35] I. M. Sobol. Global sensitivity indices for nonlinear mathematical models and their monte carlo estimates. *Mathematics and computers in simulation,* 55(1):271–280, 2001.

[36] B. Tang. Orthogonal array-based latin hypercubes. *Journal of the American Statistical Association,* 88(424):1392–1397, 1993.

[37] C. Taylor, A. Marathe, and R. Beckman. Same influenza vaccination strategies but different outcomes across us cities? *International Journal of Infectious Diseases,* 14(9):e792–e795, 2010.

[38] C. Tong. PSUADE userâĂŹs manual. *Lawrence Livermore National Laboratory (LLNL), Livermore, CA,* 109, 2005.

[39] C. Wang, Q. Duan, C. H. Tong, Z. Di, and W. Gong. A GUI platform for uncertainty quantification of complex dynamical models. *Environmental Modelling & Software,* 76:1–12, 2016.

[40] S. Wu and H. S. Mortveit. A general framework for experimental design, uncertainty quantification and sensitivity analysis of computer simulation models. In *2015 Winter Simulation Conference (WSC),* pages 1139–1150. IEEE, 2015.

[41] J.-S. Yeom, A. Bhatele, K. Bisset, E. Bohm, A. Gupta, L. V. Kale, M. Marathe, D. S. Nikolopoulos, M. Schulz, and L. Wesolowski. Overcoming the scalability challenges of epidemic simulations on blue waters. In *Parallel and Distributed Processing Symposium, 2014 IEEE 28th International,* pages 755–764. IEEE, 2014.

A Graph Partitioning Algorithm for Parallel Agent-Based Road Traffic Simulation

Yadong Xu
TUMCREATE Ltd
1 CREATE Way
Singapore 138602, Singapore
yadong.xu@tum-
create.edu.sg

Wentong Cai
Nanyang Technological
University
50 Nanyang Avenue
Singapore 639798, Singapore
aswtcai@ntu.edu.sg

David Eckhoff
TUMCREATE Ltd
1 CREATE Way
Singapore 138602, Singapore
david.eckhoff@tum-
create.edu.sg

Suraj Nair
TUMCREATE Ltd
1 CREATE Way
Singapore 138602, Singapore
suraj.nair@tum-
create.edu.sg

Alois Knoll
Technische Universität
München
Boltzmannstraße 3
85748 Garching b. München,
Germany
knoll@in.tum.de

ABSTRACT

A common approach of parallelising an agent-based road traffic simulation is to partition the road network into subregions and assign computations for each subregion to a logical process (LP). Inter-process communication for synchronisation between the LPs is one of the major factors that affect the performance of parallel agent-based road traffic simulation in a distributed memory environment. Synchronisation overhead, i.e., the number of messages and the communication data volume exchanged between LPs, is heavily dependent on the employed road network partitioning algorithm. In this paper, we propose Neighbour-Restricting Graph-Growing (NRGG), a partitioning algorithm which tries to reduce the required communication between LPs by minimising the number of neighbouring partitions. Based on a road traffic simulation of the city of Singapore, we show that our method not only outperforms graph partitioning methods such as METIS and Buffoon, for the synchronisation protocol used, but also is more resilient than stripe spatial partitioning when partitions are cut more finely.

Keywords

Neighbour-Restricting Graph-Growing; parallel simulation; agent-based traffic simulation; graph partitioning

1. INTRODUCTION

Agent-based road traffic simulation has become an important tool in the evaluation of today's and future transportation systems. It is useful in solving many severe problems

that modern large cities face such as increasing traffic congestion and high CO_2 emissions. To this end, simulating entire cities [14, 22] with thousands to millions of agents (i.e., vehicles) can give valuable insights, however, at the same time it poses a major challenge in terms of computational resources.

Parallel computing techniques can be used to speed-up these simulations. In a parallel agent-based road traffic simulation, computational workload is divided and executed by a group of Logical Processes (LPs), each of which is assigned to a physical processing unit. To maintain the correctness of the parallel simulation, inter-process communication is required due to data dependencies between LPs [4]. This is referred to as *synchronisation* and, in distributed memory environments, is typically achieved by message passing between the LPs. Due to the synchronisation between the LPs, it is crucial to consider load-balancing, so that the waiting time of each LP is reduced. The workload of traffic simulation is often dynamic, which necessitates dynamic load-balancing during simulation run-time. Inter-process communication and load imbalance are the two major factors that affect the performance of parallel simulation, and both of them are influenced by how the simulation is partitioned.

A common way to parallelise traffic simulation is to decompose the road network into multiple spatial subregions (i.e., partitions) and assign each partition to an LP. The most straightforward method of achieving this is through the use of geographical information, e.g., by cutting the network into stripes, grids, or areas of equal sizes [1, 12, 13, 23]. The downside of these methods is that they do not consider synchronisation overhead. Another approach is to convert the road network into a graph (where edges represent road segments and nodes represent connections between these segments) and then use graph partitioning algorithms [15, 20]. Graph partitioning algorithms use certain heuristics aiming to reduce edge-cut and thereby the dependencies among partitions. However, depending on the synchronisation protocol, minimising edge cut alone may not minimise the total synchronisation overhead [7].

SIGSIM-PADS 17, May 24 26, 2017, Singapore.

© 2017 ACM. ISBN 978-1-4503-4489-0/17/05. . . $15.00

DOI: http://dx.doi.org/10.1145/3064911.3064914

In this paper, we propose Neighbour-Restricting Graph-Growing (NRGG), a graph partitioning algorithm that reduces synchronisation overhead by limiting the number of neighbouring LPs, that is, LPs exchanging messages. Two partitions are called *neighbouring partitions* if there exists at least one road link that connects the two partitions, thus creating data dependencies between the two LPs that execute them. Reducing the number of neighbours for each partition can therefore reduce the required synchronisation messages, especially when an asynchronous protocol is used for synchronisation. We achieve this by developing a two-step algorithm that first partitions the road network into stripe-like shaped regions, and then refines the partitions using a modified Kernighan-Lin (KL) local search algorithm. Our contributions can be summarised as follows:

- We present Neighbour-Restricting Graph-Growing (NRGG)[1], a novel two-step graph partitioning algorithm for parallel road traffic simulation.

- We show the applicability and performance of our proposed algorithm by applying it to *double-blinded* [24], a parallel agent-based microscopic road traffic simulator for distributed memory environments.

- We compare our method to the existing algorithms and show that it is not only more scalable than stripe spatial partitioning, but also leads to fewer synchronisation messages compared to the graph partitioning methods METIS [9] and Buffoon [18].

The reminder of this paper is organised as follows: Section 2 presents the related work. Section 3 provides some preliminary information for the work in this paper, including a brief description of the agent-based traffic simulation that the partitioning algorithm operates on, and the formulation of the partitioning problem we attempt to solve. Section 4 proposes the partitioning algorithm. Then experiments are described in Section 5. Lastly, we draw conclusions and discuss future work in Section 6.

2. RELATED WORK

To split the computational workload between LPs, road networks can be partitioned in various ways. For example, the road network can be cut into stripes or grid cells using coordinate information [12,13]. The resulting subregions do not necessarily need to have the same geometric area. They are weighted, e.g., in terms of traffic density to achieve a low workload imbalance between the LPs. Another method is recursive coordinate bisection (RCB) [1, 23], where the road network is cut into two equally sized sub-regions by a plane orthogonal to one of the coordinate axes. This procedure is then recursively applied until the desired number of sub-regions are obtained. The downside of cutting the road network into stripes, grids or using RCB method is that they mainly focus on workload balancing and do not consider the minimisation of synchronisation overhead. In an environment where message passing is time-consuming, ignoring synchronisation overhead can be significantly detrimental to the performance of parallel simulation.

Graph partitioning algorithms try to not only equalise the workload of partitions, but also minimise edge cut among

[1]Source code of implementation in C++ is available at https://github.com/xu-yadong/nrgg.

partitions. Cutting an edge in a road network means that connected road segments geographically lie in two partitions, therefore requiring communication between the two responsible LPs. The graph partitioning problem is NP-hard, therefore heuristics are required to obtain approximate results. Various graph partitioning algorithms can be found in the literature [7, 9, 10, 18]. An example is the well-known multilevel partitioning approach [7, 9, 10]. In multilevel partitioning, the graph is first recursively coarsened to a smaller graph. Then a graph partitioning algorithm such as spectral bisection [16] or evolutionary algorithm [3, 17, 18] partitions the smaller graph. Finally, the smaller graph is uncoarsened back to the original graph. At each level of uncoarsening, local search refinement is commonly used to improve the quality of partitions. The Kernighan and Lin algorithm [10] is the classic algorithm for local refinement, where two vertices at the boundary of two neighbouring partitions are exchanged to reduce edge cut.

METIS is a widely used set of programs for partitioning graphs. It adopts the multi-level approach and has been used to parallelise traffic simulation [15, 20]. It was shown that graph partitioning outperforms spatial partitioning algorithms in terms of edge cut, which potentially reduces synchronisation overhead between LPs. Buffoon [18] is also a multi-level graph partitioning algorithm which uses natural cuts in road networks as a preprocessing technique to obtain a coarser graph. It is able to generate less edge cut compared to METIS for road networks. However, the algorithm is slower than METIS, which may make it unsuitable for dynamic partitioning at simulation run-time. To receive a better understanding of the performance of NRGG, we compare our proposed method to both METIS and Buffoon in Section 5.

The discussed graph partitioning algorithms in this section have in common that they aim at minimising edge cut. However, depending on the synchronisation protocol, reducing edge cut does not always lead to minimising synchronisation overhead, as also pointed out by Hendrickson and Kolda [7]. To address this problem, we extend the state of the art by also considering the number of neighbouring partitions to reduce synchronisation overhead.

3. PRELIMINARIES

In this section, we introduce the parallel agent-based traffic simulation platform that we use. The synchronisation protocol is described, which motivates our partitioning algorithm. We also formulate the partitioning problem.

3.1 Agent-based Road Traffic Simulation

3.1.1 Simulation space

A road network, containing links and nodes, is a *spatial network* that forms the simulation space. Links represent roads in the real world and can have one or more lanes, and nodes contain the connectivity information of links. Nodes possess geographical coordinate information, i.e., longitudes and latitudes. An agent always has to be situated on a link, making links effectively a container of agents.

3.1.2 Agents

An *agent* in the simulation represents a driver-vehicle unit. The behaviour of agents is usually modelled using car-following models [5,21] and lane-changing models [6,11]. Car-following models calculate the velocity and acceleration of a vehicle according to the characteristics of the driver and the vehicle, and the surrounding traffic conditions. Commonly, car-following models adjust the velocity of an agent to maintain or reach a desired safety gap to the vehicle in front. Lane-changing models calculate whether an agent should change lanes, e.g., based on the current speed and on vehicles on other lanes. These models require agents to have a *sensing range*, which is the area in the road network around the agent within which other agents may have an effect on the agent's behaviour. The agent needs to examine the traffic conditions within its sensing range to make acceleration and lane-changing decisions. This is challenging in parallel traffic simulation when the sensing range is reaching into other partitions as it then potentially requires synchronisation between the responsible LPs.

3.1.3 Agent state variables

Each agent has a *state* at a particular virtual simulation, represented by state variables. Agent states potentially change upon executing *time-stamped events* scheduled by agent models. The simulation advances by executing these events in the ascending time-stamp order. State variables can be classified into two types depending on their visibility: *Agent-based state variables* belong to the agent as a whole and are visible to other agents, e.g., velocity and geographical location; while *component-based state variables* belong only to the models inside the agent and are not visible to other agents, e.g., state-of-charge of vehicle battery. We assume that agent-based state variables are updated periodically with a fixed interval, which is called an *update interval*, a.k.a., *time-step*. The events that change agent-based state variables may have an effect on other LPs, thus they affect the synchronisation between LPs. Other events that change component-based state variables are internal to an LP.

3.2 Parallelisation and Synchronisation of Logical Processes

3.2.1 Parallelisation

To parallelise the simulation, the road network is decomposed into multiple spatial subregions, i.e., partitions. The network is divided by cutting links. Links that are cut and therefore lie in two partitions are named *boundary links*. A boundary link is evenly divided between two partitions.

An LP is responsible for executing the events for the agents (e.g., moving the agent along a link) in one subregion. An agent is *local* to an LP if it is inside the subregion that belongs to the LP.

There are data read and write dependencies between neighbouring LPs. During the simulation, when an agent moves beyond the boundary of partition i and enters the area of partition j $(i = j)$, the agent *migrates* from LP_i to LP_j. The migration of agents incurs a data *write dependency* between the two LPs. Migrated agents are destroyed in the original LP and recreated with all their state variables in the new LP. If there is an agent A in LP_i inside the sensing range of another agent B in LP_j, agent B should be aware of the agent-based state variables of agent A. To achieve this, a *proxy agent* is created in LP_j that mirrors agent A. It possesses exactly the same agent-based state variables as agent A. Hence, the agent-based state variables of agent A

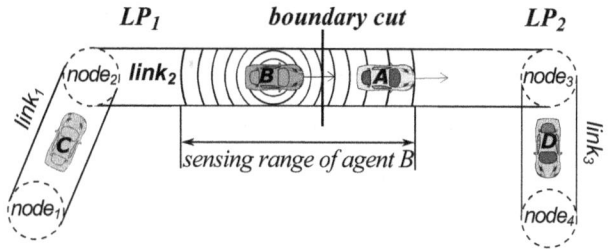

Figure 1: Road network partitioning with boundary cut on $link_2$**.**

should be sent by LP_i to LP_j to keep the state of the proxy agent updated. In this case, there is a data *read dependency* between LP_i and LP_j. The agent-based state variables of agent A are *shared states*.

An illustration of the above concepts is shown in Figure 1. $Link_2$ is a boundary link between LP_1 and LP_2. Agent A in LP_2 is inside the sensing range of agent B in LP_1, hence, the agent-based state variables of agent A are shared states. There is a proxy of agent A in LP_1. If agent B migrates into LP_2, the whole agent B, including all state variables and model parameters should be sent to LP_2 by LP_1. Agent B will be destroyed in LP_1 and recreated in LP_2. There are read and write dependencies between LP_1 and LP_2.

3.2.2 Synchronisation

Data read and write dependencies necessitate the communication between LPs. An LP should not progress the simulation over the point when a read or write dependency happens until the dependency is fulfilled by exchanging messages with the relevant LPs. In our use-case, *synchronisation* is the sending and receiving of migrating agents and shared states. We adopt a conservative approach where no violations of dependencies may ever occur during the simulation. The synchronisation between LPs is carried out using a Mutual Appointment (MA) protocol [26], which we will now briefly describe.

The progression of the simulation in LP_i using the MA protocol is shown in Algorithm 1. The simulation iteratively executes a synchronisation event and an update event for every update interval. Associated with each synchronisation event, there is a set of LPs that currently have appointments with LP_i, denoted as Syn_i^t. Syn_i^t may include all, none, or only a subset of the neighbouring LPs of LP_i. For each LP_j in the set Syn_i^t, LP_i sends one compound message containing migrating agents, shared states and lookahead. *Lookahead* of LP_i towards LP_j $(i = j)$ at simulation time t is a time interval in the simulated future within which LP_i will not have data dependencies with LP_j. LPs estimate their lookahead by predicting when there will be agents to migrate and states to be shared. When Syn_i^t is empty, no message-passing occurs for LP_i at time t. After messages are received, the next appointment is made according to the lookahead, by adding the LP to the future $Syn_i^{t+\Delta t}$ set, where Δt is the mutual lookahead.

Using the MA synchronisation protocol, the number of synchronisation messages is affected by the number of neighbouring partitions and lookahead. Communication data volume is determined by the number of migrating agents and shared states. Sending synchronisation messages requires a

---

Algorithm 1: Simulation progression in LP_i using the MA protocol.

1 Definitions:
2 $l_{i,j}^t$ lookahead from LP_i to LP_j at simulation time t
3 Syn_i^t LPs having appointments with LP_i at time t
4 T_{end} simulation ending time
5 δ update interval

6 initialise $t \leftarrow 0$;
7 initialise Syn_i^0 as all neighbouring LPs of LP_i;
8 **while** $t < T_{end}$ **do**
    `// synchronisation event`
9   **foreach** $LP_j \in Syn_i^t$ **do**
10   send migrating agents, shared states, and current lookahead (i.e., $l_{i,j}^t$) to LP_j;
11   prepare to receive a message from LP_j;
12   **end**
13   wait for all message sending and receiving to finish;
14   update the local agent set and proxy agent set;
15   **foreach** $LP_j \in Syn_i^t$ **do**
16   add LP_j to $Syn_i^{t+\Delta t}$, where $\Delta t = \min(l_{i,j}^t, l_{j,i}^t)$;
17   **end**
    `// event for updating agent-based states`
18   update the states of local agents for this update interval;
19 $t \leftarrow t + \delta$; `// time-stamp of the update event`
20 end

---

start-up time and a transmission time. More synchronisation messages will require more start-up time, and a larger data volume means longer transmission time. Therefore, synchronisation overhead should consider both the number of messages and communication data volume.

3.2.3 Dynamic load-balancing

In addition, workload imbalance also affects the performance of parallel simulation in a distributed memory environment. Workload refers to the processing of the agent events. A workload imbalance can occur if some LPs are responsible for more agents (namely, the events of the agents) than others, which in turn leads to idle waiting times at the synchronisation stage of the simulation. The way the road network is partitioned has a considerable influence on both synchronisation overhead and workload distribution. Thus, the deployed partitioning algorithm plays an essential role in the performance of parallel agent-based road traffic simulation.

Often, the workload of LPs changes in traffic simulation as new agents are created and agents migrate between LPs. This necessitates dynamic load-balancing during the simulation, which can be achieved either by completely reapplying the partitioning algorithm to partition the simulation, or by incrementally changing the shapes of partitions (i.e., diffusive methods) [19].

The problem of dynamic load-balancing is a challenge on its own and it involves additional considerations such as workload exchange and initiation rules for load-balancing operations [2]. In this paper, we focus on the partitioning problem, meaning should dynamic load-balancing be required, we reapply the partitioning algorithm to partition the road network.

3.3 Partitioning Problem

3.3.1 Preprocessing

To use a graph partitioning algorithm, the road network needs to be converted to a weighted graph $G=(E, V)$ first, where E and V are the sets of edges and vertices, respectively. One node in the road network is mapped to one vertex in the graph. The links between two nodes in the road network are mapped to one edge between two vertices. After the graph is decomposed, the partitions are then mapped back to the road network.

Each link in the road network has some workload information and data dependency information, e.g., based on the expected traffic density and flow, or the length and the number of lanes. Based on this, we add weight to vertices and edges of the graph. Edges have weights which encode the communication data volume due to data dependencies, if the the edges are cut. Traffic density and traffic flow on their corresponding links in the road network can be used for calculating the weights. Vertices have weights which encode the workload on the connecting links of their corresponding nodes. Traffic density on the links in the road network can be used for calculating the weights. For a more detailed explanation of the pre-processing steps, we refer readers to [25].

When repartitioning is required during the simulation due to dynamic workload, weights of vertices and edges are recalculated using run-time traffic density and flow information on the road network.

3.3.2 Partitioning as an optimisation problem

A graph partitioning algorithm cuts G into I disjoint partitions, $\mathcal{G} = \{G_0, G_1, ..., G_{I-1}\}$. Edges of the weighted graph are cut. Let the set of vertices in partition G_i ($0 \leq i < I$) be V_i, then $V = \bigcup_{i=0}^{I-1} V_i$ and $V_i \cap V_j = \varnothing$ ($0 \leq j < I, i \neq j$). In order to increase the performance of the parallel simulation, we consider the following three optimisation objectives during the partitioning process:

The first objective is to minimise workload imbalance. Let W_i be the total weight of the vertices in V_i. Then, the first objective can be formulated as:

$$Obj_1 = \arg \min_{\mathcal{G}} \left(\max_{0 \leq i < I}(W_i) - \overline{W} \right) \qquad (1)$$

where $\overline{W}$ is the average weight of all partitions.

The second objective is to minimise the total number of neighbouring partitions. To the best of our knowledge, this requirement has not yet been considered in other graph partitioning algorithms for traffic simulation. We minimise the number of neighbouring partitions to reduce the synchronisation overhead in road traffic simulation. Let $N=(n_{i,j})$, $0 \leq i < I, 0 \leq j < I$, be a matrix of connectivity of partitions. If G_i and G_j are neighbours, $n_{i,j}=1$. Otherwise, $n_{i,j}=0$. The, the second objective can be formulated as:

$$Obj_2 = \arg \min_{\mathcal{G}} \left(\sum_{i=0}^{I-2} \sum_{j=i+1}^{I-1} n_{i,j} \right) \qquad (2)$$

The third objective is to minimise edge cut which is the total weight of edges between all partitions. Let the weight of all edges between partition G_i and G_j be $W_{i,j}$ ($i \neq j$).

Then, the third objective is formulated as:

$$Obj_3 = \arg\min_{\mathcal{G}} \Big(\sum_{i=0}^{I-2} \sum_{j=i+1}^{I-1} W_{i,j} \Big) \qquad (3)$$

Since the optimisation problem is multi-objective and NP-hard, finding the optimal solution may be impractical. A common approach is to use heuristics to obtain a reasonably good result.

4. NEIGHBOUR-RESTRICTING PARTITIONING

We now present the main contribution of this paper, which is the graph partitioning algorithm NRGG, short for, Neighbour-Restricting Graph-Growing. It contains an initial partitioning phase and a refinement phase. The initial partitioning phase cuts the road network, trying to achieve Obj_1 and Obj_2. The refinement phase tries to achieve Obj_3, as well as improve Obj_1 if Obj_1 achieved in the initial partitioning phase is unsatisfactory, e.g., an imbalance threshold is exceeded.

4.1 Graph-grow Partitioning

4.1.1 Graph-growing algorithm

The graph generated from the road network is first partitioned by graph-growing. Starting from an initial vertex, subgraphs are grown one by one along the edges of the graph. It can be easily proven that for a 2D space, cutting the space into stripes generates the smallest number of neighbouring partitions. In order to limit the number of neighbouring partitions, we apply this idea for partitioning a graph, i.e., generate stripe-like partitions.

The graph-growing algorithm is shown in Algorithm 2. The first step is to select an initial vertex for graph-growing. The initial vertex should be an extreme point of the graph, so it is the furthest vertex along the graph-grow direction. It can be determined using the geographical coordinates of the vertex.

Then, the second step is to grow graphs starting from the initial vertex. A *priority queue* is used to control the order of vertices to be visited. The initial vertex is pushed into the priority queue (line 13) and marked as *enqueued* (line 14). Then, vertices are iteratively popped from the front of the queue (line 16). Based on the cumulative weight and the current vertex weight, it is determined whether a new partition should be initiated (lines 17 - 24). If the number of already generated partitions does not exceed the targeted total number ($i < I$), a new partition is initiated under two conditions (line 18):

1. the accumulated weight of vertices is equal to or greater than the average weight; or

2. the accumulated weight plus the weight of the current vertex is greater than the average weight, and a randomly generated number in the range $[0, 1]$ is less than 0.5 (the exact average weight cannot be achieved, thus the current vertex is assigned randomly to either the current or a new partition, i.e., a new partition is initiated with a probability of 0.5 in this case).

Then, the current or the new partition id i is assigned to the vertex (line 25). All adjacent vertices of the current

---

Algorithm 2: Partitioning a weighted graph into I partitions with graph-growing.

1 Definitions:
2 i id of the partition
3 I total number of partitions
4 W_i total weight of vertices in the partition G_i
5 $\overline{W}$ average total weight of vertices per partition
6 $\widetilde{W}$ cumulative weight of the current partition i
7 w_v weight of vertex v in the graph
8 Q priority queue in which the tuples are ordered
9   according to the partition the vertices connect to
10   and the coordinates of the vertices

11 initialise $i \leftarrow 0$, $\widetilde{W} \leftarrow 0$, $Q \leftarrow \varnothing$;
12 determine the initial vertex v_{init} for graph-growing;
13 push tuple (i, v_{init}) into Q;
14 mark v_{init} as *enqueued* ;
15 **while** Q *is not empty* **do**
16   pop a tuple from Q, and let the vertex be v;
17   generate a random double number rdm in the range $[0,1]$;
18   **if** $(\widetilde{W} \geq \overline{W} \lor (\widetilde{W} + w_v > \overline{W} \land rdm < 0.5)) \land i < I - 1$ **then**
19 $W_i \leftarrow \widetilde{W}$; // new partition is initiated
20 $\widetilde{W} \leftarrow w_v$;
21 $i \leftarrow i + 1$;
22   **else**
23 $\widetilde{W} \leftarrow \widetilde{W} + w_v$;
24   **end**
25   assign vertex v to the ith partition;
26   **foreach** *vertex u, where $e(u, v) \in E$* **do**
27   **if** *u has not been enqueued before* **then**
28   push tuple (i, u) into Q; // sorted
29   mark u as *enqueued*;
30   **end**
31   **end**
32 **end**

---

vertex that have not been enqueued before are pushed to the queue and marked as enqueued (lines 26 - 31). A vertex is enqueued together with partition id i, forming a *tuple* (lines 13 and 28). Partition id i in the tuple marks that the vertex being enqueued has an adjacent vertex that has already been assigned to partition i. This information is used to reduce neighbouring partitions (details will be explained later in this section).

Graph-growing terminates when every vertex is assigned a partition id. Graph-growing can reach all vertices, because the weighted graph is a connected graph. The complexity of this graph-growing algorithm is $O(|E| + |V| \cdot \log_2 |Q|)$, where $|E|$ and $|V|$ are the number of edges and vertices in the graph respectively, and $|Q|$ is the average queue length. Each edge or vertex is visited exactly once, so traversing the graph takes $O(|E| + |V|)$ time. The time for sorting the priority queue can be achieved in $O(\log_2 |Q|)$ whenever a tuple is pushed, thus the total time for sorting is $O(|V| \cdot \log_2 |Q|)$. Due to the low time complexity, heuristics to decrease the size of the graph for reducing the partitioning time, such as multi-level coarsening [9], are not required.

4.1.2 Sorting rules of vertices during graph-growing

The essence of graph-growing lies in sorting the vertices in the priority queue. Each item in the priority queue is in fact a tuple (i, v) consisting of the partition id a vertex is assigned to and the vertex itself. The vertices are sorted primarily according to the partition ids marked in their tuples and secondarily according to their coordinates. Rules for comparing vertices are as follows: for two tuples (i, v_a) and (j, v_b), (i, v_a) ranks in front of (j, v_b) in the queue, if

1. $i < j$; or

2. $i = j$ and $|v_a.crd - v_{init}.crd| < |v_b.crd - v_{init}.crd|$, where $v_x.crd$ is the coordinate of vertex v_x along the graph-grow direction and v_{init} is the initial vertex; or

3. $i = j$ and $|v_a.crd - v_{init}.crd| = |v_b.crd - v_{init}.crd|$ and $v_a.\lambda < v_b.\lambda$, where $v_x.\lambda$ is another attribute of vertex v_x that can break the tie between the two vertices.

The first rule has a direct effect on the number of neighbouring partitions: According to Algorithm 2, when the $(i+1)$th partition is initiated, there exists a set of vertices in the queue marked with tuple partition ids equal to (or less than) i. These vertices are adjacent to the vertices at the boundary of the previous partition (or partitions). They will be ranked higher than any vertices pushed later to the queue, namely, vertices whose adjacent vertices are in the previous partitions are popped first and grouped into as few partitions as possible.

The second rule sorts vertices by their coordinates if they have the same associated partition id in tuples. Vertices that are closer to the initial vertex along the graph-grow direction are ranked higher. The graph-grow direction, as the name indicates, is a general line along which partitions expand. The use of one-dimensional distances along this line leads to stripe-like shaped partitions. For example, if *coord* is the coordinate in the horizontal direction, resulting partitions are positioned generally next to each other along the horizontal direction.

The third rule states another customisable rule in order to deterministically sort two vertices if they have equal partition ids and coordinates. For instance, it can be the degree or the id of the vertices.

4.1.3 Comparison with stripe spatial partitioning

The presented graph-growing algorithm is different from simply cutting the graph directly into stripes. A comparison is shown in Figure 2, where a small graph is partitioned into three partitions. Each partition contains two vertices.

Figure 2(a) shows the result when applying the proposed graph-growing algorithm. Vertex 1 is the initial vertex. We assume the cutting direction to be horizontal from left to right, i.e., vertices further left rank higher than those on the right side. Hence, the vertex visiting order of our algorithm is 1, 2, 5, 4, 6, and 3. In Figure 2(b), the graph is simply cut into three partitions vertically. This straightforward approach leads to the situation where the leftmost and rightmost partitions also become neighbouring partitions due to the long edge $e(1, 4)$. This is undesirable as it would introduce additional data dependencies between the partitions. For a larger and more complex road networks, the edges in the graph may considerably differ in lengths (e.g., expressways versus smaller roads). Simply cutting the

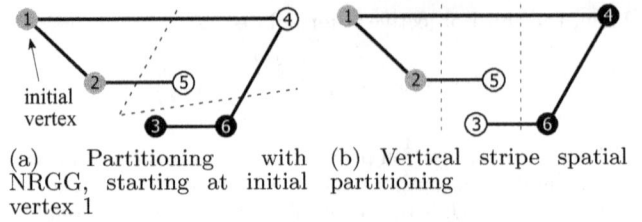

(a) Partitioning with NRGG, starting at initial vertex 1 (b) Vertical stripe spatial partitioning

Figure 2: Comparison of the proposed partitioning algorithm with stripe spatial partitioning, where a simple graph is divided into three partitions (assuming vertices have equal weights).

graph into stripes can therefore lead to a higher number of neighbouring partitions.

4.2 Refinement with Local Search

After the initial partitioning, partitions are refined in order to reduce edge cut (i.e., Obj_3), as well as to alleviate workload imbalance in case there is severe imbalance.

We propose a local search refinement heuristic similar to Karypis and Kumar's boundary refinement heuristic [8], which is a variation of the original heuristic of Kernighan and Lin [10]. A distinct feature of our proposed local search refinement heuristic is to restrict neighbouring partitions. The procedure is described below.

4.2.1 Gains of moving vertices

First, the *internal costs* and *external costs* of the vertices at the boundaries of partitions are calculated using the weights of the connected edges. For a vertex v in partition G_i, its *internal cost* is the total weight of all edges that connect vertex v and its adjacent vertices in the same partition. Let S_v be the set of adjacent vertices of v in the same partition G_i. Then, the interval cost can be calculated as:

$$I_v = \sum_{u \in S_i} w_{e(v,u)} \qquad (4)$$

where $w_{e(v,u)}$ is the weight of edge $e(v, u)$.

The *external cost* of vertex v towards partition G_j (assuming G_i and G_j are neighbouring partitions) is the total weight of the edges connecting v and its adjacent vertices in partition G_j. Let $S_v^{(j)}$ be set of adjacent vertices of v in partition G_i. Then, the external cost is calculated as:

$$E_v^{(j)} = \sum_{k \in S_v^{(j)}} w_{e(v,k)} \qquad (5)$$

A vertex can have only one internal cost, but multiple external costs if it has adjacent vertices in more than one neighbouring partitions. The external cost indicates the data volume of communication between neighbouring LPs. Therefore, the external costs of vertices should be reduced in the refinement phase.

The *gain* of moving a vertex from one partition to another is calculated according to the costs. It is the reduction of total external costs if a vertex is *moved*. To move a vertex means to change the partition id assigned to it. The gain of moving a vertex v from G_i to G_j is the difference between its external cost towards G_j and its internal cost, that is,

$$gain_v^{i \to j} = E_v^{(j)} - I_v \qquad (6)$$

When $E_v^{(j)} > I_v$, $gain_v^{i \to j} > 0$, moving vertex v from G_i to G_j can reduce the total external cost (i.e., the total weight of cut edges). However, if $E_v^{(j)} < I_v$ the gain will be negative. Gains are computed for each potential partition a vertex could be moved to.

4.2.2 Moving rules

After the gains of boundary vertices are computed, the vertices are examined for moving from their current partitions to neighbouring partitions. The order of examination is from the higher gains to the lower gains. A vertex v will be moved from its origin partition G_i to a neighbouring partition G_j in two cases: i) when the external cost can be reduced; and ii) when there is severe weight imbalance that needs to be alleviated. The first case needs to satisfy all the following criteria:

1. $gain_v^{i \to j} > 0$

2. $W_i > W_{min}$ after v is moved, where W_{min} is the minimum weight an LP must contain, that is, the weight of the origin partition is above a low threshold after moving the vertex, for example, $W_{min} = 0.9 \cdot \overline{W}$

3. $W_j < W_{max}$ after v is moved, where W_{max} is the maximum weight an LP can contain, that is, the weight of the target partition is below an upper threshold after moving the vertex, for example, $W_{max} = 1.1 \cdot \overline{W}$

4. k, l such that if $n_{i,k}=0$ and $n_{j,l}=0$ (i, j, k, l being four partition ids, and $n_{i,j}$ the indicator whether i and j are neighbours), then $n_{i,k}$ and $n_{j,l}$ have to remain 0 after v is moved, that is, moving vertex v does not create new neighbouring partitions

The second case needs to satisfy all the following criteria:

1. $W_i > W_{max}$ before the move, that is, the weight of the origin partition has exceeded an upper threshold

2. $W_j < W_i$ after v is moved, that is, the move is only from a partition with more weights to another partition with less weights

3. $w_v > 0$

4. k, l such that if $n_{i,k}=0$ and $n_{j,l}=0$, $n_{i,k}$ and $n_{j,l}$ remain to be 0 if v is moved (in line with the fourth criterion in the first case)

The fourth criterion in both cases is a neighbour-restricting constraint, which is illustrated with an example in Figure 3. G_2 is a neighbouring partition of both G_1 and G_3. Vertices 1 and 2 in G_2 have external costs with both other partitions. However, it is forbidden to move either of them to G_1 or G_3 according to the neighbour-restricting constraint, because G_1 and G_3 are not neighbouring partitions. Moving vertex 1 or 2, however, would make G_1 or G_3 neighbours.

Whenever a vertex is moved, its internal cost and external costs are updated, as well as the costs of its adjacent vertices. A *pass* of refinement is finished when all boundary vertices are examined for moving. At the end of each pass, the boundary vertex set is updated. Then, a new pass begins. This process repeats until there is no vertex movement in a pass or the number of passes has reached a pre-defined maximum value. The complexity of the refinement phase is $O(B \cdot \log_2 B \cdot P)$ where B is the number of boundary vertices and P is the maximum number of passes. The factor $\log_2 B$ is for sorting the vertices according to their gains.

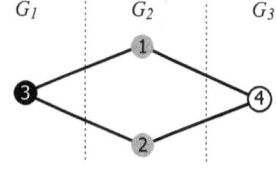

Figure 3: A simple graph in three partitions. Due to the neighbour-restricting constraint, vertices 1 and 2 are not allowed to be moved to G_1 or G_3.

5. EXPERIMENTS

The performance of the proposed partitioning algorithm was investigated in a parallel agent-based traffic simulation, *double-blinded* [24]. The simulation is implemented using C++. The communication between LPs is realised using OpenMPI. Comparison with stripe spatial partitioning, and graph partitioning methods, i.e, METIS [9] and Buffoon [18] is performed. We compare our algorithm, denoted as *NRGG*, to stripe spatial partitioning (denoted as *Stripe*), to METIS partitioning (denoted as *METIS*) and to Buffoon partitioning (denoted as *Buffoon*). Parameter settings of METIS and Buffoon are the default values provided in their software packages. Since the simulation involves stochastic elements, the simulation was run multiple times for each method.

5.1 Simulation Configuration

5.1.1 Data and models

The data used in the experiments is based on real-world data, including the road network and origin-destination matrix of agents. The experiment scenario is set up as follows: The road network is the network of Singapore city that consists of approximately 43,000 nodes and 84,000 links in our representation. The origin-destination matrix of agents is derived from the data of the 2008 Household Interview and Travel Survey (HITS). Agents move according to the intelligent driver car-following model [21] and a simple rule-based lane-changing model. The traffic of 19 hours from 5am to midnight of one day is simulated. The maximum number of agents during the peak traffic hours of the day is approximately 73,000.

5.1.2 Partitioning and dynamic load-balancing settings

We use run-time dynamic partitioning to achieve dynamic load-balancing. Workload of LPs is examined periodically every 10 minutes of simulation time. When the imbalance exceeds 500 agents (value obtained from our previous work in [25]) the road network is repartitioned by a partitioning algorithm, including recalculation of vertex and edge weights. After that, agents are re-distributed to their new partitions.

To partially solve the problem that the choice of initial vertex for graph-growing affects the partitioning result, we run the proposed partitioning algorithm twice concurrently by two LPs using two different initial vertices. One is the vertex furthest to the east, and the other is the vertex furthest to the west. The partitioning result with less edge cut is chosen as the final result.

In the refinement phase, the workload thresholds for moving vertices, W_{min} and W_{max}, are $0.9 \cdot \overline{W}$ and $1.02 \cdot \overline{W}$, re-

(a) Partitioning result using NRGG

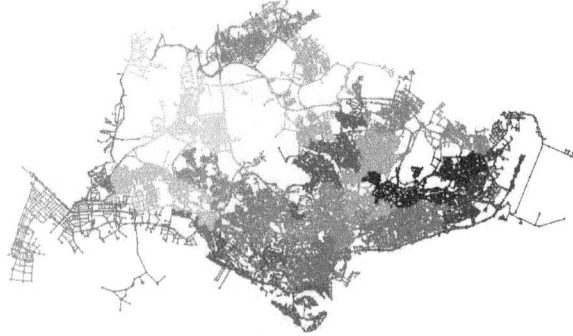

(b) Partitioning result using METIS

Figure 4: Partitioning of the Singapore road network into 16 partitions.

spectively. A maximum of 8 refinement passes are allowed, based on the observation that additional passes did not lead to significant improvement on edge cut.

5.1.3 Hardware

The experiments were run on a cluster consisting of three compute nodes each of which has the following hardware configurations: two *Octacore Intel(R) Xeon(R)* CPUs with 2.60 GHz clock frequency (i.e., 16 physical processors), and 192 GB RAM. The compute nodes are connected via 56 Gbps InfiniBand. Each LP in a parallel simulation is bonded to one physical CPU core.

5.2 Results

A visual representation of the difference between our algorithm and METIS is given in Figure 4. The road network of Singapore is divided into 16 partitions. Different colours represent different partitions. Stripe and Buffoon are not shown since they generate similar shapes as NRGG and METIS, respectively.

As expected, the partitions generated from NRGG (Figure 4(a)) are in roughly striped shapes with saw-toothed boundaries, because the vertices are sorted by their longitudes, whereas METIS (and Buffoon) create more irregular shapes (Figure 4(b)).

5.2.1 Workload Imbalance

The first indicator of the quality of partitioning algorithms is the workload imbalance of the simulation. We measure the imbalance with the number of agents assigned to the LPs, since every agent has roughly the same computational workload. The imbalance was captured every 4 seconds of simulation time. The average for the entire simulation is

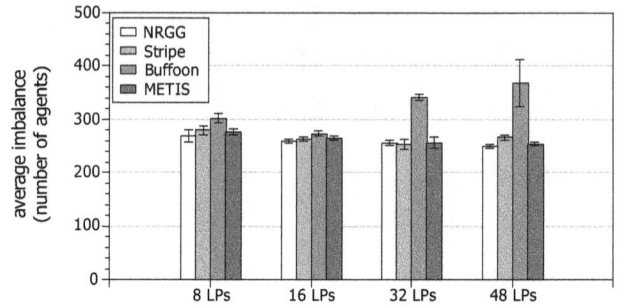

Figure 5: Average load imbalance per update interval in terms of number of agents. Smaller is better.

shown in Figure 5. We observe that all partitioning methods have achieved similar balancing results, except Buffoon that has a higher imbalance with 32 and 48 LPs. The reason is that the workload change of LPs is more severe for partitions generated by Buffoon. The load-balancing operation was also triggered more often using Buffoon as a result of a more dynamic workload, as shown in Table 1.

5.2.2 Synchronisation Messages

The second indicator is the number of messages sent throughout the simulation. The average number of neighbouring partitions per partition and the total number of synchronisation messages are shown in Figure 6.

We can observe from Figure 6(a) that the average number of neighbouring partitions increases as the number of LPs increases for all partitioning methods. NRGG has generated the smallest average number of neighbouring partitions. Stripe has a similar result for 8 LPs, but not 16 and 32 LPs. The reason is that when a spatial graph is cut into a large number of partitions using Stripe, long edges tend to span further than two partitions and lead to more neighbouring partitions (see Figure 2(b)). Thus, we conclude that NRGG is more resilient than Stripe when partitions are cut more finely. Buffoon and METIS generate a much larger number of neighbouring partitions, because they do not consider the minimisation of the number of neighbouring partitions.

Consequently, NRGG is able to keep the number of messages the lowest in all the cases above, as shown in Figure 6(b). Using Buffoon and METIS, we observe a considerable higher number of synchronisation messages, resulting from the larger number of neighbouring partitions. Looking at the lookaheads of LPs, we observe that Buffoon and METIS have around 40 percent larger lookahead than NRGG and Stripe. This is an advantage because larger lookahead leads to fewer synchronisation messages. The larger lookahead is a result of fewer boundary links between partitions, which generate less data dependencies. However, this larger lookahead did not compensate the disadvantage of the larger number of neighbouring partitions.

5.2.3 Communication Data Volume

The third indicator for the quality of partitioning algorithms is the communication data volume. It is quantified using the number of migrated agents and the number of shared states. The results are shown in Figure 7. Smaller values mean lower transmission time for synchronisation messages.

It can be observed from Figure 7(a) that NRGG has a

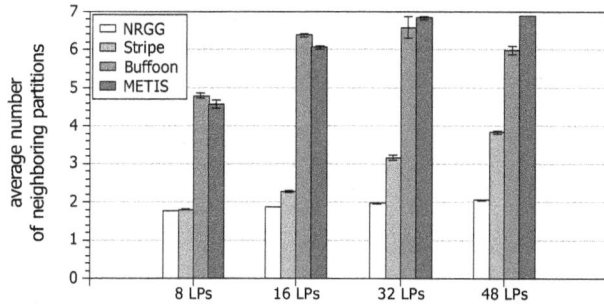

(a) Average number of neighbouring partitions

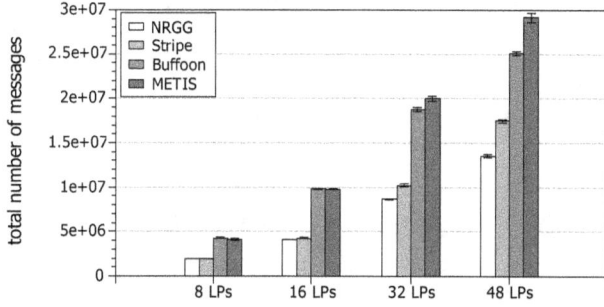

(b) Total number of exchanged messages between LPs

Figure 6: Statistics on synchronisation overhead between LPs. Smaller values are better.

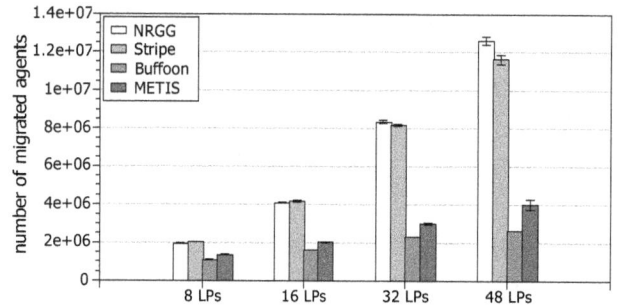

(a) Total number of migrated agents

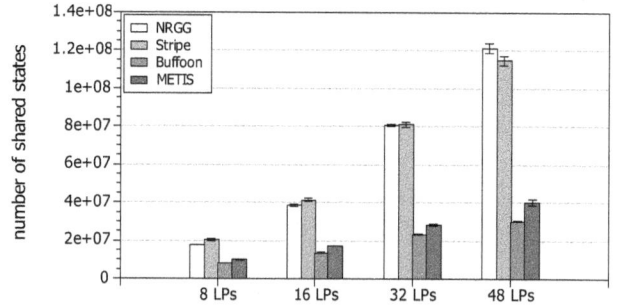

(b) Total number of shared states

Figure 7: Indicators of communication data volume, smaller is better.

considerably larger number of migrated agents and shared states than METIS and Buffoon. This is because edge cut is not minimised in the initial partitioning phase, and the local search refinement can only reduce edge cut to a certain extent. Buffoon leads to the lowest number of migrated agents and shared states in all cases, which shows that the natural cut heuristic improves the quality of edge cut in partitioning road networks. Stripe performs similar to NRGG. In the cases of 32 and 48 LPs, NRGG is slightly worse than Stripe, which shows that to restrict neighbouring partitions may sacrifice some edge cut quality.

We also investigated the possibility of using multi-level refinement to increase the search space of local search. It can reduce the number of migrated agents and shared states by approximately 10 percent when using 8 LPs. However, for a higher numbers of LPs, no obvious improvement was observed. The reason may be that for a large number of partitions, the search space cannot be increased by the multi-level approach, and the neighbour-restricting constraint limits the search space. Hence, multi-level refinement can be considered for a small number of partitions to reduce communication data volume.

In conclusion, it can be observed that NRGG trades a higher number of migrated agents and shared states to achieve a considerably lower number of neighbouring partitions and synchronisation messages. Whether this improves the overall performance of the parallel simulation compared to other algorithms depends on which indicator plays a more important role in the synchronisation overhead. The execution time of the simulation using the various partitioning methods will be presented later in this section.

5.2.4 Partitioning Overhead

The total overhead of partitioning using the partitioning methods are shown in Table 1. Results of multiple runs were recorded and the averages were taken.

Table 1 shows that the overhead of NRGG partitioning is almost negligible compared to the total execution time of the simulation, which is shown in Figure 8a. The overhead of NRGG is less than 0.5 percent for all LP configurations. This results from its low complexity. Low overhead also applies to Stripe and METIS. Stripe takes the least time since only one traverse of the vertices is needed for partitioning. The overhead of Buffoon is higher than other three methods, however, Buffoon partitioning generated the lowest edge cut. The large overhead is a result of the more complex coarsening and partitioning algorithms in Buffoon.

Table 1: Dynamic load-balancing count and total overheads of the partitioning algorithms in dynamic load-balancing.

	8 LPs	16 LPs	32 LPs	48 LPs
NRGG count	48±2	41±1	30±2	25±2
Time (s)	4.42±0.16	4.94±0.18	5.00±0.27	4.02±0.02
Stripe count	47±1	40±2	31±2	28±2
Time (s)	1.20±0.07	1.33±0.04	1.23±0.07	1.20±0.07
Buffoon count	53±3	42±2	43±5	62±3
Time (s)	91.9±2.38	94.3±3.48	185.1±11.0	421.4±25.0
METIS count	47±2	41±1	31±3	27±1
Time (s)	4.57±0.62	6.25±0.23	4.21±0.54	3.9±0.2

5.2.5 Overall Execution Time of the Simulation

The overall execution time of the parallel simulation is shown in Figure 8a. The execution time of the sequential simulation is around 9,000 seconds. The speed-up of parallel simulation relative the sequential simulation is shown in Figure 8b.

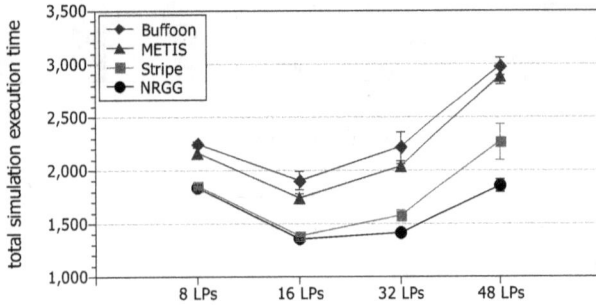

(a) Execution time of the simulation using various partitioning methods (lower is better)

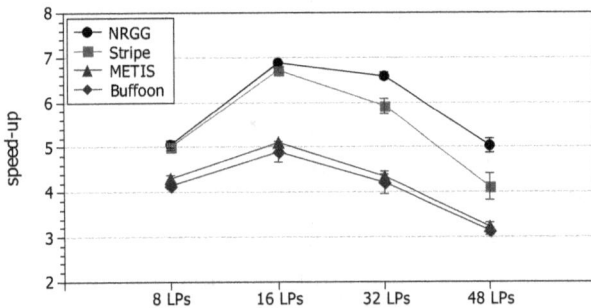

(b) Speed-up of the simulation using various partitioning methods relative to the sequential simulation

Figure 8: Overall execution time and speed-up of the simulation using various partitioning methods.

Figures 8a and 8b show that the simulation using NRGG always provides the lowest execution time and thus the best speed-up. With 8 and 16 LPs, Stripe has similar performance as NRGG. This is because Stripe is able to generate comparable neighbouring partitions as NRGG with such a small number of LPs. However, with 32 and 48 LPs, the performance of Stripe degrades faster due to the increasing number of neighbouring partitions generated by Stripe (see Figure 6(b)). Thus, NRGG has much better resilience than Stripe based on our experiment.

In our simulated road network, Buffoon had the longest execution time. Taking 16 LPs as an example, it spends approximately 40 percent more time than NRGG and 9 percent more than METIS. According to the figures of load imbalance and synchronisation overhead indicators, Buffoon should have similar performance as METIS. However, longer execution time is incurred because of its much higher overhead for dynamic partitioning (see Table 1).

5.2.6 Discussion

The performance of a parallel simulation depends on many factors: load balance, number of synchronisation messages, and data volume of communication. Compared to the existing methods, we have shown that for conventional microscopic agent-based traffic simulation, NRGG improves the overall performance of the simulation by considering the objective of reducing the number of neighbouring partitions. This demonstrates that general graph partition algorithms may not work best in some parallel applications.

NRGG emphasizes more on minimising the number of neighbouring partitions than minimising edge cut. However, there is a trade-off between the two objectives. In a setting where communication data volume plays a more critical role in the synchronisation overhead than the number of messages, METIS and Buffoon may provide better performance. One example for such a setting is that the increased communication data volume using NRGG may activate the rendezvous protocol of MPI, thereby tremendously increasing the synchronisation overhead. In addition, depending on the synchronisation protocol, the number of synchronisation messages may not be heavily affected by the number of neighbouring partitions. In these cases, NRGG may not achieve the best performance. For our microscopic agent-based traffic simulation, however, NRGG has been shown to outperform the existing approaches.

6. CONCLUSION AND FUTURE WORK

We have proposed Neighbour-restricting Graph-Growing (NRGG), a graph partitioning algorithm for reducing the total execution time of parallel agent-based road traffic simulation. In addition to minimising the imbalance of partitions and minimising edge cut, NRGG particularity focuses on reducing the number of neighbouring partitions. It makes use of a graph-growing algorithm, followed by a modified KL local search refinement algorithm. The essence of the proposed algorithm is that it tries to constrain the number of neighbouring partitions of each partition in both the graph-growing phase and the refinement phase, guided by both connectivity information and the geographical information of the road network. Our approach is able to considerably reduce the number of synchronisation messages. Experiments using our parallel agent-based traffic simulation have shown that NRGG outperforms stripe spatial partitioning and both the popular graph partitioning methods, METIS and Buffoon.

Future work can be conducted from the following aspects: i) for different settings of traffic simulation and for other types of parallel applications, the trade-off between the three objectives can be tuned for optimised performance, depending on their respective significance; and ii) for dynamic load-balancing, neighbour-restricting diffusion can be investigated, where partitions incrementally change their shapes instead of repartitioning.

7. ACKNOWLEDGEMENTS

This work was financially supported by the Singapore National Research Foundation under its Campus for Research Excellence And Technological Enterprise (CREATE) programme.

8. REFERENCES

[1] M. J. Berger and S. H. Bokhari. A Partitioning Strategy for Nonuniform Problems on Multiprocessors. *IEEE Transactions on Computers*, C-36(5):570–580, May 1987.

[2] A. Boukerche and S. K. Das. Dynamic Load Balancing Strategies for Conservative Parallel Simulations. In

Proceedings of the 11th Workshop on Parallel and Distributed Simulation, pages 20–28, Austria, June 10 - 13, 1997.

[3] D. Delling, A. V. Goldberg, I. Razenshteyn, and R. F. Werneck. Graph Partitioning with Natural Cuts. In *Proceedings of the 25th IEEE International Parallel and Distributed Processing Symposium (IPDPS 2011)*, pages 1135–1146, Anchorage, AK, USA, May 2011.

[4] R. M. Fujimoto. *Parallel and Distributed Simulation Systems*. Wiley Interscience, December 1999.

[5] P. G. Gipps. A behavioural car-following model for computer simulation. *Transportation Research Part B: Methodological*, 15(2):105–111, April 1981.

[6] P. G. Gipps. A model for the structure of lane-changing decisions. *Transportation Research Part B: Methodological*, 20(5):403–414, October 1986.

[7] B. Hendrickson and T. G. Kolda. Graph partitioning models for parallel computing. *Parallel Computing*, 26(12):1519–1534, Nov. 2000.

[8] G. Karypis and V. Kumar. A fast and high quality multilevel scheme for partitioning irregular graphs. *SIAM Journal on Scientific Computing*, 20(1):359–392, Jan. 1998.

[9] G. Karypis and V. Kumar. Multilevel k-way partitioning scheme for irregular graphs. *Journal of Parallel and Distributed Computing*, 48(1):96–129, January 1998.

[10] B. W. Kernighan and S. Lin. An efficient heuristic procedure for partitioning graphs. *The Bell system technical journal*, 49(1):291–307, February 1970.

[11] A. Kesting, M. Treiber, and D. Helbing. General Lane-Changing model MOBIL for Car-Following Models. *Transportation Research Record: Journal of the Transportation Research Board*, No. 1999(1):86–94, Jan. 2007.

[12] R. Klefstad and Y. Zhang. A distributed, scalable, and synchronized framework for large-scale microscopic traffic simulation. In *Proceedings of the 2005 IEEE Intelligent Transportation Systems Conference (ITSC 2005)*, pages 813–818, Vienna, Austria, September 2005. IEEE.

[13] D.-H. Lee. A Framework for Parallel traffic simulation using multiple instancing of a simulation program. *Journal of Intelligent Transportation Systems*, 7(3):279–294, July 2002.

[14] H. Mizuta, Y. Yamagata, and H. Seya. Large-scale traffic simualtion for Low-Carbon City. In *Proceedings of the 2012 Winter Simulation Conference (WSC'2012)*, pages 1–12, Berlin, Germany, December 2012.

[15] K. Nagel and M. Rickert. Parallel implementation of the TRANSIMS micro-simulation. *Parallel Computing*, 27(12):1611–1639, November 2001.

[16] A. Pothen, H. D. Simon, and K.-P. P. Liu. Partitioning Sparse Matrices with Eigenvectors of Graphs. *SIAM Journal on Matrix Analysis and Applications*, 11(2):430–452, 1990.

[17] T. Potuzak. Distributed/Parallel Genetic Algorithm for Road Traffic Network Division Using a Hybrid Island Model/Step Parallelization Approach. In *Proceedings of the 2016 IEEE/ACM 20th International Symposium on Distributed Simulation and Real Time Applications (DS-RT)*, pages 170–177, London, UK, September 21-23 2016.

[18] P. Sanders and C. Schulz. Distributed Evolutionary Graph Partitioning. In *Meeting on Algorithm Engineering & Experiments (ALENEX '12)*, pages 16–29, Kyoto, Japan, jan 2012.

[19] K. Schloegel, G. Karypis, and V. Kumar. Wavefront diffusion and LMSR: Algorithms for dynamic repartitioning of adaptive meshes. *IEEE Transactions on Parallel and Distributed Systems*, 12(5):451–466, 2001.

[20] T. Suzumura and H. Kanezashi. Highly Scalable X10-Based Agent Simulation Platform and Its Application to Large-Scale Traffic Simulation. In *Proceedings of the 2012 IEEE/ACM 16th International Symposium on Distributed Simulation and Real Time Applications (DS-RT 2012)*, pages 243–250, Dublin, Ireland, October 2012.

[21] M. Treiber, A. Hennecke, and D. Helbing. Congested traffic states in empirical observations and microscopic simulations. *Physical Review E*, 62(2):1805–1824, February 2000.

[22] S. Uppoor and M. Fiore. Large-scale Urban Vehicular Mobility for Networking Research. In *Proceedings of the 3rd IEEE Vehicular Networking Conference (VNC 2011)*, pages 62–69, Amsterdam, Netherlands, November 2011. IEEE.

[23] D. Wei, F. Chen, and X. Sun. An improved road network partition algorithm for parallel microscopic traffic simulation. In *Proceedings of the 2010 International Conference on Mechanic Automation and Control Engineering (MACE)*, pages 2777 – 2782, Wuhan, China, June 2010.

[24] Y. Xu, H. Aydt, and M. Lees. SEMSim: A Distributed Architecture for Multi-scale Traffic Simulation. In *Proceedings of the 26th ACM/IEEE/SCS Workshop on Principles of Advanced and Distributed Simulation (PADS'12)*, pages 178–180, Zhangjiajie, China, July 15-19 2012. IEEE.

[25] Y. Xu, W. Cai, H. Aydt, and M. Lees. Efficient graph-based dynamic load-balancing for parallel large-scale agent-based traffic simulation. In *Proceedings of the 2014 Winter Simulation Conference (WSC'14)*, pages 3483–3494, Savannah, GA, USA, December 2014. IEEE.

[26] Y. Xu, W. Cai, H. Aydt, M. Lees, and D. Zehe. An Asynchronous Synchronization Strategy for Parallel Large-scale Agent-based Traffic Simulations. In *Proceedings of the 3rd ACM SIGSIM Conference on Principles of Advanced Discrete Simulation (PADS'15)*, pages 259–269. ACM, June 2015.

Lightweight WebSIM Rendering Framework Based on Cloud-Baking

Chang Liu
Tongji University
Caoan Highway 4800
Shanghai, China
Nanchang Hangkong University
South Fenghe Road 696
Jiangxi Province, China
lcsszz@163.com

Jinyuan Jia
Tongji University
Caoan Highway 4800
Shanghai, China
jyjia@tongji.edu.cn

Qian Zhang
Shanghai Shinegraph Ltd
Hengtong road 360 Yitianxia Building 23B10
Shanghai, China
zhangqian@shxt3d.com

Lei Zhao
Nanchang Hangkong University
South Fenghe Road 696
Jiangxi Province, China
zhaolei201676@163.com

ABSTRACT

Current cloud rendering systems are expensive in terms of data storage, rendering computation, and networking transmission. In this paper, we propose a novel framework for lightweight and realistic WebSIM rendering based on cloud baking. Different from the existing cloud rendering systems that render full-frame image sequences, we propose that global illumination (GI) maps are baked occasionally at the server side. Our proposed framework consists of three key stages. First, the GI maps are re-baked only when the users change the WebSIM scene or the lighting. Then, after rebaking, these GI maps with indirect illumination are encoded and transferred to the client s web browsers using H.264. Finally, these GI maps are decoded and blended to produce rather realistic illuminating effects with WebGL direct illuminations. Compared with cloud rendering techniques, our system is lightweight, as it consumes much fewer resources at the cloud server in terms of both data and rendering. It provides a highly efficient, high-quality, and low-cost solution to WebSIM online interactive rendering. A prototype has been implemented, and we showed that it is able to achieve real-time rendering performance and satisfactory visual effects on web browsers, similar to popular offline rendering engines.

CCS Concepts

•**Computing methodologies** → **Real-time simulation;** •**Human-centered computing** → **Virtual reality;** •**Information systems** → *Multimedia information systems; Massively multiplayer online games;*

Correspondence Author

SIGSIM-PADS 17, May 24 26, 2017, Singapore, Singapore
© 2017 ACM. ISBN 978-1-4503-4489-0/17/05. . . $15.00
DOI: http://dx.doi.org/10.1145/3064911.3064933

Keywords

Cloud Baking; Lightweight Scene Preprocessing; Global Illumination Maps (GI Maps); WebSIM; Lightweight Web3D Rendering

1. INTRODUCTION

In the era of Internet+ and Simulation (SIM), the popularity of WebSIM has accelerated. WebGL is now widely supported by default in modern browsers. Tools such as xml3D [29], X3DOM [3], Cobweb [2], and three.js [14] allows developers to easily create Web3D contents. Commercial game engines such as Unity3D [17] and Unreal Engine [5] are starting to offer ways to export and publish directly to Web3D.

WebGL-based WebSIM technology is bringing a revolutionary impact on the new generation of visualization-based web services. It produces various critical applications in virtual tourism, virtual museum, virtual city, smart building, e-commerce, and so on. WebSIM can provide web visualization services over mobile internet. Now, WebSIM can run very well on portable devices such as laptops, smartphones, head-mounted display system (HMDS), etc. We believe the era of WebSIM has arrived. Increasingly, simulation applications are implemented on the web platform, for example, multi-user 3D application server OpenSimulator [18], web-based air traffic control simulator ATC-SIM [15], 3D virtual clothing [8] and so on.

The explosion of WebSIM application, however, is restricted by slow downloading and weak rendering for large-scale virtual scenes or complicated indoor space over the mobile Internet. WebSIM faces the following challenges:

1. **Slow networking transmission.** WebSIM offers require a huge amount of data to be downloaded from a server, making it impossible to transmit the data instantly based on currently available networking bandwidth and to achieve real-time interaction. According to our experience, users are willing to wait less than 5 seconds usually for initial downloading of WebSIM scenes.

2. **High demand for visual effects.** Current WebGL engines support direct lighting online only. Indirect lighting usually

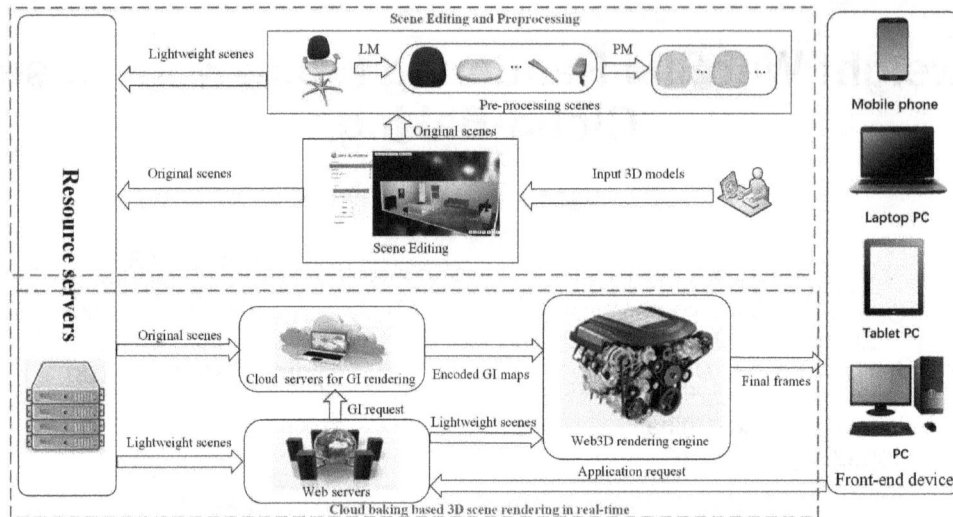

Figure 1: Overall Architecture. The two boxes with blue dashes depict the two main processes: (i) scene data pre-processing and (ii) cloud baking-based 3D scene real-time rendering. The top process describes how a scene is created, pre-processed, and stored. First, the user creates a 3D scene in an editor, possibly with some existing 3D models. We call this the original scene. The system stores two copies of the original scene: One in resource server for GI baking; The other is pre-processed into a lightweight scene and stored on the resource server for Web3D transmission. The lower diagram describes how the scene is rendered. When an application makes a rendering request through the web browser, the web server submits a GI request to the cloud server for GI baking. The cloud server retrieves the original scene from the resource server to bake and passes the baked and encoded GI maps to the Web3D rendering engine for rendering. The Web3D rendering engine blends the decoded GI maps and the lightweight scene (retrieved from the resource server) to render the final frames and transmit to the client.

requires rather expensive computation. So it cannot provide realistic visual effects to satisfy WebSIM users, especially when users change the illumination configurations.

This paper addresses the above challenges and proposes a practical, low-cost, and lightweight solution to WebSIM applications.

2. RELATED WORK

Rendering technology has been researched and developed for a long time. Many rendering engines have been commercialized, including Mental Image s Mental Ray [16], Pixar s RenderMan [10], SplutterFish s Brazil [30], and Chaos group s Vary [23]. Most of these rendering technologies focus on offline rendering. Until the Stage3D [20] and WebGL [1] emerged, web browser cannot use graphics hardware acceleration in real-time rendering. The real-time rendering of online web pages has evolved into a new phase, especially with the development and support of WebGL in modern browsers. In our literature review below, we classify online real-time web page rendering into pure server-side rendering and pure client-side rendering.

2.1 Pure server-side rendering

This rendering approach places the primary rendering task on the server and transfers the rendering results to the web in the form of image streams. The web front-end (i.e., web client) is used only to display the rendering results without participating in the rendering task. The advantages of this type of rendering are better security, supports for computationally intensive rendering effect, and lower resource requirements for the web front-end. Therefore, this approach is adopted in many related work, such as [4] (saving client resources), [25] (protecting 3D models), and [7] (cloud video game).

Remote rendering is a typical application of this type of rendering. In mobile Internet, the rendering server helps various visual devices to render in real-time with realistic lighting effects. Crassin s CloudLight system [11] is a typical pure server-side remote rendering system; we compare our cloud baking system with CloudLight in Table 1. The current trend in the gaming industry to move towards Gaming as a Service (GaaS) model adopts the same approach [6].

2.2 Pure web client-side rendering

This rendering approach places the primary rendering task on the web browser. The server transfers the 3D models, textures, and other storage resources to the web front-end without participating in any rendering task. Typical tools that adopts this approach includes Web3D engine such as three.js [14], Flare3D [19], X3DOM [3], Cobweb [2], and so on.

In the field of education, Web3D simulation has been used for the delivery of interactive 3D virtual learning environments through the Internet, potentially reaching learners worldwide [9]. For example, Ramasundaram et al.[28] developed a Web3D-based virtual field laboratory that provides students with a simulation environment to study the environmental processes in space and time that cannot be experienced through few real field trips. Nigel makes Web3D surgical simulators train clinicians and first-aid operators [22]. Hsu makes a 3D simulation-based application in tourism education [21].

Pure server-side rendering approach is limited by bandwidth and server-side hardware. On the other hand, pure web client-side rendering applications has lower quality rendering effects than the server-side approach due to the limited rendering ability of Web3D engine. Our contribution in this paper is to establish a hybrid Web-SIM rendering framework that combines the advantages of the two rendering approaches, as shown in Table 1. Our approach address the challenge of limited bandwidth through pre-processing of the

Table 1: Technical feature of Web3D rendering engines

Technical feature	CloudLight	WebGL	Cloud-Baking (ours)
Rendering type	Pure server	Pure web	Hybrid
Data volume	heavy	lightweight	middle
Calculation	heavy	lightweight	middle
Render effects	excellent	middle	excellent
Equipment cons	expensive	cheap	middle
Bandwidth cons	expensive	cheap	middle

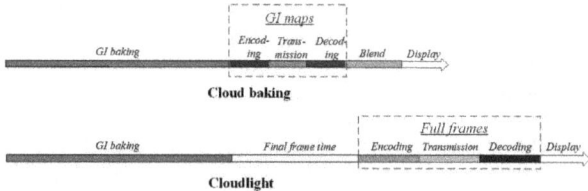

Figure 2: Frame Rendering Time Contrast. We use the length of different color bar represents the time of separate step. Both systems have the same GI baking time (red). After GI baking, our system enters the transmission phase (blue dashed box). The CloudLight system takes the final frame time to generate the full frame before entering the transmission phase (blue dashed box). The transmission phase of both systems are very similar, but the size of the full frames transmitted by the CloudLight is greater than the size of our GI baking system. So CloudLight spent more time on transmission than our system. In the web front-end, CloudLight can display the frame directly. But, our system needs to blend GI with Local Illumination before displaying the blended frame. In general, our system s frame rendering time is shorter than CloudLight s.

3D scene using *lightwighting* [27] and H.264 compression, and enhance the rendering effects using *cloud baking*.

3. PLATFORM ARCHITECTURE

The overall platform is shown in Figure 1, which consists of the follwoing two components:

1. **Scene data pre-processing.** Considering the system resource constraints of web-based applications, it is necessary to create web client-side rendering exclusive data through data pre-processing. Data pre-processing is divided into two parts: scene data processing and data deduplication (see Section 4).

2. **Cloud baking based Web3D online real-time rendering mechanism.** This rendering mechanism puts complex indirect lighting operations in the cloud while placing direct lighting calculations and rendering of lightweight scenes at the web front-end. It takes full advantage of the web front-end rendering capabilities for lightweight scene presentation while supplementing the web front-end rendering capabilities with cloud baking (see Section 5).

4. SCENE PRE-PROCESSING

4.1 Scene Architecture Construction

We divide the whole scene into subspace and classify each subspace as either indoor or outdoor. When the user roams in the scene,

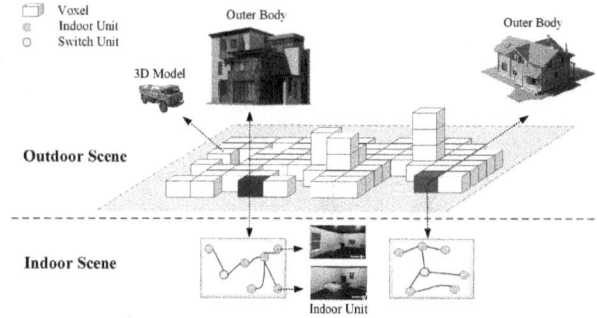

Figure 3: Scene Architecture. This figure separates indoor scenes and outdoor scenes with dashed lines. Each indoor scene is constructed by some indoor units and a connected graph that illustrates the relationship of these indoor units. The indoor switch unit is a particular indoor unit that stores indoor and outdoor switching points. Objects stored in an indoor scene must be bound to an indoor unit. The outdoor scene divides the space into voxels. A box represents a voxel. The colored box represents a particular voxel that includes indoor scene. During roaming, this voxel will appear in the form of outer body of the indoor scene.

the position of the viewpoint determines the type of scene in which it is located. After entering the scene, we subdivide the scene, build the relationship between each subspace and bind the model index and subspace as follows:

1. **Indoor scene.** We consider a completely visible and relatively confined space as an interior space unit, such as a separate room, a separate cave and so on. This scene type establishes the connectivity between the indoor units, record the connected data, and bind the indoor model index with the indoor unit index.

2. **Outdoor scene.** We voxelize the outdoor scene. Each voxel is the smallest unit of this outdoor scene. A model in the outdoor scene should belong to one or more voxels. A particular model that logically contains an indoor scene will appear only as external contour (we call it *outer body*).

We set key points in the scene where users switch from indoor to outdoor, and vice versa.

4.2 Scene data Pre-Processing

After classification, we pre-process the scene data as follows:

1. **Lightweighting.** There could be multiple duplicates parts in the 3D scene, which only differ in spatial position, scaling, or rotation. We extract the unique model from duplicate parts, and remove these duplicates from the 3D scene, thereby reducing the scene data into a set of unique models and their transformation metadata [27].

2. **Progressive mesh.** It is noted that the ability of the human eye to distinguish the object decreases as the distance between the object and the viewpoint increases. We use the method of progressive mesh (PM) to encode the model mesh into a basic mesh and a series of mesh increments [31]. The size of the mesh increment corresponds to the fineness level of the model, and the distance between the object and the viewpoint determines the fineness level of the loading model. Compared with the traditional LOD algorithm, PM achieves no redundant transmission. [26].

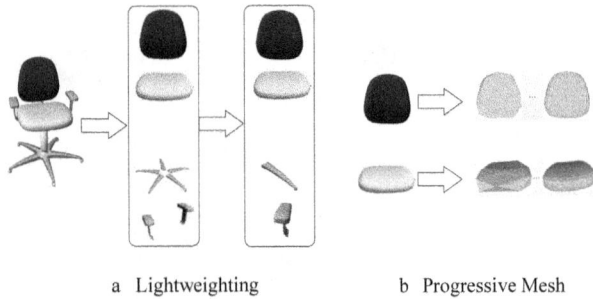

a Lightweighting   b Progressive Mesh

Figure 4: Subfigure (a) depicts reuse-based model lightweighting. Subfigure (b) depicts the method of progressive mesh (PM). Our system first pre-processes the 3D models to obtain a set of unique models and the set of transformation parameters. Then, we convert these models to progressive meshes.

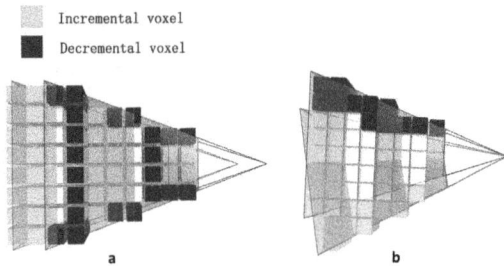

Figure 5: Green voxels are potential-visible voxels, and the blue voxels are opposite. When the current frustum (blue) moves, the pre-loaded view frustum (red) should add potential-visible voxels and delete potential-invisible voxels. Subfigure (a) depicts the movement of frustum; Subfigure (b) depicts the rotation of frustum.

5. CLOUD RENDERING MECHANISM

This mechanism is the core of our platform, formed by three modules, namely: web front-end rendering, cloud server back-end rendering, and data transmission. Figure 6 shows the complete workflow of this mechanism.

5.1 Web front-end rendering

In this stage, the web front-end directly receives the application request in the beginning and output the rendering results at the end. This module is divided into six parts, namely: lightweight scene loading and management, application monitoring and GI request, scene object information update and transmission, direct lighting calculation, GI information reception, synthesize the last map and output, as follows:

1. **Lightweight scene loading and management.** Based on the motion trajectory of the viewpoint and the view frustum, the system predicts the voxels space that will be added and load them before rendering. This pre-load method and pre-processing of the scene data are sufficient to solve the large data loading pressure problem when rendering large-scale scenes in real-time, as shown in Figure 4.

2. **Application monitoring and GI request.** This step is to monitor whether the application will modify the information in the scene (light source, camera, and model, etc.). As shown in Figure 6, the monitoring not only directly affects

the execution of Steps (3) and (4) but also affects whether or not to send GI requests to the cloud server.

3. **Scene object update and transmission.** When Step (2) is true, the Web3D rendering engine will modify the scene s object information according to the application s requirements and update the render queue to prepare for the next direct light shading. Some of the modified attributes, such as the location of the model and the light source, the matrix of the camera, etc., will be sent to the cloud server.

4. **Direct lighting calculation.** Web3D rendering engine can be efficient on the web side of the direct light for the deferred shading. When Step (2) is false, the calculation is done directly. Otherwise, it will wait for Step (3) to update the rendering queue first before calculating, which can significantly improve the deferred shading efficiency.

5. **GI information reception.** Step (2) accepts the web request; then the web front-end receives the H.264 encoded GI image frame from the cloud server at this stage and decodes it on the web front-end.

6. **Synthesize the last map and output.** The GI map frame decoded at the web front-end will be passed to the Web3D rendering engine and blended with the Local illumination (LI) map generated in Step (4). Then, our platform output the final map to the web application.

5.2 Cloud rendering

In this module, the cloud server receives GI request and scene object transformation information from the web front-end and outputs H.264 encoded GI map frames to the web front-end. The whole module includes five parts, namely: Original high-precision 3D scene loading, GI render request monitoring, scene object update, indirect lighting calculation, and GI map encoding and output, as follows:

1. **Original high precision 3D scene loading and management.** This step derives the original high-precision 3D scene from the model library and loads it into the cloud server. The loading and management method for this step is similar to Step (1) of web front-end rendering (Section 5.1).

2. **GI render request monitoring.** This step continues to monitor and wait until the web front-end sends GI requests to the cloud server.

3. **Scene object update** After receiving the GI request and the scene object change information from the web front-end, the cloud server processes separately according to the object class of the transformation information. These object categories include 3D models in the scene, cameras, and light sources. The 3D models update will reorganize the spatial space management structure of the scene, the camera update will re-cut the scene and recalculate the occlusion relationship, and the update of the light source will update all the preset GI maps;

4. **Indirect lighting calculation.** Our system uses RSM[13], LPV[24], and voxel cone tracing[12] as the real-time indirect lighting algorithms as the main GI algorithm in our platform. The calculated GI maps will be passed to Step (5).

5. **GI map encoding and output.** After receiving the GI map frames from Step (4), the cloud server encodes these map frames by H.264 and transmits it to the web front-end.

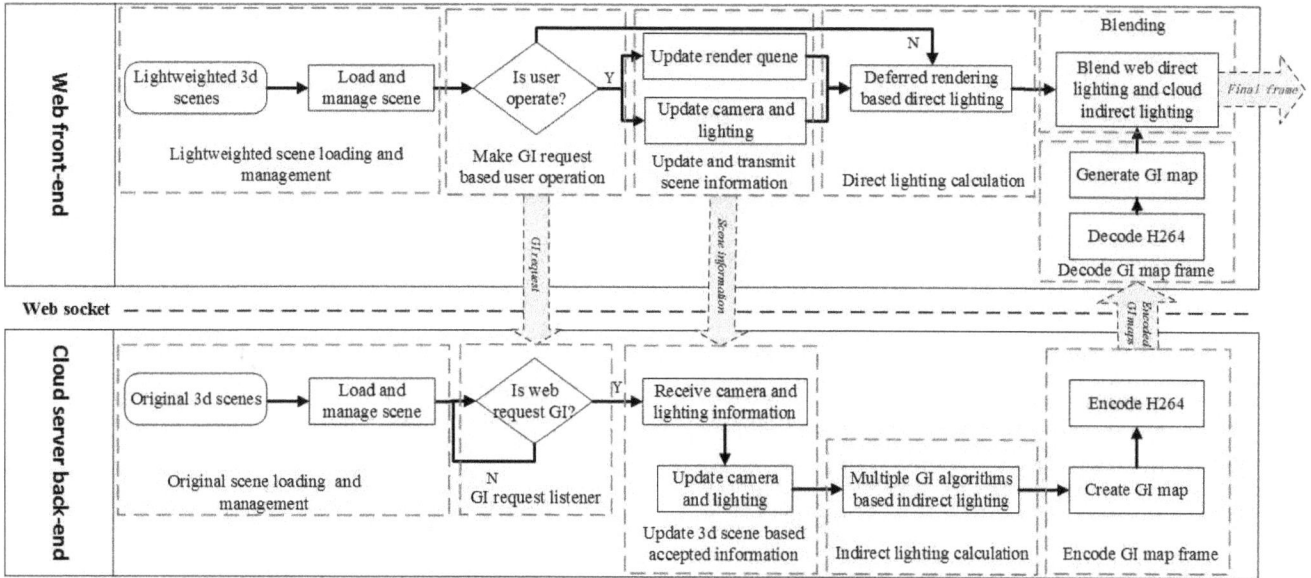

Figure 6: Data Flow Diagram of Rendering Framework. In this figure, the lightweight 3D scene and the original high-precision 3D scene, which are extracted from the model repository and have a one-to-one correspondence, are transferred to the web front-end and the cloud server back end, respectively. The web front-end will submit the GI render request to the cloud in real-time according to the needs of the application program and transmit the transformation information (position, matrix, etc.) of the camera and light source in the current scene. The cloud back-end, which receives the request, renders the GI map in real-time based on the information and requests from the front end. The information transmission and monitoring in this mechanism use the WebSocket protocol.

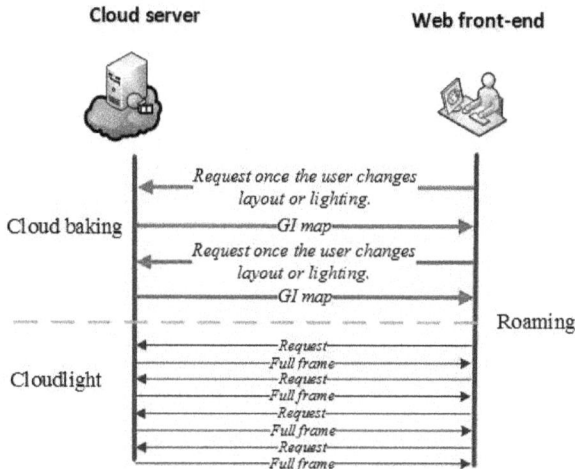

Figure 7: In our cloud baking system architecture, GI requests are made to the cloud sever once the user changes the layout and lighting. In contrast, in the CloudLight system architecture, the web front-end requests full frame at all times.

5.3 Data transmission

As shown in Figure 6, there are three types of data in this mechanism, specifically: GI request, scene object transformation information, and GI map information. Therefore, our system controls the transmission frequency of these data at the web front-end and responds to these data efficiently at cloud server.

1. **Request only when the information change.** The web front-end requests GI data from the cloud server only when the

application program modifies the scene object information related to the GI effect, such as camera attributes, dynamic light source properties, etc. Otherwise, no request is made. This strategy makes our platform different from the pure server rendering platform, which requires the server to render every frame even if it is still.

2. **Send GI map only for the latest frame.** When the cloud server sends GI map to the web front-end, if the transmission time is less than the interval between adjacent requests, we think that the transmission is smooth and there is no backlog. Otherwise, we only transmit the latest GI map, ignoring all the previous backlog. This method can greatly reduce the complexity of the server transmission, save bandwidth, and improve transmission efficiency.

$$n' = \begin{cases} n+1 & t \quad \Delta t \\ n+t/\Delta t & otherwise \end{cases} \quad (1)$$

To achieve this, we use Equation (1) to calculate n', the response index of the GI map to be send next. Here, n is the response index corresponding to the GI map currently being sent to the web front-end, t is the time it takes to send the current GI map, and Δt is the interval between the two requests. Figure 8 illustrates the process.

6. EXPERIMENT AND ANALYSIS

The verification experiment of our system uses typical rendering test scenes, such as Crytek Sponza, Sibenik Cathedral, Conference Room and Cornell Box, and some actual project scenes. The size of all these scenes ranges from 17 to 422,920 triangles, which are very representative. At the same time, we compared our system

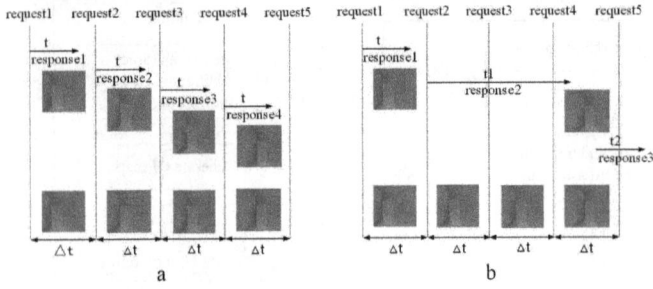

Figure 8: Data Transmission.Assume that the cloud server is sending GI data to the web front-end according to the request. The data transmission takes time t_n and the interval of the GI request is $\triangle t$. As shown in (a), if t_n is smaller than $\triangle t$, data will not accumulate. However, as shown in (b), when t_1 is greater than $\triangle t$, the front end has submitted $t_2/\triangle t$ requests to the server and generated $t_2/\triangle t$ GI maps to be transmitted. In this case, we ignore the first $t_2/\triangle t$-1 GI maps to be transmitted and transmit the latest GI map directly.

Table 2: Device configuration

Hdwe.&OS	Cloud server	web front-end
CPU	Intel Xeon E5 2640V3	Intel i7-4720
GPU	Nvidia Quadro M6000	Nvidia GeForce GTX860
Memory	128G	8G
OS	windows server 2012	windows 10

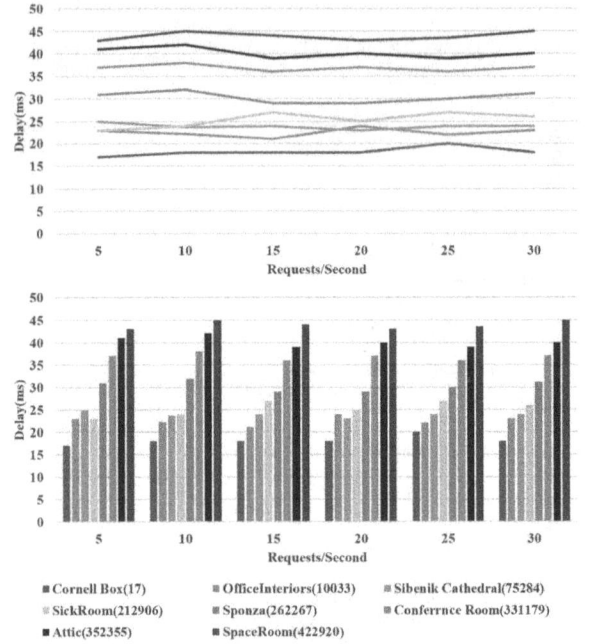

Figure 9: Rendering Delay VS Requested. Each color represents a scene with the different scale. The size of the scene range from 17 to 422,920 triangles. The requested frequency is from 5 to 30 times per second. The rendering delay per second is between 15ms and 45ms.

with CloudLight systems, which is a state-of-the-art cloud rendering system [11].

6.1 Time delay analysis

As shown in Figure 9, we measure the delay of the entire rendering process, which starts with the GI request and ends with image frame output, and discuss the relationship between the delay and the request frequency. We find that the increase request frequency (from 5 times per seconds to 30 times per second) did not affect the delay much. In other words, the cloud server rendering frequency should be 30 GI maps per second, up from 5. We believe that the stability of the delay shows that our system can fully realized GI real-time rendering. When we run our system on eight different scenes (Table 3) with different complexity , and found that as the size of the scene increases, the average delay increases. Reducing the impact of the scene size will be our future work.

6.2 Comparison and analysis

Table 3: Data size of experiment scene

Number	Model name	Triangle count
1	Cornell Box	17
2	Space Room	422,920
3	Silk Room	212,906
4	Attic	352,355
5	Sibenik Cathedral	75,284
6	Sponza	262,267
7	Conference Room	331,179
8	Office Interiors	10,033

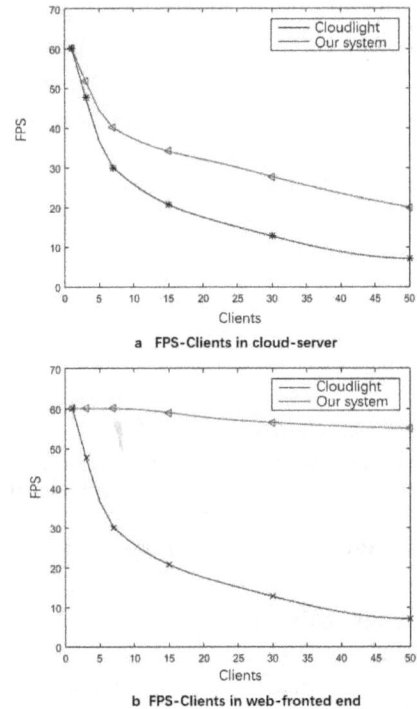

Figure 10: The relationship between the refresh rate and the number of users, comparing the performance of our system (red) and CloudLight (blue).

226

Figure 10 describes the relationship between the refresh rate and the number of customers respectively, comparing CloudLight to our system. We found the CloudLight system front-end and back-end refresh rate is very similar. The update rate of the web front-end is also the same when the update rate of the cloud back-end decreases as the number of clients increases. On the contrary, when the refresh rate of our system s cloud back-end decreases as the number of users increases, the refresh rate of the web front-end remains high. According to our analysis, the main reasons are the following:

1. Rendering in CloudLight is done only in the server the client only receives and displays the incoming frame. Therefore, when the server refresh rate decreases, the web front-end refresh rate will inevitably decline.

2. In our system, the web front-end performs rendering. The rendering in the cloud only complements the GI effect of the client, without restricting its rendering. Therefore, even when the refresh rate of the cloud server reduces, there is no impact on web front-end rendering. This is the essential difference between our system and the pure server-side rendering system such as CloudLight.

3. Our cloud server performance is also better than CloudLight system, because our rendering task is less expensive as it only renders GI map. Furthermore, our rendering requirements less as it only needs to render in particular objects activities.

7. CONCLUSION

In this paper, we build a novel WebSIM framework based on cloud baking technology, which aims to supplement Web3D s ability to render in the client with cloud rendering. The web front-end uses a lightweight version of the scene to allow interactive changes. The cloud-based renderer carries out the expensive indirect lighting computation and transmits the indirectly light frame over the network to blend with the web front-end direct lighting scene. To accommodate the need for seamless indirect lighting calculation, GI maps transformation and illumination blend in real-time. We also present some optimizing transmission strategies, such as sending request only when there is information change and send GI map only for the latest frame to avoid backlog.

The experimental results show that our framework is feasible and can run smoothly. Compared to CloudLight, a state-of-the-art cloud rendering system, our rendering architecture has the advantages in both speed and rendering quality. There are many possible research directions in our framework. For example, how to solve the constraints of the size of the scene, and how to optimize the rendering task on the GPU. We plan to answer these questions in the future.

8. ACKNOWLEDGMENTS

This work was supported by National 12th Five Years Plan for Science Technology Support (No. 2012BAC11B00-04-03), The Research Fund for the Doctoral Program of Higher Education (No. 20130072110035), Changbai Valley Talent Plan of Changchun National Hi-Tech Industrial Development Zone (No. 3-2013006), Key project in scientific and technological of Jilin province (No. 2014-0204088GX) and Tongji University Young Scholar Plan (No. 2014-KJ074), Projects of National Natural Science Foundation (No. 612-72276). We thank Wei Tsang Ooi for his comments on the earlier draft of this work.

9. REFERENCES

[1] E. Angel and D. Shreiner. *Interactive Computer Graphics with WebGL.* Addison-Wesley Professional, 2014.

[2] C. Barnes, I. Boutron, B. Giraudeau, R. Porcher, D. G. Altman, and P. Ravaud. Impact of an online writing aid tool for writing a randomized trial report: the cobweb (consort-based web tool) randomized controlled trial. *BMC medicine*, 13(1):221, 2015.

[3] J. Behr, P. Eschler, Y. Jung, and M. Zöllner. X3dom: a dom-based html5/x3d integration model. In *Proceedings of the 14th international conference on 3D web technology*, pages 127 135. ACM, 2009.

[4] K. W. Brodlie, D. A. Duce, J. R. Gallop, J. Walton, and J. Wood. Distributed and collaborative visualization. In *Computer graphics forum*, volume 23, pages 223 251. Wiley Online Library, 2004.

[5] J. Busby, Z. Parrish, and J. Wilson. *Mastering Unreal Technology, Volume I: Introduction to Level Design with Unreal Engine 3.* Pearson Education, 2009.

[6] W. Cai, M. Chen, and V. C. Leung. Toward gaming as a service. *IEEE Internet Computing*, 18(3):12 18, 2014.

[7] K.-T. Chen, Y.-C. Chang, P.-H. Tseng, C.-Y. Huang, and C.-L. Lei. Measuring the latency of cloud gaming systems. In *Proceedings of the 19th ACM international conference on Multimedia*, pages 1269 1272. ACM, 2011.

[8] L. Chittaro and D. Corvaglia. 3d virtual clothing: from garment design to web3d visualization and simulation. In *Proceedings of the eighth international conference on 3D Web technology*, pages 73 ff. ACM, 2003.

[9] L. Chittaro and R. Ranon. Web3d technologies in learning, education and training: Motivations, issues, opportunities. *Computers & Education*, 49(1):3 18, 2007.

[10] R. Cortes. *The renderman shading language guide.* Cengage Learning, 2007.

[11] C. Crassin, D. Luebke, M. Mara, M. McGuire, B. Oster, P. Shirley, and P.-P. S. C. Wyman. Cloudlight: A system for amortizing indirect lighting in real-time rendering. *Journal of Computer Graphics Techniques Vol*, 4(4), 2015.

[12] C. Crassin, F. Neyret, M. Sainz, S. Green, and E. Eisemann. Interactive indirect illumination using voxel cone tracing. In *Computer Graphics Forum*, volume 30, pages 1921 1930. Wiley Online Library, 2011.

[13] C. Dachsbacher and M. Stamminger. Reflective shadow maps. In *Proceedings of the 2005 symposium on Interactive 3D graphics and games*, pages 203 231. ACM, 2005.

[14] J. Dirksen. *Learning Three. js: the JavaScript 3D library for WebGL.* Packt Publishing Ltd, 2013.

[15] N. Dorighi. Atc sim-costs and benefits. *Airports International*, 36(9), 2003.

[16] T. Driemeyer. *Rendering with mental ray R*, volume 1. Springer, 2013.

[17] U. G. Engine. Unity game engine-official site. *Online][Cited: October 9, 2008.] http://unity3d. com*, pages 1534 4320.

[18] P. A. Fishwick. An introduction to opensimulator and virtual environment agent-based m&s applications. In *Simulation conference (WSC), proceedings of the 2009 winter*, pages 177 183. IEEE, 2009.

[19] K. Gladstien. *Flash Game Development In a Social, Mobile and 3D World.* Cengage Learning, 2013.

[20] J. GuiâAŹe. Research of display efficiency about flash

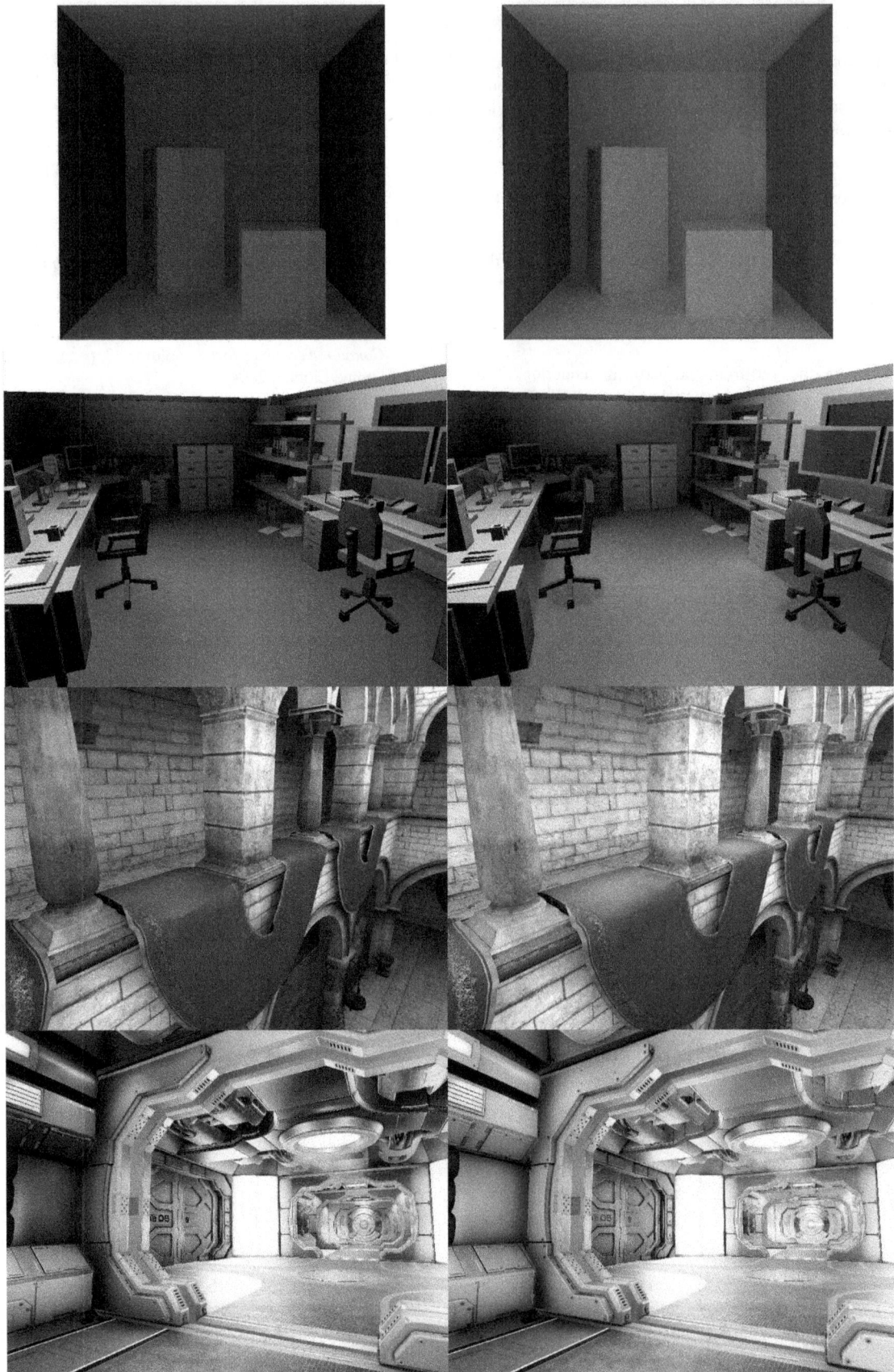

Figure 11: Local Lighting Rendering vs Final Rendering.The comparison of the local lighting rendering effect and the final rendering effect. The left part only contains local lighting, which can be achieved in the web-client side. The right part contains local lighting and global lighting, showing the obvious light bounce effect. And this is the ultimate rendering effect of our system.

applications on mobile terminal. *Microcomputer Applications*, 3:008, 2013.

[21] L. Hsu. Web 3d simulation-based application in tourism education: A case study with second life. *Journal of Hospitality, Leisure, Sport & Tourism Education*, 11(2):113 124, 2012.

[22] N. W. John. The impact of web3d technologies on medical education and training. *Computers & Education*, 49(1):19 31, 2007.

[23] A. Kämä et al. Photorealistic lighting and rendering of a small apartment interior: a case study with 3ds max and v-ray. 2016.

[24] A. Kaplanyan and C. Dachsbacher. Cascaded light propagation volumes for real-time indirect illumination. In *Proceedings of the 2010 ACM SIGGRAPH symposium on Interactive 3D Graphics and Games*, pages 99 107. ACM, 2010.

[25] D. Koller, M. Turitzin, M. Levoy, M. Tarini, G. Croccia, P. Cignoni, and R. Scopigno. Protected interactive 3d graphics via remote rendering. In *ACM Transactions on Graphics (TOG)*, volume 23, pages 695 703. ACM, 2004.

[26] M. Limper, M. Thöner, J. Behr, and D. W. Fellner. Src-a streamable format for generalized web-based 3d data transmission. In *Proceedings of the 19th International ACM Conference on 3D Web Technologies*, pages 35 43. ACM, 2014.

[27] X. Liu, N. Xie, K. Tang, and J. Jia. Lightweighting for web3d visualization of large-scale bim scenes in real-time. *Graphical Models*, 88:40 56, 2016.

[28] V. Ramasundaram, S. Grunwald, A. Mangeot, N. B. Comerford, and C. Bliss. Development of an environmental virtual field laboratory. *Computers & Education*, 45(1):21 34, 2005.

[29] K. Sons, F. Klein, J. Sutter, and P. Slusallek. The xml3d architecture. In *ACM SIGGRAPH 2015 Posters*, page 39. ACM, 2015.

[30] C. Sullivan. Brazil rendering system 1.0, splutterfish, 2003.

[31] L. Wen, N. Xie, and J. Jia. Client-driven strategy of large-scale scene streaming. In *International Conference on Multimedia Modeling*, pages 93 103. Springer, 2016.

Analyzing Emergency Evacuation Strategies for Mass Gatherings using Crowd Simulation and Analysis framework: Hajj Scenario

Imran Mahmood

Center for Research in Modeling, Simulation & Vision (Crimson), National University of Sciences and Technology, Pakistan
imran.mahmood@seecs.edu.pk

Muhammad Haris

Center for Research in Modeling, Simulation & Vision (Crimson) National University of Sciences and Technology, Pakistan

Hessam Sarjoughian

Arizona Center for Integrative Modeling & Simulation (ACIMS), School of Computing, Information, and Decision Systems Engineering, Arizona State University, USA

ABSTRACT

Hajj is one of the largest mass gatherings where Muslims from all over the world gather in Makah each year for pilgrimage. A mass assembly of such scale bears a huge risk of disaster either natural or man-made. In the past few years, thousands of casualties have occurred while performing different Hajj rituals, especially during the Circumambulation of Kaba (Tawaf) due to stampede or chaos. During such calamitous situations, an appropriate evacuation strategy can help resolve the problem and mitigate further risk of causalities. It is however a daunting research problem to identify an optimal course of action based on several constraints. Modeling and analyzing such a problem of real-time and spatially explicit complexity requires a microscale crowd simulation and analysis framework. Which not only allows the modeler to express the spatial dimensions and features of the environment in real scale, but also provides modalities to capture complex crowd behaviors.

In this paper, we propose an Agent-based Crowd Simulation & Analysis framework that incorporates the use of Anylogic Pedestrian library and integrates/interoperate Anylogic Simulation environment with the external modules for optimization and analysis. Hence provides a runtime environment for analyzing complex situations, e.g., emergency evacuation strategies. The key features of the proposed framework include: (i) Ability to model large crowd in a spatially explicit environment at real-scale; (ii) Simulation of complex crowd behavior such as emergency evacuation; (iii) Interoperability of optimization and analysis modules with simulation runtime for evaluating evacuation strategies. We present a case study of Hajj scenario as a proof of concept and a test bed for identifying and evaluating optimal strategies for crowd evacuation

CCS Concepts

• Computing methodologies → Modeling and simulation →Simulation types and techniques → Agent / discrete models. • Computing methodologies → Modeling and simulation →

Simulation support systems → Simulation tools. • Computing methodologies → Machine learning → Machine learning approaches → Bio-inspired approaches → Genetic algorithms. • Computing methodologies → Modeling and simulation → Model development and analysis → Modeling methodologies.

Keywords

Emergency Evacuation Strategies; Public Safety & Security; Agent-Based Crowd Simulation; Anylogic Simulation Software; Hajj Scenario

1. INTRODUCTION

A mass gathering, as defined by World Health Organization is: "A planned or unplanned event at a specific location, attended by a huge number of people for a common purpose. This number is sufficient enough to strain the planning and response resources of the community, state or a nation hosting that event" [1]. Mass gathering can be classified as: (i) Religious obligation like Hajj (ii) Sport events like Olympics and celebrity shows; and (iii) Political like procession and rallies or social riots. The increasing influx of large numbers of people to mass gathering events may give rise to complex disastrous situations, thus require extreme planning and operational support for Public Safety & Security (PSS) preparedness by the organizers of mass gatherings or the governmental entities in general.

Hajj is one of the largest mass gatherings, where about 3 million Muslims gather in Makkah (Saudi Arabia), from over 140 countries, each year for a minimum of five days and up to 40 days. Following an exponential rise in the past decade, Makkah becomes the site of extreme crowd densities with huge inflow of crowd and quite vulnerable to serious disasters including stampede, accidents, construction failures, fires and communicable hazards [2]. Factors that magnify these risks include: extended stays at Hajj sites, extreme heat, densities above 6 or 7 persons per square meter, individuals' inability to move at concentrated regions and jostle to find breath, groups swept along in waves, struggling to avoid falling and being trampled, thus hundreds of deaths can occur as a result. Moreover, the advanced age of many pilgrims with pre-morbid health status adds to the mortality risks. In the past, these disasters took place many times during Hajj. In July 1990, 1426 people were killed in a crowd crush as a result of improper crowd control. In 1997, 343 pilgrims were killed and 1,500 injured in a fire incident. Similarly, in 2006, 346 deaths took place in stampede in Mina valley while throwing stones at pillars. In 2015, crane fell in the courtyard of Masjid-Al-Haram (grand mosque) causing a

SIGSIM-PADS'17, May 24-26, 2017, Singapore, Singapore
© 2017 ACM. ISBN 978-1-4503-4489-0/17/05...$15.00
DOI: http://dx.doi.org/10.1145/3064911.3064924

total of 512 casualties. Again, in September 2015 more than 2000 pilgrims were crushed due to stampede at Mina [2].

The aforementioned disasters can be prevented through proper crowd management & control strategies and is usually expressed as a governmental responsibility under PSS departments. An effective PSS infrastructure for crowd management & control consists of the following key components: (i) Monitoring, (ii) Mitigation, (iii) Preparedness & Incidence Response and (iv) Recovery [3]. Monitoring involves a continuous process of observing real-world activities and supervising the crowd flow. Mitigation concerns pre-emptively preventing possible emergencies, planning exit points & escape routes etc. Preparedness deals with the timely preparations to handle dangerous situations such as firefighting, construction failures, or natural disasters. Incidence response involves timely rescue operations, emergency evacuations, crowd management, shelter and medical services during crisis. Recovery deal with the actions taken to return to a normal state. An efficient PSS infrastructure relies on smart planning and decision support systems that can provide quick and accurate identification and assessment of optimal strategies to be used for a real-world situation under a specific context.

With the advent of modern Modeling and Simulation (M&S) paradigms, there has been an increasing trend in the use of M&S in PSS planning and decision support. Simulation models are now becoming useful in replicating scenarios of safety/mission critical systems in a risk-free, low cost, time independent and harmless experimental environment where modelers can exhaust trials of different nature to gain the insights of the system, compare different alternatives or to find best design parameters [4]. Modeling and simulation plays a vital role in solving crowd evacuation problems [5]. Modeling the crowd behavior and movement of each individual in a crowd can help reduce the number of deaths that take place in a building or a public area. As the population is growing exponentially which is eventually leading to make the public places busier and causing crowd related disasters.

In recent years, M&S technologies have gained tremendous momentum in investigating crowd dynamics [5]. Crowd Simulations can be distinguished into two broader areas. The first one focuses on the realism of behavioral aspects like evacuation simulators, sociological crowd models, or crowd dynamics models. The second area aims at a high-quality visualization of crowd with a convincing visual result and an emphasis on rendering and animation methods [6]. Another classification of crowd simulations is based on the size of the crowd and the approach used. Simulated crowd sizes may vary from tens or hundreds to a couple of hundred thousand or million individuals. Usually large crowds are treated as a whole (macro-scale) where the global trend of the crowd is the focus due to high computational need. For smaller crowds (microscale), the individual behavior is modelled in detail to support investigation of crowd dynamics at individual level [5]. In this paper, we place a balance between both extremes and use an intermediate approach (mesoscale). The crowd size is reasonably large (10,000) but possess some unique individual attributes and behavior so that they can be incorporated while globally examining the crowd dynamics.

1.1 Related Work
This section projects some representative work in crowd simulation and crowd evacuation categories.

1.1.1 Crowd Simulation
In last few years, a lot of models have been proposed to simulate crowd motion. Dorine and Winnie [7] describes few of the models to simulate pedestrian movements. They focused on Cellular Automata, Social Force, Velocity-Based, and Behavioral models. Cellular Automata are microscopic models with grid-based motion decisions. Social Force models are also microscopic models, but they focus on continuous space. Velocity-based models present pedestrians actively seeking free paths through the crowd by avoiding moving objects that are in their way or field. The behavioral models have been developed to take the more psychological influences of pedestrians into account. Talib and Haron [8] proposed a model using cellular automata approach to simulate the pilgrims in a circular Tawaf movement. They claimed that most of the simulation software are not efficient to simulate circular movements in Tawaf area and they also can't handle dense crowds. Their main focus was mostly on the movement of pilgrims in the Tawaf area. Moreover, their proposed model is capable of handling thousands of pedestrians.

Sarmady and Haron [9] also simulated the crowd movements in the Tawaf area. In this work they have also focused on the characteristics and behaviors of individual pedestrian agents. In order to simulate pedestrians using multi-agent methods we need to develop a model of human movement process. For the development of human movement process psychological processes must be taken into account to simulate pedestrian behaviors. Another recent work attempts to model high-density crowd dynamic flows in autonomous and controlled scenarios. A microscopic approach was used to model and analyze pilgrims movement for the evaluation of the Tawaf capacity of the Mataf area (the courtyard) based on observed collective behavior in emergency conditions, where the detailed design of interactions is overlapped by group behavior [10].

1.1.2 Crowd Evacuation

Zhong and Cai proposed an evolutionary algorithm-based methodology for crowd evacuation. The proposed framework was developed using agent-based model and Cartesian Genetic Programming (CGP) to find out the optimal heuristic rule. The main idea was to divide the area into sub-regions and dynamically determine the exits for each sub-region. System incorporates the situation dynamically and calculates the evacuation rule and guide the pedestrians about optimal exit. The proposed methodology was experimented on different scenarios and generic solution was presented to minimize the evacuation time. The movement of agents and gaining the dynamic environment features was challenging, which was overcome by using LifeBelt device. This device is capable of receiving commands from global center and recommending individuals exit for each sub-region [11]. Ferscha and Zia [12] suggested a wearable device that silently guides the individuals in crowd to evacuate. LifeBelt is a wearable device that assists individuals to find their way towards exits during unexpected circumstances. LifeBelt contains sensors, using these sensors individuals' positions can be captured and sent to some centralized system. This device contains eight vibrators associated to belt controller; built on microcontroller board, that receives commands from global evacuation control unit. It then calculates the shortest exit paths according to the sensed situation and guide individuals to designated evacuee areas. Authors has proved that using wearable device, crowd panic and evacuation time can be reduced. A modeling framework for large-scale crowd evacuation was developed with multiple exit gates. The basic idea was to use

Genetic Algorithm (GA) to find optimal evacuation paths and Cellular Automata (CA) based simulated model to evaluate the fitness of proposed solution. They have divided the entire area into subareas and find optimal exits for each subarea. Furthermore, the delay concept was introduced to minimize the overcrowding. Each subarea was assigned a specific time to start the evacuation to avoid the congestion on evacuation paths and exit gates [13].

This paper proposes an Agent-based Crowd Simulation & Analysis framework that harness comprehensive approach: (i) to model a huge number of pedestrians as agents, and real scale environments e.g., stadium, malls, campuses and large mosques, as spatial networks; (ii) to simulate movements of high density crowd in the modeled environments using real or virtual time simulation approaches using different experimental settings; and (iii) to provide detailed assessment of different crowd management & control strategies such as emergency evacuation. Our proposed framework incorporates the use of Anylogic Pedestrian library for Agent based modeling of pedestrians at a microscale, where each agent possesses structure (attributes) and behavior (states) and can communicate with other agents through message passing. A population of agents is modeled as crowd using Pedestrian library. The crowd simulation is built in Anylogic and is integrated with our Optimization and Analysis modules and can interoperate with our framework under different experimental settings. The implementation details are discussed in Section 3. We present a case study of Hajj scenario as a proof of concept and a test bed for identifying and evaluating optimal strategies for crowd evacuation.

The rest of the paper is organized as follows. Section 2 describes the background concepts used in this paper. Section 3 describes the proposed framework. Section 4 presents the simulation studies, case study and experimental results. Finally, Section 5 frames the summary and conclusions.

2. BACKGROUND

In this section, we briefly discuss background and basic concepts of techniques used in this paper.

2.1 Anylogic Simulation Environment

Anylogic Simulation environment [14] provides both a user friendly Integrated Development Environment (IDE) and an efficient simulation engine that allows the modelers to quickly create and simulate high fidelity models of complex systems. It supports different modelling techniques such as Discrete Event, Agent Based and System Dynamics. Anylogic provides rapid prototyping through a user-friendly interface, Java-based development environment and a set of multipurpose component libraries, which all together help to speed up the modelling process [15].

2.1.1 Anylogic Pedestrian Library (APL)

Anylogic includes a pedestrian library [16] that primarily deals with different modeling aspects of crowd simulation. It is used to model microscale behavior of pedestrians using agent based approach and simulate the pedestrians flow in physical environments such as shopping mall, airport and subway stations.

Table 1: Pedestrian Library Control Blocks

Pedestrian flow Blocks

	PedSource	Generates an initial population of pedestrians with given arrival rates
	PedSink	Disposes pedestrians. Pedestrian are removed on entering PedSink
	PedEnter	Places pedestrians into an area defined by a Space markup element.
	PedExit	Removes pedestrians from an area
	PedGoTo	Directs selected pedestrians to go to a specified target, defined by a point, line or area (e.g., Exit gate).
	PedWait	Causes pedestrians to wait for a specified time in a specified location.
	PedSelectOutput	Routes the incoming pedestrians to 1/N output ports depending on a specified condition or assigned probability.

Settings Blocks

	PedConfiguration	Configures general parameters related to all objects of the Pedestrian Library
	PedGround	Defines a 2D surface in the simulated environment, representing floor on which pedestrians can walk
	PedArea	Represents an area defining physical rules and restrictions for pedestrian behavior
	PedAttractor	Allows controlling pedestrian's location when waiting.

APL also provides mechanisms for developing spatial environments using Cartesian or GIS-based coordinates systems and support graphical definition of spatial elements like walls, obstacles, gathering areas using Space Markup Elements [17]. Models created using different blocks of APL simulate pedestrians' movements in continuous or discrete space and support crowd behavior such as their reaction on obstacles, collision avoidance, movements in groups, queuing, scattering etc. all depending on the physical rules of simulation. **Error! Reference source not found.** presents an overview of selected control block classes used in the model discussed in Section 3.

3. Crowd Simulation & Analysis Framework

This section provides technical details of our proposed framework as our main contribution of this paper. Figure 1 illustrates layers and main modules of our framework. Our proposed framework consists of the following layers:

3.1 Simulation Layer

In this layer, we propose the use of Anylogic simulation environment using which a modeler can design spatial environments for any large crowd. The Space markup library provides necessary elements for developing a real-scale graphics model of a continuous space. It also provides import feature for AutoCAD floor plans or GIS shape files. Using this feature the spatial geometry can be modeled precisely up to the scale of a real-world environment. Furthermore, the modeler can use Agent based modeling approach to describe the nature of individuals and their interactions in a crowd, by defining attributes e.g., Age, Weight, Gender etc. Finally, the modeler is required to create a logical model of crowd using the Pedestrian library blocks discussed in Section 2.1.1. The library can import previously created agent population and the spatial environment and implements the flow of pedestrian as per physical rules defined by the modeler. (We present a case study of Hajj Scenario in Section 4 as an example.)

Once the model is ready and compiled successfully, the modeler can create any number of experiments. Each experiment uses input parameters and executes the model on the Anylogic simulation engine (in real or virtual time modes). The visualization module is used to show animation of the crowd dynamics.

3.2 Interface Layer

This layer enables the integration & interoperability of Simulation layer with external programs. We develop a Java based middleware that interfaces with the Simulation layer and allows the user to expose input parameters of the Simulation model as public variables which can be configured outside the simulation layer. This middleware also provides the use of Call-back functions that can be used externally for accessing model objects, periodically, at particular events or throughout the lifetime of the simulation thus become useful in allowing interleaved operations during the simulation runs.

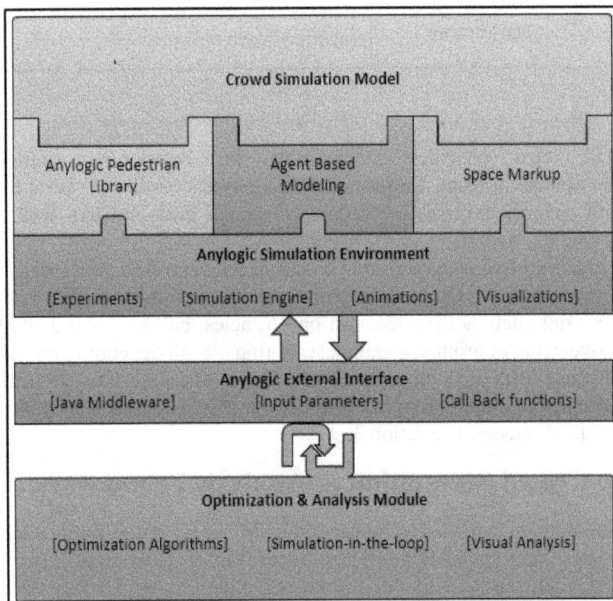

Figure 1: Crowd Simulation & Analysis framework

3.3 Optimization & Analysis Layer

The main purpose of this layer is to allow users to implement and integrate optimization algorithms or use external java frameworks for such purpose. This layer allows flexibility and independence for using any optimization approach and utilizes the interface layer for interacting with Simulation model in a variety of ways. Keeping in view high end computational requirements of optimization algorithms, we implemented multi-threaded interaction with interface layer in order to run the simulation model parallel with varied input parameters, thus contributing in high performance of the optimization process. The analysis part of this layer includes data collection during optimization process, output analysis and visualization. This layer can further be integrated with external libraries of automated analysis and visualization.

4. Simulation Study: Hajj Scenario

In this section, we present a case study of Hajj Scenario as an example to demonstrate the functionality of our framework and as a proof of concept. The scenario presents emergency evacuation of crowd from the Holly Mosque of Makkah. Following steps are used in this process:

4.1 Model Development (Simulation Layer)

The model of Hajj scenario is built in the simulation layer. It has three main constituents: (i) Spatial Environment, (ii) Agent Design and (iii) Pedestrian behavior.

4.1.1 Spatial Environment

At first the physical environment is built Figure 2 shows the top view of the environment built for the crowd simulation using Autocad drawing of Masjid Al-Haram (the grand mosque of Makkah). The mosque is divided into two parts: (i) Inner region, which is an open courtyard where the Kabba (cube) is located in the center; and (ii) the outer region which is a regular mosque building. Pedestrians (pilgrims) enter the courtyard from different entrances (archways) and perform Tawaf. In the first step of developing the crowd model, the Autocad drawing is imported in Anylogic Graphic editor and the spatial elements are used to sketch the inner region using Polylines. The polylines are converted into Walls and 12 entrance/exit points are drawn as shown in Figure 2. Some obstacles are also drawn in the center.

4.1.2 Agent Design

In the crowd simulation model development, a modeler can either use default agents or can create new types of agents with a custom physical and behavioral design. Physical structure includes attributes such as age, gender, height, weight etc. whereas behavior include states such as: normal, injured, critical, unconscious or deceased etc. Agents can also be related to each other in many ways e.g., family relations, group members, nationality. Anylogic provides several probability distributions to initialize a population of agents and randomly generate initial values of these attributes based on a selected probability distribution. The behavior of agents is controlled using state charts with time triggered or event triggered transitions. The relationships of agents can be implemented using Agent Network API. Modelers need to consider the tradeoff between level of details required for the individuals in a crowd model and the computational power required to execute the models. In our experience an agent model with greater number of details, and for a population of more than a couple of thousand individuals is not easily executed on a desktop PC, and instead requires a cloud computing platform.

4.1.3 Pedestrian Behavior
The behavioral logic of the crowd simulation is implemented using Pedestrian flow controls as shown in Figure 3. A brief description of each block shown in Figure 3 is provided in Section 2.1.1. At first the *pedConfiguration* block is used to assign types of individual entities. A modeler can select the default class of Pedestrian (Ped) or can assign user defined agents (Section 4.1.2). Then *pedGround* and *pedArea* blocks are used to configure and assign the spatial environments created previously (Section 4.1.1). The *pedAttractors* blocks are points, lines and polygons used to direct the flow of pedestrians in an open area. Figure 2 shows the concentration of pedestrians in circular orbits, due to the attractors used. When the configuration blocks are ready, the *pedSource* block is used to generate a crowd with an assigned rate of arrival. The *pedWait* block is used to keep the crowd waiting in an area, after which it moves to the *pedSink* block and is removed from the system. The *pedWait* can also be *cancelled* using a method call which will cause the pedestrians to move to *pedSelect* blocks. There are three *pedSelect* switch blocks (PS) direct selected pedestrians to designated *pedGoto* blocks (i.e., Gate1, ..., Gate12). We assigned a long *pedWait* duration (100 min) and assume that while pedestrians are in the courtyard, an alarming event occurs due to which the pedestrians will start evacuating from the Entrance/Exit archways and eventually from the mosque using four main gates. For the sake of simplicity, we only consider evacuation through the inner part of the mosque.

4.2 Simulation Experiment (Interface Layer)
In order to allow simulation interoperability of the model with external environments, a Simulation Experiment was developed using Anylogic Experiment framework [18]. It consists of the following parts:

4.2.1 Interface Parameters
It includes the definition of parameters exposed to the external environment for controlling the simulation. The details of parameters selected for external interface are presented in Section 4.5. The visibility of exposed parameters should be *public*.

4.2.2 Call Back Functions
Depending upon the needs and usage a modeler can create various types of call back functions in order to access data of model objects at different times via different events. For the external use, we implemented the following callback function:

```
public interface Callback {
    void onFinish(Main root);
}
```

This function interfaces a method *onFinish* which lets the external environment know that the simulation run is finished. We use it to collect and access the total evacuation time when all the pedestrians have exited the mosque.

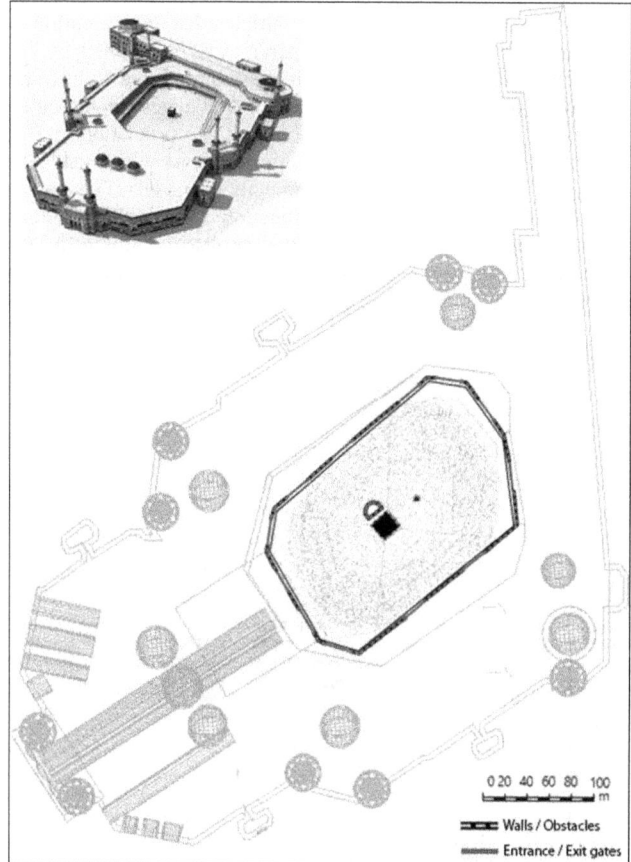

Figure 2: Masjid Al-Haram Spatial Model in Anylogic

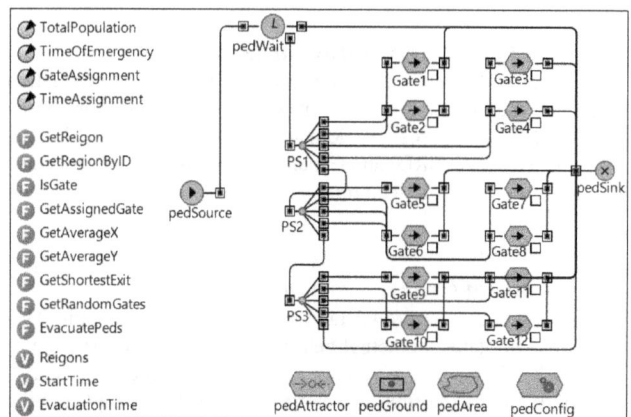

Figure 3: Pedestrian flow controls

4.3 External modules (Optimization & Analysis Layer)

For the Hajj scenario, we implemented Genetic algorithm (see Figure 4) in the Optimization & Analysis layer. The GA aims to identify the most appropriate gate assignments so as to minimize the total evacuation time. This module uses instances of Simulation Experiments via interface layer for initialization and execution of the simulations with appropriate parameters determined by the optimization algorithm optimization algorithm. Figure 4 illustrates the basic working of this layer. When GA initializes with an initial population, for each candidate solution the simulation run is performed by communicating with interface layer which sends the candidate's parameters to the simulation model. Once the simulation is finished the callback function is invoked that returns the simulation results. Based on the results, the fitness of the solution is analyzed (i.e., compared with the fittest). Then population is evolved for the next generation.

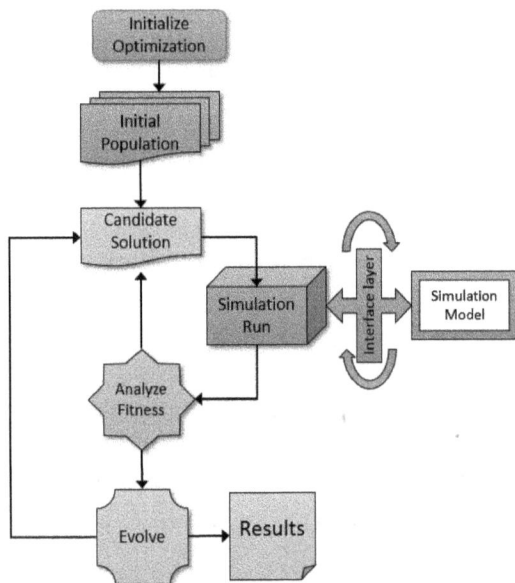

Figure 4: Optimization & Analysis Module

4.4 Emergency Evacuation Strategies

In this section, we present three variants of emergency evacuation strategies used in our simulation model. These variants are based on three different approaches: Random Crowd Evacuation, Shortest Regional Distance (SRD) and Genetic Algorithm (GA), to evacuate the crowd in Masjid-Al-Haram.

4.4.1 Random Crowd Evacuation

In this approach, the crowd randomly selects an exit path. This approach simulates the actual behavior of a crowd in the state of panic, when there is no supervisory control. When the crowd enters the courtyard, at the time of emergency, the crowd start moving towards exit gates based on random selection. That is, equal probabilities are allocated to each gate at pedSelect. Table 2 presents the proposed algorithm for Random crowd evacuation approach.

4.4.2 Shortest Regional Distance (SRD)

In this approach, we partition the entire area into logical sub-regions using polygons (see Figure 2) and divide the pedestrians in these sub-regions based on their {x, y} positions. Then, we calculate the nearest gate with respect to the mean position of pedestrians in each sub-region and the shortest path is selected for evacuation of that region. Table 3 shows the algorithm for evacuation using SRD approach.

4.4.3 Genetic Algorithm (GA)

A genetic algorithm (GA) is a metaheuristic search inspired by the process of natural selection and biological evolution. In GA, a population of candidate solutions (called individuals) is evolved toward better solutions. The evolution starts from an initial population of randomly generated individuals and evolves in multiple generations. In each generation, the fitness of every individual is evaluated. The fitness is the value of the objective function of the optimization problem. The better fit individuals are randomly selected from the population in each generation as parents, and a new individual is formed by their cross over and random mutation.

Table 2: Random Crowd Evacuation Algorithm

Algorithm I: Random Crowd Evacuation
Input: Population, Time Of Emergency
Output: Evacuation Time
1   Initialize Population ▷ Using PedSource
2   **While** (time < delay)
▷ Current time is less than Ped Wait delay
3   Population Waits in the area   ▷ using PedWait
4   **If** Time of Emergency event has occurred **then**
5   Start Time ← Current Time
6   Cancel Wait
▷ Causes pedestrians to start evacuating
7   **for** each Ped ∈ Population **do**
8   Gate ← Uniform Probability (1 to 16)
9   Goto Gate (Gate) ▷ using PedGoto
10   Remove Ped from Population ▷ using PedSink
11   End for
12   Evacuation Time = Current Time – Start Time
13   End If
14   End While
15 **Return** Evacuation Time

The new generation of candidate solutions is then used in the next iteration of the algorithm. The algorithm terminates when either a maximum number of generations has been produced, or a satisfactory level of fitness has been reached [18]. In this paper, we propose the use of GA as an optimization approach for selecting the best evacuation solution in a given scenario. In this case an individual is defined as an array of integers representing sub-regions and their values represent the assigned gate from where the pedestrians of that region will evacuate. An optimal solution will minimize the total evacuation time for the entire crowd. Table 4 presents our GA implementation.

The GA is implemented in the Optimization & Analysis layer of our proposed framework. Each time it creates an individual, it calls the Simulation Layer for the execution with the individual's gene structure as input parameters (i.e., in our case the gate assignment). The simulation is run in a thread without GUI mode and returns the output (i.e., Total Evacuation time), which is used at fitness value.

Table 3: Shortest Distance of the Region (SDR) Algorithm

Algorithm II: Shortest Regional Distance

Input: Population, Time of Emergency

Output: Evacuation Time

1	Initialize Population ▷ Using PedSource
2	**While** (time < delay)
	▷ Current time is less than Ped Wait delay
3	Population Waits in the area ▷ using PedWait
4	**If** Time of Emergency event has occurred **then**
5	Start Time ← Current Time
6	Cancel Wait
	▷ Causes pedestrians to start evacuating
7	**for** each Ped ∈ Population **do**
8	Region ← Get Region (Ped)
9	MeanXY ← Avergage(Ped.X, Ped.Y)
10	Gate ← Nearest gate from MeanXY
	▷ Gets the gate with shortest distance from the mean position of a region
11	Goto Gate (Gate) ▷ using PedGoto
12	Remove Ped from Population ▷ using PedSink
13	End for
14	Evacuation Time = Current Time – Start Time
15	End If
16	End While
17	**Return** Evacuation Time

Procedure: Get Region

Input: Ped

Output: Region

1	for each region ∈ {Polygons}
	▷ Regions are defined using polygons (fig 2)
2	{X, Y} ← {Ped.X, Ped.Y}
3	**If** region contains {X,Y} **then**
4	Region = region
5	End if
6	End for
7	**Return** Region

Table 4: Genetic Algorithm

Algorithm III: Genetic Algorithm

Input: N ▷ No of individuals in a generation

Output: Individual with Optimal Evacuation Time

1	{Population} ← **Generate Population**(N)
2	**for** Generation i = 1 to Maximum Generations
3	Fittest Individual ← Best Individual in the population
	▷ With minimum fitness value i.e., minimum evacuation time.
4	Population[0] ← Fittest Individual
	▷ Pick the best from the previous generation
5	**for** J = 1 to N ▷ Evolve population
6	{Group A} ← Tournament Selection
7	{Group B} ← Tournament Selection
	▷ Tournament selection randomly picks individuals from previous populations in to groups.
8	New Individual ←Cross Over
	▷ Crossover combines a set of genes from a parent of Group A and a parent of Group B.
9	New Individual ← Mutate
	▷ With a certain mutation probability the mutate function flips certain genes with new random values.
	Population [j] ← New Individual
10	End for
11	End for
11	**Return** Fittest Individual

Procedure: Generate Population

Input: N

Output: {Population}

1	**for** k = 1 to N
2	Individual ← Generate Chromosome (length)
	Fitness ← Calculate Individual Fitness
	▷ Run simulation model for the individual with assigned gates for each region and returns Evacuation Time as fitness value.
3	Population [k] ← Individual
4	End for
5	**Return** {Population}

Procedure: Generate Chromosome

Input: Length

Output: Individual

1	**for** k = 1 to Length
2	Gene ← Random gate ← {Gates}
	▷ Randomly selects a gate with uniform distribution
	Individual[k] ← Gene
3	End for
4	**Return** Individual

4.5 Simulation Results

This section presents the simulation results for each of the three evacuation scenarios discussed in Section 4.2. The simulations are developed in Anylogic 7 University 7.1.2 running on Intel iCore7 Windows desktop PC with 16GB RAM. The simulation design parameters for each evacuation strategy are defined as follows:

4.5.1 Random Crowd Evacuation (Random)

- Population = 10,000
- Time of Emergency = 1.3 minute
- Average Speed of the Crowd = Triangular Distribution with Min=1.0 m/s, Max = 2.0 m/s and Most likely=1.4 m/s
- No. of Simulation runs = 10

4.3.2 Random Timed Crowd Evacuation (Random-T)

- Population = 10,000
- Time of Emergency = 1.3 minute
- Average Speed of the Crowd = Triangular Distribution with Min=1.0 m/s, Max = 2.0 m/s and Most likely=1.4 m/s
- No. of Simulation runs = 10
- Time delay = 1.5
- Time delay assignment probability = 0.5

4.3.3 Shortest Regional Distance (SRD)

- Population = 10,000
- No. of Sub-regions = 16
- Time of Emergency = 1.3 minute
- Average Speed of the Crowd = Triangular Distribution with Min=1.0 m/s, Max = 2.0 m/s and Most likely=1.4 m/s
- No. of Simulation runs = 10

4.3.4 Shortest Regional Distance Timed (SRD-T)

- Population = 10,000
- No. of Sub-regions = 16
- Time of Emergency = 1.3 minute
- Average Speed of the Crowd = Triangular Distribution with Min=1.0 m/s, Max = 2.0 m/s and Most likely=1.4 m/s
- No. of Simulation runs = 10
- Time delay for all inner regions = 1.5

4.3.5 Genetic Algorithm (GA)

- Population = 10,000
- No. of Sub-regions = 16
- Time of Emergency = 1.3 minute
- Average Speed of the Crowd = Triangular Distribution with Min=1.0 m/s, Max = 2.0 m/s and Most likely=1.4 m/s
- No. of Simulation runs = 10
- Population N = 10;
- No of Generations = 50
- Cross Over Gene Selection = Uniform Distribution [0 to 6]
- Mutation Rate = 0.015
- Tournament Size = 5
- Elitism = true

5. Discussion

Figure 5 illustrates the mean plots for three types of evacuation strategies and a total of five distinct scenarios. In this paper, we assume uniform distribution of crowd across the area, common speed distribution (i.e., Triangular Distribution with Min=1.0 m/s, Max = 2.0 m/s and Most likely=1.4 m/s) and the exit gates are of same size. We also assume that all pedestrians evacuate with equal priority. Changing these initial conditions may cause variations in the results.

The bold red line represents the Time of emergency (1.3 minutes). For all the experiments the evacuation starts at this time. The worst-case scenario is Random Evacuation with a mean of 7.4 min. Whereas Random-T performs slightly better than Random with a mean of 6.0 min due to the time sequence the exit points are not completely jammed. SRD performs much better than the Random approach with a mean of 4.0 min because it allows a group of people to take their nearest exits. SRD-T performs even better than SRD with a mean of 3.6 min due to the same reason mentioned previously. GA on the other hand performs the best with a mean of 3.1 min. Initially GA is slower than SRD-T but eventually it finishes earlier.

Figure 6 presents the evolution of the fitness value achieved in 50 generations. The blue line represents fitness values at each generation whereas the red line is being used as a smoother to depict the decent. It is noticed that GA directs regions to optimal locations, whereas SDR-T may allocate two regions to one gate that delays the evacuation due to overcrowding. We have reasons to believe that GA may perform even better when there are multiple constraints i.e., some exits are closed due to danger, in which case GA can easily discard those chromosomes that consists of restricted gates; or the shortest aerial distance from the mean position of a region to an exit might not be geometrically the shortest path for evacuation.

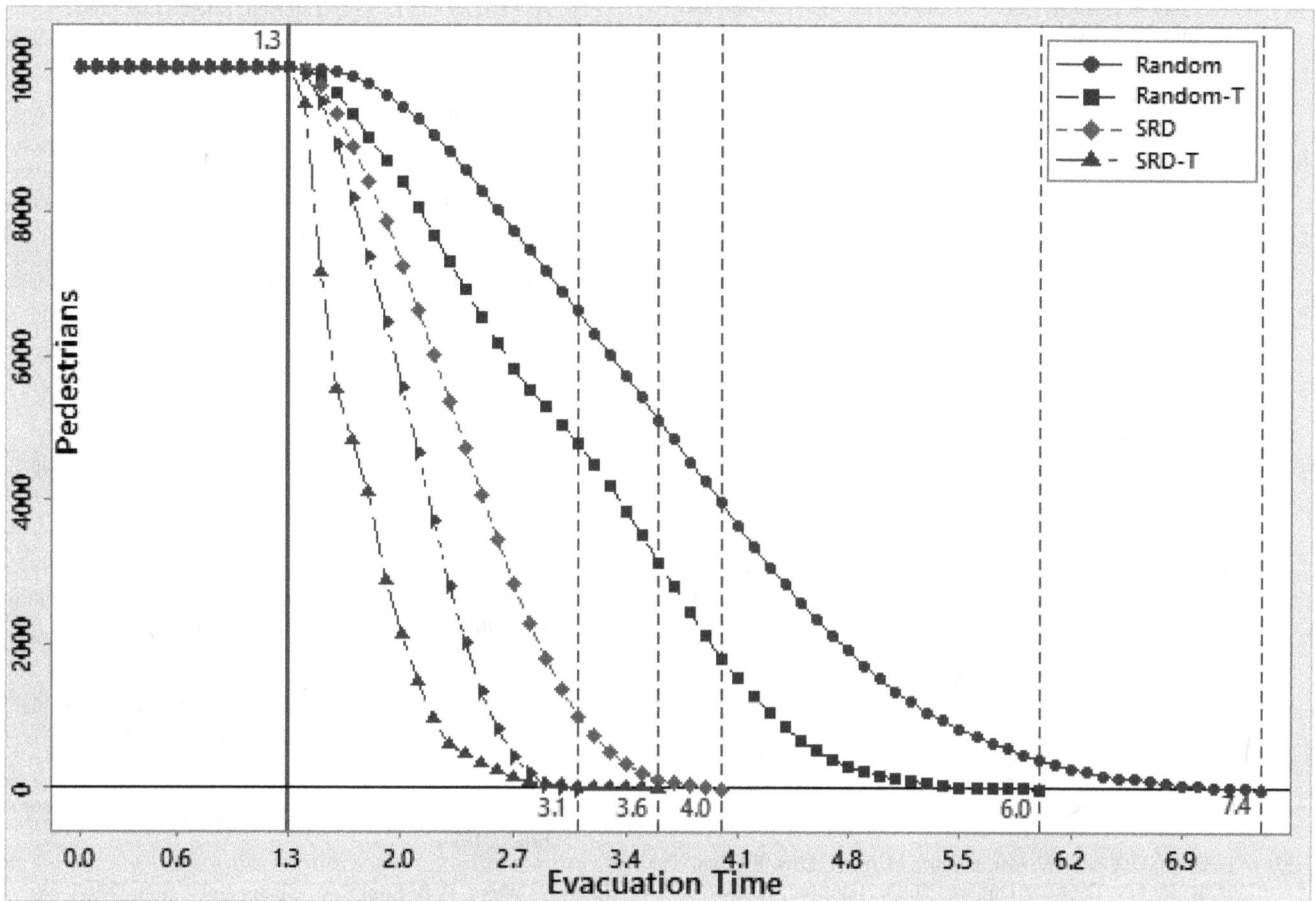

Figure 5: Mean Evacuation Time of different Strategies

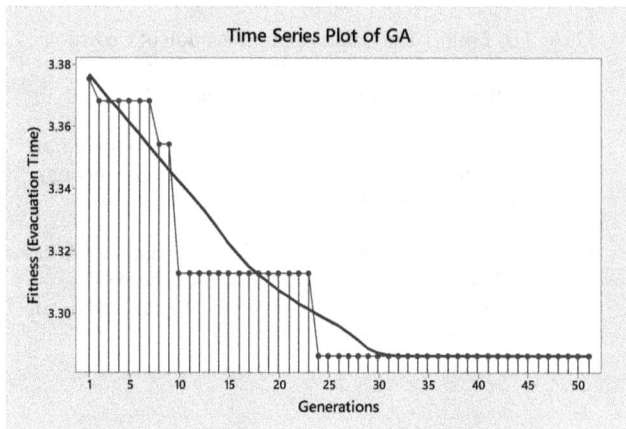

Figure 6: Evolution of Genetic Algorithm

6. CONCLUSIONS

In this paper, we discuss crowd gatherings as a potential source for resulting in natural and manmade disasters. We discuss how crowd simulation models can be useful to replicate the real-world scenarios in risk free experimental environments that allow modelers to study and analyze crowd dynamics (e.g., assessing different crowd evacuation techniques). We propose an Agent Based Crowd Simulation & Analysis framework that consists of three layers: (i) Simulation layer allows the modelers to create crowd simulation models using Anylogic simulation environment, (ii) an Interface layer extending the functionality of Anylogic with external modules and allow interaction & interoperability of crowd simulation models using Java based middleware; and (iii) an Optimization & Analysis layer that supports implementing or integrating optimization algorithms that can interact with the simulation layer via the Interface layer so that the optimization can be performed with simulation in the loop, and can be useful for the assessment of optimization approach.

We use a case study of Hajj as an example, and presented key steps in preparing a crowd simulation model and using it with our framework for the assessment of crowd evacuation strategies. We provide details of the simulation experiments and discuss their results. These results show a comparative analysis of different crowd evacuation strategies and their performance during the simulation runs for Hajj scenario. When the crowd simulation scenario becomes more complex with more physical and behavioral details, the performance of these evacuation strategies may vary.

In essence we contribute an open framework that utilizes the potential of Crowd Simulation tools like Anylogic and allow integration and interoperability of external modules for simulation, optimization and analysis. Our framework can be easily deployed

239

at Public Safety & Security (PSS) management organizations and can benefit developing decision policies.

We are further interested to extend our framework to support integration and reuse of different simulation runtime environments and optimization algorithms. Additionally, we aim to implement integration of real-world sensors and actuators for Real-world in the loop modes, where e.g., the GIS coordinates of a crowd is acquired for input and the actuators are used to manage the crowd flow for optimal evacuation.

7. REFERENCES

[1]   World Health Organization, "Communiable Disease Alert and Response for Mass Gatherings: Key Considerations," WHO Press, Geneva, 2008.

[2]   "Incidents during the Hajj," [Online]. Available: https://en.wikipedia.org/wiki/Incidents_during_the_Hajj. [Accessed January 2017].

[3]   "FDA Emergency Operations Plan," Office of crisis management, U.S Department of health and human services, 2014.

[4]   J. Banks, J. S. Carson, B. L. Nelson and D. M. Nicol, Discrete-Event System Simulation (5th Edition), 5 ed., Prentice Hall, 2009.

[5]   S. Zhou, D. Chen, W. Cai, L. Luo, M. Y. H. Low, F. Tian, V. S.-H. Tay, D. W. S. Ong and B. D. Hamilton, "Crowd Modeling and Simulation Technologies," ACM Trans. Model. Comput. Simul., vol. 20, pp. 20:1--20:35, 2010.

[6]   D. Thalmann and S. R. Musse, Crowd Simulation, London: Springer, 2007.

[7]   D. C. Duives, W. Daamen and S. P. Hoogendoorn, "State-of-the-Art Crowd Motion Simulation Models," Transportation Research Part C: Emerging Technologies, vol. 37, pp. 193-209, 2013.

[8]   S. Sarmady, F. Haron and A. Z. H. Talib, "Multi-Agent Simulation of Circular Pedestrian Moments Using Cellular Automata," in Second Asia International Conference on Modeling and Simulation, 2008.

[9]   S. Sarmady, F. Haron and A. Z. H. Talib, "Agent-Based Simulation of Crowd at the Tawaf Area," in 1st National Seminar on Hajj Best Practices Through Advances in Sciences and Technology, 2007.

[10]   M. H. Dridi, "Simulation of High Density Pedestrian Flow: Microscopic Model," arXiv preprint arXiv:1501.06496, vol. Vol. XXI, no. 1, 2015.

[11]   J. Zhong, W. Cai and L. Luo, "Crowd Evacuation Planning Using Cartersian Genetic Programming and Agent-Based Crowd Modeling," in Winter Simulation Conference, 2015.

[12]   A. Ferscha and K. Zia, "LifeBelt: Silent Directional Guidance for Crowd Evacuation," in International Symposium on Wearable Computers, Linz, 2009.

[13]   A. Abdelghany, K. Abdelghany, H. Mahmassani and W. Alhalabi, "Modeling Framework for Optimal Evacuation of Large-Scale Crowded Pedestrian Facilities," European Journal of Operational Research, vol. 237, no. 3, pp. 1105-1118, 2014.

[14]   "Anylogic Simulation Software," [Online]. Available: http://www.anylogic.com [Accessed January 2017].

[15]   A. Borshchev, The big book of simulation modeling: multimethod modeling with AnyLogic, AnyLogic North America , 2013.

[16]   "AnyLogic Pedestrian Simulation," [Online]. Available: https://en.wikibooks.org/wiki/Simulation_with_AnyLogic/ Pedestrian_Simulation. [Accessed 2017].

[17]   "Space Markup," [Online]. Available: https://help.anylogic.com/index.jsp?topic=/com.xj.anylogi c.help/html/ui/Space%20Markup%20palette.html. [Accessed 2017].

[18]   "Anylogic Experiment Framework," [Online]. Available: http://www.anylogic.com/experiment-framework. [Accessed Jan 2017].

[19]   M. Melanie, An introduction to genetic algorithms, MIT press,, 1998.

[20]   P. Wang, P. B. Lou, S.-C. Chang and J. Sun, "Modeling and Optimization of Crowd Guidance for Building Emergency Evacuation," in 4th IEEE Conference on Automation Sciences and Engineering, Washington D.C., 2008.

[21]   J. J. Fruin, "The Causes and Prevention of Crowd Disasters," in First International Conference on Engineering for Crowd Safety, London, 1993.

[22]   Y. Yang, J. Li and Q. Zhao, "Study on passenger flow simulation in urban subway station based on anylogic," Journal of Software, vol. 9, pp. 140-147, 2014.

[23]   S. Mohammad, M. S. Sunar and R. M. Hanifa, "A Review on Tawad Crowd Simulation: State-of-the-Art," International Journal of Interactive Digital Media, vol. 2, no. 11, pp. 1-6, 2014.

Online Analysis of Simulation Data
with Stream-based Data Mining

Niclas Feldkamp, Soeren Bergmann, Steffen Strassburger
Ilmenau University of Technology
P.O. Box 100565
D-98684 Ilmenau
+49 3677 - 69 4050

{niclas.feldkamp, soeren.bergmann, steffen.strassburger}@tu-ilmenau.de

ABSTRACT

Discrete event simulation is an accepted instrument for investigating the dynamic behavior of complex systems and evaluating processes. Usually simulation experts conduct simulation experiments for a predetermined system specification by manually varying parameters through educated assumptions and according to a prior defined goal. As an alternative, data farming and knowledge discovery in simulation data are ongoing and popular methods in order to uncover unknown relationships and effects in the model to gain useful information about the underlying system. Those methods usually demand broad scale and data intensive experimental design, so computing time can quickly become large. As a solution to that, we extend an existing concept of knowledge discovery in simulation data with an online stream mining component to get data mining results even while experiments are still running. For this purpose, we introduce a method for using decision tree classification in combination with clustering algorithms for analyzing simulation output data that considers the flow of experiments as a data stream. A prototypical implementation proves the basic applicability of the concept and yields large possibilities for future research.

CCS Concepts

• **Computing methodologies~Modeling and simulation**
• *Computing methodologies~Machine learning*
• *Information systems~Data stream mining*

Keywords

Simulation; Simulation output analysis; data mining; data farming; visual analytics; knowledge discovery; data stream mining.

1. INTRODUCTION

Data farming and knowledge discovery in simulation data are ongoing and popular issues in current simulation research. In short, these concepts are known as broad scale experimentation that aims

SIGSIM-PADS'17, May 24 - 26, 2017, Singapore, Singapore.
Copyright is held by the owner/author(s). Publication rights licensed to ACM.
ACM 978-1-4503-4489-0/17/05...$15.00
DOI: http://dx.doi.org/10.1145/3064911.3064915

to uncover unknown relationships and effects in the model to ultimately gain useful information about the underlying system, leading to a better understanding of the system's behavior and support decision making [6, 7, 26].

In general, data farming concepts promote efficient experimental design to reduce experimental effort. Still, in complex systems, the actual number of experiments can quickly become very large and the total computing time can add up to hours or days, especially if high performance computer clusters are not available [16].

On the analysis side, data mining methods usually provide a strong and solid basis for the discovery of knowledge in simulation data [7, 15]. Given a large total runtime due to a large number of experiments that have to be conducted, simulation experts have to defer the result analysis until the execution of all experiments is completed and all of the result data is collected. This problem becomes even more severe in situations where the analysis leads to the conclusion that additional experimentation is needed or even the experimental design has to be revamped from scratch. This is not an uncommon issue because knowledge discovery is an iterative process.

As a solution to this, we propose a concept for analyzing simulation data with online stream mining algorithms that work incrementally and allow data mining even while simulation experiments are still running. For a proof of concept, we use the Hoeffding Classification Tree [5] for building online incremental decision trees in combination with a clustering algorithm.

The remainder of this paper is structured as follows. In section 2, we present a review of related work regarding data farming and knowledge discovery in simulation data, followed by related work regarding decision trees for simulation data analysis. Additionally, we present a quick overview on data stream mining literature. In section 3, we describe our concept of simulation data analysis with data stream mining algorithms as an extension to the existing knowledge discovery in simulation data process. Section 4 presents a small prototypical case study for investigation and proof of concept. Section 5 summarizes our findings and discusses future work.

2. RELATED WORK

2.1 Data Farming and Knowledge Discovery in Simulation Data

Data farming describes a methodology for using a simulation model as data generator and efficient experimental design to maximize data yield and therefore information gain [6, 14, 15, 24].

New approaches for designing simulation experiments achieve the balance between broad scale parameter combination and variation on the one hand and manageable data volume on the other hand by abandoning inefficient n^k design patterns [18, 27]. Based on that, Feldkamp et al. [7] developed a method for finding hidden patterns and relations in large quantities of simulation data based on broad scale experimental design and visually aided analysis called knowledge discovery in simulation data as shown in Figure 1.

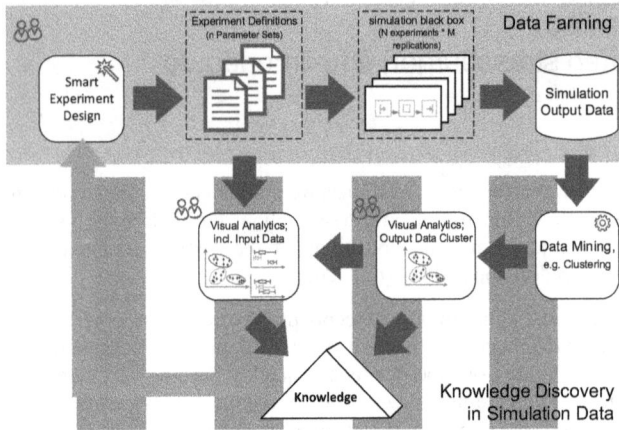

Figure 1. Knowledge discovery in simulation data [7].

Based on using data farming concepts for covering a large bandwidth of input factor values and therefore possible model behavior, data mining methods are applied onto this quantity of data. Knowledge can be gained through visual representations of data mining results combined with visualization of input/output relations.

2.2 Classification for Simulation Data Analysis

A decision tree is a supervised learning method which represents a predictive model. This model maps observations about an item to several classes of the item's target value, represented in tree branches and leaves, respectively. Visual representations of the tree tend to be readily understandable and suitable to present results to non-specialists. Additionally, tree branches can be interpreted and transformed into what-if rules for decision support [4, 22, 23].

In the context of simulation and modelling, decision trees are not an established tool for analyzing simulation data. Still, in line with the rising popularity of data mining in general, there are some papers addressing decision trees to be linked with simulation data analysis. Tercan et al. [29] investigated the applicability of classification techniques like regression and decision trees for designing industrial laser cutting processes based on simulated process data.

Tang et al. [28] used decision tree algorithms for extracting "if-then"-rules regarding tank damage over different military scenarios in combat simulations. In the context of data farming, Horne et al. [13] recommend the use of classification trees as a supporting tool in massive combat simulation data analysis for finding significant factor interactions, which is a typical issue in data farming applications. The authors emphasize that one of the main benefits of classification trees is their intuitive and comprehensible application compared to methods like stepwise regression. Giabbanelli [12] used simulation to generate network traffic and data mining techniques including classification trees for optimizing network routing.

In order to create class labels for unlabeled simulation data, clustering algorithms can be used. Feldkamp et al. [7, 8] propose a method for clustering simulation data based on selected output performance measures. Individual simulation runs are grouped into clusters of similar output performance values. As a result, simulation runs within the same cluster are similar regarding selected performance measures and can serve as a target value for decision tree classification as proposed in this paper.

2.3 Data Stream Mining

The focus of machine learning and data mining research in the last decades focused on batch learning on usually small datasets. Using a batch learning algorithm, the data has to be available in whole. The algorithm processes the data one or even multiple times before putting out a decision model. In most of today's dynamic applications, neither are datasets small enough, nor is data available at once, but collected over time. This is typically a result of the principle of automatic data generation. It describes the transition from people entering information into a computer towards computers entering data into each other [10].

A data stream is usually defined by the following features: Data elements in the stream arrive online, there is no control over the order in which elements arrive, either within a single stream or across multiple streams. Streams are potentially unlimited in size [2]. These features demand special requirements of stream mining algorithms, including sampling and randomizing techniques as well as incremental processing. Furthermore, although data streams are possibly unlimited, algorithms will have to use limited computational and bandwidth resources, and have limited direct access to the data but need to provide answers in nearly real time [9, 10]. If the data stream model allows delete and update operations, data stream mining algorithms even do have to deal with outdated information, which requires concept and drift detection mechanisms in order to maintain a trained model that still fits the learning data [19]. Current practical data stream mining applications include for example real time queries for financial stock data [30], network security [32], web site click stream analysis [17], and sensor monitoring [20].

Regarding decision trees, traditional algorithms like ID3 or CART are not suitable for application on data streams. In order to train the decision model, they need to have all training examples stored in the main memory at once, which limits the number of examples they can learn from, and an incremental construction of the tree is not possible as well. The stream based *Hoeffding Tree* algorithm serves as an alternative since it provides incremental creation of the tree as well as a one-pass processing of data [5]. This means, that it does not need the complete training data set at once in order to construct the tree. Based on the assumption that the distribution of incoming training examples stays within a certain uniformity, this algorithm leverages a statistical result known as the *Hoeffding bound* [21] which guarantees that with a high probability, an attribute chosen for a node split decision after using n examples is the same that would be chosen using infinite examples [11]. Having a constant computing time and memory consumption, it is perfectly suited for the processing a continuous data stream.

Most partitioning-based clustering algorithms like k-means are suitable for clustering data streams by default, because they commonly process data iteratively [1].

3. CONCEPTUAL PROCESS

Our proposed concept of stream mining simulation data, as shown in Figure 2, extends the existing process of knowledge discovery in simulation data. Here, the green area on top represents the conventional approach of a data farming project. The initial design of experiments determines the number of simulation runs (alias design points) that have to be carried out. After all experiments have been conducted, the analysis of simulation data can be initiated. This approach has proven to have several disadvantages.

Since we aim to cover a large bandwidth of possible input factor value combinations in order to find unknown and potential valuable hidden relations in the simulation data, in complex models we need to perform a large number of simulations runs so runtime can be very long.

If it afterwards emerges that experiment design was not sufficient for various reasons, simulation run time and therefore valuable computing time is spent in vain. Reasons for insufficient experiments may be missing input factors, too tightly or wrong chosen factor value margins, insufficient factor levels, accidently correlated factors and many more.

In a situation where the outcome of data mining application is prior unknown, shortcomings regarding input factor design oftentimes become evident after the experimentation. Additionally, knowledge discovery methods are very well suited for validation of the simulation model, because data mining algorithms can uncover odd or faulty model behavior, especially if it occurs exclusively in rare and special cases.

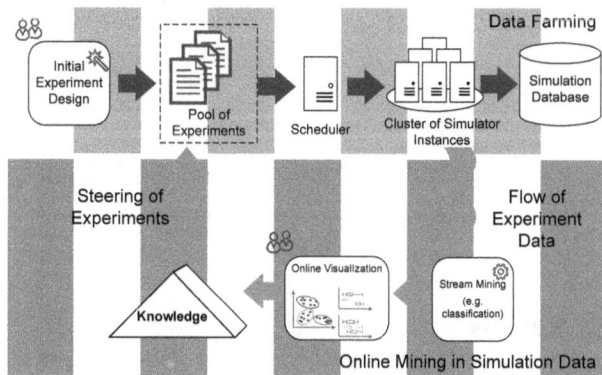

Figure 2. Conceptual process for online stream mining in simulation data.

Because of that, we propose a concept for applying data mining algorithms on the simulation data while experiments, or a proportion of experiments, are still running. The flow of finished simulation runs that are passed to the simulation database meets the characteristics of a data stream by being potentially unlimited and the interval of runs getting finished is rather unforeseeable. By using stream mining algorithms, we try to incrementally grow an understanding of the simulation data. The more fundamental a found hidden pattern or rule in the data is, the sooner it will be uncovered, even if just a small fraction of experiments has already finished.

This even yields the possibility of manipulating the pool of scheduled experiments on the fly, while the simulation is running in order to steer the experiments and the potential covered area of the response surface into a certain direction of demand. In a further development stage, we imagine a simulation model that is continuously running and adapting, creating a flow of knowledge that leads to an extremely dense data and information collection for decision support.

The process of stream mining simulation data is shown in the bottom blue area of Figure 2 and is conducted as follows:

Simultaneously to passing finished simulation runs to the database for hard storage, they are sent to an instance that feeds it to a data stream mining algorithm.

Theoretically, various data mining algorithms are adaptable for this usage including regression, classification, and machine learning, as long as they are suitable for simulation data analysis. Furthermore, they need to be capable of incremental processing of data in a way that data points can be fed to the algorithm in a sequence. Online or near real-time processing is also preferable to enable an instant analysis of results. This involves the ability of *one-pass processing*, which means that the algorithm needs to process each data point only once, which reduces memory consumption and computing time dramatically.

Potential knowledge is then created similar to the usual knowledge discovery in simulation data process by finding interesting patterns and relations through investigating the data mostly visually. Visual Analytics also enables the possibility of connecting the two dimensions of simulation input and result data, because the investigation of this connection is usually the most interesting and prolific part of simulation data analysis.

An approach for online, stream based simulation analysis imposes additional requirements regarding the visualization compared to an offline analysis. The visualization has to be highly performant, because it needs to render and adapt in real time. Furthermore, the visualization ideally offers a dynamic component that enables the user to track the integration of incoming data points and changes in the data mining results over the course of finished experiments.

The idea behind our approach is not only to have results at an earlier stage. Furthermore, if shortcomings to the experimental design or a need for re-focusing the area of investigation becomes apparent, we also need to enable the user to actively shift the response surface into a desired direction if needed, which is called experiment steering. This can be achieved by creating and feeding additional experiments to the experiment scheduler as well as deleting potentially obsolete experiments from the pool. The challenge here is to maintain important features guaranteed by the initial experimental design, like orthogonality and absent of correlation between input factors.

Additionally, we assume that the order in which experiments are conducted influences the prospects of success for an online mining of simulation data approach. An essential difference between computer and real world experiments has always been the fact that the order in which computer experiments are executed is irrelevant. In contrast to real world experiments, there can not occur a systematic bias in a sequence of computer experiments. By aiming to analyze partial result sets of the complete experiment design, which will be the case in our stream mining approach, bias may very well occur though. Imagine an experimental design, sorting the values of an input factor from low too high in line with the execution order. If this input factor has a directly correlated relation with one or more output parameters, of course results will be biased if we are looking only at subparts of the result set. To prevent this effect, implementing bias-protecting methods from traditional, real world experimental design theory, like blocking and randomizing experiments, can be implemented. This becomes even more challenging, if the experimental design incorporates any form of factor crossing, which data farmers usually do to evaluate scenario robustness [13].

In the next section, we discuss a simple prototypical use case in order to prove the general applicability of data stream mining for simulation data analysis.

4. USE CASE SCENARIO

4.1 Prototype Architecture

For a demonstration of our approach, we used an enhanced single server model. Here, seven different types of products with each of them having a distinct processing and setup time, enter a manufacturing system through a single source. Process and setup times slightly vary in very small proportion to add some random variation to the model. Additionally, each job is assigned a unique due date when entering the system. Jobs are sorted before entering the processing station, whereas five different sorting strategies have been implemented. Figure 3 shows a screenshot of the model, which has been implement in Siemens Plant Simulation.

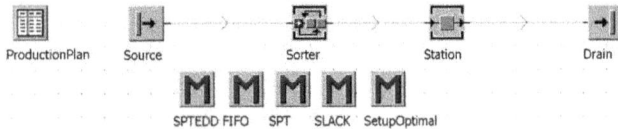

Figure 3. Screenshot of the Plant Simulation model.

The input parameters for experimental design include the inter arrival time of jobs, capacity and strategy of the sorter and mixture of product types. Each experiment is also replicated 10 times due to random variation. Table 1 shows a summary for input factors and their margins for the experimental design.

Table 1. Input factors for experimental design.

Input Factor	Margins
Inter arrival time	60s – 240s
Sorter Capacity	10 – 1000
Sorter Strategy	5 Strategies
Product Mixture (Seven product types)	0 – 100% per product
Random Number Stream	*1 – 10*

Starting from the table of input factors, we created two experimental design sheets, one for the product mixture and one for the remaining factors. Those sheets have been created with the Nearly Orthogonal Latin Hypercube Design method [25], that features an efficient design regarding number of experiments and coverage of parameter value combinations among other preferable properties like minimal correlation between input factors [31]. Afterwards we crossed both design sheets in order to analyze the robustness of product mixture combinations against variations in the remaining input factors. The final experimental design consists of nearly half a million simulation runs. Furthermore, we randomized the order of experiments to prevent the occurrence of systematic bias during online analysis.

Simulation runs have been parallelized on ten machines. A simulation worker is then processing the data as a vector of input and output parameter values in a simple csv format which is further streamed in small blocks of files to a dedicated Hadoop Distributed File System (HDFS) Server. Hence a constant flow of data is established and the simulation data matches the characteristics of a data stream.

For clustering data on the stream, we used the *streaming k-means package* from the Apache Spark Computing Framework [33]. The streaming k-means application is monitoring the HDSF directory and automatically picks up new data on arrival so that the underlying cluster model updates iteratively.

After being labeled by allocation to a cluster, the simulation data is then passed to a streaming decision tree algorithm instance in order to iteratively train a decision tree model. For this purpose we used the Hoeffding Tree Implementation by the *Massive Online Analysis* software framework (MOA) [3].

In contrast to the first stage, now the simulation input data is used to feed the mining algorithm. To be precise, we let the algorithm map the input data to the tree nodes, whereas the output data is mapped at the tree leafs, representing the output data as cluster allocation number. Each branch of the tree then represents an if-then rule regarding simulation input/output relations. Figure 4 shows how the simulation stream data is processed.

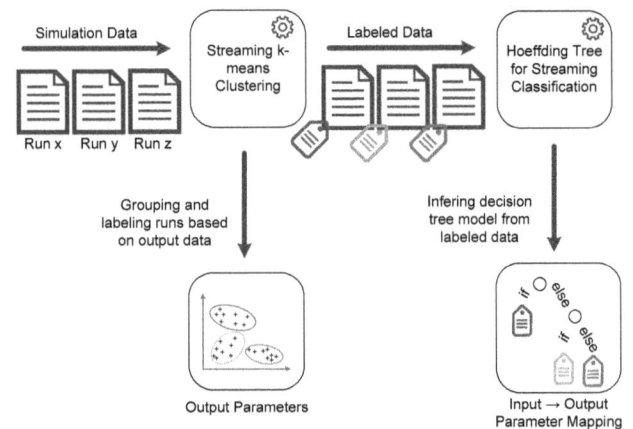

Figure 4. Stream mining procedure of the prototypical implementation.

4.2 Results

In our prototypical implementation, we let the clustering algorithm compute on the three output parameters *Throughput*, *Utilization* (station utilization in percent) and *SetupProp* (the proportion of time in which the station is blocked by setup processes). Figure 5 and Figure 6 show a comparison of the results for clustering on those three dimensions after 10% of simulations runs have passed as well as the final clustering result after all experiments have finished respectively.

In addition, we added the input factor *ArrivalTime* (inter arrival time of jobs in the systems) to the plot in order to investigate the distribution of this input factor among output parameters clusters. Apparently, the experiments that compose cluster 3 (purple) represent the overall best performance, with a high throughput, high utilization of 80% or higher and a relatively low proportion of setup times. In contrast, cluster 1 (orange) consist of opposite values and therefore consist of mostly bad performance runs. If we compare the 10% data set against the full data set, the overall distributions are very similar.

In fact, the *mediod points*, which represent the center of each cluster, do barely change. Once a point has been allocated to a cluster it rarely changes its allocation over the course of incoming finished experiments over time. The histograms of the three output parameters show that the overall distribution of output parameter values barely changes also. This effect is likely because of the beneficial properties of the NOLH-design method. This experiment design method provides an appropriate coverage of the response surface, even if only subsets of the design are considered. Furthermore, the input factor *ArrivalTime* is nearly uniformly distributed even at 10% of data, which also comes from the beneficial properties of the chosen experiment design method.

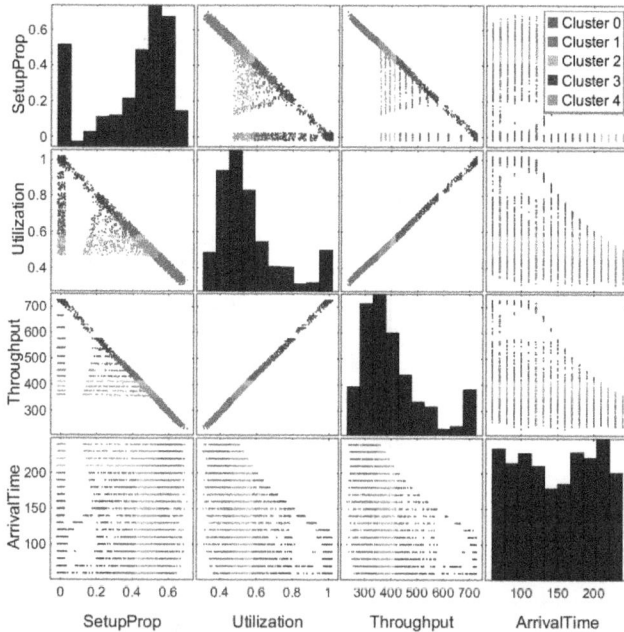

Figure 5. Clustering results for 10% of simulation runs.

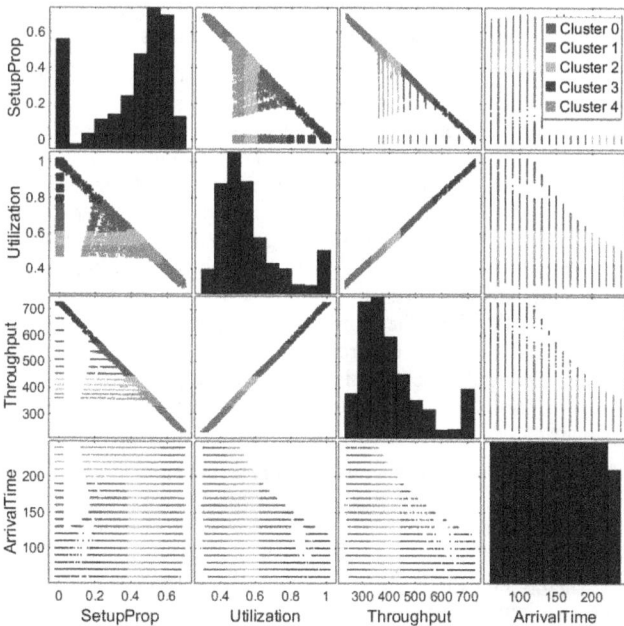

Figure 6. Clustering results for 100% of simulation runs.

Since cluster centers and data distribution stay consistent, coarse but fundamental knowledge and assumptions about the system can be gained early during experiments. On the other hand, conclusions get more precise when new data is added to the decision model.

Looking at the input factor *ArrivalTime* in Figure 7, short arrival times are dominant in the good performance cluster (cluster number 3). On the other hand, inter arrival time is perfectly equally distributed on the bad performance cluster (cluster number 1), so

there is no evidence that on the other hand longer inter arrival times lead to bad performance cluster allocation. The boxplots in Figure 7 change just slightly from 10% to 100% of simulation runs, therefore those assumptions can safely be made at already 10% of simulation runs. The most noticeable change is the slight decrease of maximum und median value of the cluster 3, which means that more simulation runs with very short inter arrival times have been allocated to this cluster which pushes down the average value of inter arrival time. Figure 5 and Figure 6 show that there is a gap around arrival time 100s that is filled with data points allocated to cluster 3 once 100% of simulation experiments is reached.

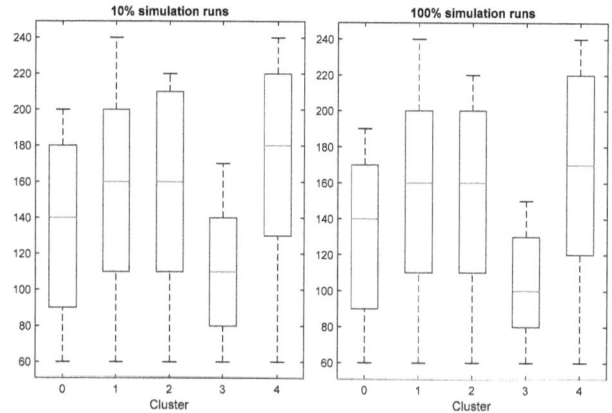

Figure 7. Comparison of the distribution of parameter values for input factor inter arrival time among different clusters.

To get a more in-depth analysis of the distribution of input parameter values to corresponding cluster allocation and therefore output parameter distribution, we can use the second stage of classification with decision trees. For the validation of our concept, we took snapshots of the tree at multiple levels of experiments completion or different points of run time, respectively.

The full test set of data (100% of simulations runs), which was generated prior for evaluation purpose, was applied to every tree snapshot in order to generate classifier evaluation measures, which is shown in Figure 8. This figure shows the correctness and precision measures for cluster 1 and 3 as well as for the data in total. Correctness or accuracy means the number of correct classifications divided by the number of total classifications made. Precision on the other hand describes the number of correct class predictions divided by the total number of class values predicted (true positives / (true positives + false positives)). The more data from completed simulation runs is added to the decision model, the more does the overall goodness of the model increase. The evaluation measures for individual classes/clusters varies heavily.

In general, the prediction goodness for good and bad performance cluster is high, whereas it is rather mediocre among the other clusters, which is why the overall total prediction goodness drops. As such, predicting a good or bad system performance is easier than predicting runs whose performance is average. In addition, these clusters are much better separable to each other. The number of runs in cluster 1 that are mistakenly predicted as being in cluster 3 and vice versa is zero even at 10% of data.

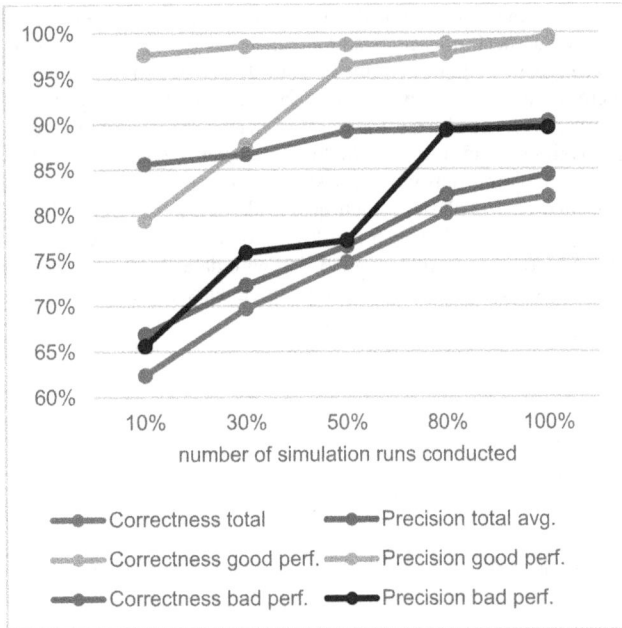

Figure 8. Accuracy of decision model for total data and also good and bad performance clusters.

Looking at the actual decision tree model structure, the overall model stays the same, at least regarding the split nodes at the top. The first split decision is *ProdMix*, which is a measurement for the homogeneity of the product mixture. The higher the value of *ProdMix*, the more dominant the proportion of a distinct product type is in mix. On the other hand, a low value of *ProdMix* indicates a uniform distribution of product types. Since this parameter is the tree's top split decision, the composition of the product mixture apparently is the most influential factor for cluster allocation and therefore system performance in this model, followed by inter arrival time and sorter strategy. Figure 9 shows an extract of the tree visualization after 10% of the simulation data was processed.

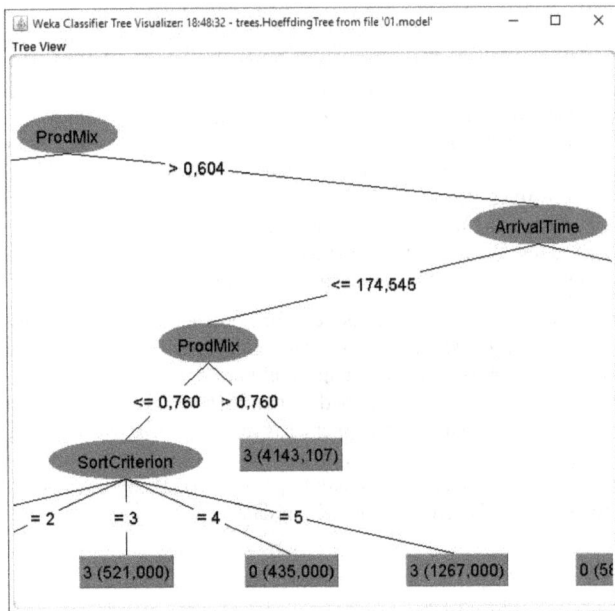

Figure 9. Detail extract of Hoeffding Tree at 10% data.

As more data flows into the model, the depth of the tree increases up to branches with a length of 12, because more detailed split nodes are added, covering more exceptions and special cases as the response surface gets more dense and existing gaps get filled with data. Table 2 shows exemplary tree branches that have been transformed into tabulated what-if rules. Those rules describe input factor values that lead to good performance cluster allocation. Note how split decision node values only slightly adapt from 10% to 100% percent of simulation data.

Table 2. Selected decision tree branches.

Stream	Input Factors			Prediction
	Prod. mixture	Arrival time	Sorting strategy	Cluster
10% data	> 0.76	< 174.55s	-	3
	< 0.76 and > 0.604	< 174.55s	Setup optimal	3
100% data	> 0.734	< 141.8s	-	3
	< 0.734 and > 0.604	< 141.8s	Setup optimal	3

5. DISCUSSION AND SUMMARY

We successfully showed how a knowledge discovery process can be applied on simulation data even if not all experiments have been conducted, through considering simulation experiments as a data stream and using online stream mining technologies.

In our prototypical experiment, we were able to successfully gain valid assumptions about the underlying system even at 10% of experiment completion. While more simulation data is added, the possible insights and knowledge gets more complex and detailed. However, since this paper is ongoing research and the model used for the prototypical investigation was very simple more research on this topic is needed. Randomizing the order of simulation experiments worked surprisingly well, since we expected to run into problems of biased findings caused by the crossed experimental design. Therefore, more complex simulation models and the application of experimental designs with broader factor value limits need to be investigated. Additionally, different stream mining algorithms besides clustering and decision trees should be evaluated.

This paper serves as a general proof and demonstration of concept. Therefore, the third part of our concept, the dynamic steering and manipulation of experiments, was not part of our prototypical investigation. Considering the findings of our work, this topic yields large implications for future research in order to actively be able manipulate the investigated area of the response surface without having to restart experimentation from scratch, especially regarding the experiment design, which needs to maintain important features like orthogonality and correlation reduction.

Regarding the visualization of results, true real time dynamic visualizations would enhance the usability of the workflow dramatically.

Furthermore, we demonstrated the general applicability of decision trees in combination with clustering algorithms for simulation output analysis. Decision trees are very well suited for mapping input/output relations in the simulation model. Having massive amounts of data for training the decision model, the tree gets very large in size and depth though, which limits readability and usability for human cognition. Regarding the iterative stream constructed Hoeffding Tree, tracking and monitoring tree branches visually over the course of simulation time possibly proves to be difficult to some extent. More sophisticated methods for pruning branches and mining and transforming what-if rules should be investigated in future work.

6. References

[1]   Alpaydin, E. 2010. *Introduction to Machine Learning*. Adaptive computation and machine learning. MIT Press, Cambridge, Mass.

[2]   Babcock, B., Babu, S., Datar, M., Motwani, R., and Widom, J. 2002. Models and issues in data stream systems. In *Proceedings of the twenty-first ACM SIGMOD-SIGACT-SIGART Symposium on Principles of Database Systems*. ACM Press, New York, NY, 1–16. DOI=10.1145/543613.543615.

[3]   Bifet, A., Holmes, G., Kirkby, R., and Pfahringer, B. 2010. MOA: Massive Online Analysis. *The Journal of Machine Learning Research* 11, 1601–1604.

[4]   Breiman, L. 1984. *Classification and Regression Trees*. Chapman & Hall/CRC; Chapman & Hall, New York.

[5]   Domingos, P. and Hulten, G. Mining high-speed data streams. In *the sixth ACM SIGKDD international conference*, 71–80. DOI=10.1145/347090.347107.

[6]   Elmegreen, B. G., Sanchez, S. M., and Szalay, A. S. 2014. The Future of Computerized Decision Making. In *Proceedings of the 2014 Winter Simulation Conference*, 943–949. DOI=10.1109/WSC.2014.7019954.

[7]   Feldkamp, N., Bergmann, S., and Strassburger, S. 2015. Knowledge Discovery in Manufacturing Simulations. In *Proceedings of the 2015 ACM SIGSIM PADS Conference*, 3–12. DOI=10.1145/2769458.2769468.

[8]   Feldkamp, N., Bergmann, S., and Strassburger, S. 2015. Visual Analytics of Manufacturing Simulation Data. In *Proceedings of the 2015 Winter Simulation Conference*, 779–790.

[9]   Gaber, M. M., Zaslavsky, A., and Krishnaswamy, S. 2005. Mining data streams. *SIGMOD Rec.* 34, 2, 18–26.

[10]   Gama, J. 2010. *Knowledge discovery from data streams*. Chapman & Hall/CRC data mining and knowledge discovery series. Chapman & Hall/CRC, Boca Raton, FL.

[11]   Gama, J., Rocha, R., and Medas, P. 2003. Accurate decision trees for mining high-speed data streams. In *Proceedings of the ninth ACM SIGKDD international Conference on Knowledge Discovery and Data Mining*. ACM, New York, NY, USA, 523. DOI=10.1145/956750.956813.

[12]   Giabbanelli, P. J. 2010. Impact of complex network properties on routing in backbone networks. In *2010 IEEE Globecom Workshops. GC'10, Workshops: Dec 5, 2010 to Dec 10, 2010 in Miami, Florida, USA*. IEEE, [Piscataway, N.J.], 389–393. DOI=10.1109/GLOCOMW.2010.5700347.

[13]   Horne, G., Åkesson, B., Meyer, T., and Anderson, S. 2014. *Data farming in support of NATO. Final Report of Task Group MSG-088*. STO technical report TR-MSG-088. North Atlantic Treaty Organisation, Neuilly-sur-Seine Cedex.

[14]   Horne, G. E. and Meyer, T. 2010. Data farming and defense applications. In *MODSIM World Conference and Expo*.

[15]   Horne, G. E. and Meyer, T. E. 2005. Data Farming: Discovering Surprise. In *Winter Simulation Conference, 2005*, 1082–1087.

[16]   Kallfass, D. and Schlaak, T. 2012. NATO MSG-088 Case Study Results to demonstrate the Benefit of using Data Farming for Military Decision support. In *Proceedings of the 2012 Winter Simulation Conference*, 1–12. DOI=10.1109/WSC.2012.6465132.

[17]   Kaushal, C. and Singh, H. 2015. Comparative Study of Recent Sequential Pattern Mining Algorithms on Web Clickstream Data. In *2015 IEEE Power, Communication and Information Technology Conference (PCITC)*, 652–656. DOI=10.1109/PCITC.2015.7438078.

[18]   Kleijnen, J. P., Sanchez, S. M., Lucas, T. W., and Cioppa, T. M. 2005. State-of-the-Art Review: A User's Guide to the Brave New World of Designing Simulation Experiments. *INFORMS Journal on Computing* 17, 3, 263–289.

[19]   Lemaire, V., Salperwyck, C., and Bondu, A. 2015. A Survey on Supervised Classification on Data Streams. In *eBISS 2014. Lecture Notes in Business Information Processing*, E. Zimányi and R.-D. Kutsche, Eds. Springer, Heidelberg, 88–125.

[20]   Madden, S. and Franklin, M. J. 2002. Fjording the Stream: An Architecture for Queries over Streaming Sensor Data. In *Proceedings of the 2002 Intl. Conf. on Data Engineering*. IEEE, Piscataway, NJ, 555–566. DOI=10.1109/ICDE.2002.994774.

[21]   Oded Maron and Andrew W. Moore. Hoeffding Races: Accelerating Model Selection Search for Classification and Function Approximation.

[22]   Quinlan, J. R. 1987. Simplifying decision trees. *International Journal of Man-Machine Studies* 27, 3, 221–234.

[23]   Rokach, L. and Maimon, O. 2008. *Data mining with decision trees. Theory and applications*. Series in machine perception and artificial intelligence v. 69. World Scientific, Singapore.

[24]   Sanchez, S. M. 2007. Work Smarter, Not Harder: Guidelines for Designing Simulation Experiments. In *Proceedings of the 2007 Winter Simulation Conference. December 9 - 12, 2007, Washington, DC, U.S.A.* IEEE, Piscataway, N.J., 84–94. DOI=10.1109/WSC.2007.4419591.

[25]   Sanchez, S. M. 2011. *NOLHdesigns spreadsheet*. http://harvest.nps.edu/. Accessed 1 February 2015.

[26]   Sanchez, S. M. 2014. Simulation Experiments: Better Data, Not Just Big Data. In *Proceedings of the 2014 Winter Simulation Conference*, 805–816.

[27]   Sanchez, S. M. and Wan, H. 2009. Better than a petaflop: The power of efficient experimental design. In *Proceedings of the 2009 Winter Simulation Conference (WSC 2009). (WSC 2009) : Austin, Texas : 13-16 December 2009*. IEEE Service Center, Piscataway, N.J., 60–74. DOI=10.1109/WSC.2009.5429316.

[28]   Tang, Z., Xue, Q., Zhao, M., and Wei, Y. 2009. Decision Tree Algorithm for Tank Damage Analysis in Combat Simulation Tests. In *9th International Conference on Electronic Measurement & Instruments (ICEMI 2009)*, 3-830-3-835. DOI=10.1109/ICEMI.2009.5274185.

[29]   Tercan, H., Al Khawli, T., Eppelt, U., Büscher, C., Meisen, T., and Jeschke, S. 2016. Use of Classification Techniques to Design Laser Cutting Processes. *Procedia 5CIRP6* 52, 292–297.

[30]   Tsay, R. S. 2010. *Analysis of financial time series*. Wiley series in probability and statistics. Wiley, Hoboken, NJ.

[31]   Vieira, H., Sanchez, S. M., Kienitz, K. H., and Belderrain, M. C. N. 2011. Improved efficient, nearly orthogonal,

nearly balanced mixed designs. In *Proceedings of the 2011 Winter Simulation Conference (WSC 2011)*, 3600–3611. DOI=10.1109/WSC.2011.6148054.

[32] Yoshida, K. 2007. Sampling-Based Stream Mining for Network Risk Management. In *New Frontiers in Artificial Intelligence. JSAI 2006 conference and workshops, Tokyo, Japan, June 5-9, 2006 ; revised selected papers*. Lecture notes in computer science Lecture notes in artificial intelligence 4384. Springer, Berlin, New York, 374–386. DOI=10.1007/978-3-540-69902-6_32.

[33] Zaharia, M., Franklin, M. J., Ghodsi, A., Gonzalez, J., Shenker, S., Stoica, I., Xin, R. S., Wendell, P., Das, T., Armbrust, M., Dave, A., Meng, X., Rosen, J., and Venkataraman, S. 2016. Apache Spark. *Commun. ACM* 59, 11, 56–65.

Spatial and Temporal Charging Infrastructure Planning Using Discrete Event Simulation

Marco Pruckner
University of
Erlangen-Nuremberg
Martensstr. 3
91058 Erlangen
Germany
marco.pruckner@fau.de

Reinhard German
University of
Erlangen-Nuremberg
Martensstr. 3
91058 Erlangen
Germany
reinhard.german@fau.de

David Eckhoff
University of
Erlangen-Nuremberg
Martensstr. 3
91058 Erlangen
Germany
david.eckhoff@fau.de

ABSTRACT

The switch from gasoline-powered vehicles to electric vehicles (EVs) is an important step to reduce greenhouse gas emissions. To this end, many European countries announced EV stock targets, e.g., Germany aims to have one million EVs on the roads by 2020. To achieve these goals and to handle the range limitation of EVs, a widespread publicly accessible charging infrastructure is needed. This paper provides a dynamic spatial and temporal simulation model for the building of charging infrastructure on a municipality scale. We evaluate empirical data about the timely utilization of different charging stations in the German federal state of Bavaria. This data is used to derive empirical models for the start time and duration of charging events as well as the popularity of charging stations. We develop a lightweight discrete event simulation model which can be used to investigate different expansion strategies, e.g., based on the load of charging stations or the number of successful and failed charging attempts. We show the applicability of our model using the German federal state of Bavaria as a use case.

Keywords

Discrete Event Simulation; Charging Infrastructure Planning; Electric Vehicles; Electromobility; Charging stations

1. INTRODUCTION

According to the Global EV Outlook 2016 [1] fourteen countries have announced EV stock targets, aiming to bring thirteen million EVs on the road in the near future. For instance, the German government aims to have one million EVs on German roads by the end of 2020. One major challenge for achieving these numbers is overcoming the main disadvantage of EVs, namely their limited range of approximately 150 km [8]. One way to mitigate this shortcoming is to provide a widespread, publicly accessible charging infrastructure.

Permission to make digital or hard copies of all or part of this work for personal or classroom use is granted without fee provided that copies are not made or distributed for profit or commercial advantage and that copies bear this notice and the full citation on the first page. Copyrights for components of this work owned by others than ACM must be honored. Abstracting with credit is permitted. To copy otherwise, or republish, to post on servers or to redistribute to lists, requires prior specific permission and/or a fee. Request permissions from permissions@acm.org.

SIGSIM-PADS 17, May 24 26, 2017, Singapore.

© 2017 ACM. ISBN 978-1-4503-4489-0/17/05. . . $15.00

DOI: http://dx.doi.org/10.1145/3064911.3064919

According to the Progress Report and Recommendations of Charging Infrastructure for Electric Vehicles in Germany 2015 [7], there will be a need of about 16,000 charging stations by 2020. In more details, 5,700 additional fast charging points and 10,000 normal AC charging stations (meaning 20,000 additional normal charging points) will be needed until 2020. In the federal state of Bavaria alone (consisting of 71 administrative districts and 25 independent cities) there are plans to build as many as 7,000 publicly accessible charging stations [2]. There exist various programs to meet these requirements [7], however, at this point it is unclear where and when new charging stations should be built. Stakeholders and decision makers could benefit from reliable predictions based on detailed statistics about the utilization of today's charging infrastructure.

In order to provide such predictions and recommendations, we develop a novel methodology for charging infrastructure planning using empirical data and discrete event simulation.[1] We evaluate the available empirical data including charging information about 394 charging stations in Bavaria over a four month period. This information is used to describe charging events with regard to their start time and duration. Under the additional consideration of an exponential growth of EVs until the end of 2020, we model the increasing number of charging events on publicly accessible charging stations. We define different output parameters such as the probability of successful charging attempts, the utilization of a charging station, as well as a theoretical waiting time in order to assess different scenarios regarding the expansion of charging infrastructure. Given different expansion strategies, we derive a spatial and temporal expansion schedule for each subregion in the federal state.

The remainder of the paper is organized as follows. In Section 2 we give an overview of related work in the field of charging infrastructure planning. We explain our system model in Section 3, followed by Section 4 where we describe the developed methodology, input modeling and the implementation of our discrete event simulation model. In Section 5 we present results for the use case study carried out using data for the federal state of Bavaria. Section 6 provides a discussion about our model and Section 7 concludes the paper with a short summary and an outlook on future work.

---

[1]The empirical data was provided by CIRRANTiC GmbH, a company which provides enhanced data streams to users and information management tools for EV infrastructure.

2. RELATED WORK

There exist several publications on charging infrastructure planning on an abstract level. For instance, Germany's report on Charging Infrastructure for Electric Vehicles [7] provides an overview of the current status of Germany's charging infrastructure. The authors mentioned that the expansion in normal charging infrastructure has been slowing since 2012 due to poor cost-efficiency, whereas the ramp-up of EVs is much more pronounced. Nevertheless, it is important that the number of publicly accessible charging stations grows with the number of EVs on German roads. This fact is also mentioned in a position paper by the Bavarian state government and Bavarian car manufacturers [2]. Although in Germany's report at least a rough schedule for expansion in charging infrastructure is given, only the Bavarian position paper provides a hard target number of 7,000 in total. Detailed schedules and spatial distributions of the presented total number of charging stations is not available. This is a major concern for stakeholders and infrastructure planners since they don't know where and when the expansion of new charging stations is necessary.

Literature pertaining to charging infrastructure planning relevant to the subject of this paper is also focused on spatial and temporal distribution.

Wirges [11] developed detailed models for charging infrastructure planning. He refines the planning not only for regions but also for the street level and presented different application areas of his model. In a second step, he developed a simulation model for the long-term development (until 2020) of charging infrastructure based on the increasing number of EVs, calculated quotas of charging points per EV and also inter-municipal commuter data for the German city of Stuttgart. His simulation results showed that only 1.2 % of all charging points were public charging points. Brost et al. [3] developed a site selection model for electric charging infrastructure based on origin-and-destination traffic generation, different user groups, and their trip behavior. Further input parameters include the zone-specific points of interest (POI) and information with regard to the duration of stay. Based on a vehicle ownership model and current charging infrastructure, the number of possible charging cycles can be determined. The results can be used by local planners to make micro-location plans for expansion of the charging infrastructure. Both publications have in common that they don't use empirical data for the modeling of charging events.

In Bi et al. [9] the authors developed an optimal charging station deployment model under the consideration of different charging behavior. To this end, they used an agent-based sub-microscopic city-scale traffic simulation which allows the investigation of different charging behavior under the assumption that charging stations are placed at existing gas stations. Results show that charging behavior has an influence on the charging infrastructure of the city-state Singapore. However, a charging infrastructure plan from a temporal perspective is not given.

Authors of [10] investigate where the state of charge would reach a critical level and, from that, they infer candidate locations for charging stations. They also took into account parking lots and driving behavior. The optimal placement of charging stations is also addressed in Lam et al. [5]. They define an optimization problem by finding the best locations to construct charging stations in a city by solving the EV charging station placement problem. The authors are

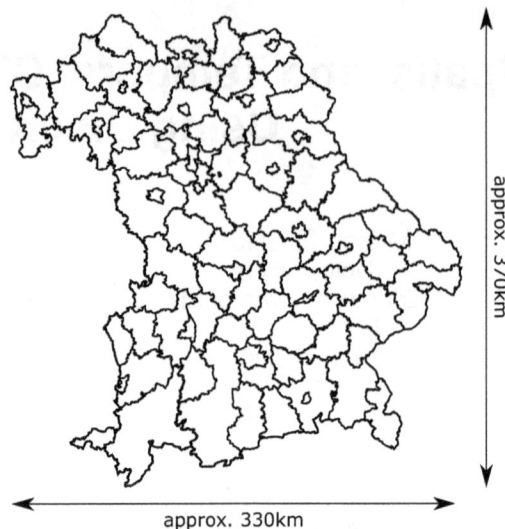

Figure 1: Scale of simulation: map of Bavaria, Germany with municipality borders.

focused on the complexity of these kinds of problems and propose four different solution methods. A temporal plan of charging stations placement is not given in detail.

There also exist several publications investigating the effect of electromobility on the power grid. In Dharmakeerthi et al. [4] the authors applied a particle swarm optimization-based approach for the planning of EV infrastructure on a distribution feeder level. They suggest to promote public charging stations in order to reduce electricity network upgrade requirements to accommodate EV charging on low voltage networks.

The idea of this work is to present a lightweight discrete event simulation model for the spatial and temporal charging infrastructure planning based on empirical data about the utilization of the existing charging infrastructure and the ramp-up of EVs as an input. Our model allows to derive detailed spatial and temporal expansion plans for different regions. The applicability of our model is shown for the German federal state of Bavaria. However, our approach can be applied to any other region worldwide as long as sufficient input data is available.

3. SYSTEM MODEL

The goal of the simulation is to give spatial and temporal recommendations for the building of charging infrastructure on the municipality scale. Figure 1 provides a visual reference for the scale of the simulation. It shows the German federal state of Bavaria with municipality borders. In total, Bavaria is divided in 96 municipalities. The outcome of the simulation is a recommendation for when to build charging stations at a temporal resolution of one week and a spatial resolution on the municipality level.

To achieve this, we have to make several assumptions. First, we want to abstract away from microscopic driver models, charging behavior, and mobility altogether by utilizing empirical data collected by today's charging stations. Creating realistic microscopic traffic demand, traffic assignments, and psychological driver models, combined with specific local features of the vicinity of a charging station is infeasible at the scale of a federal state spanning more than $70,000 \text{ km}^2$. By utilizing existing real-world charging data, we bypass the necessity for these complex and possibly inaccurate models, as the empirical data already inherently includes the results that would be obtained using these models. The empirical data used in this study includes the number of electric vehicles per municipality, the number and location of charging stations, as well as detailed information about *charging events* in the federal state of Bavaria. We define a charging event as the triple of the charging station, the start time, and the charging duration.

From the empirical distribution of charging events, we derive charging events in the simulation. This means we do not model state of charge and trip distances, we assume that all charging events are of opportunistic nature, that is, if a charging station is occupied, the driver will not wait. Each charging station is assumed to have two outlets. As the charging duration is derived from real-world data, we do not model charging speeds. We assume that the charging stations about which we do not have empirical data behave the same as the ones we do have data about. This means that we assume charging stations about which we have data to be representative. With communication capabilities added to more and more charging stations, this assumption naturally becomes less critical.

For the building of new charging stations, we assume that charging stations can be built instantly. We do not consider the profitability of publicly accessible charging stations, nor do we assume that there will be a different distribution of charging station popularity after new ones are added. This is done to keep our model lightweight and to avoid unjustified assumptions. We also do not consider restrictions regarding the underlying power system. The main reason for this is that we do not recommend the exact position where the stations should be built. Such recommendations would naturally have to consider the power grid.

As for the scenario, we assume that a total number of 200,000 electric vehicles in Bavaria will be reached by the end of 2020. We assume the distribution of electric vehicles among the different municipalities to be the same over the simulation time.

4. METHODOLOGY

In this section we describe the applied methodology. First, we present the modeling of input parameters, including the progress of the number of EVs over time and the implemented expansion strategies for charging infrastructure. Subsequently, we briefly discuss the development of the discrete event simulation model.

An overview of our simulation is given in Figure 2. A large part of the input consists of empirical data that has to be processed and prepared to be used in the simulation environment. Additionally, we define different expansion strategies for the building of charging infrastructure.

In order to account for incomplete and missing data, we make use of the empirical distribution of the input data. Based on this, the discrete event simulation will derive charging events (start time and duration in the resolution of minutes), add infrastructure on a weekly basis, and also gradually increase the numbers of electric vehicles in the system. Based on the success rate, the load of the charging stations, and the expansion strategy, we can then give recommendations for the building of charging infrastructure.

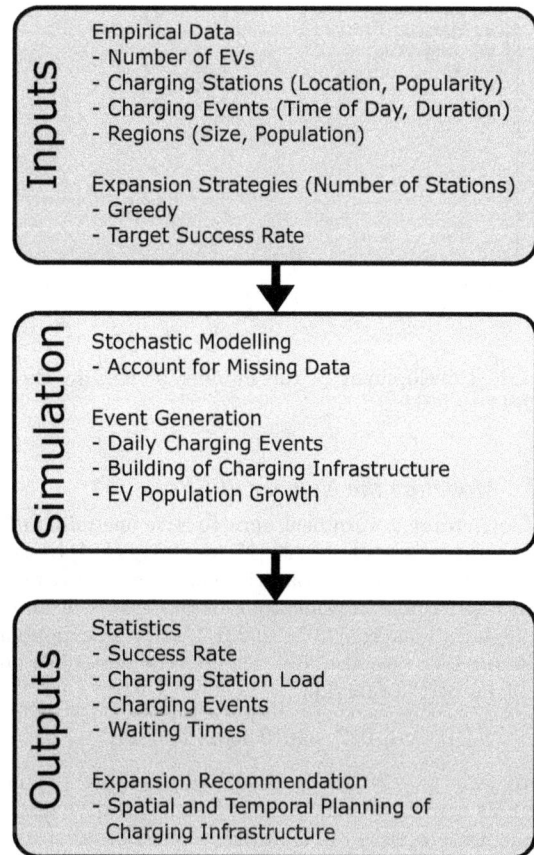

Figure 2: Inputs and outputs of the developed simulation engine.

4.1 Input Modeling

4.1.1 Regions

Input data for each municipality in the federal state of Bavaria includes the number of electric vehicles, the population, the area size, and the type of municipality (e.g., city, town, rural, etc.). For some of the investigated areas, there was no available information about the number of charging events. Developing a linear model, based on population, area size, and number of EVs to determine the number of daily charging events per region was not possible (R^2 0.5). We conclude that at this rather early stage of electric vehicle market introduction, local characteristics of municipalities (e.g., the presence of a car manufacturer) have a higher impact on the EV market share of a region, making the number of daily charging events hard to predict. We therefore decided to apply hierarchical clustering, and arrived at 15 different clusters for the 96 municipalities. We validated the clustering result by again applying a linear model to determine the cluster for each region and arrived at an R^2 value of 0.9 and higher. This means that some regions have common characteristics in terms of EVs, population and daily charging events. Others, even though they are the same type of municipality, are considerably different. We assume that regions belonging to the same cluster will share common characteristics in terms of charging events, allowing us to also model regions where only limited empirical data is available.

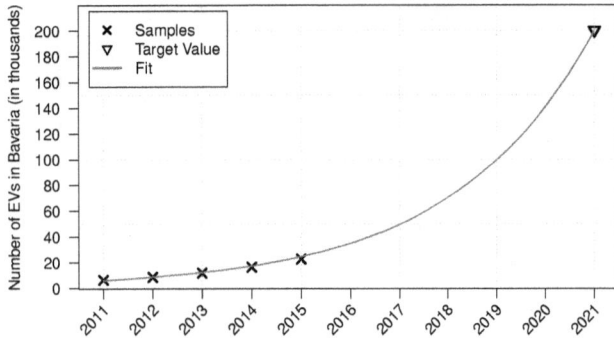

Figure 3: Development of the number of EVs in Bavaria from 2011 to 2021.

4.1.2 Modeling the Number of EVs

As the German government aims to have one million EVs on the road by the end of 2020 [1], we derive that, based on today's share of vehicles, Bavaria will have approximately 200,000 EVs. Under consideration of the historical number of EV registrations from 2011 to 2015, we fit an exponential increase for EVs (see also [6]). The fit is depicted in Figure 3 and given by the function

$$EV(t) = 6,027 \cdot \exp\left(0.3502 \cdot (t - 2012)\right), \qquad (1)$$

wherein year $t \geq 2012$. In order to distribute the number of EVs across different regions (administrative districts and independent cities) in Bavaria, we use official statistics of vehicle registration authorities and derive a distribution factor $\beta_i \in (0,1)$ for each region i. The development of EVs in region i is given by

$$EV_i(t) = \beta_i \cdot EV(t). \qquad (2)$$

Thereby, we assume that the share of EVs within each region with regard to the total number of EVs to be constant over the next years.

4.1.3 Modeling of Charging Stations

As of today, there exist approximately 1,250 charging stations in Bavaria, however, only 394 of them have a back-end connection that allows to collect statistics. These charging stations store information about each charging event, that is, the start time and the duration. For each region we derived the following information for a period of four months:

- Histogram over start times of charging events in a fifteen minute resolution
- Histogram over duration of charging events in a fifteen minute resolution
- Histogram over popularity of charging stations

An example histogram over the start time of charging events is shown in Figure 4a for a small city in Bavaria. We observed similar features for almost all charging stations. It can be seen that most of the charging events on publicly accessible charging stations take place between 08:00 and 18:30. The peak at about 17:00 can be explained as this is a common time to finish work in Germany.

In Figure 4b the histogram for the duration of charging events is given. Most of the charging events last between fifteen and ninety minutes, mainly caused by people charg-

ing their vehicle while shopping. Longer charging durations could be observed at long-term parking lots and locations where people change to public transport. We also observe that vehicles occupying a charging station for over 24 hours is not uncommon.

Figure 5 depicts an example histogram for the popularity of charging stations, showing that two charging stations are considerably more popular than the remaining eleven. These two stations experience more charging events than the rest of the back-end stations in this municipality combined. This is similar to what we observed for many regions, meaning there is no gradually decreasing popularity but rather only two types of charging stations: popular and considerably less popular. In this example, the number of charging stations with a back-end connection was 13, the overall number of stations in this region, however, was 38. Assuming the missing charging stations behave similar to the ones with a back-end connection, we add them based on the existing popularity distribution. This is a strong assumption, especially when the number of back-end charging stations is low. We make equal-probability random selections between charging stations with back-end connection (cf. charging station ID in Figure 5), multiply the given number of charging events with a Gaussian distributed parameter ($\mu = 0, \sigma = 0.15$), and add the new charging station to the histogram. Figure 5a shows the histogram over the popularity of charging stations after the expansion of the original histogram to the total number of charging stations within this region.

4.1.4 Number of daily charging events

From the total number of charging events in a certain region i, we derive the mean number of daily charging events ϕCE_i^{day} by dividing the total number of charging events by the number of days within the four month period. In order to determine the number of daily charging events within a certain region we have also to consider charging events that occurred on charging stations without back-end connection. We assume the same utilization of charging stations without back-end connection using the ratio between charging station in total CS_i^{total} and with back-end connection CS_i^{conn}. The utilization depends also on the number of EVs, meaning we also take into account the ratio of the number of EVs at the simulation start time $EV_i(0)$ and the number of EVs $EV_i(t)$ at time t.

For a certain region i the number of daily charging events $CE_i(t)$ is given by

$$CE_i(t) = \phi CE_i^{\mathrm{day}} \cdot \frac{CS_i^{\mathrm{total}}}{CS_i^{\mathrm{conn}}} \cdot \frac{EV_i(t)}{EV_i(0)}. \qquad (3)$$

As in the real world the number of daily charging events is not a deterministic number we also consider stochastic influences modeled by a Gaussian distributed parameter α ($\mu = 0, \sigma = 0.15$). Thus, further influences such as holidays, seasons or special events (e.g., sporting events) can be described. We acknowledge that, ideally, this should be derived from the empirical data as well, however, the low sample size of charging events for public holidays and other special occasions did not allow us to draw conclusions.

The modeled number of daily charging events is given by

$$\widehat{CE}_i(t) = (1 + \alpha) \cdot CE_i(t). \qquad (4)$$

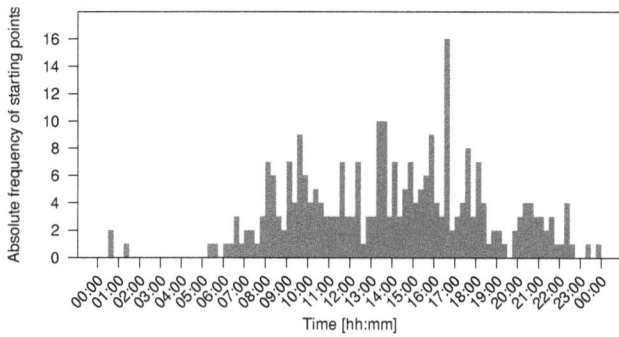

(a) Example histogram for the distribution of starting points of charging events.

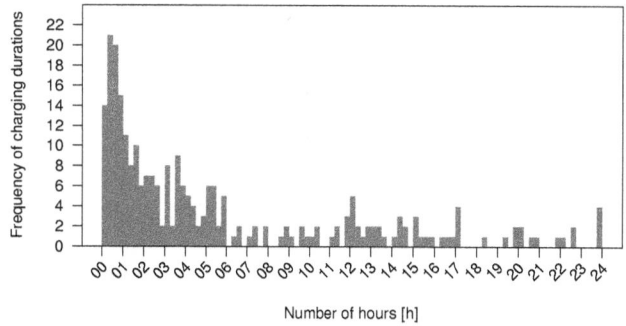

(b) Example histogram for the distribution of duration of charging events.

Figure 4: Example charging events recorded for a small town.

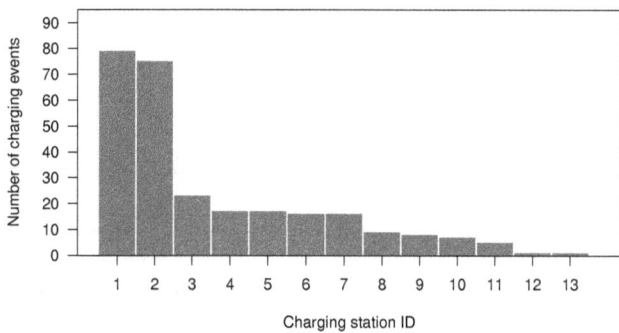

(a) Example histogram for popularity of charging stations within a small city in Bavaria.

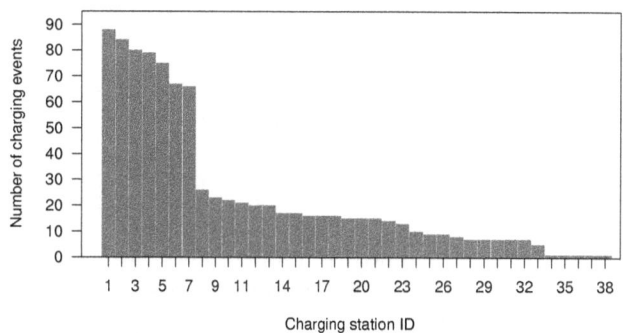

(b) Example histogram of popularity of charging stations including charging stations without internet connection.

Figure 5: Empirical and synthetic charging station popularity for a small city.

4.1.5 Expansion strategies for charging infrastructure

The Bavarian state government aims to have up to 7,000 publicly accessible charging stations installed by the end of 2020. For the expansion of charging infrastructure we consider two different expansion strategies: *Success* and *Target*. In the simulation, the decision to build new charging stations is made on a weekly basis. In order to catch up with the exponential growth of EVs and the fast increasing charging station demand, we double the number of newly built charging stations per region if this region was already selected for expansion in the previous week.

The first expansion strategy, denoted as *Success*, is based on the percentage of successful charging events (cf. Equation 5). We treat every region in Bavaria as stand-alone, meaning that the number of new charging stations is independent from the number of new charging stations in another region. If the percentage of successful charging events drops under a threshold τ (e.g., under 0.95), then new charging stations will be constructed in this region. The overall number of built stations in the scenario then solely depends on τ, i.e., no upper bound for the number of new charging stations is considered. In Algorithm 1 the principal idea of this expansion strategy is shown. When a new station is added to a

region, its popularity will be determined in the same manner as non-back-end stations are added (cf. Subsection 4.1.3).

The second expansion strategy, denoted as *Target*, assumes that the number of charging stations should also grow exponentially to serve the exponentially growing number of EVs (cf. Figure 3). Based on this function, we determine the number of available charging stations per week. Compared to the *Success* strategy, *Target* is more of a centralized approach, meaning that there is a total weekly limit of charging stations which can be built. To this end, we sort all regions within the simulated area by the percentage of successful charging events in an ascending order. Then we add charging stations until all available stations have been assigned a region. To catch up with increasing demand, the number of newly built charging stations is doubled for regions that already experienced an expansion in the week before. The working principle of *Target* is given in Algorithm 2

The main difference between the two expansion strategies lies within what they try to achieve. *Success* gives information about how many charging stations are required to achieve a certain success probability, whereas *Target* distributes a predetermined number of charging stations in a manner so that the average success probability between regions is maximized.

Algorithm 1: *Success* expansion strategy.

1 **Definitions:**
2 t The current week
3 $p_i^{\text{succ}}(t)$ The percentage of successful charging attempts
4   in region i during week t
5 $\text{new}_i(t)$ The number of stations to be built
6   in region i in week t
7 τ The threshold for the construction of new
8   stations

9 **foreach** *region i* **do**
10   **if** $(p_i^{succ}(t-1) < \tau)$ **then**
11      $\text{new}_i(t) = 2^{\text{new}_i(t-1)}$
12   **else**
13      $\text{new}_i(t) = 0$
14   **end**
15   **Build** $\text{new}_i(t)$ charging stations in region i
16 **end**

Algorithm 2: *Target* expansion strategy.

1 **Definitions:**
2 t The current week
3 $CS(t)$ Number of charging stations that can be built
4   in week t based on exponential growth function
5 $p_i^{\text{succ}}(t)$ The percentage of successful charging attempts
6   in region i during week t
7 $\text{new}_i(t)$ The number of stations to be built
8   in region i in week t

9 **sort** all regions i into stack L according to $p_i^{\text{succ}}(t)$
10 **var** $avail = CS(t)$
11 **while** *(avail > 0)* **do**
   // Region with lowest success probability is
     on top of stack
12    $i = $ **pop** L
13    $\text{new}_i(t) = 2^{\text{new}_i(t-1)}$
14   **Build** $\min(avail, \text{new}_i(t))$ charging stations in region
     i
15    $avail = avail - \text{new}_i(t)$
16 **end**

4.2 Simulation Model

The simulations were conducted using the discrete-event simulator OMNeT++, a component-based C++ simulation library and framework. It provided the event scheduling engine and the required statistical tools.

4.2.1 Description of a single charging event

The exponential growth of EVs combined with the input distributions based on the empirical data determines the number of charging events per day per region. For each region, the simulation maintains three distributions, i.e, one over the start times, one for the charging durations, and one for the popularity of stations.

The simulation will schedule an event every day at 0:00 to determine the charging events for the next day. Based on the three stored distributions per region, we draw $n = 3 \cdot \widehat{CE_i}(t)$ random numbers. Each triple of start time, duration, and charging station describe a charging event. The events are sorted by start time and processed one by one to determine whether a charging attempt was successful. If there is an outlet available at the randomly determined charging station, then this outlet is set to occupied for the duration. The charging event is set to successful. Should there be no available outlet for a charging event, then we define this charging event to be failed.

For an example region of Bavaria an excerpt of an event list sorted in chronological order regarding starting times is given in Table 1. It can be seen that most of the charging events are successful. However, charging events 11 and 14 failed because both outlets of the target charging stations were already occupied by earlier events.

4.2.2 Output measures

Simulating at charging event level allows us to derive various output measures to assess the overall performance of the charging infrastructure. Let $\#CE^{\text{succesful}}$ be the number of all successful charging events, and $\#CE^{\text{total}}$ the total number of all events, then the overall success probability $p^{\text{succ}}(t)$ can be given as:

$$p^{\text{succ}}(t) = \frac{\#CE^{\text{successful}}(t)}{\#CE^{\text{total}}(t)} \qquad (5)$$

This probability can be computed for every time window and for each region by only considering the respective charging events.

From an economic perspective, the load of a charging station might be the decisive factor for profitable operation. Let $CE(t)$ be the charging events in a given time interval t and $\#CS(t)$ the overall number of charging stations (each with 2 outlets) in this interval, then the overall system load can be computed as:

$$Load(t) = \frac{\sum_{e \in CE(t)} \text{duration of } e}{\text{total time} \cdot \#CS(t) \cdot 2} \qquad (6)$$

Again, statistics for single regions or single charging stations can be computed by only considering the respective subset of $CE(t)$.

Table 1: Excerpt of an event list of charging events for a certain region (sorted in chronological order regarding starting times).

ID	Start [hh:mm]	Duration in [hh:mm]	Char. Station	Outlet	Status
1	14:35	01:25	1	1	successf.
2	14:55	00:23	3	2	successf.
3	15:23	00:59	7	1	successf.
4	15:33	04:20	6	1	successf.
5	15:39	02:35	5	2	successf.
6	15:55	01:15	1	2	successf.
7	16:03	01:08	16	2	successf.
8	16:11	03:25	2	1	successf.
9	16:25	00:28	1	1	successf.
10	16:34	00:33	6	2	successf.
11	16:39	02:11	1	1	failed
12	16:47	00:48	2	2	successf.
13	17:08	00:59	4	1	successf.
14	17:11	14:15	2	1	failed
15	17:27	04:25	3	2	successf.

Load and success probability give an indication of how well the charging infrastructure operates. As a last output measure, we propose the theoretical waiting time, that is, the duration a driver would have to wait until one outlet of the charging station becomes available. For this, we assume that each vehicle will queue in front of the charging station, regardless of queue length, time of day, and charging duration of vehicles in front. This output measure is purely theoretical, however, it will react more sensitively to a mismatch between supply and demand as waiting times will quickly grow. The average theoretical waiting time $\phi wait(t)$ is simply the waiting time of all individual charging events normalized by the number of charging stations $\#CS(t)$ (each with 2 outlets) for a given time interval t.

$$\phi wait(t) = \frac{\sum_{e \in CE(t)} \text{wait time of } e}{\#CS(t) \cdot 2} \quad (7)$$

5. RESULTS

In this section we present example simulation results as a demonstration of the capabilities of our simulation model. We simulated the federal state of Bavaria from 2016-01-01 to 2020-12-31.

We analyzed three different expansion scenarios: The first one is a scenario where no new publicly accessible charging stations are built (denoted as *No Expansion*). This serves as a benchmark in order to understand the effect of a growing number of EVs on today's charging infrastructure. We additionally simulated the *Success* and *Target* expansion strategies (see Section 4.2). The threshold τ for *Success* was set to 0.95. For the *Target* strategy, we assume a target number of 7,000 charging stations for the entire federal state.

Due to the variety of regions (71 administrative districts and 25 independent cities) it is not possible to show results for every single municipality. As an example, we choose a small independent city in Bavaria and present different results including the number of daily charging events, percentage of successful charging events, the mean load of charging station, the theoretical waiting time, and finally the expansion of charging stations until the end of 2020.

Figure 6 shows the number of daily charging events for the entire simulation period. As expected, an exponentially increasing number of EVs leads to an exponentially growing number of charging events (cf. Equation 3). The variations originate from the applied Gaussian noise.

In Figure 7 the percentage of successful charging events according to Equation 5 is depicted. In the *No Expansion* scenario it can be observed that the percentage of successful charging events declines from 95 % in 2016 to approximately 55 %. Hence, this scenario is useful to see the consequences when no new charging stations are built.

The *Success* strategy (blue line) was able to successfully ensure a 95 % success rate, showing only minor fluctuations around the fixed threshold τ throughout the entire observation period. For the *Target* expansion strategy (red line), the success rate drops under 90 % between the years 2017 and 2018. This is a direct effect from the competition of the city with other regions within Bavaria regarding the allocation of charging infrastructure. In this period there were other regions with a lower percentage of successful charging events, receiving priority for newly built charging stations. These are mainly regions that already today do not have a sufficient number of charging stations. Once enough charg-

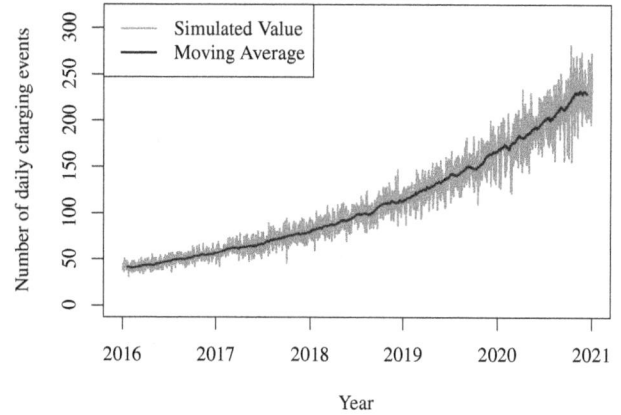

Figure 6: Number of daily charging events until 2020 for a small independent city in Bavaria.

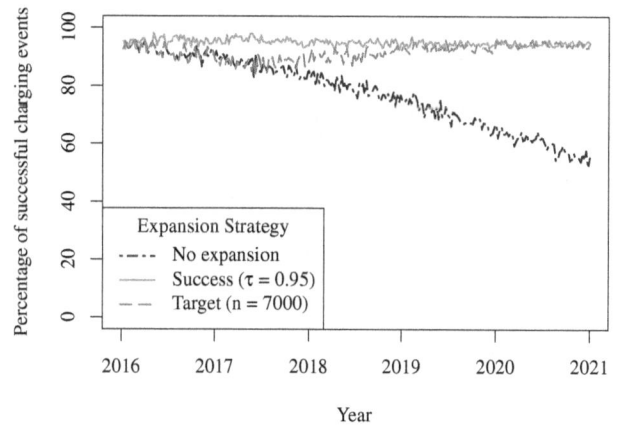

Figure 7: Percentage of successful charging events from 2016 to 2021 for a small independent city in Bavaria.

ing stations are deployed in these regions (after 2018), the success percentage for the presented city approximates 95 %.

Investigating the mean load of charging stations (Figure 8), we observe that the high success probabilities achieved using the *Success* and *Target* strategies come at the price of mostly idle charging stations. In both scenarios (red and blue lines), the average load of charging stations did not exceed 20 %, arriving at values as low as 10 % at the end of 2020. Even without building new infrastructure (black line), the load did not exceed 40 %. This is caused by low demand after work until the next day, further affected by standard trading hours in Bavaria (06:00 - 20:00) (cf. Figure 4a). From an operator perspective, it might be more logical to achieve a higher average load rather than high success rates. Our model design also allows to define expansion strategies with regard to the mean load of charging stations to arrive at a more economical expansion plan.

The average theoretical waiting time is depicted in Figure 9. Without building new charging stations, the theoretic waiting time grows exponentially. For instance, in the end of 2020 the theoretical waiting time amounts to over 50.000 minutes per charging attempt, which is more than 34

Figure 8: Mean load of charging stations from 2016 to 2021 for a small independent city in Bavaria.

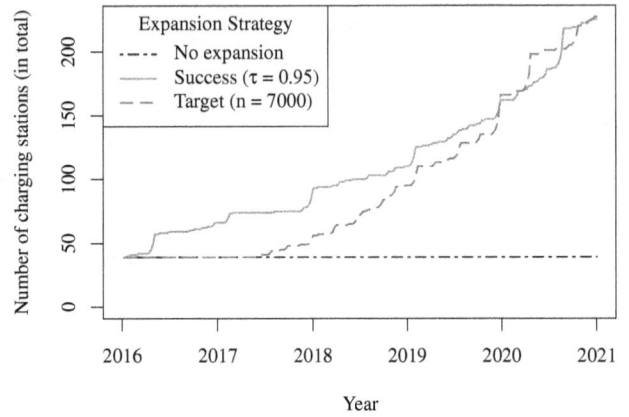

Figure 9: Average theoretical waiting time from 2016 to 2021 for a small independent city in Bavaria (y axis is in log scale).

days. Consequently, a significant mismatch between supply and demand is identified. The *Success* strategy contributes to keep the theoretical waiting time on a constant level of approximately 40 minutes. In the *Target* strategy, the theoretical waiting time increases to approximately two hours until mid 2017. After that, we observe an average theoretical waiting time of approx. 40 minutes.

The core output of our simulation is the spatial and temporal charging infrastructure plan, i.e. for a certain region we obtain a temporal expansion plan for building charging stations.

Figure 10 shows the expansion of charging stations in a weekly resolution. For both the *Success* and *Target* scenarios, we observe that the building of only one charging station per week is not sufficient to catch up with the growing demand of electric vehicles. At some times, it was necessary to build the double, fourfold, or eightfold etc. number of charging stations in the subsequent week (cf. blue line at 2018 or red line at 2020 in Figure 10). Both strategies coincidentally arrive at a similar number of charging stations by the end of 2020, however, the building schedule strongly differs.

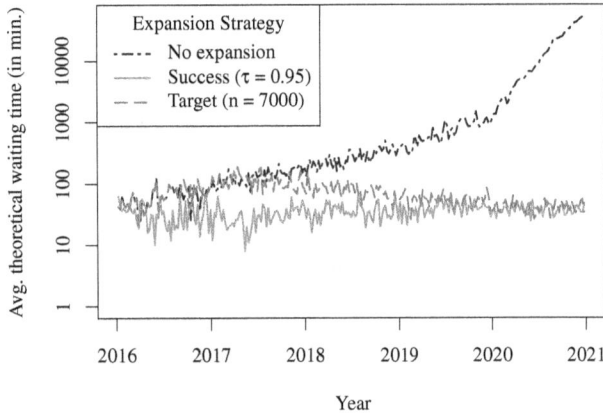

Figure 10: Temporal construction of charging stations from 2016 to 2021 for a small independent city in Bavaria.

Please note, that different values for τ would lead to a different number of charging stations. The centralized *Target* strategy prioritized other under-supplied regions, delaying the beginning of building new stations until mid 2017. This delay leads to a steeper increase compared to the *Success* strategy where charging stations are added right from the beginning.

6. DISCUSSION

The presented simulation model is mostly of empirical nature and intended to assist stakeholders and policy makers in planning the building of charging infrastructure. The most challenging part for such a model is validation. Unfortunately, the data needed for validation is not yet available as electromobility and statistical data collection of charging stations is a rather new domain. Therefore we did not attempt to model charging behavior of individual vehicles, but assume that the utilization of today's charging stations is a direct result from a complex set of parameters that, without large amounts of data, it is not possible to model. By sticking closely to the distributions of the empirical input data, we abstract away from these parameters.

To achieve at least some level of validation, all models and results were discussed with domain experts. According to these experts the current differences in the utilization of charging stations located in independent cities and administrative districts are represented adequately by the provided empirical data.

The sparseness of data also required us to make various assumptions (see Section 3). The way the input data is used, however, allows the simulation to scale with the data quality of the input. The more information about charging stations and charging events is available, the more accurate we assume the predictions will become. We therefore recommend to iteratively use this modeling approach as soon as higher quality input data is available.

7. CONCLUSIONS

EVs contribute to more sustainable future transportation systems. In order to meet the announced EV targets, a significant number of publicly accessible charging stations is required. Therefore, many countries worldwide define expansion targets for charging stations. However, determining when and where new charging stations should be built is a challenging task.

In this paper we addressed this issue and developed a spatial and temporal charging infrastructure planning tool using discrete event simulation. Based on comprehensive analysis of empirical data about the utilization of charging stations, we derived models for the starting time and duration of charging events. Our simulation model allows to evaluate different expansion strategies with regard to various output metrics such as the likelihood of charging attempts to be successful, the average load of charging stations, and the theoretical waiting time, a measure that quickly reacts to a mismatch between supply and demand. As a proof of concept, we demonstrate the capabilities of our model for a city in the German federal state of Bavaria, where it is already used to assist stakeholders and policy makers.

Future work includes the investigation of different scenarios and an iterative application of the presented modeling approach. As more and more charging stations become equipped with a back-end connection, the picture that can be drawn from the collected data becomes more complete. This data could also be used to evaluate how the share of electric vehicles and the utilization of charging infrastructure will develop over time. This would allows us to derive specific scenarios for different regions to develop more accurate models for the observed charging behavior. The data could also be used for backtesting to validate the proposed approach.

8. ACKNOWLEDGMENTS

The authors would like to thank the Bavarian State Government, Bayern Innovativ GmbH and CIRRANTiC GmbH for providing the data.

9. REFERENCES

[1] I. E. Agency. Global EV Outlook 2016 - Beyond one million electric cars, 2016. https://www.iea.org/publications/freepublications/publication/Global_EV_Outlook_2016.pdf.

[2] Bavarian State Government. Gemeinsame Position der Bayerischen Staatsregierung und der bayerischen Automobilhersteller zur Elektromobilität, 2015. https://www.stmwi.bayern.de/fileadmin/user_upload/stmwivt/Themen/Initiativen/Dokumente/2016-01-26-Gemeinsame_Position_der_Bayerischen_Staatsregierung.pdf.

[3] W. Brost, T. Funke, and D. Vallee. SLAM - Schnellladenetz für Achsen und Metropolen. In *DVWG Jahresverkehrskongress 2016: Elektromobilität - aktuelle Chancen und Risiken der Umsetzung*, pages 1–3, 2016.

[4] C. H. Dharmakeerthi, N. Mithulananthan, and T. K. Saha. Planning of electric vehicle charging infrastructure. In *2013 IEEE Power Energy Society General Meeting*, pages 1–5, July 2013.

[5] A. Y. S. Lam, Y. W. Leung, and X. Chu. Electric vehicle charging station placement: Formulation, complexity, and solutions. *IEEE Transactions on Smart Grid*, 5(6):2846–2856, Nov 2014.

[6] G. Mauri and A. Valsecchi. Fast charging stations for electric vehicle: The impact on the mv distribution grids of the milan metropolitan area. In *2012 IEEE International Energy Conference and Exhibition (ENERGYCON)*, pages 1055–1059, Sept 2012.

[7] Nationale Plattform Elektromobilität. Charging Infrastrucutre for Electric Vehicles in Germany - Progress Report and Recommendations 2015, 2015. http://nationale-plattform-elektromobilitaet.de/fileadmin/user_upload/Redaktion/AG3_Statusbericht_LIS_2015_engl_klein_bf.pdf.

[8] N. Pearre, W. Kempton, R. Guensler, and V. Elango. Electric vehicles: How much range is required for a days driving? *Transportation Research Part C: Emerging Technologies*, 19(6):1171–1184, December 2011.

[9] R. Bi and J. Xiao and V. Viswanathan and A. Knoll. Influence of Charging Behaviour Given Charging Station Placement at Existing Petrol Stations and Residential Car Park Locations in Singapore. *Procedia Computer Science*, 80:335 – 344, 2016.

[10] V. Viswanathan, D. Zehe, J. Ivanchev, D. Pelzer, A. Knoll, and H. Aydt. Simulation-assisted exploration of charging infrastructure requirements for electric vehicles in urban environments. *Journal of Computational Science*, 12:1–10, 2016.

[11] J. Wirges. *Planning the Charging Infrastructure for Electric Vehicles in Cities and Regions.* KIT Scientific Publishing, Karlsruhe, Germany, 2016.

Towards a Benchmark for the Quantitative Evaluation of Traffic Simulators

Priya Toshniwal
Nanyang Technological
University
50 Nanyang Avenue,
Singapore
TOSH0001@ntu.edu.sg

Masatoshi Hanai
Nanyang Technological
University
50 Nanyang Avenue,
Singapore
mhanai@acm.org

Elvis S. Liu
Nanyang Technological
University
50 Nanyang Avenue,
Singapore
elvisliu@ntu.edu.sg

ABSTRACT

Smart city projects, infrastructure planning, and traffic engineering are some of the applications where traffic simulations are playing an increasingly important role. Although many traffic simulators, commercial or open-sourced, are available at our disposal today, choosing the one that best fits a user's requirements is usually not possible by taking into account only the qualitative aspects and features of the simulator. In resource-constrained simulation platforms, performing traffic simulations with less memory usage and faster execution time is always highly coveted. In this paper, we propose a quantitative benchmarking approach for evaluating the performance of traffic simulator, based on commonplace scenarios and real-life city maps.

Keywords

Traffic simulation; performance comparison

1. INTRODUCTION

Traffic simulation is a tool that can help city planners and researchers to understand complex traffic dynamics. With the recent explosion in the research of urban development, smart cities, and traffic planning, traffic simulations have become an essential part of urban planning, finding their use for myriad purposes. Sustainable development, Intelligent Transportation Systems (ITS) [1], traffic control strategies, traffic patterns in urban and sub-urban areas, feasibility of infrastructure implementation, vehicle emission patterns, impacts of blocked roads, accidents and natural calamities are examples of some current topics of interest that justify the growing importance of traffic simulations for transportation planners.

To serve various intentions of research and study about traffic systems and urban mobility, a number of open-sourced and commercial traffic simulators have been developed over the years. Some representative examples of these simulators

SIGSIM-PADS '17, May 24–26, 2017, Singapore.

© 2017 ACM. ISBN 978-1-4503-4489-0/17/05. . . $15.00

DOI: http://dx.doi.org/10.1145/3064911.3064928

are MATSim [2], Simulation of Urban MObility (SUMO) [3], and TRANSIMS [4, 5]. Choosing a suitable simulator is one of the major concerns of conducting traffic simulations [6]. Factors such as runtime performance, features, file formats, interoperability with other simulators, scalability, availability of Graphical User Interface (GUI), etc. should all be considered before starting with a simulator.

In the literature, several analytical studies have been done to evaluate various traffic simulators [5, 7, 8, 9, 10]. These studies, however, are largely qualitative and only compare the features of simulators such as their feasibility and potential of inclusion of transportation of electric vehicles. This is clearly insufficient since today's traffic simulators are expected to perform simulations on a large area like a big city or a country; therefore, quantitative evaluations are essential to assess the performance of the simulators such as runtime efficiency and scalability since they are very crucial if we wish to simulate traffic system on a country-scale or beyond. Nevertheless, the needs of a quantitative benchmarking platform to evaluate the performance of simulators and their capabilities to simulate large-scale networks have largely been unmet by the existing work.

In this paper, we concentrate on the development of a quantitative benchmarking platform for traffic simulators. This platform would make it easier for the users to select the most suitable simulators that meet their performance requirements. It will also save the efforts and time being invested in various comparative analyses in the traffic simulation domain. Our approach can be extended to evaluate the run-time efficiency and scalability of the simulators based on real-life road networks and several realistic case scenarios.

2. RELATED WORK

Traffic simulators are seen as an integral part of smart city planning today and are mostly used to simulate and plan changes within a traffic network. Since there are quite many simulators available, choosing the right one to use is not a simple task. The challenge is to have reliable models which can accommodate the dynamic conditions of cities and urban areas. Over the years, a number of traffic simulator analyses have been done based on features like supported operating systems and whether they are open-sourced. In [9], review on the features of traditionally used macroscopic and microscopic traffic simulation models has been done with a comparative analysis to evaluate the models' suitability on congested networks, large urban and regional networks, and integration of ITS, etc., suggesting the researchers to evaluate the state-of-the-art simulators and find out tools or approaches suited for the local conditions pertaining to Saudi Arabia.

In a study conducted by Kotusevski *et al.* [8], the simulators chosen were compared based on parameters such as CPU and memory consumption, operating system portability, modes of transport supported, software documentation, and user interfacing. This work acknowledges the fact that the greatest hurdle is choosing a simulator for one's requirements; however, most of its metrics of comparison were qualitative capabilities of the simulators. Although the study mentions that most of the reviewed simulators have the ability to cope up with large networks, it does not discuss whether the time taken to simulate these networks is realistic or not and there is no information provided about how large a network can these simulators cope up with.

Similarly, in the study conducted by Allan *et al.* [5], a qualitative analysis was conducted on different open-source simulators, namely MATSim, TRANSIMS, and SUMO, based on their default simulation examples. The performance evaluation was conducted using criteria such as physical structure, physical and control behaviours, and implementation of software. Similar to the analytical studies we have reviewed so far, this analysis is qualitative and focuses mainly on the feasibility of transportation-electrification.

In [11], Suzumura *et al.* have developed a microscopic simulator and have performed traffics simulations for greater Dublin region. The simulations involve private cars, public buses, and trains and leverage real data sets available about the activity of the population, bus and train routes, timings, and origin-destination information. Here, the travel times of public transport and private cars was evaluated by creating a simulation of about 4 hours and these simulated travel time values were benchmarked based on the real travel time values.

Considering the fact that much effort and time have been put on various analyses of available traffic simulators, a detailed quantitative benchmarking platform of these simulators would help the researchers in the areas of traffic simulation and engineering. Quantitative benchmarking will answer questions like 'what is the best possible time we can get with a traffic simulator?' and 'how large a network can we actually simulate in real-time?'. In this paper, we propose a benchmarking strategy for available traffic simulators to evaluate their performance and capabilities. We decided to start with microscopic simulators [7] because it is more realistic and can model the detailed behaviours of every vehicle and its interaction with other vehicles and its environment. In microscopic simulators, amongst the various choices, we chose to start with SUMO [12] for our benchmarking evaluation study for two reasons: first, SUMO is an open-sourced tool and second, it is well-documented.

3. OVERVIEW OF BENCHMARKING

A good benchmarking strategy is the one that comprises of a comprehensive list of metrics used for the benchmarking process. In our approach, we have designed a couple of benchmarking scenarios that can be used for evaluation and grading of the simulators. These scenarios are realistic and common cases and are completely unbiased. They represent every day situations, complexities of road networks, and the interaction of the population with these networks and other infrastructure.

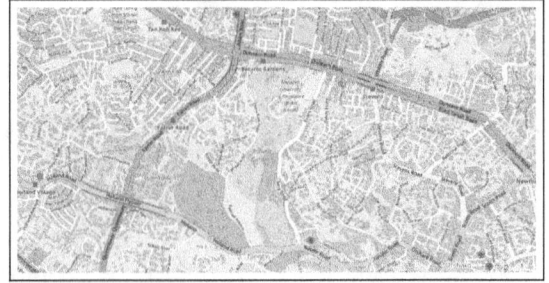

Figure 1: A section from the OpenStreetMap of the city of Singapore

The proposed scenarios ensure direct comparison of various traffic simulators. In the benchmarking process, a candidate simulator is tested against these benchmarking scenarios and graded based on the benchmarking metrics.

In the following sub-sections, the scenarios are briefly described, along with the motivation to choose these scenarios. For all scenarios, we wish to carry out the simulation with passenger cars first and include other modes of transport gradually.

3.1 Benchmarking Scenarios

We obtained the city map from OpenStreetMap (OSM) of Singapore[13] and converted this to SUMO input network using NETCONVERT tool available in SUMO [14].

Available python script 'randomTrips.py' in SUMO package was used to generate random trips due to the unavailability of origin-destination data. Every scenarios was simulated for a time of 1 hour. We first set up a reference scenario. In this scenario, the road network spans over an area of 6.8 km^2 with 2067 edges, 1283 nodes, and total edge length of 130.8 km. In addition, the vehicle density (number of vehicles per total edge length) is set to 37.44 vehicles/km.

The total execution time taken to simulate the population demand of 5,000 vehicles in the reference scenario was 52 seconds and the memory usage was 4.7 Megabytes. With respect to this reference scenario, we change different scenario characteristics as described below, in order to further investigate the performance of the simulator.

3.1.1 Scenario 1: High Road Density

To test the simulator for urban and regional networks, we should be able to simulate a highly dense road networks. Therefore, the initial road density of scenario was changed using NETEDIT application available in SUMO. More edges and nodes were added into the reference network. Scenario 1 contains 2304 edges, 1418 nodes and total edge length of 151.72 km.

Moreover, to keep the vehicle density the same as reference scenario, we simulated Scenario 1 with 5640 vehicles. Finally, the simulation was run and the time and memory usage were noted on completion of the simulation.

Figure 1 shows a section of the actual city map of Singapore that is used in the benchmarking process, while Figure 2 shows the same section of the city map generated by NETEDIT.

3.1.2 Scenario 2: High Vehicle Density

In this scenario, we intend to evaluate the appropriateness of the simulator for modelling congested arterial street con-

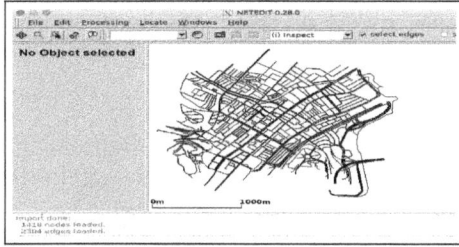

Figure 2: Scenario 1 generated from the reference network using NETEDIT

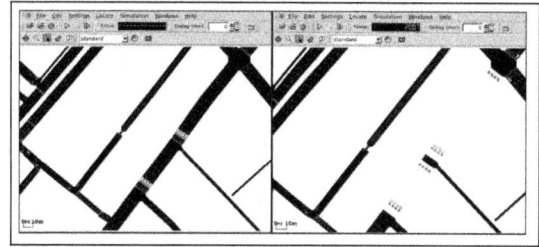

Figure 3: The edges on the left-side have been blocked in the right-side image from t=2000 seconds to t=3000 seconds

ditions, which is a common problem faced in many countries. We believe that scalability in terms of supported population is very important as it determines how large a population dimension can a simulator cope up with. This is peculiarly crucial for microscopic simulators since a computing system has restricted memory and CPU resources, and microscopic simulators are more detailed and hence require more memory for storage. Furthermore, we are interested in the results of the simulation in real time, since some simulators might cope up with large demand but may take long execution time for the production of the output results. For this scenario, using the same reference network, we increased the vehicle population in the same area to 150% of the original 5,000 vehicles. Hence, this scenario was simulated for 1 hour with 7,500 vehicles.

3.1.3 Scenario 3: Large network

In some cases, traffic networks that are being examined maybe of a very large scale, like a downtown area of a large city or may be even a city as a whole. The size of the network is another very important property to be evaluated. Therefore, the scenario must be big enough to show the standard congestion pattern visible in modern cities, yet small enough to permit simulations in a justifiable amount of time. To simulate a large network, we chose a map over a larger area from the same OSM of Singapore, spanning over $8.82km^2$ and consisting of 2816 nodes and 6148 edges. This scenario is simulated with a population demand of 8645 vehicles to keep the vehicle density constant (37.17 vehciles/km; approximates to 37 vehicles/km).

3.1.4 Scenario 4: Skewed Vehicle Distribution

In many real-life cases, not every road in the network will have a uniform distribution of vehicles. It is highly probable that some roads experience more traffic congestion compared to rest of the roads. To simulate skewed vehicle distribution, SUMO provides 3 options to work with edge probability selection—edge length, number of lanes, and edge speed. For the purpose of making a skewed distribution scenario, the probability of selection of an edge was varied based on the length of the edge. This option of selection is available while running the 'randomTrips.py' script.

3.1.5 Scenario 5: Closing of an edge/edges

Road networks often get jammed due to road closures or traffic accidents. The ability for a traffic simulator to compute dynamic traffic assignments is an integral requisite for proper simulation of urban and rural areas. For this scenario, we simulate a road closure in the same reference network that is synonymous to an accident by closing 2 edges

in the simulation from the time period t=2,000 to t=3,000 seconds (see Figure 3). Vehicles arriving on these edges will get a new route (the probability for vehicle rerouting is 1) and the algorithm for selecting a new route is, by default, the Dijkstra's algorithm. Traffic reassignments in the simulation affect the average travel time and travel length of the vehicles, depending on the underlying routing algorithms.

3.2 Benchmarking Metrics

The proposed quantitative benchmarking focuses on evaluating the run-time performance of the traffic simulators. For this purpose, CPU execution time and memory usage are adopted as the metrics for evaluation.

In the benchmarking process, we obtain the simulator's performance based on the time taken and memory consumed by the simulating system to process and complete the entire simulation over a period of time. These metrics are important since CPU execution time can have implications on other system performance characteristics such as power consumption and resource profile (usage of resources). Moreover, since today's users tend to simulate large traffics in real-time. The lesser the simulation time, the better and more useful the simulation results. Furthermore, the memory of a computing system is also an important resource to support large-scale highly dense simulations.

4. EXPERIMENTAL RESULTS

All benchmarking scenarios were run on a machine with a 2.9 Ghz Intel Core i5 2-core processor and 8GB RAM. For all scenarios, a time value of 1000 seconds was used for teleporting the vehicles in the case of traffic jams. Figure 4 shows the time usage profile in different scenarios and Figure 5 shows the memory usage profile.

From the results, it is observed that, in Scenario 1, increasing the road density from 19.8 km/km^2 to 22.31km/km^2, led to the total execution time increased to 3.4 times that of the reference scenario, keeping the vehicle density constant. In Scenario 2, increasing the population density to 1.5 times the original led to a 8.09 times increase in the total execution time. The total execution time was the largest with the case of large network simulation (Scenario 3), as one would intuitively expect. Although the road network was increased only by 1.3 times the reference road network size, the total time taken had nearly a 24.3 times increase. In scenario 4, keeping both the vehicle density as well as network size constant and altering only the distribution of the vehicles, the time taken had only 2.21 times increase compared to the original time. In the last scenario, the time taken was 2.24 times the original time.

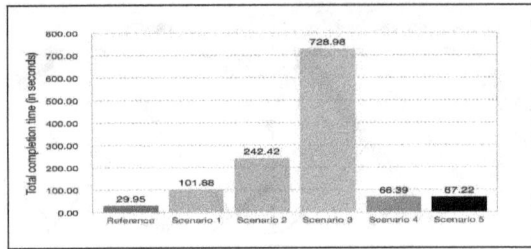

Figure 4: Execution Time.

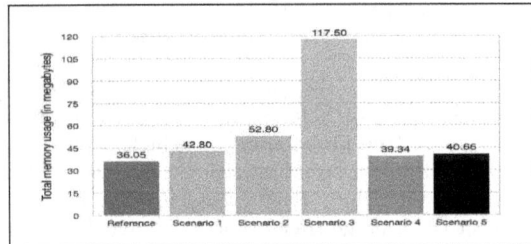

Figure 5: Memory Usage.

Clearly, Scenario 3 has the largest completion time. In this case, to simulate one hour with the given vehicle density, it takes 728.98 seconds. Therefore, the simulator can complete 4.93 times faster than real time, which is not a very good value. To simulate a scenario for an entire day, it would take a minimum of 4.85 hours, which is not a very desirable value.

In case of memory usage, Scenario 1, Scenario 4, and Scenario 5 do not vary significantly. However, in the case of Scenario 3, the memory consumption is 3.25 times that of the reference scenario. This may account for the storage of large road network and the route trip information of the increased population over this network.

5. CONCLUSION AND FUTURE WORK

In this paper, we presented an approach to benchmark traffic simulators quantitatively. The aim of this proposal is to move towards the establishment of a benchmark platform to evaluate the existing simulators based on some common and realistic scenarios, and assess them according to performance metrics such as execution time and memory usage. A benchmarking standard will provide a competitive edge to the available traffic simulators and help us decide the best fit for our purpose. We started with SUMO and evaluated its performance in every scenario that has been proposed in this paper and the performance values have been compared based on a reference scenario. The simulator performed differently in different cases, consuming the most amount of time in the simulation of a large network.

For simulation of real networks of the scale of a city or beyond, the performance obtained from SUMO in our experiments would not be enough. Nevertheless, this approach will be extended to include more traffic simulators and compare their performance by using the proposed benchmark. Although we started with microscopic simulators, this benchmarking approach can be applied across any abstraction level of traffic simulation modelling. Future work may include inclusion of more simulators for comparing and benchmarking them. Other metrics, in addition to the ones used

in this paper, will be included in the future for performance evaluation.

6. REFERENCES

[1] L. R. Rilett and J. Zietsman. An Overview of the Transims Micro-Simulation Model: Application Possibilities for South Africa. *20th South African Transport Conference on Meeting the Transport Challenges in Southern Africa*, 2001.

[2] Benjamin Kickhofer, Daniel Hosse, Kai Turnera, and Alejandro Tirachinic. Creating an Open MATSIM Scenario from Open Data:The Case of Santiago de Chile. *VSP Working Paper 16-02; TU Berlin Transport Systems Planning and Transport Telematics*, March 2016.

[3] Laura Bieker, Daniel Krajzewicz, AntonioPio Morra, Carlo Michelacci, and Fabio Cartolano. Traffic Simulation for All: A Real World Traffic Scenario from the City of Bologna. In *Proceedings of 2nd SUMO Conference on Modeling mobility with open data*, 2015.

[4] TRANSIMS. https://code.google.com/archive/p/transims/.

[5] Deema Fathi Allan and Amro M. Farid. A Benchmark Analysis of Open Source Transportation-Electrification Simulation Tools. In *Proceedings of IEEE 18th International Conference on Intelligent Transportation Systems*, 2015.

[6] Lara Codeca, Raphael Frank, and Thomas Engel. Lust: A 24-hour scenario of luxembourg city for sumo traffic simulations. In *Proceedings of the SUMO 2015, Intermodal Simulation for Intermodal Transport*, 2015.

[7] Zafeiris Kokkinogenis, Lucio Sanchez Passos, Rosaldo Rossetti, and Joaquim Gabriel. Towards the Next-Generation Traffic Simulation Tools: A First Evaluation. In *Proceedings of 6th Iberian Conference on Information Systems and Technologies*, 2011.

[8] G. Kotusevski and K.A. Hawick. A Review of Traffic Simulation Software. *Research Letter in Information and Mathematical Science*, 13, 2009.

[9] Nedal T. Ratrout and Syed Masiur Rahman. A Comparative Analysis of Currently Used Microscopic and Macroscopic Traffic Simulation Software. *The Arabian Journal for Science and Engineering*, 34(1B), 2009.

[10] Michael Maciejewski. A comparison of microscopic traffic flow simulation systems for an urban area. 5, 2010.

[11] Toyotaro Suzumura, Gavin McArdle, and Hiroki Kanezashi. A High Performance Multi-Modal Traffic Simulation Platform and its Case Study with the Dublin City. In *Proceedings of IEEE 2015 Winter Simulation Conference*, 2015.

[12] SUMO. http://www.sumo.dlr.de/userdoc/index.html.

[13] OpenStreetMap. http://wiki.openstreetmap.org/wiki/WikiProject_Singapore/.

[14] Daniel Krajzewicz, Jakob Erdmann, Michael Behrisch, and Laura Bieker. Recent Development and Applications of SUMO -Simulation of Urban MObility. *International Journal on Advances in Systems and Measurements*, 5(3,4), 2012.

Automatic State Saving and Rollback in ns-3

Euna Kim and George Riley
Department of Electrical and Computer Engineering
Georgia Institute of Technology
Atlanta, GA. USA
euna.kim,riley@gatech.edu

ABSTRACT

When designing, implementing and executing large-scale distributed simulation codes it is well-known the so-called *optimistic* time synchronization methods often lead to better overall performance as compared to the so-called *conservative* methods. Particularly when the model being simulated suffers from small *lookahead* between two or more of the logical processes working on the overall simulation execution. However, the design and implementation of simulation model codes intended to be executed using optimistic approach is often daunting, especially when working with existing codes which were designed and implemented to be used in a conservative approach. When executing simulation events, optimistic simulation models must first save any existing state in the model prior to executing codes that change that state, and furthermore must implement *rollback* code which restores that state to the original value. The necessity for such extra software functionality is often a barrier to the complete implementation of an optimistic-based simulation model and the corresponding improved performance.

However, recent work by Lawrence Livermore National Laboratory *(LLNL)* shows promise toward easing the burden of state-saving and rollback which will ultimately lead to simulation models that include state-saving and rollback *automatically* with little or no extra effort on the part of the model developer. This work, known as *Backstroke*, uses the C or C++ source code of the simulation model and generates both the forward-direction *state-saving* and the reverse-direction *rollback* prior to executing any simulation event. In this work, we demonstrate that the Network Simulator 3 *(ns-3)* model code, instrumented by Backstroke, can successfully execute scenario to some arbitrary time T, and then *roll back* to simulation time $T0$, restoring previously saved state for all modified *ns-3* events and resulting in identical model state to that created in the original prior to the execution of the very first model event. Finally, we measure and report on the amount of wall-clock time overhead incurred by the *ns-3* execution required by the Backstroke state saving and restoration, and compare that time to the execution time of the original unmodified *ns-3* model codes.

SIGSIM-PADS '17 May 24–26, 2017, Singapore, Singapore

© 2017 ACM. ISBN 978-1-4503-4489-0/17/05. . . $15.00

DOI: http://dx.doi.org/10.1145/3064911.3064925

Keywords

ns-3, Backstroke, rollback, network simulation, scalability

1. INTRODUCTION

Due to the tremendous growth of large-scale complex networks, the importance of network simulator speedup using parallel and distributed simulation techniques is increasingly significant. Illustrating this trend, we see that many parallel programming techniques (e.g. MPI or OpenMP) and distributed system specific approaches (e.g. massively parallel computing with OpenCL or CUDA) are being developed or have already been deployed in network simulators.

1.1 Motivation

Of the network simulators in use, ns-3 is an open-source, discrete-event network simulator under GNU GPLv2 license, which is primarily used in academic research; Conservative lookahead mechanism is already available within ns-3 and is implemented using Message Passing Interface (MPI) [4] (Pelkey 2011). However, conservative synchronization is known to work poorly where a simulation runs with a small lookahead value, which leads to a decreasing set of safe events to run by suppressing a LBTS (Lower Bound on the Time Stamp), thereby degenerating performance. This prevents all LPs(Logical Processes) in the simulation from exploiting parallelism and eventually yields poor performance [2] (Fujimoto 1989). Applications associated with the Internet of Things (IoT), such as smart grid and intelligent transportation, are thriving. As those revolutionary services developed in Wireless Network or Wireless Sensor Network (WSN) flourish, the need for performance enhancement to emulate the enormous amount of LPs via a network simulator is paramount. Network protocols similar to WSN are generally designed with small lookahead values in simulations due to their node proximity and low-energy constraints. Indeed, optimistic synchronization may be an attractive alternative method to run simulation in parallel and distributed with those network models.

1.2 Related work

Time Warp [3] (Jefferson 1985) is the first and best known optimistic synchronization protocol. Contrary to conservative protocols, Time Warp allows LPs to proceed to execute events without ensuring causality violations and recover from them when causality errors are found. As a result of this, it is not critically influenced by defining lookahead value to achieve a higher degree of parallelism of the simulation model and, it does not have to deal with frequent global synchronization to calculate GVT (Global Virtual Time).

Although it has clear advantages, optimistic synchronization has often not been applied to commodity simulation software due to the impediment in offering reversible code to model developers and the overhead of saving states and performing rollback. Various attempts to store state information for later use in a rollback phase have been proposed since the rollback-based synchronization approach was first conceived. These attempts have included methods which require huge memory usage to maintain the state information (the snapshot restoration or incremental check pointing) and approaches to save extra information to restore the prior state (control flow saving and reverse code generation). More details about related work in the past can be found in [5] (Schordan 2015). Using reverse computation instead of restoring snapshot for rollback was suggested in [1] (Carothers 1999), and implemented in Rensselaer's Optimistic Simulation System (ROSS) (which was based on Time Warp algorithm, with manually written reverse code offered by a programmer).

1.3 Backstroke

Although optimistic synchronization is an effective and useful option for specific domains in large-scale distributed event simulation, historically this has required developers to provide manually written reverse codes in order to reap the benefits of parallelism. This requirement is cumbersome and prone to human error especially where the design and implementation of software has already been completed.

LLNL's recent achievement, *Backstroke* [5], which can generate reversible-forward code and restore-state-saving code during rollback automatically, is an important step towards lessening a model developer's workload and making use of the optimistic mechanism in ns-3 a tenable option. Backstroke can automatically generate both forward code and reverse library corresponding to the original C++ source file without a programmer's intervention. The Backstroke generated forward code is a source-to-source conversion, thereby providing model developers with the opportunity to verify and improve if necessary. This forward code functions identically to the original code except for the addition of state-saving code on each memory access to modify the value. Generated reverse library is invoked during rollback phase in order to restore the LP's state so the model's state is identical to the state of any previously executed events.

By measuring the overhead of state-saving in forward-direction execution with automatically generated code by Backstroke, we will reveal the potential value of employing optimistic synchronization using the automatic conversion tool. Performance experiments using point-to-point campus network topology have been conducted by scaling the number of nodes from 1076 to 4303, processing nearly 1 million events. In section 2, we will describe the modification of ns-3 core source code to employ state-saving and the preparation of forward code and reverse library of network model code created by Backstroke. The result of measuring state-saving overhead and analysis will be presented in Section 3. Finally in section 4, we will discuss our conclusion and the future work of this research.

2. IMPLEMENTATION

2.1 Setup to use Backstroke

In order to use Backstroke, both ROSE and Boost must be leveraged. ROSE is an open source compiler infrastructure that can build source-to-source transformation developed by LLNL. Boost is a collection of open source libraries that extends the functionality of C++. Initially, an inquiry of compatibility among versions of Boost, ROSE and GCC will be necessary.

2.2 Modifications in ns-3

In order to use Backstroke in ns-3 there are two major alterations required. One, the simulator in the core will now activate backstroke to record all memory manipulation histories during invoking events. Two, the model code will be transformed as forward code and reverse/commit methods automatically via backstroke. Forward code allows backstroke to store the states of simulation in order to restore the variables during rollback.

2.2.1 Modifications in ns-3 core

In order to successfully perform optimistic synchronization, the simulatorImpl in the core must leverage functions of Run, Rollback and Commit. Backstroke is activated to start and to finish storing the memory changes during a simulation's Run. When a straggler event is found while running a simulation rollback will be executed. During rollback, Backstroke's revert function is called until the simulation time of the event queue becomes the straggler's timestamp. In ns-3, all allocated memory (which heretofore has been deallocated immediately upon such construct) is now simply registered as such upon the traditional construct and deallocated only subsequent to confirmation that same is not needed within a rollback process commensurate to that time in the commit phase according to GVT.

The GVT calculation and outgoing message annihilation is a unique method to realize optimistic synchronization in the simulation. In the calculation algorithm, GVT is similar to LBTS in conservative synchronization. The differentiation is that GVT in optimistic synchronization is not utilized as lookahead value to proceed with parallel simulation, but as a trigger for retrieving dynamic memory via commit. Anti-message is introduced in [3] as an approach to cancel messages already sent to a separate LP. The positive or negative sign field of a message is used to invalidate the original message in the event queue when receiving the paired message of opposite sign.

2.2.2 Generation of forward and reverse code

Backstroke creates a deque (double ended queue) for each event. When the event implementation is invoked, Backstroke starts recording all indicated memory manipulations as newly generated forward code. Backstroke then inserts that information into their own deque and same is removed during either commit or rollback. There is no explicit source-to-source transformed code for reverse and commit in Backstroke. Reverse and commit processes are now in a library form of the module sharing implementation of forward code and realizing the Forward-Reverse-Commit approach. State-saving is performed by restoring previous values triggered upon acknowledgement of assignment operator during program execution. Forward code does not change a program's original intent, logic or control flow.

```
1  UdpL4Protocol::UdpL4Protocol ()
2   : m_endPoints (new Ipv4EndPointDemux ()), m_endPoints6 (
       new Ipv6EndPointDemux ())
3   {   NS_LOG_FUNCTION_NOARGS (); }
4  void UdpL4Protocol::DoDispose (void) {
```

```
5     if (m_endPoints != 0) {
6         delete m_endPoints;
7         m_endPoints = 0;
8     }
9  }
10 void OnOffApplication::SetMaxBytes (uint32_t maxBytes) {
11     NS_LOG_FUNCTION (this << maxBytes);
12     m_maxBytes = maxBytes;
13 }
14
```

Listing 1: Original Code

```
1  UdpL4Protocol::UdpL4Protocol ()
2    : m_endPoints ((xpdes::registerAllocationForRollbackT(new
        Ipv4EndPointDemux ()))), m_endPoints6 ((xpdes::
        registerAllocationForRollbackT(new Ipv6EndPointDemux
        ())))
3  {  NS_LOG_FUNCTION_NOARGS (); }
4  void UdpL4Protocol::DoDispose (void) {
5      if (m_endPoints != 0) {
6          (xpdes::registerDeallocationForCommitT(m_endPoints));
7          (xpdes::avpushT(m_endPoints)) = 0;
8      }
9  }
10 void OnOffApplication::SetMaxBytes (uint32_t maxBytes) {
11     NS_LOG_FUNCTION (this << maxBytes);
12     (xpdes::avpushT(m_maxBytes)) = maxBytes;
13 }
14
```

Listing 2: Reversible Forward Code

In Listing 1 and 2 we show the original code and forward code memory allocation (*xpdes::registerAllocationForRollbackT()*) and manipulation of variables and registration (*xpdes::avpush()*) for later commit as deferred memory deallocation (*xpdes::register Deallocation-ForCommitT()*). Monitoring, as noted by *(xpdes:: avpushT(m_maxBytes))=maxBytes* stores the subsequent value changes in that particular memory location within the data structure internal to Backstroke. At this point in the process we have prepared new forward code having prefix "rose_" in its file name. During compilation, new forward codes are generated according to the files indicated within makefile and substituted for the correlating ns-3 source code. Obsolete original source code is no longer used. Once object files are created, future compilations occur upon changed files exclusively. ns-3 libraries and application programs by model programmers are now created from forward code.

3. EXPERIMENT AND ANALYSIS

Measuring performance of this distributed parallel simulation in ns-3 was conducted with campus networks topology shown in Figure 1. Multiple campus networks were created with point-to-point connection, while each had four subnet connections among routers, servers and client nodes through various speed and bandwidth of LAN and non-LAN links. By setting the number of 42 clients on each LAN node, the total number of nodes engaged by the campus networks topology used in our experiment ranged from 1076 to 4303 nodes.

Our implementation in ns-3 code base includes Default-SimulatorImpl modification for adding state-saving while running simulation, as well as, invoking revert_events function in Backstroke while executing rollback. Forward codes and reversible library are automatically generated by Backstroke and used for experiments. Software refactoring for rollback-friendly behavior in ns-3 is occurring. Generated

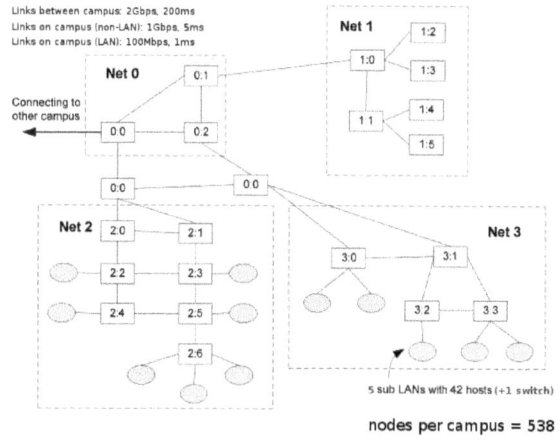

Figure 1: The campus network topology is comprised of net0, net1, net2 and net3. Each of the 12 ovals represent a combination of local area networks containing 42 nodes. Link speed inside of the LAN is 100Mbps with 1ms delays and the connections between the LANs have 1Gbps speed with a delay of 5ms. The number of campus networks is easily increased by duplicating and connecting across the network's symmetric topology.

forward codes examined for our performance analysis were partially restricted in core, network and Internet modules, resulting in 81 forward codes built in less than 5 minutes for initial compilation.

3.1 Overhead for state-saving

Memory usage and wall-clock elapsed time were both used to measure potential performance decrease resulting from state-saving during forward code execution. We contrived a scenario where the simulation starts at 0.0 second and rollback initiates at simulation time 50.00 second, reverting to simulation time at 40.00 second. When rollback is completed at 40.00 second, all events which have a timestamp after 40.00 seconds in the processed event list are popped, thereby triggering Backstroke to restore the variables' values from the 40.00 second mark. In this test, commit for memory deallocation is not performed. With the topology described above, our 50 second simulation included a transfered size of 5000 bytes and generated 947167 events. Each node schedules packet sending events at random time during simulation.

3.1.1 Time

We found execution time of forward code to be faster than execution time of original code as shown in Figure 2 (a). We attribute this positive result to deferred deallocation policy negating the need for frequent delete[] functions execution in many small base objects in ns-3. Also, cache locality effect and lower memory fragmentation are plausible reasons for the results. An overall implication being that a subject machine used for optimistic simulation can be optimized for available memory and period of GVT. Also, rollback execution time is relatively negligible, but rescheduling takes as long as the initial simulation time. Therefore severe rollback throttling will need to be managed accordingly.

3.1.2 Memory usage

The amount of used memory with and without activating state-saving is shown in Figure 2 (b). With state-saving

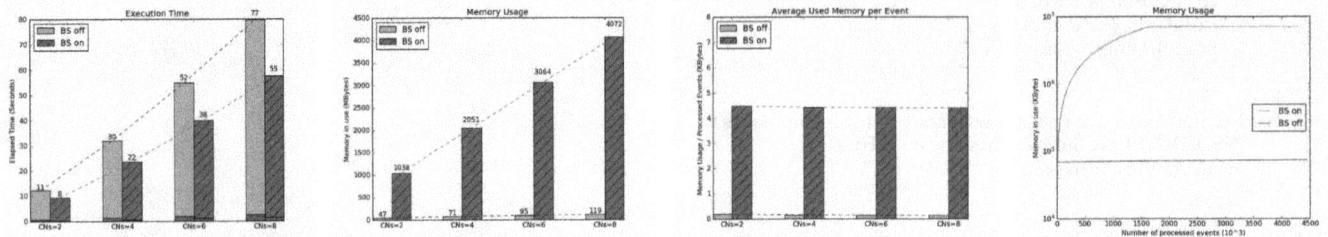

(a) Execution Time (init+run) (b) Memory Usage (c) Memory usage per Event (d) Memory Usage, # of events

Figure 2: The relationship of simulation runtime, memory usage and the number of processed events is tested by scaling Campus network 2,4,6,8 increased the number of nodes involved in communication 1076, 2152, 3228, 4304 respectively

Figure 3: Simulation runtime, memory usage and number of processed events tested by scaling simulation size as follows: number of CNs/total nodes/total events 2/1076/236516, 4/2152/474871, 6/3228/711896, 8/4304/947167.

disabled the memory usage is saturated at 400MB regardless of the number of events. Whereas, with state-saving enabled memory usage increases commensurate to the available hardware memory in the system. In Figure 2 (d) we see that processing 1.5 million events utilizes 8GB memory. We can observe a relationship between topology size, communication type, network protocol, simulation run time, number of processed events and resulting memory usage. The current implementation does not contain the GVT calculation, which is designed to guarantee the safe time to perform commit. Once we implement commit to retrieve memory, the memory requirement will decrease. Backstroke execution has revealed minor memory leak thus far. We anticipate memory usage reduction with further development of Backstroke.

3.2 Verification

To ensure the automatically generated reverse library and forward codes are working as intended we implemented test suites. The test suites are designed to schedule events utilizing various data objects in ns-3 and c++ standard built-in data type. The test suites are also designed to start and stop at any time and rollback to any prior arbitrary time within the simulation. Upon rollback completion the simulation re-runs and begins processing scheduled events.

3.2.1 Forward code generation

In order to verify forward code from a functional perspective, the simplest method is to retrieve the simulation log files and contrast those against the correlating log files of the original program without backstroke. The result should be identical trace files as Backstroke does not affect functionality in original logic and, in our simulation, this was achieved.

3.2.2 Rollback correctness

We check rollback correctness in two ways. First, by determining if the values of state-saved variables have restored their old values after rollback. Second, by comparing the ns-3 trace files of the initial simulation run versus re-run after rollback. If the entire program status is successfully restored after rollback, then the two trace files should be identical. ns-3 source code refactoring is yet to be completed and limitations of forward code generation within the current implementation of Backstroke leads to temporarily incomplete results. Nonetheless, our trace files present with a highly reflective behavior pattern.

4. CONCLUSIONS AND FUTURE WORK

We have shown the impact of state-saving with automatically generated reversible forward code and its overhead in simulation time. State-saving is the essential functionality to actualize optimistic synchronization in parallel simulation within our approach. Because of this, evaluating the performance degeneration caused by state-saving is important to investigating the feasibility of deploying this technology. Although the results indicate fairly heavy workloads, we cannot deny the advantages of a reversible computation mechanism of existing source code, through an automatic source transformation tool. Our ultimate goal is to deploy optimistic synchronization in ns-3 using Backstroke. In order to do this, existing ns-3 source code must be modified and refactored in a rollback-friendly form to prevent potential conflicts with Backstroke. In addition, key features for realizing optimistic synchronization such as GVT calculation and Time Warp should be implemented within the ns-3 core module. Software compatibility and system constraints prevented us from conducting a larger scale simulation. However, our results indicate the possibility of optimistic synchronization winning execution time performance in certain contexts. Lastly, the current version of Backstroke has limitations in forward file generation and memory management. Once this work is complete, model programmers will be able to feasibly exploit parallelism with little or no extra effort.

5. REFERENCES

[1] C. D. Carothers, K. S. Perumalla, and R. M. Fujimoto. Efficient optimistic parallel simulations using reverse computation. *ACM Trans. Model. Comput. Simul.*, 9(3):224–253, July 1999.

[2] R. M. Fujimoto. Parallel discrete event simulation. *Commun. ACM*, 33(10):30–53, Oct. 1990.

[3] D. R. Jefferson. Virtual time. *ACM Trans. Program. Lang. Syst.*, 7(3):404–425, July 1985.

[4] J. Pelkey and G. Riley. Distributed simulation with mpi in ns-3. In *Proceedings of the 4th International ICST Conference on Simulation Tools and Techniques*, SIMUTools '11, 2011.

[5] M. Schordan, T. Oppelstrup, D. Jefferson, P. D. Barnes, Jr., and D. Quinlan. Automatic generation of reversible c++ code and its performance in a scalable kinetic monte-carlo application. In *Proceedings of the 2016 Annual ACM Conference on SIGSIM Principles of Advanced Discrete Simulation*, SIGSIM-PADS '16, 2016.

Author Index

www.ingramcontent.com/pod-product-compliance
Lightning Source LLC
Chambersburg PA
CBHW061352210326
41598CB00035B/5963